CHILD ABUSE AND NEGLECT

CHILD ABUSE AND NEGLECT

DEFINITIONS, CLASSIFICATIONS, AND A FRAMEWORK FOR RESEARCH

edited by

Margaret M. Feerick, Ph.D.

John F. Knutson, Ph.D.

Penelope K. Trickett, Ph.D.

and

Sally M. Flanzer, Ph.D.

·P A U L·H·
BROOKES
PUBLISHING C⁰ ®

Baltimore • London • Sydney

Paul H. Brookes Publishing Co.
Post Office Box 10624
Baltimore, Maryland 21285-0624

www.brookespublishing.com

"Paul H. Brookes Publishing Co." is a registered trademark of
Paul H. Brookes Publishing Co., Inc.

Typeset by A.W. Bennett, Inc., Hartland, Vermont.
Manufactured in the United States of America by
Versa Press, Inc., East Peoria, Illinois.

Cover photograph by Don Smith / Alamy.

Library of Congress Cataloging-in-Publication Data

Child abuse and neglect : definitions, classifications, and a framework for research / edited
by Margaret M. Feerick [et al.].
    p.   cm.
Includes bibliographical references and index.
ISBN-13: 978-1-55766-759-5
ISBN-10: 1-55766-759-4
    1. Child abuse—United States. 2. Child abuse—Investigation—United States.
I. Feerick, Margaret Mary, 1967– II. Title.
HV6626.52.F44 2006
362.760973—dc22
                                                          2006013377

British Library Cataloguing in Publication data are available from the British Library.

CONTENTS

I   CLASSIFICATION OF CHILD ABUSE AND NEGLECT

II   DEFINITION AND THEORY IN CHILD ABUSE
AND NEGLECT

ABOUT THE EDITORS

Margaret M. Feerick, Ph.D., Psychologist and Independent Consultant, Feerick Consulting, Laytonsville, MD 20882. Dr. Feerick holds a bachelor's degree in English and a master's degree in developmental psychology from Columbia University and a doctorate in developmental psychology from Cornell University. Early in her career, Dr. Feerick worked as a language arts teacher and director of development/contributions at an independent junior high school in New York City while also working as a freelance editor/reader for Penguin Books, U.S.A. She has also served in research and statistical consultant positions on several federally funded research projects at St. Luke's–Roosevelt Hospital in New York City, the New York State Research Institute on Alcoholism and Addictions, and the National Data Archive on Child Abuse and Neglect and has published articles and book chapters addressing various aspects of child maltreatment and family violence. Dr. Feerick has received numerous fellowships and awards, including an individual National Research Service Award from the National Institutes of Health (NIH) and a Society for Research in Child Development Executive Branch Policy Fellowship. From 1998 to 2004, Dr. Feerick served as a Health Scientist Administrator/Program Director at the National Institute of Child Health and Human Development, where she directed a large research and training program in child development, family processes, and child maltreatment and violence. In addition she has served on numerous inter-agency work groups and committees, including the Federal Interagency Work Group on Child Abuse and Neglect, the NIH Child Abuse and Neglect Working Group (which she co-chaired), the Inter-Agency Work Group on Children Exposed to Violence (which she developed and chaired), and the Technical Advisory Group for the Fourth National Incidence Study (NIS-4) of the Office on Child Abuse and Neglect in the Children's Bureau of the Administration for Children and Families at the U.S. Department of Health and Human Services. Dr. Feerick is currently working as an independent consultant; a freelance science writer; a Liaison for the Section on Child Maltreatment of the Division on Children, Youth, and Families of the American Psychological Association; and a reviewer for several peer-reviewed journals, while completing a respecialization program in clinical psychology at Fielding Graduate University and raising her two children. She recently co-edited (with Gerald B. Silverman) the book *Children Exposed to Violence* (Paul H. Brookes Publishing Co., 2006).

John F. Knutson, Ph.D., Professor, Department of Psychology, The University of Iowa, Iowa City, IA 52242. Dr. Knutson holds a bachelor's degree in psychology from Augustana College, Rock Island, Illinois, and a master's degree in psychology and a doctorate in clinical psychology from Washington State University. After completing a postdoctoral fellowship in Medical Psychology at The University of Oregon Medical School, he joined the faculty at Iowa, where he was a recipient of the Regents' Award for Faculty Excellence in 1999. He has served two tours of duty as Director of Clinical Training at Iowa, and he directed the Department's training clinic for 10 years. He has held editorial positions on *Journal of Abnormal Psychology, Journal of Clinical Child and Adolescent Psychology*, and *Aggressive Behavior*, and he is a fellow of the American Psychological Association and the American Psychological Society. He recently ended his third term as Treasurer of the International Society for Research on Aggression. Dr. Knutson's early research career focused on basic processes underlying the development of aggression, with his research on child maltreatment commencing in the late 1970s. He has also devoted considerable effort to research on psychological factors, including family relations, in the outcome of cochlear implants with deaf adults and children. Dr. Knutson has published more than 100 journal articles and book chapters on aggression, physical child abuse, neglect, the association between abuse and disabilities, cochlear implants, and methodology pertaining to the assessment of child maltreatment. Recently Dr. Knutson served on two federal committees focused on research definitions of child maltreatment and he was a member of the Technical Advisory Group for the Fourth National Incidence Study (NIS-4) of the Office on Child Abuse and Neglect in the Children's Bureau of the Administration for Children and Families at the U.S. Department of Health and Human Services. His current actively supported research projects are examining the role of supervisory and care neglect in the development of young children's aggression and the influence of exposure to domestic violence on young children's social adjustment.

Penelope K. Trickett, Ph.D., David Lawrence Stein/Violet Goldberg Sachs Professor of Mental Health, School of Social Work; and Professor of Psychology, College of Arts, Letters, and Sciences, University of Southern California, Montgomery Ross Fisher Building, Los Angeles, CA 90089. Dr. Trickett earned her doctorate from the New School for Social Research, New York. She is a developmental psychologist whose research, for more than two decades, has focused on the developmental consequences of child abuse and neglect on children and adolescents and on the characteristics of families in which such abuse occurs. She has received an Independent Scientist Award from the National Institute of Mental Health. In addition, Dr. Trickett is conducting a longitudinal study, now in its 18th year, of the psychobiological impact of familial sexual abuse on girls and female adolescents. She is also the Principal Investigator of a longitudinal study of the impact of neglect on adolescent development funded by the National Institutes of Health. She served as member, and then Chair, of the Committee on Children, Youth, and Families of the American Psychological Association (APA) from 1992 to 1995 and was member-at-large of the Executive Committee of the Section on Child Maltreatment of APA's Division of Child, Youth, and Family Services. She is a Fellow of APA's Division 7 (Developmental Psychology). Dr. Trickett also directs a university-wide interdisciplinary violence research initiative at the University of Southern California.

Sally M. Flanzer, Ph.D., currently Human Protections Administrator/Health Scientist Administrator, Agency for Healthcare Research and Quality (AHRQ), 540 Gaither Road, Rockville, Maryland 20850. Dr. Flanzer earned a bachelor's degree with honors in liberal arts from the University of Illinois–Chicago Circle Campus; a master's degree in educational counseling from Northwestern University, Evanston, Illinois; and a doctorate in Human Development from the Catholic University of America, Washington, D.C. Dr. Flanzer was the Director of the Division of Data, Research and Innovation at the Children's Bureau, Administration on Children, Youth and Families, Administration for Children and Families, U.S. Department of Health and Human Services (DHHS; 1997–2003), after having worked at the National Center on Child Abuse and Neglect from 1993 to 1997. Prior to working for the federal government, Dr. Flanzer worked for several consulting firms in the Washington, D.C., area, conducting program evaluations and research on child maltreatment, runaway and homeless youth, family violence, domestic violence, foster care, and foster care parenting and discipline. Dr. Flanzer has made numerous presentations on these topics to professional and lay audiences. In her present position, Dr. Flanzer oversees the human protections program for intramural research at AHRQ and serves as a consultant to the extramural research program. She also serves on many committees and working groups in DHHS, including serving as an ex officio member of the Secretary's Advisory Committee on Human Research Protections, the inter-agency Human Subjects Research Subcommittee (HSRS) of the National Science and Technology Council Committee on Science under the auspices of the President's Office of Science and Technology Policy, and on the Social and Behavioral Research Working Group of the HSRS. While serving at the Children's Bureau, Dr. Flanzer also participated in the Federal Interagency Work Group on Child Abuse and Neglect, the National Institutes of Health Child Abuse and Neglect Working Group, the Federal Child Neglect Research Consortium, and the Child Welfare League of America's National Council on Research in Child Welfare (1991–2003). She is an occasional reviewer for *Child Abuse & Neglect: The International Journal, Child Maltreatment,* and *The Journal of the Professional Society on the Abuse of Children.* She serves as a member of the Institutional Review Board at Caliber, an ICF International company in Fairfax, Virginia, and she is a member of PRIM&R (Public Responsibility in Medicine and Research)/ARENA (Applied Research Ethics National Association), the professional association for human research protection program practitioners.

ABOUT THE CONTRIBUTORS

Jill Antonishak, Ph.D., Department of Psychology, The University of Virginia, Post Office Box 400400, Charlottesville, VA 22904. Dr. Antonishak is a researcher in the Department of Psychology at The University of Virginia. She received her undergraduate degree from Goucher College and her doctorate from The University of Virginia. Her research focuses on adolescent risk taking and problem behavior, with an emphasis on peer relations. Other research interests include the application of developmental psychology to law and public policy, especially juvenile justice and media issues.

Marla R. Brassard, Ph.D., Associate Professor of Psychology and Education, Programs in School Psychology, Teachers College, Columbia University, TC Box 63, New York, NY 10027. Dr. Brassard obtained her doctorate in school psychology from Columbia University. Her research focuses on the mental injuries and behavioral problems that result from parental psychological maltreatment and the contextual factors that moderate the effects of maltreatment, particularly the role of schools, teachers and peer relationships. She has co-edited/authored two books on this topic, *Psychological Maltreatment of Children and Youth* (1987, with Stuart Hart & Robert Germain, Pergamon Press) and *Psychological Maltreatment of Children* (2001, with Nelson Bingelli & Stuart Hart, Sage Publications), and many articles, chapters, special issues of journals, and pamphlets for parents and educators. Her co-authored book, *Preschool Assessment: Principles and Practices* (with Ann Boehm, Guilford Press), is due out in 2006. Since 1995, Dr. Brassard has been a consultant to the National Board of Medical Examiners and the New York State Bar Examiners on applicant requests for accommodations on their exams for learning disabilities.

Rosemary Chalk, B.A., Director, Board on Children, Youth, and Families, The National Academies, 500 Fifth Street, NW, Washington, DC 20016. Ms. Chalk received her bachelor's degree in foreign affairs at the University of Cincinnati and completed several years of graduate study in science and public policy at The George Washington University. She has worked with the National Research Council and the Institute of Medicine as a study director since 1987, where she has been an editor or senior contributor to reports on child abuse and neglect, family violence, youth development, the financing of vaccines and public health, and research ethics. Ms. Chalk is the editor of the collection of readings titled *Sci-*

ence, Technology, and Society, published in 1988 by the American Association for the Advancement of Science. She is a former Exxon Research Fellow at the Science, Technology, and Society Program at the Massachusetts Institute of Technology.

David S. DeGarmo de Martinez, Ph.D., Research Scientist, Oregon Social Learning Center, 10 Shelton McMurphey Boulevard, Eugene, OR 97401. Dr. DeGarmo received his doctorate at The University of Akron in family sociology and subsequently served as a postdoctoral fellow of the National Institute of Mental Health Family Research Consortium focusing on risk and resilience. Dr. DeGarmo's work focuses on family interaction and family adjustment to stressful events and socially disadvantaged environments and their impacts on children's developmental outcomes. He is currently working on a 4-year study focusing on social support processes for divorced fathers and adjustment of their children funded by the National Institute of Child Health and Human Development (NICHD). Dr. DeGarmo serves as a reviewer for the NICHD Population Sciences Subcommittee and is a member of the American Sociological Association, the National Council on Family Relations, and the Society for Prevention Research.

Kera L. Donovan, Ed.M., PSI: Partners for Success & Innovation, Post Office Box 468, Twinsburg, OH 44087. Mrs. Donovan is a school psychologist assistant working for a charter high school that serves at-risk youth and an advanced doctoral student in the school psychology program at Teachers College Columbia University. Her research interests include the role of youths' perceptions of parental psychological maltreatment in predicting social and mental heath functioning during middle childhood/adolescence and the harmfulness of psychological maltreatment at differing levels of severity.

Howard Dubowitz, M.D., M.S., Professor, University of Maryland School of Medicine, 520 W. Lombard Street, Baltimore, MD 21201. Dr. Dubowitz is a Professor of Pediatrics and Co-director of the Center for Families at the University of Maryland, Baltimore. He is on the Executive Council of the International Society for the Prevention of Child Abuse and Neglect. He served two terms on the Board of the American Professional Society on the Abuse of Children and has chaired the Committee on Child Maltreatment, American Academy of Pediatrics, Maryland Chapter. Dr. Dubowitz is a clinician, researcher, and educator, and he is active in the policy arena. He edited *Neglected Children: Research, Practice and Policy* and co-edited the *Handbook for Child Protection Practice*, both published by Sage Publications.

Diana J. English, Ph.D., Child Welfare League of America, 440 First Street, NW, Third Floor, Washington, DC 20001. Dr. English is the Director of Research and Evaluation for the Child Welfare League of America, a public child welfare research center conducting research on the identification of child abuse and neglect, decision-making in child protective services, effective interventions for child maltreatment victims, foster care services, independent living and adoption. For the past 17 years Dr. English has been the Office Chief of Research, Children's Administration, Washington State Department of Social and Health Services. Dr. English completed her doctorate in social welfare in 1985 at The University of Washington. Since the mid-1990s she has participated in numerous national and state child welfare commissions and committees, and she has published numerous articles and reports on child welfare issues.

Jeffrey J. Haugaard, Ph.D., Associate Professor, Department of Human Development, Cornell University, Martha Van Rensselaer Hall, Ithaca, NY 14853. After receiving his bachelor's degree, Professor Haugaard worked for 10 years at a boarding school in California, where he was also a foster parent for 6 years. He returned to graduate school in 1984 and received his doctorate in clinical psychology from The University of Virginia in 1990. He has served on several national committees focused on child maltreatment and was the founding president of the section on Child Maltreatment of the American Psychological Association. He has also served on the Council of Representatives of the American Psychological Association. Professor Haugaard has served on the editorial boards of three journals, was an Associate Editor of *Child Maltreatment* and *Law and Human Behavior,* and was the editor of special issues of *Law and Human Behavior* and the *American Psychologist.* He has published four books and many articles and book chapters and is in the midst of completing a textbook on child psychopathology. He has won many awards for teaching and advising during his tenure at Cornell.

Deanna Heckenberg, J.D., Department of Psychology, The University of Iowa, Iowa City, IA 52242. Ms. Heckenberg received a bachelor of arts degree in psychology and sociology, with distinction and honors in psychology, from The University of Iowa. Following graduation, Mrs. Heckenberg worked full time as a research assistant on a multisite project investigating the relation between childhood aggression and neglectful parenting. Ms. Heckenberg received her law degree from The University of Iowa College of Law. During law school she interned for Iowa Legal Aid and the Cook County (Illinois) Office of the Public Guardian, where her work focused on family law cases and representing abused and neglected minors in court. In addition, in 2005 she was a Bergstrom Fellow and participated in child welfare law training at The University of Michigan College of Law.

Maryfrances R. Porter, Ph.D., Department of Psychiatry, The University of Virginia, Charlottesville, VA 22904. Dr. Porter is a postdoctoral resident at The University of Virginia School of Medicine. She received a bachelor of arts from

Emory University in 1996 and her doctorate in clinical psychology from The University of Virginia in 2005. Her research interests include the role of attachment organization in adolescent development and peer relationships, as well as the integration of developmental psychology in child/family policy and program evaluation.

Sharon G. Portwood, J.D., Ph.D., Executive Director, Institute for Social Capital; Professor of Health Behavior and Administration, University of North Carolina at Charlotte, 9201 University City Boulevard, Charlotte, NC 28223. Dr. Portwood received her juris doctor from the University of Texas School of Law in 1985 and, after more than 10 years as a practicing trial attorney, received her doctorate in psychology from The University of Virginia in 1996. Her research reflects an integration of her training and practice in law, community psychology, and developmental psychology applied to a broad spectrum of issues involving social policy, particularly as it affects children, youth, and families at the systems level. Dr. Portwood has conducted training sessions on program evaluation and research at the invitation of the U.S. Department of Health and Human Services, the American Bar Association, the Missouri Department of Mental Health, and the American Professional Society on the Abuse of Children. From 2001 to 2005, she served as Program Director for the Kansas City Metro Child Traumatic Stress Program, part of the National Child Traumatic Stress Network. Dr. Portwood currently is President of the American Psychological Association's Section on Child Maltreatment.

John B. Reid, Ph.D., Senior Research Scientist, Oregon Social Learning Center, 160 E. 4th Avenue, Eugene, OR 97401. Dr. Reid's career has focused on understanding, treating, and preventing youth antisocial and delinquent behavior. Dr. Reid is a founder and immediate past Executive Director of the Oregon Social Learning Center, a nonprofit research center that was formed in 1975 to conduct research on the development of aggression, delinquency, and violent behavior. He is the director of the Oregon Prevention Research Center, founded in 1990, and the Pathways Home-Reducing Risk in the Child Welfare System Center, founded in 2003. Since receiving his doctoral degree from the University of Oregon in 1967, Dr. Reid has dedicated his career to the investigation of factors promoting and preventing antisocial behavior, the development of observation methodologies, and the design of randomized intervention trials. His prevention program, Linking the Interests of Families and Teachers, has received national recognition as a Promising Program for Safe and Drug Free Schools. Dr. Reid has served on private, state, and federal task forces to study the most effective interventions for delinquency and antisocial behavior. Most recently, he has served on the National Academy of Sciences Committee on the Representation of Minority Children in Special Education and on the Planning Board and Peer Review section of the Surgeon General's Report on Youth Violence and was a contributing expert to the National Institute of Mental Health report, *Taking Stock of Risk Factors for Child/Youth Externalizing Behavior Problems.*

N. Dickon Reppucci, Ph.D., Professor, Department of Psychology, The University of Virginia, Post Office Box 400400, Charlottesville, VA 22904. Dr. Reppucci has been Professor of Psychology at The University of Virginia since 1976. He received his doctorate from Harvard University in 1968 and was Assistant and Associate Professor at Yale University from 1968 to 1976. He is author, co-author, or editor of more than 135 books, chapters, and articles. His major research interests include children; families; the law, especially juvenile justice and adolescent development; and the prevention of child abuse and neglect.

Desmond K. Runyan, M.D., Dr.Ph., Professor, University of North Carolina School of Medicine, Department of Social Medicine, CB #7240, Chapel Hill, NC 27599. Dr. Runyan is the chair of the Department of Social Medicine and professor of Social Medicine, Pediatrics, and Epidemiology at the University of North Carolina at Chapel Hill. Dr. Runyan joined the faculty at the University of North Carolina (UNC) in 1981 after completing medical school and a residency in pediatrics at the University of Minnesota and both the Dr.Ph. degree and the Robert Wood Johnson Clinical Scholars Program at the University of North Carolina. In 1996, he co-founded the Center for Child and Family Health–North Carolina, a joint UNC, Duke University, and North Carolina Central University center for child abuse evaluation, treatment, and research. Dr. Runyan has conducted research into myriad aspects of maltreatment, including physical abuse and neglect, sexual abuse, Munchausen Syndrome by Proxy, Shaken Baby Syndrome, and the impact of social capital. He currently directs a multisite longitudinal study of the consequences of child abuse that is in its 15th year and is involved in collaborative research on child abuse in five developing countries. Dr. Runyan serves on the NGO Advisory Panel for the Secretary-General's International Study of Children and Violence as a representative of the International Society for the Prevention of Child Abuse and Neglect and on the Biobehavioral and Behavioral Sciences Review Group of the National Institute of Child Health and Human Development.

Cassandra Simmel, M.S.W., Ph.D., Assistant Professor, School of Social Work, Rutgers University, 502 George Street, Room 206, New Brunswick, NJ 08901. Dr. Simmels's research interests include child maltreatment, child welfare services, child and youth mental health, and research ethics. She has published several articles and chapters on these topics.

Kyle L. Snow, Ph.D., Program Director, Early Childhood Education, Research Triangle Institute (RTI) International, 6110 Executive Blvd., Suite 902, Rockville, MD 20852. Dr. Kyle Snow is Program Director for Early Childhood Education at RTI International. In this position he serves as Principal Investigator for the Early Childhood Longitudinal Study–Birth Cohort (ECLS-B), a prospective longitudinal study following a nationally representative cohort of children from birth to kindergarten entrance. Dr. Snow was previously the Director of the National Institute of Child Health and Human Development (NICHD) Program in Early Learning and School Readiness, where he had responsibilities for developing initiatives to support research on the processes and contexts of early learning. Prior to joining NICHD, Dr. Snow was a research analyst in the education studies division at Westat, a contract research firm in Rockville, Maryland. Dr. Snow has also held a faculty appointment at Wilkes University in Pennsylvania, and taught courses at Cornell University, American University, and Seton Hall University. Dr. Snow holds a bachelor of arts in psychology from Castleton State College in Vermont, and a master of arts and doctorate in developmental psychology from Cornell University. He is co-editor with Robert C. Pianta and Martha J. Cox of the forthcoming *School Readiness and the Transition to Kindergarten in the Era of Accountability* (Paul H. Brookes Publishing Co.).

David Watson, Ph.D., Department of Psychology, The University of Iowa, 11 Seashore Hall, Iowa City, IA 52242. Dr. Watson is the F. Wendell Miller Professor of Psychology at The University of Iowa. Dr. Watson received his doctorate in personality research and assessment from the University of Minnesota, working under the supervision of his graduate advisor, Auke Tellegen. Prior to joining the faculty of The University of Iowa in 1993, Dr. Watson worked for 9 years at Southern Methodist University in Dallas, Texas. He has conducted a wide range of research studies in the areas of personality, mood and temperament, and psychopathology. Dr. Watson has published a number of papers on measurement, scale construction, and factor analysis, and he has created a number of popular assessment instruments, including measures of mood and trait affectivity, basic dimensions of temperament, obsessive-compulsive symptoms, specific and social phobia, dissociative tendencies, hypochondriasis, and mood and anxiety symptoms. He currently is the principal investigator on a 5-year study funded by the National Institute of Mental Health that has led to the creation of a new set of factor-analytically derived symptom measures, the Iowa Depression and Anxiety Scales. Dr. Watson has served on a number of editorial boards and currently is the Editor-in-Chief of the *Journal of Abnormal Psychology*.

Mary Bruce Webb, Ph.D., Director of the Division of Child and Family Development, Office of Planning, Research and Evaluation, Administration for Children and Families, U.S. Department of Health and Human Services (DHHS), 370 L'Enfant Promenade, Washington, DC 20447. Dr. Webb currently directs the Division of Child and Family Development in the Office of Planning, Research and Evaluation, Administration for Children and Families at DHHS. Her research interests are in early childhood development, child maltreatment, and services for high-risk children and families.

Ying-Ying T. Yuan, Ph.D., Senior Vice President and Director of National Programs of Walter R. McDonald & Associates, Inc., 12000 Twinbrook Parkway, Suite 310, Rockville, MD 20852. Dr. Yuan received her doctoral degree from the Department of Social Relations, Harvard University. Dr. Yuan is the Technical Team Director of the National Child Abuse and Neglect Data System, which collects national statistics on child maltreatment from all state public child welfare agencies. In this role she leads the technical assistance efforts to help states use their automated information systems to report on child abuse and neglect. She is also the Principal Investigator of the Initiative Level Evaluation of SPARK, an early education systems reform initiative of the W.K. Kellogg Foundation. She recently completed the National Study of Child Protective Services Systems and Reform Efforts for the U.S. Department of Health and Human Services. Her primary area of interest is in improving outcomes for children, with particular attention to definitional, measurement, and evaluation issues.

FOREWORD

Although concern with the mistreatment of children goes back centuries (Bakan, 1971; Ross, 1980) modern interest in the phenomenon dates from Kempe et al.'s famous "The Battered Child Syndrome" (Kempe, Silverman, Steele, Droege-mueller & Silver, 1962). I first became involved with child abuse as a scientific and social policy issue in the early 1970s when I was Chief of the Children's Bureau in the United States. The bureau sponsored a conference at which Henry Kempe proposed a program of mandatory home visiting as a preventative to child maltreatment, ignoring the conflict between the child's right not to be victimized and the family's right to privacy. The bureau's interest culminated in my working closely with Senator Walter Mondale and Congressman John Brademas in drafting the first national legislation dealing with child abuse in 1974, the legislation that authorized the Center for Child Abuse and Neglect (placed in the Children's Bureau) and the subsequent national conferences dealing with child maltreatment.

This book makes available to both scholars and policy makers the proceedings of two major conferences sponsored by a number of federal agencies. The circumscribed task covered by the chapters in this volume deals with the intellectually demanding effort involved in defining, classifying and measuring the various forms of child maltreatment. Given the centrality of definition and classification (or taxonomy) to any scientific discipline, there is no more important or challenging task. The authors make no pretense that they are presenting us with the long-awaited final solution to the definitional and classificatory dilemma that has confronted the field since its modern inception in the 1960s. Instead these leading workers provide us with a methodologically and theoretically sophisticated status report on current views and recommended solutions to the dilemma of definition and classification. The authors thus view this volume as providing the field a solid base from which scholars can safely venture forth to the next (if not final) stage in the effort to define and categorize child maltreatment. In this vein the introductory chapter presents an excellent history of the efforts prior to this book that attempted to resolve the definition and classification issue. Upon reading through the well-organized chapters and the final chapter, in which conclusions and future research directions are presented, I concluded that the authors had accomplished their circumscribed goal in an extremely impressive fashion.

The definition issue, addressed in this important book, has remained unresolved for far too long. The need for the field to reach a consensus on the definition of child abuse was emphasized in my keynote address to the First National Conference on Child Abuse and Neglect (Zigler, 1976). I emphasized the definitional dilemma and the toll it takes in advancing our understanding of child abuse again in a keynote address at another conference a few years later (Zigler, 1980).

Our inability as a field to reach a clear consensus of the definition of abuse may well be a factor in the failure of our society to demonstrably reduce the incidence of child abuse. In 1974 when the first federal child abuse act was passed, the best estimate of reported cases of abuse and neglect was approximately 750,000. In recent years, reported cases were approximately 3 million (with about 1 million confirmed). Many insist this increase reflects an increase in reporting rather than an increase in true incidence. Antithetically some consensus has been reached that as stress on families increases, so does abuse. There is little question that as a result of poverty, welfare reform, and variegated lacunae in our national system of family supports, many families are experiencing distress, which in turn increases abuse in these families. Scholars in the field have now argued for years about whether we should adopt a narrow definition, confining abuse to cases involving severe physical abuse and sexual abuse, or a broad definition in which any act that compromises the child's optimal development constitutes abuse (Zigler, 1980). Indeed the field is not fully clear as to the exact point at which normative and accepted behavior (e.g., corporal punishment) becomes child abuse. In regard to the critical measurement issue, this volume makes clear that such oft-used categories as neglect and emotional maltreatment (unlike physical and sexual abuse) are lacking in acceptable levels of reliability and validity. Nevertheless as the years go by the field keeps adding types of maltreatment. As noted in this book we now have "educational neglect" and "medical neglect."

It would be well for the field to remember that a legal authority in championing parents' rights stated that "child neglect, as distinguished from actual physical abuse, is one of the most subjective and amorphous concepts known to law" (Uviller, 1980, p. 151). Compounding the difficulty of this issue is the intricate relation between child neglect and poverty and the well-known fact that governmental intrusion into the home is much more likely for low socioeconomic status families as compared with more affluent families. Workers in this area today should be aware of views of earlier leading thinkers regarding this broad versus narrow definition issue. Nick Hobbs, a past president of the American Psychological Association (APA), argued convincingly that as a label invariably produces some negative effect, no child (and by extension, no family) should be labeled unless the label results in receiving enough helpful services to offset the negative consequences of the label itself. This view inheres in the position advanced by Al Solnit, one of the world's great child psychiatrists and an authority on the legal rights of both children and families. In his seminal chapter, "Too Much Reporting, Too Little Service" (1980), Solnit argued the state should intrude on the family only in cases of physical or sexual abuse and such intrusions should invariably be accompanied with a panoply of worthwhile services. Citing the danger of false positives, another past president of the APA, George Albee (1980) echoed Solnit's view that the term *abuse* be defined narrowly.

I was chair of the conference where the Solnit and Albee papers were delivered. The Solnit remarks resulted in an odd reaction from social workers working primarily in state government agencies having the responsibility for enforcing state child abuse laws. A delegation from this group insisted on meeting with me to discuss the Solnit paper. At this meeting they made clear their preference that neglect be included in any definition of maltreatment. They also requested that the Solnit paper not be included in the proceedings of the conference (Gerbner, Ross, & Zigler, 1980). It should be remembered that government agencies are allocated resources commensurate with the magnitude of the problem with which they are dealing. Thus there is some incentive for children's protective services to generate more and more cases without great concern about the services needed by each case.

As a scholar who has worked at the intersect of our field's knowledge base and social policy, I was particularly pleased by the inclusion in this book of a section on social policy that explicitly deals with contextual issues and how a scientific definition and categorization system must be made useful to child protective service workers, prosecutors and policy makers. In a cogent analysis Porter, Antonishak, and Reppucci present the requirements necessary to produce such synergism between science and social action a reality. Chapter 12 points out how different definitions of maltreatment are employed for different purposes. Whereas an early group of scholars endorsed multiple definitions to be employed for different purposes (Ross & Zigler, 1980), Feerick and Snow in their concluding chapter note the problems inherent in different definitions of the same phenomenon. If such unanimity is to be achieved, we should follow Bevan's (1980) advice (also cited in Chapter 12) and build much stronger bridges to the social policy community. For a comprehensive discussion of this issue, see Cicchetti and Toth (1993).

In summary we have here a comprehensive, must-read volume prepared by leading scholars explicating the current status of the child maltreatment field's effort to define and categorize phenomena of major importance both to our science and society at large.

Edward Zigler, Ph.D.
The Edward Zigler Center in Child
Development and Social Policy, Yale University

REFERENCES

Albee, G. (1980). Primary prevention and social problems. In G. Gerbner, C. Ross, & E. Zigler (Eds.), *Child abuse: An agenda for action.* New York: Oxford University Press.

Bakan, D. (1971). *Slaughter of the innocents.* San Francisco: Jossey-Bass.

Bevan, W. (1980). On getting in bed with a lion. *American Psychologist, 35*, 779–789.

Cicchetti, D., & Toth, S.L. (Eds.). (1993). *Child abuse, child development and social policy: Advances in applied developmental psychology* (Vol. 8). Norwood, NJ: Ablex Publishing Corporation.

Gerbner, G., Ross, C., & Zigler, E. (Eds.). (1980). *Child abuse: An agenda for action.* New York: Oxford University Press.

Kempe, C.H., Silverman, F.N., Steele, B.F., Droegemueller, W., & Silver, H.K. (1962). The battered child syndrome. *Journal of the American Medical Association, 181,* 17–24.

Ross, C. (1980). The lessons of the past: Defining and controlling child abuse in the United States. In G. Gerbner, C. Ross, & E. Zigler (Eds.), *Child abuse: An agenda for action.* New York: Oxford University Press.

Ross, C., & Zigler, E. (1980). An agenda for action. In G. Gerbner, C. Ross, & E. Zigler (Eds.), *Child abuse: An agenda for action.* New York: Oxford University Press.

Solnit, A. (1980). Too much reporting, too little service. In G. Gerbner, C. Ross, & E. Ziglcr (Eds.), *Child abuse: An agenda for action.* New York: Oxford University Press.

Uviller, R. (1980). Save them from their saviors: The constitutional rights of the family. In G. Gerbner, C. Ross, & E. Zigler (Eds.), *Child abuse: An agenda for action.* New York: Oxford University Press.

Zigler, E. (1976). [Keynote address to the First National Conference on Child Abuse and Neglect.] Proceedings reported by the U.S. Department of Health, Education and Welfare.

Zigler, E. (1980). Controlling child abuse: Do we have the knowledge and/or the will? In G. Gerbner, C. Ross, & E. Zigler (Eds.), *Child abuse: An agenda for action.* New York: Oxford University Press.

FOREWORD

The Children's Bureau in the Administration on Children, Youth and Families (ACYF) in the Administration for Children and Families (ACF) in the U.S. Department of Health and Human Services (DHHS) is the oldest federal agency for children. Our programs assist states in the delivery of child welfare services to protect children and strengthen families. The agency provides grants to states, tribes, and communities to operate a range of child welfare services, and it makes major investments in staff training, technology, and innovative programs on a foundation of knowledge developed through funded research, service demonstration, and program evaluation grants. Other federal agencies also support work on child maltreatment, including other agencies of DHHS, the U.S. Department of Defense, the U.S. Department of Justice, and the U.S. Department of Education.

There is a history of interagency collaboration on definitions in the child maltreatment field, and the impetus for this volume springs from one particular collaboration within the DHHS. Beginning in 1994, members of the Research Subcommittee of the Federal Interagency Task Force on Child Abuse and Neglect worked on developing a system of core variables that could be used by researchers to describe children's maltreatment experiences. This work was prompted by a 1993 report of the National Research Council (NRC), *Understanding Child Abuse and Neglect,* which concluded that "research definitions of child maltreatment are inconsistent, and the breadth and quality of instrumentation for child maltreatment studies are seriously incomplete"(p. 31). The report stated, "Improved definitions and instrumentation will facilitate the development of small and large scale epidemiological investigations" (p. 31). In response to this conclusion, Dr. Kathleen Sternberg from the National Institute of Child Health and Human Development (NICHD) emerged as the key developer of the instrument which came to be known as The Child Maltreatment Log (see Sternberg et al., 2005).

In 1997, the National Institutes of Health (NIH) established a Working Group on Child Neglect in response to a directive by both the House and Senate Committees on Appropriations, which requested that NIH report on NIH efforts, accomplishments, and future plans for research on child abuse and neglect. The group, chaired at the time by Peter S. Jensen, M.D., issued a report in 1997 (DHHS, 1997), based on both an analysis of the NIH portfolio as well as on the 1993 NRC report, *Understanding Child Abuse and Neglect*; the 1998 Institute of Medicine report, *Violence in Families: Assessing Prevention and Treatment Programs* (NRC, 1998); recommendations from the October 1997 National Institute of

Justice Child Abuse and Neglect Interventions Strategic Planning Meeting; and a June 1993 National Center for Child Abuse and Neglect–sponsored symposium on chronic neglect. Dr. Jensen took a pragmatic approach, creating a grid of the 17 NRC recommendations along the vertical axis and federal agencies and funding sources along the horizontal, populating the cells with "current" or ongoing funding activities and revealing, in the process, the lack of progress and specific gaps. This made targeting future activities relatively straightforward, though no less challenging.

Three specific activities were designed to begin filling in those gaps— competition for "K awards" (career development/mentorship grants), creation of a research portfolio centered around a consortium of grantees exploring child neglect (now known as the Federal Child Neglect Research Consortium), and a series of meetings on research definitions of child abuse and neglect. The NIH Child Abuse and Neglect Working Group (CANWG), an offspring of the original National Institutes of Health Working Group on Child Neglect and also considered the "reconstituted" research arm of the Federal Interagency Work Group on Child Abuse and Neglect, took the leadership role for each of these activities.

During the years following Dr. Jensen's analysis of the NIH research portfolio, the CANWG, subsequently under the direction of Cheryl Boyce, Ph.D., of the National Institute of Mental Health, and Margaret M. Feerick, Ph.D., of the NICHD, met monthly to coordinate federal research efforts in child abuse and neglect. While the Children's Bureau Office on Child Abuse and Neglect and NIH shouldered the majority of these efforts, many other agencies participated, including the U.S. Department of Justice (National Institute of Justice and the Office of Juvenile Justice and Delinquency Prevention), and the U.S. Department of Education. Their joint activities have included clarifying institute/ agency responsibilities in areas of overlap, identifying research needs, and planning future activities. The CANWG also sponsored a number of workshops to stimulate child abuse and neglect research. The workshops focused on developing new investigators in the area of child abuse and neglect research, research-based assessments of physical injuries, targeted announcements of funding available for research, and optimal approaches to the definition and measurement of child abuse and neglect.

While no comprehensive review of the responses to the NRC report on child abuse has yet been undertaken, the increase in attention to and work on maltreatment is good evidence of the impact alone. This new book sits squarely in the foundational work and guidance provided by the NRC report, the CANWG, and the continuing interest of the federally funded research community. The problem of inadequate and competing definitions continues to hamper our ability to identify, treat, and prevent child maltreatment. Existing definitions, or classifications, are not standardized and have, in fact, developed in three distinct use-targeted realms. Definitions exist based on statute and regulation and are usually state specific. Agencies serving children and families develop their own classification systems, often based on needs and risk assessments, designed primarily for case management and service planning. Researchers, pursuing different goals, have created assessment and measurement instruments to develop both a priori and empirical definitions and classifications. Many of us believe that developing generalizable knowledge, advancing science, and promoting evidence-influenced practice improvements and policy that speak to actual child-centered, family- and community-based needs require a more coordinated approach to creating definitions and classifications. This volume represents the fine work of many talented thinkers as it explores the background and future for taking those next steps. The efforts of the authors of the chapters of this book and your interest, now and in the future, are greatly appreciated.

Catherine Nolan, M.S.W., ACSW
Director, Office on Child Abuse and Neglect
Administration on Children, Youth and Families
Administration for Children and Families
U.S. Department of Health and Human Services

REFERENCES

National Research Council. (1993). *Understanding child abuse and neglect*. Washington, DC: National Academies Press.

National Research Council. (1998). *Violence in families: Assessing prevention and treatment programs*. Washington, DC: National Academies Press.

Sternberg, K.J., Knutson, J.F., Lamb, M.E., Baradaran, L.P., Nolan, C., & Flanzer, S. (2004). The Child Maltreatment Log: A PC-based program for describing research samples. *Child Maltreatment*, 9, 30–48.

U.S. Department of Health and Human Services, National Institutes of Health. (1997). *NIH research on child abuse and neglect: Current status and future plans*. Retrieved from http:// www.nimh.gov/canwg/nihabuse.cfm

PREFACE

Over the past few decades, the field of child abuse and neglect has grown considerably, as child maltreatment has come to be recognized as one of the most pressing social problems facing children today. Official statistics indicate that approximately 3 million children are reported to child protective services agencies for abuse or neglect each year (U.S. Department of Health and Human Services, 2005), whereas the National Incidence Study (NIS-3), a congressionally mandated study designed to estimate the occurrence of child abuse in the population, suggests that at least 40 children per 1,000 are harmed or endangered by abuse and neglect annually (Sedlak & Broadhurst, 1996). At the same time, child abuse and neglect remains one of the least understood threats to child health and development today. Despite several decades of research on this topic, little consensus exists about how best to prevent this problem, intervene with maltreated children and their families, and ameliorate the long-term harmful consequences of maltreatment on child health and development. To a large extent, this is due to the fact that despite the enormity of the problem, child maltreatment has received less funding, less concerted federal research effort, and less commitment on the part of funding agencies than other significant risks to children today (see, e.g., Putnam, 2001; Theodore & Runyan, 1999; Thompson & Wilcox, 1995). For example, although the incidence rate of child abuse and neglect in the United States is approximately 10 times as high (40 children per 1,000 children per year) as the incidence rate for all forms of cancer in the population (3.9 individuals per 1,000 individuals per year), the 2001 budget for the National Cancer Institute was $3.74 billion, whereas funding for the Child Abuse and Prevention Treatment Act (CAPTA) state grants, CAPTA discretionary grants, and CAPTA Community Based Grants combined was only $72 million (Child Welfare League of America, 2001). This state of the field, however, is also due to the fact that much of the research on child abuse and neglect has been plagued by a number of methodological problems that seriously undermine scientific, political, and public confidence in the findings and their application. These include inconsistent definitions of abuse and neglect; inadequate measurement approaches and instruments; lack of theory-based and integrative models of maltreatment; and complex legal, public policy, and ethical constraints on investigations.

Although in recent years, there have been several advances in many of these areas (see, e.g., Cicchetti & Manly, 2001), the editors and authors of this volume believe that if we are to ultimately understand child abuse and neglect from a scientific perspective, the first and most important step is that the field must undertake a systematic effort to establish clear and precise valid and reliable definitions of the problem and a theoretically based classification system that is open to empirical scrutiny. Such a classification system not only must provide a valid framework for researchers and clinicians to identify different types of abuse and neglect, but also it must be robust enough to recognize the distinctions and relations among different types of abuse and neglect and among abuse and neglect and other threats to child health and well-being. These are not easy goals to accomplish, as attested to by the literature on the history and current status of research on child abuse and neglect, much of which is reviewed in this volume. Nevertheless, the field must not be limited or constrained by the past, and future efforts to develop new conceptualizations that provide clear and empirically supported descriptions and characterizations of abuse and neglect should not be deterred. Rather, they should be based on a thorough understanding of what we currently know, the best available methods, and a careful analysis of contemporary approaches to defining and classifying abusive and neglectful experiences.

In an attempt to address these issues, the National Institutes of Health Child Abuse and Neglect Working Group and the Children's Bureau of the Administration on Children, Youth and Families convened two meetings designed to address key challenges in defining and classifying child abuse and neglect, measuring key constructs associated with child maltreatment, and developing a research agenda that could move the field of child abuse and neglect forward. The first of these meetings was held in December 1999, in Bethesda, Maryland. The senior scholars who were invited to this conference were charged with three major goals: 1) to identify the current classification and definitional strategies that have been adopted and are in use, 2) to determine the strengths and weaknesses within current classification and definitional practices that support or impede research and the translation of research to practice, and 3) to develop an action plan that identifies strategic goals to guide a research initiative resulting in a coherent classification system and definition for child abuse and neglect.

In attempting to accomplish these goals, the workshop participants noted that developing a precise definition and classification system for research in child abuse and neglect would require an understanding of the fundamental characteristics of classification systems as well as of the different assumptions underlying them, key theories and assumptions underlying different definitional approaches, and social and political factors that influence and/or constrain current definitional approaches. They also noted that to develop a robust classification and definition system for child abuse and neglect would require a significant and concerted federal effort to advance the field forward, including the development of a working group that could help formulate specific goals in support of the initiative, a review of current and historical definitional approaches used in child abuse and neglect research, and the development of a workshop/conference focused on measurement issues in child abuse and neglect.

A second workshop, focused broadly on measurement issues in child abuse and neglect, was held in September 2000 in Bethesda, Maryland, to expand and build upon the recommendations from the first workshop. The purpose of the second workshop was to develop a strategic plan for the development of an internally and externally valid classification system and operational definitions of child abuse and neglect. The goals of the workshop were to 1) identify adequate and effective measurement strategies and instruments for assessing child maltreatment and 2) propose measurement standards and procedures to guide research and practice. The broader goal of the meeting was to develop recommendations for how child maltreatment research should be conducted to ensure that future studies of child maltreatment can be integrated and help inform clinical practice, public policy, service delivery, and the training of both researchers and clinicians. In addressing these goals, participants noted that the field could benefit from a critical review and analysis of existing definition and classification approaches, current sampling and measurement models and tools, and relevant theoretical and analytic approaches. They also noted the need for a concerted federal research program to improve future child abuse and neglect research.

This book and the workshops on which it is based reflect our initial attempts to address some of these issues and to suggest new directions for research that are based on an analysis of the current state of the field. In developing this volume, it is our goal to provide professionals and students interested in child abuse and neglect with a state-of-the-art review of critical issues in the definition and classification of child abuse and neglect; a consideration of current measurement approaches; and an identification of the significant social and public policy issues that are related to research in the area. The contents of the book are based on the premise that scientific and clinical advances in the field of child abuse and neglect must be based on an understanding of the key conditions that must be in place if we are to define and classify child abuse and neglect in a reliable and valid manner, develop theories and models that lend themselves to empirical testing, and develop effective and empirically supported interventions for maltreated children within the varied social contexts in which they live.

The book is organized in four sections. The chapters in Section I are concerned with addressing critical issues and needs in defining and classifying child abuse and neglect for research purposes. The chapters in this section are focused on critically examining the history of classification and definition efforts in child abuse and neglect and determining the essential components necessary for the development of classification frameworks that can aid in the recognition of distinctions and relations among different types of abuse and neglect experiences and other childhood risks. In addition, the content in this section provides a comparison and contrast between classification methodologies for practitioners, policy makers, and researchers, providing a basis for the work discussed in other sections in this volume. The chapters in Section II review and appraise existing theory and definitions relevant to different abusive and neglectful experiences, providing specific suggestions for future empirical work and theory development. The focus of the chapters in this section is on the limitations and strengths of current definitions and classification approaches and the conditions necessary for the development of more valid and reliable definitions and measurement approaches in the field. In Section III, the authors have provided an overview and analysis of existing measurement tools used in research. While these chapters are not meant to be exhaustive, they provide an introduction to key issues and considerations in measuring child abuse and neglect and the limitations of specific approaches. Taken together, the chapters in this section argue for multi-method, multi-source approaches and research frameworks that can help overcome the limitations of any one measurement approach. Finally, the chapters in Section IV address how prevailing social and policy trends and practices influence both research and practice in child abuse and neglect and how they can advance or impede scientific progress in this area. In this regard, it is our contention that scientists and practitioners involved with work related to maltreated children must appreciate how contextual forces and factors may not only influence research on child abuse and neglect but how this work may be used and interpreted in developing more scientifically informed public policy. If the social contexts and public policy influences are ignored by researchers, the science in this area is likely to have little practical value.

It should be noted that although the structure of this volume would seem to indicate that the editors are embracing the current classification system that distinguishes among physical abuse, sexual abuse, neglect, and psychological or emotional abuse, we are merely treating that "system" as a convenient heuristic reflecting current research methodologies. We make no assumptions as to whether future empirical work will blur or eliminate those distinctions, or whether new classifications will emerge. To ignore the current state of the field and blur those distinctions at the present time would yield an unwieldy and, perhaps, redundant review of the literature. To advance an alternative approach in the absence of an empirical base would certainly not advance the field. Thus, we felt obliged to continue to link the work to the current framework, recognizing that it might not stand the test of time.

This book is intended for a wide range of audiences that include researchers, students, practitioners, administrators, and policy makers. It is the goal of this book to provide a starting point for future classification and definition efforts in child abuse and neglect research that reflect a critical understanding of the factors necessary for useful, valid, reliable, theoretically derived, and empirically sound classification approaches. As such, this book is intended to stimulate future discussion, analysis, and empirical work in the area.

REFERENCES

Child Welfare League of America. (2001, August 2). *Child Protection*. Testimony submitted to the House Subcommittee on Select Education of the Committee on Education and the Workforce for the hearing on CAPTA: Successes and Failures at Preventing Child Abuse. Retrieved August 12, 2005, from the Child Welfare League of America Web site, http://www.cwla.org/advocacy/childprot080201.htm

Cicchetti, D., & Manly, J.T. (Eds.). (2001). Operationalizing child maltreatment: Developmental processes and outcomes [Special issue]. *Development and Psychopathology, 13(4)*.

National Research Council. (1993). *Understanding child abuse and neglect*. Washington, DC: National Academies Press.

Prevent Child Abuse America. (2001). *Total estimated cost of child abuse and neglect in the United States: Statistical evidence*. Retrieved August 12, 2005, from http://www.preventchildabuse.org/learn_more/research_docs/cost_analysis.pdf

Putnam, F.W. (2001). Why is it so difficult for the epidemic of child abuse to be taken seriously? In K. Franey, R. Geffner, & R. Falconer (Eds.), *The cost of child maltreatment: Who pays? We all do*. San Diego: Family Violence & Sexual Assault Institute.

Sedlak, A.J., & Broadhurst, D.D. (1996). *Third national incidence study of child abuse and neglect: Final report*. Washington, DC: U.S. Department of Health and Human Services.

Theodore, A.D., & Runyan, D.K. (1999). A medical research agenda for child maltreatment: Negotiating next steps. *Pediatrics, 104(1)*, 168–177.

Thompson, R.A., & Wilcox, B.L. (1995). Child maltreatment research: Federal support and policy issues. *American Psychologist, 50*, 789–793.

U.S. Department of Health and Human Services, Administration for Children and Families. (2005). *Child maltreatment 2003*. Washington, DC: U.S. Government Printing Office. Retrieved from http://www.acf.dhhs.gov/programs/cb/publications/cmreports.htm

ACKNOWLEDGMENTS

We wish to extend our deep appreciation to a number of individuals who contributed significantly to the development and completion of this book. Our sincere thanks go out to Catherine Nolan, Peter Jensen, and Reid Lyon for their continued support of this work and their leadership in the formulation and development of the workshops on which this book is based. We also cannot thank enough all of those who participated in and contributed to the two National Institutes of Health/Children's Bureau workshops held on defining and classifying child abuse and neglect and to this volume. The workshops were actually intense working meetings, where participants were asked to devote several days of their time to analyzing significant issues and needs in child abuse and neglect research. Similarly, we cannot thank enough the authors whose ideas and information appear in the following chapters.

Clearly, the contents of this book would not be available to the public without the dedication and support of the acquisitions, production, and marketing staff at Paul H. Brookes Publishing Co. Without their commitment to this area of science and to this particular area of work, this book would not be a reality.

Finally, we wish to thank our families, colleagues, and friends for their ongoing support through what turned out to be a much longer process than originally expected. We owe them our heartfelt appreciation and gratitude for their encouragement and personal support in the completion of this work.

To the memory of Kathleen Sternberg,
a pioneer and leader
in the area of child maltreatment definitions

I

CLASSIFICATION OF CHILD ABUSE AND NEGLECT

DEFINITION AND CLASSIFICATION play a critical role in creating operationally meaningful and useful accounts of human behavior and experience. Without clear definitions and descriptions of phenomena of interest, attempts to understand and explain particular behaviors and experiences are limited at best, and not replicable and generalizable at worst. Thus, the development of clear, useful, theoretically informed, and empirically grounded definitions and classifications is fundamental to the scientific enterprise. Any attempt to develop a particular area of research first requires a clear description of the phenomena of interest, operational definitions of that phenomena, and reliable and valid measurement approaches.

For a number of reasons discussed in the chapters in Section I, the field of child abuse and neglect could benefit from the appropriate application of classification efforts. For example, it has become increasingly clear that the general category of abuse and neglect represents an extremely diverse population of children who have experienced a wide variety of events, the characteristics and consequences of which most likely fall on a continuous distribution. Unless well-designed studies are developed to classify this diverse group of children into relatively homogeneous subgroups and to distinguish them from persons with other hypothesized risk factors and experiences, research findings will continue to be confounded by other factors associated with unexplained heterogeneity. The classification of abused and neglected children also could provide insight into the measurement of useful dimensions and categories that might lead to more effective treatments and interventions for children who have been maltreated and their families. Moreover, identification of specific patterns of behaviors and/or experiences within longitudinal designs could enhance knowledge of meaningful developmental continuities and their relation to long-term outcomes.

The chapters in this first section are devoted to examining, in depth, the advantages of developing taxonomies and the application of classification methodology to the identification and description of child abuse and neglect. In Chapter 1, Feerick and Snow discuss the background for a classification approach to child abuse and neglect research, providing a brief overview of the state of the field and describing two federally-sponsored workshops focused on issues of definition and classification in child abuse and neglect research. They discuss the goals and summary recommendations from these workshops and present an overview of different classification models discussed at the workshops as a framework for this work. In Chapter 2, Chalk describes the history of the search for consensus in defining child abuse and neglect experiences, describing in detail the major recommendations made by the National Academy of Sciences in 1993. Finally, in Chapter 3, Haugaard presents an overview of the history of definitions of child abuse and neglect, analyzing how social and professional values have influenced the development of both legal and research definitions. He argues for a new look at child abuse and neglect definitions that might allow researchers to reap the benefits of current definitions while eliminating many of their shortcomings. In particular, he raises the question of whether the field is ready for a new look at definitional issues and a critical appraisal of past and current practices.

1

An Examination of Research in Child Abuse and Neglect

Past Practices and Future Directions

MARGARET M. FEERICK AND KYLE L. SNOW

THE FIELD OF CHILD ABUSE and neglect has grown considerably since child maltreatment was first recognized by the federal government as a public policy issue with the passing of the Child Abuse Prevention and Treatment Act of 1974 (CAPTA; PL 93-247).[1] At the same time, however, child maltreatment remains one of the least understood social problems facing children today. Indeed, as attested to by the authors of this volume and through several recent appraisals of the literature (e.g., Cicchetti & Manly, 2001; Freyd et al., 2005; Manly, 2005; Theodore & Runyan, 1999), the field has been and continues to be plagued by a number of persistent problems regarding definition and classification, measurement and assessment practices, ethics, and public policy, all of which have hampered our ability to achieve consensus regarding how best to prevent maltreatment, intervene with children who have been maltreated and their families, and ameliorate the long-term consequences of child maltreatment on child health and development.

Although there are clearly numerous reasons—many presented throughout the chapters of this book—for the field's persistent struggles and challenges, it is the premise of this book that one of the major obstacles to progress in child maltreatment research has been the lack of consistent, clear, reliable, and valid definitions and classifications of abusive and neglectful experiences. As articulated by Besharov in 1981, the lack of clear definitions of child abuse and neglect has led to a limited ability to compare studies, even of the same construct; a tendency to take reliability without validity; and "a lack of taxonomic delineation

---

[1] Although the federal government's recognition of child abuse actually began earlier, when states were encouraged by the Children's Bureau and with the promise of federal monies to pass laws requiring the reporting of child abuse and neglect to social services agencies by medical professionals and other mandated reporters, the CAPTA legislation was responsible for the creation of a U.S. Advisory Board on Abuse and Neglect and the establishment of the National Center on Child Abuse and Neglect in the U.S. Department of Health and Human Services (see, e.g., Heins, 1984; Theodore & Runyan, 1999; Wissow, 1995).

with the grouping of cases on the basis of the outcome of abuse rather than classification on the basis of hypothesized cause" (Gough, 1996, p. 996).

Thus, it is the belief of this chapter's authors that the field could greatly benefit from a careful analysis of where it has been with respect to defining and classifying child abuse and neglect, current measures and methodologies that are available for defining and measuring key constructs and variables, and where the field needs to go to advance the understanding of this significant social problem. This chapter's authors further believe, and it is a premise of this book, that the field is at a critical juncture in which an examination of the basic constructs, concepts, operational definitions, and measurement practices that have been the basis of current thinking about child abuse and neglect is in order, and the need for a coherent framework to capture these constructs is pressing (see, e.g., Gough, 1996).

It is not unusual for fields of science to undergo such critical self-examination with regard to their basic definitions and concepts. Broad areas of developmental and social sciences have undergone this process during their developments as fields. Certainly, the fields of psychiatry and clinical psychology have frequently had to reexamine their basic constructs and definitions, each time revising the *Diagnostic and Statistical Manual* (*DSM*), now in its fourth edition with revised text (*DSM-IV-TR*; American Psychiatric Association, 2000), to provide conceptual clarity within the complex collection of terms and concepts within the psychopathology literature. Similarly, the field of learning disabilities has had to undertake such self-examination in developing agreed-on definitions (see Lyon, 1995, and Lyon, Gray, Kavanagh, & Krasnegor, 1993, for reviews). Both of these literatures contribute models that may help the field of child abuse and neglect frame a discourse on common definitions for research purposes. In many respects, efforts undertaken within the learning disabilities field do map onto needed efforts in the field of child abuse and neglect in important ways, not the least of which is the similarity between the two fields in the roles of public policy and public sentiment in shaping how key concepts are defined.

The science of child abuse and neglect has evolved to its current state of readiness to inform, rather than react to, public policies pertaining to child maltreatment. No longer can the science of child abuse and neglect take a back seat to the social and political forces that have shaped the field to date. Rather, what is needed is a targeted, science-driven plan for change and new directions for understanding the complexities inherent in child abuse and neglect so that a systematic research agenda can be undertaken. At its core, this effort requires a firm grounding in classification methodology, including the construction of theory-driven hypotheses, the selection and development of tools and measures to test these hypotheses, a determination of the reliability and validity of measures and methodologies, and the external validation of findings. This agenda should include studies conducted within a developmental, longitudinal framework, in which the same children are repeatedly observed and studied without the need for a priori assumptions about which of them are maltreated children, particularly if such children are studied from the youngest ages and are followed over time.

In this chapter, the authors attempt to provide a brief context for the need to entertain new research directions and methodologies in child abuse and neglect, with particular attention paid to scientific and social factors that have influenced the field to date. In so doing, the authors hope to present a clear message that the field must examine many of the basic assumptions on which it is based before it can move forward, both as a scientific enterprise and as a scientific force that can shape and sharpen public policies designed to protect children.

WHERE HAVE WE BEEN?

Concerns about child abuse and neglect have long been driven by the relative weighing of societal concern for the best interests of the child, society's responsibility to protect children (*parens patriae*), and efforts undertaken to ameliorate the potential negative consequences of what is believed to be an adverse experience on the one hand and a belief in the privacy and sanctity of families on the other.[2] The early history of research on child maltreatment is marked by changes in the relative balance between these potentially competing concerns. Zimring noted that a belief in the privacy rights of the family dominates the legal system, but that "the imminent threat to the life or health of a minor child . . . trigger[s] the law's willingness to penetrate the privacy of family life because the family privacy considerations are outweighed by other important public goals" (1989, p. 553). As this concern has been articulated through federal and state laws, cultural and societal forces have led to classifications of actions directed at children (or not directed at children, as in neglect cases) that have been guided more by ethical and moral concerns than by a scientific understanding of the ramifications of these behaviors (or lack of behaviors) for the developing child. In addition, changes in societal views and values have continued to play a role in how we expect children to be treated. For example, prior to compulsory education laws, keeping a child from school was often advantageous to a family, especially one involved in the agrarian economy in which children were often needed to tend to crops or livestock. However, shifts in our expectations concerning the need for children to attend school (and indeed, the state's obligation to provide education to all children) have led to new concepts of parental obligations as well as the consequences of a lack of fulfillment of these obligations (e.g., the concept of educational neglect). In part, and throughout the earliest history of research on child abuse and neglect, such an approach has not been terribly problematic insofar as the debate has occurred largely outside of the realm of rigorous scien-

---

[2]See also Chapter 3 by Jeffrey J. Haugaard for a more detailed examination of the sociohistory of child maltreatment research.

tific inquiry. Thus, although there has been considerable debate about some aspects of child abuse and neglect (e.g., corporal punishment, the validity of differing forms of child neglect), the field has achieved some consensus about broad categories of abuse and neglect (Bensley et al., 2004; Portwood, 1999). Still, there continues to be considerable disagreement in definitions, based, in part, on demographic characteristics (Craft & Staudt, 1991; Korbin, Coulton, Lindstrom-Ufuti, & Spilsbury, 2000) and cultural factors (Collier, McClure, Collier, Otto, & Polloi, 1999; Hong & Hong, 1991; Korbin, 1981; Rose & Meezan, 1995, 1996), as well as a disconnect between professional judgments and reports from parents and children (Boehm, 1964; Cruise, Jacobs & Lyons, 1994; McGee, Wolfe, Yuen, Wilson, & Carnochan, 1995).

In the legal realm, these disputes have been resolved largely by state child and protective services systems, which employ a range of definitions and parameters to identify child maltreatment (Bulkley, 1985; Burns & Lake, 1983; Straus & Moore, 1990). Certainly, states have the right to define their legal and criminal codes within federal guidelines, a right often affirmed by the U.S. Supreme Court, and it is not unusual that two contiguous states would have differing laws pertaining to the same set of behaviors (e.g., speed limits, public smoking, blood alcohol levels). The relativism that this presents in local definitions of child maltreatment is in many ways the antithesis to the objectivity demands of scientific inquiry. However, when there is a growing body of scientific data about the impact of behaviors that are (presumably) within legal authority, that data should be brought to bear in an examination of those laws. Indeed, Manly concluded a commentary on research comparing current classification systems by noting that "utilizing a classification system with objective criteria that transcends variability in state laws and local policies will increase comparability across laboratories and improve research in the field" (2005, p. 431). Still, there remains a divide between research definitions and legal definitions of child maltreatment (Barnett, Manly, & Cicchetti, 1993). In their commentary on the American Psychological Association's handling of the controversy following publication of the meta-analysis on the effects of sexual abuse conducted by Rind, Tromovitch, and Bauserman (1998), Sher and Eisenberg pointed out that " . . . current definitions of CSA [child sexual abuse] are based primarily on sociolegal foundations, not on scientific ones, and there may be places where scientific and sociolegal terminology diverge as a function of their intended uses" (2002, p. 207).

The science of child abuse and neglect has evolved a great deal during its long history (see Lynch, 1985). Although it is not the authors' intent here to give a full recounting of the history of the field, there are several notable events (and their historical contexts) that warrant mention. First, it must be recognized that although most contemporary work in the field traces its roots to the seminal paper "The Battered Child Syndrome," by Kempe, Silverman, Steele, Droegemueller, and Silver (1962), which introduced the phrase "battered child" to general and medical vocabulary in America, physicians had long made observations about child injuries and the likelihood that they were not accidental in nature (Labbe, 2005; Lynch, 1985). A historical linkage between Kempe and colleagues' work and earlier work was made explicit when Silverman (1972) directly related the findings of the battered child syndrome to the earlier work of Ambroise Tardieu. In a review on the life of French physician Tardieu, Labbe (2005) noted that although even respected members of the medical community (e.g., Tardieu) were active in identifying and studying child maltreatment, social beliefs dominant at the time (in this case, 19th-century France) favored family privacy and did not typically grant many rights to children. Similarly, although it was not until the early 1900s that state legislatures passed statutes criminalizing abusive and neglectful behavior and specifying procedures for meeting the concerns of maltreated children, concerns about the welfare of children and specialized institutions to serve them existed as early as the 18th century in the United States (Miller-Perrin & Perrin, 1999; Stein, 1991). However, it was not until the 19th century and the changes that came with industrialization that there was clear identification of child maltreatment as a social problem and the development of social and legal mechanisms to address it. These began with efforts to correct "errant and destitute children" and concerns about the moral development of children growing up in impoverished families and only later included specific legislation and institutions focused on the concerns of abused and neglected children (Giovannoni, 1989, p. 5).

In the United States, concern about child maltreatment rapidly intensified, however, when Kempe et al. (1962) published the aforementioned work "The Battered Child Syndrome," which created "a stir in the medical profession as well as in the people of the nation to take action against child maltreatment in the United States" (Theodore & Runyan, 1999, p. 170). By 1967 all 50 states had child abuse reporting laws, and in 1974 CAPTA (PL 93-247) was passed, establishing state-implemented services for at-risk children and families. Child Protective Services (CPS)[3] was established as the primary lens through which child maltreatment was defined (Bartol & Bartol, 1994). Around that same time, public awareness of child maltreatment exploded; Wolfe (1985) reported that only about 10% of respondents in national polls in 1970 considered child abuse a serious problem, but by 1983 that percentage had climbed to more than 90% (see also Chapter 3). It was also around this time that Giovannoni and Becerra (1979) published the first concerted study of varying definitions of what constitutes child maltreatment.

By the early 1980s, concern about child abuse and neglect led to large-scale, publicly funded scientific efforts to determine the scope of the problem. The most influential of these efforts was the first National Incidence Study (NIS-1) com-

---

[3]Throughout this chapter, the term *child protective services*, or CPS, is used to refer generally to the range of service agencies established by states in response to CAPTA to provide surveillance of child maltreatment through reporting and investigation or substantiation systems.

missioned by the U.S. Department of Health and Human Services (DHHS; 1981). This landmark study and its two subsequent iterations (DHHS, 1988; Sedlak & Broadhurst, 1996) set the tone for how child abuse and neglect were operationalized and counted, and they continue to be a dominant force in how the field approaches definitions of child maltreatment. However, in conducting the National Incidence studies with the intention of making national estimates, researchers had to reconcile in some way the variability among state definitions for events that would establish these national estimates.

By the early 1990s, the field of child maltreatment research underwent a period of reappraisal as professionals in the field began to closely examine the definitions that had guided their work. In 1990, Hutchinson published a paper with the provocative title "Child Maltreatment: Can it Be Defined?" During this time, a number of papers were published attempting to define various types of child maltreatment, including general child neglect (Dubowitz, Black, Starr, & Zuravin, 1993; Rose & Meezan, 1993), emotional abuse and neglect (O'Hagan, 1995; Stevenson, 1996), psychological abuse and neglect (Barnett, Manly, & Cicchetti, 1991; Brassard, Germain, & Hart, 1987; McGee & Wolfe, 1991), and even physical abuse (Oldershaw, Walters, & Hall, 1989; Whipple & Richey, 1997).

In 1993, the National Research Council (NRC) published its authoritative work recounting where the field of child abuse and neglect had been and describing where it needed to go. One important need identified by the NRC was "the formulation of research definitions of child maltreatment [which] should be guided by four key principles: consideration of specific objectives the definition must serve; division into homogenous sub-types; conceptual clarity; and feasibility" (1993, p. 5). In the same year, Barnett, Manly, & Cicchetti (1993) published the Maltreatment Classification System (MCS), a framework for reviewing CPS records that would be adopted by many professionals in the child abuse and neglect research community, creating the opportunity for inferred understanding based on a degree of commonality and cross-site reliability to CPS reports used as research data. The MCS utilizes CPS reports and classifies incidents into broader categories than typically had been used by the field, while also providing an ordinal scoring system within categories to provide more rich information about events.

Over the past several decades, a large body of specific studies concerning different aspects of child maltreatment, including antecedents and consequences, has grown to the point in which research syntheses and meta-analyses are available (e.g., Cicchetti, 1996; Hildyard & Wolfe, 2002; Trickett & McBride-Chang, 1995). Behl, Conyngham, and May (2003) examined the peer-reviewed literature on child abuse and neglect published in the years 1977 through 1998 in a set of six journals of most relevance to the field. In addition to charting tremendous growth in the number of articles published (from 51 in 1977 to 344 in 1998), as well as the emergence of several specialty journals focused on emotional abuse and sexual abuse (among other specialties), Behl and colleagues noted a shift from theoretical papers to empirical papers, an increasing tendency for articles to identify specific types of maltreatment, and a relative underrepresentation of child neglect and emotional abuse in a literature in which childhood sexual abuse had become the largest and fastest growing body of work.

In recent years, a large body of more complex, ambitious studies has been undertaken to more fully explore the complexities of child maltreatment, including long-term follow-up of maltreated children (e.g., Horowitz, Widom, McLaughlin, & White, 2001; Malinosky-Rummell & Hansen, 1993; Perez & Widom, 1994; Putnam, 2003; Widom, 1989; Wolfe & McGee, 1994), intergenerational studies (e.g., Ertem, Leventhal, & Dobbs, 2000; Kaufman & Zigler, 1989; Oliver, 1993), prospective developmental studies (e.g., Bagley & Mallick, 2000; Brown, Cohen, Johnson, & Salzinger, 1998; Runyan et al., 1998), intervention and prevention studies for families and/or children at risk (e.g., Duggan et al., 2004; Macmillan et al., 2005; Olds et al., 1997; see also Geeraert, Van den Noortgate, Grietens, & Onghena, 2004, and MacLeod & Nelson, 2001, for meta-analytic reviews), treatment studies (e.g., Cohen & Mannarino, 1998; Donohue & Van Hasselt, 1999; Greenwalt, Sklare & Portes, 1998; Kolko, 1996; Toth & Cicchetti, 1993; Wolfe & Wekerle, 1995), and studies of children's psychobiological responses to maltreatment (e.g., Cicchetti & Rogosch, 2001; DeBellis, 2001, 2005; Glaser, 2000; Teicher et al., 2003). This latter group of studies is especially noteworthy because the studies target the consequences and/or antecedents of the maltreatment event itself rather than focusing on a group of children who have experienced that type of event. As discussed later in this chapter, the need to specify both discrete events as well as children who experience these events creates a great deal of complexity for any classification system. As a group, this wide range of studies has provided a growing understanding of the causes and consequences of child maltreatment despite the lack of field consensus (or even general agreement) with regard to labels and definitions.

As the field has continued to grow as a science, however, the occasional conflict between a scientific approach to child abuse and neglect research and social and political assumptions or beliefs has created controversy. This especially has been the case where the definitions used in research on child abuse and neglect have not yet incorporated important event characteristics into the definitions of abuse (e.g., the various forms of coercion in sexual activity) and in definitions that do not clearly differentiate maltreatment from experiences within the normal range (e.g., physical punishment). For example, when Rind et al. (1998) published their meta-analysis on the long-term effects of childhood sexual abuse, a flurry of reaction in the public press indicated how scientific evidence may fare and be abused or misinterpreted when it conflicts with particular social and political agendas (Sher & Eisenberg, 2002; see also Garrison & Kobor, 2002, and Lillienfeld, 2002, for detailed accounts of the events surrounding publication of this article). A similar, but less severe, crisis occurred following Gershoff's (2002) publication of a meta-analysis regarding the effects of corporal punishment, drawing some professional commentary (e.g., Baumrind, Larzelere, & Cowan, 2002; Benjet & Kazdin, 2003) as well as coverage in popular media. (It should be noted that when any of the countless literature reviews or meta-analyses concerning the deleterious effects of various forms of child maltreatment for which there is broad general agreement as to the potential for harm were published in the peer-reviewed literature, little to no public attention was paid to these important papers). Such controversy underscores the continuing need for clear definitions and classification of child abuse and neglect both for research and research-informed public policy. It also highlights the challenges inherent in the field of child abuse and neglect as the science advances to address questions that may challenge social or political assumptions.

What is clear in this history of the field of child abuse and neglect is that as the science of child abuse and neglect continues to evolve and address more and more complex and refined questions, many of the social and political assumptions about child abuse and neglect are exposed. In some cases, the science is likely to substantiate these widely held beliefs, but in others the scientific findings may conflict with commonly held beliefs as well as political or ideological positions. It is critical, therefore, that as scientists continue to study child maltreatment, they assume a scientific (as opposed to legal, political, or societal) view of the phenomena under study and, to the extent possible, that this scientific view be uninfluenced by political and societal pressures. This will require bringing the considerable scientific tools in the field, many of them described and explored in this book, to bear.

CURRENT CHALLENGES IN THE STUDY OF CHILD ABUSE AND NEGLECT

A number of unique challenges exist in the conduct of sound research on child abuse and neglect. These are generally known in the field and are not explored in great detail in this chapter. Rather, they are presented briefly in an effort to identify the set-point for the field. To move the field forward, these challenges must be regularly reconsidered and previous efforts to overcome them examined. In cases in which the challenges have been overcome, the ameliorative practices should be identified and maintained as the field grows. In cases in which the challenges have not been overcome, efforts must be redoubled to meet them or to develop strategies that otherwise avoid or circumvent these challenges.

The central theme of this book is that the critical challenge in the field now is an inadequate definition and classification structure, the presence of which would allow the field to overcome many of its other obstacles. To date, efforts at classification have been largely built around CPS reporting, either using reported and/or substantiated CPS cases directly or by applying a framework such as the MCS (Barnett et al., 1993) to CPS data. It is time, however, to reconsider this reliance on CPS data for research purposes (Dubowitz et al., 2005; Runyan et al.,

2005). First, for a number of reasons, not all children who are maltreated are brought to the attention of CPS, even as an initial report (Gracia, 1995; Waldfogel, 1998). Second, there is some data to suggest that reporting and/or substantiation of maltreatment may be racially or socioeconomically biased (e.g., Ards, Chung, & Myers, 1998; Ards, Myers, Chung, Malkis, & Hagerty, 2003; Drake & Zuravin, 1998; Eckenrode, Powers, Doris, Munsch, & Bolger, 1988; Fluke, Yuan, Hedderson, & Curtis, 2003; Lu et al., 2004), although the interpretation of these findings, especially in light of the presence of additional risk factors, remains challenging (e.g., Hines, Lemon, Wyatt, & Merdinger, 2004) and the presence of a discrepancy is itself still contentious in the field (e.g., Ards & Harrell, 1993). In addition, although reports and substantiations have critical differences in meaning and resultant action within the CPS system, Hussey et al. (2005) have presented data suggesting that when predicting outcomes, there is little difference between children for whom CPS reports are substantiated and children for whom CPS reports are made (substantiated or not). This finding, in need of replication and further exploration, suggests the need for a different strategy, not relying solely on CPS data insofar as it could be expected that substantiated maltreatment will have a differential developmental impact on children. As Slack, Holl, Altenbernd, McDaniel, and Stevens noted, "sole reliance on system indicators, created for bureaucratic and tracking purposes as opposed to research purposes, does not substantially move us toward a better understanding of the underlying child maltreatment phenomena" (2003, p. 101).

Finally, Runyan et al. (2005; see also Chapter 10) compared the three most common classification systems: CPS labels, the MCS, and criteria used in the second National Incidence Study. Although Runyan and colleagues found relatively high concordance among the three systems in parsing the universe of cases and events in instances of physical or sexual abuse, there was less concordance across reports of neglect and emotional maltreatment. In their random telephone survey of adults in Washington state, Bensley et al. (2004) found a similar pattern, with very high agreement as to what constitutes sexual abuse and severe physical abuse, somewhat less consensus about forms of child neglect, and little consensus about emotional abuse. Bensley et al. did report, however, that among those items in the survey that mapped onto CPS codes, there was greater than 95% agreement, except for items categorized by CPS as medical neglect. This reliability across coding systems and respondents for at least some forms of maltreatment is not only encouraging, but also indicative of those types of maltreatment for which we are far from reaching agreement.

Another central challenge to the field is its focus on a wide range of behaviors. Often, the central behavior of concern is one of omission (e.g., neglect) rather than commission (e.g., abuse), and these behaviors tend not to occur publicly or in directly accessible ways. As a result, professionals in the field are seldom able to observe the behaviors of concern but rather must rely on reports of these behaviors (either self-report from the perpetrator, recollections of the victim, or reports to referral agencies from others) and frequently must infer the behaviors from the apparent proximal consequences (i.e., a bruise may indicate an unseen abusive behavior or it may indicate an accidental injury). In addition, because abuse and neglect carry with them social stigma, and victims may be threatened not to reveal their experiences. Under such circumstances, collecting data on actual events and matching for outcomes and effects is indeed challenging.

WHERE DO WE NEED TO GO?

In 1999, the National Institutes of Health (NIH), together with the Children's Bureau in the Administration on Children, Youth and Families, responded to many of these challenges by initiating a major effort to develop a research agenda focused on defining and classifying child abuse and neglect. At the urging of Congress, the NIH had created a Child Abuse and Neglect Working Group (CANWG) in 1997. As the CANWG developed initiatives to better understand child abuse and neglect, it became increasingly clear that limitations in the definition and classification of this complex topic were hindering scientific progress in this area. Therefore, a series of workshops was organized to solicit advice from the scientific and clinical communities working in the field of abuse and neglect with the ultimate goal of operationally defining abuse and neglect while taking into account legal, clinical, and privacy issues. The goal of these meetings was to develop an action plan for a research agenda that would lead to data collection efforts that could inform the development of an empirically based classification system.

The first workshop, held in December 1999, brought together researchers to review and summarize the knowledge base and gaps relevant to defining and classifying child abuse and neglect and to develop plans for a research agenda in this area. During the course of this meeting, the early work of Harvey Skinner (1977, 1979, 1981) on classification systems, especially his focus on the importance of construct validity and incorporating both theory and data in the development of classification systems, was highlighted to provide a framework for subsequent discussion.

The second workshop was held in September 2000. The purpose of this workshop was to develop an action plan for the development of an internally and externally valid classification system and an operational definition of child abuse and neglect. Specifically, the workshop was organized to 1) identify adequate and effective measurement strategies and instruments for assessing child maltreatment and 2) propose measurement standards and procedures to guide research and practice. The overall goal of the meeting was to develop specific recommendations for a research agenda on definitional issues in child maltreatment so that future studies on child maltreatment would be comparable and would help to inform research, clinical practice, policy decisions, service delivery, and training programs for both researchers and clinicians.

Although these two meetings led to a number of recommendations for future research that are summarized in the concluding chapter of this book, two specific outcomes of these meetings are worthy of mention here. First, meeting participants clearly desired to develop a science-driven classification effort that would identify and describe key categories of abuse and neglect. Second, in order to successfully pursue such an effort, participants agreed that there must be movement toward consensus on key constructs and measures in the field. Participants at both meetings felt that the field of child abuse and neglect could benefit greatly from a careful consideration of classification frameworks as a starting point for the field and, then, from a review of key concepts, definitions, theories, and methodological approaches as a means of charting future directions. The remainder of this chapter addresses the first of these recommendations by providing a brief overview of classification approaches. The remaining chapters of this volume address the second recommendation through a careful analysis of existing definitional and measurement approaches and significant needs for future research.

A CLASSIFICATION FRAMEWORK FOR CHILD MALTREATMENT

The field of child abuse and neglect has been plagued by a history of diverse definitions of what constitutes maltreatment in general and by the issue of which specific categories of maltreatment are important for study. The diversity in definitions, however, has not been without its advantages; as Gough argued, "A lack of specificity allows everyone to be against abuse" (1996, p. 994). During the course of contemporary study of child maltreatment (see also Kempe, 1978), researchers in the field have expanded the scope of maltreatment experiences to include new categories that were not widely considered to be relevant during the early history of child abuse and neglect research, such as psychological abuse (e.g., McGee & Wolfe, 1991; Navarre, 1987; O'Hagan, 1995), educational neglect (e.g., Yudof, Kirp, Levin, & Moran, 2002), and even medical neglect (e.g., Bross, 1982) that goes beyond failure to thrive (Barbero & Shaheen, 1967; Elmer, Gregg, & Ellison, 1969). The emergence of these new categories has led to critical questions about what constitutes maltreatment, especially in contrast with suboptimal parenting (e.g., Barnett et al., 1993; Roscoe, 1990).

Psychology, and philosophy before it, has made inroads in studying how categories are formed and maintained by people to organize the world around them (see De Boeck, Wilson, & Acton, 2005; Murphy & Medin, 1985). Several themes that have emerged from this history should be considered as a classification system and categorical structure to guide research in child abuse and neglect is contemplated. First, classification systems lead to categorical structures that lend coherence to the component discrete categories. One theory of conceptual coherence argues that categories are constructed based on similarities between as-yet uncategorized events (or objects, or concepts) and exemplars (e.g., Cohen

& Murphy, 1984; Rosch & Mervis, 1975), similar to Plato's ideal forms. In the context of child abuse and neglect, such an approach would require that there be exemplary instances of different kinds of child maltreatment against which events and experiences could be matched to indicate a maltreatment event. A second approach argues that categories are based on a common set of attributes that are shared (either in total or in part according to some predetermined minimum) among members of the category (e.g., Smith & Medin, 1981). Murphy and Medin (1985) proposed a third possibility: that categories are formed and coherence achieved through personal theories about how the world is organized, suggesting that we do not use categories to make sense of the world around us but instead have a theory about the world around us that generates categories within which we maintain our view of the world (see, e.g., Quine, 1977). Skinner (1981) underscored the importance of the continuing evolution of classifications through the interaction between theory and empirical analysis. Through such interactions, Skinner (1977) proposed, emerges a "Modal Profile" of fundamental concepts and categories.

In addition to considering how categories are identified and maintained, researchers in the field of child abuse and neglect must develop scientifically based definitions and classification systems based on an implicit understanding of the goals of classification. First, a classification system allows for consistent communication among users of the information. When there is consistent classification of groups, users of the information can reliably and accurately communicate with each other about these groups. Meehl has cautioned that this need should not "produce an obsession with reliability instead of construct validity" (1995, p. 267), as it is construct validity that is the central concern in psychological research (Cronbach & Meehl, 1955; Skinner, 1981). At its best, a classification system allows for few but clear boundaries between groups to minimize ambiguity in membership (Meehl, 1992). For example, a reliable classification system for employment allows all states to report (and the media to provide commentary on and policy makers to formulate policy about) the number of employed and unemployed people in their states. Without a clear classification, such communication would not be possible. A classification system also allows researchers, service providers, and policy makers greater ability to predict the unifying event or events of interest, understand its etiology and its consequences, and formulate treatments or interventions. To achieve these goals over time, classification systems tend to become much more complex relative to the depth of knowledge in relevant areas. In developing a classification scheme, an inherent tension exists between the desire to establish fewer categories, to facilitate communication, and the desire to create more sufficiently distinct categories to capture all interactions among attributes of interest. For example, the most commonly reported statistics for child abuse are based on either reported or substantiated CPS incidents. This allows for fewer categories and easier communication, even though there is variability in what leads to either a CPS report or a substantiated report. To capture these distinctions, allowing for a more fine-tuned understanding of child abuse, requires more categories and a proportionate change in the ease of communication, clarity, comprehensiveness, and specificity.

In science this tension between broad-band and narrow-band classification is resolved, in part, through hypothesis testing. Regardless of the number of categories classification systems employ, all such systems have implicit (if not explicit) hypotheses, some of which may be connected to a larger underlying theory, that suggest the attributes and their parsing to create categories within the system. For example, in the study of poverty, we may have a range of categories for income (e.g., wages; investments; in-kind, nonmonetary subsidies), but we do not include all of the categories that are possible because we do not have theories that generate hypotheses about relationships to other attributes (e.g., money found on the street). In developing a classification scheme, a critical judgment is made about those attributes considered most relevant. Although such judgments should be theory-driven, a range of tools available to measure those attributes helps researchers delineate important constructs. For example, the use of cluster modeling techniques reveals how attributes tend to co-occur (i.e., cluster) within individuals, creating groups of individuals that are internally homogenous (at least as far as the attributes included in the model are concerned), yet different from individuals that may fall into other groups.

There is mounting evidence that a number of key attributes of events may be meaningful in the study of child abuse and neglect. Cicchetti and Rizley (1981) were among the first to argue that child maltreatment encompassed a heterogeneous blending of characteristics, etiologies, developmental impacts, and responses to treatment. It is important to note that data have accumulated demonstrating individual differences in child response to maltreatment (called multifinality; see Cicchetti & Rogosch, 1996). Thus, as called for as early as 1991 by Cicchetti and Barnett, a classification system for child maltreatment would involve multiple critical attributes, a requirement served by several classification frameworks. Dimensional, multiaxial, and vector schemes allow for simultaneous consideration of multiple attributes. Although dimensional schemes acknowledge several attributes at once, these may be seen as largely independent dimensions along which behaviors or individuals vary, and decisions for categorization require judgments about demarcation points along each continuum, the decisions of which must again be independent from each other. The most common multiaxial scheme is used in the *DSM* of the American Psychiatric Association. Similar to a dimensional frame, a multiaxial scheme allows for the dimensions to be related, and frequently, as is the case with the *DSM,* has clear indications as to when an array of characteristics would lead to group membership. Classification built around vectors, or change over time, are much less common but have an inherent developmental component that acknowledges that attributes may change over time. A vector scheme may be particularly relevant to child abuse and neglect because of the importance of the developmental timing and duration of maltreatment (e.g.,

Hildyard & Wolfe, 2002; Manly, Kim, Rogosch, & Cicchetti, 2001; Trickett & McBride-Chang, 1995).

In determining which classification scheme to apply to the field of child maltreatment, consideration of the strengths and weaknesses of each approach must be considered, including an examination of the degree to which research is available to inform the resultant design. It may be the case that extant data create a limiting factor in setting a classification scheme to guide further research. However, given the availability of data, a range of data analytic techniques are available to allow for the development and testing of hypotheses (e.g., Skinner, 1979). Lau and her colleagues (Lau et al., 2005) used the Longitudinal Studies of Child Abuse and Neglect (LONGSCAN) data, a multisite longitudinal study of abused children and children at risk for abuse (see also Chapters 5 and 10), to test the predictive validity (against a set of outcomes associated with maltreatment, including behavior problems, evidence of trauma, and adaptive functioning) of three classification schemes built around types of maltreatment. Although limited to type of maltreatment as the single dimension in the scheme, this initial study may become an important model for how classification work will proceed in the future. Lau et al. noted that "it appears that different ways of classifying predominant types of maltreatment yield varying levels of predictive validity" (2005, p. 547).

The use of the current literature on concept formation and coherence, introduced earlier as a jumping-off point, is limited, however, in that it is based largely on the study of how individuals process events internally. In the language of research methods, this literature is based on a single-informant, single-measure design. The literature on child abuse and neglect, however, can be characterized as one that uses a variety of informants and measures, although most individual studies use a single-source, single-method approach. As a result, in developing a classification system to generate meaningful, coherent categories, or definitions, for child abuse and neglect, consideration must be given to the diverse methods used by the field. One of the biggest limiting factors in the research community is the ability to measure the key attributes and phenomena in question. As indicated previously, most instances of child maltreatment are not directly observed, creating a reliance on self-report or third party inference. Although such approaches may allow for a valid classification of acts and victims, they do little to address what are believed to be other key attributes, such as age of onset, duration of maltreatment experiences, relationship between perpetrator and child, and even specific information about the type of maltreatment experienced.

Although estimates of the prevalence of child maltreatment do suggest it is a serious public health problem, the frequency of maltreatment behaviors is still relatively rare, and these behaviors may be especially difficult to observe in the context of a sound research design. Certainly strong social desirability demands may tend to reduce the incidence of behaviors the observed individuals might consider unacceptable. The inability to directly observe the attributes or events of interest contributes to the need for inference previously discussed, but it also creates a reliance on self-report of unobserved behaviors. In the past few decades, a burgeoning literature has arisen that raises concerns about reliance on contemporaneous reports of victimized children, especially very young children (see Ceci & Bruck, 1995, for a review). The most typical approach to obtaining data on childhood maltreatment experiences is a reliance on retrospective reports, a methodology that has been examined extensively in general psychological research (e.g., Henry, Moffitt, Caspi, Langley, & Silva, 1994; Yarrow, Campbell, & Burton, 1970) as well as in the field of child abuse specifically (Ornstein, Ceci, & Loftus, 1998). As the field has grown, a number of studies allow for a comparison between retrospective reports and either parent report (e.g., Tajima, Herrenkohl, Huang, & Whitney, 2004), CPS records (e.g., Brown et al., 1998; Widom & Morris, 1997; Widom & Shepard, 1996), previous home observations (Prescott et al., 2000), and even previous self-reports and records (e.g., Femina, Yeager, & Lewis, 1990). This lack of comparability across informants and sources of information creates a great challenge to consistent classification across methods or studies (Kaufman, Jones, Stieglitz, Vitulano, & Mannarino, 1994; Kinard, 1998). However, it also suggests that a useful classification framework for child abuse and neglect might be derived from a combination of these multiple information sources and methods as a means of empirically testing different hypotheses about groups, subgroups, and relevant constructs and dimensions.

In subsequent chapters of this volume, the contributors to this work review previous efforts to define and classify child abuse and neglect experiences, paying attention to historical, social policy, and practical considerations. In doing so, they attempt to highlight many of the implicit assumptions that have been present in the field and the underlying classification models that have framed much of the field to date. Although, taken together, they offer no one classification or definitional approach as the standard for the field, they do point to a number of promising frameworks and methodologies that should help shape future discourse and research in this area.

SUMMARY AND OVERVIEW OF THE BOOK

In summary, much of our research thinking about child abuse and neglect has been based on information obtained from ambiguously defined samples of children. These samples have typically been identified by CPS as having experienced varied kinds of abuse and neglect and generally have been measured at one point in time, using one primary definitional approach or framework. Moreover, much of the work in the field has been based on a number of assumptions that have been derived more from historical or social policy influences than science-driven classification efforts. The result is that the field of child abuse and neglect lacks a logically consistent, easily operationalized, and empirically valid and reliable definition and classification system. Thus, it has been difficult for the field to make specific predictions and recommendations concerning the treatment of mal-treated children, the prevention of this problem, and the best approaches to pro-moting optimal functioning of maltreated children over time and in different cir-cumstances and settings. It is the premise of this book that these issues need to be addressed in an informed and systematic fashion, and the contributors to this book are hopeful that their chapters provide a first step in this direction.

The overarching goal of this book is to identify research definitions and methodologies that have a high probability of establishing a useful, scientific framework for the field of child abuse and neglect. It is important, however, that such definitions and methodologies be considered within the legal, social, and political contexts that have always accompanied and informed the field of child abuse and neglect. The authors of the chapters in this volume present what can be considered state-of-the-art evidence about 1) linkages between theory and the development of a valid and reliable definition and classification system for child abuse and neglect, 2) current approaches to definition and measurement in this area, and 3) the role the legal system and public policy play in setting priorities for research and practice. In doing so, the authors attempt to come to terms with the major obstacles to establishing a reliable and valid definition and classifica-tion system for research in this area and to identify the conditions that must be in place if the field of child abuse and neglect is to move forward in establishing a clear definitional, theoretical, conceptual, and methodological base on which to advance as a scientific area.

The chapters in this book have been organized into four sections. The first section consists of Chapters 1 through 3 and addresses critical issues in and his-torical approaches to defining and classifying child abuse and neglect. In this chapter (Chapter 1) the authors have sought to provide a brief overview of the field and present a rationale for entertaining new research directions in child maltreatment. In Chapter 2, Rosemary Chalk provides a detailed overview of the history of the search for consensus in the field by discussing the development and conclusions of the NRC's (1993) report "Understanding Child Abuse and Ne-glect." In doing so, she points to the progress that has been made in the field as well as the key issues with which the field continues to grapple. In Chapter 3, Jeffrey J. Haugaard presents a socio-legal history of child abuse and neglect def-initions, examining the role of historical influences, public sentiment, and the-ory in informing the development of the field and concluding that it may be time for a new look at child abuse and neglect definitions.

The second section is composed of Chapters 4 through 8 and addresses the current state of the field and critical issues with respect to defining different types of abuse and neglect experiences. In Chapter 4, John F. Knutson and Deanna Heckenberg review historical and public policy influences on past and current definitions of child physical abuse, identifying the underlying compo-nents or assumptions of research definitions in this area and key issues in defin-ing and operationalizing physical abuse. In so doing, they suggest a number of

conditions that good operational definitions should meet and outline several recommendations for future research. Howard Dubowitz's work in Chapter 5 presents a similar analysis of research definitions of child neglect by reviewing a
number of general, conceptual, and operational issues in defining and measuring
neglect and by discussing several specific and composite measures that have been
developed for work in this area. He then presents a number of recommendations
for future research, suggesting that, at a minimum, researchers need to fully
specify the conceptual basis and operational definition used to measure neglect.

In Chapter 6, Penelope K. Trickett critically reviews the literature with
respect to definitions of sexual abuse, documenting a number of problems that
have plagued this literature and presenting original data on differences in the
impact of sexual abuse as a result of different types or characteristics of abuse. She
then presents several recommendations for how issues in definition and classification can be better addressed in future research, arguing that to move the field
forward it is necessary for research to be more explicitly theory-based and for
researchers to focus more on the definition of sexual abuse, the independent variable in this research. In Chapter 7, Marla R. Brassard and Kera L. Donovan
review the status of major research definitions of psychological maltreatment,
examine the degree to which these research definitions are embedded in clinical
diagnostic and research instruments, and evaluate empirical support for each definition by age of the child. They then make a number of recommendations with
respect to finalizing definitions in this area and to the development of measurement instruments that can operationalize these definitions. They conclude that
much definitional and empirical work in psychological maltreatment already
exists that can serve as a strong foundation on which to make empirically supported policy recommendations and that can be used to guide future research.

The final chapter in the second section, Chapter 8, presents an overview of
how basic concepts and principles of psychological measurement can be used to
define child maltreatment. In this chapter, David Watson outlines the evolution
of psychometric thinking over the course of the 20th century, noting that construct validity has emerged as the central unifying concept in contemporary psychometrics. He then reviews the basic stages of construct validation in an effort
to show how it can be applied to establish research definitions of child maltreatment. He concludes by summarizing how a focus on construct validity has
changed our understanding of many psychometric concepts, indicating that they
need to be applied flexibly to match theoretical specifications of the target construct. He further indicates that this emphasis on construct validity underscores
the need to develop clear, precise definitions of the key constructs in the area of
child maltreatment, noting that psychological measurement involves a constant
interplay between theory and empirical data.

The third section consists of Chapters 9 through 11. Each of these chapters
addresses one of three major approaches to measurement in child maltreatment:
self-report approaches, case record reviews, and observation and analogue mea-

sures. In Chapter 9, Sharon G. Portwood provides a background for evaluating self-report approaches to child maltreatment research, discussing the benefits and limitations of self-reports; reviewing a sampling of existing measures for use with children, adolescents, and adults; and outlining special considerations for each of these populations. In Chapter 10, Desmond K. Runyan and Diana J. English present a similar overview of major case record review approaches, presenting original data comparing three major definitional approaches: CPS records, the National Incidence Study, and the Maltreatment Classification System. Chapter 11 concludes this section with an analysis of direct observations and analogue measures by David S. DeGarmo, John B. Reid, and John F. Knutson, in which the authors discuss the roles of observational and laboratory measurements in research on child maltreatment, identify and describe some powerful and specific methods, and make recommendations about when and where the methods can be used most effectively. In presenting this analysis, the authors provide a framework for the development of measurement and analytic models, present examples of naturalistic and structured observations and analog laboratory tasks, and employ constructs derived from these approaches to illustrate the study of linkages among theoretical constructs measuring child physical abuse and neglect. They conclude with a discussion of how research on maltreatment can be advanced by adopting a multimethod/multisource approach to operationally defining key constructs in child physical abuse and neglect.

In the fourth and final section of the book, consideration is given to a number of social policy issues relevant to research definitions and measures of abuse and neglect. This section begins with Chapter 12, by Maryfrances R. Porter, Jill Antonishak, and N. Dickon Reppucci, in which the authors review the purposes of current federal and state policy definitions of child maltreatment and discuss the ways in which empirical and policy definitions may inform each other to strengthen child protection practices. In Chapter 13, Sally M. Flanzer, Ying-Ying T. Yuan, and Diana J. English examine the impact of information technology on defining and classifying child abuse and neglect, describing a number of ways in which information technology can be used to assist researchers in their efforts to advance the science. In Chapter 14, Cassandra Simmel, Sally M. Flanzer, and Mary Bruce Webb examine a number of ethical issues in child maltreatment research that have emanated from the conduct of research on this topic. In this chapter, the authors underscore the challenges that continue to face researchers in the field of child abuse and neglect by presenting a number of research studies to depict the range of solutions that various researchers have used to deal with these ethical issues. The authors conclude with a number of suggestions for dealing with these ethical challenges in the future.

In the final chapter of this section, Chapter 15, Margaret M. Feerick and Kyle L. Snow summarize common themes across the chapters of this volume regarding promising directions for future research. They then present an agenda for future research relevant to defining, classifying, and measuring child abuse and neglect that is based on the summary recommendations from the two federal workshops that were held on these topics.

In closing, it is the hope of the authors that the following chapters serve as a useful framework to guide future research in this area. In particular, the authors hope that they will encourage further discussion, thought, and empirical work focused on definition, classification, and measurement of child abuse and neglect.

REFERENCES

American Psychiatric Association. (2000). *Diagnostic and statistical manual of mental disorders* (4th ed., text revision). Washington, DC: Author.

Ards, S., Chung, C., & Myers, S.L., Jr. (1998). The effects of sample selection bias on racial differences in child abuse reporting. *Child Abuse & Neglect, 22,* 103–115.

Ards, S., & Harrell, A. (1993). Reporting of child maltreatment: A secondary analysis of the national incidence surveys. *Child Abuse & Neglect, 17,* 337–344.

Ards, S.D., Myers, S.L., Jr., Chung, C., Malkis, A., & Hagerty, B. (2003). Decomposing black-white differences in child maltreatment. *Child Maltreatment, 8,* 112–121.

Bagley, C., & Mallick, K. (2000). Prediction of sexual, emotional, and physical maltreatment and mental health outcomes in a longitudinal cohort of 290 adolescent women. *Child Maltreatment, 5,* 218–226.

Barbero, G.J., & Shaheen, E. (1967). Environmental failure to thrive: A clinical view. *Journal of Pediatrics, 71,* 639–644.

Barnett, D., Manly, J., & Cicchetti, D. (1991). Continuing towards an operational definition of psychological maltreatment. *Development and Psychopathology, 3,* 13–30.

Barnett, D., Manly, J., & Cicchetti, D. (1993). Defining child maltreatment: The interface between policy and research. In D. Cicchetti & S. Toth (Eds.), *Child abuse, child development, and social policy: Vol. 8. Advances in applied developmental psychology* (pp. 7–73). Norwood, NJ: Ablex.

Bartol, C.R., & Bartol, A.M. (1994). *Psychology and law: Research and application* (2nd. ed.). Belmont, CA: Wadsworth.

Baumrind, D., Larzelere, R.E., & Cowan, P.A. (2002). Ordinary physical punishment: Is it harmful? Comment on Gershoff (2002). *Psychological Bulletin, 128,* 580–589.

Behl, L.E., Conyngham, H.A., & May, P.F. (2003). Trends in child maltreatment literature. *Child Abuse & Neglect, 27,* 215–229.

Benjet, C., & Kazdin, A.E. (2003). Spanking children: The controversies, findings, and new directions. *Clinical Psychology Review, 23,* 197–224.

Bensley, L., Ruggles, D., Simmons, K.W., Harris, C., Williams, K., Putvin, T., et al. (2004). General population norms about child abuse and neglect and associations with childhood experiences. *Child Abuse & Neglect, 28,* 1321–1337.

Besharov, D.J. (1981). Towards better research on child abuse and neglect: Making definitional issues an explicit methodological concern. *Child Abuse & Neglect, 5,* 383–391.

Boehm, B. (1964). The community and the social agency define neglect. *Child Welfare, 43,* 453–464.

Brassard, M.R., Germain, R., & Hart, S.N. (Eds.). (1987). *Psychological maltreatment of children and youth.* New York: Pergamon Press.

Bross, D.C. (1982). Medical care neglect. *Child Abuse & Neglect, 6,* 375–381.

Brown, J., Cohen, P., Johnson, J., & Salzinger, S. (1998). A longitudinal analysis of risk factors for child maltreatment: Findings of a 17-year prospective study of officially recorded and self-reported child abuse and neglect. *Child Abuse & Neglect, 22,* 1065–1078.

Bulkley, J. (1985). Analysis of civil child protection statutes dealing with sexual abuse. In J. Bulkley (Ed.), *Child sexual abuse and the law* (5th ed.). Washington, DC: American Bar Association.

Burns, G.E., & Lake, D.E. (1983). A sociolegal perspective on implementing child abuse legislation in education. *Interchange, 14,* 33–49.

Child Abuse Prevention and Treatment Act of 1974, PL 93-247, § 88 Stat 4, codified as amended at 42 U.S.C. § 5101–5120 (1996).

Ceci, S.J., & Bruck, M. (1995). *Jeopardy in the courtroom: A scientific analysis of children's testimony.* Washington, DC: American Psychological Association.

Cicchetti, D. (1996). Child maltreatment: Implications for developmental theory and research. *Human Development, 39,* 18–39.

Cicchetti, D., & Barnett, D. (1991). Toward the development of a scientific nosology of child maltreatment. In W. Grove & D. Cicchetti (Eds.), *Thinking clearly about psychology: Essays in honor of Paul E. Meehl: Vol. 2. Personality and psychopathology* (pp. 346–377). Minneapolis: University of Minnesota Press.

Cicchetti, D., & Manly, J.T. (Eds.). (2001). Operationalizing child maltreatment: Developmental processes and outcomes [Special issue]. *Development and Psychopathology, 13*(4).

Cicchetti, D., & Rizley, R. (1981). Developmental perspectives on the etiology, intergenerational transmission, and sequelae of child maltreatment. *New Directions for Child Development, 11,* 32–59.

Cicchetti, D., & Rogosch, F.A. (1996). Equifinality and multifinality in developmental psychopathology. *Development and Psychopathology, 8,* 597–600.

Cicchetti, D., & Rogosch, F.A. (2001). Diverse patterns of neuroendocrine activity in maltreated children. *Development and Psychopathology, 13,* 677–694.

Cohen, B., & Murphy, G.L. (1984). Models of concepts. *Cognitive Science, 8,* 27–58.

Cohen, J.A., & Mannarino, A.P. (1998). Factors that mediate treatment outcome of sexually abused preschool children: Six- and 12-month follow-up. *Journal of the American Academy of Child and Adolescent Psychiatry, 37,* 44–51.

Collier, A.F., McClure, F.H., Collier, J., Otto, C., & Polloi, A. (1999). Culture-specific views of child maltreatment and parenting styles in a Pacific-island community. *Child Abuse & Neglect, 23,* 229–244.

Craft, J.L., & Staudt, M.M. (1991). Reporting and founding of child neglect in urban and rural communities. *Child Welfare, 70,* 359–370.

Cronbach, L.J., & Meehl, P.E. (1955). Construct validity in psychological tests. *Psychological Bulletin, 52,* 281–302.

Cruise, K.R., Jacobs, J.E., & Lyons, P.M. (1994). Definitions of physical abuse: A preliminary inquiry into children's perceptions. *Behavioral Science and the Law, 12,* 35–48.

DeBellis, M.D. (2001). Developmental traumatology: The psychobiological development of maltreated children and its implications for research, treatment, and policy. *Development & Psychopathology, 13,* 539–564.

DeBellis, M.D. (2005). The psychobiology of neglect. *Child Maltreatment, 10,* 150–172.

De Boeck, P., Wilson, M., & Acton, G.S. (2005). A conceptual and psychometric framework for distinguishing categories and dimensions. *Psychological Review, 112,* 129–158.

Donohue, B., & Van Hasselt, V.B. (1999). Development and description of an empirically based ecobehavioral treatment program for child maltreatment. *Behavioral Interventions, 14,* 55–82.

Drake, B., & Zuravin, S. (1998). Bias in child maltreatment reporting: Revisiting the myth of classlessness. *American Journal of Orthopsychiatry, 68,* 295–304.

Dubowitz, H., Black, M., Starr, R.H., & Zuravin, S. (1993). A conceptual definition of child neglect. *Criminal Justice and Behavior, 20,* 8–26.

Dubowitz, H., Pitts, S.C., Litrownik, A.J., Cox, C.E., Runyan, D., & Black, M.M. (2005). Defining child neglect based on child protective services data. *Child Abuse & Neglect, 29,* 493–511.

Duggan, A., MacFarlane, L., Fuddy, L., Burrell, L., Higman, S.M., Windham, A., et al. (2004). Randomized trial of a statewide home visiting program: Impact in preventing child abuse and neglect. *Child Abuse & Neglect, 28,* 597–622.

Eckenrode, J., Powers, J., Doris, J., Munsch, J., & Bolger, N. (1988). Substantiation of child abuse and neglect reports. *Journal of Consulting and Clinical Psychology, 56,* 9–16.

Elmer, E., Gregg, G.S., & Ellison, P. (1969). Late results of the *failure to thrive* syndrome. *Clinical Pediatrics, 8,* 584–589.

Ertem, I.O., Leventhal, J.M., & Dobbs, S. (2000). Intergenerational continuity of child physical abuse: How good is the evidence? *Lancet, 356,* 814–819.

Femina, D.D., Yeager, C.A., & Lewis, D.O. (1990). Child abuse: Adolescent records vs. adult recall. *Child Abuse & Neglect, 14,* 227–231.

Fluke, J.D., Yuan, Y.T., Hedderson, J., & Curtis, P.A. (2003). Disproportionate representation of race and ethnicity in child maltreatment: Investigation and victimization. *Children and Youth Services Review, 25,* 359–373.

Freyd, J.J., Putnam, F.W., Lyon, T.D., Becker-Blease, K.A., Cheit, R.E., Siegel, N.B., et al. (2005). The science of child sexual abuse. *Science, 308,* 501.

Garrison, E.G., & Kobor, P.C. (2002). Weathering a political storm: A contextual perspective on a psychological research controversy. *American Psychologist, 57,* 165–175.

Geeraert, L., Van den Noortgate, W., Grietens, H., & Onghena, P. (2004). The effects of early prevention programs for families with young children at risk for physical child abuse and neglect: A meta-analysis. *Child Maltreatment, 9,* 277–291.

Gershoff, E.T. (2002). Corporal punishment by parents and associated child behaviors and experiences: A meta-analytic and theoretical review. *Psychological Bulletin, 128,* 539–579.

Giovannoni, J. (1989). Definitional issues in child maltreatment. In D. Cicchetti & V. Carlson (Eds.), *Child maltreatment: Theory and research on the causes and consequences of child abuse and neglect* (pp. 3–37). New York: Cambridge University Press.

Giovannoni, J., & Becerra, R. (1979). *Defining child abuse.* New York: Free Press.

Glaser, D. (2000). Child abuse and neglect and the brain—a review. *Journal of Child Psychology and Psychiatry, 41,* 97–116.

Gough, D. (1996). Defining the problem. *Child Abuse & Neglect, 20,* 993–1002.

Gracia, E. (1995). Visible but unreported: A case for the *not serious enough* cases of child maltreatment. *Child Abuse & Neglect, 19,* 1083–1093.

Greenwalt, B.C., Sklare, G., & Portes, P. (1998). The therapeutic treatment provided in cases involving physical child abuse: A description of current practices. *Child Abuse & Neglect, 22,* 71–78.

Heins, M. (1984). The *Battered Child* revisited. *Journal of the American Medical Association, 251,* 3295–3300.

Henry, B., Moffitt, T.E., Caspi, A., Langley, J., & Silva, P.A. (1994). On the remembrance of things past: A longitudinal evaluation of the retrospective method. *Psychological Assessment, 6,* 92–101.

Hildyard, K.L., & Wolfe, D.A. (2002). Child neglect: Developmental issues and outcomes. *Child Abuse & Neglect, 26,* 679–695.

Hines, A.M., Lemon, K., Wyatt, P., & Merdinger, J. (2004). Factors related to the disproportionate involvement of children of color in the child welfare system: A review and emerging themes. *Children and Youth Services Review, 26,* 507–527.

Hong, G.K., & Hong, L.K. (1991). Comparative perspectives on child abuse and neglect: Chinese versus Hispanics and Whites. *Child Welfare, 70,* 463–475.

Horowitz, A.V., Widom, C.S., McLaughlin, J., & White, H.R. (2001). The impact of child-hood abuse and neglect on adult mental health: A prospective study. *Journal of Health and Social Behavior, 42,* 184–201.

Hussey, J.M., Marshall, J.M., English, D.J., Knight, E.D., Lau, A.S., Dubowitz, H., et al. (2005). Defining maltreatment according to substantiation: Distinction without a differ-ence. *Child Abuse & Neglect, 29,* 479–492.

Hutchinson, E.D. (1990). Child maltreatment: Can it be defined? *Social Science Review, 64,* 1–78.

Kaufman, J., Jones, B., Stieglitz, E., Vitulano, L., & Mannarino, A. (1994). The use of mul-tiple informants to assess children's maltreatment experiences. *Journal of Family Violence, 9,* 227–248.

Kaufman, J., & Zigler, E. (1989). The intergenerational transmission of child abuse. In D. Cicchetti & V. Carlson (Eds.), *Child maltreatment: Theory and research on the causes and con-sequences of child abuse and neglect* (pp. 129–150). New York: Cambridge University Press.

Kempe, C.H. (1978). Recent developments in the field of child abuse. *Child Abuse & Neglect, 2,* 2261–2277.

Kempe, H., Silverman, F., Steele, B., Droegemueller, W., & Silver, H. (1962). The battered child syndrome. *Journal of the American Medical Association, 181* (1), 17–24.

Kinard, E.M. (1998). Classifying types of child maltreatment: Does the source of informa-tion make a difference? *Journal of Family Violence, 13,* 105–112.

Kolko, D.J. (1996). Individual cognitive behavioral treatment and family therapy for phys-ically abused children and their offending parents: A comparison of clinical outcomes. *Child Maltreatment, 1,* 322–342.

Korbin, J. (Ed.). (1981). *Child abuse and neglect: Cross-cultural perspectives.* Berkeley, CA: Uni-versity of California Press.

Korbin, J.E., Coulton, C.J., Lindstrom-Ufuti, H., & Spilsbury, J. (2000). Neighborhood views on the definition and etiology of child maltreatment. *Child Abuse & Neglect, 12,* 1509–1527.

Labbe, J. (2005). Ambroise Tardieu: The man and his work on child maltreatment a century before Kempe. *Child Abuse & Neglect, 29,* 311–324.

Lau, A.S., Leeb, R.T., English, D., Graham, J.C., Briggs, E.C., Brody, K.E., et al. (2005). What's in a name? A comparison of methods for classifying predominant type of mal-treatment. *Child Abuse & Neglect, 29,* 533–551.

Lilienfeld, S.O. (2002). When worlds collide: Social science, politics, and the Rind et al. (1998). Child sexual abuse meta-analysis. *American Psychologist, 57,* 176–188.

Lu, Y.E., Landsverk, J., Ellis-Macleod, E., Newton, R., Ganger, W., & Johnson, I. (2004). Race, ethnicity, and case outcomes in child protective services. *Children and Youth Services Review, 26,* 447–461.

Lynch, M.A. (1985). Child abuse before Kempe: An historical literature review. *Child Abuse & Neglect, 9,* 7–15.

Lyon, G.R. (Ed.). (1995). *Frames of reference for the assessment of learning disabilities: New views on measurement issues.* Baltimore: Paul H. Brookes Publishing Co.

Lyon, G.R., Gray, D.B., Kavanagh, J.F., & Krasnegor, N.A. (Eds.). (1993). *Better understand-ing learning disabilities: New views from research and their implications for education and public policies.* Baltimore: Paul H. Brookes Publishing Co.

MacLeod, J., & Nelson, G. (2001). Programs for the promotion of family wellness and the prevention of child maltreatment: A meta-analytic review. *Child Abuse & Neglect, 24,* 1127–1149.

Macmillan, H.L., Thomas, B.H., Jamieson, E., Walsh, C.A., Boyle, M.H., Shannon, H., et al. (2005). Effectiveness of home visitation by public-health nurses in prevention of the recurrence of child physical abuse and neglect: A randomized controlled trial. *Lancet, 365,* 1786–1793.

Malinosky-Rummell, R., & Hansen, D.J. (1993). Long-term consequences of childhood physical abuse. *Psychological Bulletin, 114,* 68–79.

Manly, J.T. (2005). Advances in research definitions of child maltreatment. *Child Abuse & Neglect, 29,* 425–439.

Manly, J.T., Kim, J.E., Rogosch, F.A., & Cicchetti, D. (2001). Dimensions of child maltreatment and children's adjustment: Contributions of developmental timing and subtype. *Development and Psychopathology, 13,* 759–782.

Meehl, P.E. (1992). Factors and taxa, traits and types, differences of degree and differences in kind. *Journal of Personality, 60,* 117–174.

Meehl, P.E. (1995). Bootstrap taxometrics: Solving the classification problem in psychopathology. *American Psychologist, 50,* 266–275.

McGee, R.A., & Wolfe, D.A. (1991). Psychological maltreatment: Toward an operational definition. *Development and Psychopathology, 3,* 3–18.

McGee, R.A., Wolfe, D.A., Yuen, S.A., Wilson, S.K., & Carnochan, J. (1995). The measurement of maltreatment: A comparison of approaches. *Child Abuse & Neglect, 19,* 233–249.

Miller-Perrin, C., & Perrin, R.D. (1999). *Child maltreatment: An introduction.* Thousand Oaks, CA: Sage Publications.

Murphy, G.L., & Medin, D.L. (1985). The role of theories in conceptual coherence. *Psychological Review, 92,* 289–316.

National Research Council. (1993). *Understanding child abuse and neglect.* Washington, DC: National Academies Press.

Navarre, E.L. (1987). Psychological maltreatment: The core component of child abuse. In M.R. Brassard, R. Germain, & S.N. Hart (Eds.), *Psychological maltreatment of children and youth* (pp. 45–56). New York: Pergamon Press.

O'Hagan, K.P. (1995). Emotional and psychological abuse: Problems of definition. *Child Abuse & Neglect, 19,* 449–461.

Oldershaw, L., Walters, G.C., & Hall, D.K. (1989). A behavioral approach to the classification of different types of physically abusive mothers. *Merrill-Palmer Quarterly, 35,* 255–279.

Olds, D.L., Eckenrode, J., Henderson, C.R., Jr., Kitzman, H., Powers, J., Cole, R., et al. (1997). Long-term effects of home visitation on maternal life course and child abuse and neglect: Fifteen-year follow-up of a randomized trial. *Journal of the American Medical Association, 278,* 637–643.

Oliver, J.E. (1993). Intergenerational transmission of child abuse: Rates, research, and clinical implications. *American Journal of Psychiatry, 150,* 1315–1324.

Ornstein, P.A., Ceci, S.J., & Loftus, E.F. (1998). Adult recollections of childhood abuse: Cognitive and developmental perspectives. *Psychology, Public Policy, & Law, 4,* 1025–1051.

Perez, C.M., & Widom, C.S. (1994). Childhood victimization and long term intellectual and academic outcomes. *Child Abuse & Neglect, 18,* 617–633.

Portwood, S.G. (1999). Coming to terms with a consensual definition of child maltreatment. *Child Maltreatment, 4,* 56–68.

Prescott, A., Bank, L., Reid, J.B., Knutson, J.F., Burraston, B.O., & Eddy, J.M. (2000). The verdicality of punitive childhood experiences reported by adolescents and young adults. *Child Abuse & Neglect, 24,* 411–423.

Putnam, F.W. (2003). Ten-year research update review: Child sexual abuse. *Journal of the American Academy of Child & Adolescent Psychiatry, 42,* 269–278.

Quine, W.V.O. (1977). Natural kinds. In S.P. Schwartz (Ed.), *Naming, necessity, and natural kinds* (pp. 155–175). Ithaca, NY: Cornell University Press.

Rind, B., Tromovitch, P., & Bauserman, R. (1998). A meta-analytic examination of assumed properties of child sexual abuse using college samples. *Psychological Bulletin, 124,* 22–53.

Rosch, E., & Mervis, C.B. (1975). Family resemblances: Studies in the internal structure of categories. *Cognitive Psychology, 7,* 573–605.

Roscoe, B. (1990). Defining child maltreatment: Ratings of parental behaviors. *Adolescence, 99,* 517.

Rose, S.J., & Meezan, W. (1993). Defining child neglect: Evolution, influences, and issues. *Social Service Review, 67,* 279–293.

Rose, S.J., & Meezan, W. (1995). Child neglect: A study of the perceptions of mothers and child welfare workers. *Children and Youth Services Review, 17,* 471–486.

Rose, S.J., & Meezan, W. (1996). Variations in perceptions of child neglect. *Child Welfare, 75,* 139–160.

Runyan, D.K., Cox, C.E., Dubowitz, H., Newton, R.R., Upadhyay, M., Kotch, J.B., et al. (2005). Describing maltreatment: Do child protective service reports and research definitions agree? *Child Abuse & Neglect, 29,* 461–477.

Runyan, D.K., Curtis, P.A., Hunter, W.M., Black, M.M., Kotch, J.B., Bangdiwala, S., et al. (1998). Longscan: A consortium for longitudinal studies of maltreatment and the life course of children. *Aggression and Violent Behavior, 3,* 275–285.

Sedlak, A.J., & Broadhurst, D.D. (1996). *Third national incidence study of child abuse and neglect: Final report.* Washington, DC: U.S. Department of Health and Human Services.

Sher, K.J., & Eisenberg, N. (2002). Publication of Rind et al. (1998): The editors' perspective. *American Psychologist, 57,* 206–210.

Silverman, F.N. (1972). Unrecognized trauma in infants, the battered-child syndrome, and the syndrome of Ambroise Tardieu. *Radiology, 104,* 337–353.

Skinner, H.A. (1977). *The eyes that fix you:* A model for classification research. *Canadian Psychological Review, 18,* 142–151.

Skinner, H.A. (1979). Dimensions and clusters: A hybrid approach to classification. *Applied Psychological Measurement, 3,* 327–341.

Skinner, H.A. (1981). Toward the integration of classification theory and methods. *Journal of Abnormal Psychology, 90,* 68–87.

Slack, K.S., Holl, J., Altenbernd, L., McDaniel, M., & Stevens, A.B. (2003). Improving the measurement of child neglect for survey research: Issues and recommendations. *Child Maltreatment, 8,* 98–111.

Smith, E.E., & Medin, D.L. (1981). *Categories and concepts.* Cambridge, MA: Harvard University Press.

Stein, T.W. (1991). *Child welfare and the law.* New York: Longman Publishing Group.

Stevenson, O. (1996). Emotional abuse and neglect: A time for reappraisal. *Child and Family Social Work, 1,* 13–18.

Straus, M.A., & Moore, D.W. (1990). Differences among states in child abuse rates and programs. In D.J. Besharov (Ed.), *Family violence: Research and public policy issues* (pp. 150–163). Washington, DC: The AEI Press.

Tajima, E.A., Herrenkohl, T.I., Huang, B., & Whitney, S.D. (2004). Measuring child maltreatment: A comparison of prospective parent reports and retrospective adolescent reports. *American Journal of Orthopsychiatry, 4,* 424–435.

Teicher, M.H., Anderson, S.L., Polcari, A., Anderson, C.M., Navalta, C.P., & Kim, D. (2003). The neurobiological consequences of early stress and childhood maltreatment. *Neuroscience and Biobehavioral Reviews, 27,* 33–44.

Theodore, A.D., & Runyan, D.K. (1999). A medical research agenda for child maltreatment: Negotiating the next steps. *Pediatrics, 104*(1), 168–177.

Toth, S.L., & Cicchetti, D. (1993). Child maltreatment: Where do we go from here in our treatment of victims? In D. Cicchetti & S.L. Toth (Eds.), *Child abuse, child development, and social policy* (pp. 399–438). Norwood, NJ: Ablex.

Trickett, P., & McBride-Chang, C. (1995). The developmental impact of different forms of child abuse and neglect. *Developmental Review, 15,* 311–337.

U. S. Department of Health and Human Services. (1981). *Study findings: National study of the incidence and severity of child abuse and neglect* (DHHS Publication No. OHDS 81-30325). Washington, DC: Government Printing Office.

U.S. Department of Health and Human Services. (1988). *Study findings: Study of national incidence and prevalence of child abuse and neglect* (DHHS Publication No. ADM 20-01099). Washington, DC: Government Printing Office.

Waldfogel, J. (1998). Rethinking the paradigm for child protection. *The Future of Children, 8*(1), 104–119.

Whipple, E.E., & Richey, C.A. (1997). Crossing the line from physical discipline to child abuse: How much is too much? *Child Abuse & Neglect, 21,* 431–444.

Widom, C.S. (1989). Does violence beget violence? A critical examination of the literature. *Psychological Bulletin, 106,* 3–28.

Widom, C.S., & Morris, S. (1997). Accuracy of adult recollections of childhood victimization: Part 2. Childhood sexual abuse. *Psychological Assessment, 9,* 34–46.

Widom, C.S., & Shepard, R.L. (1996). Accuracy of adult recollections of childhood victimization: Part 1. Childhood physical abuse. *Psychological Assessment, 8,* 412–421.

Wissow, L. (1995). Child abuse and neglect. *New England Journal of Medicine, 332,* 1425–1431.

Wolfe, D.A. (1985). Child-abusive parents: An empirical review and analysis. *Psychological Bulletin, 97,* 462–482.

Wolfe, D.A., & McGee, R. (1994). Child maltreatment and adolescent adjustment. *Development and Psychopathology, 6,* 165–181.

Wolfe, D.A., & Wekerle, C. (1995). Treatment strategies for child physical abuse and neglect: A critical progress report. *Clinical Psychology Review, 13,* 473–500.

Yarrow, M., Campbell, J.D., & Burton, R.V. (1970). Recollections of childhood: A study of the retrospective method. *Monographs of the Society for Research in Child Development, 35* (5, Serial No. 138).

Yudof, M., Kirp, D., Levin, B., & Moran, R. (2002). *Educational policy and the law.* Belmont, CA: Wadsworth.

Zimring, F.E. (1989). Toward a jurisprudence of family violence. In L. Ohlin & M. Tonry (Eds.), *Family Violence: Vol. 11. Crime and justice: An annual review of research* (pp. 547–570). Chicago: University of Chicago Press.

2

Defining Child Abuse and Neglect

A Search for Consensus

ROSEMARY CHALK

In 1991, Dr. Wade Horn, then Commissioner for the Administration on Children, Youth and Families (ACYF) in the U.S. Department of Health and Human Services (DHHS), asked the National Academy of Sciences to develop a research agenda that could guide future studies of child maltreatment. Several factors prompted his request. The research community had long expressed interest in developing a synthesis of findings from the extensive research literature that had emerged since the passage of the Child Abuse Prevention and Treatment Act of 1974 (PL 93-247). In addition, program staff within DHHS were concerned with the quality of the future child maltreatment research program. Their objective was to develop a set of programmatic research priorities that could offer protection against persistent congressional efforts to set aside, or "earmark," funds in the federal child abuse research program for special interest service delivery projects. Up to that time, child abuse and neglect research projects within the ACYF were largely responsive to immediate and programmatic information needs within the child protection and child welfare services practice community and were generally uninformed by conceptual or disciplinary frameworks. The result was a fragmentary and patchwork research field that had second-class status within the scientific community when compared with theory-driven research sponsored by the National Institute of Child Health and Human Development (NICHD), the National Institute of Mental Health (NIMH), and other components of the National Institutes of Health (NIH). Furthermore, stakeholders within the federal government and the research community were hopeful that the development of a coherent rationale and research agenda on child maltreatment would lead to the expansion of funds available to support studies in the area.

In response to the Commissioner's request, the National Academy of Sciences (NAS) convened a study panel, referred to as the Panel on Research on Child Abuse and Neglect, within the National Research Council (NRC), the operating arm of the NAS that was responsible for ad hoc studies. The panel was chaired by Anne C. Petersen, Ph.D., a well-known researcher in the field of adolescent

---

The author recognizes the research contributions of Purva Rawal in developing this chapter.

development who was then Vice President for Research and Dean of the graduate school at the University of Minnesota. The 16 panel members included distinguished researchers in the field of child abuse and neglect, as well as others who were not directly associated with this field but who presented solid credentials and expertise in the areas of epidemiology, statistics, pediatric medicine, child development, and sociology.[1]

The composition of the NRC panel was designed to mix researchers who had expertise in the field with others who could critique the quality and coherence of child abuse and neglect studies by comparing this research literature with other areas of child and family studies. The NRC panel conducted its work through a series of public and private deliberations, an extensive review of the research literature, the development of commissioned papers, and a survey of leading organizations in child maltreatment research.

The purpose of the panel was to perform a comprehensive examination of the theoretical and pragmatic research needs in the field of child abuse and neglect. More specifically, the study was designed to 1) review and assess research on child abuse and neglect, including work previously conducted by the ACYF and other public and private agencies; 2) identify research relevant to the child abuse and neglect field; and 3) outline research priorities for the upcoming decade. Research priorities that were identified included shaping building blocks for knowledge development in child maltreatment, finding new research avenues that could be funded by public and private agencies, and suggesting research areas within the field that might no longer be funding priorities.

The report of the panel, *Understanding Child Abuse and Neglect* (NRC, 1993), is now considered a landmark synthesis of child abuse and neglect research. It provided a foundation that has since guided many discussions about the importance of developing a common conceptual framework, research definitions, rigorous classification, and empirical measurement in the field of child maltreatment. The panel's study also represented a pivotal moment in shifting the field from a patchwork effort of applied research studies to a more cohesive set of activities striving to improve theory, instrumentation, measurement, and data collection efforts.

One result of the NRC panel's report was that the NIH and the Children's Bureau in the Administration on Children, Youth and Families convened two

---

[1]The members of the National Research Council Panel on Research on Child Abuse and Neglect were Anne C. Petersen (chair), University of Minnesota; J. Lawrence Aber, Columbia University; Andrew Billingsley, University of Maryland; Jeanne Brooks-Gunn, Columbia University; Donald Cohen, Yale University; Michael I. Cohen, Albert Einstein College of Medicine; Jon Robert Conte, University of Washington; Byron Egeland, University of Minnesota; E. Mavis Hetherington, University of Virginia; Sara McCue Horwitz, Yale University; Jill Korbin, Case Western Reserve University; Dorothy Otnow Lewis, New York University; Roderick J.A. Little, University of California at Los Angeles; Murray A. Straus, University of New Hampshire; Cathy Spatz Widom, University of New York at Albany; and Gail Wyatt, University of California at Los Angeles. The author of this chapter was the study director.

workshops focused on defining and classifying child abuse and neglect (the first in December 1999 and the second in September 2000) that were the inspiration for this book. Therefore, it is useful to reexamine the basic framework and approach adopted by the NRC panel and to consider their relevance for contemporary discussions of classification, theory, measurement, and definitions of child abuse and neglect.

SHIFTING FRAMEWORKS FOR RESEARCH ON VIOLENCE AND CHILD DEVELOPMENT

The work of the NRC panel was influenced indirectly by other studies that were underway within the NRC in the late 1980s and early 1990s. In 1988, a consortium of federal agencies—the National Institute of Justice, the National Science Foundation, and the Centers for Disease Control—had asked the NAS to assess the state of scientific knowledge about violence, to consider the implications of that understanding for preventive interventions, and to design research and evaluation studies that could improve the understanding and the control of violence. In response, the NAS created the NRC Panel on the Understanding and Control of Violent Behavior, chaired by sociologist Albert Reiss from Yale University. The Reiss panel eventually published a four-volume series of reports that included a summary report as well as a series of background papers commissioned by the committee (NRC, 1993/1994).

Although the activities of these two studies occurred at the same time, the two groups did not meet, nor did they share research materials. However, the conceptual framework that evolved from the Reiss panel was "in the air" at the time the Petersen panel was convening, and it helped to guide discussions that focused on how to move the field of child abuse away from an applied research orientation toward one that was grounded more firmly in theory, measurement, classification, and data. One important contribution from the Petersen panel was the recognition of the need for multiple classification schemes in addressing violent events as well as of the inherent limits of using administrative data records to guide empirical and scientific studies. Because research on child abuse and neglect had often depended (and continues to depend) on records from child protective and child welfare agencies rather than from population-based, longitudinal, or experimental studies, the need to disaggregate different types of child abuse and neglect into new categories based on a theory-driven classification scheme acquired central importance in the Petersen panel.

The studies on violence research and child abuse were the first in what would become a series of reports on other aspects of family violence published by the NRC. Subsequent publications included "Understanding Violence against Women" (1996); "Violence in Families: Assessing Prevention and Treatment Programs" (1998); and, in 2002, "Confronting Chronic Neglect: The Education and Training of Health Professionals on Family Violence." Each report had its own study committee, study sponsor, and study director, and each report considered separate research literatures. Nevertheless, the research literatures examined in these multiple reports showed a movement toward a gradual acceptance of the importance of conceptual frameworks and the need for stronger theory to guide the discovery of fundamental processes in the study of complex human behavior, parenting practices, and family systems.

Two influential lines of research were emerging within the child development literature that drew child maltreatment studies toward a broader ecological framework of parent–child interactions. The first, ecological systems theory, developed by Urie Bronfenbrenner (1979) and others, has had a profound influence on research in child development. Ecological systems theory, as described by Bronfenbrenner, asserts that child development occurs through a complex process of interactions between the immediate environment of the child and broader environmental layers, such as the family, school, church, community, and larger society and cultural norms. Development is shaped at the microsystem level by family and local community factors, at the mesosystem level by intermediate societal factors and institutions, and at the macrosystem level by national and global factors. Disruption at any one of these layers affects the others as well. Thus, child development is a complex interaction between the child's biology and proximal and distal environmental influences (Bronfenbrenner, 1979).

Second, studies of violence in the latter part of the 20th century moved toward an analysis of biobehavioral actions within social settings and studies of child development and parental caregiving. These shifts were influenced by transitions in new theories that sought to account for the role of social and cultural factors in human behavior and interpersonal relationships (Garbarino, 1977; Wolfe, 1991). Researchers began conceptualizing child maltreatment from a transactional perspective, in which factors associated with families, communities, and the larger society and culture acquired greater importance in examining processes that contributed to child maltreatment as well as child development. The result was a de-emphasis on personal factors, such as parental psychopathology, and greater attention to the examination of interactions among individual, family, and community stressors (Belsky, 1980; Cicchetti & Lynch, 1993). The increasing level of sophistication in consideration of multiple causal pathways and processes was characteristic of other social policy studies at the time.

New paradigms were created to reconcile the nature and sources of aggression and violence in human relationships with emerging theory describing stages of child development, parental caregiving and disciplinary practices, and family interactions in coping with stress and conflict. The result was a significant shift in both the field of violence research and the field of child development, away from a narrow focus on mechanistic models that isolated individual psychiatric and psychological factors toward a more expansive, yet still poorly conceptualized, approach that put greater emphasis on settings, cultural forces, and dynamics in child development and their role in multiple pathways to abuse and neglect

(Cicchetti & Lynch, 1993; Wolfe, 1991). Greater research attention was devoted to understanding the role of risk and protective factors in the social environment; the processes of resiliency; and the ways in which the presence or absence of psychological, social, and cultural supports within the family and community help to mediate or influence certain types of stressful interactions involving care for children, particularly those who are young (Belsky, 1980; Egeland, Breitenbucher, & Rosenberg, 1980; Polansky, Gaudin, & Kilpatrick, 1992).

These and other research developments influenced the Petersen panel to adopt an ecological, developmental perspective in examining the etiology, incidence, and consequences of child maltreatment. For instance, Egeland et al. (1980) conducted a prospective study of the antecedents of child maltreatment in which they compared families that had been reported for child maltreatment with high-risk families that appeared to provide adequate levels of care. Results demonstrated that the association between risk level in families and whether children were maltreated was far from linear; in fact, many mothers who were considered high-risk for maltreating their children did not do so, and many incidents of maltreatment occurred among mothers judged to be at low risk (Egeland et al., 1980). This study demonstrated the complexity of the relationships among parental characteristics, environmental stressors, and the occurrence of child maltreatment.

The shift in research paradigms had profound implications for the definition and classification of child abuse and neglect experiences. In addition, recognition of the variations and gaps associated with legal and administrative definitions of child maltreatment emerged within policy and programmatic fields, fostering more receptivity to research-based definitions and measurement. However, the research field itself was changing and rearranging conceptual frameworks (Belsky, 1980; Cicchetti & Lynch, 1993). For instance, Garbarino (1977) and Belsky (1980) created ecological models of child maltreatment based largely on Bronfenbrenner's work. Cicchetti and Lynch (1993) later created transactional and interactive models of child maltreatment, in which combinations of risk factors and protective factors were assumed to interact across all ecological levels to contribute to the occurrence of child maltreatment behaviors. The result of these new frameworks was greater ambiguity and confusion as to how to define the principal elements of abuse and neglect and how to align science-based definitions with legal standards and administrative records. However, this ambiguity should not be viewed as a step backwards. Indeed, it acted as a precursor to a deeper understanding of the critical elements of abuse and neglect, and it offered an opportunity to reframe definitions that could subsequently guide policy and practice by focusing on the most critical aspects of child maltreatment as well as those behaviors that might be most amenable to change.

One other body of research literature deserves mention here, although it did not receive major consideration in the NRC study on child abuse and neglect. In the mid-1980s, public health agencies on injury began to form more rigorous classification and definitional standards to improve the quality of surveillance and epidemiological studies of injury. In 1985, a NRC study, "Injury in America: A Continuing Public Health Program," summarized these efforts, recommending improving the systematic collection of injury data to strengthen prevention strategies. The report concluded, among other things, that significant uncertainties and gaps in the epidemiology of injury occurrence impeded scientific understanding of the causes and consequences of assaultive injuries. Most importantly for the child maltreatment field, the report recommended that funding for research on the prevention of injury and maltreatment of children should be proportionate to its status as the largest cause of death and disability in youth.

The public health injury surveillance system began to pay attention to child abuse and neglect within the category of "intentional injuries," and it eventually developed a detailed classification scheme that is now part of the International Classification of Disease (ICD) codes. Newer versions of the ICD codes include "E-codes," which classify external causes of injury, such as the use of guns or knives in assault injuries. It is noteworthy that the child development and violence research literatures are still explaining how to adapt the detailed ICD classification scheme to provide additional injury-specific information, such as identifying the time of day or locations where injuries occur or their association with particular actions such as feeding or disciplinary behaviors.

MOVING BEYOND
LEGAL CATEGORIES OF ABUSE AND NEGLECT

The 1974 Child Abuse and Prevention Treatment Act (CAPTA; PL 93-247) stipulated that the new National Center on Child Abuse and Neglect (NCCAN) investigate the incidence of child abuse and neglect across the country. CAPTA and the research that emerged from it led to more specific classification of child abuse and neglect. At the time that the Petersen panel began its work, four general categories of child maltreatment—a result of CAPTA—were commonly recognized in the research literature: physical abuse, sexual abuse, neglect, and emotional or psychological maltreatment. Most research studies had focused on physical and sexual abuse. The amount of attention focused on neglect in the research community was limited, despite the fact that cases of child neglect constituted more than half of the reports received annually by child protection agencies, were widely recognized as the most common individual type of maltreatment. The second National Incidence Study (NIS-2; DHHS, 1988) also demonstrated that neglect was involved in 63% of the reported cases. Wolock and Horowitz, commenting on this phenomenon, wrote about "the neglect of neglect" in a 1984 paper.

Recognizing that these four categories encompassed a broad range of behaviors, the NRC report "Understanding Child Abuse and Neglect" (1993) stated that although broad consensus might exist around extreme forms of child abuse and neglect (e.g., beatings, disfigurement, and sexual abuse), less severe manifestations presented more complicated issues with respect to definition and classification. Furthermore, a classification scheme by types of abuse might be useful for pragmatic or legal reasons, but it lacked the conceptual constructs that could help research studies differentiate the pathways to and outcomes associated with abuse and neglect. Co-occurrence of different types of maltreatment was common, blurring even the appearance of mutually exclusive sequelae by type. The "types of abuse" typology also provided little support in comparing research findings across studies or in explaining the sequence, timing, or relationship of maltreatment to other family processes and social behaviors. Therefore, the panel was searching for alternative frameworks and definitions that could address these limitations and help to improve data collection efforts that would strengthen the overall field of child abuse and neglect research.

LIMITATIONS OF SERVICE-BASED DEFINITIONS

In the absence of universal definitions of child abuse and neglect, different service sectors and the research community had developed separate and multiple criteria and classification frameworks for each of the four traditional categories of child maltreatment: physical abuse, sexual abuse, neglect, and emotional or psychological maltreatment. Definitions of child abuse and neglect were largely driven by state laws and regulations, creating inconsistencies and variations that impeded the use of standardized assessment instruments. Additional complications were associated with high caseloads and gaps in social services, inaccurate or incomplete information, and limited services for affected families (Hoaglin, Light, McPeek, Mosteller, & Stoto, 1982; Leventhal, 1990). The NRC report reviewed these approaches, indicating that although service-oriented definitions were necessary for delivery, practice, and policy purposes, they were characterized by fragmentation and inconsistencies that represented serious impediments to improving the quality of data and knowledge in this field. Medical and clinical definitions, social services definitions, and legal and judicial definitions are reviewed in the following sections.

Medical and Clinical Definitions

For decades, physicians had recognized child abuse and neglect as a disturbing and sometimes unique set of physical conditions, frequently characterized by fractures, burns, scars, other injuries, and parental deprivation of medical care. In the early 1990s, however, no universal medical definition of child abuse and neglect, much less of physical abuse per se, existed. If physicians thought in terms beyond injury and treatment, their classifications were likely to be hindered by state definitions that included ambiguous terms such as *substantial, unjustified,* and *allowable* (Johnson, 1990). Over time, health professionals acquired greater expertise through clinical experience and improved instrumentation in detecting signs of abuse or neglect. For example, in the case of "shaken baby syndrome," physicians began to search for physical signs of shaking (e.g., bruises, retinal hemorrhaging) and for more moderate symptoms, including poor feeding history or flu-like symptoms in the absence of diarrhea or fever (Palmer, 2000). Other tell-tale signs of abuse and/or neglect included discrepant or vague explanations of child injuries, delay in seeking care, a family crisis or history of abuse, trigger behaviors by the child, unrealistic expectations of the child by the parents (often involving personal hygiene, feeding, or emotional regulation), isolation of the family, and the parent's own history of abuse (Krugman, 1983).

In the area of sexual abuse, the medical literature focused predominantly on physical findings, such as chafing, abrasions, bruising of the inner thighs and genitalia, scarring in specific genital areas, and specific abnormalities of the hymen (American Academy of Pediatrics, 1991). According to a report published by the Office of Juvenile Justice and Delinquency Prevention, the presence of certain sexually transmitted diseases also often served as the first indicator of sexual abuse, especially among young children (Hammerschlag, 2001).

The NRC report indicated that although the medical diagnosis of child abuse had improved, especially in the area of physical abuse, research in this area was retrospective, clinical, and frequently derived from observation of individuals from one institution. A major shortcoming in the development of medical definitions of abuse was the absence of prospective and population-based studies that could describe the routine as well as extreme range of physical conditions that occur during the development of young children within different racial and ethnic groups. These physical conditions include sexual development and the array of injuries that may be particularly damaging at certain critical developmental periods for infants, toddlers, and preschoolers, regardless of their origins.

Social Services Definitions

Most of the data associated with child maltreatment studies is derived from case records and administrative data collected by child protective services (CPS) and child welfare agencies. In the early 1990s, with support from Congress, NCCAN began a series of initiatives to standardize the application of definitions and classification guidelines within the child protection and child welfare administrative datasets and the state data collection systems that were used to track and report individual cases. These initiatives included the development of the National Child Abuse and Neglect Data Systems (NCANDS), the State Automated Child Welfare Information System, and, more recently, the Adoption Foster Care Analysis and Reporting System (DHHS, 2006).

The development of standardized case definitions and classification criteria was challenged by the long-standing tradition of child protection and child welfare as a state-based responsibility within the United States. This fragmentation and the absence of a separate data system to guide scientific studies hampered progress in developing generalizable knowledge and theory. In seeking to upgrade the quality of state information and tracking systems, federal agencies needed to respect and accommodate significant variations in state law, reporting requirements, and administrative capacity at the local and county levels. Through a series of conferences and technical assistance and consensus-building efforts, the quality of the NCANDS data and the automated child protection and child welfare information systems began to improve; however, major shortcomings that continue to deter classification efforts still remain in the areas of incomplete or missing data, duplicated cases, and inconsistent reporting practices.

One important limitation in using administrative datasets to define and classify child abuse and neglect cases is the variation that is introduced by uncontrolled methods of case detection and selection into those datasets. The resource limitations within the child protection and child welfare fields contribute to case selection strategies that are comparable to the clinical bias that exists in medical settings. CPS samples rarely include mild forms of child maltreatment, because such cases are routinely screened out when physical evidence to support allegations is lacking. The frequency of contacts between social services agencies and poor children may contribute to overrepresentation of these populations in the CPS case records. As noted in the NRC report, regional or chronological differences in maltreatment rates may reflect different patterns and standards of reporting and selection criteria as well as differences in agency resources, rather than true differences in underlying rates of occurrences of abuse and neglect.

Legal and Judicial Definitions

The NRC report also reviewed the role of legal and judicial standards in developing early definitions of child abuse and neglect. The panel noted that legislative acts, such as CAPTA (1974), began to broaden the study of prohibited behaviors by moving attention beyond the precise characteristics of abusive acts themselves to include greater consideration of their consequences for the child. Broader legal definitions of child abuse included emotional injury, neglect, lack of provision of medical services by parents, and factors damaging children's moral development, in addition to physical abuse (Cicchetti & Barnett, 1991). The Juvenile Justice Standards Project used three major categories to define child abuse: physical harm, emotional damage, and sexual abuse, with strict standards within each of the three categories (Wald, 1977). In the absence of empirical definitions, the law and the courts drew on evidentiary standards derived from legislative guidelines, professional opinion, and customary practice. These definitions were intended to guide legal interventions, not long-term treatment or prevention efforts or research studies, and their focus was often more stringent than the approaches used in medical, social services, or research settings, searching out the aspects of the report or event that made the best evidence for a successful prosecution.

For example, in the Juvenile Justice Standards Project (Wald, 1977), the following definitions were used:

- Physical harm is defined as disfigurement, impairment of bodily functions, or other serious physical injury.

- Emotional damage is evidenced by severe anxiety, depression or withdrawal, or untoward aggressive behavior toward self or others; and the child's parents are unwilling to provide treatment for him or her.

- Sexual abuse is limited to those cases in which the child is seriously harmed physically or emotionally thereby. Such a definition excludes many cases in which consequences are not immediately apparent but may emerge at later points in the developmental cycle.

RECONCEPTUALIZING THE FIELD THROUGH A DEVELOPMENTAL AND ECOLOGICAL APPROACH

The discussion of definitions in the 1993 NRC report, "Understanding Child Abuse and Neglect," symbolized a significant shift in the traditional paradigms that had guided the field of child maltreatment studies and data collection. Frustration with the shortcomings and fragmentation of medical, social services, and legal definitions was driving the research field toward a unified and integrated approach that could replace the multiple and separate frameworks focused on types of abuse and neglect in different service and policy settings.

The panel concluded that empirical research in this field was weakened by inconsistent definitions of the phenomenon under study and the tremendous variation and differences introduced by different selection criteria and research samples. As noted in the report,

Definitions are . . . essential in order to develop measures to compare and generalize results of different studies on the effects of maltreatment on the primary, secondary, or tertiary prevention of maltreatment. In the absence of consensus about child maltreatment measures, existing studies employ an array of different measures that can yield results that conflict or are hard to interpret. (NRC, 1993, p. 59)

The study committee also observed that a fundamental role of conceptual frameworks is to guide measurement and data collection. The framework and theory should offer guidance as to what is important to measure and how to measure it. The report stated,

A classification scheme of great conceptual elegance is of limited utility in empirical research unless it can be operationalized. That is, the conceptual definition has to be converted into specific behaviors that can be measured by observation, interview, or some other practical means. (NRC, 1993, p. 63)

Yet, it is difficult to create science-based frameworks, classifications, and definitions in the absence of reliable and valid measures. For example, a precursor framework and theory might offer guidance about what is important to measure and how to measure it, but it is the measures themselves that will empirically guide the complex framework.

In reaching for greater conceptual strength that could guide future measurement and data collection efforts, the NRC panel was strongly influenced by research on child development and family relations and the desire to bring this theoretical and empirical work to bear on child abuse and neglect studies. Earlier conceptual work by Urie Bronfenbrenner (1979) and the later transactional and ecological theories developed by James Garbarino (1977), Dante Cicchetti, (Cicchetti & Barnett, 1991; Cicchetti & Carlson, 1989), Jay Belsky (1980), and others had all sought to put forward a child developmental framework based on empirical observations of relationships among children, families, and their social environments. The NRC panel drew heavily on this literature and sought to integrate child maltreatment studies within an ecological, transactional, developmental framework that was focused on parent–child interactions. Garbarino (1977) has described this reconceptualization as an approach that considers child abuse and neglect as one part of a wider category of unhealthy patterns of parent–child relations. This approach was desirable because it could help explain typical patterns as well as disruptions in parental and other nurturing behaviors and also examine the management of stress and conflict within families as part of a larger continuum of parent–child relationships. The NRC panel gave particular emphasis to the relationship of social and cultural factors to parenting and caregiving behaviors and the systemic forces that could mitigate or exacerbate family processes and relationships, thus contributing to child protection and nurturance as well as child abuse and neglect.

The panel did not consider the role of genetic or biological factors in its effort to define and classify child abuse and neglect. Indeed, research implicating such factors had not yet been published at the time of the panel's deliberations from the fall of 1991 into the summer of 1993 (NRC, 1993). In its review of adult personality characteristics associated with abuse and neglect, the panel observed that "a consistent profile of parental psychopathology or a significant level of mental disturbance has not been supported" (NRC, 1993, p. 111). The NRC panel further rejected the use of single-factor or unicausal theories that might purport to explain the origins of child abuse and neglect, noting that they "have not been able to identify specific mechanisms that influence the etiology of child maltreatment" (p. 139).

PRINCIPLES UNDERLYING RESEARCH DEFINITIONS

The NRC panel did not develop its own definitions of child abuse and neglect, but drew instead on an earlier definition developed by a 1989 conference convened by the NICHD. The NICHD conference recommended that maltreatment be defined as

> Behavior towards another person, which (a) is outside the norms of conduct, and (b) entails a substantial risk of causing physical or emotional harm. Behaviors included will consist of actions and omissions, ones that are intentional and ones that are unintentional. (Christoffel et al., 1992)

Child maltreatment, under this definition, included those behaviors that involved risk for the child as well as harm.

This definition had the advantage of incorporating all categories of abuse and neglect, reaching beyond the issue of intent, and including behaviors that represented risk as well as evidence of actual harm. Yet it was still not quite right. Terms such as *norms of conduct, substantial risk,* and *physical or emotional harm* were still significantly open to subjective interpretation. No attention was given to chronicity or severity of harm (apart from risk assessment). The definition seemed more suited to active forms of maltreatment (i.e., physical or sexual abuse) rather than the more difficult to address area of child neglect. The definition did not consider the frequency of comorbidity or co-occurrence of different types of abuse. Finally, the definition offered little guidance as to the specific behaviors or categories of risk that could represent the beginnings of an index to classify a range of cases.

Therefore, in seeking to move the child abuse and neglect research field beyond service-based definitions and the classification of different types of abuse and neglect based on presenting conditions, the NRC panel offered guidance as to how a more complete and operational definition might be developed. In so doing, the panel initially drew on four basic principles described by Zuravin (1991):

1. *Definition must serve specific objectives.* Aber and Zigler (1981) had proposed that distinct definitions be used for legal settings, care management settings, and research. Although this represented an initial pragmatic approach, Cicchetti and Barnett (1991) urged researchers to take advantage of the evolution of the field and to be vigilant in identifying areas in which convergences might appear within these setting-specific definitions. They indicated that if significant correlations or even causality could be established from the harm or effects that resulted from certain types of abuse, then new conceptual arrangements might be necessary and possible to address the commonalities among the service-based and research definitions.

2. *Homogenous subtypes divided.* The classification system required the recognition of subtypes within the broad categories of physical abuse, sexual abuse, emotional or psychological maltreatment, or neglect. The use of these subtypes was helpful in examining specific consequences of and pathways to abuse and neglect. As certain similarities or significant differences emerged among the subtypes, the panel pointed to new conceptual arrangements that organized the cases by criteria that were not immediately self-evident, such as chronicity, frequency, severity, or contextual factors.

3. *Conceptual clarity.* Zuravin (1991) had observed that a reliable and valid classification system needed to clearly state every criterion that a behavior must meet for consistent identification across different settings and time periods.

4. *Operational translations.* Elegant conceptual schemes offered limited utility if they could not be translated into classification measures and sorting instruments that could be used by multiple observers. As stated in the NRC report,

> The panel believes strongly that progress on child maltreatment research requires not only the development of intelligent classification schemes, but also the development of standardized field instruments, such as clinical checklists or structured survey questionnaires, with documented psychometric properties. In other words, instruments need to be developed, together with associated documentation such as training manuals; interrater reliability studies need to be conducted to document consistency together with studies of construct validity and (in the longer term) predictive validity; culturally sensitive versions of these instruments need to be developed for ethnic subpopulations; and consideration for literacy or English as a foreign language needs attention. (NRC, 1993, p. 63)

BUILDING BLOCKS FOR NEW RESEARCH-BASED DEFINITIONS OF CHILD ABUSE AND NEGLECT

Using these guiding principles, the NRC panel introduced a set of core elements to guide future definitional efforts. The core elements represented a roadmap of issues that needed to be resolved to improve the quality of definitions and classification of child abuse and neglect. However, the report recognized that these elements involved significant methodological challenges and urged that they be addressed through research and consensus-building efforts.

The core elements, or specific definitional issues identified by the panel (NRC, 1993) included 1) endangerment versus demonstrable harm, 2) severity of acts, 3) frequency of acts, 4) class of potential perpetrators, 5) intent to harm and culpability, 6) developmental level, and 7) culturally informed definitions. Each of these issues is discussed next.

Endangerment versus Demonstrable Harm

Zuravin (1991) and others had identified inconsistencies regarding emphasis on harm or risk in state-based and survey definitions of child abuse and neglect. Some definitions relied on a standard of demonstrable harm, which required evidence of injuries or adverse consequences to the child. Definitions based on a standard of endangerment, however, encompassed a wider set of activities, such as hitting, shoving, choking, or threatening behaviors that might not result in physical injury. The NRC panel agreed with Zuravin that the endangerment standard was the more appropriate criterion "since it places emphasis on the act itself rather than the uncertain consequence of the act" (1993, p. 64).

Severity of Acts

Recognizing that certain survey instruments of child abuse and neglect had included both mild and severe forms of physical assaults on children (e.g., spanking or other forms of corporal punishment), the NRC panel (1993) urged that
new empirical definitions include indices that could assign higher weights to
more severe acts. For instance, the Center for Epidemiologic Studies Depression
Scale (CES-D; Radloff, 1977), developed by the NIMH, was used to operationalize the concept of clinical depression. The CES-D included cut-off scales to identify borderline behaviors and moods that were closely related to conditions that
warranted treatment but represented milder forms of the disorder. In definitions
of child abuse and neglect, such indices could be adjusted to account for age-
related differences that could contribute to severity ratings. In addition to the
benefits these kinds of indices would bring to the research enterprise, they also
would have significant potential for improving practice and service matching.

Frequency of Acts

Definitions of child maltreatment should distinguish between acts that constitute "chronic behavioral patterns" and "infrequent explosive episodes" (Widom,
1988, p. 263). The NRC report (1993) noted that a consensus strategy for defining chronicity or persistence would enhance the comparability of results across
studies. Relatively minor episodes that would not meet the threshold of severity
to warrant abuse or neglect might acquire new meaning if they were part of a
chronic behavior pattern of maltreatment.

Class of Potential Perpetrators

Assaults on children committed by nonfamilial members were generally not
regarded as abuse or neglect. However, the panel (NRC, 1993) decided that special circumstances arose when a live-in member of the household (e.g., a mother's
boyfriend) was the perpetrator. Similarly, charges of abuse or neglect could arise
when a parent left a child under the supervision of another adult, depending on
the extent to which the designated caregiver could be expected to act responsi-
bly. Further complicating matters were variations in state law that created inconsistencies in administrative data.

Intent to Harm and Culpability

The intention of the perpetrator was at one time a strict criterion for abuse and
neglect. Zuravin (1991) observed, however, that research definitions of abuse and
neglect did not generally involve intent or motivation. Yet the second National
Incidence Study (NIS-2; DHHS, 1988) indicated that hazardous housing condi-

tions were *not* (emphasis added) considered neglect when they could be attributed to poverty or other lack of financial resources, posing lack of intent as an exclusion criteria.

Developmental Level

The NRC report (1993) urged that definitions of abuse and neglect consider the age and developmental status of a child, because long-term sequelae from certain types of acts might be more likely to occur when a child is very young or when an adult perpetrator has a significant caregiving relationship with the child. Aber and Zigler (1981) noted that separation and loss might cause severe emotional damage, particularly during a child's earliest years. Similarly, standards for child supervision are very different for 3-year-olds and 12-year-olds. The panel concluded that developmental status might be a key factor in defining the severity of abusive or neglectful acts; thus, it should be considered in determining intent and formulating standards of harm or endangerment.

Culturally Informed Definitions

Although general consensus existed around the standards to be used in extreme cases of abuse and neglect, the panel acknowledged that genuine cultural differences might complicate assessments of less severe reports. Recognizing that considerable variation exists among child care practices, the panel noted that definitions of abuse and neglect needed to seek a balance between accommodating this diversity while also avoiding the creation of different standards of care for children based on race, ethnicity, or economic class. Similarly, the panel observed that a desire to achieve scientific comparability and uniformity of definition should be balanced with the need to accommodate differences in cultural perspectives and practices. The NRC report commented that information on the cultural parameters of child maltreatment was lacking, particularly in terms of how families from different backgrounds judged the severity or appropriateness of certain supervisory, disciplinary, or other caregiving practices, as well as how children interpreted, incorporated, or were shaped by particular contextualized events (NRC, 1993).

RESEARCH RECOMMENDATIONS

The NRC report proposed 17 research priority recommendations, 3 of which dealt with concerns involving definitions, classification, and measurement to improve understanding of the nature and scope of child maltreatment. The first priority recommendation from the list of 17 was the need to establish a consensus on research definitions for each form of child abuse and neglect. As stated in the report,

> The development of consensus requires a major federal and professional commitment to a dynamic, evolutionary process, guided by a series of expert multidisciplinary panels and developed in conjunction with existing agencies that could review existing work on research definitions. (NRC, 1993, p. 31)

The panel further elaborated that the development of a consensus definition would require convening a series of expert multidisciplinary panels to review existing work and to coordinate the development of research definitions with case-report and legal definitions of child abuse and neglect. The research definitions should be developmentally appropriate and culturally sensitive, provide clear inclusion and exclusion criteria, adopt unified subtyping schemes, and provide clear guidelines on issues of severity, duration, and frequency. This guidance was derived directly from the initial principles articulated by Zuravin (1991) and the core components described in this chapter.

The second and third priority recommendations dealt with measurement and epidemiological studies. The NRC panel recommended that reliable and valid clinical-diagnostic and research instruments for the measurement of child maltreatment were needed to operationalize the consensus definitions (second priority recommendation). Once these tools were developed, the panel also encouraged their use in epidemiological studies on the incidence and prevalence of child abuse and neglect, as well as the inclusion of research questions about child maltreatment in other national surveys (third priority recommendation).

In addition to these research priorities, the NRC panel offered guidance to the field in the form of other research recommendations. Two areas received particular attention: 1) the need to improve the detection process that leads to the identification of child abuse and neglect cases within social services agencies and 2) the need to conduct empirical research on the physical indicators of child sexual and physical abuse that can assist physicians in their diagnostic efforts. In each area, the NRC panel recommended pilot studies of clinically based instruments with large populations and attention to physical presentation and healing in different ethnic groups. The panel commented that longitudinal studies of processes of puberty in large populations of children and youth would be informative, as would be research on physical conditions that mimic abusive head trauma or malnutrition. The panel cautioned, however, that such research could raise important ethical dilemmas and complex informed consent issues, and the panel noted the need to encourage participation from many families while also protecting children when signs of abuse or neglect were detected.

SUMMARY

In 1993, the NRC published a report on child abuse and neglect research that recommended the development of uniform and consistent definitions to guide future measurement and data collection efforts. The report described the limitations of using descriptive or service-based definitions of child abuse and neglect and indicated that the quality of research in this field would continue to be impaired until clear, reliable, valid, and useful definitions of child abuse and neglect could be developed. Building from emerging theory and new conceptual frameworks in the fields of violence research and child development, the NRC study emphasized the need to view child maltreatment within an ecological and developmental context. This approach focused on the interactions among parent–child behaviors and the social and cultural factors that foster or inhibit stress and conflict within families. Such frameworks had the potential to deepen our understanding of the pathways to and prevention of abuse and neglect, but they also added new complexities that impeded the development of rigorous definitions.

In the decade since the publication of the NRC report, additional analysis and consensus-building efforts have sought to reconcile these factors. In addition, improvements in public health injury classification systems have offered promise in standardizing components of child maltreatment that are directly linked to intentional harm. Yet, even as we are better prepared to address aspects of maltreatment associated with physical harm and endangerment, we are learning more about the more hidden forms of abuse and neglect, such as emotional maltreatment, that have insidious and severe consequences for the child (Garbarino & Vondra, 1987; Hart & Brassard, 1987; Hart, Germain, & Brassard, 1987). The fundamental importance of nurturance, authoritative guidance, and loving support for children and youth, in addition to protecting their safety and meeting their physical concerns, still looms large (NRC, 1993). Achieving a definition that can address the essential behaviors that are necessary for child health and well-being and still meet society's expectations for focusing on the most severe and demonstrable forms of abuse and neglect remains a persistent challenge.

REFERENCES

Aber, J.L., & Zigler, E. (1981). Developmental considerations in the definition of child maltreatment. In R. Rizley & D. Cicchetti (Eds.), *Developmental perspectives on child maltreatment: New directions for child development* (pp. 1–29). San Francisco: Jossey-Bass.

American Academy of Pediatrics. (1991). Committee on child abuse and neglect: Guidelines for the evaluation of sexual abuse of children. *Pediatrics, 87,* 254–259.

Belsky, J. (1980). Child maltreatment: An ecological integration. *American Psychologist, 35,* 320–335.

Bronfenbrenner, U. (1979). *The ecology of human development: Experiments by nature and design.* Cambridge, MA: Harvard University Press.

Child Abuse Prevention and Treatment Act of 1974, PL 93-247, § 88 Stat 4, codified as amended at 42 U.S.C. § 5101-5120 (1996).

Christoffel, K.K., Scheidt, P.C., Agram, P.F., Kraus, J.F., McLoughlin, E., & Paulson, J.A. (1992). Standard definitions for childhood injury research: Excerpts of a conference report. *Pediatrics, 89,* 1027–1034.

Cicchetti, D., & Barnett, D. (1991). Toward the development of a scientific nosology of child maltreatment. In D. Cicchetti & W. Grove (Eds.), *Thinking clearly about psychology: Essays in honor of Paul E. Meehl* (pp. 346–377). Minneapolis, MN: University of Minnesota Press.

Cicchetti, D., & Carlson, V. (Eds.). (1989). *Child maltreatment: Theory and research on the causes and consequences of child abuse and neglect.* New York: Cambridge University Press.

Cicchetti, D., & Lynch, M. (1993). Toward an ecological/transactional model of community violence and child maltreatment: Consequences for children's development. *Psychiatry, 56,* 96–118.

Egeland, B, Breitenbucher, M., & Rosenberg, D. (1980). A prospective study of the significance of life stress in the etiology of child abuse. *Journal of Clinical and Consulting Psychology, 48,* 195–205.

Garbarino, J. (1977). The human ecology of child maltreatment: A conceptual model for research. *Journal of Marriage and the Family, 39,* 721–735.

Garbarino, J., & Vondra, J. (1987). Psychological maltreatment: Issues and perspectives. In R. Germain & S.N. Hart (Eds.), *Psychological maltreatment of children and youth* (pp. 24–44). New York: Pergamon Press.

Hart, S.N., & Brassard, M.R. (1987). A major threat to children's mental health: Psychological maltreatment. *American Psychologist, 42,* 160–165.

Hart, S.N., Germain, R., & Brassard, M.R. (1987). *The challenge: To better understand and combat the psychological maltreatment of children and youth.* New York: Pergamon Press.

Hammerschlag, M.R. (2001). *Sexually transmitted diseases and child sexual abuse. Portable guides to investigating child abuse.* Washington, DC: Office of Juvenile Justice and Delinquency Prevention, Department of Justice. Retrieved March 22, 2004, from http://www.ncjrs.org/txtfiles/stdandab.txt

Hoaglin, DC, Light, R.J., McPeek, F., Mosteller, F., & Stoto, M. (1982). *Data for decisions: Information strategies for policymakers.* Cambridge, MA: Abt Books.

Johnson, C.F. (1990). Inflicted injury versus accidental injury. *Pediatric Clinics of North America, 37,* 791–814.

Krugman, R.D. (1983). Child abuse and neglect: The role of the primary care physician in recognition, treatment, and prevention. *Primary Care, 11,* 527–534.

Leventhal, J.M. (1990). Epidemiology of child sexual abuse. In R.M. Oates (Ed.), *Understanding and managing child sexual abuse* (pp. 18–41). Sydney, Australia: Harcourt Brace Jovanovich.

National Research Council. (1985). *Injury in America: A continuing public health problem.* Washington, DC: National Academies Press.

National Research Council. (1993). *Understanding child abuse and neglect.* Washington, DC: National Academies Press.

National Research Council. (1993/1994). *Understanding and preventing violence* (Vols. 1–4). Washington, DC: National Academies Press.

National Research Council. (1996). *Understanding violence against women.* Washington, DC: National Academies Press.

National Research Council. (1998). *Violence in families: Assessing prevention and treatment programs.* Washington, DC: National Academies Press.

National Research Council. (2002). *Confronting chronic neglect: The education and training of health professionals on family violence.* Washington, DC: National Academies Press.

Palmer, S. (2000). *Shaken baby syndrome.* Retrieved March 22, 2004, from http://thearc.org/faqs/Shaken.html

Polansky, N., Gaudin, J., & Kilpatrick, A. (1992). Family radicals. *Children and Youth Services Review, 14,* 19–26.

Radloff, L.S. (1977). The CES-D Scale: A self-report depression scale for research in the general population. *Applied Psychological Measurement, 13,* 385–401.

U.S. Department of Health and Human Services. (1988). *Study findings: Study of national incidence and prevalence of child abuse and neglect* (DHHS Publication No. ADM 20-01099). Washington, DC: Government Printing Office.

U.S. Department of Health and Human Services. (2006). *Administration for Children and Families.* Statistics and Research. [on-line]. Retrieved February 20, 2006, from http://nccanch.acf.hhs.gov/general/stats/index.cfm

Wald, M. (1977). Juvenile justice standards project. In M. Wald (Ed.), *Standards relating to abuse and neglect.* Cambridge, MA: Ballinger.

Widom, C.S. (1988). Sampling biases and implications for child abuse research. *American Orthopsychiatric Association, 58,* 260–270.

Wolfe, D. (1991). *Preventing physical and emotional abuse of children.* New York: Guilford Press.

Wolock, I., & Horowitz, B. (1984). Child maltreatment as a social problem: The neglect of neglect. *American Journal of Orthopsychiatry, 54,* 530–543.

Zuravin, S.J. (1991). Research definitions of child physical abuse and neglect: Current problems. In R. Starr & D. Wolfe (Eds.), *The effects of child abuse and neglect: Issues and research.* New York: Guilford Press.

3

Characteristics of Child Maltreatment Definitions

The Influence of Professional and Social Values

JEFFREY J. HAUGAARD

THE INITIAL GOAL of this chapter was to describe the ways in which theory has influenced the definitions of *child maltreatment*[1] that are currently used in research, public policy, and clinical practice. After spending a considerable amount of time reading the early clinical and research literatures on child maltreatment, talking with colleagues, and talking with the editors of this volume, I came to the conclusion that although theory has had a fundamental influence on society's views of childhood and how children should be treated by their parents and social institutions, other issues such as the values and goals of researchers, the way in which research is conducted, and legal issues have had a greater impact on definitions of child maltreatment than has theory; consequently, this chapter focuses on these issues.

This chapter first examines briefly the ways in which thinking in the United States about child maltreatment and the interventions that are appropriate for children who have been maltreated and their families has changed during the past few hundred years. I then explore the ways in which psychological theories, in particular psychoanalytic, behavioral, and attachment theories, influenced this thinking. The discussion then moves on to an exploration of the development of legal and research definitions of child maltreatment. I argue that several issues related to research strategies and the social climate in the 1970s and 1980s led to research definitions of child maltreatment that are 1) broad and inclusive and 2) divided by the types of behaviors of those perpetrating the maltreatment (e.g., sexual, physical, neglectful). I then explore some historical and legal influences that have resulted in more narrow definitions of maltreatment when it is used in legal contexts and describe some results of the conflict that ensues when the

---

[1]Most authors in the field divide the broad category of child maltreatment into four basic components: physical abuse, sexual abuse, emotional or psychological maltreatment, and neglect. In this chapter, the term *child maltreatment* will be used to describe the broad category of maltreatment. Specific terms (e.g., *physical abuse, neglect*) are used when it is necessary to refer to a specific type of maltreatment.

broader definitions used by researchers and the narrower definitions used in legal contexts collide.

It is important to note at the beginning of this chapter that I have approached it more as an historian approaches a chapter than as a social science researcher might. Although the research of historians and social scientists involves the same process of gathering and then interpreting data, my personal view is that historical research requires more interpretation of data than does social science research. Social scientists often design research to minimize the interpretation of data; for example, they may design a series of small studies to eliminate competing interpretations of data so that, in the end, only one interpretation appears appropriate. Historical researchers, however, often are required to interpret data consisting of the writings of those who are now deceased and therefore are often unable to test competing interpretations of those writings. The data for this chapter are the writings of many researchers in the fields of psychology, sociology, medicine, and the law about child maltreatment. My conclusions are based on my interpretations of what these individuals have written and should be taken as such.

A BRIEF HISTORICAL REVIEW

Commonly held views in the United States regarding what constitutes physical abuse of children and what constitutes appropriate punishment or discipline for children have changed dramatically over the past 100 years. As discussed later, at the first meeting of the New York Society for the Prevention of Cruelty to Children in the late 1800s, it was argued that "wholesome flogging" of children was an important part of good parenting, and yet, less than 100 years later, Belsky expressed alarm at a study showing that "more than 10% of [educators, police officers, and clerics] believed that the use of belts, straps, and brushes was acceptable for maintaining control [of children]!" (1980, p. 329). It is hard to imagine anyone at a meeting of psychologists or child welfare workers today claiming that flogging is good for children; in fact, it seems much more likely that expressions of alarm similar to Belsky's would be heard. How did we come so far in our thinking during the past 100 years?

Child Protection Through the 1800s

Beginning from the earliest history of the United States, services for children who are dependent or who have been maltreated have been provided by government agencies or private charities. Laws pertaining to dependent children in colonial America were based on the Elizabethan Poor Law of 1601 (Trattner, 1979; for extended review, see Cox & Cox, 1985). Care was provided mainly through indentured servitude, in which dependent children were legally bound to adults as apprentices until they were between the ages of 18 and 24 (Bremner, 1970). Some communities used *vendue,* or the procedure of obtaining publicly funded care for a child by auctioning the child to the person willing to provide the care for the least amount of money. The social importance of work and discipline during this time period was reflected in officials' abilities to remove children from parents who allowed them to grow up in "idleness or ignorance" and place them in a setting where they could learn the value of hard work (Bremner, 1970). Thus, it appears that very early definitions of maltreatment focused on neglect of children's moral upbringing rather than physical or sexual abuse.

In the early 1800s, the first legislative definitions of child maltreatment began to emerge. Children who were maltreated included those whose parents behaved in ways to endanger their moral development, life, or health, thus broadening the definition to include abuse as well as neglect (Giovannoni, 1989). However, there was little public concern about child maltreatment. Only the most egregious cases received attention, and these were handled by the courts rather than social services agencies (Nelson, 1984). The principal intervention with maltreated children was to remove them from their homes and place them in institutions, many of which also housed destitute, physically ill, and mentally ill adults (Geiser, 1973). Children were removed from families because of society's opposition to providing support directly to maltreating parents; it was believed that such support would promote their laziness and dependence (Bremner, 1970).

During the late 1800s, beliefs about maintaining children in their families changed. This resulted in the settlement house movement, a movement that promoted working with families to prevent removing children from them. Many private charities developed settlement houses in tenement areas, staffed by workers who provided education, support, and aid directly to parents and other caregivers. Rather than placing children who could not be maintained in their families into large institutions, efforts were made to place them in foster families that were funded by local governments and private charities (Cox & Cox, 1985).

The Society for the Prevention of Cruelty to Children was established in New York City during the late 1800s in response to the well-publicized case of Mary Ellen—a terribly abused child for whom no governmental intervention was allowed because her mother had not been convicted of a crime (Giovannoni, 1989; Wolfe, 1999). Within several years, similar societies appeared in many cities and they eventually were incorporated into the national American Humane Association. The American Humane Association became the principal advocate for social change for children who had been maltreated and their families and has remained a strong force in this area since (Giovannoni, 1989). However, even from the beginning of this movement to help abused children, disagreements about the definition of child abuse emerged. Nelson noted that at the first meeting of the New York Society for the Prevention of Cruelty to Children, one member took exception to the characterization of a father who beat his children as a "brute," stating "that while anxious to protect children from undue severity . . . he was in favor of a good wholesome flogging, which he often found most efficacious" (1984,

p. 55). Although flogging would be seen as abusive by most in the United States today, differentiating between appropriate parental discipline and abusive behavior continues to be a focus of debate even among those who are advocates for children.

Changes in Attitudes About Children and Governmental Intervention

Nelson (1984) suggested that important changes in beliefs about children occurred throughout the second half of the 1800s and through the 1900s and that these new beliefs formed the foundation of our current view of childhood and our willingness to intervene in families not providing adequate care for children. Early changes in belief can be traced to the period during and after the Civil War, when there was a reawakening of the debate about the natural rights of all citizens, including children. During this time, many individuals began to view childhood as a time during which future citizens were to be nurtured instead of viewing children as individuals to be used primarily as labor. The importance of childhood as a time of learning was advocated by many members of the societies for the protection of children. These individuals generally belonged to urban middle- and upper middle-class families in which children could be raised without working. Many members of the societies used the manner in which they raised their children as a model for how all children should be raised.

Another important change that influenced society's view of child maltreatment occurred during the 1930s and 1940s, as federal and state governments began taking on more direct responsibility for the welfare of citizens. This increased responsibility was seen in government programs to aid veterans returning from World War I and World War II and in the government's aid to families during the Great Depression (Beirne-Smith, Ittenbach, & Patton, 2002). During this time, the Social Security Act of 1935 (PL 74-271) established a variety of programs for dependent children (Nelson, 1984).

The Role of Child Development Theory

Several psychological theories that have their roots in the early to mid-1900s influenced views on how children should be raised and continued the movement, begun in the mid-1800s, to make childhood a time for learning the types of attitudes, beliefs, and behaviors that would make individuals competent and healthy children, adolescents, and adults. Psychoanalytic theory emphasized the importance of the socialization of children and the role that parents and others had, beginning very early in a child's life, in helping the child manage and redirect his or her sexual and aggressive instincts in directions that were appropriate for living in society. Childhood was seen as a critical time in a person's development. Aggressive or sexual behaviors directed at children by parents or other adults were believed to disrupt the child's socialization and possibly permanently harm the child's individual development.

Behavioral theories also demonstrated the importance of the proper care and training of children. John Watson's famous demonstration with Little Albert showed that fear and anxiety could be induced in a young child by adult behaviors (Wilson, 1989). The work of Skinner and others in the field of operant conditioning demonstrated that children would produce a wide range of socially acceptable and socially unacceptable behaviors based on the schedules of reinforcements and punishments they received (Skinner, 1953). Bandura's social learning theory described how children learn behaviors by observing the reinforcements and punishments received by others (Bandura, 1977). As such, many behaviorists demonstrated the ways in which abusive or neglectful parenting could influence a range of behaviors in children that would later result in impairment for them and problems for society.

Finally, Bowlby's (1958, 1969) attachment theory demonstrated how neglectful or abusive parenting could result in problematic attachments between a young child and his or her parents and how the internal working model of relationships that developed as part of the child's initial attachment influenced the child's future attachments. The work of Ainsworth and her colleagues (e.g., Ainsworth, Blehar, Waters, & Wall, 1978) showed how insecure attachments can have substantial negative influences on the lives of children and how the disorganized style of attachment, which is often present in abused and neglected children, can substantially impede their ability to form future attachments.

The Discovery by Society of Child Maltreatment

It can be argued that by the 1960s, many professionals working with children had learned through their professional training of the vital role that a nurturing childhood can have on individuals' development and on the ways in which individuals live in and influence society. Also, at that time, the civil and women's rights movements brought the issues of equality and human rights to the forefront of the minds of many Americans (Finkelhor, 1996). In addition, the Supreme Court decision in *In re Gault* (1967) made it clear that children's rights were guaranteed by the Constitution. Each of these events helped to focus attention on the rights of children to be free from abuse and neglect and on the role that governments at local, state, and federal levels had in ensuring their safety.

The publication of an article by Kempe, Silverman, Steele, Droegemueller, and Silver (1962) titled "The Battered Child Syndrome" was a critical event in the "discovery" by many in our society of the physical abuse of children. This article ignited a strong social movement, initially by physicians and individuals from other professions who joined them, to raise public and governmental awareness of child physical abuse. One outcome of this movement was action by the U.S. Congress. Although Congress had created the Children's Bureau in 1912, the focus of the Bureau was on general child welfare issues: strengthening families, reducing problematic parenting, and intervening with children when needed. In 1973, Congress took up what would later become the Child Abuse Prevention and Treatment Act (CAPTA; PL 97-243) of 1974. Initial action was in the Senate, with Senator Walter Mondale taking a lead role with the legislation. Mondale was particularly interested in distinguishing efforts to prevent and treat child abuse from efforts in general child welfare (Nelson, 1984). This resulted in a strong focus on physical abuse, which was described as a problem occurring throughout our society, and a minor focus on child neglect, which was primarily considered a child welfare issue associated with low-income families. Because antipoverty programs were not in favor in the nation during the Nixon administration, Mondale's goal was to maintain CAPTA's focus on physical abuse and avoid having CAPTA become an antipoverty program. The definitions of physical abuse were kept narrow to avoid confrontations with more conservative members of Congress who, although concerned about child abuse, were also concerned about the expansion of the role of the federal government in family functioning— particularly in mandates from the federal government about what constituted appropriate parental discipline (Nelson, 1984).

Although the initial goal of Kempe and his colleagues (1962) was to create laws requiring the reporting of physical abuse, their efforts expanded over the next decade to include emotional abuse and neglect (Helfer, 1974). Thus, the breadth of acts that were defined as abusive increased far beyond the narrow definitions used in CAPTA. Research on the prevalence of child sexual abuse in the 1970s by Finkelhor (1979) and later by others (e.g., Russell, 1983; Wyatt, 1985) brought the issue of child sexual abuse into the public spotlight. It may be reasonable to argue that although the public was bothered by reports of physical abuse of children, they were shocked by the reports of sexual abuse. Child advocates used the burgeoning research on child abuse and neglect and the public outcry against it to create a wide range of programs to prevent abuse and neglect and to intervene on behalf of children who were being abused or neglected. Despite the increased awareness of child physical, emotional, and sexual abuse, few definitions of these types of abuse existed. The ways in which research and professional values shaped those definitions is the topic of the next few sections of this chapter.

PROFESSIONAL VALUES AND THE CREATION OF CATEGORIES OF CHILD MALTREATMENT

One aspect of the definition of child maltreatment has become so ingrained in how we think about it that it is almost not noticed: its division into categories based on the behavior of the person who initiates the maltreatment. The most enduring categories have been physical abuse, sexual abuse, emotional or psychological abuse, and neglect (although even these categories have been subdivided by some [e.g., into emotional neglect, medical neglect, and educational neglect]). It is hard to consider the division of child maltreatment into other categories, but others are conceivable. For example, categories could be based on the amount of pain or injury involved. Nonpainful maltreatment might be one category (e.g., sexual abuse involving fondling, neglecting a child's educational needs), maltreatment that caused pain that did not require medical intervention might be a second category (e.g., hitting a child with a belt, digital penetration of adolescents), and maltreatment requiring medical intervention might be a third (e.g., penile penetration of young children, keeping an infant malnourished and confined in a filthy crib for weeks).

Definitions of maltreatment used in the 1800s and early 1900s did not use the categories used today. Decisions to intervene with families were often made on the totality of the experience of a child's maltreatment, which often included physical abuse, neglect, emotional abuse, and possibly sexual abuse (Nelson, 1984). Even the description of Mary Ellen—the girl who had been repeatedly beaten by her stepmother—included information about her lack of nutrition and cleanliness (Wolfe, 1999).

An important influence on our current strategy for categorizing child maltreatment can be traced to the article by Kempe and colleagues (1962) on the battered child syndrome. The use of the term *syndrome* and the initial involvement of physicians in identifying and treating children who had been battered brought the strategies used in physical medicine to the field of child maltreatment (Giovannoni, 1989). Battered child syndrome, for example, which was diagnosed based on radiological evidence showing broken bones and other injuries, was seen as a syndrome distinct from other forms of maltreatment that a child might experience. Because the battered child syndrome was brought to light early in the emerging public awareness of maltreatment and in the development of the research and clinical literatures on child maltreatment, seeing specific types of child maltreatment as discrete syndromes had an important and lasting influence on the field. Even today, although it is understood that many children experience multiple forms of maltreatment, the tendency remains to view them as experiencing multiple discrete types of maltreatment; just as a child with the flu and strep throat is viewed as experiencing two discrete physical disorders, a child who is sexually abused and neglected is viewed as experiencing two discrete forms of child maltreatment.

As noted previously, public policy efforts such as the initial passage of CAPTA further delineated physical abuse from other forms of maltreatment. Initially, physicians were seen as those primarily responsible for identifying and treating physical abuse, whereas child welfare professionals were responsible for identifying and treating neglect and other forms of problematic family life. Work by Finkelhor (1979), Russell (1983), Wyatt (1985), and others who concentrated their research efforts on child sexual abuse focused attention on yet another discrete category of maltreatment. The separateness of sexual abuse from the other forms of maltreatment can be seen in the lack of discussion in the early research on sexual abuse about the presence of physical abuse or neglect in the lives of children who had been sexually abused.

The initial division of child maltreatment was, and continues to be, reinforced by researchers and clinicians. Researchers, following the dictum of studying a small issue and studying it thoroughly, focused their research efforts on one or more categories of child maltreatment. Specific samples of children and adults who had experienced one of the forms of child maltreatment were studied separately, and studies that employed children who had experienced a range of maltreatment divided their samples into those who had experienced individual or combined forms of maltreatment (Eckenrode, Laird, & Doris, 1993). In addition, in the 1980s and 1990s, a wide variety of therapeutic strategies were developed for children who had experienced specific forms of maltreatment—primarily for children who had been abused sexually (Saywitz, Mannarino, Berliner, & Cohen, 2000; Wolfe, 1999). A variety of these strategies described the emotional, cognitive, and behavioral outcomes of each type of maltreatment, reinforcing beliefs about the value of viewing each form of maltreatment as a discrete experience and then providing treatment for that experience (again, as continues to be done in physical medicine).

The result of this specialization of research and clinical work was that a considerable amount was learned about each category of maltreatment. Another consequence, however, was that each category became defined as a specific type of child maltreatment, and few efforts were made to conceptualize child maltreatment in other ways. As researchers and clinicians created a body of literature based on the initial categories of maltreatment, that strategy for categorizing maltreatment became established. As these researchers and clinicians trained new generations of researchers and clinicians, many of whom focused on one category of maltreatment, the divisions became strengthened. This made it increasingly difficult for other possible ways of categorizing maltreatment to emerge and inhibited work using other types of categories that might provide new or different insights on the development or consequences of maltreatment in its various forms.

CHILD MALTREATMENT AS A SOCIAL MOVEMENT AND THE CREATION OF BROAD DEFINITIONS

Beginning in the 1960s, research, clinical intervention, and community action in the area of child maltreatment took on the characteristics of a social movement or, as Finkelhor (1996) describes it, a moral transformation. The legal and moral rights of children to be free from adult behavior that caused them anguish and impeded their development were supported by research and public policy. Child maltreatment as a social movement influenced the breadth of the definitions of the various types of abuse and neglect that were used by researchers and clinicians, and, in turn, these broad definitions helped to focus and maintain child maltreatment as a social movement.

The Development of Broad Definitions

Once social concern about child maltreatment expanded beyond the most egregious cases and the narrowly defined battered child syndrome, many researchers began to dramatically broaden the realm of behaviors that were considered child abuse. As discussed in the following sections, it appears that while different strategies were used to create the definitions of sexual abuse and physical abuse, each resulted in broad definitions. Two reasons for this trend were 1) researchers' hesitancy to impose definitions of sexual abuse or physical abuse on those who believed they had been abused and 2) the value that broad definitions had on child maltreatment as a social movement (Finkelhor, 1996).

The Definition of Sexual Abuse
Based on Research Participant Conceptualizations

Early researchers in the field of child sexual abuse struggled with the issue of how narrowly or broadly to define sexual abuse (Finkelhor, 1979). Apparently, researchers felt comfortable determining the characteristics that would define the word *child* and the word *abuse,* but they had more difficulty determining which types of behaviors should be classified as sexual. Consequently, rather than defining the term *sexual,* researchers asked participants (who were all adults) to report all behaviors that they believed were sexual. For example, in one of the first studies of sexual victimization of children, Finkelhor asked undergraduates to report on "sexual experiences you had while growing up. By sexual we mean a broad range of things, anything from playing doctor to sexual intercourse—in fact, anything that might have seemed sexual to you" (1979, p. 49). The reluctance to limit the behaviors considered sexual may have been due to the researchers' desire to avoid imposing the definitions devised by "experts" on highly personalized experiences such as sexual behavior. The researchers then applied specific criteria that they had developed to determine whether the sexual activity constituted child abuse. The most common criteria were the age of the child when the sexual activity occurred (commonly before age 16, 17, or 18), the difference in age between the child and the other participant in the sexual activity (a common criteria, for example, was a difference of 5 or more years), and whether the sexual activity was desired by the child (typically, sexual activity desired by older children was not considered abuse) (Finkelhor, 1979; Russell, 1983; Wyatt, 1985).

The result of this process for defining child sexual abuse was that although the criteria used to determine if a behavior was abusive were circumscribed, the behaviors considered sexual ranged broadly—in some studies from an invitation to do something sexual, to seeing an exhibitionist, to being fondled, to intercourse

(Haugard & Reppucci, 1988). Although some early studies limited the types of behaviors considered sexual, for example, to those involving physical contact, most early studies did not limit the types of behaviors considered to be sexual.

Researchers defining child sexual abuse may have felt fewer constraints in determining which behaviors in their studies were abusive than those researchers defining physical abuse for research or public-policy purposes. Most people consider sexual activity between a child and an older person as wrong. Therefore, if a behavior between a child and an older individual is considered sexual, it can be considered abusive. Thus, kissing that is considered sexual by a child can be defined as abusive with relative ease. However, as discussed above, considerable debate continues in our society about the appropriateness of adults being physical with a child. Thus, a parental behavior considered physical by a child—for example, spanking a child—may not automatically be considered abusive.

The Definition of Physical Abuse
Based on Researchers' Conceptualizations

The definitions of physical abuse or family violence used by researchers also encompassed a wide range of behaviors, from those with a clear potential for causing physical harm to children to those in which the potential for harm was much less apparent, such as pushing, grabbing, or hitting (Emery & Laumann-Billings, 1998). However, in contrast to the ways in which acts were defined as sexual by researchers in the area of child sexual abuse, most early researchers in the area of physical abuse have generated their own broad definitions. For example, in one of the first major epidemiological studies, Gil defined physical abuse as "the intentional, nonaccidental use of physical force, or intentional, nonaccidental acts of omission, on the part of a parent or other caretaker interacting with a child in his care, aimed at hurting, injuring, or destroying that child" (1970, p. 6). Thus, physical abuse included acts that ranged from those that caused pain to those that resulted in death.

Several other researchers chose to use terms such as *violence* or *family violence* rather than *physical abuse* to avoid confusing the types of acts on which their research focuses with those that might meet the legal definition of physical abuse. The definitions of violence are often broader than those meeting the legal definitions of physical abuse. Gelles, for instance, defined *violence* as "an act carried out with the intention, or perceived intention, of physically injuring another person. The injury can range from slight pain, as with a slap, to murder" (1979, p. 78). This broad definition was chosen, as stated by Gelles, "because we wanted to draw attention to the issue of people hitting each other in families; we have defined this behavior as 'violent' in order to raise controversy and call the behavior into question" (pp. 78–79). For example, in some of the best known studies of family violence, minor violence included acts such as slapping or spanking a child, and severe violence included kicking, beating up, and using a knife or a gun on a child (Straus & Gelles, 1986). The value of using terms other than *physical abuse* can be seen in a study by Berger, Knutson, Mehm, and Perkins (1988). Although 6% of a large sample of undergraduates reported that they had been punched by a parent, 3% that they had been choked, and 2% that they had been severely beaten, and although about 5% had been significantly injured (i.e., they had broken bones or head injuries), only 2.9% of the sample reported that they had been physically abused as a child.

The Ongoing Use of Early, Broad Definitions

Although the definitions used in research after these initial studies of child sexual abuse, physical abuse, and family violence changed somewhat, these differences were often minor (Haugaard & Reppucci, 1988). As is often true in social science research, the definitions used by early researchers are used by later researchers so that comparisons between the results of the studies can be made (Nelson, 1984). A consequence of this process is that the early definitions often become generally accepted by researchers. In the field of child abuse, the early definitions, which were broad and based on the values and beliefs of the early researchers, became accepted as the definitions of the various types of abuse. As more research was completed, the definitions became more firmly entrenched because of their increased use, making it increasingly difficult for them to be changed by future researchers.

The Benefits of Broad Definitions for the Social Movement

From a social activist perspective, broad definitions of child maltreatment help to create an environment in which social action to reduce child maltreatment is more likely. Narrow definitions of child maltreatment that encompass only the most egregious cases, such as those used in the 1800s, are less likely to attract concern from a wide range of the public. Rare and egregious abuse that may be viewed as occurring primarily in poverty-stricken, large urban areas may be easily ignored by most people—even if they find the cases shocking. However, when broader definitions are used to identify children who are being abused and communities in which the abuse is occurring, it becomes clearer to many in society that the types of children who are the victims of maltreatment may be children with whom they have regular contact and perhaps even their own children. For example, studies of community samples showing that 50% of girls experience some type of sexual abuse (e.g., Wyatt, 1985) and studies of undergraduates showing that up to 30% of women have experienced child sexual abuse (e.g., Finkelhor, 1979) suddenly make the issue of child sexual abuse salient to all parents; it becomes difficult for them to assume that sexual abuse only occurs to children living in circumstances far removed from the circumstances of their own children. It seems reasonable to assume that the broad public concern about child maltreatment has been propelled, in some degree, by the increased understanding of many in our society that children they know may be the victims of maltreatment, broadly defined.

CHILD MALTREATMENT DEFINED AS AN INDIVIDUAL ISSUE RATHER THAN A SOCIETAL ISSUE

As noted in the historical discussion at the beginning of this chapter, child maltreatment consistently has been defined as an individual issue in our society rather than a societal problem (Zigler, 1979). Regardless of how narrowly or broadly child maltreatment is defined, it is most commonly seen as a failure on the part of individual parents or caregivers (Aber & Zigler, 1981). Several aspects of the characteristics of research on child maltreatment also show that it is defined as an individual issue. Although some research has focused on social influences on child maltreatment, such as the role of poverty in physical abuse and neglect (Gil, 1970), most has focused on the experiences of individual children and the adults who abuse or neglect them. Studies of the causes of child sexual and physical abuse, for example, often focus on the characteristics of the perpetrators of the abuse (e.g., Boney-McCoy & Finkelhor, 1995; Gil, 1970; Siegel, Sorenson, Golding, Burnam, & Stein, 1987). In addition, a variety of studies have searched for the ways in which parents and other adults develop into the type of people who would sexually or physically abuse a child (Wolfe, 1999). Finally, many efforts to reduce child maltreatment have focused on prevention strategies to keep individual parents from physically abusing or neglecting their children (Wekerle & Wolfe, 1996) and to assist individual children in developing the knowledge and skills to avoid becoming a victim of sexual abuse (Reppucci & Haugaard, 1989).

In his article "Controlling Child Abuse in America: An Effort Doomed to Failure," Zigler took the opposite view and argued that child maltreatment should be defined as a social problem: "I have looked closely at who is guilty of child abuse and have discovered it is I" (1979, p. 47). He argued that little progress would be made in reducing child maltreatment as long as social policy and attitudes stayed the same and 1) homemaker services remained unavailable to many parents who would benefit from them, 2) quality child care remained unavailable to many parents who need it, 3) corporal punishment remained a viable strategy for disciplining children, and 4) physical restraint of children in social institutions, such as residential treatment and juvenile detention facilities, remained rampant. Fundamental changes in social policy, he argued, will provide the foundation on which changes in the frequency of child maltreatment would be made. These changes are unlikely to be made as long as child maltreatment is defined as an individual issue.

THE RELATIVE NARROWNESS OF LEGAL DEFINITIONS

The historical section at the beginning of this chapter shows that early attention to child maltreatment focused on egregious cases of abuse and neglect by family members and others who provided care for children and that efforts to help children who were maltreated were usually limited to removing the children from their families. As the government became more involved in the lives of families in which children were being maltreated, however, it became necessary to balance government intervention that focused on removing children from the homes in which they were being maltreated with the strongly held legal and social values that, except under extreme circumstances, parents should be allowed to raise their children as they saw fit (e.g., *Meyer v. Nebraska*, 1923; *Santosky v. Kramer*, 1982). In other words, government agencies could not remove a child from a parent's care based on the accusation that the parents were not providing ideal care. However, if a child's basic welfare was being threatened, the government was required to use their *parens patriae* powers to intervene and protect that child. The requirement that government agencies determine that a child's welfare was in jeopardy before removing the child from his or her home led to an important component of legal definitions of child abuse and neglect: Harm, or the threat of imminent harm, must be present for parental behaviors to be considered abuse or neglect. For example, the definition of child abuse and neglect in the original CAPTA legislation was as follows:

> Child abuse and neglect means the physical or mental injury, sexual abuse, negligent treatment, or maltreatment of any child under the age of eighteen by a person who is responsible for the child's welfare under circumstances that indicate the child's health or welfare is harmed or threatened thereby. (PL 93-247, 1974, section 2)

The requirement for harm remains in most legal definitions of abuse and neglect today. For example, current law in New York (NY Family Court Act of 2004) defines child abuse as follows:

(e) "Abused child" means a child less than eighteen years of age whose parent or other person legally responsible for his care,
  (i) inflicts or allows to be inflicted upon such child physical injury by other than accidental means which causes or creates a substantial risk of death, or serious or protracted disfigurement, or protracted impairment of physical or emotional health, or protracted loss or impairment of the function of any bodily organ, or
  (ii) creates or allows to be created a substantial risk of physical injury to such child by other than accidental means which would be likely to cause death or serious or protracted disfigurement, or protracted impairment of physical or emotional health, or protracted loss or impairment of the function of any bodily organ. (NY CLS Family Ct Act § 1012, 2004)

New York State law defines child neglect as follows:

(f)   "Neglected child" means a child less than eighteen years of age

   (i)   whose physical, mental or emotional condition has been impaired or is in imminent danger of becoming impaired as a result of the failure of his parent or other person legally responsible for his care to exercise a minimum degree of care

      (A)   in supplying the child with adequate food, clothing, shelter or education in accordance with the provisions of part one of article sixty-five of the education law, or medical, dental, optometrical or surgical care, though financially able to do so or offered financial or other reasonable means to do so; or

      (B)   in providing the child with proper supervision or guardianship, by unreasonably inflicting or allowing to be inflicted harm, or a substantial risk thereof, including the infliction of excessive corporal punishment; or by misusing a drug or drugs; or by misusing alcoholic beverages to the extent that he loses self-control of his actions; or by any other acts of a similarly serious nature requiring the aid of the court (NY CLS Family Ct Act § 1012, 2004).

It is worth noting that in New York, both abuse and neglect include acts of commission and acts of omission. What distinguishes them is that abuse involves more serious acts than neglect.

In a series of influential writings, Goldstein, Freud, and Solnit also have argued for limitations on the state's ability to intervene in cases of suspected abuse or neglect in families. They suggest that intervention should be limited to 1) "conviction, or acquittal by reason of insanity, of a sexual offense against one's child" (1979, p. 62) and 2) "serious bodily injury inflicted by parents upon their children, and attempts to inflict such injury, or the repeated failure of parents to prevent their child from suffering such injury" (p. 72). They would not even allow an investigation of a family unless one of the criteria discussed were alleged.

As indicated in previous sections, the requirement that harm be present or imminent has not been a part of many definitions of abuse that have been created by researchers. Consequently, discrepancies exist between the definitions of abuse and neglect that are used in many legal situations and those that are used by researchers and clinicians. An important example of this discrepancy can be seen in the controversial assertions made by Rind, Tromovitch, and Bauserman (1998) that, because their meta-analysis of the consequences of child sexual abuse from studies involving undergraduates showed little harm resulting from much of that contact, certain types of sexual contact between adults and children should not be labeled abuse. The analyses on which Rind et al. based their conclusions have spurred sharp debate. Controversy has also ensued about whether harm must occur in order for an act to be considered abusive (Haugaard, 2000). These debates highlight the differences between definitions of abuse and neglect that are based on legal requirements and that include the criteria of harm or imminent harm to children, and those that are based on social deviance (Aber & Zigler, 1981) and thus include behaviors that cause or may cause harm to children as well as behaviors that are considered improper by society. Although researchers and clinicians may feel comfortable using the second definition, it is much more difficult for an agency of the government to use that definition when it might result in the government intruding into the life of a family.

This discrepancy also has created difficulty in using the terms *abuse* or *maltreatment* in a variety of contexts; common usage of the terms does not always imply that some type of harm must occur for situations to be labeled as abuse or maltreatment. For example, common usage of the term *abuse* includes 1) a corrupt practice or custom; and 2) improper or excessive use or treatment (Agnes, 1999). Similarly, the term *maltreatment* comes from the French word *maltraiter*— to treat roughly, unkindly, or brutally (Agnes, 1996). Thus, in broad use, both terms encompass a wide range of behaviors, from those that are improper or unkind, to those that are brutal and harmful. Consequently, although an act may not be considered abuse by some because it fails to meet the standard of creating harm or the likelihood of harm (based on legal definitions), others consider that same act to be abuse or maltreatment based on social deviance definitions. As a result of this controversy, there is often strong pressure to label a wide range of improper behaviors as abuse and not to declare that these behaviors are not abuse; to do so may indicate to some that these behaviors are not improper. For example, even though seeing an exhibitionist one time may cause no demonstrable harm to the development of a 14-year-old girl, we are loathe to declare that the act is not abusive; this declaration may imply to some that the behavior is not improper.

SUMMARY

The premise of this chapter is that our definitions of child abuse and neglect, and the entire way we conceptualize the field of abuse and neglect, are based on the values and interests of early researchers and on the tendency of researchers to use definitions employed in research that has already been published. Society's definitions and conceptualizations of child abuse and neglect are so well established at this point that we have almost become oblivious to the limitations they present (e.g., the definitions used by researchers are seldom useful in legal settings). At issue is whether we can stop and reconsider current definitions and toy with the idea of creating a new set of definitions. The new definitions might allow us to continue to experience the benefits of the current definitions while eliminating some of their shortcomings. Unfortunately, new definitions often create trauma in a field, as researchers worry about the potential consequences of the new definitions. It is clear that an effort to redefine child abuse and neglect would have to be carefully organized and well funded and involve leaders in the field;

one or two clinicians or researchers calling for an exploration of possible new definitions can easily be dismissed. Whether researchers in the field of child abuse and neglect are ready to proceed in new directions remains to be seen.

REFERENCES

Aber, J.L., & Zigler, E. (1981). Developmental considerations in the definition of child maltreatment. In R. Rizley & D. Cicchetti (Eds.), *Developmental perspectives on child maltreatment: New directions in child development* (pp. 1–29). San Francisco: Jossey-Bass.

Agnes, M.E. (Ed.). (1996). *Webster's new world dictionary.* Cleveland, OH: World Publishing.

Agnes, M.E. (Ed.). (1999). *Webster's new world college dictionary.* New York: Random House.

Ainsworth, M.D.S., Blehar, M.C., Waters, E., and Wall, S. (1978). *Patterns of attachment: A psychological study of the strange situation.* Mahwahn, NJ: Lawrence Erlbaum Associates.

Bandura, A. (1977). *Social learning theory.* Upper Saddle River, NJ: Prentice Hall.

Beirne-Smith, M., Ittenbach, R., & Patton, J.R. (2002). *Mental retardation* (6th ed.). Upper Saddle River, NJ: Prentice Hall.

Belsky, J. (1980). Child maltreatment: An ecological integration. *American Psychologist, 35,* 320–335.

Berger, A.M., Knutson, J.F., Mehm, J.G., & Perkins, K.A. (1988). The self-report of punitive childhood experiences of young adults and adolescents. *Child Abuse & Neglect, 12,* 251–262.

Boney-McCoy, S., & Finkelhor, D. (1995). Psychosocial sequelae of violent victimization in a national youth sample. *Journal of Consulting and Clinical Psychology, 63,* 726–736.

Bowlby, J. (1958). The nature of the child's tie to his mother. *International Journal of Psychoanalysis, 39,* 350–373.

Bowlby, J. (1969). *Attachment and loss: Vol. 1. Attachment.* (2nd ed.) New York: Basic Books.

Bremner, R.H. (1970). *Children and youth in America* (Vol. 1). Cambridge, MA: Harvard University Press.

Child Abuse Prevention and Treatment Act of 1974, PL 93-247, § 88 Stat 4, codified as amended at 42 U.S.C. § 5101-5120 (1996).

Cox, M.J., & Cox, R.D. (1985). A brief history of policy for dependent and neglected children. In M.J. Cox & R.D. Cox (Eds.) *Foster care: Current issues, policies, and practices* (pp. 1–25). Norwood, NJ: Ablex Publishing.

Eckenrode, J., Laird, M., & Doris, J. (1993). School performance and disciplinary problems among abused and neglected children. *Developmental Psychology, 29,* 53–62.

Emery, R.E., & Laumann-Billings, L. (1998). An overview of the nature, causes, and consequences of abusive family relationships. *American Psychologist, 53,* 121–135.

Finkelhor, D. (1979). *Sexually victimized children.* New York: Free Press.

Finkelhor, D. (1996). Introduction. In J. Briere, L. Berliner, J. Bulkley, C. Jenny, & T. Reid (Eds.), *The APSAC handbook on child maltreatment* (pp. iii–ix). Thousand Oaks, CA: Sage Publications.

Geiser, R.L. (1973). *The illusion of caring.* Boston: Beacon Press.

Gelles, R.J. (1979). *Family violence.* Beverly Hills: Sage Publications.

Gil, D.G. (1970). *Violence against children.* Cambridge, MA: Harvard University Press.

Giovannoni, J. (1989). Definitional issues in child maltreatment. In D. Cicchetti & V. Carlson (Eds.), *Child maltreatment: Theory and research on the causes and consequences of child abuse and neglect* (pp. 3–37). New York: Cambridge University Press.

Goldstein, J., Freud, A., & Solnit, A. (1979). *Before the best interests of the child.* New York: Free Press.

Haugaard, J.J. (2000). The challenge of defining child sexual abuse. *American Psychologist,* *55,* 1036–1039.

Haugaard, J.J., & Reppucci, N.D. (1988). *The sexual abuse of children.* San Francisco: Jossey-Bass.

Helfer, R. (1974). The responsibility and role of the physician. In R. Helfer & C.H. Kempe (Eds.), *The battered child* (pp. 89–97). Chicago: University of Chicago Press.

In re Gault, 387 U.S. 1 (1967).

Kempe, C.H., Silverman, F., Steele, B., Droegemueller, W., & Silver, H. (1962). The battered child syndrome. *Journal of the American Medical Association, 181,* 17–24.

Meyer v. Nebraska, 262 U.S. 390 (1923).

Nelson, B.J. (1984). *Making an issue of child abuse.* Chicago: University of Chicago Press.

NY CLS Family Ct Act § 1012 (2004).

Reppucci, N.D., & Haugaard, J.J. (1989). The prevention of child sexual abuse: Myth or reality? *American Psychologist, 44,* 1266–1275.

Rind, B., Tromovitch, P., & Bauserman, R. (1998). A meta-analytic examination of assumed properties of child sexual abuse using college samples. *Psychological Bulletin, 124,* 22–53.

Russell, D. (1983). The incidence and prevalence of intrafamilial and extrafamilial sexual abuse of female children. *Child Abuse & Neglect, 7,* 133–146.

Santosky v. Kramer, 455 U.S. 745 (1982).

Saywitz, K., Mannarino, A.P., Berliner, L., & Cohen, J.A. (2000). Treatment for sexually abused children and adolescents. *American Psychologist, 55,* 1040–1050.

Siegel, J.M., Sorenson, S.G., Golding, J.M., Burnam, M.A., & Stein, J.A. (1987). The prevalence of childhood sexual assault. *American Journal of Epidemiology, 126,* 1141–1153.

Skinner, B.F. (1953). *Science and human behavior.* New York: Macmillan.

Social Security Act of 1935, PL 74-271, 42 U.S.C. §§ 301 *et seq.*

Straus, M.A., & Gelles, R.J. (1986). Societal change and change in family violence from 1975–1985. *Journal of Marriage and the Family, 48,* 465–479.

Trattner, W.I. (1979). *From poor law to welfare state.* New York: Free Press.

Wekerle, C., & Wolfe, D. (1996). Child maltreatment. In E. Mash & R. Barkley (Eds.), *Child psychopathology* (pp. 492–540). New York: Guilford Press.

Wilson, G.T. (1989). Behavior therapy. In R. Corsini & D. Wedding (Eds.) *Current psychotherapies* (pp. 241–282). Itasca, IL: Peacock Publishing.

Wolfe, D.A. (1999). *Child abuse: Implications for child development and psychopathology.* Thousand Oaks, CA: Sage Publications.

Wyatt, G. (1985). The sexual abuse of Afro-American and White American women in childhood. *Child Abuse & Neglect, 10,* 231–240.

Zigler, E. (1979). Controlling child abuse in America: An effort doomed to failure. In D. Gill (Ed.), *Child abuse and violence* (pp. 39–48). New York: AMS Press.

II

DEFINITION AND THEORY
IN CHILD ABUSE AND NEGLECT

THE FIELD OF CHILD ABUSE and neglect has been persistently impeded in its development because of difficulties in formulating operational definitions that apply consistently to the heterogeneous types of experiences subsumed in the broad category of child abuse and neglect. In many ways, this lack of definitional clarity can be attributed to the number of disciplines and advocacy and professional groups that are interested in studying and helping children who have been maltreated as well as the variety of statutory, legal, and applied definitions that exist in practice and policy settings. This multidisciplinary view of child abuse and neglect has led to definitions that vary by setting (e.g., legal, services, policy), purpose, and goals as well as across specific research projects. Although definitions should and do serve different purposes, the variety of definitions used in the literature have led to difficulties in comparing and replicating specific research findings and have prevented the development of clear and valid descriptions of the phenomena that would help foster understanding and communication of the essential features of abuse and neglect and the characteristics of abused and neglected children.

In addition, this limited definitional clarity is accompanied by limitations in the development of theories that can account for and predict the behaviors and characteristics observed in children who have been maltreated. Therefore, the dynamic relationship that should exist between theory and definition in the field of child abuse and neglect is mostly lacking, and the field continues to struggle with definitional issues.

The chapters in Section II seek to examine these issues and to provide reasonable directions for progress in the development of robust definitions and theories. Although the chapters in this section are organized by type of abuse, as has been common in the literature, this is done for heuristic purposes only, to reflect current methodologies. Whether this classification approach will be useful in the future or whether new classifications will emerge remains to be seen as the field of child abuse and neglect continues to advance as a science.

In Chapter 4, Knutson and Heckenberg initiate the discussion by examining the history of the construct of child physical abuse and analyzing the operational definitions and measures that have been used in this area. They then suggest criteria for future operational definitions and present a model of how multimethod approaches to defining physical abuse could be used to advance the research in this area. In Chapter 5, Dubowitz reviews the literature on child neglect definitions, examining a number of general, conceptual, and operational issues in defining and measuring neglect and discussing several measurement instruments that have been developed for work in this area. He then outlines a number of recommendations for future research, suggesting that, given the shortcomings of any one measurement approach, the best strategy for defining and measuring neglect may involve combining data from multiple sources and employing or integrating a variety of methods. In Chapter 6, Trickett provides an overview of the research literature on child sexual abuse, evaluating the two major approaches used in research in this area: cross-sectional studies of children and adult retrospective studies. She underscores the limitations of research using each of these approaches, indicating that to get beyond these limitations requires the development of theoretical models and the testing of hypotheses derived from these models. As an example for how this might occur, Trickett presents original data and results from a series of multivariate analyses from her longitudinal study of girls who have been sexually abused. She concludes with a number of recommendations for future research, underscoring that to move the field of sexual abuse forward will require more explicit, multidimensional definitions. In Chapter 7, Brassard and Donovan analyze the literature on child psychological abuse, discussing the barriers that have impeded the development of consensual definitions, the history of specific efforts to define psychological maltreatment, and definitions that have been put forth by a variety of agencies, organizations, and researchers. They then examine instruments that have been developed to assess this type of maltreatment and evaluate the degree to which they align with the definitions that have been developed. The chapter concludes with a discussion of where consensus has been achieved, areas of disagreement, and recommendations for future research. Finally, in Chapter 8, Watson provides an overview of basic concepts and principles of psychological measurement, demonstrating how these may be used in defining child maltreatment. Specifically, he describes the process of construct validation, providing examples relevant to child abuse and neglect research. He concludes with a discussion of how different theoretical schemes can be incorporated into the development of initial item pools so they can be subjected to empirical scrutiny, underscoring the constant interplay between theory and empirical data.

4

Operationally Defining Physical Abuse of Children

JOHN F. KNUTSON AND DEANNA HECKENBERG

THE TWO FOCI of this chapter are a consideration of strategies adopted by researchers to operationally define the physical abuse of children and the development of some recommendations as to how future investigators might operationalize physical abuse in research. To develop this chapter, the chapter authors started with a reconsideration of one author's comprehensive review of the research on the physical abuse of children published prior to 1993 (see Knutson & Schartz, 1997). That review had as its focus the possibility of including abuse and neglect as a relational diagnosis in the *Diagnostic and Statistical Manual of Mental Disorders, Fourth Edition (DSM-IV;* American Psychiatric Association, 1994). Although Knutson and Schartz's review evaluated the evidence pertaining to the possibility of a clinical diagnosis of physical abuse, the literature forming the basis of that review included all of the research literature extant at the time. At approximately the same time that the review was being prepared, the National Academy of Sciences established an expert panel to review the existing literature on child maltreatment, assess the quality of that research, and make recommendations for future research and supporting public policy. In large measure, this chapter (and other chapters in this volume) can be seen as an index of how far the field has progressed since the National Research Council (NRC; 1993) and others (e.g., Knutson & Schartz, 1997; Widom, 1988) raised questions about the methodological rigor used to operationally define child physical abuse and other forms of maltreatment. Although it is clear that some progress has been made, the fact that this volume is being prepared reflects, to some extent, that the field has not achieved a gold standard against which operational definitions of physical abuse and other forms of maltreatment can be judged.

Because of the logical positivist tradition that dominated social science and biomedical research in the 20th century, it would seem that as long as scholars adopt operational definitions that are clear, unambiguous, and public, there are

This work was supported, in part, by research grant MH61731, funded by the National Institute of Mental Health and the Administration on Children, Youth and Families, through the Neglect Consortium; and, in part, by research grant HD046789, funded by the National Institute of Child Health and Human Development.

many different approaches to operationally defining physical abuse that are defensible and potentially useful for empirical work. Unlike those research domains that are anchored to laboratory phenomena in which direct extrapolations to applied contexts are not considered to be important, research purported to be studying the physical abuse of children is presumed to relate in some fundamental fashion to clinical phenomena that occur in the natural habitat of children. Hence, even while embracing a logical positivist approach, a scholar doing research on physical abuse is obligated, to some extent, to provide some justification that the operational definition used relates to clinical phenomena. Thus, whether operational definitions are based on theory or empirical referents and whether the research contributes to our understanding of the clinical phenomenon of physical abuse will depend, at least in part, on the degree to which the operational definition can be linked to some clinical phenomenon.

In considering operational definitions of physical abuse, it is important to distinguish between the events that are operationalized as abusive and the methodology used to measure those events. That is, there are two dimensions on which to consider the development of operational definitions. One dimension is the basis (i.e., theory or empirical work) on which an act, an event, or a consequence of the act is considered to be abusive, and the second dimension pertains to how an investigator chooses to measure the caregiver act that is considered to be abusive. It is important to note that research literature on the physical abuse of children has adopted operational definitions that focus more on how the physical abuse is assessed than the specifics of the event that is being measured. Indeed, in some contexts the critical event is not actually measured but is presumed on the basis of a child's name being present in a child protective services (CPS) registry.

One critical issue that was raised by the NRC (1993), as well as by others, is the degree to which investigators have based their operational definitions of child maltreatment on information that is largely relegated to decisions by external agencies that have established the maltreatment status of participants enrolled in research. In some respects, this is a criticism of how an investigator assesses the presence of the circumstance of physical abuse, rather than the criterion as to what event is judged to be abusive. Although it is the case that in some circumstances the basis for judging an event to be abusive and how the information was obtained are so inextricably entwined that the two dimensional considerations noted here are largely obscured. Whenever possible, the authors of this chapter will attempt to distinguish "the how" from "the what" in this review.

HISTORICAL AND PUBLIC POLICY CONSIDERATIONS

The physical abuse of children, as a research topic, was largely ignored until the publication of "The Battered Child Syndrome" (Kempe, Silverman, Steele, Droegemueller, & Silver, 1962). Although this paper resulted in a dramatic growth in professional interest in child abuse, perhaps more importantly, the paper attracted popular media attention to the problem, thereby setting the occasion for a new child-related political agenda (Nelson, 1984). This political agenda has had far-reaching implications for the way in which many researchers have defined physical abuse during the last four decades. The impact of the political agenda on research was largely a consequence of the Child Abuse Prevention and Treatment Act (CAPTA) of 1974 (PL 93-247), the federal statute that formed the basis for many federal research initiatives on maltreatment. Perhaps more importantly, CAPTA also charged states with the responsibility to develop standards for defining abuse, the obligation to establish mandatory reporting of suspicions of maltreatment, and the necessity of identifying the state agency responsible for investigating abuse allegations. Those three charges to the states led to legislative action at the state level that has had both direct and indirect effects on the operational definitions of physical abuse used by many investigators.

Subsequent to CAPTA, legislation in each state was developed that provided statutory definitions of child maltreatment as well as provisions to attempt to meet the needs of children who had been maltreated and their families. Although the statutory definitions were not necessarily expected to control research definitions, in practice these statutory definitions had a great impact on how researchers within specific jurisdictions defined physical abuse of children. Although the scope of abuse legislation has been expanded (e.g., Title I of the Child Abuse Prevention and Treatment and Adoption Reform Act of 1978, PL 95-266; the Child Abuse Amendments of 1984, PL 98-457),[1] it was those early federal and state legislative actions that had the greatest impact on how researchers operationally defined physical abuse. With continuing legislative activity (e.g., Child Abuse Prevention, Adoption, and Family Services Act of 1988, PL 100-294)[2] that can set research agendas, it is clear that defining child physical abuse is likely to continue to be embedded in public policy debates and legislative initiatives.

One of the most important legislative influences on research definitions has been the establishment of mandatory reporting laws and their effects on both the operational definitions of abuse and the development of research samples. Because abuse victims and their families often come to the attention of researchers through the mandatory reporting system, much of the early research on physical abuse was largely determined by the mandatory reporting statutes in the jurisdictions in which the researchers were working. Mandatory reporting statutes typically identify specific professions or occupational roles that are required to report sus-

---

[1] The Child Abuse Prevention and Treatment and Adoption Reform Act of 1978 (PL 95-266) and the Child Abuse Amendments of 1984 (PL 98-457) amended the Child Abuse Prevention and Treatment Act of 1974 (PL 93-247) to allocate additional federal funds for research on child abuse.

[2] The Child Abuse Prevention, Adoption, and Family Services Act of 1988 (PL 100-294) established the National Center on Child Abuse and Neglect and a national clearinghouse designated to serve as a repository for information related to child abuse. The Act provides for the allocation of additional federal funds to states that meet delineated requirements for the investigation and reporting of suspected abuse.

picions of maltreatment of a child and the specific agency that is charged with the responsibility of investigating the veridicality of any abuse allegation. However, some states (e.g., see N.C. Gen Stat. § 7B-301, 1999) consider all individuals and institutions to be mandatory reporters. Such jurisdictional differences in the statutory identification of mandatory reporters results in nonprofessional and untrained individuals submitting reports in some jurisdictions and primarily professionals submitting mandatory reports in other jurisdictions. Substantiation rates and case level handling differ as a function of whether the report is submitted by a professional or nonprofessional (e.g., Eckenrode, Powers, Doris, Munsch, & Bolger, 1988). Thus, when CPS records are used for research, data can differ as a function of who is identified as a mandatory reporter.

Because the laws were motivated by the desire to aid children who might be at risk for being harmed, the statutes for mandatory reporting specify relatively low standards of evidence necessary to evoke suspicion, with higher standards being required for substantiation of an allegation by an investigating agency. In turn, these standards for substantiating maltreatment by a CPS agency are less stringent than the judicial standards in juvenile court proceedings for establishing the occurrence of abuse (i.e., "preponderance of evidence"). However, even judicial standards of evidence of abuse can reflect considerable variance in public policy considerations. For example, if the child in question were a Native American with tribal rights, because of the Indian Child Welfare Act (ICWA) of 1978 (PL 95-608),[3] a more stringent evidential standard of "clear and convincing" would need to be met. Thus, when researchers develop operational definitions based on judicial procedures, because of the mandates of the ICWA, the data on abuse among Native Americans in administrative data or on out-of-home placements may not be comparable to the data from other ethnic groups in the United States (see Kessel & Robbins, 1984; Limb, Chance, & Brown, 2004; Wichlacz & Wechsler, 1983). In addition, there is considerable variability among states in their abuse definitions (see Flango et al., 1988; Hartley, 1981). In short, if researchers depend on mandatory reporting to establish their samples, or if they use statutory definitions, the operational definitions of physical abuse may not be comparable across jurisdictions even if the researchers adopt the same methodologies for accessing the administrative records.

When research definitions are placed in the context of public policy or statutory considerations, questions may be raised as to whether the criterion for defining physical abuse should be identical to standards for suspicions in mandatory reporting statutes or should require a more stringent standard (i.e., substantiation). This is an example in which the operational definition of physical abuse is somehow linked to political and public policy contexts, regardless of how a researcher chooses to measure the abuse. Related to these issues, a distinction can

---

[3]The Indian Child Welfare Act (IWCA) of 1978 (PL 95-608) establishes standards for adoptive and foster care placements of Native American children.

be made between a "harm" standard and an "endangerment" standard. Although endangerment might be sufficient for establishing a suspicion, substantiation of maltreatment may require the standard of harm, depending on the jurisdiction and the circumstances of the assessment. A prominent research example of the difference between the harm criterion and the endangerment criterion is reflected in the Second National Incidence Study (NIS-2; Department of Health and Human Services [DHHS], 1988) and the Third National Incidence Study (NIS-3; Sedlak & Broadhurst, 1996), in which epidemiological data were provided that distinguished between children who met the endangerment criteria and children who met the harm criteria. When researchers use policy-based decisions, harm or endangerment standards are not necessarily clearly specified.

Adding to the complexity of using definitions of physical abuse that are based on state statute is the inherent vagueness in the statutory definitions and the variability among states in that degree of vagueness. Statutory vagueness typically is justified because statutes are designed to subsume a remarkably broad range of endangering or harmful acts directed at children. Although the vagueness of statutory definitions has long been criticized because of the clinical and legal implications (e.g., Christophersen, 1983; Wald, 1975, 1976, 1982; Wasserman & Rosenfeld, 1985), that vagueness has research implications as well. It is of interest to note that although some researchers have lamented the effects of these vague definitions on research (e.g., Besharov, 1981; Giovannoni & Becerra, 1979; Mele-Sernovitz, 1980) and called for more narrow definitions of abuse, others have argued in favor of broad, nonspecific definitions (e.g., Gelles, 1982). In his considerations of the implications of abuse statutes, Wald (1975, 1976, 1982) argued for statutes that adopt very stringent standards for defining abuse in terms of the harmful consequences (i.e., tissue damage) of the abusive act. However, arguments such as those offered by Wald do not seem to have been persuasive in state legislatures and are rarely embraced by researchers. Indeed, the broad and nonspecific approach to defining abuse in child protection statutes continues as the typical contemporary state statute. As a consequence, when researchers attempt to use a statute-based definition, they either have to live with relatively vague operational definitions or they have to refine their definitions from the information that is available to them in state records (e.g., Barnett, Manly, & Cicchetti, 1993). However, whenever researchers attempt to anchor their operational definitions to statutory considerations, both the definition and the measurement strategy can be controlled more by public policy decisions than considerations of scientific rigor.

The apparent public support for corporal punishment in homes or the schools illustrates how public policy could determine the classification of specific acts as physically abusive in some jurisdictions when state administrative data are used to establish an operational definition of abuse or when researchers attempt to link their research to statutory definitions of particular states (Reitman, 1988). For example, corporal punishment by parents that is "reasonable in manner and moderate in degree" is explicitly excluded from abuse criteria in some states (e.g., see S.C. Code Ann.§ 20-7-490, 2003), whereas in other states the maltreatment statutes are silent on corporal punishment by parents (e.g., see Iowa Code Ann. § 232.68, 2000). Still other jurisdictions include in their abuse statutes corporal punishment that is cruel, prolonged, or circumstantially excessive (e.g., see Ohio Rev. Code Ann. § 2919.22, 2004). Thus, when CPS records are used to define the occurrence of physical abuse in Iowa (e.g., Hartley, 2002), Ohio (e.g., Mraovich & Wilson, 1999), or other states (e.g., Drake & Pandey, 1996; Fantuzzo, McDermott, Manz, Hampton, & Burdick, 1996; Fantuzzo et al., 1996; Haskett, Scott, Grant, Ward, & Robinson, 2003; Way, Chung, Jonson-Reid, & Drake, 2001), the decision to include or exclude some forms of corporal punishment in the definition of physical abuse can depend more on where the research is conducted than on theory or empirical referents. Although it is recognized that circumstances may exist in which researchers must attempt to anchor their operational definitions of physical abuse to the statutory or judicial context in which they are conducting research, it is cautioned that using those bases to establish operational definitions of physical abuse virtually assures operational definitions that will not generalize across jurisdictions. In addition, the statutory wording of mandatory reporting requirements can have a direct impact on whether professionals report circumstances to CPS agencies (Brosig & Kalichman, 1992). Thus, the statutes can influence the base rate of reporting as well as the way in which a case might be handled by an agency.

Not only do state statutes differ on matters pertaining to corporal punishment by parents, but also inconsistencies exist among states as to whether corporal punishment in the schools is sanctioned. That is, corporal punishment in the schools is prohibited by statute in some states; however, the codes of most states are either silent on the matter of corporal punishment in the schools or explicitly authorize it. When the laws of a state do not prohibit corporal punishment in the schools, the courts have treated statutory silence as tacit support for the use of corporal punishment in the schools (Connors, 1979). In 2004, the statutes of 23 states in the United States addressed corporal punishment in the schools, but only 2 of those states explicitly prohibited such corporal punishment (Purver, 2004). This circumstance can result in an ironic situation in which specific acts meted by parents in their homes could be considered abusive while comparable acts in the schools would not constitute physical abuse. Thus, when state statute forms the basis for a research definition, the event would be less important than the agent of that act. A Department of Education survey estimated that there were more than 1.4 million episodes of corporal punishment in U.S. schools in 1980 (Van Dyke, 1983). The use of corporal punishment was most common in southern and southeastern states and least common in the northeastern states (McCluney, 1987; Van Dyke, 1983). With widespread support for the use of corporal punishment in the schools, diagnostic standards for physical abuse by parents could be influenced by the standards of corporal punishment established for school personnel in those states. The guidelines for corporal punishment, however, also are often vague or nonexistent (McCluney, 1987), and the limits on corporal punishment in the schools have been based largely on judicial decisions.

Two Supreme Court decisions have been pivotal in establishing guidelines for the use of corporal punishment in the schools. These decisions may have implications for some operational definitions of physical abuse. In a five to four decision, the 1977 *Ingraham v. Wright* ruling established that corporal punishment in the schools is not cruel and unusual punishment and, therefore, is not a violation of the Eighth Amendment. Moreover, the ruling established that the corporal punishment experienced by the child in that case did not violate due process standards and that a hearing prior to the imposition for corporal punishment was not required. In *Baker v. Owen* (1976), the Supreme Court affirmed without opinion a district court ruling that outlined the minimal due process requirements of corporal punishment in the schools. Essentially, unless the transgressions are extreme, corporal punishment should not be applied on a first-offense basis, students should be apprised of the corporal consequences of their offenses, punishment should be administered in the presence of another school official, and parents may request a written explanation of the reasons for the punishment and who was present during its administration. These guidelines do not directly address the issue of severity of the punishment and the possible tissue damaging consequences of the acts.

Based on a review of relevant statutes, state and local regulations, and judicial decisions, Hudgins and Vacca (1985) provided guidelines for corporal punishment in the schools that could have implications for some operational definitions of physical abuse by parents and/or guardians in some jurisdictions when administrative data are used for research. First, the goal of the punishment should be for "correction" and be the best means for achieving child obedience; thus, the punishment should not involve any malice. This specification of a goal for the discipline is not unlike some abuse statutes that exclude parental corporal punishment that is "perpetrated for the sole purpose of restraining or correcting the child" (e.g., S.C. Code Ann.§ 20-7-490 [2][a][ii], 1981). Such a standard invokes the dubious notion that the putative intentions of parents or school personnel can be unequivocally assessed. Second, the punishment should not be considered "cruel and unusual." In that context, the dissenting opinion in *Ingraham v. Wright* noted that the injurious punishment experienced by the plaintiff in that case would clearly be unacceptable in criminal proceedings. Moreover, in a family court context in many jurisdictions, the injurious consequences of discipline considered acceptable in *Ingraham v. Wright* would almost certainly have been seen as abusive. In short, if standards of school-based corporal punishment were applied to physical abuse definitions in some jurisdictions, severe corporal punishment would fall outside the domain of physical abuse if the researcher were to base operational definitions on standards in those jurisdictions.

According to Hudgins and Vacca (1985), corporal punishment in the schools that would meet contemporary standards of "acceptability" would have the following characteristics: appropriate for the age and sex of the child, resulting in no lasting or permanent injury, and incorporating an appropriate instrument at an appropriate locus of impact. Similarly, Connors (1979) indicated that guidelines for excessive corporal punishment in the schools establish standards that specify more than three blows with a paddle, blows that left bruises or marks, blows applied anywhere other than the buttocks, or discipline that resulted in temporary or permanent physical injury.

In recent years, efforts have been made by some researchers to argue for the inclusion of any corporal punishment in a broadened domain of physical abuse (e.g., Straus, 2000). Other researchers (e.g., Baumrind, 1996; Baumrind, Larzelere, & Cowan, 2002; Larzelere, 2000) have advanced the notion that normative corporal punishment (i.e., spanking) is an appropriate component of parents' disciplinary armamentarium, a view that is vigorously debated (e.g., Gershoff, 2002; Holden, 2002). Public policy support for physical discipline in the schools and statutory support for parental corporal punishment in some states, coupled with widespread public support for physical discipline in the home (e.g., Erlanger, 1974) caused Zigler (1979) to express pessimism about the prospects of reducing physical abuse of children in their homes. Although the experiences of the Nordic countries after World War II would suggest that the base rate of corporal punishment could be reduced (e.g., Durrant, 1999), it is also clear that noninjurious corporal punishment such as spanking would not meet a statistical atypicality criterion for inclusion in an operational definition of physical abuse. Also, it is important to note that some "normative" corporal punishment will necessarily be included in some operational definitions of physical abuse when the methodologies used to operationally define that abuse do not include a means of systematically excluding corporal punishment.

Methods Based on Administrative Data

Aside from state statutes as a basis of definitional variation, another of the critical aspects of public policy and state statute that has influenced defining physical abuse was the development of state central registries. The establishment of central registries was a corollary of the mandatory reporting statutes, because the registries were conceptualized as a vehicle for establishing epidemiological data and for providing a context in which clinical decisions could be made on the basis of repeated referrals. Because of the mandate of CAPTA, all of the states established some version of a state central registry. Although among states there are differences in criteria for reports to be entered into the central registry, differences in expungement criteria, and differences in determining who has access to those records, the apparent availability of the central registry data to bona fide researchers has caused some researchers to adopt the criteria for reporting to central registries as the primary component for establishing samples as abused (in the registry) or not abused (not in the registry) in the United States (e.g., Cerezo, D'Ocon, & Dolz, 1996; Feldman, Salzinger, Rosario, & Alvarado, 1995; Mraovich

& Wilson, 1999; Salzinger, Feldman, Ng-Mak, Mojica, & Stockhammer, 2001; Salzinger et al., 2002) and the United Kingdom (e.g., Gillham et al., 1998). Using this same general strategy, some investigators have detailed the statutory basis of the definitions and provided a general breakdown of how the sample met various criteria in the statute. For example, Haskett et al. (2003) indicated the percentage of the sample that was in the registry because of "physical abuse" and "improper discipline." Similarly, Salzinger, Feldman, Hammer, and Rosario (1993) noted the distribution of those who incurred injuries or experienced excessive corporal punishment at the hands of parents or guardians (not school personnel) in which different statutes and different standards uniformly existed across jurisdictions. Using this approach, the operational definition of physical abuse is limited to an event that was sufficient to cause a record to be entered into the central registry of that jurisdiction. Such an approach, of course, runs the risk of operationalizing physical abuse in a manner that is idiosyncratic to the setting in which the research is being conducted. Although the approach anchors research to the clinical context of the setting in which the research is conducted, such an approach can greatly compromise the generalizability of findings beyond the jurisdiction in which the research was conducted.

A related strategy designed to reduce this idiosyncratic contextualizing and improve generalizability has been to use central registry information or CPS records as the primary source of information about the abuse status of a participant and then to use a researcher-based framework to classify the events reflected in the actual CPS record. In this strategy for operationalizing abuse, the researcher does not rely on the registry classification but attempts to classify the abuse through an abstracting or coding of the CPS records. Of course, such an approach is limited by the degree to which the record is sufficiently detailed (e.g., Salzinger et al., 1993). Benedict, Zuravin, Somerfield, and Brandt (1996) used evidence of injury (i.e., cuts, bruises, long bone fractures, and unexplained bruises) in CPS records to establish physical abuse while children were in foster care.

Perhaps the most widely used approach to classify abusive experiences from CPS records is the Barnett et al. (1993) Maltreatment Classification System (MCS). The MCS uses CPS records to determine the types of maltreatment a child has experienced and provides an ordinal scale rating (1–5) for each type of maltreatment. Within the MCS, the detailing of child experiences is more complete in the area of physical abuse, with a number of studies establishing its utility in research on physical abuse (e.g., Klorman, Cicchetti, Thatcher, & Ison, 2003; Macfie, Cicchetti, & Toth, 2001; Pollak, Cicchetti, Hornung, & Reed, 2000; Sullivan & Knutson, 1998, 2000). The ordinal scale of the MCS provides the possibility of parsing endangerment from harm, using participants with a higher MCS score when an injury (i.e., harm) standard is adopted (e.g., Smetana et al., 1999). Although data from users and the developers of the MCS have established the reliability of record coding by trained coders, the MCS is useful but also limited by the ordinal scale and the fact that more complete records (more information) will yield higher scores. In view of the fact that CPS records can be decidedly uneven, this association between record completeness and the MCS score is a limitation in the use of the MCS.

Alternative CPS record-coding systems have been described that extract information about the caregiver acts that are classified as abuse in the records. For example, Ezzell, Swenson, and Brondino (2000) reported as abused participants who had been hit with objects; burned "impulsively;" hit, punched, or kicked; or shaken or pushed. Thus, in this scheme, the participants who had been physically abused were identified by the acts that were reported in the records to have been perpetrated by a child's caregiver.

The record review with the MCS scale strategy used by Ezzell et al. (2000) is similar to a strategy adopted by researchers who use CPS records as the source of information but use the Conflict Tactics Scales (CTS; Straus, Gelles, & Steinmetz, 1980) to classify the events experienced by the child as abusive or not, depending on where the act or acts would fall on the Violence Scale of the CTS. The original CTS was not designed to measure parent–child interactions, but the use of the CTS as a framework for evaluating CPS records as an extension of a standardized self-report measure, rather than establishing it as a record-abstracting tool, has been justified largely on the normative data obtained with the CTS in telephonic survey work (e.g., Ross, 1996; Wolfner & Gelles, 1993). The Parent–Child CTS (Straus, Hamby, Finklehor, Moore, & Runyan, 1998) might make a better structure for operationalizing physical abuse from CPS records, but such an approach seems not to have been adopted. Yet another approach was used by Raiha and Soma (1997), in which the records of the Army Family Advocacy Central Registry were evaluated by a multidisciplinary team who made a determination of abuse status by "preponderance of available evidence," an approach that would be difficult to replicate.

In addition to using CPS records or central registry files, another approach to using administrative data to operationally define physical abuse is to use a judicial decision standard. In such research, the researchers operationalize abuse by using the adjudication standard for the jurisdiction in which they conduct research. Widom has used such an approach in both short-term (e.g., Rivera & Widom, 1990; Widom, 1989) and long-term (e.g., Colman & Widom, 2004; Horwitz, Widom, McLaughlin, & White, 2001; Raphael, Widom, & Lange, 2001; Widom & Shepard, 1996) assessments of the outcomes of abuse. Similarly, using juvenile court records, Garland, Landsverk, Hough, and Ellis-MacLeod (1996) defined physical abuse in terms of bruising, burns, or other injuries incurred by a child. Like other administrative data, the operationalization of physical abuse from court records could reflect both the jurisdiction in which the data were collected and the time frame in which the judicial decision was reached.

Another factor of concern that relates to operational definitions derived from administrative records is the inclusion of a recency criterion (Kolko, 1996). In studies of children who have been physically abused, to ensure that a minimum of intervening events occur between the circumstance of abuse and the research itself, limiting a sample to children who were identified as abused within a relatively short period of time could be important in terms of inferring consequences from outcomes.

Self-Report Approaches to Defining Physical Abuse

Although Chapter 9 in this volume is devoted to self-report indices of maltreatment, some consideration of that methodology specifically related to operationalizing physical abuse needs to be considered in this chapter as well. The use of self-report indices of physical abuse are second only to the use of CPS administrative data in research. Self-report indices have been used with child (e.g., Benbenishty, Zeira, & Astor, 2002; Ney, Fung, & Wickett, 1994), adolescent (e.g., Tyler & Cauce, 2002), and adult (e.g., Jasinski, Williams, & Siegel, 2001; Knutson & Selner, 1994; Raine et al., 2001; Thakkar, Gutierrez, Kuczen, & McCanne, 2001) participants of childhood physical abuse research, and they have been used with parents who are asked to describe their own current or recent parenting practices (e.g., Connelly & Straus, 1993; Dodge, Pettit, Bates, & Valente, 1996; Epstein & Bottoms, 2002; Mahoney, Donnelly, Boxer, & Lewis, 2003; Mahoney, Donnelly, Lewis, & Maynard, 2000; Weiss, Dodge, Bates, & Pettit, 1992).

When self-report is used to operationally define physical abuse, investigators have used a wide range of idiosyncratic or standardized measures with known or unknown evidence of reliability and validity (see Chapter 8). It is interesting to note that some investigators have merely asked participants if they have been physically abused at any time in their lives (e.g., Feerick & Haugaard, 1999; Silverman, Reinherz, & Giaconia, 1996), or adoptive parents have been asked about the abusive experiences of children prior to adoption (Erich & Leung, 2002). In such approaches, the operational definition of physical abuse is essentially a standard that the participant applies to his or her own experiences. Thus, the criterion for abuse is essentially based on the normative standards of the participants as they define the boundary conditions of abusive and nonabusive disciplinary experiences. Evidence that participants apply normative standards that are based, in part, on their own specific experiences (Bensley et al., 2004; Berger, Knutson, Mehm, & Perkins, 1988; Bower & Knutson, 1996; Bower-Russa, Knutson, & Winebarger, 2001), and that they either may be overly harsh or may underreport actions classified as abusive by other criteria leads to less rigor in the data for researchers. When investigators operationally define physical abuse by asking participants if they have been physically abused, they risk an operational definition that is more a reflection of the idiosyncratic views of the participants rather than the investigator's own criterion.

There are many examples of operational definitions based on self-reports of specific acts or parenting events. Friedrich, Tally, Panser, Fett, and Zinsmeister (1997) used a questionnaire to ask participants whether an older person had hit, kicked, or beaten them. In a similar approach, Wind and Silvern (1993) used questions to determine whether participants had been punched, kicked, bitten, beaten up, or threatened with a weapon. Wind and Silvern included being struck by an object more than once per month as an index of physical abuse, whereas Perkins and Jones (2004) defined abuse as hitting that resulted in persistent soft tissue damage more than two times per year. McGee, Wolfe, and Wilson (1997) used visual analog scales and verbal prompts from the Ratings of Past Life Events Scale (McGee, 1990) to define abuse in terms of various acts of physical discipline. Ryan, Kilmer, Cauce, Watanabe, and Hoyt (2001) first asked a screening question as to whether anyone had hurt the participant physically. Physical abuse was then defined as experiencing a "serious" injury, "excessive" corporal punishment by someone at least 5 years older, or actions leading to a CPS report. Thakkar et al. (2001) also established a physical abuse classification by combining self-reports of disciplinary acts and injurious consequences.

Other investigators have invited participants to indicate whether they have experienced disciplinary injuries or specific acts of parenting in the context of an interview or a self-report questionnaire. For example, Jasinski et al. (2001) asked whether a parent had hit, kicked, punched, tied up, or did "something even worse" as the index of physical abuse. Welch and Fairburn (1996) defined participants who had been abused as those who reported deliberate contact that resulted in injury, with severe physical abuse limited to burns, fractures, and injuries to the head or face. In similar work, Epstein and Bottoms (2002) asked participants if they had experienced injuries such as welts, bruises, or bleeding, as well as whether they had experienced specific potentially injurious disciplinary acts. Epstein and Bottoms also asked participants if they had been a "victim of child abuse." Chaffin, Kelleher, and Hollenberg (1996) based their operational definition on the participants answering yes to any of five questions in the antisocial personality disorder section of the Diagnostic Interview Schedule (Robins, Helzer, Croughan, & Ratliff, 1981), in which reports of injury in the form of bruising or worse consequences were acknowledged.

Equally vague definitions of abuse are statements such as "an overt act of physical aggression directed toward a child " (Francis, Hughes, & Hitz, 1993, p. 675). It is important to note that the use of such single-item characterizations of childhood experiences of abuse continue to be used to operationally define physical abuse in contemporary research published in archival journals (e.g., Perkins & Jones, 2004). An alternative single self-report question is one that inquires about any disciplinary acts that resulted in injuries, coupled with a listing of examples of injuries such as bruises, welts, cuts, burns, broken bones, dental injuries, or head injuries (Leitenberg, Gibson, & Novy, 2004). Although less likely to be influenced by personal normative standards, from a psychometric standpoint (see Chapter 8), the single item approach is likely to be associated with reduced reliability and validity.

In an approach that blends self-report indices of abuse with administrative data, Caselles and Milner (2000) recruited parents from among those who had been identified as abusive through a social services investigation or those who had joined Parents Anonymous, a self-help group for parents who see themselves as abusive. In addition, the participants had to score above a cut-off score of 215 on the Child Abuse Potential Inventory (CAPI; Milner, 1986) to be identified as abusive parents. Although some data exist to support the use of the CAPI as a risk-screening inventory, it is more a representation of the participant's background than of their abusive behavior at the time of completion, as the scale represents a large number of personal history items, especially those pertaining to the subjects' own childhoods. Moreover, Baumann and Kolko (2002) reported that abusive and nonabusive mothers in a high-risk sample did not differ on their CAPI scores, raising questions about CAPI scores as a self-report index of contemporaneous physical abuse.

Among the more common approaches to obtaining self-report indices of physically abusive experiences or acts is the original CTS (Straus et al., 1980) and the newer Parent–Child Conflict Tactics Scales (Straus et al., 1998). These instruments are either administered as self-report questionnaires or as interviews (e.g., Kuyken & Brewin, 1996; Tyler & Cauce, 2002), with physical abuse typically defined as acts falling on the Violence Scale or acts that are deemed to be potentially injurious. It should be noted that although the CTS provides an act-based approach to defining physical abuse, it does not represent the full range of parenting acts that can injure children or acts that are represented in CPS records that parents have used to harm children. In addition, some investigators have elected not to use some of the items (e.g., the use of a knife or gun) because they are associated with a very low base rate (zero or approaching zero in most child studies), and they have been deemed to be off-putting to research participants (e.g., Molnar, Buka, Brennan, Holton, & Earls, 2003). As an example of how widespread use of the CTS as a measure of child physical abuse has become, Bugental and Happaney (2004) used it as a self-report measure by mothers of 1-year-old infants. Thus, a measure designed to assess adult couple interactions has been used in an unjustified manner in research on mother–infant interactions reported in a respected archival journal.

Used as a self-report measure of punitive and abusive discipline, the Assessing Environments III questionnaire developed by Berger et al. (1988) has been used to assess the childhood experiences of adult and adolescent participants drawn from clinical (e.g., Meyerson, Long, Miranda, & Marx, 2002; Miller & Knutson, 1997; Rorty, Yager, & Rossotto, 1995; Varia, Abidin, & Dass, 1996; Worling, 1995; Worling & Curwen, 2000; Zaidi & Foy, 1994) and nonclinical (e.g., Gauthier, Stollak, Messe, & Aronoff, 1996; Knutson & Selner, 1994; Lopez & Heffer, 1998) populations. In this approach, participants are classified as abused if they endorse more than a minimum criterion on a physical discipline scale (some studies used a criterion of > 3 and others used a criterion of > 4). The scale includes a number of potentially injurious, injurious, and noninjurious disciplinary acts, some of which involve striking with objects, as well as blows characterized by a specific response topography or target loci. Thus, the operational definition of physical abuse used in this approach is essentially endorsing a sufficient number of different disciplinary acts and/or consequences to reach a cutoff score that distinguishes abused and nonabused participants (judicial criterion; Berger et al., 1988) or that is associated with theoretically consistent outcomes (e.g., Zaidi, Knutson, & Mehm, 1989).

Another self-report measure of physical abuse is the Child Physical Abuse Scale, developed by Briere and Runtz (1990). In this questionnaire, participants rate the occurrence of 8 parental behaviors on a 5-point Likert scale indicating whether acts never occurred or occurred more than 20 times. In addition, the Briere and Runtz questionnaire provides for experiencing injurious consequences from the parental acts. Thus, in studies based on this measure (e.g., Runtz & Schallow, 1997), physical abuse is operationalized as self-reports of parental acts and injurious consequences. The Childhood Trauma Questionnaire (CTQ; Bernstein et al., 1994) is a similar instrument in which participants respond to 7-point Likert scale items on the Physical Abuse Scale. When the CTQ was used by Feerick, Haugaard, and Hien (2002), physical abuse was defined in terms of acts leaving marks or bruises or requiring medical services. In addition, blows severe enough to be noticed by others or the frequent use of belts, boards, cords, or hard objects were classified as abuse. Thus, the self-report criterion reflected either injuries or some specific disciplinary acts. Others using the CTQ have used the total scale score as an index of abuse (e.g., Wolfe, Wekerle, Scott, Straatman, & Grasley, 2004). Scher, Forde, McQuaid, and Stein (2004) defined physical abuse with a CTQ cutoff score derived from work by Walker et al. (1999). In the Walker et al. work, the cutoffs were developed using receiver-operating curve (ROC) methodology and clinical interviews with the participants as the criterion. Thus, the empirically derived cutoff score was based on a single-source methodology rather than an effort to use the ROC methodology with an independent criterion.

When used with parents, one question that is raised about self-report indices of physical abuse is the degree to which participants would be willing to disclose potentially incriminating information as well as whether mandatory reporting obligations of researchers in some jurisdictions would compromise the researcher's capacity to ask about physically abusive events. Some researchers have adopted an approach that actually warns participants about the mandatory reporting requirements before parents are interviewed (e.g., Dodge et al., 1996; Weiss et al., 1993). Moreover, some laboratories have operationally defined physical abuse as maternal reports of minor injuries, such as bruising, because there is an assumption that mothers will have a bias to report less severe injuries (e.g., Keiley, Howe, Dodge, Bates, & Pettit, 2001). There is, however, no systematic published research on the matter of parental underreporting. Yet, anecdotal reports shared by researchers at meetings suggest that parents will report seemingly self-incriminating acts because they do not see those acts as atypical, harmful, abusive, or reportable. That is, of course, another circumstance in which the participant's own norms may influence how he or she responds. Based on conversations with experienced investigators, and based on research with more than 600 high-risk mothers, this concern that parents will be unwilling to disclose punitive and injurious acts seems overstated. Indeed, with data suggesting that many parents do not share the same norms for discipline as the investigators (e.g., Bower & Knutson, 1996) or do not share normative standards with the general public (e.g., Bensley et al., 2004; Sapp & Carter, 1978), it is possible that research participants are likely to disclose acts that might seem to be self-incriminating. That is not inconsistent with data suggesting that some participants who minimize (i.e., fail to classify their severely punitive experiences as abusive) also show evidence of significant social and psychological adjustment problems (Varia et al., 1996).

Related to the matter of reporting or underreporting biases, a number of studies have shown that participants from clinical and nonclinical samples are much less likely to report experiencing "physical discipline" than they are to report "spanking" (Berger et al., 1988; Knutson & Selner, 1994; Lopez & Heffer, 1998). Such data suggest that physical discipline is not seen as a superordinate category in which spanking would be a member. Such data also underscore the importance of understanding response biases when developing self-report indices of physical abuse as well as considering how questions regarding discipline are phrased.

Although researchers have legitimate concerns about the use of self-report indices of physical abuse, data also exist suggesting that the self-reports of adults can be reliable across time (e.g., Dube, Williamson, Thompson, Felitti, & Anda, 2004). In addition, data also exists that supports the veridicality of some self-report indices of harsh and punitive discipline during childhood (e.g., Prescott et al., 2000) if the questions reflect discrete objective behavioral events rather than characterizations of the nature of those experiences (i.e., as abusive). In addition, there are data to suggest some degree of correspondence between self-report measures in adulthood and administrative data based on childhood events (see Chapter 9). However, it is also the case that some studies have shown that participants' self-reports are not entirely congruent with independently established information about their disciplinary or abusive experiences (e.g., Kolko, Kazdin, & Day, 1996; Stein & Lewis, 1993). Such studies underscore potential problems in relying exclusively on self-report measures.

Multimethod/Multisource Approaches

Although the use of administrative data and a child's presence or absence in CPS records have been the most widely used approaches to operationally defining physical abuse, and although self-report measures are also widely used, increasingly researchers have turned to multimethod or multisource strategies to operationally define physical abuse. Kolko (1996) combined CPS referral information, caseworker reports, and interviews with parents to assess harsh discipline as well as founded incidents of physical abuse. Yates, Dodds, Sroufe, and Egeland (2003) used a combination of home observations, interviews, and CPS records as sources of information and then used a case conference methodology to integrate the material, with the criterion for physical abuse being parental acts that resulted in "physical damage" to the child, such as bruising, cuts, and burns. Pollak's laboratory (e.g., Pollak & Sinha, 2002; Pollak & Tolley-Schell, 2003) has selected children who have experienced "direct physical abuse" using a combination of the substantiation of physical abuse by the county Department of Human Services office coupled with the parents' completion of the Parent–Child CTS (Straus et al., 1998). Similarly, Johnson et al. (2002) used central registry data (abuse prior to age 8) coupled with the CTS administered when the child was age 6. The child attesting to abuse identified in CPS records, coupled with parent/caregiver confirmation, was used by Ackerman, Newton, McPherson, Jones, and Dykman (1998). Shields and Cicchetti (2001) interviewed parents about maltreating events and then examined CPS records using the MCS (Barnett et al., 1993). All of these studies tried to compensate for the limitations of a single source by attempting to obtain confirmatory information from a second source, with abuse operationalized as concordant information from two or more sources.

In a similar approach, Brown and Kolko (1999) used a combination of the Child Abuse Incident Report (Kolko, 1996), the Child Abuse Survey Report (Kazdin, Moser, Colbus, & Bell, 1985) and the Violence Scale of the CTS (Straus et al., 1980) to classify the physically abusive experiences of children in the 6- to 13-year age range. A multisource, if not multimethod, approach was used by Naar-King, Silvern, Ryan, and Sebring (2002) by using an interview format with adolescents, their therapists, and their social services caseworkers. Physical abuse was physical discipline other than spanking and was categorized on a 3-point ordinal scale, with mild abuse involving an absence of injuries and no striking with a closed fist, moderate abuse consisting of being struck by objects or fists or incurring marks and bruising, and severe abuse involving injuries that required medical services.

In a study of pediatric head trauma, Ransom, Mann, Vavilala, Haruff, and Rivara (2003) established abuse using the following criteria: 1) caregiver confession; 2) police investigation; 3) medical examiner ruling the child's death a homicide; 4) CPS records; 5) retinal hemorrhages; and 6) injuries inconsistent with the reported mechanism of injury. With the exception of the confession, physical abuse was confirmed when three of the remaining five criteria were met. Although all criteria were based on injury data, the researchers used a six-source methodology.

Cantos, Neale, O'Leary, and Gaines (1997) operationally defined abusive mothers as those who had injured their children, but the extent or the locus of the injuries were unspecified. Similarly, physical abuse was operationalized by

Dodge et al. (1996) when a mother reported injuring her child by her actions or the interviewer reached a determination that the child was probably harmed by the parental acts.

Most of the multisource/multimethod approaches are essentially a fail-safe system whereby the child is judged to have been physically abused, or the parent is judged to be physically abusive, if at least one or some minimum number of indices reflect a positive finding. Considering physical abuse to be a reflection of extreme discipline, some researchers have attempted to develop multimethod/multisource abuse constructs using structural modeling strategies (e.g., Knutson, DeGarmo, Koeppl, & Reid, 2005; Knutson, DeGarmo, & Reid, 2004). In this approach, theoretically or empirically based indicators of the construct are aggregated mathematically to achieve a continuous measure of harsh parenting or physical abuse. Chapter 11 by DeGarmo, Reid, and Knutson provides examples as to how adding indicators to the construct can improve the explanatory capacity and the variance that can be accounted for in a theoretical model.

Implications for Future Research

Since Kempe et al.'s paper was published in 1962, the research literature on the physical abuse of children has reflected a wide range of operational definitions adopted by researchers. As suggested by the material reviewed previously, coupled with earlier reviews (e.g., Knutson & Schartz, 1997), it should not be surprising that some operational definitions of physical abuse are a direct reflection of statutes, regulations, or local policies, while other definitions reflect the methodological or theoretical positions of investigators. Some seem to be reflections of convenience. It is important to note that advocates for various approaches to defining physical abuse have often advanced strong arguments in favor of their particular approaches, or they have attempted to anchor them to a research tradition (e.g., Besharov, 1981; Finkelhor & Korbin, 1988; Gelles, 1982; Giovannoni & Becerra, 1979; O'Toole, Turbett, & Nalepka, 1983; Parke, 1977; Parke & Collmer, 1975; Rosenthal, 1988; U.S. Deptartment of Health and Human Services, 1988). However, none of those arguments seem to have been sufficiently persuasive to move the field in a particular direction. Indeed, although there has been considerable consistency across time in the manner with which individual researchers have chosen to operationally define abuse, at the time this book is being written, there is no generally agreed-upon approach. This variance in operational definitions, although troubling, is of perhaps less concern than the lack of specificity that almost certainly precludes replication and the development of a systematic corpus of knowledge. The authors of this chapter believe that the most critical remedy is to adopt operational definitions that are sufficiently detailed and clear so as to assure replicability across laboratories and jurisdictions and to support analyses and understanding across studies.

KEY ISSUES IN DEFINING
AND OPERATIONALIZING PHYSICAL ABUSE

Although it is unlikely that a single and highly specific operational definition of child physical abuse will be adopted in the near future, the existing literature provides a framework for identifying a number of key issues that researchers should consider in developing definitions of abuse.

Abuse as a Parental Act

In general, physical abuse of children is considered to be an act (or acts) of commission by a parent or a parent proxy, such as a child care provider, a household resident, or someone who is charged by a parent or an agency to provide care for a child. These acts of commission are to be distinguished from acts of omission, which would typically be subsumed under those aspects of maltreatment that are deemed neglect (see Chapter 5). In short, operational definitions of physical abuse in the reviewed literature have typically specified, or assumed, that the abusive event was a purposive act directed at the child rather than a parental act that was not specifically directed at the child. Indeed, in both self-report strategies and in CPS data, virtually all of the physically abusive acts that have been specified have been placed in a disciplinary context.

When abusive actions are defined within the context of parental discipline, there is usually some distinction between those acts that are considered to be abusive and those acts that are not considered to be abusive. Thus, some researchers have considered parental acts that have specific response topographies (e.g., striking with a closed fist) to be abusive acts, while other response topographies (e.g., striking with an open hand) might be deemed corporal punishment but not abuse. Similarly, the particular target loci of a disciplinary act (e.g., striking the head or abdomen) might be considered abusive while other target loci (e.g., buttocks) would not be considered abusive. Striking with objects is yet another example of characteristics of a parental act that might cause that act to be considered abusive. Some researchers have considered striking with any object to be abusive, whereas others have distinguished between striking with some specific objects as abusive (e.g., coat hangers, electrical cords) and other objects (e.g., wooden spoons, rulers, spatulas) as nonabusive. Other researchers have referred to generic characteristics of the objects (e.g., hard objects). These response characteristics and target loci also can be qualified by a consideration of the amplitude of the caregiver response. That is, blows struck with a short and/or slow excursion of the limb would be considered nonabusive, whereas long and rapid excursions of the limb would be considered abusive. Sometimes the categorization is delimited by frequency of occurrence.

The use of act-based definitions of physical abuse are reflected in research that incorporates variations of the CTS and other act-based instruments noted in this chapter. In such research, some of the identified acts have been deemed physically abusive, and others have not been classified as abuse. In all of the research reviewed, the basis for classifying the acts is either unspecified or is linked to some information on the prevalence of the acts in the population, a presumption of statistical atypicality, or some other normative standards.

Atypicality also can be related to defining physical abuse as a specific set of responses based on estimates of contemporary social norms. Social norms can be inferred from statute and public policy, such as those pertaining to corporal punishment in the schools, but they can also be determined through surveys of general population groups. For example, Sapp and Carter (1978) surveyed a representative sample of Texans and established their personal definitions of abuse by asking respondents to classify parent–child acts as abusive or nonabusive. If the criteria for physical abuse were based on a majority of respondents from the Sapp and Carter survey, striking children with some objects (e.g., belts, wooden paddles) would not be abuse, and striking children with other objects (e.g., coat hangers, belt buckles) would be abuse. According to a majority of surveyed Texans, any acts that resulted in injury to the child would also be considered abuse. In view of the regional differences in the acceptability of corporal punishment in the schools, it might be expected that there would be regional differences in rating different parenting behaviors as abusive, which would confound definitions that are purported to be generalizable. It should be noted, however, that an assessment of community subcultural differences in ratings of parental acts as maltreatment did not identify any major group differences (Dubowitz, Klockner, Starr, & Black, 1998; Polansky, Ammons, & Weathersby, 1983). It is also of interest that surveys similar to that of Sapp and Carter with university students in the midwest yielded ratings of parental acts that were generally comparable to those from Sapp and Carter (Bower & Knutson, 1996; Bower-Russa et al., 2001). It is important to note that when individuals reported experiencing a specific disciplinary act in childhood, they were significantly less likely to label that act as physical abuse, unless they incurred an injury from that form of discipline (in which case they were more likely to rate it as abusive).

Occasionally, researchers are confronted with behaviors that are outside their experiences and outside the domain of their catalogs of disciplinary acts. As reflected in inquiries from researchers on various abuse-related listservs (e.g., the ISPCAN list and the CHILD-MALTREATMENT-RESEARCH-L Listserv), when those atypical behaviors are displayed by a member of an ethnic minority group, questions are raised as to whether some specific responses (e.g., striking children on their teeth with a knife handle or spanking on the soles of the feet) might be uniquely common and even acceptable in some subcultures. Such questions intimate that there could be acts that would be abusive in some subcultures and not in others. Responses from others on the Listservs typically provide evidence or opinion that the idiosyncratic responses are either not typical or not acceptable in the identified subcultures. Such circumstances underscore the problems with developing catalogs of acceptable and unacceptable disciplinary acts in the absence of some evidence of harm or endangerment. The essential point here is that researchers who attempt to operationally define physical abuse in terms of specific parental acts, or attempt to anchor their work to the opinion of the general public do not necessarily enhance the clarity of their definitions. Such attempts can, however, increase the apparent relevance of the work in public policy or popular media contexts.

One of the problems with defining child physical abuse as a set of specific parental acts is that it becomes virtually impossible to catalog all of the acts that parents might use in the context of discipline. Even if a researcher were to develop a listing of specific parental acts that are abusive by some explicit criteria, it is a virtual certainty that some acts will be omitted from the list. In addition, without a theoretical or empirical framework to classify the acts, defining physical abuse as specific acts runs the risk of being an excessively arbitrary approach.

Abuse as the Consequences of Parenting

An alternative to defining physical abuse in terms of parental acts is to define abuse in terms of the consequences of parental behavior, without any specification of the act or acts that occasioned the consequences. When the definition of abuse is based on consequences of parental behavior, as noted in the literature previously reviewed, some tissue damage is the prototypical defining characteristic. The injurious consequences of an act or acts can range from red marks that persist for a matter of hours to bruises, other soft tissue injuries, or fractures. The locus of a particular injury can also be a qualifying consideration; for example, red marks on the face might be considered to be abuse, but red marks on the buttocks or legs might not. A related criterion could be the need for medical services or even that a life-threatening injury has been experienced by the child. Examples of the injurious consequences approach are included in parts of the Barnett et al. (1993) MCS method of classifying CPS records and in other studies that have used that approach to establish the prevalence of physical abuse in their samples (e.g., Sullivan & Knutson, 1998, 2000). Although the consequences approach to defining abuse seems straightforward, setting defining criteria for abuse in terms of degree of tissue damage is only superficially simple (see Wald, 1982). Moreover, sometimes the source of an injury is not so clear as to permit an unequivocal determination as to whether the injury can be attributed to parental behavior. Thus, merely defining child physical abuse as injurious acts by parents can also be associated with ambiguity and a lack of specificity that is undesirable in most research contexts.

The developmental status of the recipient is also a qualification that can be applied to an injury criterion for operationally defining physical abuse. Such an approach has rarely been specified in the research literature reviewed, but it almost certainly plays a role in the decision process when parenting consequences are used to determine reporting under mandatory reporting statutes. That is, a particular level of tissue damage incurred by an infant that results in reporting might be ignored in an older child. Researchers who attempt to operationally define physical abuse in terms of consequences must also link those consequences to the developmental status of the recipient.

Another approach to operationally defining abuse in terms of consequences is to incorporate the emotional or psychological sequelae of acts that have not resulted in significant tissue damage or that might not meet a physical endangerment standard. Although this approach has been criticized for its vagueness (e.g., Browne & Penny, 1974; Nelson, 1984; Wald, 1982), some investigators (e.g., Garbarino & Stocking, 1980; Hart & Brassard, 1987; Rohner & Rohner, 1980) have argued that psychological consequences are at the heart of all maltreatment and could serve as the defining characteristics of physical abuse as well (e.g., Garbarino & Gillian, 1980). Some authors even have argued that the presence of some psychiatric symptoms, such as multiple personality disorder in children, are prima facie evidence of abuse (e.g., Elliott, 1982). Unfortunately, in the context of determining the consequences of maltreatment, or in studies of the comorbidity of behavior problems with maltreatment, defining abuse in terms of psychological consequences will confound outcomes, presenting problems, and the operational definitions of abuse. Moreover, research has yet to establish any behavioral or psychiatric markers of physical abuse with acceptable specificity and reliability. Thus, the authors of this chapter believe that physical abuse should not be operationalized in terms of putative psychological sequelae. Understanding the psychological consequences of parental acts might be a suitable goal for research and is clearly germane to treatment planning, but operational research definitions should not be tied to global psychological sequelae.

Abuse as Acts Plus Consequences

As an alternative to the consequences approach to operationally defining physical abuse, researchers can adopt operational definitions that reflect a combination of parental acts and the injurious consequences of those acts. That is, for an act to be abusive, it must result in an injurious consequence; and for an injurious event to be classified as abuse, there must be some behavioral antecedent. There are at least two advantages to this approach. First, it provides a somewhat objective indication as to whether the parental act was actually a high-amplitude act. That is, a blow struck with a wooden spoon or spatula would be classified as an abusive act if it resulted in some injurious consequence. If the blow did not result in an identifiable injury, it would not constitute an abusive act. Second, this approach makes it possible for researchers to separate injurious childhood experiences that are not attributable to parental acts of commission from those that are. For example, rough and tumble play or playing catch could result in injurious consequences to a child that do not necessarily reflect a purposive child-directed act. However, injuring a child with a thrown ball could be a parental act of commission when the act is one of discipline or punishment rather than play.

Another example of how a combination of behavioral events or setting contexts can be used to operationally define physical abuse is the strategy adopted by Duhaime et al. (1992) for distinguishing abusive head trauma from accidental head trauma in young pediatric patients. In this approach, the associated medical evidence (e.g., radiologic evidence) is used in conjunction with information from caregivers and historical information about the event to distinguish between abuse-induced head trauma and head trauma that is presumed abuse or suspicious of abuse. The approach has been used in recent research to assess outcomes and medical costs of abusive head trauma in comparison to head trauma from other causes (e.g., Ettaro, Berger, & Songer, 2004).

Efforts to operationalize physical abuse as a set of specific acts combined with a set of specified outcomes does not eliminate the need to develop catalogs of the specific acts and specific injuries that are associated with defining abuse as an act or an injury alone. However, in the absence of a strong developmental theory or solid empirical referents, a researcher's catalog based on acts and consequences is as likely to be arbitrary as a catalog based on acts alone.

Because of difficulty in setting a tissue damage standard coupled with a catalog of behavioral acts considered to be abusive and because of difficulties in documenting some injurious consequences when time has elapsed between an act and an investigator's contact with a research participant, some research has based a definition of physical abuse on the degree to which an act by a caregiver could occasion risk to the child. Such an approach was consistent with the Straus et al. (1980) criterion for abuse. This "endangerment" standard was incorporated in the NIS-2 (DHHS, 1988) and NIS-3 (Sedlak & Broadhurst, 1996) and provides a framework for operationally defining physical abuse. Such an approach is based on the notion that some acts pose a clear and present danger to the child, even if those acts might not have actually resulted in injury, whereas other acts might only meet the criterion for physical abuse if actual injury is incurred by the child. The endangerment criterion would presumably be based on some normative data as to the likelihood that certain acts would be associated with injuries, thus a probabilistic model is implied. In addition, acts that are not necessarily injurious but exceedingly painful (e.g., electric shock from stock prods) might be included. The authors of this chapter believe that an act-plus-consequences approach that includes an endangerment standard has distinct advantages over operational definitions based only on acts or operational definitions based only on harmful consequences.

Intentionality of Acts and Consequences

One of the major issues in defining physical abuse for research, practice, and legal proceedings has been the importance of the intentionality of the acts. In a study of hospital personnel and their ratings of events as abusive, Snyder and Newberger (1986) demonstrated that the intentionality of the alleged perpetrator was important in determining whether physicians, social workers, psychologists, and nurses classified events as abuse. Intention is typically considered as a goal to harm the victim. Because perpetrators often attempt to convince others that their intentions were socially acceptable or provide an explanation of unknown veracity for a child's injury, determining that an injury was purposive is a challenging enterprise (e.g., Johnson, 1990).

In court proceedings, the presumed intention of an abuse perpetrator is crucial. For example, youngsters could be brought to medical attention because of a subdural hemotoma or retinal hemorrhages that are the direct result of shaking (e.g., Alexander, Crabbe, Sato, Smith, & Bennett, 1990; Alexander, Sato, Smith, & Bennett, 1990; Caffey, 1972; Levin, Magnusson, Rafto, & Zimmerman, 1989). If the act were determined to have been perpetrated in a disciplinary context, it would be viewed as physical abuse; however, if the act were determined to have occurred during a playful interaction, it is unlikely to be labeled physical abuse. The health consequences to the child would be indistinguishable, but whether CPS agencies would intervene might well be a function of a determination of the intention of the perpetrating parents. In such a circumstance, whether the family would be identified as a potential physical abuse research participant could also be conditional on making a determination of the intentions of the parents. Finkelhor and Korbin (1988) argued that abuse should be defined as injurious acts that are proximal, proscribed, and preventable. Moreover, according to Finkelhor and Korbin, the intentionality of the acts is critical for them to be termed abuse. It is of interest to note that in *Estelle v. McGuire* (1991), the Supreme Court ruled that prior injuries are considered to be probative in determining the intention of parents. Such an approach has not been explicitly operationalized in research contexts, although it could be incorporated in the case conference methodology adopted in some laboratories (e.g., Yates et al., 2003).

This core question regarding parental intentionality is a central component of some operational definitions of physical abuse. Intentionality is different than asking whether an adult intended to strike a child; instead, intentionality pertains to whether the blows being struck were to inflict pain and injury or to affect some desired change in the child's behavior. However, the authors of this chapter still believe that adding harmful intent does not improve operational definitions of physical abuse. Whether the purported goal of striking a child in a disciplinary context is to alter the child's behavior in a prosocial fashion or to inflict pain or harm the child does not materially affect an operational definition of physical abuse. Specifying an act and the consequence of that act would be sufficient. Arguing that intentionality is central to defining physical abuse ignores the critical question as to how a researcher establishes unequivocally that a parent's intention can be reliably assessed. In the context of clinical work, forensic evaluations, and research, one of the authors of this chapter has conducted interviews with a large number of parents who have injured their children; during these interviews, not a single parent ever indicated that they had intended to harm or injure the child. Thus, the intention of the parent must be inferred by the researcher rather than assessed directly, and such inferences introduce additional noise, variation, or even potential bias in an operational definition.

That is not to say that parents never engage in acts designed to harm or even kill their children. Frankly homicidal acts directed at children and stepchildren are represented in both the research literature (e.g., Daly & Wilson, 1994; Gauthier, Chaudoir, & Forsyth, 2003; Haapasalo & Petaejae,1999; Kunz, & Bahr, 1996; Wissow, 1998) and popular media. It is important to note, however, that under circumstances of nonaccidental death, the context, the psychological state of the parent, and other factors often suggest that intentionality to harm may not be present. It is the distinction between nonaccidental injurious death and frankly homicidal death that has been considered important in understanding the contribution of socio-economic factors in serious child maltreatment (e.g, Nixon, Pearn, Wilkey, & Petrie, 1981). The main point here is not that intentionally harmful acts do not occur; it is that researchers cannot unequivocally assess them, and the base rate appears to be so low as to not be critical in developing operational definitions of physical abuse.

It should be noted that this concern for assessing the intention of a participant in operational definitions has a long history in aggression research (see Buss, 1961; Dollard, Doob, Miller, Mowrer, & Sears, 1939; Feshback, 1971; Knutson, 1973). There are those who have argued that aggression must be defined in terms of the intentionality of the actor (e.g., Berkowitz, 1983; Kaufman, 1970) and those who have argued that intentions cannot be assessed unequivocally and, therefore, should not be the determining factor in whether an act is considered aggressive (Buss, 1961; Knutson, 1973). By the latter approach, whether an act is defined as aggressive would not be a function of caveats based on expressions of social desirability or subjective ratings of inadvertence. Knutson (1978, 1988) advanced the same argument in a consideration of defining physical abuse. Following the precedent of a parallel approach in aggression research, according to Knutson, the expressed social desirability of a perpetrator (i.e., the goal of improved behavior of the child) would be ignored in defining physical abuse. Similarly, the possible accidental nature of an injurious event would be determined probabilistically through an assessment of the setting context in which the event occurred rather than through the assertions of the actors. Thus, if an injury were to occur when rule-consistent activity was being followed (e.g., struck by a pitched ball during a game of softball), the probability of the injury being an accident would be enhanced. It also has been suggested that base rate information regarding accidents could be derived from consumer product safety data to distinguish between the probability of a particular injury occurring as an accident and the probability that it could have occurred in an episode of discipline and coercion (see, e.g., Wissow & Wilson, 1988). In this case, injuries that are judged to be improbable based on the correspondence between the locus and severity of the injuries and the product safety information would be judged probabilistically to be abusive rather than accidents.

Continuous versus Categorical Approaches

One assumption underlying the very notion of doing research related to the physical abuse of children is that an act can be categorized and that categories are useful in describing and delineating mutually exclusive sets for research purposes. Some acts by child caregivers are harmful and, by definition, deviant. Thus, there is also the assumption that researchers can establish a criterion that separates deviant parenting from nondeviant parenting, with deviant being abusive and nondeviant being nonabusive. Although such an assumption typically is made to develop categorical operational definitions of abuse, it is not necessarily the case that continuous models are not possible. That is, some researchers (e.g., Greenwald, Bank, Reid, & Knutson, 1997; Knutson & Bower, 1994) have advocated placing physical abuse at the extreme end of a continuum of physical discipline. It should be noted that spirited arguments regarding continuous versus categorical models have been long-standing in domains of psychopathology, and many of the same positions can be advanced in the context of physical abuse. At the present time, most of the research on physical abuse explicitly adopts a categorical model. That is, even when an approximation of a continuous model could be developed using various ordinal measures (e.g., Barnett et al., 1993), researchers often treat physical abuse as an all-or-nothing phenomenon.

When physical abuse is defined as the distributional extreme on a continuum of physical discipline, it places the definition in a probabilistic model that is conditional on the sample that is recruited. That is, the definition of physical abuse becomes a function of the list of acts and consequences that are included as indicators of harsh discipline and the distribution of scores that are present in the sample studied. When the samples represent an adequate range of scores, this approach can yield theoretically meaningful approaches for an operational definition of physical abuse as "harsh discipline" (e.g., Knutson et al., 2005). In the modern era, in which multivariate statistical strategies are available and structural modeling can be accomplished, there is considerable apparent utility in developing continuous measures of discipline, with extreme scores considered to be physically abusive. Again, the utility of this approach will depend on the indicators selected and the distribution of scores in the sample, but the approach combines key aspects of other strategies in a particularly value-added way. It offers an alternative, and usefully coherent organizing principle, and it may be more representative of how people seem to actually sort and sift evidence.

Referral Source Limitations

In much of the physical abuse literature, investigators have left operational definitions of abuse or neglect to a referral source or the source of administrative data rather than making independent assessments. Although the use of direct assessments of case-level information has improved in the last decade, the ease of access and the frequency of use means that operational definitions of physical abuse based on administrative data persist despite the relatively large body of research that suggests standards for reporting suspicions of physical abuse and neglect differ between professionals and nonprofessionals and among geographical locations (e.g., Alter, 1985; Deitrich-MacLean & Walden, 1988; Dukes & Kean, 1989; Giovannoni & Becerra, 1979; Misener, 1986; O'Toole et al., 1983; Snyder & Newberger, 1986; Wolock, 1982). Thus, the referral source approach may not be reliable when operationally defining abuse. Similarly, differences between suspicions of abuse and substantiation of abuse can be considerable, and that distinction is not always made by researchers when referral sources determine the abuse or neglect status of participants with, as previously described, important differences among jurisdictions in setting criteria for abuse. Just as aggregating types of maltreatment may limit the utility of research, aggregating referral sources (e.g., courts, CPS agencies, and Parents Anonymous) can yield samples that combine unlike realities and obscure the influence of important variables.

Dependency on a referral source to define a sample also can result in sampling bias. This is one of many causes of sampling bias discussed by Widom (1988) in a review paper focusing on the implications of sampling biases and the resulting limitations of the knowledge base in the area of child abuse. According to Widom, there are two basic biasing influences: method selection and criterion selection. In the former, the common methodologies adopted by abuse investigators (e.g., using agency records, emergency rooms, families in treatment, self-report measures) yield data of unknown generality. When samples are selected on the basis of some criterion-related events (e.g., neurological impairment, biological family members), biased data on abuse-related events may result. Because of such problems in sampling bias, Browne and Finklehor (1986) have argued for using "natural collectivities." Such an approach has been used in some laboratories (e.g., Berger et al., 1988; Goldston, Turnquist, & Knutson, 1989) but is not widely implemented.

One of the fundamental principles in experimental design is that a control group has none of the independent variable—in this case, that the members of the control group have not been physically abused. To unequivocally make that determination, it is important that the sample has an equal opportunity to display the requisite behavior and be detected. Too often, the level of scrutiny applied to the comparison or control group in child maltreatment research might not match the level applied to those who have been "detected" as having been maltreated. Too often, researchers continue to use the absence of a child or a family in a central registry, a CPS record, or a self-defined abuse group (e.g., Parents Anonymous) as a suitable index of the absence of abuse. The referral source can be used to define the absence of abuse as well as its presence. Unfortunately, as noted by several surveys reported over the decades (e.g., American Humane Association, 1979, 1983, 1988; Flango et al., 1988; National Center on Child Abuse and Neglect, 1980), remarkable variability exists among state registries, and the utility of those registries for detecting nonabused samples is quite limited. For example, in most states, central registries are not likely to include events involving extrafamilial maltreatment because such events typically proceed through law enforcement agencies. Law enforcement agencies do not routinely submit reports to central registries in most states (Flango et al., 1988). When law enforcement records are included in studies, based on administrative data (e.g., Ricci, Giantris, Merriam, Hodge, & Doyle, 2003; Sullivan & Knutson, 1998, 2000), the nonoverlap in information and the presence of different types of information is apparent. This is another example of a weakness in single-method, referral-source definitional approaches and another argument for the multimethod/multisource strategies for operationalizing physical abuse.

Absence of Fathers

Although CPS data indicate that fathers, or other males in the household, are well represented as perpetrators of physical abuse, as Martin (1984) and Bradley and Lindsay (1987) noted some time ago, males are poorly represented in the research literature. Indeed, Knutson and Schartz (1997) noted that mothers even have participated as participants in studies of maltreating parents when the perpetrator was the father or a domestic partner. Haskett, Marziano, and Dover (1996) also noted the paucity of data regarding male perpetrators of physical abuse. It is unlikely that the operational definitions utilized by researchers necessarily cause an underrepresentation of males in studies; however, by relying on CPS records, in which the focus more often is on the person responsible for the care of the child, that person most often being the mother, the method or source factor in the operational definition could result in samples that essentially exclude access to male perpetrators. This is another basis for arguing for multimethod/multisource operational definitions and investigator-established methods rather than referral source operational definitions.

Comorbidity

Researchers engaged in research on physical abuse cannot ignore the high rate of comorbidity among various forms of maltreatment (Barnett et al., 1993; Dong et al., 2004; Knutson et al., 2005; Sullivan & Knutson, 2000). Indeed, establishing clear operational definitions of physical abuse requires concomitant operational definitions of other forms of maltreatment. An alternative strategy has been to use a hierarchical priority system for establishing operational definitions. For example, using administrative CPS data, Drake and Pandey (1996) used a priority system to place children into maltreatment-type classes. Though interesting, such an approach also obscures information that could be important in understanding outcomes or circumstances of covariation among forms of maltreatment and disadvantage.

CONCLUSIONS AND RECOMMENDATIONS

It is clear from reviewing more than 4 decades of research on the physical abuse of children that the existent empirical and theoretical work does not lead to satisfaction with the utility of any single approach to operationally defining physical abuse. It is clear that no single methodology to secure the critical information has been satisfactory. Problems in the use of administrative data persist, but limitations in self-report data are no less thorny. Direct assessments and analog measures (see Chapter 11) hold promise, but they too are not without limitations. In short, the authors of this chapter believe that the field will advance most effectively if investigators adopt a multimethod/multisource approach. In addition, it is their belief that an act plus consequence approach is superior to either a consequence-only or act-only criterion.

If operational definitions of abuse are based solely on acts, there is a potential problem in selecting the range of acts that constitute abuse. That is, investigators are confronted with either limiting the domain on the basis of prior empirical work, making a priori decisions about what constitutes abuse, or adopting theory-based classifications. With limitations in the existing body of knowledge, an alternative is to attempt to catalog more fully the parental acts that participants in research studies experience, using a structure such as that in the Child Maltreatment Log (Sternberg et al., 2004). By fully detailing the experiences of the participants, hypothesized links between specific acts and outcomes can be tested. Thus, parenting acts in the context of discipline are detailed and the putative consequences assessed empirically.

To develop a useful corpus of knowledge, a science of behavior requires replicability of findings. Sadly, even in contemporary archival journals, operational definitions of physical abuse often are described so vaguely or are so dependent on the unique circumstances of the jurisdictions in which the work was conducted that other researchers could not possibly reproduce the findings. Editors need to become more demanding of investigators and not permit "off-label" use of instruments without empirical justification, and they need to insist that operational definitions of physical abuse are presented in sufficient detail that other scholars can reproduce them. This is particularly important when the possibility of secondary analyses is considered. With federally funded research being archived (e.g., National Data Archive on Child Abuse and Neglect, Cornell University, Ithaca, New York), creative new strategies of analysis might be permitted and data sets aggregated. If operational definitions of physical abuse are not developed with an eye toward replication, the data will not be useful for aggregated secondary analyses and good science will not be served.

REFERENCES

Ackerman, P.T., Newton, J.E., McPherson, W.B., Jones, J.G., & Dykman, R.A. (1998). Prevalence of posttraumatic stress disorder and other psychiatric diagnoses in three groups of abused children (sexual, physical, and both). *Child Abuse & Neglect, 22,* 759–774.

Alexander, R., Crabbe, L., Sato, Y., Smith, W., & Bennett, T. (1990). Serial abuse in children who are shaken. *American Journal of Diseases of Children, 144,* 58–60.

Alexander, R., Sato, Y., Smith, W., & Bennett, R. (1990). Incidence of impact trauma with cranial injuries ascribed to shaking. *American Journal of Diseases of Children, 144,* 724–726.

Alter, C.F. (1985). Decision making factors in cases of child neglect. *Child Welfare, 64,* 99–111.

American Humane Association. (1979). *Child protective services entering the 1980s: A nationwide survey.* Englewood, CO: Author.

American Humane Association. (1983). *Annual report, 1981: Highlights of official child neglect and abuse reporting.* Denver, CO: Author.

American Humane Association. (1988). *Highlights of official child neglect and abuse reporting, 1986.* Denver, CO: Author.

American Psychiatric Association. (1994). *Diagnostic and statistical manual of mental disorders* (4th ed.). Washington, DC: Author.

Baker v. Owen, 395 F. Supp. 294 (M.D.N.C), aff'd, 423 U.S. 907 (1976) (mem.).

Barnett, D., Manly, J., & Cicchetti, D. (1993). Defining child maltreatment: The interface between policy and research. In D. Cicchetti & S.L. Toth (Eds.), *Advances in applied developmental psychology: Child abuse, child development and social policy* (pp. 7–73). Norwood, NJ: Ablex Publishing Co.

Bauman, B.L., & Kolko, D.J. (2002). A comparison of abusive and nonabusive mothers of abused children. *Child Maltreatment, 7,* 369–376.

Baumrind, D. (1996). A blanket injunction against disciplinary use of spanking is not warranted by the data. *Pediatrics, 98,* 828–831.

Baumrind, D., Larzelere, R.E., & Cowan, P.A. (2002). Ordinary physical punishment: Is it harmful? Comment on Gershoff (2002). *Psychological Bulletin, 128,* 580–589.

Benbenishty, R., Zeira, A., & Astor, R.A. (2002). Children's reports of emotional, physical and sexual maltreatment by educational staff in Israel. *Child Abuse & Neglect, 26,* 763–782.

Benedict, M.I., Zuravin, S., Sumerfield, M., & Brandt, D. (1996). The reported health and functioning of children maltreated while in family foster care. *Child Abuse & Neglect, 20,* 561–571.

Bensley, L., Ruggles, D., Wynkoop Simmons, K., Harris, C., Williams, K., Putvin, T., et al. (2004). General population norms about child abuse and neglect and associations with childhood experiences. *Child Abuse & Neglect, 28,* 1321–1337.

Berger, A.M., Knutson, J.F., Mehm, J.G., & Perkins, K.A. (1988). The self-report of punitive childhood experiences of young adults and adolescents. *Child Abuse & Neglect, 12,* 251–262.

Berkowitz, L. (1983). Aversively stimulated aggression: Some parallels and differences in research with animals and humans. *American Psychologist, 38,* 1135–1144.

Bernstein, D.P., Fink, L., Handelsman, L., Foote, J., Lovejoy, M., Wenzel, K., et al. (1994). Initial reliability and validity of a new retrospective measure of child abuse and neglect. *American Journal of Psychiatry, 151,* 1132–1136.

Besharov, D.J. (1981). Toward better research on child abuse and neglect: Making definitional issues an explicit methodological concern. *Child Abuse & Neglect, 5,* 383–390.

Bower, M.E., & Knutson, J.F. (1996). Attitudes toward physical discipline as a function of disciplinary history and self-labeling as physically abused. *Child Abuse & Neglect, 20,* 689–699.

Bower-Russa, M.E., Knutson, J.F., & Winebarger, A. (2001). Disciplinary history, adult disciplinary attitudes, and risk for abusive parenting. *Journal of Community Psychology, 29*(3) 219–240.

Bradley, E.J., & Lindsay, R.C. (1987). Methodological and ethical issues in child abuse research. *Journal of Family Violence, 2,* 239–255.

Briere, J., & Runtz, M. (1990). Differential adult symptomatology associated with three types of child abuse histories. *Child Abuse & Neglect, 14,* 357–364.

Brosig, C.L., & Kalichman, S.C. (1992). Child abuse reporting decisions: Effects of statutory wording of reporting requirements. *Professional Psychology: Research & Practice, 23*(6), 486–492.

Brown, E.J., & Kolko, D.J. (1999). Child victims' attributions about being physically abused: An examination of factors associated with symptom severity. *Journal of Abnormal Child Psychology, 27,* 311–322.

Browne, A., & Finkelhor, D. (1986). Impact of child sexual abuse: A review of the research. *Psychological Bulletin, 99,* 66–77.

Browne, E.W., & Penny, L. (1974). *The non-delinquent child in juvenile court: A digest of case law.* Reno, NV: National Council of Juvenile and Family Court Judges.

Bugental, D.B., & Happaney, K. (2004). Predicting infant maltreatment in low-income families: The interactive effects of maternal attributions and child status at birth. *Developmental Psychology, 40,* 234–243.

Buss, A.H. (1961). *The psychology of aggression.* New York: Wiley.

Caffey, J. (1972). On the theory and practice of shaking infants. *American Journal of Diseases of Children, 124,* 161–169.

Cantos, A.L., Neale, J.M., O'Leary, K.D., & Gaines, R.W. (1997). Assessment of coping strategies of child abusing mothers. *Child Abuse & Neglect, 21,* 631–636.

Caselles, C.E., & Milner, J.S. (2000). Evaluations of child transgressions, disciplinary choices, and expected child compliance in a no-cry and a crying infant condition in physically abusive and comparison mothers. *Child Abuse & Neglect, 24,* 477–491.

Cerezo, M.A., D'Ocon, A., & Dolz, L. (1996). Mother–child interactive patterns in abusive families versus nonabusive families: An observational study. *Child Abuse & Neglect, 20,* 573–587.

Chaffin, M., Kelleher, K., & Hollenberg, J. (1996). Onset of physical abuse and neglect: Psychiatric, substance abuse, and social risk factors from prospective community data. *Child Abuse & Neglect, 20,* 191–203.

Child Abuse Amendments of 1984, PL 98-457, 42 U.S.C. §§ 5101 *et seq.*

Child Abuse Prevention, Adoption and Family Services Act of 1988, PL 100-294, 42 U.S.C. § 5101 *et seq.*

Child Abuse Prevention and Treatment Act of 1974, PL 93-247, 42 U.S.C. § 5101 *et seq.*

Child Abuse Prevention and Treatment and Adoption Reform Act of 1978, PL 95-266, 42 U.S.C. § 5101 *et seq.*

Christophersen, R.J. (1983). Public perception of child abuse and the need for intervention: Are professionals seen as abusers? *Child Abuse & Neglect, 7,* 435–442.

Colman, R.A., & Widom, C.S. (2004). Childhood abuse and neglect and adult intimate relationships: A prospective study. *Child Abuse & Neglect, 28,* 1133–1151.

Connelly, C.D., & Straus, M.A. (1993). Mother's age and risk for physical abuse. *Child Abuse & Neglect, 16,* 709–718.

Connors, E.T. (1979). *Student discipline and the law.* Bloomington, IN: Phi Delta Kappa Educational Foundation.

Daly, M., & Wilson, M.I. (1994). Some differential attributes of lethal assaults on small children by stepfathers versus genetic fathers. *Ethology & Sociobiology, 15,* 207–217.

Deitrich-MacLean, G., & Walden, T. (1988). Distinguishing teaching interactions of physically abusive from nonabusive parent–child dyads. *Child Abuse & Neglect, 12,* 469–479.

Dodge, K.A., Pettit, G.S., Bates, J.E., & Valente, E. (1996). Social information-processing patterns partially mediate the effect of early physical abuse on later conduct problems. *Journal of Abnormal Psychology, 104,* 632–643.

Dollard, J., Doob, L.W., Miller, N.E., Mowrer, O.H., & Sears, R.R. (1939). *Frustration and aggression.* New Haven: Yale University Press.

Dong, M., Anda, R.F., Felitti, V.J., Dube, S.R., Williamson, D.F., Thompson, T.J., et al. (2004). The interrelatedness of multiple forms of childhood abuse, neglect, and household dysfunction. *Child Abuse & Neglect, 28,* 771–784.

Drake, B., & Pandey, S. (1996). Understanding the relationship between neighborhood poverty and specific types of child maltreatment. *Child Abuse & Neglect, 20,* 1003–1018.

Dube, S.R., Williamson, D.F., Thompson, T., Felitti, V.J., & Anda, R.F. (2004). Assessing the reliability of retrospective reports of adverse childhood experiences among adult HMO members attending a primary care clinic. *Child Abuse & Neglect, 28,* 729–737.

Dubowitz, H., Klockner, A., Starr, R.H., & Black, M.M. (1998). Community and professional definitions of child neglect. *Child Maltreatment, 3,* 235–243.

Duhaime, A.C., Alario, A.J., Lewander, W.J., Schut, L., Sutton, L.N., Seidl, T.S., et al. (1992). Head injury in very young children: Mechanisms, injury types, and ophthalmologic findings in 100 hospitalized patients younger than 2 years of age. *Pediatrics, 90,* 179–185.

Dukes, R.L., & Kean, R.B. (1989). An experimental study of gender and situation in the perception and reportage of child abuse. *Child Abuse & Neglect, 13,* 351–360.

Durrant, J.E. (1999). Evaluating the success of Sweden's corporal punishment ban. *Child Abuse & Neglect, 23,* 435–448.

Eckenrode, J., Powers, J., Doris, J., Munsch, J., & Bolger, N. (1988). Substantiation of child abuse and neglect reports. *Journal of Consulting and Clinical Psychology, 56,* 9–16.

Elliott, D. (1982). State intervention and childhood multiple personality disorder. *Journal of Psychiatry and Law, 10,* 441–456.

Epstein, M.A., & Bottoms, B.L. (2002). Explaining the forgetting and recovery of abuse and trauma memories: Possible mechanisms. *Child Maltreatment, 7,* 210–225.

Erich, S., & Leung, P. (2002). The impact of previous type of abuse and sibling adoption upon adoptive families. *Child Abuse & Neglect, 26,* 1045–1058.

Erlanger, H.S. (1974). Social class differences in parents' use of physical punishment. In S.K. Steinmetz & M.A. Straus (Eds.), *Violence in the family* (pp. 150–158). New York: Harper & Row.

Estelle v. McGuire, 502 U.S. 62 (1991).

Ettaro, L., Berger, R.P., & Songer, T. (2004). Abusive head trauma in young children: Characteristics and medical charges in a hospitalized population. *Child Abuse & Neglect, 28,* 1099–1111.

Ezzell, C.E., Swenson, C.C., & Brondino, M.J. (2000). The relationship of social support to physically abused children's adjustment. *Child Abuse & Neglect, 24,* 641–651.

Fantuzzo, J.W, McDermott, P.A, Manz, P.H., Hampton, V.R., & Burdick, N.A. (1996). The Pictorial Scale of Perceived Competence and Social Acceptance: Does it work with low-income urban children? *Child Development, 67,* 1071–1084.

Fantuzzo, J., Sutton-Smith, B., Atkins, M., Meyers, R., Stevenson, H., Coolahan, A.W., et al. (1996). Community-based resilient peer treatment of withdrawn maltreated preschool children. *Journal of Consulting & Clinical Psychology, 64,* 1377–1386.

Feerick, M.M., & Haugaard, J.J. (1999). Long-term effects of witnessing marital violence for women: The contribution of childhood physical and sexual abuse. *Journal of Family Violence, 14,* 377–398.

Feerick, M.M., Haugaard J.J., & Hien D.A. (2002). Child maltreatment and adulthood violence: The contribution of attachment and drug abuse. *Child Maltreatment, 7,* 226–240.

Feldman, R.S., Salzinger, S., Rosario, M., & Alvarado, L. (1995). Parent, teacher, and peer ratings of physically abused and nonmaltreated children's behavior. *Journal of Abnormal Child Psychology, 23,* 317–334.

Feshbach, S. (1971). Dynamics and morality of violence and aggression: Some psychological considerations. *American Psychologist, 26,* 281–292.

Finkelhor, D., & Korbin, J. (1988). Child abuse as an international issue. *Child Abuse & Neglect, 12,* 3–23.

Flango, V.E., Casey, P., Dibble, T., Flango, C.R., Rubin, H.T., & Bross, D. (1988). *Central registries for child abuse and neglect: A national review of records management, due process safeguards, and data utilization.* Williamsburg, VA: National Center for State Courts.

Francis, C.R., Hughes H.M., & Hitz, L. (1993). Physically abusive parents and the 16-PF: A preliminary psychological typology. *Child Abuse & Neglect, 16,* 673–691.

Friedrich, W.N., Talley, N.J., Panser, L., Fett, S., & Zinsmeister, A.R. (1997). Concordance of reports of childhood abuse by adults. *Child Maltreatment, 2,* 164–171.

Garbarino, J., & Gillian, G. (1980). *Understanding abusive families.* Lexington, MA: Lexington Books.

Garbarino, J., & Stocking, S.H. (1980). *Protecting children from abuse and neglect: Developing and maintaining effective support systems for families.* San Francisco: Jossey-Bass.

Garland, A.F., Landsverk, J.L., Hough, R.L., & Ellis-MacLeod, E. (1996). Type of maltreatment as a predictor of mental health service use for children in foster care. *Child Abuse & Neglect, 20,* 675–688.

Gauthier, D.K., Chaudoir, N.K., & Forsyth, J. (2003). A sociological analysis of maternal infanticide in the United States, 1984–1996. *Deviant Behavior, 24,* 393–404.

Gauthier, L., Stollak, G., Messe, L., & Aronoff, J. (1996). Recall of childhood neglect and physical abuse as differential predictors of current psychological functioning. *Child Abuse & Neglect, 20,* 549–559.

Gelles, R.J. (1982). Toward better research on child abuse and neglect: A response to Besharov. *Child Abuse & Neglect, 6,* 487–496.

Gershoff, E.T. (2002). Corporal punishment, physical abuse, and the burden of proof: Reply to Baumrind, Larzelere, and Cowan (2002), Holden (2002), and Parke (2002). *Psychological Bulletin, 128,* 602–611.

Gillham, B., Tanner, G., Cheyne, B., Freeman, I., Rooney, M., & Lambie, A. (1998). Unemployment rates, single parent density, and indices of child poverty: Their relationship to different categories of child abuse and neglect. *Child Abuse & Neglect, 22,* 79–90.

Giovannoni, J.M., & Becerra, R.M. (1979). *Defining child abuse.* New York: Free Press.

Goldston, D.B., Turnquist, D.C., & Knutson, J.F. (1989). Presenting problems of sexually abused girls receiving psychiatric services. *Journal of Abnormal Psychology, 98,* 314–317.

Greenwald, R.L., Bank, L., Reid, J.B., & Knutson, J.F. (1997). A discipline-mediated model of excessively punitive parenting. *Aggressive Behavior, 23,* 259–280.

Haapasalo, J., & Petaejae, S. (1999). Mothers who killed or attempted to kill their child: Life circumstances, childhood abuse, and types of killing. *Violence & Victims, 1,* 219–239.

Hart, S.N., & Brassard, M.R. (1987). A major threat to children's mental health: Psychological maltreatment. *American Psychologist, 42,* 160–165.

Hartley, C.C. (2002). The co-occurrence of child maltreatment and domestic violence: Examining both neglect and child physical abuse. *Child Maltreatment, 7,* 349–358.

Hartley, E.K. (1981). American state intervention in the parent–child legal relationship. *Child Abuse & Neglect, 5,* 141–145.

Haskett, M.E., Marziano, B., & Dover, E.R. (1996). Absence of males in maltreatment research: A survey of recent literature. *Child Abuse & Neglect, 20,* 1175–1182.

Haskett, M.E, Scott, S.S., Grant, R., Ward, C.S., & Robinson, C. (2003). Child-related cognitions and affective functioning of physically abusive and comparison parents. *Child Abuse & Neglect, 27,* 663–686.

Holden, G.W. (2002). Perspectives on the effects of corporal punishment: Comment on Gershoff (2002). *Psychological Bulletin, 128,* 590–595.

Horwitz, A.V., Widom, C.S., McLaughlin, J., & White, H.R. (2001). The impact of childhood abuse and neglect on adult mental health: A prospective study. *Journal of Health & Social Behavior, 42*(2), 184–201.

Hudgins, H.C., Jr., & Vacca, R.S. (1985). *Law and education: Contemporary issues and court decisions,* (2nd ed.). Charlottesville, VA: The Mitchie Company.

Indian Child Welfare Act of 1978, PL 95–608, 92 Stat. 3069 (1978).

Ingraham v. Wright, 430 U.S. 651 (1977).

Iowa Code Ann. § 232.68 (West 2000).

Jasinski, J.L., Williams, L.M., & Siegel, J. (2001). Childhood physical and sexual abuse as risk factors for heavy drinking among African-American women: A prospective study. *Child Abuse & Neglect, 24,* 1061–1071.

Johnson, C.F. (1990). Inflicted injury versus accidental injury. *Pediatric Clinics of North America, 37*(4), 791–814.

Johnson, R.M., Kotch, J.B., Catellier, D.J., Winsor, J.R., Dufort, V., Hunter, W., et al. (2002). Adverse behavioral and emotional outcomes from child abuse and witnessed violence. *Child Maltreatment, 7,* 179–86.

Kaufman, H. (1970). *Aggression and altruism.* New York: Holt, Rinehart, & Winston.

Kazdin, A.E., Moser, J., Colbus, D., & Bell, R. (1985). Depressive symptoms among physically abused and psychiatrically disturbed children. *Journal of Abnormal Psychology, 94,* 298–307.

Keiley, M.K., Howe, T.R., Dodge, K.A., Bates, J.E., & Pettit, G.S. (2001). The timing of child physical maltreatment: A cross-domain growth analysis of impact on adolescent externalizing and internalizing problems. *Development & Psychopathology, 13,* 891–912.

Kempe, C.H., Silverman, F.N., Steele, B.F., Droegemueller, W., & Silver, H.K. (1962). The battered child syndrome. *Journal of the American Medical Association, 181,* 17–24.

Kessel, J.A., & Robbins, S.P. (1984). The Indian Child Welfare Act: Dilemmas and needs. *Child Welfare, 63,* 225–232.

Klorman, R., Cicchetti, D., Thatcher, J.E., & Ison, J.R. (2003). Acoustic startle in maltreated children. *Journal of Abnormal Child Psychology, 31,* 359–370.

Knutson, J.F. (1973). Aggression as manipulable behavior. In J.F. Knutson (Ed.), *Control of aggression: Implications from basic research* (pp. 253–295). Chicago: Aldine-Atherton.

Knutson, J.F. (1978). Child abuse research as an area of aggression research. *Pediatric Psychology, 3,* 20–27.

Knutson, J.F. (1988). Physical abuse and sexual abuse of children. In D.K. Routh (Ed.), *Handbook of pediatric psychology.* (pp. 32-70). New York: Guilford Press.

Knutson, J.F., & Bower, M.E. (1994). Physically abusive parenting as an escalated aggressive response. In M. Potegal & J.F. Knutson (Eds.), *The escalation of aggression in dyads and groups: Biological and social processes* (pp. 195–225). Hillsdale, N.J: Lawrence Erlbaum Associates.

Knutson, J.F., DeGarmo, D., Koeppl, G., & Reid, J.B. (2005). Care neglect, supervisory neglect and harsh parenting in the development of children's aggression: A replication and extension. *Child Maltreatment, 10,* 92–107.

Knutson, J.F., DeGarmo, D.S., & Reid, J.B. (2004). Social disadvantage and neglectful parenting as precursors to the development of antisocial and aggressive child behavior: Testing a theoretical model. *Aggressive Behavior, 30,* 187–205.

Knutson, J.F., & Schartz, H.A. (1997). Physical abuse and neglect of children. In T.A. Widiger, A.J. Frances, H.A. Pincus, R. Ross, M.B. First, & W. Davis (Eds.), *DSM-IV sourcebook* (Vol. 3, pp. 713–804). Washington, DC: American Psychiatric Association Press.

Knutson, J.F., & Selner, M.B. (1994). Punitive childhood experiences reported by young adults over a 10-year period. *Child Abuse & Neglect, 18,* 155–166.

Kolko, D.J. (1996). Clinical monitoring of treatment course in child physical abuse: Psychometric characteristics and treatment comparisons. *Child Abuse & Neglect, 20,* 23–43.

Kolko, D.J., Kazdin, A.E., & Day, B.T. (1996). Children's perspectives in the assessment of family violence: Psychometric characteristics and comparisons to parent report. *Child Maltreatment, 1,* 156–167.

Kunz, J., & Bahr, S.J. (1996). A profile of parental homicide against children. *Journal of Family Violence, 11,* 347–362.

Kuyken, W., & Brewin, C.R. (1996). Autobiographical memory functioning in depression and reports of early abuse. *Journal of Abnormal Psychology, 104,* 585–591.

Larzelere, R.E. (2000). Child outcomes of nonabusive and customary physical punishment by parents: An updated literature review. *Clinical Child and Family Psychology Review, 3,* 199–221.

Leitenberg, H., Gibson, L.E., & Novy, P.L. (2004). Individual differences among undergraduate women in methods of coping with stressful events: The impact of cumulative childhood stressors and abuse. *Child Abuse & Neglect, 28,* 181–192.

Levin, A.V., Magnusson, M.R., Rafto, S.E., & Zimmerman, R.A. (1989). Shaken baby syndrome diagnosed by magnetic resonance imaging. *Pediatric Emergency Care, 5,* 181–186.

Limb, G.E., Chance, T., & Brown, E.F. (2004). An empirical examination of the Indian Child Welfare Act and its impact on cultural and familial preservation for American Indian children. *Child Abuse & Neglect, 28,* 1279–1289.

Lopez, M.A., & Heffer, R.W. (1998). Self-concept and social competence of university student victims of childhood physical abuse. *Child Abuse & Neglect, 22,* 183–195.

Macfie, J., Cicchetti, D., & Toth, S.L. (2001). The development of dissociation in maltreated preschool-aged children. *Development & Psychopathology, 13,* 233–254.

Mahoney, A., Donnelly, W.O., Boxer, P., & Lewis, T. (2003). Marital and severe parent-to-adolescent physical aggression in clinic-referred families: Mother and adolescent reports on co-occurrence and links to child behavior problems. *Journal of Family Psychology, 17,* 3–19.

Mahoney, A., Donnelly, W.O., Lewis, T., Maynard, C. (2000). Mother and father self-reports of corporal punishment and severe physical aggression toward clinic-referred youth. *Journal of Clinical Child Psychology, 29,* 411-423.

Martin, J.A. (1984). Neglected fathers: Limitations in diagnostic and treatment resources for violent men. *Child Abuse & Neglect, 8,* 387–392.

McCluney, R.S. (1987). *The legal aspects of corporal punishment in American public schools.* Unpublished doctoral dissertation, University of North Carolina, Greensboro.

Mele-Sernovitz, S. (1980). Some problems of vagueness and overbreadth in criminal child abuse statutes. In D.C. Bross (Ed.), *In advocacy for the legal interests of children* (pp. 375–380). Denver, CO: The National Association of Counsel for Children.

McGee, R.A. (1990). *The Ratings of Past Life Events Scale.* Unpublished manuscript, University of Western Ontario.

McGee, R.A., Wolfe, D.A., & Wilson, S.K. (1997). Multiple maltreatment experiences and adolescent behavior problems: Adolescents' perspectives. *Development & Psychopathology, 9*(1), 131–149.

Meyerson, L.A., Long, P.L., Miranda, R., Jr., & Marx, B.P. (2002). The influence of childhood sexual abuse, physical abuse, family environment, and gender on the psychological adjustment of adolescents. *Child Abuse & Neglect, 26,* 387–405.

Miller, K.S., & Knutson, J.F. (1997). Reports of severe physical punishment and exposure to animal cruelty by inmates convicted of felonies and by university students. *Child Abuse & Neglect, 21,* 59–82.

Milner, J.S. (1986) *The Child Abuse Potential Inventory: Manual* (2nd ed.). Webster, NC: Psytec.

Misener, T.R. (1986). Toward a nursing definition of child maltreatment using seriousness vignettes. *Advances in Nursing Science, 8*(4), 1–14.

Molnar, B.E., Buka, S.L., Brennan, R.T., Holton, J.K., & Earls, F. (2003). A multilevel study of neighborhoods and parent-to-child physical aggression: Results from the Project on Human Development in Chicago neighborhoods. *Child Maltreatment, 8*(2), 84–97.

Mraovich, L.R., & Wilson, J.F. (1999). Patterns of child abuse and neglect associated with chronological age of children living in a midwestern county. *Child Abuse & Neglect, 23,* 899–903.

Naar-King, S., Silvern, V., Ryan, V., & Sebring, D. (2002). Type and severity of abuse as predictors of psychiatric symptoms in adolescence. *Journal of Family Violence, 17,* 133–149.

National Center on Child Abuse and Neglect. (1980). *Child abuse and neglect: State reporting laws.* (DHHS Publication No. OHDS 80-30265). Washington, DC: U.S. Government Printing Office.

National Research Council. (1993). *Understanding child abuse and neglect.* Washington, DC: National Academies Press.

N.C. Gen. Stat. §7B-301 (1999).

Nelson, B.J. (1984). *Making an issue of child abuse: Political agenda setting for social problems.* Chicago: The University of Chicago Press.

Ney, P.G., Fung, T., & Wickett, A.R. (1994). The worst combinations of child abuse and neglect. *Child Abuse & Neglect, 18,* 705–714.

Nixon, J., Pearn, J., Wilkey, I., & Petrie, G. (1981). Social class and violent child death: An analysis of fatal non-accidental injury, murder, and fatal child neglect. *Child Abuse & Neglect, 5,* 111–116.

Ohio Rev. Code Ann. § 2919.22 (West 2004).

O'Toole, R., Turbett, P., & Nalepka, C. (1983). Theories, professional knowledge, and diagnosis of child abuse. In D. Finkelhor, R.J. Gelles, G.T. Hotaling, & Strauss, M.A. (Eds.), *The dark side of families: Current family violence research* (pp. 349–362). Beverly Hills, CA: Sage Publications.

Parke, R.D. (1977). Socialization into child abuse: A social interactional perspective. In J.L. Tapp & F.J. Levine (Eds.), *Law, justice, and the individual in society: Psychological and legal issues* (pp. 1–49). New York: Holt, Rinehart & Winston.

Parke, R.D., & Collmer, C.W. (1975). Child abuse: An interdisciplinary analysis. In E.M. Hetherington (Ed.), *Review of Child Development Research* (Vol. 5, pp. 1–102). Chicago: University of Chicago Press.

Perkins, D.F., & Jones, K.R. (2004). Risk behaviors and resiliency within physically abused adolescents. *Child Abuse & Neglect, 28,* 547–563.

Polansky, N.A., Ammons, P.W., & Weathersby, B.L. (1983). Is there an American standard of child care? *Social Work, 28*(5), 341–346.

Pollak, S.D., Cicchetti, D., Hornung, K., & Reed, A. (2000). Recognizing emotion in faces: Developmental effects of child abuse and neglect. *Developmental Psychology, 36,* 679–688.

Pollak, S.D., & Sinha, P. (2002). Effects of early experience on children's recognition of facial displays of emotion. *Developmental Psychology, 38,* 784–791.

Pollak, S.D., & Tolley-Schell, S.A. (2003). Selective attention to facial emotion in physically abused children. *Journal of Abnormal Psychology, 112,* 323–338.

Prescott, A., Bank, L., Reid, J.B., Knutson, J.F., Burraston, B.O., & Eddy, J.M. (2000). The veridicality of retrospective reports of punitive childhood experiences. *Child Abuse & Neglect, 24* 411-423.

Purver, J.M. (2004). Teachers' use of excessive corporal punishment. In Lawyers Cooperative Publishing Company (Ed.), *American jurisprudence proof of facts* (2nd ed., p. 511). Bancroft-Whitney Co.: San Francisco.

Raiha, N.K., & Soma, D.J. (1997). Victims of child abuse and neglect in the U.S. Army. *Child Abuse & Neglect, 21,* 759–768.

Raine, A., Park, S., Lencz, T., Bihrle, S., LaCasse, L., Widom, C.P., et al. (2001). Reduced right hemisphere activation in severely abused violent offenders during a working memory task: An MRI study. *Aggressive Behavior, 27*(2), 111–129.

Ransom, G.H., Mann, F.A., Vavilala, M.S., Haruff, R., & Rivara, F.P. (2003). Cerebral infarct in head injury: Relationship to child abuse. *Child Abuse & Neglect, 27,* 381–392.

Raphael, K.G., Widom, C.S., & Lange, G. (2001). Childhood victimization and pain in adulthood: A prospective investigation. *Pain, 92*(1–2), 283–293.

Reitman, A. (1988). Corporal punishment in the schools: The ultimate violence. *Children's Legal Rights Journal, 9,* 6–13.

Ricci, L., Giantris, A., Merriam, P., Hodge, S., & Doyle, T. (2003). Abusive head trauma in Maine infants: Medical, child protective, and law enforcement analysis. *Child Abuse & Neglect, 27,* 271–283.

Rivera, B., & Widom, C.S. (1990). Childhood victimization and violent offending. *Violence and Victims, 5*(1), 19–35.

Robins, L.N., Helzer, J.E., Croughan, J.L., & Ratcliff, K.S. (1981). National Institute of Mental Health diagnostic interview schedule: Its history, characteristics, and validity. *Archives of General Psychiatry, 38,* 381–389.

Rohner, R.P., & Rohner, E.C. (1980). Antecedents and consequences of parental rejection: A theory of emotional abuse. *Child Abuse & Neglect, 4,* 189–198.

Rorty, M., Yager, J., & Rossotto, E. (1995). Aspects of childhood physical punishment and family environment correlates in bulimia nervosa. *Child Abuse & Neglect, 19,* 659–667.

Rosenthal, J.A. (1988). Patterns of reported child abuse and neglect. *Child Abuse & Neglect, 12,* 263–271.

Ross, S.M. (1996). Risk of physical abuse to children of spouse abusing parents. *Child Abuse & Neglect, 20,* 589–598.

Runtz, M.G., & Schallow, J.R. (1997). Social support and coping strategies as mediators of adult adjustment following childhood maltreatment. *Child Abuse & Neglect, 21,* 211–226.

Ryan, K.D., Kilmer, R.P., Cauce, A.M., Watanabe, H., & Hoyt, D.R. (2001). Psychological consequences of child maltreatment in homeless adolescents: Untangling the unique effects of maltreatment and family environment. *Child Abuse & Neglect, 24,* 333–352.

Salzinger, S., Feldman, R., Ng-Mak, D.S., Mojica, E., Stockhammer, T., & Rosario, M. (2002). Effects of partner violence and physical child abuse on child behavior: A study of abused and comparison children. *Journal of Family Violence, 17,* 23–52.

Salzinger, S., Feldman, R.S., Hammer, M., & Rosario, M. (1993). The effects of physical abuse on children's social relationships. *Child Development, 64*(1), 169–187.

Salzinger, S., Feldman, R.S., Ng-Mak, D.S., Mojica, E., & Stockhammer, T.F. (2001). The effect of physical abuse on children's social and affective status: A model of cognitive and behavioral processes explaining the association. *Development & Psychopathology, 13,* 805–825.

Sapp, A.D., & Carter, D.L. (1978). *Child abuse in Texas: A descriptive study of Texas residents' attitudes.* Huntsville, TX: Sam Houston State University.

S.C. Code Ann. § 20-7-490 (Law. Co-op. 2003).

Scher, C.D., Forde, D.R., McQuaid, J.R., & Stein, M.B. (2004). Prevalence and demographic correlates of childhood maltreatment in an adult community sample. *Child Abuse & Neglect, 28,* 167–180.

Sedlak, A.J., & Broadhurst, D.D. (1996). *Third national incidence study of child abuse and neglect: Final report.* Washington, DC: U.S. Department of Health and Human Services.

Shields A., & Cicchetti D. (2001). Parental maltreatment and emotion dysregulation as risk factors for bullying and victimization in middle childhood. *Journal of Clinical Child Psychology, 30,* 349–363.

Silverman, A.B., Reinherz, H.Z., & Giaconia, R.M. (1996). The long-term sequelae of child and adolescent abuse: A longitudinal community study. *Child Abuse & Neglect, 20,* 709–723.

Smetana, J.G., Daddis, C., Toth, S.L., Cicchetti, D., Bruce, J., & Kane, P. (1999). Effects of provocation on maltreated and nonmaltreated preschoolers' understanding of moral transgressions. *Social Development, 8,* 335–348.

Snyder, J.C., & Newberger, E.H. (1986). Consensus and difference among hospital professionals in evaluating child maltreatment. *Violence and Victims, 1*(2), 125–129.

Stein, A., & Lewis, D.O. (1993). Discovering physical abuse: Insights from a follow-up study of delinquents. *Child Abuse & Neglect, 16,* 523–531.

Sternberg, K.J., Knutson, J.F., Lamb, M.E., Baradaran, L.P., Nolan, C., & Flanzer, S. (2004). The Child Maltreatment Log: A PC-based program for describing research samples. *Child Maltreatment, 9,* 30–48.

Straus, M.A. (2000). Corporal punishment and primary prevention of physical abuse. *Child Abuse & Neglect, 24,* 1109–1114.

Straus, M.A., Gelles, R.J., & Steinmetz, S.K. (1980). *Behind closed doors: Violence in the American family.* Garden City, NY: Anchor Press/Doubleday.

Straus, M.A., Hamby, S.L., Finkelhor, D., Moore, D.W., & Runyan, D. (1998). Identification of child maltreatment with the Parent–Child Conflict Tactics Scales: Development and psychometric data for a national sample of American parents. *Child Abuse & Neglect, 22,* 249–270.

Sullivan, P.M., & Knutson, J.F. (1998). The association between child maltreatment and disabilities in a hospital-based pediatric sample. *Child Abuse & Neglect, 22,* 271–288.

Sullivan, P.M., & Knutson, J.F. (2000). Maltreatment and disabilities: A population-based epidemiological study. *Child Abuse & Neglect, 24,* 1257–1274.

Thakkar, R.R., Gutierrez, P.M., Kuczen, C.L., & McCanne, T.R. (2001). History of physical and/or sexual abuse and current suicidality in college women. *Child Abuse & Neglect, 24,* 1345–1354.

Tyler, K.A., & Cauce, A.M. (2002). Perpetrators of early physical and sexual abuse among homeless and runaway adolescents. *Child Abuse & Neglect, 26,* 1261–1274.

U.S. Department of Health and Human Services. (1988). *Study findings: Study of national incidence and prevalence of child abuse and neglect* (DHHS Publication No. ADM 20-01099). Washington, DC: Government Printing Office.

Van Dyke, H. (1983). Corporal punishment in our schools. *Phi Delta Kappa, 65,* 287–292.

Varia, R., Abidin, R.R., & Dass, P. (1996). Perceptions of abuse: Effects on adult psychological and social adjustment. *Child Abuse & Neglect, 20,* 511–526.

Wald, M.S. (1975). State intervention on behalf of neglected children: A search for realistic standards. *Stanford Law Review, 27,* 985.

Wald, M.S. (1976). State intervention on behalf of *neglected* children: Standards for removal of children from their homes, monitoring the status of children in foster care, and termination of parental rights. *Stanford Law Review, 28,* 623–707.

Wald, M.S. (1982). State intervention on behalf of endangered children: A proposed legal response. *Child Abuse & Neglect, 6,* 3–45.

Walker, E.A., Gelfand, A., Katon, W.J., Koss, M.P., Von Korff, M., Bernstein, D., et al. (1999). Adult health status of women with histories of child abuse and neglect. *The American Journal of Medicine, 107,* 332–339.

Wasserman, S., & Rosenfeld, A. (1985). Decision making in child abuse and neglect. *Bulletin of the American Academy of Psychiatry and the Law, 13*(3), 259–271.

Way, I., Chung, S., Jonson-Reid, M., & Drake, B. (2001). Maltreatment perpetrators: A 54-month analysis of recidivism. *Child Abuse & Neglect, 25,* 1093–1108.

Weiss, B., Dodge, K.A., Bates, J.E., & Pettit, G.S. (1992). Some consequences of early harsh discipline: Child aggression and a maladaptive social information processing style. *Child Development, 63,* 1321–1335.

Welch, S.L., & Fairburn, C.G. (1996). Childhood sexual and physical abuse as risk factors for the development of bulimia nervosa: A community-based case control study. *Child Abuse & Neglect, 20,* 633–642.

Wichlacz, C.R., & Wechsler, J.G. (1983). American Indian law on child abuse and neglect. *Child Abuse & Neglect, 7,* 347–350.

Widom, C.S. (1988). Sampling biases and implications for child abuse research. *American Journal of Orthopsychiatry, 58*(2), 260–270.

Widom, C.S. (1989). Child abuse, neglect, and adult behavior: Research design and findings on criminality, violence, and child abuse. *American Journal of Orthopsychiatry, 59*(3), 355–367.

Widom, C.S., & Shepard, R.L. (1996). Accuracy of adult recollections of childhood victimization: Part 1. Childhood physical abuse. *Psychological Assessment, 8*(4), 412–421.

Wind, T.W., & Silvern, L.E. (1993). Type and extent of child abuse as predictors of adult functioning. *Journal of Family Violence, 7,* 261–281.

Wissow, L.S. (1998). Infanticide. *New England Journal of Medicine, 339,* 1239–1241.

Wissow, L.S., & Wilson, M.H. (1988). The use of consumer injury registry data to evaluate physical abuse. *Child Abuse & Neglect, 12,* 25–31.

Wolfe, D.A., Wekerle, C., Scott, K., Straatman, A.L., & Grasley, C. (2004). Predicting abuse in adolescent dating relationships over 1 year: The role of child maltreatment and trauma. *Journal of Abnormal Psychology, 113,* 406–415.

Wolfner, G.D., & Gelles, R.J. (1993). A profile of violence toward children: A national study. *Child Abuse & Neglect, 17,* 197–212.

Wolock, I. (1982). Community characteristics and staff judgments in child abuse and neglect cases. *Social Work Research and Abstracts, 18*(2), 9–15.

Worling, J.R. (1995). Adolescent sibling-incest offenders: Differences in family and individual functioning when compared to adolescent nonsibling sex offenders. *Child Abuse & Neglect, 19,* 633–643.

Worling, J.R., & Curwen, T. (2000). Adolescent sexual offender recidivism: Success of specialized treatment and implications for risk prediction. *Child Abuse & Neglect, 24,* 965–982.

Yates T.M., Dodds, M.F., Sroufe L.A., & Egeland B. (2003). Exposure to partner violence and child behavior problems: A prospective study controlling for child physical abuse and neglect, child cognitive ability, socioeconomic status, and life stress. *Development & Psychopathology, 15*(1), 199–218.

Zaidi, L.Y., & Foy, D.W. (1994). Childhood abuse experiences and combat-related PTSD. *Journal of Traumatic Stress, 7,* 33–41.

Zaidi, L.Y., Knutson, J.F., & Mehm, J.G. (1989). Transgenerational patterns of abusive parenting: Analog and clinical tests. *Aggressive Behavior, 15,* 137–152.

Zigler, E. (1979). Controlling child abuse in America: An effort doomed to failure? In R. Bourne & E.H. Newberger (Eds.), *Critical perspectives on child abuse* (pp. 171–213). Lexington, MA: Lexington Books.

5

Defining Child Neglect

HOWARD DUBOWITZ

ACCORDING TO the U.S. Department of Health and Human Services (DHHS; 2004), neglect is the most frequently identified form of child maltreatment; however, a lack of conceptual agreement on its definition as well as difficulties operationalizing and measuring neglect have impeded research on this problem (Zuravin, 2001). Building the knowledge base on child neglect requires a clear definition (Aber & Zigler, 1981; Cicchetti & Barnett, 1991; National Research Council, 1993). Despite Besharov's (1981) recommendation that researchers clearly describe how maltreatment was defined in their studies, Zuravin (1999) found in her review of the neglect literature that relatively few had done so. This chapter first considers a number of important, general issues regarding operationalizing and defining neglect. Next, several conceptual dilemmas will be addressed, followed by a discussion of operational issues in defining neglect and a look at specific and composite measures of child neglect.

GENERAL ISSUES

It is possible that there will never be a single definition of neglect given the multiplicity of purposes for defining neglect. For example, a pediatrician may have a rather low threshold for considering a situation as neglect, whereas a child protective services (CPS) worker, guided by state law and limited agency resources, usually has a higher threshold. A prosecutor, in turn, is likely to have the highest threshold, pursuing only the most serious cases of neglect. Alternatively, one can imagine a single, broad definition of neglect that takes into account the differing purposes it may serve, and accordingly allows for varying responses. Specific criteria could be established, for example, for a subset of cases in which criminal prosecution appears warranted.

The general, common goal in defining neglect is to help ensure adequate care of children. An ideal definition of neglect would be based on empirical data demonstrating the actual or likely harm to children associated with a certain cir-

This work was supported by grants from the Office on Child Abuse and Neglect (Grant No. 90CA1401, 90CA2481, 90CA1569, 90CA1681) and the National Institute of Child Health and Human Development (Grant No. SR01HD39689102).

cumstance (e.g., not receiving adequate emotional support). Although evidence-based definitions are a worthy goal, they can be difficult to achieve—at least regarding some types of neglect. This is due in part to the fact that adequacy of care of children exists on a continuum, without natural cut-off points. This makes it difficult to determine at what point inadequate household sanitation, for example, is associated with harmful outcomes. In addition, children's health and development occur within a complex ecology, with many interacting influences, making it difficult to disentangle the impact of a single risk factor, such as inadequate cognitive stimulation. Even a relatively concrete area such as establishing the daily requirement for specific nutrients is not straightforward, and it is difficult to measure the extent to which these requirements are met. The context of children's experiences also influences the possible impact of a certain circumstance; a mature 9-year-old, for example, may do well left alone for a few hours, whereas a child with a fire-setting problem is a different proposition. Also, in some areas, it is questionable whether data are really needed to document harm (e.g., hunger, homelessness, being abandoned). It seems self-evident that these conditions risk children's safety, health, and development.

Another issue is the political, policy, cultural, and economic context in which neglect is defined. For example, in many cultures, young children help care for their younger siblings. This is both a necessity and considered important in the child's learning to be responsible. Yet, others may view the practice as unreasonably burdensome for the child caregiver and too risky an arrangement. There is no easy resolution to such a debate, and, as a result, awkward, clinical dilemmas can arise with new immigrants to the United States. Clearly, the risks and supports of having a young child care for his or her younger siblings in the United States might be very different from the risks and supports in the country of origin. There is a need to recognize the importance of the contexts and the way in which they influence the meaning and consequences of experiences for children. It is, however, also important to recognize that just because a certain practice is normative within a culture does not mean that it may not harm children (Korbin & Spilsbury, 1999). One needs to be careful to avoid glibly accepting or respecting all culturally accepted practices; some may be clearly harmful and should not be sanctioned.

Another salient issue concerns the strong link between poverty and child neglect. For example, in the Third National Incidence Study, neglect was 44 times more likely to be identified in families earning less than $15,000 per year compared with those earning more than $30,000 per year (Sedlak & Broadhurst, 1996). In addition, ample data demonstrate that poverty jeopardizes children's health, development, and safety (Parker, Greer, & Zuckerman, 1988). The child protection system focuses narrowly on parental or caregiver omissions in care, and in many states' laws on neglect, circumstances attributable to poverty are explicitly excluded. A suggested approach is to have a broad definition of neglect that would include conditions tied to poverty while identifying a subset of circumstances as the responsibility of CPS. Alternative strategies, or agencies other than CPS, could be more appropriate for other types or levels of neglect (e.g., homelessness).

Another key issue concerns the distinction between research goals that center on enhancing an understanding of neglect and goals for clinical practice in which "real world" decisions must be made. These goals can be compatible. Researchers can focus on the situations that clinicians are addressing. To a large extent this has happened, with much of the research on neglect based on families involved with CPS. Researchers are interested in examining the impact of existing social policies and practices, and studies of families involved with CPS can serve this purpose well. Some difficulty arises due to the biases in who is identified to, reported to, and investigated and substantiated by CPS, limiting research to a skewed subset of those experiencing neglect (English, 1997). Many important questions pertaining to neglect, therefore, require more representative samples from the community in general. There is thus a need for research on both CPS and general populations. There is also interest in the research community in examining aspects of neglect that may not be within the realm of CPS, such as whether a certain circumstance of possible neglect is indeed harmful to children. Such a research goal does not necessarily fit with current legal or CPS definitions. Given the previous discussion of general issues, the following sections present several conceptual dilemmas pertaining to defining neglect.

CONCEPTUAL ISSUES

A Parent-Focused versus a Child-Focused Definition of Neglect

There have been two broad approaches to defining child neglect. Some researchers have argued that neglect should be viewed as occurring when a child's basic needs are not adequately met, resulting in actual or potential harm (Dubowitz, Black, Starr, & Zuravin, 1993). This child-focused perspective is in contrast to prevailing CPS definitions of neglect, which are based on parental omissions in care (DePanfilis, 2000). There are several advantages to the child-focused approach. First, it fits with a primary goal of helping to ensure children's safety, health, and development. Second, it is less blaming and more constructive. Third, it draws attention to other potential contributors, aside from parents, and encourages a broader response to the problems underpinning neglect. Clearly, however, not all circumstances within this broad view of children's unmet needs will meet criteria for CPS involvement; therefore, alternative interventions must be considered. Again, it is possible to develop criteria for a subset of neglect circumstances in which CPS involvement would be appropriate.

What Are Children's Basic Needs?

Over time and across societies, views have varied regarding what should be considered the basic needs of children. The level of consensus, however, in the United Nations Convention on the Rights of the Child attests to a remarkable degree of agreement. *Basic* refers to a critical need that, if not met, would likely result in significant harm (e.g., inadequate food). Basic needs are distinct from wants or luxuries. Empirical evidence supports several needs as basic, including having adequate food, health care, shelter, education, supervision/protection, and emotional support and nurturance (Asser & Swan, 1998; Grantham-McGregor & Fernald, 2002; Huebner & Howell, 2003; NICHD Early Child Care Research Network, 2002; Scaramella, Conger, Simons, & Whitbeck, 1998; Stoneman, Brody, Churchill & Winn, 1999). Other needs, such as adequate hygiene or sanitation and adequate clothing, emerge from a societal consensus, although empirical support may be lacking. As children develop, naturally their needs change. Several researchers have noted the need for different neglect definitions to factor in children's age or developmental level (Barnett, Manly, & Cicchetti, 1991, 1993). In addition to the needs identified above, there is the normal variation among children, with specific needs differing substantially.

It is also interesting to note that new awareness of children's needs may emerge with advances in knowledge. For example, ample data document the benefits of using car seat restraints (Klein & Waltz, 1991), and a child not so protected could be considered neglected. Similarly, not long ago, treatment for some medical conditions, such as HIV and AIDS, was experimental. Today, however, the benefits are well established (Thorne & Newell, 2003), and not receiving appropriate care could prove fatal and therefore be viewed as neglect. A third example is that of exposure to secondhand smoke, especially for children with underlying respiratory disease (Nelson, 2002); an asthmatic exposed to smoke at home may be seen as having the need for adequate health care not being met.

The Extent to Which a Need is Met Exists on a Continuum

Seldom is a need met perfectly or not at all. Generally, the extent to which children's needs are met exists on a continuum. Herein lies a problem for a categorical approach to defining neglect. Usually cut-off points are quite arbitrary. For some research questions, such as examining the influence of parental support on children's development, it may be preferable to examine the extent to which the need is met as a continuous variable.

Clinical practice typically is based on more categorical approaches, such as determining that a specific circumstance or level of inadequacy of care constitutes neglect. Researchers can help provide empirical support for a categorical definition of neglect by examining different cut-points of independent variables. This also can serve the different purposes in defining neglect. Typically CPS has a rather high threshold, to reflect relatively serious neglect. However, if the goal is to offer help, without necessarily involving CPS, a lower threshold may be appropriate. For example, a pediatrician may be concerned about an asthmatic child's parent's smoking and urge cessation. This can be seen as "low-severity" neglect, and a CPS report would be unlikely.

Neglect is a Very Heterogeneous Phenomenon

It is evident that the different types of unmet needs children may experience represent quite different circumstances. In addition to types of neglect, other characteristics also may vary, such as the duration (or chronicity) of the neglect, the number of incidents, the severity of the neglect, and the context in which the neglect occurs. It seems clear that research on neglect needs to examine these dimensions of the problem in a refined manner rather than simplistically examining neglect as a unitary phenomenon.

Actual versus Potential Harm

Most state legal definitions of neglect include circumstances of potential harm in addition to actual harm. However, approximately one third of states restrict their practice to circumstances involving actual harm (Zuravin, 2001). The issue of potential harm is of special concern because the impact of neglectful circumstances may only be apparent years later. In addition, the goal of prevention is served by addressing neglect even if no harm is apparent. A difficulty, however, is that it is often difficult to predict the likelihood and nature of future harm. In some instances, epidemiological data are useful. For example, we can estimate the increased risk of a serious head injury from a fall off a bicycle when not wearing a helmet compared with when wearing a helmet (Wesson, Spence, Hu, & Parkin, 2000). In contrast, predicting the likelihood of harm when an 8-year-old is left home alone for a few hours is very difficult. Indeed, such circumstances often only come to light when harm ensues. In addition, even when the risk can be estimated, opinions may vary as to how seriously to weigh the risk. For example, some might argue that a relatively remote risk does not justify intervention. In addition to the likelihood of harm, the nature and severity of the potential harm should be considered. A high likelihood of minor harm (e.g., bruising from short falls) might be acceptable whereas a low likelihood of severe harm (e.g., fatal drowning) would not be. The cost and discomfort of raising concerns of neglect may be a factor, although intervention could be offered without mentioning neglect. Another consideration is that inclusion of potential harm substantially broadens the scope of child neglect, and many families may be investigated, further overwhelming already limited CPS resources. Alternatively, specific criteria could be established for CPS involvement, and other interventions may be appropriate for less severe circumstances.

OPERATIONAL ISSUES IN DEFINING NEGLECT

Having discussed several general and conceptual issues pertaining to neglect, the next section focuses on a number of operational issues.

Establishing Cut-Points for Neglect

As mentioned earlier, the phenomenon of neglect mostly occurs on a continuum, making it difficult and rather arbitrary to discern a cut-point for neglect. Alternatively, examination of the measure as a continuous variable allows one to discern whether there exists a relationship to a child outcome of interest. Receiver operating curves are useful for balancing the sensitivity and specificity of a screening or diagnostic measure to detect a dichotomous outcome (or diagnosis) (Fletcher, Fletcher, & Wagner, 1996). For example, levels of parental monitoring can be assessed against the likelihood of adolescent risk behaviors or school failure.

Disentangling Neglect from Abuse

Much of the research on child neglect has not disentangled it from potentially co-occurring abuse. This is especially problematic because different types of maltreatment do often co-occur. However, an interest in examining potentially unique aspects of neglect demands that careful efforts be made to identify possible abuse and to address this issue in sampling strategies or statistical analyses. An optimal approach is to identify children who have experienced only neglect and not abuse. Sample size may be a limiting factor, however, requiring the combination of a "pure neglect" group with a group of individuals who have been neglected and physically abused.

Different Dimensions of Neglect

A crude categorical approach of defining neglect as "neglect" or "no neglect" is patently simplistic, obscuring the heterogeneity of neglect experiences. Given the heterogeneity of neglect, it is important to characterize its key dimensions: type, severity, chronicity, frequency, and child's age/developmental level (Manly, Kim, Rogosch, & Cicchetti, 2001).

Several classifications that list multiple types of neglect have been suggested (e.g., Sedlak & Broadhurst, 1996). Often, these multiple types of neglect are later consolidated into physical, psychological, and educational neglect. There is also the dilemma of how to classify children who have experienced multiple types of neglect, in one or multiple incidents. One approach is to code all types of neglect experienced across all reports and to sum the number of times each type occurred, a crude proxy for severity (Dubowitz et al., 2005).

Several other attempts have been made to consider the severity of neglect experiences. Some have tried to differentiate between the severity of the act versus that of the actual or potential consequences (Barnett et al., 1993). This appears to be an artificial distinction in that concern about acts or omissions is inherently tied to its implications. It does not seem helpful to consider the severity of an act or experience per se; rather, consideration of the act or experience together with the actual or potential consequences is more useful. Hence, a severe form of neglect is one in which a child's inadequate care results in serious, actual or potential, harm. One effort at rating severity involved four or five levels for several types of neglect and asked an expert panel of professionals in the field to rate the severity of each level (Magura & Moses, 1986). In this way, a scale of 0–100 was developed for each type of neglect, with 0 representing the most severe neglect. Another example is the rating system used in the Maltreatment Classification System (MCS; Barnett et al., 1993) in which each type of maltreatment was coded with a severity rating, based on the authors' perspectives of what seemed a more serious or harmful experience. Litrownik and colleagues (in press) used the severity ratings of the MCS to examine different strategies for measuring severity in which there might be multiple types of neglect and abuse within a single report and in which there might be multiple reports. They examined four approaches: 1) maximum severity within each of five maltreatment types, 2) overall maximum severity across the five types, 3) total severity, or the sum of the maximum severity for each of the five types, and 4) mean severity, or the average severity, for the types of alleged maltreatment. The findings supported the first approach via its association with children's later functioning at age 8. An alternative approach was used by Dubowitz and colleagues (2005), in which the number of times neglect was coded from CPS reports was used as an admittedly crude proxy measure of severity, an approach supported by the work of McGee, Wolfe, Yuen, Wilson, and Carnochan (1995). To date, no research has been conducted that specifically examines the outcomes of children experiencing what is thought to be varying degrees of neglect to offer empirical support for rating severity.

Chronicity, a pattern of omissions over time, is challenging to measure. Some experiences of neglect are usually only worrisome when they occur repeatedly (e.g., poor hygiene, sanitation). Thus, chronicity may be important in considering whether a particular experience constitutes neglect. Separately, it can be a dimension of the neglect experience. A crude proxy measure of chronicity is to consider the duration of CPS involvement, the period of time from when the first report was opened until the last report was closed, as the period of time when maltreatment was occurring. The problems are obvious. A CPS report mostly captures when the problem was identified, and it is highly speculative to assume what transpired during periods between reports. The challenge of assessing chronicity by self-report is also clear, as respondents may choose not to disclose socially undesirable information.

Frequency can be estimated by the number of CPS reports or by self-report; both methods have their limitations. CPS reports mostly offer data limited to incidents that have been identified, reported, and screened. Self-report measures have the limitation of respondents feeling uncomfortable disclosing socially undesirable information.

English, Graham, Litrownik, Everson, and Bangdiwala (2005) found that a definition of chronicity based on children's developmental stages predicted child outcomes. They examined patterns of reports across four developmental periods within the first 8 years of life. Some children were reported in each period, others in just one, and others in two or three periods that may have been contiguous. The outcomes were children's functioning at age eight, including behavior problems, trauma-related symptoms (reported by the child), and adaptive functioning.

Self-Report Measures

Self-report measures, whether completed by parent or child, are problematic; often, the parent or child responds to questions with what he or she believes to be a socially desirable response or exhibits recall bias (Marlowe & Crowne, 1964). This is especially the case with such a sensitive issue as the measurement of neglect. It is inevitable that self-report measures will yield conservative estimates of neglectful behavior. Recent approaches asking youth and young adults to consider possible neglect during their childhood may be limited by recall bias, given a possible inclination to view one's childhood positively or negatively (Straus, Kinard, & Williams, 1995). Clearly, self-report measures of neglect should avoid using emotionally charged terms such as *neglect* or *deprivation* and should instead focus on specific experiences and behaviors, such as not having had enough food. This approach may be promising, especially when directly interviewing children about their experiences.

Observational Measures

Direct observation offers an opportunity to objectively assess children's experiences and the care they receive. However, this approach also may be affected by social desirability because participants wish to "look good" (i.e., the Hawthorne effect), making it difficult for researchers to observe certain forms of neglect (Crocker & Algina, 1986). Nevertheless, the chapter author's experience is that it is remarkable what people may or may not do, even when observed. For example, the author and his colleagues have videotaped very worrisome behavior with the camera in full view, a few feet away. Research assistants conducting planned visits have found homes in enormous disarray, with terribly unsanitary conditions, and occasionally young children are home alone. Thus, direct observation can be a rich source of data, albeit yielding a conservative estimate of neglect. An obvious obstacle to observational approaches is the considerable effort and cost involved, making it prohibitive for some studies.

Validating Measures of Neglect

The outcomes of neglect, including children's health, development, and safety, are highly complex phenomena, influenced by a multiplicity of interacting risk and protective factors. Similarly, neglect itself is often the result of multiple and interacting risk and protective factors (Belsky, 1980, 1993). This complex interaction of factors makes it difficult to validate a measure of neglect by linking a discrete experience to a deleterious outcome. This is especially challenging for psychosocial and long-term outcomes. The harm resulting from a neglectful experience (e.g., not feeling emotionally supported by a parent) may become apparent long after the experience itself. Not surprisingly, neglect alone may explain a relatively modest amount of the variance in outcomes. This problem is compounded by research on very high-risk families in which community stressors, family dysfunction, parental depression, and the often accompanying burdens of poverty may be the predominant explanatory variables, with neglect adding little to an already deeply troubled situation. There are, however, some circumstances in which an outcome can clearly be attributed to neglect, such as when a child is admitted to a hospital due to a complication related to not receiving prescribed medications or when an unsupervised infant drowns in a bathtub. However, it is generally difficult to validate measures of neglect, and several attempts have found only modest associations between neglect and child outcomes (Dubowitz, Papas, Black, & Starr, 2002).

SPECIFIC MEASURES OF CHILD NEGLECT

This section briefly discusses specific measures of neglect that have been and continue to be used in research studies.

Child Protective Services Data

Researchers have relied heavily on CPS data to identify samples of neglected children. As discussed earlier, CPS samples are very appropriate for questions pertaining to children in the child welfare system. They are also suitable for research related to current policy questions. One dilemma, however, is whether to use all reports or only substantiated ones. Several studies have found few differences between these groups, suggesting the use of all those reported regardless of substantiation (e.g., Hussey et al., in press).

CPS data also have certain limitations. They capture only a fraction of the neglect (and abuse) experienced; professionals have been found to report only one to two thirds of the maltreatment they identified (Sedlak & Broadhurst, 1996). Reports to CPS probably reflect more severe forms of neglect; less severe experiences are less likely to be reported, investigated, or substantiated (English, 1997).

For example, many children have health problems due to not receiving prescribed medical care, but only the "neglect" label is applied, and a CPS report possibly generated, in the most egregious circumstances. Another concern is that laws, regulations, and practices vary considerably among and within states and over time, precluding easy comparisons across studies. Indeed, enormous variability in practice may exist within the same agency (Barnett et al., 1993). In addition, CPS reports and findings may not accurately or completely reflect children's maltreatment experiences. For example, uncertain evidence of sexual abuse may instead be labeled as neglect, based on inadequate supervision (D. Runyan, personal communication, April, 2005). McGee et al. (1995) compared CPS records, CPS caseworker ratings, and adolescent self-ratings of maltreatment. Findings showed fairly large discrepancies regarding neglect, with CPS records and CPS caseworkers agreeing with the adolescents only 59% and 65% of the time, respectively.

Despite these shortcomings, CPS data do reflect an important, albeit incomplete and biased, aspect of neglect. CPS reports do reflect concerns of suspected neglect that are investigated by professionals trained to apply state laws and regulations. Despite deficits in what gets documented and likely biases, CPS may still provide documentation of experiences of child maltreatment. Clearly, the use of CPS data, including the narrative information, is very appropriate for research on neglect as it is addressed in the child welfare system at the time of this book's printing. CPS records include specific details such as the nature of the alleged maltreatment, the date it was observed, whether the report was substantiated, how long the agency was involved, and information on interventions implemented. CPS definitions of neglect, rooted in state laws, have prioritized "Failure to Provide" (an MCS neglect type), mostly with regard to inadequate nutrition, medical care, cleanliness, and supervision (S. Berry, personal communication, March, 2002). Another important concern has been "Lack of Supervision" (another MCS neglect type), in which children are left in the care of compromised or dangerous substitute caregivers.

Zuravin (2001) and others have recommended an approach to optimize the use of CPS data and circumvent some of the above limitations. This approach requires researchers to develop clear, a priori definitions of maltreatment. CPS records are then reviewed, rigorously applying the maltreatment definitions. Although reliance on CPS documentation remains an issue, this approach's attention to data quality enhances the reliability of the measurements of neglect and its subtypes provided in the CPS records. The following are two examples of coding schemas developed to abstract useful and consistent data from CPS records.

Maltreatment Classification System

Barnett et al. (1993) developed a coding scheme, the MCS, for measuring types of child maltreatment based on CPS records. CPS databases often include a final designation of just one or two types of maltreatment. In contrast, the MCS takes advantage of the details in the CPS narrative record, permitting multiple types and characteristics of maltreatment to be coded. Careful review of the narratives in the CPS records enables one to determine whether the circumstances in the narrative fit the preset criteria for specific definitions of subtypes of neglect (e.g., medical neglect, lack of supervision). The authors also developed a severity scale for each type of maltreatment, based on their experience and thought about which characteristics and circumstances constitute increasingly serious experiences of abuse and neglect.

The MCS was modified by the Longitudinal Studies of Child Abuse and Neglect (LONGSCAN; Runyan et al., 1998) consortium to code several subtypes of neglect, to enhance the specificity regarding severity, and to improve reliability (English, Bangdiwala, & Runyan, 2005). The LONGSCAN coding schema has been referred to as the modified MCS (MMCS). Two broad neglect types, mentioned previously, were defined by the MCS and the MMCS: Failure to Provide (FTP) and Lack of Supervision (LOS). FTP includes the neglect subtypes of "Food," "Clothing," "Shelter," "Medical/Dental/Mental Health Care," and "Hygiene and Sanitation." LOS includes three subtypes: "Supervision" (i.e., failing to ensure that a child is engaged in safe activities; inadequate supervision), "Environment" (i.e., failing to ensure that a child is playing in a safe area), and "Substitute Care" (i.e., failing to provide adequate substitute care in a caregiver's absence). Modest validation of these subtypes has been found (Dubowitz, Pitts, & Black, 2004).

Record of Maltreatment Experiences

The Record of Maltreatment Experiences (ROME) was developed by McGee, Wolfe, and Wilson (1990). The 87-item instrument attempts to measure a child's history of victimization. Its five scales measure 1) constructive parenting practices, 2) psychological maltreatment, 3) exposure to family violence, 4) sexual abuse, and 5) physical abuse. The lack of constructive parenting may be construed as psychological or physical neglect. Respondents rate the occurrence of specific parental behaviors on a 4-point scale, from never occurring to occurring very often. The measure is completed by a review of CPS records and possible discussion with caseworkers. One problem with the scale is that no specific guidance is offered regarding how to rate or measure items on the scale (e.g., instruction on how to rate the adequacy of a child's diet). Inclusion of such items, at least, may help remind CPS workers of the need to assess particular issues; unfortunately, how to measure these items remains uncertain. Ratings can be made for three developmental periods: early childhood, middle childhood, and adolescence. Severity ratings are based on the number of times each maltreatment type occurred and can be rated for each age period.

Child Well-Being Scales

The Child Well-Being Scales (CWBS; Magura & Moses, 1986) was developed for CPS caseworkers to track families' progress. The measure includes 43 scales pertaining to physical aspects of the home, functioning of the parent and child, and the child–parent relationship. Each scale includes four or five severity ratings ranging from adequate to grossly inadequate care. The authors then had a panel of experts rate the seriousness of each of these described levels of severity on a scale of 0–100 to allow summing of scores and comparisons across scales. Once again, no specific guidance is given on how information for a specific scale should be obtained, although there is a general reliance on observation by workers who may be very familiar with the family. This poses a challenge, however, for research assistants who have limited knowledge of the family and may only have a single home visit to rate the scales. A possible solution is to only use those scales that are amenable to being rated under such limited circumstances. Seaberg (1988) questioned the validity of the scales, although Gaudin, Polansky, and Kilpatrick (1992) found good internal consistency and concurrent validity using 17 of the scales.

Neglect Scale

Straus et al. (1995) developed the Neglect Scale to provide a retrospective, easily administered, standardized measure of neglect. A pool of 63 items was generated based on expertise in the area of child maltreatment and on existing measures of child maltreatment; 40 items from the pool were selected for the test development. Respondents rate the degree to which they agree with each item on a 4-point Likert scale (1 = *strongly agree* to 4 = *strongly disagree*). The 40-item version was administered to a sample of 377 mostly Caucasian undergraduates at a New England state university. Approximately half their fathers were college educated, and 72% were from households with both biological parents.

Item analyses were conducted to select a subset of 20 items by eliminating half of the items least highly correlated with the total score of the respective scales. Internal consistency reliability was very good, with alphas of .80 to .89 for the four subscales and .93 for the full 20-item scale. Orthogonal (Varimax) rotation yielded two components. Twelve items had loadings of .41 or greater on the first component (Emotional/Cognitive) and eight items had loadings of .40 or greater on component two (Supervision/Physical). All emotional and cognitive needs items loaded below .40 on the second component. Harrington, Zuravin, DePanfilis, Dubowitz, and Ting (2003), however, were not successful in replicating the factor structure on a different sample of mostly African American, low-income urban mothers. They did however find an alternative model that worked well, concluding that the measure was promising.

Childhood Level of Living Scale

The Childhood Level of Living Scale (Polansky, Chalmers, Buttenweiser, & Williams, 1978) was the first observational measure of neglect developed to be completed by child welfare workers or other professionals who know the family well.

Defining Child Neglect   119

The requirement for considerable familiarity with the family has not been conducive to its use in research studies.

Multidimensional Neglect
Scale for Child Self-Report

Kantor and colleagues (in press) are developing the Multidimensional Neglect Scale for Child Self-Report (MNS-CR). This measure focuses on the child's perspective and is broadly conceptualized, including several types of child neglect (physical, emotional, supervisory, and cognitive) as well as circumstances that would not concern child welfare agencies (e.g., a parent not reading to the child). It therefore targets a wide audience that is interested in optimizing children's development. There is, however, a focus on parental omissions in care, thus excluding other circumstances in which children's needs are not met (e.g., exposure to community violence).

Two versions of the MNS-CR have been developed: a young child version for children ages 6–9 and an older child version for children ages 10–15. The instruments utilize Audio Computer Assisted Self Administered Interview (ACASI) computer programs, which read the questions aloud to the child participating in the study and allow the child to respond using a touch screen. The pictorial scale versions reflect the age and gender of the child and the gender of the primary caregiver.

Kantor et al. (in press) have been evaluating the instrument on a mostly Caucasian clinical sample of 215 children whose parents have been suspected of maltreatment (mostly abuse). A comparison community sample of 70 children was recruited from aftercare programs. Preliminary analyses of the full version of the MNS-CR showed high internal consistency reliability for both age groups. Factor analyses did not confirm the conceptual four types of neglect, and the authors have recommended using the total score instead. The authors found support for construct validity in associations between neglect and depression and lower cognitive scores in both age groups. Older children with high neglect scores were more likely to have had CPS involvement. In addition, the clinical sample had higher neglect scores than the community group. The LONGSCAN consortium has adapted the Straus et al. (1995) self-report measure for use in 12- and 14-year-olds, and evaluation of this measure is underway. A different measure was developed for 16-year-olds and is being used by LONGSCAN at the time of this book's printing.

Miscellaneous Measures of Neglect

Trocme's (1996) Child Neglect Index is based on the legal definition of neglect in Ontario, Canada. It was developed to assist child welfare workers in substantiating cases and to assist researchers using the Ontario legal standards. McGee et al. (1995) and Rohner (1986) have developed self-report measures of neglect, but little subsequent development and evaluation of these measures has occurred. Slack and colleagues (Slack, Holl, Altenbernd, McDaniel, & Stevens, 2003) have suggested strategies for measuring neglect via survey research.

Alternative Measures of Neglect

Neglect also can be measured using related measures or variables. The following are examples of how different measures may capture the adequacy of children's care without focusing explicitly on child neglect. The Home Observation for Measurement of the Environment (HOME; Caldwell & Bradley, 1979) referred to later in this chapter is a good example. Another example is a measure of food security (Bickel, Nord, Price, Hamilton, & Cook, 2000) that assesses the extent to which a family and children might not have adequate food. This can be used as a measure of nutritional neglect. Some have used trends in children's growth parameters to diagnose failure to thrive or inadequate growth, a possible measure of nutritional neglect (Bithoney, Dubowitz, & Egan, 1992). Another example is a measure of children's perceived emotional support (e.g., Harter & Pike, 1984).

Environmental Neglect

If children's needs include living in a safe, supportive environment, one might conceptualize living in a dangerous neighborhood as a form of environmental neglect (Dubowitz et al., 2001; Linares et al., 2001). Environmental neglect was operationalized as living in a neighborhood characterized by crime, lack of civility, and few resources for children and families. This can be measured using the Perceived Neighborhood Scale (PNS), which includes 17 positive and 11 negative characteristics of a neighborhood. The PNS has been validated and shown to have excellent psychometric properties (Martinez, 2000; Martinez, Black, & Starr, 2001). Mothers rated each statement based on their perceptions of their neighborhoods using a 5-point scale (from 1 = *strongly agree* to 5 = *strongly disagree*). A Negative Neighborhood subscale was developed by summing the responses to the 11 items that describe negative characteristics such as open drug abuse; fear of being raped, robbed, mugged, or murdered; and property damage. The internal consistency of this measure was high (Cronbach's alpha = .93). A z score was computed using the sample mean and standard deviation of the Negative Neighborhood subscale. This measure by itself was not found to be predictive of children's behavior at age 3 (Dubowitz et al., 2002), but measured at age 5, it was associated with internalizing and externalizing behavior problems at age 6 (Dubowitz et al., 2004).

COMPOSITE MEASURES OF NEGLECT

Given the shortcomings of any single measure of neglect, one strategy is to combine data from different measures, ideally from different sources. This approach can be used both for characterizing specific types of neglect as well as for establishing a general index of neglect. At the University of Maryland School of Medicine, the author of this chapter and his colleagues have participated in the LONGSCAN consortium, a 20-year study of the antecedents and outcomes of child maltreatment.

The author and his colleagues have developed scales to measure physical and psychological neglect using the HOME (Caldwell & Bradley, 1979) and the CWBS (Magura & Moses, 1986). The HOME and the CWBS assessments were completed by research assistants following a 1-hour home visit that included an interview and checking where the child "plays, eats and sleeps."

The HOME (Caldwell & Bradley, 1979) consists of 45 items and six subscales concerning the quality and child-centeredness of the home environment, including emotional and verbal responsiveness of the mother, avoidance of restriction and punishment, organization of the physical and temporal environment, provision of appropriate play materials, maternal involvement with the child, and opportunities for variety in daily stimulation. Interrater reliability, assessed by having two trained research assistants jointly code 25% of home visits, was maintained at greater than .90.

Two factors were derived from a factor analysis of the HOME subscales: 1) a psychological care factor, including the subscales of emotional and verbal responsiveness of the mother, avoidance of restriction and punishment, maternal involvement with the child, and opportunities for variety in daily stimulation; and 2) a physical care factor, including organization of the physical environment and provision of appropriate play materials subscales. These factors were examined first as continuous variables, with low scores representing relatively inadequate care within the sample. An alternative approach focused on the lowest quartile (25%) of the overall score. These homes reflected the least adequate home environments and were construed as neglectful.

Fourteen of the scales from the CWBS (Magura & Moses, 1986) were rated by research assistants following a home visit. Those scales that were relatively easy to rate by someone not familiar with the family were selected. Five of the selected scales refer to physical aspects of the home (Furnishings, Overcrowding, Sanitation, Utilities, and Safety), two involve observations of the child (Clothing and Hygiene), and seven pertain to maternal behavior toward the child (Supervision, Child Care, Acceptance, Approval, Expectations, Discipline, and Stimulation). Seriousness (or severity) scores, based on ratings by an expert panel consulting to the measure's authors, ranged from 0 to 100 (optimal) and were used as a continuous measure. The interrater reliability was greater than .90. A categorical approach also was used in which a score less than 60 on any scale was considered inadequate care or neglect, except for the safety category, in which a cutoff of 50 was used to adjust for children's age. In keeping with a child-focused definition of neglect, some of the scales (e.g., Utilities) include conditions experienced by the children that do not require parental responsibility.

Psychological and physical factors also were derived from a factor analysis of the CWBS. Five items loaded on the physical factor—Overcrowding, Furnishings, Hygiene, Clothing, and Sanitation (Cronbach's alpha = .69). Four items loaded on the psychological factor—Acceptance, Approval, Expectations, and Stimulation (Cronbach alpha = .79).

The author of this chapter and his colleagues have been interested in examining the parent–child relationship by videotaping their interactions during semistructured play (Dubowitz, Black, Kerr, Starr, & Harrington, 2000). Maternal nurturance, for example, was coded from videotaped observations of mothers playing with their 3-year-olds for approximately 10 minutes. Large blocks and a "find the picture" book were provided, and mothers were asked to play with their children using these materials; a video camera was visible, but an operator was not present. The videotapes were coded by research assistants who were blinded to the children's risk status. A schema based on parenting style (Baumrind, 1971) was used to rate the interaction between the parent and child (Pratt, Kerig, Cowan, & Cowan, 1988). Individual items were coded using ordinal scores based on behaviorally defined anchors, with high scores representing the most positive interactions. Interrater reliability of at least 90% was maintained through weekly reviews. Four factors were derived: warmth, engagement, structure, and negative emotion, each with an alpha > .80. The first three factors were highly correlated and were averaged to form a construct representing parent nurturance, with good internal consistency (Cronbach's alpha = .82). This measure was used both continuously and categorically, with the lowest quartile representing neglect (Dubowitz et al., 2002).

Both psychological and physical neglect were operationalized using the derived factors from the HOME and the CWBS; they were defined as the average of the HOME and CWBS subscales. The author and his colleagues also have attempted to incorporate the ratings of the videotaped mother–child interaction into the Psychological Neglect subscale. Scores on relevant subscales were standardized into z scores using the sample mean and standard deviation separately prior to being averaged to create the neglect subtypes. In one study, only Psychological Neglect, which also included a rating of mother–child interaction, was predictive of children's internalizing and externalizing behavior problems at age 3 (Dubowitz et al., 2002).

In general, the author and his colleagues have found the neglect subtypes, particularly physical and psychological neglect, to be moderately correlated (r = 0.50) (Dubowitz et al., 2004). In this later study, both psychological (not including mother–child interaction) and physical neglect were related to teachers' reports of problematic peer relationships in 6-year-olds. However, physical neglect was no longer significant after controlling for psychological neglect.

The author and his colleagues also have developed a categorical Cumulative Neglect Index (Dubowitz et al., 2002), including physical, psychological, and environmental neglect. If the neglect score was lower than 1.5 standard deviations below the mean, the child was considered to be experiencing that form of neglect. Thus, a child could experience zero to three types of neglect. Cumulative Neglect was predictive of children's internalizing behavior problems at age 3 (Dubowitz et al., 2002). General Neglect has been operationalized as the mean of physical, psychological, and environmental neglect (Dubowitz et al., 2004), using standardized scores for each type. However, the author and his colleagues found General Neglect to be less strongly associated with children's functioning at age 6 compared with its component neglect subtypes.

Finally, in a study examining the associations between father involvement and neglect (Dubowitz et al., 2000), the author and his colleagues developed a 3-point, composite Neglect Index based on categorical definitions from the CWBS, HOME, and the videotaped mother–child interaction, together with CPS data. It was scaled as follows:

- *Probable neglect:* CPS data indicating neglect plus two other measures, or no CPS data but three other measures indicating neglect
- *Possible neglect:* CPS data indicating neglect and either no or one other measure, or no CPS data but two other measures indicating neglect
- *Unlikely neglect:* No CPS data indicating neglect and either no or one other measure indicating neglect.

Environmental neglect was not included in the composite Neglect Index. In families in which a father was interviewed, a longer duration of his involvement ($p < .01$), a greater sense of his parenting efficacy ($p < .01$), more involvement with household tasks ($p < .05$), and less involvement with child care ($p < .05$) were associated with less neglect. The overall model explained 26.5% of the variance in child neglect. The counterintuitive finding regarding child care may be explained by the mother's coping well; fathers may have been doing less because less was asked or needed of them.

RECOMMENDATIONS FOR FUTURE RESEARCH

First, there is a need to carefully consider the general and conceptual issues discussed in this chapter. There is to date no single, strong recommendation for a definition or specific measure of child neglect. Given varying objectives, it appears inevitable that several definitional approaches and measures are needed. For some objectives, a refined approach using CPS data appears reasonable. For other questions pertaining to the examination of possible neglect and the validation of neglect measures, it is necessary to capture children's experiences and test their associations with later outcomes. Given the inherent shortcomings of any one measure, this problem is partly circumvented by combining data from multiple sources, employing a variety of methods. Second, there remains the challenge of how best to integrate such data. More recently, direct questioning of children appears promising in assessing their experiences, including possible neglect. In addition, there is room for creativity in applying measures originally designed to capture related phenomena (e.g., quality of the home environment). At a minimum, it is important for researchers to fully specify the conceptual basis and operational definition used to measure neglect. There remains a need to refine our understanding of neglect. This requires disentangling neglect from abuse and attempting to characterize children's experiences as comprehensively as possible, taking into account the type of neglect, severity, chronicity, and frequency, as well as contextual variables.

CONCLUSION

This chapter has attempted to present key conceptual and methodological issues pertaining to research definitions of child neglect. A number of approaches and measures were described. It is clear, however, that defining and measuring neglect remains challenging, the optimal approach is not clear, and much remains to be done to improve our measurement of this complex phenomenon.

REFERENCES

Aber, J.L., & Zigler, E. (1981). Developmental considerations in the definition of child maltreatment. In R. Rizley & D. Cicchetti (Eds.), *Developmental perspectives on child maltreatment: New directions for child development* (pp. 1–29). San Francisco: Jossey-Bass.

Asser, S., & Swan, R. (1998). Child fatalities from religion-motivated medical neglect. *Pediatrics, 101,* 625–629.

Barnett, D., Manly, J.T., & Cicchetti, D. (1991). Continuing toward an operational definition of psychological maltreatment. *Development and Psychopathology, 3,* 19–29.

Barnett, D., Manly, J.T., & Cicchetti, D. (1993). Defining child maltreatment: The interface between policy and research. In D. Cicchetti & S.L. Toth (Eds.), *Child abuse, child development, and social policy* (pp. 7–73). Norwood, NJ: Ablex.

Baumrind, D. (1971). Current theories of parental authority. *Developmental Psychology Monograph, 4*(1, Pt. 2).

Belsky, J. (1980). Child maltreatment: An ecological integration. *American Psychologist 35*(4), 320–335.

Belsky, J. (1993). Etiology of child maltreatment: A developmental-ecological analysis. *Psychological Bulletin, 114*(93), 413–434.

Besharov, D. (1981). Toward better research on child abuse and neglect: Making definitional issues an explicit methodological concern. *Child Abuse & Neglect, 5,* 383–390.

Bickel, G., Nord, M., & Price, C., Hamilton, W., & Cook, J. (2000, March). *Measuring food security in the United States: Guide to measuring household food security. Revised 2000.* Alexandria, VA: U.S. Department of Agriculture, Food and Nutrition Service, Office of Analysis.

Bithoney, W.G., Dubowitz, H., & Egan, H. (1992). Failure to thrive/growth deficiency. *Pediatrics in Review, 13,* 453–459.

Caldwell, B.M., & Bradley, R.H. (1979). *Home Observation for Measurement of the Environment: Administration manual.* Little Rock: University of Arkansas at Little Rock.

Cicchetti, D., & Barnett, D. (1991). Toward the development of a scientific nosology of child maltreatment. In W. Grove & D. Cicchetti (Eds.), *Thinking clearly about psychology: Essays in honor of Paul E. Meehl: Personality and psychopathology* (Vol. 2, pp. 346–377). Minneapolis: University of Minnesota Press.

Crocker, L., & Algina, L. (1986). *Introduction to classical and modern test theory.* New York: Holt, Reinhart and Winston.

DePanfilis, D. (2000). How do I determine if a child is neglected? In H. Dubowitz & D. DePanfilis (Eds.), *Handbook for child protection practice* (pp. 121–126). Thousand Oaks, CA: Sage Publications.

Dubowitz, H., Black, M., Kerr, M., Starr, R., & Harrington, D. (2000). Fathers and child neglect. *Archives of Pediatrics and Adolescent Medicine, 154*(2), 135–141.

Dubowitz, H., Black, M., Starr, R., & Zuravin, S. (1993). A conceptual definition of child neglect. *Criminal Justice Behavior, 20,* 8–26.

Dubowitz, H., Kerr, M., Hussey, J., Black, M., Starr, R., & Morrel, T. (2001). Type and timing of mothers' victimization: Effects on mothers and children. *Pediatrics, 107*(4), 728–35.

Dubowitz, H., Papas, M.A., Black, M.M., & Starr, R.H. (2002). Child neglect: Outcomes in high-risk urban preschoolers. *Pediatrics, 109*(6), 1100–1107.

Dubowitz, H., Pitts, S., & Black, M. (2004). Measurement of three major subtypes of child neglect. *Child Maltreatment, 9*(4), 344–356.

Dubowitz, H., Pitts, S., Litrownik, A., Cox, C.E., Runyan, D., & Black, M. (2005). Defining child neglect based on child protective services data. *Child Abuse & Neglect, 29*(5), 461–477.

English, D., Bangdiwala, K., & Runyan, D. (2005). The dimensions of maltreatment: Introduction. *Child Abuse & Neglect, 29*(5), 441–460.

English, D.J. (1997). Current knowledge about CPS decision-making. In T.D. Morton & W. Holder (Eds.), *Decision-making in children's protective services: Advancing the state of the art* (pp. 56–74). Atlanta, GA: Child Welfare Institute.

English, D.J., Graham, J.C., Litrownik, A.J., Everson, M., & Bangdiwala, S.I. (2005). Defining maltreatment chronicity: Are there differences in child outcomes? *Child Abuse & Neglect, 29*(5), 575–595.

Fletcher, R.H., Fletcher, S.W., & Wagner, E.M. (1996). *Clinical epidemiology: The essentials* (3rd ed.). Baltimore: Lippincott, Williams & Wilkins.

Gaudin, J.M., Polansky, N.A., & Kilpatrick, A.C. (1992). The Child Well-Being Scales: A field trial. *Child Welfare, 71*(4), 319–328.

Grantham-McGregor, S.M., & Fernald, L.C. (2002). Nutritional deficiencies and subsequent effects on mental and behavioral development in children. *Pediatrics, 110*(4), e41.

Harrington, D., Zuravin, S.J., DePanfilis, D., Dubowitz, H., & Ting, L. (2003). Neglect Scale: Confirmatory factor analysis in a low-income sample. *Child Maltreatment, 18,* 29–41.

Harter, S., & Pike, R. (1984). The pictorial scale of perceived competence and social acceptance for young children. *Child Development, 55,* 1969–1982.

Huebner, A.J., & Howell, L.W. (2003). Examining the relationship between adolescent sexual risk-taking and perceptions of monitoring, communication, and parenting styles. *Journal of Adolescent Health, 33*(2), 71–78.

Hussey, J.M., Marshall, J.M., English, D.J., Knight, E.D., Lau, A.S., Dubowitz, H., et al. (in press). Defining maltreatment according to substantiation: Distinction without a difference? *Child Abuse & Neglect.*

Kantor, G.K., Brown, W., Drach, K., Holt, M., Macallum, C., Mebert, C., et al. (in press). Development and preliminary psychometric properties of the Child Self-Report Multidimensional Neglect Scale (MNS-CR). *Child Maltreatment.*

Klein, T.M., & Walz, M.C. (1991). Child passenger restraint use and motor vehicle-related fatalities among children—United States, 1982-1990. *MMWR, 40,* 600–602.

Korbin, J.E., & Spilsbury, J.C. (1999). Cultural competence and child neglect. In H. Dubowitz (Ed.), *Neglected children: Research, practice, and policy* (pp. 69–88). Thousand Oaks, CA: Sage Publications.

Linares, L.O., Heeren, T., Bronfman, E., Zuckerman, B., Augustyn, M., Tronick, E., et al. (2001). A mediational model for the impact of exposure to community violence on early child behavior problems. *Child Development, 72*(2), 639–652.

Magura, S., & Moses, B.S. (1986). *Outcome measures for child welfare services: Theory and applications.* Washington, DC: Child Welfare League of America.

Manly, J.T., Kim, J., Rogosch, F., & Cicchetti, D. (2001). Dimensions of child maltreatment and children's adjustment: Contributions of developmental timing and subtype. *Development & Psychopathology, 13,* 759–782.

Marlowe, D., & Crowne, D. (1964). *The approval motive.* New York: Wiley.

Martinez, L.M., Black, M.M., & Starr, R.H., Jr. (2001). Factorial structure of the Perceived Neighborhood Scale (PNS): A test of longitudinal invariance. *American Journal of Community Psychology, 30,* 23–43.

Martinez, M.L. (2000). *Neighborhood context and the development of African American children.* New York: Garland.

McGee, R.A., Wolfe, D.A., & Wilson, S.K. (1990). *A record of maltreatment experiences.* Unpublished manuscript.

McGee, R.A., Wolfe, D.A., Yuen, S.A., Wilson, S.K., & Carnochan, J. (1995). The measurement of maltreatment: A comparison of approaches. *Child Abuse & Neglect, 19,* 233–249.

National Research Council. (1993). *Understanding child abuse and neglect.* Washington, DC: National Academies Press.

Nelson, R. (2002). Smoking outside still causes second-hand smoke exposure to children. *Lancet, 11,*(9318), 1675.

NICHD Early Child Care Research Network. (2001). Parenting and family influences when children are in child care: Results from the NICHD Study of Early Child Care. In J.G. Borkowski, S.L. Ramey, & M. Bristol-Power (Eds.), *Parenting and the child's world: Influences on academic, intellectual, and social-emotional development. Monographs in Parenting* (pp. 99–123). Mahwah, NJ: Lawrence Erlbaum Associates.

Parker, S., Greer, S., & Zuckerman, B. (1988). Double jeopardy: The impact of poverty on early child development. *Pediatric Clinics of North America, 35,* 1227–1240.

Polansky, N.A., Chalmers, M.A., Buttenwieser, E., & Williams, D. (1978). Assessing adequacy of child caring: An urban scale. *Child Welfare, 57*(7), 439–449.

Pratt, M.W., Kerig, P., Cowan, P.A., & Cowan, C.P. (1988). Mothers and fathers teaching 3-year-olds: Authoritative parenting and adult scaffolding of children's learning. *Developmental Psychology, 24,* 832–839.

Rohner, R.P. (1986). *The warmth dimension: Foundations of parental acceptance-rejection theory.* Beverly Hills, CA: Sage Publications.

Runyan, D.K., Curtis, P.A., Hunter, W.M., Black, M.M., Kotch, J.B., Bangdiwala, S., et al. (1998). LONGSCAN: A consortium for longitudinal studies of maltreatment and the life course of children. *Aggression and Violent Behavior, 3,* 275–285.

Scaramella, L.V., Conger, R.D., Simons, R.L., & Whitbeck, L.B. (1998). Predicting risk for pregnancy by late adolescence: A social contextual perspective. *Developmental Psychology, 34,* 1233–1245.

Seaberg, J.R. (1988). Child Well-Being Scales: A critique. *Social Work Research and Abstracts, 24,* 9–15.

Sedlak, A.J., & Broadhurst, D.D. (1996). *Third national incidence study of child abuse and neglect: Final report.* Washington, DC: U.S. Department of Health and Human Services.

Slack, K.S., Holl, J., Altenbernd, L., McDaniel, M., & Stevens, A.B. (2003). Improving the measurement of child neglect for survey research: Issues and recommendations. *Child Maltreatment, 8*(2), 98–111.

Stoneman, Z., Brody, G.H., Churchill, S.L., & Winn, L.L. (1999). Effects of residential instability on Head Start children and their relationships with older siblings: Influences of child emotionality and conflict between family caregivers. *Child Development, 70,* 1.

Straus, M.A., Kinard, E.M., & Williams, L.M. (1995, July 23). *The Multidimensional Neglect Scale, Form A: Adolescent and Adult-Recall Version.* Presented at the Fourth International Conference on Family Violence Research, Durham, NH.

Thorne, C., & Newell, M.L. (2003). Mother-to-child transmission of HIV infection and its prevention. *Current HIV Research, 1*(4), 447–62.

Trocme, N. (1996). Development and preliminary evaluation of the Ontario child neglect index. *Child Maltreatment, 1*(2), 145–155.

U.S. Department of Health and Human Services, Administration on Children, Youth and Families (2004). *Child Maltreatment 2002.* Washington, DC: U.S. Government Printing Office.

Wesson, D., Spence, L., Hu, X., & Parkin, P. (2000). Trends in bicycling-related head injuries in children after implementation of a community-based bike helmet campaign. *Journal of Pediatric Surgery, 35*(5), 688–689.

Zuravin, S.J. (1999). Child neglect: A review of definitions and measurement research. In H. Dubowitz (Ed.), *Neglected children: Research, practice and policy* (pp. 24–46). Thousand Oaks, CA: Sage Publications.

Zuravin, S.J. (2001). Issues pertinent to defining child neglect. In T.D. Morton & B. Salovitz (Eds.), *The CPS response to child neglect: An administrator's guide to theory, policy, program design and case practice* (pp. 2.1–2.22). Duluth, GA: National Resource Center on Child Maltreatment.

6

Defining Child Sexual Abuse

PENELOPE K. TRICKETT

ONLY IN THE LAST 2 decades has society come to realize that the sexual abuse of children in America occurs frequently. Formerly, such abuse was thought to occur only very rarely. In addition, only as society has come to realize that sexual abuse is not a rare phenomenon have researchers turned their attention to studying the impact it might have on child development and adult outcomes. Sexual abuse research is thus of recent vintage. Despite this, much research has been devoted to sexual abuse, as attested to by a large number of reviews of the research (e.g., Beitchman, Zucker, Hood, daCosta, & Akman, 1991; Beitchman et al., 1992; Kendall-Tackett, Williams, & Finkelhor, 1993; Trickett, Kurtz, & Noll, 2005; Trickett & McBride-Chang, 1995; Trickett & Putnam, 1998).

It becomes clear in reading these reviews that definitional problems, which have so plagued the research on child maltreatment in general (National Research Council, 1993), have also afflicted research on sexual abuse. The number and range of these problems is staggering. Especially bothersome is the variability and vagueness of definitions, problems that have greatly contributed to confusing and inconsistent research findings. Often, particularly in early studies of sexual abuse, very little detail has been provided on the nature of the sexual abuse, and thus it is not clear what the child experienced. For example, it has not been clear whether the sexual abuse described involved repeated vaginal penetration, was one occasion of exposure to pornography, was rape brought about with physical violence and threats, was perpetrated by a parent, or was any of a number of other experiences that could be regarded as sexual abuse.

In research on the impact of sexual abuse on development, it is useful to realize that sexual abuse is the independent variable, and generally the design of the research is quasi-experimental. In such a design, usually two groups are formed—one composed of children who have experienced sexual abuse and a control sample made up of children not known to have experienced such abuse. (Usually, in selecting the control sample, there is some effort to select children who are comparable to the sample of abused children.) Just as it is important in experimental research to define variations in the independent variable that can be compared, tested, and described in such detail that the experiment can be replicated, so too is it important to clearly define the independent variable in the quasi-experimental research on sexual abuse. Operational definitions of the independent variable determine the inclusion criteria for selection into both the sample of abused children and the sample of comparison children. It is thus critical that sexual abuse be defined fully and clearly if there is to be an advance in the scientific understanding of the impact of sexual abuse on human development.

Most of the research on sexual abuse has examined its impact on child, adolescent, and/or adult development, and it is these studies that are the focus of this chapter. Other types of sexual abuse research do exist—in particular, research that tries to clarify the frequency (i.e., annual incidence or lifetime prevalence) of sexual abuse in our society. In this type of research, definitions of sexual abuse are very important as well, for how sexual abuse is defined relates to the rates that are determined. (See Bolen & Scannapieco, 1999, for a discussion of some of these issues.)

This chapter describes the definitions of sexual abuse that have been used in research, points to problems solved and not solved with these definitions, and examines how these definitions have affected the state of our knowledge. It also provides findings from a study that examined how variations in the nature of sexual abuse were related to developmental outcomes. Finally, this chapter makes recommendations for how issues in definition and classification can be better addressed in future research.

HISTORICAL CONTEXT

As long ago as the earliest recorded history, humankind has been aware of the existence of incest, commonly defined as "sexual intercourse between persons too closely related to marry legally" (*Webster's New World Dictionary,* 1977, p. 378); and, almost universally across cultures, there has been a strong taboo against such behavior. In fact, society enacted laws criminalizing this behavior at least as early as the early part of the 20th century, despite the fact that the behavior was considered extremely rare. In the 1913 edition of the Funk and Wagnalls *New Standard Dictionary of the English Language,* it was stated that

> In 1908 the Punishment of Incest Act was passed in England under which sexual intercourse of a male with granddaughter, daughter, sister, or mother (a consenting female being equally liable) was declared punishable with penal servitude for not less than 3 or more than 7 years. In the United States incest is not an indictable offense at common law, but almost all the states have rendered it punishable by statute. (p. 1239)

Societal awareness of the frequency of what we now call child abuse, both physical and sexual, has been much more recent—within the last 40 years. The awareness of physical abuse came first, in the 1960s, when doctors discovered that children were being physically injured by their parents. This discovery led Kempe, Silverman, Steele, Droegemueller, and Silver to write their landmark paper "The Battered Child Syndrome" (1962). About a decade following the publication of Kempe and colleagues' paper, society recognized that the sexual abuse of children also was not the extremely rare phenomenon it had been previously thought to be.

Out of this awareness came federal legislation, in 1974, in the form of the Child Abuse Prevention and Treatment Act (CAPTA; PL 93-247) and the establishment of the National Center on Child Abuse and Neglect. CAPTA provides the basis for the legal definitions of abuse and neglect used by each state. CAPTA defines sexual abuse as

> The employment, use, persuasion, inducement, enticement, or coercion of any child to engage in, or assist any other person to engage in, any sexually explicit conduct or simulation of such conduct for the purpose of producing a virtual depiction of such conduct; or the rape, and in cases of caretaker or inter-familial relationships, statutory rape, molestation, prostitution, or other forms of sexual exploitation of children, or incest with children. (National Center on Child Abuse and Neglect, 1996)

State statutes vary in the detail and breadth of their definitions, but essentially all derive from the above definition and include *sexual activity* with a child and *sexual exploitation,* meaning not only such acts as forcing or encouraging a child to take part in prostitution or the production of pornography, but also forcing a child to witness pornography, sexual activity, or "lewdness."

It is significant to note that the sexual activity described in CAPTA is much broader, and one might say more vague, than the "sexual intercourse" referred to in the earlier incest laws. It is also significant to note that the linking of sexual abuse to parental behaviors or even familial behaviors is weak. This is in sharp contrast to the accepted definitions of child physical abuse and neglect (see Chapter 4, by Knutson and Heckenberg, and Chapter 5, by Dubowitz) in which, with some exceptions, the perpetrators of the abuse or neglect are parents or parent surrogates. In the case of sexual abuse, it would seem that rape or sexual exploitation by a stranger or acquaintance could, in a number of jurisdictions at least, be considered sexual abuse. (Most state statutes do require, however, that the perpetrator be at least 4–5 years older than the victim.)

The nature of these definitions of sexual abuse is important because, as is shown in the following sections, most research studies have either explicitly or implicitly used the "child protection" definition of sexual abuse. Thus, it is important to realize that even though the legal definition of sexual abuse is consistent among different jurisdictions across the United States, there is considerable breadth in the experiences that might have taken place. As a result, if a research study just describes the sample as having experienced "substantiated sexual abuse," this definition is vague and could include anything from witnessing sexual activity or pornography to repeated violent rapes. Moreover, the perpetrators could be parents, other family members, acquaintances, or strangers.

DEFINITIONS OF SEXUAL ABUSE USED IN EXISTING RESEARCH

With a few notable exceptions, two basic approaches have been adopted in research focusing on the impact of sexual abuse on development. The first approach involves follow-up with children or adolescents for whom sexual abuse has been officially identified or disclosed and focuses on the short-term or acute impact of abuse on these samples. The second approach uses retrospective designs to study the long-term impact of sexual abuse in samples of adults (and occasionally adolescents) who report themselves as having been abused as children. There are important differences in these two approaches. In the retrospective studies, the information used to classify research participants as abused is based entirely on participants' memories, perceptions, and willingness to disclose; whereas in the follow-up research, classification may depend to some extent on a child's willingness to disclose, but it depends most critically on the abuse coming to the attention of some person or agency apart from the child. This person or agency may be a parent or teacher, child protective services, the court system, or any other such agency that determines the presence of abuse based on a number of sources of evidence including, but not limited to, self-report. Thus, in most research studies involving children, the official definition of sexual abuse, as defined by law in a given jurisdiction, is used and has been substantiated by the investigative methods used in that jurisdiction.

Cross-Sectional Studies of Children

The cross-sectional studies of child victims of sexual abuse cited in the reviews previously listed (e.g., Beitchman et al., 1991; Trickett et al., 2005) vary in the details provided about the sexual abuse. Some just state that sexual abuse was substantiated. For example, Friedrich, Beilke, and Urquiza stated that their inclusion criterion was "substantiation by at least two mandated agencies, for example, police, welfare office, sexual assault center, courts, of at least one incident of sexual abuse of the child by an adult (18 years and older) in the past 18 months" (1987, p. 394). Others, for example, Cosentino, Meyer-Bahlburg, Alpert, and Gaines, have been more specific about the nature of the sexual abuse: "Criteria for inclusion in the sexually abused group were: female children who . . . had at least one sexually abusive experience involving oral, anal, vaginal intercourse, or genital fondling, with a person who was at least 5 years older" (1992, p. 941). These researchers elaborated, as follows, on the nature of the sexual abuse experienced by their sample:

> The mean age of onset of the abuse was 6.8 years, and the mean duration of the abuse was 2.2 years. Sixty percent of the sexually abused girls experienced some form of intercourse (vaginal, anal, or both). The majority of girls (90%) were abused within the family, by fathers, father surrogates, or other family members (male cousins, uncles and grandparents). Twenty-five percent had more than one abuser. (p. 942)

Some studies, however, have provided sparse detail. For example, White, Halpin, Strom, and Santilli stated only that

> Mothers of known sexually abused children . . . were contacted through the hospital's sexual abuse program and through the Parenting Program. The sexual abuse was thought to have occurred within the previous 6 months. Specific characteristics of

the sexual abuse were unavailable in some cases, so a detailed accounting of abuse-related variables was not possible. (1988, p. 54)

Similarly, Wonderlich et al. reported that the children in their sample

> Were referred by county social workers or law enforcement officials who determined that there was sufficient evidence to suggest that the children had been sexually abused. . . . The definition of sexual abuse for inclusion in the study included either intrafamilial sexual activity . . . or extrafamilial sexual activity that was unwanted or that involved another person 5 or more years older than the subject. (2000, p. 1278)

Unlike some studies of physical abuse, in which the nature or degree of physical injury is sometimes part of the definition used to select samples, sexual abuse research does not take into account physical or medical evidence of the abuse. None of the studies reviewed in Trickett and McBride-Chang (1995), Trickett and Putnam (1998), or Trickett et al. (2005) considered physical or medical evidence of sexual abuse as part of the inclusion criteria, although this evidence may well have contributed to the substantiation of the sexual abuse. Despite this fact, one would not want to rely on physical evidence of sexual abuse for substantiation (or inclusion in a sample): Research shows that for the vast majority of sexual abuse cases, there is, in fact, no such physical evidence. For example, in a sample of almost 2,400 children referred to a county hospital for medical evaluation after reports of sexual abuse, fully 96% had a normal medical examination (Heger, Ticson, Velasquez, & Bernier, 2002).

In sum, what is seen from these studies is that the definitions of sexual abuse used in research usually have been tied to the "child protection" definitions of the jurisdictions where the abuse took place; and, as such, substantiation has been based not only on disclosure of the victims but also on other forms of evidence as well. In addition, it is clear from these studies that little detail has been provided in published reports on the nature of the abuse, and, because child protection definitions are themselves vague, the exact nature of the abuse experienced by the child in these studies is not known. Thus, in many cases of sexual abuse, the only known fact is that the child experienced some sexual activity or exploitation that was perpetrated by an individual at least 4 or 5 years older than the child. Physical harm has not been a prerequisite for an act to be considered sexual abuse. Nor, for that matter, has emotional or psychological harm, which appears to be implicitly assumed. It may well be that the strength of the centuries-old incest taboo has contributed to this widely held, implicit assumption.

Adult Retrospective Studies

As noted in this chapter, for adult retrospective studies, as compared with cross-sectional child studies, there are differences in how sexual abuse has been defined and, consequently, in how samples have been attained. For the most part, in these studies, a large group of individuals has been surveyed, by mail questionnaires or telephone or in-person interviews and then asked some screening questions

Table 6.1. Sample inclusion criteria for 20 retrospective sexual abuse studies

Source	Nature of abuse criterion	Age criterion	Perpetrator criterion
Abdulrehman and De Luca (2001)	Childhood sexual experience	Childhood	5 years older than victim or in a position of power
Bifulco, Brown, and Adler (1991)	Sexual contact before age 17, excluding willing contact with nonrelated peers	< 17	None
Buist and Janson (2001)	Unclear	Childhood	Unclear
Garnefski and Diekstra (1997)	"Have you ever been sexually abused? For example, forced to perform sexual acts, assaulted, or raped?"	Sample was 12–19	None
Gutierrez, Thakkar, and Kuczen (2000)	Range from "invitation" to intercourse	< 15	5 years older than victim
Harrison, Hoffman, and Edwall (1989)	"Has anyone in your family been sexual with you? Has anyone else sexually abused you?"	Adolescents in substance abuse rehabilitation	None
Herrenkohl, Herrenkohl, Egolf, and Russo (1998)	"A question . . . identified who had been sexually abused" (p. 294).	Sample was comprised of adolescents	None
Hunter (1991)	Physical contact of a sexual nature	< 18	At least 3 years older than victim
Kamsner and McCabe (2000)	Ranged from "request for sexual engagement" to vaginal or anal intercourse	< 13	At least 5 years older than victim
Krahe, Scheinberger-Olwig, Waizenhofer, and Kolpin (1999)	"Have you been sexually abused?"	Child or young adolescent	None
Lipovsky, Saunders, and Murphy (1989)	Sexual abuse involving physical contact	< 18	Adult in parental role
Messman-Moore and Long (2000)	Nonvoluntary sexual contact	< 17	Relative, forced, or 5 years older than the victim
Mullen, Martin, Anderson, and Romans (1994)	"Unwanted sexual advances"	< 16	None
Mullen, Martin, Anderson, Romans, and Herbison (1996)	Penetration and/or genital contact more than 10 times	< 16	None

Nash, Hulsey, Sexton, Harralson, and Lambert (1993)	At least genital manipulation to orgasm	< 17	5 years older than victim
Nereo, Farber, and Hinton (2002)	Forced or somewhat forced sexual experience	Childhood	Forced or 5 years older than victim
Perkins and Luster (1999)	"Have you ever been sexually abused?"	Not mentioned	None
Runtz and Briere (1986)	Sexual contact	< 15	At least 5 years older than victim
Stein, Golding, Siegel, Burnam, and Sorenson (1988)	Sexual contact, forced	< 16	None
Whiffen, Thompson, and Aube (2000)	Nonconsenting sexual hug to intercourse	< 14	At least 5 years older than victim
Zuravin and Fontanella (1999)	Unwanted sexual contact or intercourse	< 14	None

about their sexual abuse experiences. Then, based on their responses, participants have been placed in the "sexual abuse" group, the comparison group, or, in some cases, neither group. Thus, the screening questions have determined how sexual abuse has been defined in these studies.

Table 6.1 lists inclusion criteria based on the screening information for 20 adult (or occasionally adolescent) retrospective studies that were reviewed in Trickett and Gordis (2004) and/or Trickett et al. (2005). As can be seen, these 20 studies varied considerably with regard to how sexual abuse was defined in the screening questions. Although in a few cases there were specific criteria such as penetration and/or genital contact that occurred more than 10 times (Mullen, Martin, Anderson, Romans, & Herbison, 1996) or "at least genital manipulation to orgasm of, or by, the child" (Nash, Hulsey, Sexton, Harralson, & Lambert, 1993, p. 277), for the most part what has been reported has been nonspecific or general. The terminology used includes "ever been sexually abused?" (e.g., Garnefski & Diekstra, 1997; Krahe, Scheinberger-Olwig, Waizenhofer, & Kolpin, 1999; Perkins & Luster, 1999); "anyone been sexual with you?" (Harrison, Hoffman, & Edwall, 1989); sexual contact (e.g., Bifulco, Brown, & Adler, 1991; Runtz & Briere, 1986; Stein, Golding, Siegel, Burnam, & Sorenson, 1988); sexual experience (Abdulrehman & De Luca, 2001; Nereo, Farber, & Hinton, 2002); and sexual advances (Mullen, Martin, Anderson, & Romans, 1994). In addition, a number of these studies had definitions that encompassed a broad range of behaviors, from "invitation" (Gutierrez, Thakkar, & Kuczen, 2000), "request for sexual engagement" (Kamsner & McCabe, 2000), or "non-consenting sexual hug" (Whiffen, Thompson, & Aube, 2000) to intercourse. There was also wide variability in the retrospective studies of how or whether they specified how "childhood" was defined. That is, some asked about experiences that occurred during childhood, and some specified an upper bound for age (at least one study indicated before age 14, 15, 16, 17, or 18). One study, seemingly, did not mention childhood or any age at all (Perkins & Luster, 1999). Finally, Table 6.1 indicates a lot of variability in whether these studies included criteria for perpetrator characteristics. Many indicated that the perpetrator had to be older than the victim (usually by 5 years). Only one study indicated that inclusion criteria included a perpetrator who was in the parental role (Lipovsky, Saunders, & Murphy, 1989), and two others differentiated between intrafamilial and extrafamilial perpetrators (Harrison et al., 1989; Messman-Moore & Long, 2000). For the rest of the studies, no information was obtained regarding who the perpetrator was and whether he or she was a family member.

Although most of these studies did not explicitly use a "child protection" definition of sexual abuse, the implicit definitions used were very similar in many cases—sexual activity of some sort vaguely defined, occurring during childhood (or adolescence), and perpetrated by someone older than the child or adolescent. It is striking how little detail was provided by the studies listed in Table 6.1. In almost all cases, nothing was presented in the published reports about the age of the child when the abuse took place or the duration of the abuse; whether there was violence involved; or whether the perpetrators were known to the victims or were family members. In a number of instances, it was not at all clear what the sexual activity was and to what degree the definition used meant the same or different things to the different respondents. For example, what is a "sexual invitation" or a "non-consenting sexual hug"? It is quite possible that different acts would be judged to qualify as sexual abuse by the different participants, resulting in a group of people with quite heterogeneous experiences, labeled sexually abused, being compared with another group, potentially equally heterogeneous, labeled not abused. The result is an inadequate quasi-experimental design with the independent variable defined (or at least described) in such a way that there is not a clear distinction between the experimental and comparison groups and that cannot be subject to replication.

What difference does this make? It most certainly contributes to the inconsistency and variability in the findings of sexual abuse research, which have left the field with predominantly generic knowledge about the impact of childhood sexual abuse on later development and with little knowledge about the mechanisms responsible for that impact. Many group main effects have been found, indicating, on average, poorer psychosocial adjustment or mental health of the sexual abuse groups as compared with the nonabused groups. However, most of these studies have demonstrated considerable overlap of the groups, and, as noted, there has been much variability and inconsistency in these findings.

To get beyond this generic knowledge, it is important to be able to develop theoretical models and test hypotheses derived from these models. A number of theories can be brought to bear on this endeavor. Developmental theory, for example, would suggest that the age at onset of the abuse and the developmental period or periods through which the abuse continues would have significant effects on the impact of sexual abuse on later development. Developmental theory would also suggest that, given the importance of parental influence and parent–child relationships on child development, whether a perpetrator was a child's parent would be influential in the outcomes for the child. Trauma or stress theory would posit that the degree to which the abuse was accompanied by great fear and/or pain, or was a chronic stressor, would predict later negative outcomes, including posttraumatic stress disorder (PTSD), dissociation, or cortisol dysregulation. Unfortunately, if all that is known is that research participants answered affirmatively to the question "Have you ever been sexually abused," hypotheses based on these theories cannot be examined. What is clearly needed is a multidimensional approach to defining sexual abuse for research.

CHARACTERISTICS OF SEXUAL ABUSE AS PREDICTORS OF IMPACT

Some research has been conducted that attempts to examine the importance, as mediators of impact, of varying characteristics of sexual abuse; for example, the severity of the abuse (often defined as penetration), the age at which the abuse began, its duration and/or frequency, the relationship of the victim to the perpetrator, and whether the sexual abuse was accompanied by violence. The findings of these studies have been quite inconsistent. For example, a number of studies have found an association between abuse perpetrated by a father or father figure and the severity of negative impact (Adams-Tucker, 1982; Briere & Runtz, 1987; McLeer, Deblinger, Atkins, Foa, & Ralphe, 1988; Sirles, Smith, & Kusama, 1989; Tsai, Feldman-Summers, & Edger, 1979). However, some studies have not shown this association (Einbender & Friedrich, 1989; Kiser et al., 1988; Mennen, 1993). In terms of the impact of duration or frequency of abuse, a number of studies have indicated that abuse that takes place over a longer period of time (Bagley & Ramsey, 1986; Sirles et al., 1989; Tsai et al., 1979) or more frequently (Friedrich, Urquiza, & Beilke, 1986) results in more severe negative outcomes. As before, other studies have not shown this association (Einbender & Friedrich, 1989; Tufts New England Medical Center, Division of Child Psychiatry, 1984). Other abuse characteristics have shown even more inconsistency.

The variables that have been most consistently associated with more adverse impact are longer duration of the abuse, force or violence accompanying the abuse, and father or father-figure as perpetrator of the abuse. It is important to realize that this research has, for the most part, considered one variable at a time; that is, it cannot be considered multidimensional. In addition, in all of the studies described in this chapter, the research has been concerned with the severity of impact. The theory behind these studies, sometimes implicit, is trauma theory, and the hypothesis being tested is that a characteristic of the abuse—father as abuser, or duration, or violence—results in greater trauma and, thus, greater severity of mental health problems.

None of the above studies examined differences in impact; that is, the emergence of different types of problems being associated with different types or characteristics of abuse. Two studies, so far, have used a multidimensional approach to investigate this area. One was conducted by Mennen and Meadow (1995). This was a study in which several characteristics of abuse were considered simultaneously as predictors of adverse developmental outcomes in a sample of 134 girls and adolescents. Mennen and Meadow found that severity of abuse, as indicated by penetration, predicted outcomes on a variety of measures indicating depression, low self-esteem, and other mental health problems. There was also an interaction effect between force and the perpetrator's identity—father or father figure versus non–father figure. Girls abused with force by a non–father figure had much higher levels of distress than those abused by a non–father figure without force. Force did not predict more serious outcomes in girls abused by father figures. There was not a statistical main effect for identity of the perpetrator, and neither age at onset of abuse nor duration of abuse were predictive of symptom levels.

The second study, conducted by Trickett and colleagues, is described in detail in the remainder of this chapter. The findings described in the sections that follow come from data collected as part of a program of research on the psychobiological impact of sexual abuse on female development begun by Putnam and Trickett in 1987 (see Putnam & Trickett, 1993; Trickett & Putnam, 1993). As illustrated in Figure 6.1, the basic tenets of this research are, first, that sexual abuse experienced during childhood is generally very stressful and appropriately considered traumatic, although the degree of trauma will vary depending on certain characteristics of the abuse; second, this abuse will produce both psychological distress and physiological stress that will affect the adjustment and adaptation of abused girls; and third, these outcomes may be mediated by 1) other experiences, especially the provision of support by the mother and other family members, peers, and professionals (e.g., in the form of psychotherapy), and 2) by developmental factors, especially the passage through puberty and the transition into and through adolescence. At the time of this book's printing, this research has completed six rounds of data collection, having assessed the sample of sexually abused girls and a demographically similar comparison group at median ages of 11, 12, 13, 18, 20, and 25 years.

Based on a review (in the mid-1980s) of the extant research on the impact of sexual abuse, Trickett and Putnam (1993) had concluded that one of the reasons for the marked inconsistency in findings was the variability in the definitions of sexual abuse used by researchers. Thus, from the inception of their research, Trickett and her colleagues were concerned with this issue, which led them, first, to specify clearly the eligibility or inclusion criteria for the sexual

Trauma   Acute   Modifiers   Outcomes
                Responses

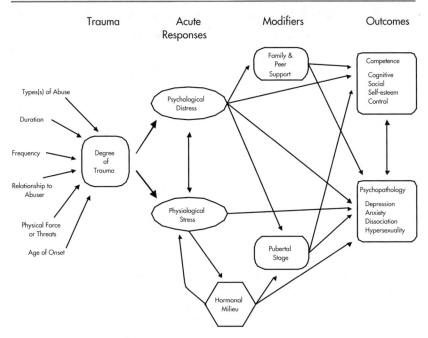

Figure 6.1. Conceptual model for research study on the psychobiological impact of sexual abuse on females.

abuse group and, second, to obtain as much detail as possible about the abuse experienced by each participant. Families were referred by and were under the active supervision of protective services agencies in the greater Washington, D.C., metropolitan area. Eligibility criteria for referral to the study were as follows: 1) The child victim was a female between 6 and 16 years of age at the time of her entry in the study, 2) the initial or most recent disclosure of the sexual abuse occurred within 6 months of referral, 3) the sexual abuse involved genital contact and/or penetration, 4) the identified perpetrator was a family member broadly defined (e.g., parent, stepparent, older sibling, uncle, mother's live-in boyfriend), and 5) a nonabusing parent or guardian was available and willing to participate in the project.

Information about the characteristics of the abuse experienced by the participants was obtained from the Caseworker Abuse History Questionnaire, a 22-item questionnaire developed for this research study (included in the appendix in Trickett, Horowitz, Reiffman, & Putnam, 1997). This questionnaire obtained information about the abuse—which in each case had resulted in referral to protective services agencies—including information regarding the age of onset of the abuse, the nature of the abusive acts, and the identity of the perpetrators. In addition, information was obtained on how the abuse was disclosed, on the disposition of the cases (e.g., arrest of the perpetrator or foster placement), on

Table 6.2. Characteristics of sexual abuse trauma

Characteristics	Percentage/Mean
Severity of abuse	
Penetration	70
Abuse count (mean)	2.81
Age of onset (mean)	7.9 years
Duration (mean)	26.23 months
Relationship to perpetrator	
Biological father	23.5
Other father figure	35.0
Other relative	41.5
Physical violence	51.9
Multiple perpetrators	41.6

other instances of sexual abuse experienced by the child, and on whether there was also a history of physical abuse and/or neglect for this child. This questionnaire was mailed to the caseworkers assigned to each family participating in the study. In many cases, research workers made follow-up telephone calls to the caseworkers or reviewed case files to obtain more complete information.

From this information, Trickett and colleagues were able to describe the nature of the sexual abuse experienced on average by the girls in the sample (see Table 6.2). Seventy percent of the sample had experienced penetration of some type (vaginal intercourse, anal intercourse, or digital penetration [vaginal or anal]). The average age at abuse onset was almost 8 years, and the average duration was slightly more than 2 years. Almost one quarter of the perpetrators were the children's biological fathers, and another 35% were stepparents (in all but one case, stepfathers) or the mothers' live-in boyfriends. The remaining 41.5% were other relatives, including uncles, cousins, older siblings, or grandfathers. Slightly more than half of the sample experienced physical force and/or threats accompanying the sexual abuse or physical abuse. More than 40% of the sample was also sexually abused by one or more adults besides the perpetrator of the referred abuse.

There was a considerable amount of variability in the characteristics of the sexual abuse experienced by the sample that the averages in the table do not clearly indicate. For example, the average age of onset was about 8 years, but the standard deviation was more than 3 years. The average duration of the abuse was 2 years, but the standard deviation 2 1/2 years. Figure 6.2 vividly illustrates the heterogeneity of the sexual abuse experienced by this sample. Other information learned from this examination of the characteristics of the sexual abuse concerned interrelationships among these characteristics (for a full description, see Trickett et al., 1997). In brief, the age of onset of abuse was found to be related to both the severity and the duration of the abuse: The younger the child at abuse onset, the more severe the abuse, in terms of the number of types of abuse experienced, and the longer the duration of the abuse. These latter two characteristics also were correlated. Abuse by a biological father was associated with longer duration and, to a lesser degree, to earlier onset. Abuse by a nonbiological father figure was associated with later onset and shorter duration. Physical violence was associated with multiple perpetrators. It was also found that, for this sample, both ethnic minority status (primarily African American) and socioeconomic status (SES) were related to certain abuse characteristics. Ethnic minority status was strongly associated with later rather than earlier onset of abuse and moderately related to shorter duration. Higher SES in this sample was associated with greater severity of abuse, earlier onset, and longer duration.

Because of these interrelationships among the characteristics of the abuse experienced by participants in this sample, multiple regression analyses were used to investigate the relationships among early onset of abuse, abuse severity, duration, use of force, and the identity of perpetrator and measures of adverse impact (Trickett et al., 1997). In these analyses, when the predictive power of each of these variables was considered while controlling for the others, abuse severity (essentially whether there was penetration) and abuse by a biological father were found to be the most important predictors of negative impact. Abuse severity predicted amount of depression and hallucinatory symptoms. Abuse by a biological father (but not "other father figures," such as stepfathers or mothers' live-in boyfriends) was predictive of aggression, delinquency, and other "acting out" externalizing behavior problems. When controlling for abuse severity and identity of perpetrator, the other variables included in the analyses—age at onset of abuse, duration, and use of force—were not significant predictors of developmental outcomes.

In other analyses, Trickett and colleagues have developed "profile groups," based on cluster analysis, that subdivide the abuse group into three subgroups based on the dimensions of the abuse characteristics described above. (This procedure is described in detail in Trickett, Noll, Reiffman, & Putnam, 2001.) In brief, the *profile 1* subgroup included girls whose abuse involved multiple perpetrators, none of whom were the biological father; and the duration of abuse extended over a relatively short period of time but often occurred with physical violence. Abuse by a single perpetrator who was not the biological father characterized the girls of the *profile 2* subgroup. Duration of the abuse for this subgroup was relatively short, and violence was not frequent. The third subgroup, *profile 3,* was characterized by abuse by the primary father (in all but three cases the biological father) over a long period, beginning at a relatively young age. In 45% of these cases, there was also sexual abuse by another perpetrator. The amount of violence for *profile 3* was intermediate to that of the other two profile subgroups.

Trickett et al. (2001) described in detail analyses comparing these three profile groups with each other and with the comparison group on nine measures

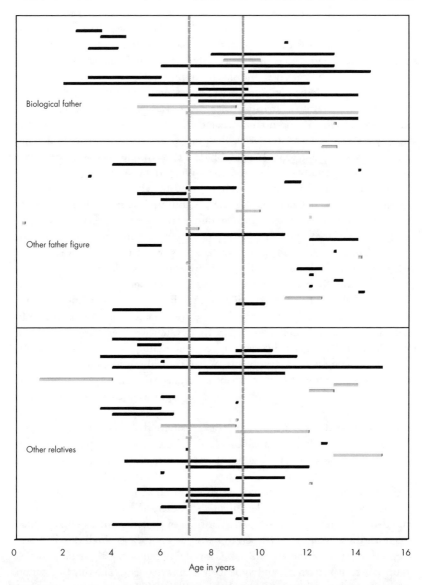

Figure 6.2. Age of onset and duration of abuse for sample of sexually abused females. Each horizontal line indicates one individual in the sample. The left end of the line indicates the age of onset of the abuse, and the length of the line indicates the duration of the abuse. The black lines indicate abuse with penetration and the gray lines abuse without penetration. The vertical line on the left indicates the average age of onset of the abuse, and the vertical line on the right marks the point indicating a 2-year duration.

indicating depression and anxiety, dissociation, delinquent and aggressive behaviors, perceived competence, and physical problems. Trickett et al. looked at short-term ("Time 1") and long-term ("Time 4") development. To summarize briefly, they found that, at Time 1, *profile 1* participants differed from the comparison group on five of the nine outcome variables; *profile 2* differed from the comparison group on four of the outcome variables; and *profile 3* differed from the comparison group on all nine outcome variables. In addition, *profile 3* had scores that were elevated relative to *profile 1* or *profile 2* on eight of the nine outcome variables. In short, all three abuse profile groups could be distinguished from a nonabused comparison group shortly after disclosure of the abuse, but *profile 3* participants—those abused by their biological father for a long duration—showed the most extreme pattern of behavior problems and maladjustment.

At Time 4, about 7 years on average after the disclosure of the abuse, *profile 1* participants were not significantly different from the comparison group on any of the outcome variables. *Profile 2* participants differed from the comparison group on four outcome variables and *profile 3* on five. In short, 7 years after the disclosure of the sexual abuse, participants from all three profile groups were not as different from the comparison group as they were shortly after the disclosure. In fact, *profile 1* could not be distinguished from the comparison group on any of the outcome variables. *Profile 3* participants continued to be the most different from the comparison group, and, interestingly, over time, *profile 2* participants became more similar to *profile 3* participants.

Differences among the profile groups also have been found in some other analyses as well. For example, Sickel, Noll, Moore, Putnam, and Trickett (2002) found that *profile 1* individuals reported the greatest number of gynecological and/or gastrointestinal health problems; whereas *profile 3* participants showed the greatest health care utilization and number of hospitalizations as compared with the other profile groups and the comparison group. Noll, Trickett, and Putnam (2003) determined that, about 9 years after disclosure of the sexual abuse (at "Time 5"), *profile 3* participants expressed stronger attitudes of sexual aversion and ambivalence than the other profile groups or the comparison group. Noll, Trickett, Susman, and Putnam (2006) found that the *profile 2* subgroup reported the most sleep disturbances close to 10 years postdisclosure, even after PTSD symptoms and depression were controlled.

In sum, these analyses indicated that, within this sample, variability in the nature of the sexual abuse experienced was associated with different degrees and types of adverse outcomes. In general, for this sample, although there were important exceptions, it seems that the most important characteristics of the abuse were the identity of the perpetrator (especially distinguishing a biological father from other familial perpetrators), whether there was a single or multiple perpetrators, and the severity of the abuse (especially whether penetration occurred).

It is important to remember that the findings reported here are for one particular sample and may well not generalize to other samples of children who have been sexually abused. All of the girls were abused by a relative—for the majority of the sample, by a father or father figure. Many sexual abuse samples include children abused by nonrelated perpetrators as well. On average, this sample was severely abused. Most experienced penetration of some sort. The sample was all female. (Clearly, more research needs to be conducted with male victims of child sexual abuse.) In addition, this sample had certain ethnic and social class characteristics that may well differentiate it from other research samples. This is clearly important because both ethnic minority status and SES were found to be correlated with certain abuse characteristics (e.g., Trickett et al., 1997). The point here, however, is that even in a sample selected to be rather homogeneous as compared with many sexual abuse samples—all instances of substantiated, intrafamilial, contact sexual abuse—there were discernible associations between characteristics of the abuse and the nature and degree of adverse impact.

CONCLUSIONS AND RECOMMENDATIONS

It seems clear that to move the field of sexual abuse research ahead, it is necessary for the research to be more explicitly theory-based, and that doing so further requires more explicit, multidimensional definitions of sexual abuse, the independent variable in this research. Historically, the research on the impact of sexual abuse has provided neither sufficient clarity about the nature of the abuse experienced by individuals in the samples nor a multidimensional perspective. This is true whether samples involved children, recently abused and under the supervision of protective services agencies, or adults who were queried retrospectively about their experiences.

Future research needs to obtain reliable information on the details of the sexual abuse. What seems most important to ascertain is information on each incident of sexual abuse with details on the nature of the abusive acts, the identity of the perpetrator(s), the individual's age at the onset of the abuse, the duration and/or frequency of incidents, and the presence of threats and/or violence. It also seems critical to obtain information about other forms of maltreatment experienced by those in the sample and other related "contextual" information, such as exposure to neighborhood violence.

Existing measurement tools are available to assess sexual abuse multidimensionally. Many of these are described elsewhere in this book (see Chapter 9, by Portwood, and Chapter 11, by DeGarmo and colleagues). Details of abuse have been extracted using the Maltreatment Classification System (Barnett, Manly, & Cicchetti, 1993), the Child Maltreatment Log (Sternberg et al., 2004), and the Caseworker Abuse History Questionnaire (Trickett et al., 1997) discussed in this chapter. Self-report measures include the Childhood Sexual Abuse Interview (CSAI) developed by Wyatt (1985) and modified for use in questionnaire format (Feerick & Snow, 2005; Miller, 1990); the Comprehensive Trauma Interview (Horowitz, 1999; Noll et al., 2002) used in the research described in this chapter; and a measure designed to be used specifically with adolescents (Wolfe & McGee, 1994). There is some evidence of both reliability and validity of these measures. In the administration of these tools, it is critical to consider the sensitive nature of the information and the potentially vulnerable status of the respondents for the measurement to be good. As discussed in other chapters in this volume, when possible, a multimethod approach to gathering this data (e.g., case record abstraction; self-report data) is likely best, though often not feasible.

It seems likely that to move the field ahead both new prospective research with children and retrospective research with adults are needed. Reliable information about the abuse is more likely obtainable from prospective studies in which the abuse occurred relatively proximal to the onset of the study and information is obtainable not only from self-report but also from case records and other informants. However, in retrospective research with adult samples, it is much easier to get the large samples needed to have adequate power to discern the expected complex, multivariate relationships. In addition, different analytic approaches probably are needed. The "profile" approach, described in this chapter, is a strategy for dealing with the complex data resulting from the measurement approaches promulgated above. Certainly, other approaches are needed as well. What seems certain is that a unidimensional, linear composite approach to capture the severity of sexual abuse is not a successful strategy.

What is being proposed, then, is, in a sense, to bring sexual abuse research back in the fold of other child abuse and neglect research, in which different theoretical models are being developed, often focusing on child development in the context of the family and on how abuse and neglect distorts and disrupts this development.

REFERENCES

Abdulrehman, R.Y., & De Luca, R.V. (2001). The implications of childhood sexual abuse on adult social behavior. *Journal of Family Violence, 16,* 193–203.

Adams-Tucker, C. (1982). Proximate effects of sexual abuse in children: A report on 28 children. *American Journal of Psychiatry, 139,* 1252–1256.

Bagley, C., & Ramsey, R. (1986). Sexual abuse in childhood: Psychosocial outcomes and implications for social work practice. *Journal of Social Work and Human Sexuality, 4,* 33–47.

Barnett, D., Manly, J.T., & Cicchetti, D. (1993). Defining child maltreatment: The interface between policy and research. In D. Cicchetti & S.L. Toth (Eds.), *Advances in applied developmental psychology: Child abuse, child development and social policy* (pp. 7–73). Norwood, NJ: Ablex Publishing Co.

Beitchman, J.H., Zucker, K.J., Hood, J.E., daCosta, G.A., & Akman, D. (1991). A review of the short-term effects of child sexual abuse. *Child Abuse & Neglect, 15,* 537–556.

Beitchman, J.H., Zucker, K.J., Hood, J.E., daCosta, G.A., Akman, D., & Cassavia, E. (1992). A review of the long-term effects of child sexual abuse. *Child Abuse & Neglect, 16,* 101–118.

Bifulco, A., Brown, G.W., & Adler, Z. (1991). Early sexual abuse and clinical depression in adult life. *British Journal of Psychiatry, 159,* 115–122.

Bolen, R.M., & Scannapieco, M. (1999). Prevalence of child sexual abuse: A corrective meta-analysis. *Social Service Review, 73*(3), 281–313.

Briere, J., & Runtz, M. (1987). Post sexual abuse trauma: Data and implications for clinical practice. *Journal of Interpersonal Violence, 2,* 367–379.

Buist, A., & Janson, H. (2001). Childhood sexual abuse, parenting and postpartum depression—a 3-year follow-up study. *Child Abuse & Neglect, 25,* 909–921.

Child Abuse Prevention and Treatment Act of 1974, PL 93–247, 42 U.S.C. § 5101 *et seq.*

Cosentino, C.E., Meyer-Bahlburg, H.F.L., Alpert, J.L., & Gaines, R. (1992). Cross-gender behavior and gender conflict in sexually abused girls. *Journal of the American Academy of Child and Adolescent Psychiatry, 32,* 940–947.

Einbender, A.J., & Friedrich, W.N. (1989). Psychological functioning and behavior of sexually abused girls. *Journal of Consulting and Clinical Psychology, 57,* 155–157.

Feerick, M.M., & Snow, K.L. (2005). The relationships between childhood sexual abuse, social anxiety, and symptoms of posttraumatic stress disorder in women. *Journal of Family Violence, 20*(6), 409–419.

Friedrich, W., Urquiza, A., & Beilke, R. (1986). Behavior problems in young, sexually abused children. *Journal of Pediatric Psychology, 19,* 155–164.

Friedrich, W.N., Beilke, R.L., & Urquiza, A.J. (1987). Children from sexually abusive families: A behavioral comparison. *Journal of Interpersonal Violence, 2,* 391–402.

Funk, I.K. (Ed.). (1913). *Funk and Wagnalls new standard dictionary of the English language.* New York: Funk and Wagnalls Company.

Garnefski, N., & Diekstra, R.F.W. (1997). Child sexual abuse and emotional and behavioral problems in adolescence: Gender difference. *Journal of the American Academy of Child and Adolescent Psychiatry, 36,* 323–329.

Gutierrez, P.M., Thakkar, R.R., & Kuczen, C. (2000). Exploration of the relationship between physical and/or sexual abuse, attitudes about life and death, and suicidal ideation in young women. *Death Studies, 24,* 675–688.

Harrison, P.A., Hoffman, N.G., & Edwall, G.E. (1989). Sexual abuse correlates: Similarities between male and female adolescents in chemical dependency treatment. *Journal of Adolescent Research, 4,* 385–399.

Heger, A., Ticson, L., Velasquez, O., & Bernier, R. (2002). Children referred for possible sexual abuse: Medical findings in 2384 children. *Child Abuse & Neglect, 26,* 6–7.

Herrenkohl, E.C., Herrenkohl, R.C., Egolf, B.P., & Russo, J.M. (1998). The relationship between early maltreatment and teenage parenthood. *Journal of Adolescence, 21,* 291–303.

Horowitz, L. (1999). *The relationship of childhood sexual abuse to revictimization: Mediating variables and developmental processes.* Unpublished doctoral dissertation, The Catholic University of America, Washington, DC.

Hunter, J.A. (1991). A comparison of the psychosocial maladjustment of adult males and females sexually molested as children. *Journal of Interpersonal Violence, 6,* 205–217.

Kamsner, S., & McCabe, M.P. (2000). The relationship between adult psychological adjustment and childhood sexual abuse, childhood physical abuse, and family-of-origin characteristics. *Journal of Interpersonal Violence, 15,* 1243–1261.

Kempe, C., Silverman, F., Steele, B., Droegemuller, W., & Silver, H. (1962). The battered child syndrome. *Journal of the American Medical Association, 181,* 17–24.

Kendall-Tackett, K.A., Williams, L.M., & Finkelhor, D. (1993). Impact of sexual abuse on children: A review and synthesis of recent empirical studies. *Psychological Bulletin, 113,* 164–180.

Kiser, L.J., Ackerman, B.J., Brown, E., Edwards, N.B., McColgan, E., Pugh, R., et al. (1988). Post-traumatic stress disorder in young children: A reaction to purported sexual abuse. *Journal of the American Academy of Child and Adolescent Psychiatry, 27,* 645–649.

Krahe, B., Scheinberger-Olwig, R., Waizenhofer, E., & Kolpin, S. (1999). Childhood sexual abuse and revictimization in adolescence. *Child Abuse & Neglect, 23,* 383–394.

Lipovsky, J.A., Saunders, B.E., & Murphy, S.M. (1989). Depression, anxiety, and behavior problems among victims of father–child sexual assault and nonabused siblings. *Journal of Interpersonal Violence, 4,* 452–468.

McLeer, S.V., Deblinger, E., Atkins, M.S., Foa, E.B., & Ralphe, D.L. (1988). Posttraumatic stress disorder in sexually abused children. *Journal of the American Academy of Child and Adolescent Psychiatry, 27,* 650–654.

Mennen, F.E. (1993). Evaluation of risk factors in childhood sexual abuse. *Journal of the American Academy of Child and Adolescent Psychiatry, 32,* 934–939.

Mennen, F.E., & Meadow, D. (1995). The relationship of abuse characteristics to symptoms in sexually abused girls. *Journal of Interpersonal Violence, 10,* 259–274.

Messman-Moore, T.L., & Long, P.J. (2000). Child sexual abuse and revictimization in the form of adult sexual abuse, adult physical abuse and adult psychological maltreatment. *Journal of Interpersonal Violence, 15,* 489–502.

Miller, B.A. (1990). *Child Sexual Abuse Interview.* Buffalo: New York State Research Institute on Alcoholism and Addictions.

Mullen, P.E., Martin, J.L., Anderson, J.C., & Romans, S.E. (1994). The effect of child sexual abuse on social, interpersonal and sexual function in adult life. *British Journal of Psychiatry, 165,* 35–47.

Mullen, P., Martin, J., Anderson, J., Romans, S., & Herbison, G. (1996). The long-term impact of the physical, emotional, and sexual abuse of children: A community study. *Child Abuse & Neglect, 20,* 7–20.

Nash, M.R., Hulsey, T.L., Sexton, M.C., Harralson, T.L., & Lambert, W. (1993). Long-term sequelae of childhood sexual abuse: Perceived family environment, psychopathology, and dissociation. *Journal of Consulting and Clinical Psychology, 61,* 276–283.

National Center on Child Abuse and Neglect. (1996). *Third study of national incidence and prevalence of child abuse and neglect (preliminary findings).* Washington, DC: U. S. Department of Health and Human Services.

National Research Council. (1993). *Understanding child abuse and neglect.* Washington, DC: National Academies Press.

Nereo, N.E., Farber, B.A., & Hinton, V.J. (2002). Willingness to self-disclose among late adolescent female survivors of childhood sexual abuse. *Journal of Youth and Adolescence, 31,* 303–310.

Noll, J.G., Horowitz, L.A., Norris, J.A., Bonanno, G.A., Trickett, P.K., & Putnam, F.W. (2002, March). *The impact of childhood sexual abuse on revictimization and self-harm.* Poster presented at the 18th annual meeting of the International Society of Traumatic Stress Studies, Baltimore.

Noll, J.G., Trickett, P.K., & Putnam, F.W. (2003). A prospective investigation of the impact of childhood sexual abuse on the development of sexuality. *Journal of Consulting and Clinical Psychology, 71,* 575–586.

Noll, J.G., Trickett, P.K., Susman, E.J., & Putnam, F.W. (2006). Sleep disturbances and childhood sexual abuse. *Journal of Pediatric Psychology, 31,* 241–242.

Perkins, D.F., & Luster, T. (1999). The relationship between sexual abuse and purging: Findings from community-wide surveys of female adolescents. *Child Abuse & Neglect, 23,* 371–382.

Putnam, F.W., & Trickett, P.K. (1993). Child sexual abuse: A model of chronic trauma. *Psychiatry, 58,* 82–95.

Runtz, M., & Briere, J. (1986). Adolescent "acting-out" and childhood history of sexual abuse. *Journal of Interpersonal Violence, 1,* 326–334.

Sickel, A.E., Noll, J.G., Moore, P.J., Putnam, F.W., & Trickett, P.K. (2002). The long-term physical health and healthcare utilization of women who were sexually abused as children. *Journal of Health Psychology, 7*(5), 583–597.

Sirles, E.A., Smith, J.A., & Kusama, H. (1989). Psychiatric status of intrafamilial child sexual abuse victims. *Journal of the American Academy of Child and Adolescent Psychiatry, 28,* 225–229.

Stein, J.A., Golding, J.M., Siegel, J.M., Burnam, M.A., & Sorenson, S.B. (1988). Long-term psychological sequelae of child sexual abuse: The Los Angeles Epidemiologic Catchment Area Study. In G.E. Wyatt & G.J. Powell (Eds.), *Lasting Effects of Child Sexual Abuse* (pp. 135–154). Newbury Park, CA: Sage Publications.

Sternberg, K.J., Knutson, J.F., Lamb, M.E., Baradaran, L.P., Nolan, C., & Flanzer, S. (2004). The Child Maltreatment Log: A PC-based program for describing research samples. *Child Maltreatment, 9,* 30–48.

Trickett, P.K., & Gordis, E. (2004). Aggression and antisocial behavior in sexually abused females. In K. Bierman & M. Putallez (Eds.), *Aggression, antisocial behavior and violence among girls: A developmental perspective* (pp. 162–202). New York: Guilford Press.

Trickett, P.K., Horowitz, L., Reiffman, A., & Putnam, F.W. (1997). Characteristics of sexual abuse trauma and the prediction of developmental outcomes. In D. Cicchetti & S.L. Toth (Eds.), *Rochester symposium on developmental psychopathology. Volume VIII: The effects of trauma on the developmental process* (pp. 289–314). Rochester, NY: University of Rochester Press.

Trickett, P.K., Kurtz, D.A., & Noll, J.G. (2005). The consequences of child sexual abuse for female development. In D.J. Bell, S.L. Foster, & E.J. Mash (Eds.), *Handbook of behavioral and emotional disorders in girls* (pp. 357–379). New York: Kluwer Academic/Plenum.

Trickett, P.K., & McBride-Chang, C. (1995). The developmental impact of different forms of child abuse and neglect. *Developmental Review, 15,* 311–337.

Trickett, P.K., Noll, J.G., Reiffman, A., & Putnam, F.W. (2001). Variants of intrafamilial sexual abuse experience: Implications for long term development. *Development and Psychopathology, 13*(4), 1001–1019.

Trickett, P.K., & Putnam, F.W. (1993). The impact of sexual abuse on female development: Toward a developmental, psychobiological integration. *Psychological Science, 4,* 81–87.

Trickett, P.K., & Putnam, F.W. (1998). The developmental impact of sexual abuse. In P.K. Trickett & C. Schellenbach (Eds.), *Violence against children in the family and the community* (pp. 39–56). Washington, DC: APA Books.

Tsai, M., Feldman-Summers, S., & Edger, M. (1979). Childhood molestation: Variables related to differential impacts on psychosocial functioning in adult women. *Journal of Abnormal Psychology, 88,* 407–417.

Tufts New England Medical Center, Division of Child Psychiatry. (1984). *Sexually exploited children: Service and research project* (Final report for the Office of Juvenile Justice and Delinquency Prevention). Washington, DC: U.S. Department of Justice.

Webster's New World Dictionary of the American Language, 2nd Concise Edition. (1977). New York: Collins World.

Whiffen, V.E., Thompson, J.M., & Aube, J.A. (2000). Mediators of the link between childhood sexual abuse and adult depressive symptoms. *Journal of Interpersonal Violence, 15,* 1110–1120.

White, S., Halpin, B.M., Strom, G.A., & Santilli, G. (1988). Behavioral comparisons of young sexually abused, neglected, and nonreferred children. *Journal of Clinical Child Psychology, 17,* 53–61.

Wolfe, D.A., & McGee, R. (1994). Dimensions of child maltreatment and their relationship to adjustment. *Development and Psychopathology, 6,* 165–181.

Wonderlich, S.A., Crosby, R.D., Mitchell, J.E., Roberts, J.A., Haseltine, B., DeMuth, G., et al. (2000). Relationship of childhood sexual abuse and eating disturbance in children. *Journal of the American Academy of Child & Adolescent Psychiatry, 39,* 1277–1283.

Wyatt, G.E. (1985). The sexual abuse of Afro-american and white-american women in childhood. *Child Abuse & Neglect , 9,* 507–519.

Zuravin, S.J., & Fontanella, C. (1999). The relationship between child sexual abuse and major depression among low-income women: A function of growing up experiences? *Child Maltreatment, 4,* 3–12.

7

Defining Psychological Maltreatment

MARLA R. BRASSARD AND KERA L. DONOVAN

WHEN THE NATIONAL Research Council's Panel on Child Abuse and Neglect published its findings in 1993, its first research priorities focused on 1) the development of consensus research definitions for each form of child abuse and neglect and 2) the development of reliable and valid clinical and research instruments for the measurement of child maltreatment to operationalize the definitions that were developed. The purpose of this chapter is to 1) review the status of major research definitions for the area of psychological maltreatment (also known as emotional abuse and neglect, emotional maltreatment, or psychological abuse and neglect), 2) assess the degree to which the research definitions are embedded in clinical and research test instruments, 3) evaluate empirical support for each definition by age of child, and 4) make recommendations with respect to finalizing definitions in this area and further developing psychometric instruments that effectively operationalize the agreed-on definitions.

The chapter begins with a discussion of barriers that have impeded and continue to impede the development of consensual research and clinical/legal definitions of psychological maltreatment. This is followed by a brief history of efforts to define psychological maltreatment and a review of major definitions, including subtypes that have been put forth by governmental agencies, professional organizations, and individual researchers. The definitional framework published by the American Professional Society on the Abuse of Children (APSAC; 1995) as the *Guidelines for Suspected Psychological Maltreatment of Children and Youth,* is used to organize the subtypes of the major definitions for purposes of comparison (see Figure 7.1). This framework was chosen because it was developed with input from many of the leading researchers in the field and has been refined empirically, it has been used repeatedly in forensic settings, and the first author of this chapter was involved in its development. The chapter then examines instruments that have been developed or used to assess suspected psychological maltreatment in children and adolescents and the degree to which they align with the definitions that have been developed. Empirical support for each subtype of psychological maltreatment is then evaluated by age of the child. Finally, areas of consensus on essential criteria for research definitions and remaining areas of disagreement are presented along with recommendations for future research.

WHY HAS IT BEEN SO HARD
TO DEFINE PSYCHOLOGICAL MALTREATMENT?

Psychological maltreatment should be easy to observe and identify. Many parents make little attempt to hide their behavior so psychological maltreatment often is in public, performed unlike sexual and physical abuse (Davis, 1996; Glaser, 2002). In addition, psychological maltreatment is not embedded in poverty like physical neglect, where it can be difficult to discern whether the lack of appropriate care is the parent's fault. There is a great deal of lay and professional consensus that psychological maltreatment is a form of abuse and neglect (Burnett, 1993; Giovannoni & Becerra, 1979; Korbin, Coulton, Lindstrom-Ufuti, & Spilsbury, 2000; Portwood, 1999; Schaefer, 1997). Despite early cautions that there might not be a distinct group of children with emotional maltreatment apart from those already identified by child protective services (CPS), mental health agencies, and police records (Sternberg & Lamb, 1991), there is now clear evidence that psychological abuse occurs frequently with and without other forms of maltreatment and that it has a unique detrimental impact on child development (see Binggeli, Hart, & Brassard, 2001, for a review of the literature). Finally, psychological maltreatment is very common. For example, by the time their children had reached 2 years of age, 90% of parents surveyed in a telephone interview using random digit dialing reported having used at least one or more forms of overt psychological aggression toward their children in the last year (e.g., they called the child dumb, lazy, or some other name) (Straus & Field, 2003). A number of other studies using similar methodology, as well as retrospective studies of adults, also point to a very high level of psychological abuse and neglect. The best estimate of the overall rate of psychological abuse is about 30% of the population, if parental behavior, excluding harm to the child, is the sole criterion used to determine whether a child has been maltreated (Binggeli et al., 2001).

Despite the relative ease of observation, the prevalence, the occurrence alone as well as with other forms of maltreatment, and the consensus as to what it is, psychological maltreatment often goes unidentified and, therefore, comes to the attention of CPS less frequently than other forms of maltreatment (e.g., Claussen & Crittenden, 1991; Crittenden, Claussen, & Sugarman, 1994). Also, researchers have studied psychological maltreatment less than other forms of abuse (although this is changing rapidly), and there have been no treatment studies that have focused on this form of abuse specifically. Hamarman, Pope, and Czaja (2002) noted that although the fourth edition of the *Diagnostic and Statistical Manual of Mental Disorders* (American Psychiatric Association, 1994) provided diagnostic criteria for parent–child relational problems, physical abuse, sexual abuse, and neglect, there were no criteria for psychological maltreatment.

What accounts for this lack of clinical and research attention? There are a number of possible explanations. The very frequency of psychological maltreatment makes legal and mental health professionals question its harmfulness (e.g., many claim, "My parents did that to me, and I turned out okay"). Its chronic, as opposed to acute, nature reduces a sense of immediate urgency with regard to intervention and confuses reporters and evaluators who are limited in their observations of the parent–child relationship. Many parents make unkind, hurtful comments once in a while or occasionally may be emotionally distracted and unavailable. What frequency or duration is needed to establish that a harmful pattern exists? What types of psychological maltreatment are most damaging? As Straus and Hamby (1997) pointed out, an often accepted belief is that some degree of psychological aggression is normative and expected in families. Further, as Glaser (2002) noted, the fact that the perpetrator is almost always the parent/caregiver puts professionals in the difficult position of protecting the child and blaming the caregiver, who may not be trying to harm the child and may even believe that his or her behavior is motivated by love. If protection necessitates removing a child from his or her home environment, professionals worry about the effects of disrupting the attachment relationship on the child's later development, especially if there is another, nonabusive, parent who, although unable to protect the child, may still be a beloved, supportive figure in the child's life (Glaser, 2002). Finally, the embeddedness of psychological maltreatment in relationships demands interventions that go well beyond what is typically offered by a crisis intervention–oriented CPS system. Parents can be threatened with the removal of their children if they do not stop hitting them or sexually assaulting them; parents cannot be ordered to change the very nature of the relationships they have with their children. Even if a parent were to agree that there are significant problems in the parent–child relationship, changing a harsh or uninvolved parenting style into one that is sensitive and protective would be a time consuming endeavor that requires a skilled clinician, high-quality program, and committed parent(s). Thus, professional hesitancy in developing consensual definitions with regard to psychological maltreatment may have to do with adults' ambivalence regarding the parenting they received as children, beliefs that some degree of psychological maltreatment is typical, the low risk of lethality resulting from the maltreatment, and real dilemmas faced by an already overwhelmed CPS system that is not set up to address the problems presented by inadequate and destructive parent–child relationships.

DEFINING PSYCHOLOGICAL MALTREATMENT: A HISTORY

Psychological maltreatment, the term used in this chapter to refer to the affective and cognitive aspects of child maltreatment, including both acts of omission and commission, has been the last form of child abuse and neglect to receive full attention from CPS and researchers. The section text that follows describes the development of definitional frameworks over the past 30 years.

Figure 7.1 organizes each of the nine definitional systems reviewed in this section relative to the presence or absence of content included in the APSAC definition (1995). To develop this table, the authors of this chapter independently classified the degree to which each of the other definitional frameworks included the subcomponents of the APSAC definitions. Using a 4-point system, the categories were a) in system and called psychological maltreatment, b) in system but not called psychological maltreatment, c) not conclusive, or d) no coverage. They then met and discussed areas of disagreement, reaching a consensus as reflected in Figure 7.1. In making these ratings, full definitional systems were reviewed to ensure that credit was given regardless of where in a system specific acts were addressed. However, as seen in Figure 7.1, a distinction was made between subtypes that were covered within the psychological maltreatment section versus other sections. The reason for doing this was twofold. First, it highlights the general level of agreement across definitional systems regarding parental behaviors considered to be maltreatment, and, second, it draws attention to the variability that exists regarding where specific acts are categorized within these systems. A list of categories that were difficult to rate and a list of content that was included in other definitional systems, but not in the APSAC definitions, was made indicating a need to expand or refine the definition. These are discussed at the end of this section.

Early Research

Although psychological abuse was recognized as an aspect of maltreatment soon after Kempe, Silverman, Steele, Droegemueller, and Silver's (1962) landmark paper on the battered child syndrome (see Laury & Meerloo, 1967) and is listed as "mental injury" in the Child Abuse Prevention and Treatment Act of 1974 (PL 93–247), it was not defined through the presentation of descriptive categories or examples, and it received minimal agency or research attention.

At the second National Conference on Child Abuse and Neglect, Lourie and Stefano (1978) presented a workshop on the topic of defining psychological maltreatment as part of their federally encouraged efforts in this area. They provided a list of examples of emotional abuse, which included scapegoating, denigration, ridicule, shaming, ambivalence, inappropriate expectations for behavior/performance, threatened withdrawal of love, threats to safety/health, physical abuse, sexual abuse, substance abuse, and psychosis.

Following the conference, research on emotional maltreatment began in earnest with the publication of two important pieces of work, one definitional and one ethnological. To develop definitions of child maltreatment, Giovannoni and Becerra (1979) surveyed both professionals (i.e., lawyers, social workers, pediatricians, police) and lay people using vignettes representing 13 hypothesized categories that depicted parental actions that potentially could be considered abusive. They were interested in obtaining information regarding concordance or discordance among groups' perceptions of the seriousness of various forms of maltreatment, including emotional maltreatment. Vignettes depicting emotional maltreatment obtained disparate seriousness ratings among the professional groups, with the highest ratings (indicating that the emotional maltreatment depicted in the vignettes were serious) coming from social workers. Emotional maltreatment uniformly was viewed by professionals as the least serious category of maltreatment. Although professionals differed in their judgments of the seriousness of the depicted acts, they agreed on the general categories these acts fell into and the relative severity of these categories in relation to one another. A comparison of the ratings of the professionals with those of community members revealed much agreement, although the community members rated all categories of maltreatment as more serious than did the professionals. Principal components factor analyses on both sets of ratings yielded nine categories of maltreatment detected by the professional group (i.e., physical abuse, sexual abuse, fostering delinquency, supervision, emotional mistreatment, alcohol/drugs, failure to provide, education, parental mores) and five categories of maltreatment detected by the community member group (i.e., physical abuse, sexual abuse, failure to provide, supervision, drugs/sex), which related well to the initial 13 categories as well as to each other. Although emotional maltreatment emerged as a distinct category for the professional groups, it was subsumed by failure to provide in the community group. The disparity between professionals and lay people appeared to be due to differences in the way these groups distinguished between types of maltreatment, with professionals seeming able to make finer distinctions because of their knowledge and experience (which also varied among professional groups).

Rohner (1975; Rohner & Rohner, 1980) used the Human Relations Area Files at Yale University to investigate parental rejection as displayed in 101 geographically and culturally disparate societies. He identified two patterns: 1) hostility toward the child as demonstrated in behavioral aggression and 2) indifference as displayed in the neglect of children's emotional and physical needs. Despite the large differences in these cultures, the researchers were able to identify a consistent set of social and economic factors that were related to rejection of children and a consistent set of negative outcomes for children related to each of the parental forms of rejection. Their groundbreaking research suggested that emotional abuse and neglect may well be a cross-cultural phenomenon of tremendous power.

Rohner's research studies have had a formative impact on definitional constructs and have reinforced their validity. Giovannoni and Becerra's (1979) categories have served as the foundation for a number of the best assessment tools in use today (e.g., the Maltreatment Classification System [MCS]; Barnett, Manly, & Cicchetti, 1993) and were the first of a number of efforts to establish the existence of a professional and lay consensus on what constitutes child maltreatment, including psychological maltreatment, reinforcing a policy mandate to address the problem. Rohner's work built on this by demonstrating not only that were

APSAC categories	Subcategories of parental/caregiver behavior toward child	NIS Sedlak and Broadhurst (1996)	Barnett, Manly, and Cicchetti (1993)	Baily and Baily (1986)	Glaser (2002)	McGee and Wolfe (1991)	Garbarino, Guttman, and Seely (1986)	Moran, Bifulco, Ball, Jacobs, and Bendim (2002)	Giovannoni and Becerra (1979)	AAP Kairys, Johnson, and AAP Committee on Child Abuse and Neglect (2002)
Spurning	Belitling, denigrating, or other rejecting	✓	✓	✓	✓	✓	✓	✓	✓	✓
	Ridiculing for showing normal emotions	✓		?	✓	✓	✓	✓		✓
	Singling out	✓		✓	✓	✓	✓	✓	✓	✓
	Humiliating in public	✓			✓	✓	✓	✓		✓
Terrorizing	Placing in unpredictable/chaotic circumstances	*	✓	✓	✓	✓	✓		*	✓
	Placing in recognizably dangerous situations	*	*		✓	*	✓			✓
	Having rigid/unrealistic expectations accompanied by threats if not met		?	✓	?	✓	✓		*	✓
	Threatening/perpetrating violence against child	✓	✓	✓	✓	✓	✓	✓		✓
	Threatening/perpetrating violence against child's loved ones/objects—includes exposure to domestic violence	✓	✓		✓	✓		✓	✓	✓
Isolating	Confining within environment	✓	✓	✓				✓	*	✓
	Restricting social interactions in community	✓	✓	✓	✓		✓	✓	?	✓

Figure 7.1. Content of major maltreatment definitions organized by APSAC definitions for suspected psychological maltreatment. (Key: ✓ = in system and called psychological maltreatment [abuse or neglect]; * = in system but not called psychological maltreatment; ? = not conclusive/partially covered.)

Exploiting/corrupting	Modeling, permitting, or encouraging antisocial behavior	✓	*	✓	✓	✓	✓	*	✓
	Modeling, permitting, or encouraging developmentally inappropriate behavior	✓	✓	✓	✓	✓	✓	✓	✓
	Restricting/undermining psychological autonomy	✓	✓	✓	?	✓	?		✓
	Restricting/interfering with cognitive development	*	*	✓	*	✓	*	*	✓
Denying emotional responsiveness	Being detached from child or uninvolved due to parent's incapacity or lack of motivation	✓	✓	✓	?	✓	?	✓	✓
	Interacting only when necessary	✓	?	?	?	✓			✓
	Failing to show affection, caring, love	✓	✓	✓	*	✓	✓	✓	✓
Mental health/ medical/ educational neglect	Parent/caregiver ignores or refuses to allow/provide treatment for child's . . .	✓	*	✓				*	✓
	. . . serious emotional/behavior problems/needs	*				*		*	✓
	. . . serious physical health problems/needs	*	*			*		*	✓
	. . . serious educational problems/needs	*		✓					✓

professionals and the lay public in the United States in agreement about what constitutes unacceptable parental behavior but also that these unacceptable behaviors could be reliably identified in disparate cultures and were associated with poor child development outcomes cross-culturally. These two findings indicated that psychological maltreatment was not solely a sociological construct, influenced by transient notions of appropriate parenting, instead, the findings suggested a universal human pattern of hostility toward and/or neglect of offspring that was related to developmental impairment and, thus, of justifiable concern to the community and the state.

The National Incidence Studies

In 1981, the federal government became involved in defining psychological maltreatment and collecting data on its incidence. The National Center on Child Abuse and Neglect (1981) recommended the following general definition of mental injury as a guide to states in developing their standards:

> "Mental injury" means an injury to the intellectual or psychological capacity of a child as evidenced by an observable and substantial impairment in the child's ability to function within a normal range of performance and behavior, with due regard to the child's culture. (Landau, Salus, Stiffarm, & Kalb, 1980, p. 2)

An early definition of psychological maltreatment, called emotional abuse and emotional neglect, was developed for the first National Incidence Study (NIS-1; U.S. Department of Health and Human Services [DHHS], 1981), a congressionally mandated study that attempted to provide current estimates of the incidence of child abuse and neglect in the United States and changes in those estimates over time. The NIS-1 was conducted in 1979–1980 and published in 1981; the second NIS (NIS-2; DHHS, 1988) was conducted in 1986–1987 and published in 1988; and the most recent NIS (NIS-3; Sedlak & Broadhurst, 1996) was conducted in 1993–1995 and published in 1996. The methodology of the NIS involved collecting data over a 3-month period in 42 counties across the United States. Researchers attempted to include all cases investigated by CPS as well as cases encountered by agencies other than CPS, including law enforcement agencies, juvenile probation centers, public health agencies, hospitals, schools, daycare centers, and mental health and social services agencies (Sedlak & Broadhurst, 1996). The NIS categories for emotional abuse and emotional neglect included *verbal and emotional assault, close confinement, inadequate nurturance/affection,* and *knowingly permitting maladaptive behavior.*

At the same time, the American Humane Association, charged with the responsibility of gathering national data on a yearly basis regarding child abuse and neglect within the United States, developed its own definitions of emotional abuse and emotional neglect to guide states in organizing their reports. They defined emotional abuse as "active, intentional berating, disparaging or other abusive behavior towards the child, which impacts upon the emotional well being of the child" and emotional neglect as "passive or passive/aggressive inattention to the child's emotional needs, nurturing, or emotional well being" (1980, pp. 3.36–3.37).

American Professional Society on the Abuse of Children and Garbarino Definitions

The next major attempt at operationally defining psychological maltreatment was the result of the International Conference on Psychological Abuse in Children and Youth, held in Indianapolis by the Office for the Study of the Psychological Rights of the Child (Brassard, Germain, & Hart, 1987; Hart & Brassard, 1990). When the conference was held in 1983, there was widespread dissatisfaction with the definitions that had been put forward previously. States were finding it difficult to define and apply the mental injury category (see Corson & Davidson, 1987). The conference conveners cited as problematic

> The lack of sufficient definitions and unclear standards of evidence associated with the mental injury category of the federal statute . . . [and] the lack of guidance provided for state laws and child protective services, and the possibilities that application of law could lead to unfair intrusions on family life and to remedies which might prove more destructive than the conditions they were meant to correct. (Hart, Germain, & Brassard, 1987, p. 5)

Major researchers and representatives of associations whose professionals were involved in the study of child maltreatment (e.g., American Academy of Pediatrics, National Association of Social Workers) were invited to participate in the conference. Building on Garbarino and Gilliam's definition of maltreatment as "acts of omission or commission by a parent or guardian that are judged by a mixture of community values and professional experience to be inappropriate and damaging" (1980, p. 7), conference participants endorsed the following working definition:

> Psychological maltreatment of children and youth consists of acts of omission and commission, which are judged on the basis of a combination of community standards and professional expectations to be psychologically damaging. Such acts are committed by individuals, singly or collectively, who by their characteristics (e.g., age, status, knowledge, and organizational form) are in a position of differential power that renders the child vulnerable. Such acts damage immediately or ultimately the behavioral, cognitive, affective, or physical functioning of the child. Examples of psychological maltreatment include acts of rejecting, terrorizing, isolating, exploiting, and missocializing. (Hart, Germain, & Brassard, 1983, p. 2)

Subsequent to that conference, Garbarino, who was a speaker at the conference (Garbarino, Guttman, & Seely, 1986), and Brassard and colleagues (Brassard et al., 1987) published the first books on the topic of psychological maltreatment. Garbarino and his colleagues proposed the categories of *isolating, missocializing, terrorizing, rejecting,* and *ignoring* and used illustrations of how each subtype would be displayed in each of four developmental periods: infancy, early childhood, school age, and adolescence.

Influenced by the work of Egeland and Erickson (1987), who had also presented at the conference, Hart and Brassard (1991) added to the five subtypes identified in the conference the definition category of *denying emotional responsiveness,* identified by Egeland and Erickson as an extremely damaging form of care in their prospective study of high-risk families. Using these six definitions, Hart and Brassard engaged in an extensive process of multidimensional scaling that included having graduate students, social workers, psychologists, and teachers sort descriptions representing each of the six subtypes of maltreatment, as well as constructive parenting, into categories generated by the sorters and into the seven categories identified by the researchers. On the basis of this, they discovered that *rejecting* broke into either a very hostile, active rejection of a child or into the *denying emotional responsiveness* category, consistent with the findings of Rohner and Rohner (1980). They also found that they could not write items that sorters were able to discriminate into clear categories of *corrupting* and *exploiting;* thus, they collapsed these into one category. Finally, they asked their group of sorters to take the 16 preschool/latency definitions developed by Baily and Baily (1986; see a description of their later work in this chapter) and see if they could sort them into the categories of *spurning, terrorizing, isolating, corrupting/exploiting,* and *denying emotional responsiveness.* The neat separation of all the items describing parental rejection into either *denying emotional responsiveness* or the category later named *spurning* further confirmed the need to distinctly separate these two forms of rejection and supported the final list of categories. The category *medical/mental health/educational neglect* was added in the early 1990s, although proposed earlier (Hart, 1985). See Figure 7.1 for the categories included in the APSAC guidelines.

Using these same constructs, Brassard, Hart, and Hardy (1993) then developed the Psychological Maltreatment Rating Scales (PMRS), an observational measure of parent–child interaction. They included the above five categories and a variety of measures of supportive, competent parenting developed by Egeland and Sroufe (n.d.), as well as some additional measures of competent parenting that they developed themselves. They used a sample of cases identified through CPS as being physically abusive or neglectful, which also met criteria using the NIS-2 for emotional abuse and/or neglect, and compared parent–child dyads from these cases with a control group of parent–child dyads, matched on gender, ethnicity, and SES, selected from the classrooms of the children who were being mistreated. They found that the PMRS accurately identified 92% of CPS families versus control families in this overly matched sample. Furthermore, when CPS identification was controlled, the degree of psychological maltreatment experienced by these children predicted whether these children had any friends, as rated by their classroom teachers (Hart & Brassard, 1991); CPS status accounted for little variance when the PMRS were added to the regression equation.

An exploratory factor analysis of the PMRS identified a very clear factor structure in both the infant/toddler sample and in the preschool/early–school-age sample. This consisted of a Psychological Abuse factor that included *spurning, terrorizing,* and *corrupting/exploiting* and two factors of competent parenting; a Maternal Emotional Support factor that included *denying emotional responsiveness* and a Facilitation of Cognitive and Social Development factor, which included *quality of maternal instruction* and *support for child's autonomy.* The *isolating* observational scale proved to be a weak measure of *denying emotional responsiveness.* This may well have been the result of the parent–child interaction task, which provided little opportunity for observing this particular characteristic.

This study made clear that a 15-minute mother–child observation by blind observers can be a powerful tool in assessing the quality of the parent–child relationship. Interrater agreement was acceptable and discrimination was quite good, considering that the control sample also was a very high-risk sample; in fact, a number of children in the control group had to be eliminated when their names matched cases reported to CPS or maltreatment was observed on the home visit. This study also suggested that the best way to assess psychological neglect was with measures of constructive parenting practices in determining harm (see also McGee, Wolfe, Yuen, Wilson, & Carnochan, 1995).

Concurrent with this process, Hart and Brassard cochaired the American Professional Society on the Abuse of Children (APSAC) Task Force on Psychological Maltreatment, a group charged with developing guidelines for the psychosocial assessment of suspected psychological maltreatment of children and youth. Task force participants were Dante Cicchetti, Patricia Crittenden, Byron Egeland, Martha Erickson, James Garbarino, Sheree Toth, and Ann Tyler, with editorial support by John Myers. The committee not only reviewed the APSAC definitions, but also proposed the use of developmental milestones as a way of assessing the presence or absence of endangerment and harm in addition to traditional measures of psychopathology. Thus, the APSAC guidelines not only consist of the psychological maltreatment subtypes presented in Figures 7.1 and 7.2 in abbreviated form, but they also recommended the use of the Individuals with Disabilities Education Act (commonly known as PL 94-142) Severe Emotional Disturbance definitions to assess harm (see 34 Code of Federal Regulations § 300.7 [9]), as well as indicators of the lack of achievement of developmental milestones.

Baily and Baily Definitions

In the mid 1980s, Baily and Baily (1986) embarked on a federally funded project to develop operational definitions of emotional abuse and neglect. The goal of the project was to involve professionals from five states and from a wide variety of occupations that involved child abuse and neglect in responding to nine questionnaires (which were continuously revised) during a 1-year period. The plan was to use the first four questionnaires to develop general statements of parental behaviors of psychological maltreatment, the next four to develop probable child consequences of maltreatment, and the last to evaluate the combined parent/child behaviors to determine whether maltreatment had, indeed, occurred and, if so, the degree of societal response that should result. Descriptions of parental behaviors were developed for the preschool period, ages birth to 5; the latency period, ages 6–12; and the adolescent period, ages 13–17. The questionnaires resulted in 15 developmental clusters or subtypes for the adolescent age group and 16 for the preschool and latency age groups. The authors also asked the participants if emotional maltreatment could be defined by parental behavior alone without consideration of the harm experienced by the child. A majority of 85.3% said yes, 6.7% gave a qualified yes, and 8.0% said no. This was an early indication that standards of care by parents would be preferred over an emphasis on evidence of harm to children in defining psychological maltreatment.

Comprehensive Research Definitions of the 1990s

In the 1990s, two independent research groups created a comprehensive set of theoretically driven definitions of all forms of child abuse and neglect, including psychological maltreatment. Barnett and his colleagues (Barnett et al., 1993) developed the Maltreatment Classification System (MCS) for coding CPS case records. Building on the early work of Giovannoni and Becerra (1979), the authors defined emotional maltreatment as persistent or extreme thwarting of children's basic emotional needs in a persistent manner or to an extreme degree. They included parental acts that were harmful because they were insensitive to the child's developmental level, including the child's psychological safety and security, which included the need for a stable attachment figure and a family environment free of marked hostility and violence. They also included as emotional maltreatment a family environment that fails to provide acceptance and self-esteem with regard to a child's particular level of functioning, with excessive criticism or unrealistic standards. Finally, they included a failure to provide age-appropriate autonomy or the opportunity to explore the environment and engage in relationships outside of the family. This also incorporated as a form of emotional maltreatment a failure to foster the child's individuality while providing structure and boundaries, without developmentally inappropriate responsibility or constraints. Barnett and colleagues' categories for emotional maltreatment included *isolating,* in the form of postconfinement and binding, as well as confining and isolating the child; *role reversals and infantilization* of the child; *rejection or inattention* to the child's need for affection and positive regard; *exposure to marital violence and/or threats to injure, abandon, or kill the child;* and *general verbal aggression or spurning* directed at the child. A separate category labeled *moral/legal/educational maltreatment* included what the APSAC guidelines would call *corrupting and ex-*

ploiting, and Garbarino and colleagues would call *missocializing,* such as modeling or encouraging the child to participate in illegal behavior and truancy. There are separate ratings in the MCS for duration and frequency/chronicity as well as a severity rating based on professional and lay ratings. The age of the child, the number of separations/placements, and the identity of the perpetrator also are coded.

McGee et al. defined psychological maltreatment as "parental communications that could be damaging to the child's development" (1995, p. 249). They grouped *mild psychological maltreatment* to include "indirect communications that represent lapses in adequate parenting" (p. 249). These generally included acts of spurning, such as belittling the child's feelings. Moderate psychological maltreatment referred to "indirect communications regarding the child's worth" (p. 249) and, again, this included a variety of parental behaviors, such as blaming the child, denying the child's reality, placing a child in role reversal, ridiculing the child, exposing the child to criminal influences, being unpredictable in discipline, and threatening other family members, which would include spurning, corrupting/exploiting, and terrorizing. Severe psychological maltreatment was "considered those parental acts that represent direct attacks on the child's sense of self or safety" (p. 249). Such acts included telling the child he or she was unwanted, destroying something the child valued, or threatening to kill or abandon the child, which would fall into the APSAC guidelines as generally terrorizing or spurning. Exposure to family violence was a separate category that included "exposure to physical violence between parents and/or parents and their partners" (p. 249). *Neglect* was defined according to Zuravin's (1991) definition as "acts of omission that deprive the child of fundamental needs" (McGee et al., 1995), with mild neglect "conceptualized as lapses in parenting that could be painful for the child" (p. 249), including not assisting the child with important tasks, not showing respect for the child's opinion, not encouraging peer activities, and not offering comfort, all of which would fall under the APSAC guidelines category of *denying emotional responsiveness* and, possibly, *isolating. Moderate neglect* items were those "acts of omission that put the child at risk for developmental deviation, and concerned parental consistency, and availability" (p. 249). These included failing to provide regular routines and stimulation, failure to ensure attendance at school, or failure to follow through on opportunities to enhance the child's development (e.g., therapy), which would fall under the various APSAC categories of denying emotional responsiveness and mental health/medical/educational neglect. The APSAC guidelines do not do a good job of capturing the provision of regular routines or stimulation included in this definitional framework. The severe neglect category includes those "parental acts of omission that put the child at physical risk for harm" (p. 249), including behaviors traditionally considered to be physically neglectful, such as a *failure to provide protection from dangerous situations* including abusive adults, failure to provide proper medical attention, and lack of supervision.

Clinically Informed Definitions in the 2000s

Glaser (1993, 2002) also has proposed a definition of psychological maltreatment based on a conceptual framework that is informed by clinical practice and treatment. Specifically, she defined psychological or emotional abuse and neglect as follows:

- A relationship between the parent and the child (rather than an event or a series of repeated events occurring within the parent/child relationship);

- The interactions of concern pervade or characterize the relationship (at the time);

- The interactions are actually or potentially harmful by causing impairment to the child's psychological/emotional health and development;

- Emotional abuse and neglect includes omission as well as commission; and

- Emotional abuse and neglect requires no physical contact. (Glaser, 2002, p. 702)

Based on this definition, Glaser included five subtypes:

1) *emotional unavailability, unresponsiveness, and neglect;*

2) *negative attributions and misattributions to the child,* including hostility toward, and denigration and rejection of the child who is perceived as deserving these;

3) *developmentally inappropriate or inconsistent interactions* with the child, including expectations of the child beyond the child's developmental capabilities, over-protection/limitation of exploration and learning, and exposure to confusing or traumatic events or interactions;

4) *failure to recognize or acknowledge the child's individuality and psychological boundary,* including using the child for the parent's psychological needs and an inability to distinguish between the child's reality and the adult's beliefs and wishes, which would include factitious disorder by proxy; and, finally,

5) *failing to promote the child's social adaptation,* including promotion of missocialization and psychological neglect including failure to provide adequate cognitive stimulation and opportunities for experiential learning. (Glaser, 2002, p.702)

Glaser noted that her classification system has clinical and research applicability because her categories address "a different aspect of the child's existence and needs, and is also determined by different motivations and psychological states of the parents in respect to the child" (2002, p. 704). She offers the following criticisms of the APSAC definitions: 1) a single incident may be classified by meeting a number of the categories simultaneously (see also McGee & Wolfe, 1991); 2) they lack a theoretical/conceptual basis; and 3) whereas the examples in each category are quite clear, it is not always obvious why they are included in a particular category (e.g., restricting or interfering with cognitive development is included under *exploiting/corrupting*).

Glaser's (2002) category of *emotional unavailability* clearly corresponds with the APSAC category of *denying emotional responsiveness,* and her category of *negative attributions and misattributions* corresponds with the APSAC category of *spurn-*

ing. The category of *developmentally inappropriate or inconsistent interactions* with the child corresponds to the APSAC categories of *corrupting/exploiting* and *terrorizing.* Glaser's categories of *failure to recognize and acknowledge the child's individuality and psychological boundary* would be placed in *corrupting/exploiting,* while *failing to promote the child's social adaptation* is a combination of *corrupting/exploiting* and *isolating.*

In 2002, the American Academy of Pediatrics produced a technical report on psychological maltreatment and put forth a definition of psychological maltreatment and categories that are identical to those in the APSAC guidelines, with the exception of three categories that they broke out from the six APSAC categories (Kairys, Johnson, & American Academy of Pediatrics Committee on Child Abuse and Neglect, 2002). These three categories are *rejecting (avoiding or pushing away), unreliable or inconsistent parenting (contradictory and ambivalent demands),* and *witnessing intimate partner violence (domestic violence).* The APSAC guidelines include witnessing intimate partner violence under *terrorizing* and, as previously mentioned, divide rejecting into either *spurning* or *denying emotional responsiveness.* The APSAC guidelines do not have a category for unreliable or inconsistent parenting unless the behavior places the child in unpredictable/chaotic circumstances.

Finally, Moran, Bifulco, Ball, Jacobs, and Benaim (2002) generated definitions of psychological abuse as an extension of the Childhood Experience of Care and Abuse Scale (CECA) that Bifulco, Brown, Neubauer, Moran, and Harris (1994) had developed previously. The CECA is a semistructured, investigator-based interview designed to gather retrospective accounts of adverse childhood experiences with adults. The definitions that they generated were gathered through interviews with 301 women drawn from a community sample. Focusing on caregiver behaviors, the authors generated the following definition:

> Psychological abuse is concerned with cruelty demonstrated by verbal and non-verbal acts, repeated or singular, intended or not, from a close other in a position of power or responsibility over the child. These have potential for damaging the social, cognitive, emotional, or physical development of the child and are demonstrated by behaviors, which are humiliating/degrading, terrorizing, extremely rejecting, depriving of basic needs or valued objects, inflicting marked distress/discomfort, corrupting/exploiting, cognitively disorienting, or emotionally blackmailing. Perpetrator behaviors involved in psychological abuse exclude physical or sexual attack, although psychological abuse may accompany these. They also exclude those forms of maltreatment identified as neglect, antipathy, role reversal, high discipline, or lax supervision, as these fall into alternative categories. (Moran et al., 2002, p. 220)

The authors noted that their definition may be controversial in that antipathy, which they describe as "a negative ongoing relationship with the parent where the latter is critical, cold, hostile, or rejecting on a day-to-day basis" (Moran et al., 2002, p. 220), is specifically excluded from their definition. In their opinion, it overlaps with typical family behavior and is rarely relevant for mandated intervention and child protection. Readers will also note, from reviewing Figure 7.1, that their definition excludes all the categories of *denying emotional responsiveness,* the category of parental behaviors that has been empirically associated with the most developmental damage and delay early in life in humans (Egeland, Sroufe, & Erickson, 1983) and other mammals (Glaser, 2000). They also exclude much of what is included in *spurning,* unless it rises to a level of meeting severe rejection. Similarly, *role reversal* is also excluded for the reasons mentioned. The authors specifically "decided to set a high threshold for inclusion of abusive behaviors, relevant to long-term effects, and to psychopathological outcomes, and to differentiate them from those already covered in related scales" (Moran et al., 2002, p. 225). Although intent was not necessary for the determination of psychological abuse, the authors note that "malevolent intent often appeared evident in the detailed descriptions of childhood experiences" (p. 225).

In general, while excluding a number of categories considered essential under other definitions, the definition set forth by Moran and colleagues (2002) makes a contribution by focusing on the most serious examples of psychologically abusive behavior by parents, many of them examples of sadistic behavior resembling hostage taking and psychological torture. This includes *cognitive disorientation,* which Moran and colleagues described as follows:

> A number of techniques aimed at confusing and disorienting a child in terms of: 1) his or her belief in the evidence of his or her senses (e.g., repeatedly telling the child she had misunderstood a command, which had in fact been correctly followed), 2) memory (e.g., enforcing a belief that the child could not recall valued experiences in the past), or 3) sense of identity (e.g., convincing the child that a biological parent was not the child's parent or that a separated parent was dead). In extreme instances, strategies akin to brainwashing are utilized. (p. 227)

In reviewing the definitions included in Table 7.1, it quickly becomes clear that although authors use different descriptions of subcategories of psychological maltreatment, the actual content is remarkably similar. The greatest agreement across definitions lies in the constructs of *belittling; singling out; public humiliation; placing in an unpredictable or chaotic environment; threatening a child and/or his or her loved one(s); modeling or permitting antisocial and developmentally inappropriate behavior;* and *failing to show affection, caring, and love.* These constructs are included in and labeled as psychological maltreatment in most definitions. There was the least agreement with regard to the category of *placing children in recognizably dangerous situations,* which was typically categorized as neglect, not psychological maltreatment. The category of *mental health, medical, and educational neglect* was omitted from many definitions.

Several constructs appeared in one or more definitional systems but not in the APSAC definition. *Deliberately withholding food, water, light, and access to the toilet* in order to create distress and/or discomfort was included in the NIS-3 (Sedlak & Broadhurst, 1996) and Moran et al. (2002) definitions and in two of the instruments reviewed. *Lack of protection of the child from abusive adults* was included in the McGee and Wolfe (1991) definition and in two of the instruments: the Child Well-Being Scales (CWBS; Magura & Moses, 1986) and the Multidimensional Neglectful Behavior Scale, Form A: Adolescent and Adult–Recall Version (Straus, Kinard, & Williams, 2001).

In creating Table 7.1, the most difficulty was with the APSAC subcategories 3 and 4 of *exploiting/corrupting* and subcategories 1 and 2 of *denying emotional responsiveness*. Subcategory 3 of *exploiting/corrupting* —restricting/ undermining psychological autonomy—reads in full in the APSAC definition as "encouraging or coercing abandonment of developmentally appropriate autonomy through extreme overinvolvement, intrusiveness, and/or dominance (e.g., allowing little or no opportunity or support for the child's views, feelings, and wishes; micromanaging the child's life)" (1995, p. 7). McGee et al. (1995) included *denying a child's reality* in their definition, and Moran et al. (2002) included a category called *cognitive disorientation*. It was difficult determining whether these two constructs fit into subcategory 3 as they seemed to suggest something more, such as a deliberate and, possibly, sadistic attempt to distort how a child perceives the world. Similarly, Baily and Baily (1986) included an item on confusing a child's sexual identity, and Glaser (2002) had a category titled "failure to recognize a child's psychological boundary" under which she included factitious disorder by proxy. Although all of these constructs seem related to subcategory 3 of APSAC's *exploiting/corrupting* category, they describe parental behaviors that seem to go further in degree or severity than the behaviors encompassed by the APSAC subcategory (e.g., trying to remake a child as another gender, attempting to fundamentally distort how a child sees the world and/or him- or herself, deliberately making a child ill or labeling a child as ill when he or she is not). This suggests that subcategory 3 of the *exploiting/corrupting* category could be further expanded.

Subcategory 4 of APSAC's *exploiting/corrupting* category —restricting/interfering with cognitive development—also was problematic. This category can be construed as a very broad category that ranges from not allowing a child to go to school to aspects of neglect, such as not reading to a child or extreme deprivation of intellectual stimulation. It might also cover the *lack of provision of regular routines,* a category McGee et al. (1995) included under neglect. This important construct is not adequately covered by the APSAC definition or, for that matter, by any of the other definitions. One of the first tasks that an infant–parent dyad faces is to help the child become physiologically and, thus, psychologically, regulated through the provision of regular routines for eating, sleeping, and social interaction (Greenspan, DeGangi, & Wieder, 2001). Such regulation facilitates an integration of mental states and a sense of self (Putnam, 1993) and makes an infant available for social and cognitive interaction with his or her caregiver, thus shaping neural development (Schore, 1994). Denying a child regular routines could be construed as consisting of both psychological maltreatment and physical neglect.

Denying emotional responsiveness subcategory 1—parent detached/uninvolved due to incapacity or lack of motivation—and subcategory 2—interacting only when necessary—originally were designed to capture the characteristics of Egeland, Sroufe, and Erickson's (1983) psychologically unavailable caregivers, who provided competent physical care and a structured environment but were often mechanistic in their ministrations. Most systems captured some aspect of such detached interactions, usually subcategory 3—failing to show affection, caring, love—but lacked a more nuanced description, making it hard to code the other subcategories of this type of psychological maltreatment.

Finally, the *exploiting/corrupting* subcategory 1—modeling, permitting, or encouraging antisocial behavior—raised an unanticipated challenge. Could this category be scored if a caregiver engaged in any form of maltreatment? Social learning theory highlights the role of modeling in the social development of children (Patterson, 1982). Parents are the first models of social behavior that children are exposed to and continue to provide a point of reference for children throughout life. Further, research related to the intergenerational transmission of abuse (Egeland, Jacobvitz, & Sroufe, 1988; Kaufman & Zigler, 1989) has documented that individuals who are maltreated as children are more likely than those not maltreated to abuse their own children, suggesting that these individuals have learned this behavior. Given this evidence, it seems that when parents maltreat their children in any form, they may be both actively affecting their children's psychological and/or physical well-being and passively teaching them more global lessons about interacting in relationships and existing in society. These lessons guide the development of the children and, without the influence of forces that counteract their impact, may influence their social competence and quality of life indefinitely. This is clearly an issue that cannot be reconciled without further exploration and debate, particularly as it relates to the development of definitions; however, the issue seemed worthy of comment in the current discussion.

MEASURES OF SUSPECTED PSYCHOLOGICAL MALTREATMENT OF CHILDREN AND ADOLESCENTS

Figure 7.2 presents prospective or concurrent measures for use with children and adolescents suspected of being psychologically maltreated. The authors of this chapter went to great lengths to obtain every extant measure of psychological maltreatment as well as measures of child maltreatment that included psychological maltreatment, emotional abuse, or emotional neglect as part of the instrument. This was done through a search of the PsycINFO, Medline, and Mental Measurements Yearbook databases and Columbia University library holdings; by checking reference lists of every measure and article in the authors' personal libraries on psychological maltreatment; and by communicating with authors of resources on psychological maltreatment. The following criteria were set for inclusion of measures in the figure: 1) the measures are not retrospective, meaning they are intended for use with children and adolescents to assess current abuse experiences; 2) the measures provide significant coverage of psychological mal treatment, meaning that they have several items tapping this form of maltreatment; 3) reliability and validity data are available; and 4) items are based on reports and/or observations of parental behaviors rather than subjective judgments of being abused.

As can be seen in Figure 7.2, the five observational measures focus primarily on the infant, toddler, and early school-age groups, with only two of the measures extending into adolescence. This probably is due to the fact that younger children are very dependent on their caregivers and cannot reliably report on their experiences, leaving researchers and clinicians in need of an independent source of data other than parent report. The CARE-Index (Crittenden, 2001) is for infants and toddlers. The PMRS (Brassard, et al., 1993) and the Childhood Level of Living Scale (CLL; Polansky, Chalmers, Buttenweiser, & Williams, 1981) are for preschool and early school-age children, and the CWBS (Magura & Moses, 1986) and the Home Observation for Measurement of the Environment (HOME; Caldwell & Bradley, 1984) are for children ranging in age from infancy to adolescence. In addition to the wide age range, with an emphasis on infancy through the preschool years, the observational measures vary a great deal in terms of the aspects of psychological maltreatment on which they focus. Similar to the definitions in Figure 7.1, the measures in Figure 7.2 are organized as to the presence or absence of items that assess each subcomponent of the definitions used in the APSAC guidelines. Most of the measures do a good job of assessing direct verbal attacks and threats, restricting/interfering with cognitive development, and failing to show involvement, affection, caring, and love. The CWBS is the most comprehensive measure and has acceptable psychometric characteristics. The HOME is particularly good at assessing neglect and cognitive neglect but does a good job of assessing verbal assaults as well. Its combination of observation and interview techniques offers some of the advantages of both formats. The CLL is the most restricted in content, and some items are now dated and culturally circumscribed based on the authors' review of item content (e.g., a prayer is said before some meals, mother expresses pride in daughter's femininity or son's masculinity).

In terms of the self-report measures, four have been developed by Straus and his colleagues at the Family Research Laboratory at the University of New Hampshire for telephone interviews: the Conflict Tactics Scales (CTS; Straus, 1979), The Parent–Child Conflict Tactics Scales (CTSPC; Straus, Hamby, Finkelhor, Moore, & Runyan, 1998), the Multidimensional Neglectful Behavior Scale, Form A: Adolescent and Adult–Recall Version (Straus et al., 2001), and the Picture-Card Version for Young Children of the Parent-to-Child Conflict Tactics Scales (Merbert & Straus, 2002). These are screening measures developed for parent report and then modified for use with children and adolescents. Straus's initial interest was physical abuse, and he developed a highly successful strategy of asking parents about how they resolved conflicts with their children or their spouses, focusing on physical aggression. The parenting and psychological aggression items were designed to lead parents into questions about using physi-

Table comparing measures of psychological maltreatment (APSAC categories) across assessment tool types.

APSAC categories	Subcategories of parental/caregiver behavior toward child	Interview — Herrenkohl (child/adolescent) Herrenkohl, Herrenkohl, and Egolf (1991); Herrenkohl, Herrenkohl, and Toedter (1982)	Rating Scales — ROME (birth to 16 years) Wolfe and McGee (1994); McGee, Wolfe, and Wilson (1990)	Rating Scales — Ontario CNI (child/adolescent) Trocme (1992, 1996)	Record Rev. — MCS (child/adolescent) Barnett, Manly, and Cicchetti (1993)	Record Rev. — Child Maltreatment Log (< 18 years) Sternberg, Knutson, Lamb, Baradaran, Nolan, and Flanzer (2004)	Self-Report — PARQ (7–12 years) Rohner, Saavedra, and Granum (1978)	Self-Report — Picture Card Version of CTS (6–9 years) Merbert and Straus (2002)	Self-Report — CTSPC (child/adolescent) Straus, Hamby, Finkelhor, Moore, and Runyan (1998)	Self-Report — CTS (adult version, used with children) Straus (1979); Straus and Hamby (1997)	Self-Report — Multidimensional Neglectful Behavior Scale (6 years to adult) Straus, Kinard, and Williams (2001)	Observational — CWBS (families with children) Magura and Moses (1986)	Observational — CLL (4–7 years) Polansky, Chambers, Buttenweiser, and Williams (1981)	Observational — HOME (birth to 15 years) Caldwell and Bradley (1984)	Observational — PMRS (3–8 years) Brassard, Hart, and Hardy (1993)	Observational — CARE-Index (birth to 24 months) Crittenden (2001)
Spurning	Belittling, denigrating, or other rejecting	✓	✓		✓	✓	✓	✓	✓	✓		✓		✓	✓	✓
	Ridiculing for showing normal emotions											✓		✓	✓	✓
	Singling out	✓	✓		✓		✓				P	✓				
	Humiliating in public	✓	✓	?			✓									
Terrorizing	Placing in unpredictable/chaotic circumstances		✓	✓	✓	✓						✓				
	Placing in recognizably dangerous situations		✓		✓	✓						✓	✓	✓		
	Having rigid/unrealistic expectations accompanied by threats if not met		✓									✓			✓	
	Threatening/perpetrating violence against child	✓	✓		✓		✓	✓		✓	P			?	✓	✓
	Threatening/perpetrating violence against child's loved ones/objects—includes exposure to domestic violence	✓	✓		✓	✓	✓					✓				

170

Figure 7.2. Measures of psychological maltreatment organized by APSAC definitions for suspected psychological maltreatment. (*Key:* P = parent version; ✓ = covered by measure; ? = not conclusive/partially covered.)

Category	Item
Isolating	Confining within environment
	Restricting social interactions in community
Exploiting/corrupting	Modeling, permitting, or encouraging antisocial behavior
	Modeling, permitting, or encouraging developmentally inappropriate behavior
	Restricting/undermining psychological autonomy
	Restricting/interfering with cognitive development
Denying emotional responsiveness	Being detached/uninvolved from child due to parent's incapacity or lack of motivation
	Interacting only when necessary
	Failing to show affection, caring, love
Mental health/medical/educational neglect	Parent/caregiver ignores or refuses to allow/provide treatment for child's . . .
	. . . serious emotional/behavior problems/needs
	. . . serious physical health problems/needs
	. . . serious educational problems/needs

cally abusive behaviors as conflict resolution strategies. As such, there was never an attempt to be comprehensive in assessing psychological abuse, and the telephone interview format of data collection placed strict limits on the number of items that could be used. The fifth self-report measure, the Parental Acceptance-Rejection Questionnaire (PARQ), was developed by Rohner, Saavedra, and Granum (1978) for cross-cultural research on parental rejection. The PARQ, which has both parent and child report forms, assesses children's experiences of being hostilely rejected, ignored, or accepted by their parents; it includes both descriptions of specific parental behaviors that cover a number of categories in the APSAC guidelines and evaluative statements about the parent–child relationship. Clearly, there is considerably more work that can be done with parent, self-, and collateral report measures in terms of making them more comprehensive and behaviorally descriptive. However, this format is an efficient way of screening for and identifying problematic, if not abusive, parent–child relationships. Adult self-report measures exist that are good models for further work in this area (e.g., the Childhood Maltreatment Questionnaire; Demaré, 1995).

In terms of record reviews, the MCS (Barnett et al., 1993) has the field to itself. Barnett and his colleagues have developed this widely used system for classifying parental behavior using CPS records. Although the MCS inherently assumes all the strengths (e.g., multiple sources of information and social validity) and weaknesses (e.g., much maltreatment goes unreported, maltreatment by noncaregivers is not included) of those records, it is nonetheless a reliable and comprehensive system that includes not only psychological maltreatment but also other forms of child abuse and neglect as well.

The Child Maltreatment Log, developed in 2004 by Sternberg and colleagues (2004), also was classified as a record review, although it is really a system of cataloguing all known maltreatment experiences derived from any source of information. It does a very extensive job of requesting information on children's witnessing of family violence and modeling, permitting, or encouraging antisocial behavior, but it does not address issues of denying emotional responsiveness, restricting/undermining psychological autonomy, restricting/interfering with cognitive development, restricting social interactions in community, or scapegoating.

In the area of social worker ratings (based on case records and the social worker's knowledge of the case), the Record of Maltreatment Experiences (ROME; McGee et al., 1995) is a comprehensive measure that would easily lend itself to a parent report measure for all ages and a child report measure for latency age and adolescent children. The ROME assesses psychological maltreatment, constructive parenting practices, exposure to family violence, sexual abuse, and physical abuse for three age ranges: birth to 6 years, 7–12 years, and 13–16 years. This measure also collects information on the perpetrator as well as on the severity and frequency of maltreatment at these three age levels.

The Ontario Child Neglect Index (CNI; Trocme, 1992, 1996) is a one-page rating scale designed to help child welfare workers and researchers gather information regarding the type and severity of neglect experienced by children. Ratings of severity are made on six scales: Supervision, Physical Care (Food/Nutrition, Clothing, and Hygiene), Provision of Health Care (Physical Health Care, Mental Health Care, Developmental, and Educational Health Care). The Provision of Health Care scale provides thorough coverage of the areas addressed under APSAC's *mental health/medical/educational neglect* category and the Supervision scale covers subcategory 2 of terrorizing. Other acts that could be considered psychological neglect, such as those falling under APSAC's *isolating* category, are not included in this rating scale.

Finally, only one interview could be identified, developed by Herrenkohl and his colleagues (Herrenkohl, Herrenkohl, & Toedter, 1982; Herrenkohl, Herrenkohl, & Egolf, 1991). This measure was used to gather more detailed information about parental disciplinary practices used in families whose cases were already substantiated by CPS. This interview covers quite a few, but not all areas, of the APSAC definition. Interviews are an underdeveloped format for assessing child maltreatment. Structured interviews have been successfully developed to assess psychopathology (e.g., Diagnostic Interview Schedule for Children-IV [DISC-IV]; Shaffer, Fisher, Lucas, Dulcan, & Schwab-Stone, 2000) through child and parent report, and Moran and colleagues (2002) have developed a semistructured interview to retrospectively assess adults' adverse childhood experiences. A promising format for a comprehensive interview of maltreatment experiences is the model set forth by the Childhood Disorders Version of the Structured Clinical Interview for DSM-IV Childhood Diagnoses, or the KID-SCID (Hien et al., 1999). This measure is designed to be used as an interview but with a coding system based on the investigator's assessment of all known information. Such a system would permit the assessor to gather detailed information in a format that allows for probing that cannot be done in questionnaires, and incorporation of all available information, yet it still provides some structure to ensure that evaluations are comprehensive.

In summary, a review of existing measures of suspected psychological maltreatment reveals several strengths and limitations. In general, most measures do a fairly good job of assessing more commonly recognized forms of psychological maltreatment such as belittling, denigrating, and other forms of active rejection; threatening/perpetrating violence against a child or a child's loved ones/objects; modeling, permitting, or encouraging antisocial behavior; and failing to show affection, caring, and/or love. However, when it comes to more nuanced subtypes there is greater variation in coverage, as would be expected. Observational scales appear to be the most adept at gathering information about the subtypes of each general subtype of maltreatment; rating scales and record review procedures also seem to do a good job of this. Self-report measures are especially lacking with regard to capturing the gradations within general subtype; this is likely due to the small number of items included in the majority of the self-report measures (e.g., the CTS by Straus & Hamby, 1997). Another reason for the variance in assessment of subtypes may be the lack of agreement on a set of subtypes to assess, which could lead to the inconsistent coverage seen across these measures.

Research on psychological maltreatment is best facilitated by gathering information from multiple sources using multiple methods and measures with demonstrated reliability and validity. This allows researchers to create and evaluate the validity of latent constructs of definitional subtypes. Subtypes that emerge from this process are likely to be replicable across time. As can be seen from the review of measures, there is already a strong foundation of instruments available for conducting this type of research. With further refinement of existing measures and development of new ones that address current weaknesses, future definitional and research efforts will become increasingly construct valid, which will lead to greater clarity in theoretical and clinical work.

EMPIRICAL EVIDENCE FOR THE EFFECTS OF PSYCHOLOGICAL MALTREATMENT SUBTYPES

Although agreement among researchers, mental health professionals, and the lay public about what constitutes psychological maltreatment provides essential social validation for definitions, the ultimate standard is empirical evidence that a parenting practice as employed in most contexts results in unacceptable harm to a child. The goal for the present review is to begin to bring together the evidence of actual harm to a child that exists in relation to each subtype of psychological maltreatment, by age or developmental period, if known. In order to identify research studies to include in this review, a search was conducted on PsycINFO using the following search terms: *psychological maltreatment, emotional abuse, psychological abuse, emotional maltreatment, emotional neglect, psychological neglect,* and *verbal abuse.* Additional studies were identified from citation lists of selected articles or chosen by the authors based on their knowledge of the literature. Due to the large number of citations compiled, the group of studies reviewed was limited to those that utilized child/adolescent samples and were published in peer-reviewed journals or books. Several articles could not be obtained due to their publication in journals that were difficult to locate (e.g., *The Arab Journal of Psychiatry*). Further, there are many relevant studies that exist in related research literatures (e.g., see Repetti, Taylor, & Seeman, 2002) for a review of research examining suboptimal family environments); however, due to space and time constraints, such a thorough review was not possible.

Table 7.1 presents a list of empirical studies that provide evidence of the harmfulness of psychological maltreatment as well as information regarding the age groups of the children that were studied, whether a community or clinical sample was used, the source of the data, the method that was used to obtain the data, the subtypes of psychological maltreatment that were measured, and the outcomes that were documented. When constructing this table, the authors of this chapter chose to use several broad categories to represent the major outcome domains that have been evaluated in the literature. The rationale was that this would be an effective method for summarizing the extant literature in a way that would identify gaps in research and allow conclusions to be drawn regarding the degree of evidence that exists for the harmfulness of each subtype of psychological maltreatment.

The *cognitive/achievement* domain encompasses outcomes related to intelligence or cognitive problems (e.g., declines in IQ score seen with lack of emotional responsiveness in early childhood, attentional problems, learning problems) and outcomes related to academic achievement (e.g., poor academic achievement). The *internalizing* domain includes problems that are related to the overcontrol of negative emotions, which, when turned inward, result in psychologically distressing symptoms such as anxious or depressive symtomatology, low self-esteem, and a negative view of self or the world. The *externalizing* domain includes outcomes representative of the undercontrol of negative emotions, which may be expressed in the form of behaviors such as aggression and delinquency. The *medical* domain was used to represent outcomes related to physical health, such as illnesses, somatic complaints, and growth problems. Last, the *social* domain encompasses relational problems, such as poor social competence and interpersonal difficulties. In certain cases, the authors chose to report the major outcome found to be associated with the psychological maltreatment, as particular outcomes (e.g., suicide attempts) were felt to carry more gravity than could be represented by any one of the categories or were difficult to categorize effectively (e.g., substance use, dissociative symptoms, personality disorder symptoms/diagnosis).

A great deal of work has been accomplished to date in the area of documenting the negative outcomes frequently associated with psychological abuse and neglect or similar parental behavior at less severe levels (see Rohner & Nielsen, 1978, for an extensive and exhaustive review and annotated bibliography as of more than 25 years ago; see Bingelli et al., 2001, for a review as of 5 years ago). Given the amount of information covered, Table 7.1 does not capture the quality of the research designs used or the nuances and power of the findings. To assist the reader in making sense of the findings, the following sections will briefly integrate the findings by age of the child.

Birth to 2 Years

Infants and toddlers with psychologically unavailable caregivers show remarkable drops in developmental quotients even when receiving adequate physical care, despite being assessed as competent infants at birth and in the first months of life (Egeland et al., 1983; Kaler & Freeman, 1994; Spitz, 1945; see Bowlby, 1966, for a review of early findings). Both psychologically unavailable care and

Table 7.1. Empirical evidence for the effects of psychological maltreatment

Child/adolescent samples	Age group(s)[a]			Sample[b]		Source[c]			Method[d]				Subtypes of psychological maltreatment (PM)[e]						Outcomes[f]				
	1	2	3	Com	Clin	S	P	O	Q	I	O	R	1	2	3	4	5	6	Cog/ ach.	Int.	Ext.	Med.	Soc.
Brassard, Hart, and Hardy (1993); Hart and Brassard (1990)	X	X		X	X	X		X	X		X	X	X	X	X	X	X	X	X				X
Brody, Ge, Kim, Simons, Gibbons, et al. (2003)	X	X		X			X		X				X	X			?				X		
Brown (1984)	X		X	X		X			X				X			X	X				X		
Brunner, Parzer, Schuld, and Resch (2000)			X		X		X	X	X			X	X				X			Dissociative symptoms			
Campo and Rohner (1992)			X+	X	X	X			X			X	X				X					Substance use	
Chang, Schwartz, Dodge, and McBride-Chang (2003)	X			X			X		X			X	X	X		X					X		
Claussen and Crittenden (1991)	X			X	X	X			X	X	X	X	X	X	X	X	X	X	Level of treatment required				
Crittenden, Claussen, and Sugarman (1994)		X			X	X	X		X	X	X	X	X	X	X	X	X		X	X	X		
Dance, Rushton, and Quinton (2002)		X			X	X	X		X		X		X						X	X	X		X
Dubowitz, Papas, Black, and Starr (2002)	X			X		X	X				X	X	X				X			X	X		
Dykeman (2003)		X			X	X			X				X	X							X		
Egeland, Sroufe, and Erickson (1983)	X			X			X	X		X	X		X				X			X	X		
Egeland, Yates, Appleyard, and van Dulmen (2002)	X	X	X	X	X	X		X			X	X	X				X		?		Ext. but not with PA in model	X	
Eron (1982)	X	X		X		X			X				?								X		
Fleming, Jory, and Burton (2002)			X	X	X	X			X				X								X		

Study																	
Glueck and Glueck (1950); Sampson and Laub (1993) (analyses of same data set)	X	X	X	X	X	X	X	X	X	X	X	X	X	X	X	X	X
Herrenkohl, Herrenkohl, Toedter, and Yanushefski (1984)	X	X	X	X	X	X	X	X	X								X
Herrenkohl, Egolf, and Herrenkohl (1997)	X	X	X	X	X	X	X						X				
Herrenkohl, Herrenkohl, Egolf, and Wu (1991)	X	X	X	X	X	X	X	X	X	X	X	X	X	X	X	X	X
Higgins and McCabe 2003): Study 1	X	X	X		X	X	X	X	X		X[g]			
Higgins and McCabe (1998)	X	X	X	X	X	X	X	X	X	X	X	X	X		
Johnson, Cohen, Smailes, et al. (2001)	X	X	X	X[h]	X	X	X		Personality disorder symptoms/diagnosis				
Johnson, Smailes, Cohen, Brown, and Bernstein (2000)	X	X	X	X	X	X	X	X	X	X	X	X	Personality disorder symptoms/diagnosis				
Johnson, Cohen, Gould, Kasen, Brown, and Brook (2002)	X	X	X		X	X	X	X				X	X
Kaufman (1991)	X		X	X	X	X	X	X	X				X
Kim, Ge, Brody, Conger, and Gibbons (2003)	X	X	X	X	X	X				X	X
Kingree, Phan, and Thompson (2003)	X	X	X	X	X	X	X	X			X
Krugman and Krugman (1984)	X	X	X	X	X	X					X	X
Lavoie, Tremblay, Vitaro, Vezina, and McDuff (2002)	X	X	X	X	X	X	X				X	X

(continued)

Table **7.1.** (continued)

Child/adolescent samples	Age group(s)[a]			Sample[b]		Source[c]			Method[d]				Subtypes of psychological maltreatment (PM)[e]						Outcomes[f]				
	1	2	3	Com	Clin	S	P	O	Q	I	O	R	1	2	3	4	5	6	Cog/ach.	Int.	Ext.	Med.	Soc.
Lipschitz, Winegar, Nicolau, Hartnick, Wolfson, and Southwick (1999)			X		X	X			X	X			X	X			X			Suicidal behaviors			
Litrownik, Newton, Hunter, English, and Everson (2003)	X			X			X		X				X	X			X			X	X		
Lochner, du Toit, Zungu-Dirwayi, Marais, Vandrdenburg, Curr, et al. (2002)			X+	X	X	X			X				X	X			X			X			
Lyon, Benoit, O'Donnell, Getson, Silber, and Walsh (2000)		X	X	X				X	X					X			X			Suicide attempt			
MacKinnon-Lewis, Starnes, Volling, and Johnson (1997)		X		X				X			X		X	X			?				X		X
Magee (1999)			X+	X		X			X				X	X			?						X Phobia
Manly, Kim, Rogosch, and Cicchetti (2001)		X		X				X				X	X	X	X	X	X	X		X	X		
Maughan, Pickles, and Quinton (1995)		X	X+	X		X	X	X	X	X		X	X	X	?	?	X	X	Work		X		X
McCord and McCord (1959); McCord (1983)		X	X	X		X	X					X	X	?	?						X		
McGee, Wolfe, Yuen, Wilson, and Carnohan (1995)			X	X		X	X	X	X			X	X	X	X					X	X		
Miller and Baruch (1948)	X	X	X		X	X	X		X	X			X				X					X	
Moore and Pepler (1998)		X	X	X	X	X	X		X		X		X	X			X			X	X		

Moran, Vuchinich, and Hall (2004)

Ney, Fung, and Wickett (1994)

Olivan (2003)

Ringwalt, Greene, and Robertson (1998)

Rohner (1975); Rohner and Rohner (1980)

Solomon and Serres (1999)

Spillane-Grieco (2000)

Spitz (1945)

Thompson and Kaplan (1999)

Vissing, Straus, Gelles, and Harrop (1991)

Wolfe and McGee (1994)

Note: A question mark indicates not conclusive/partially covered.

[a] Age group(s): 1, = birth to 5 years; 2 = 6–12 years; 3 = adolescent (X+ indicates that adult subjects were included).

[b] Sample: Com, community; Clin, clinical.

[c] Source of information used to assess psychological maltreatment: S, self; P, parent; O, other (e.g., case worker).

[d] Method used to identify psychological maltreatment: Q, questionnaire; I, interview; O, observation; R, record review (includes substantiated cases).

[e] Subtypes of psychological maltreatment: 1, spurning; 2, terrorizing; 3, isolating; 4, exploiting/corrupting; 5, denying emotional responsiveness; 6, mental health/medical/educational neglect.

[f] Outcome labels: Cog./ach., cognitive/achievement; Int., Internalizing; Ext., externalizing; Med., medical; Soc., social.

[g] No unique predictors were found, but psychological maltreatment was significant in combination with other forms of abuse/neglect.

[h] Self-report data were collected only during third wave of study.

179

harsh/verbally abusive parenting are related to attachment insecurity and/or disorganization at 12 and 18 months (Egeland & Erickson, 1987; Lyons-Ruth, Connell, & Zoll, 1989) as well as significant internalizing and externalizing problems that are not present in children who have been solely physically neglected (Dubowitz, Papas, Black, & Starr, 2002). Emotional maltreatment in infancy and toddlerhood, as classified by the MCS, is related to externalizing behaviors, behavioral ratings of aggression, and lower ego resiliency (Manly, Kim, Rogosch, & Cicchetti, 2001). Although not listed in Table 7.1, experimental studies confirm profound social and emotional problems in nonhuman primates separated from, or emotionally neglected by their mothers at early and critical stages of development (Harlow & Harlow, 1971; Sackett, 1965; Suomi, Eisele, & Grady, 1975).

Preschool-Age

By preschool, children with a psychologically unavailable caregiver look worse (i.e., exhibit more psychopathological behaviors based on teacher/caregiver ratings) than other high-risk controls, as do children with physically abusive, physically neglectful, or hostile/verbally aggressive caregivers. They, along with other children who have been maltreated, are significantly more noncompliant, avoidant, and negative in affect with the caregiver and less persistent and enthusiastic in learning (Egeland & Erickson, 1987; Pianta, Egeland, & Erickson, 1989). Studies that have included measures of physical abuse and neglect (Claussen & Crittenden, 1991; Herrenkohl & Russo, 2001) and witnessing marital violence (Litrownik, Newton, Hunter, English, & Everson, 2003) have found verbal aggression or a combination of psychological abuse and neglect to be more predictive of adjustment and/or treatment needs than these other forms of maltreatment. The children who have experienced verbal aggression from a caregiver or the combination of psychological abuse and neglect display significant levels of internalizing and externalizing symptoms. Manly et al. (2001) found that emotional maltreatment (as classified by the MCS) was related to ratings of aggression and peer reports of fighting in preschool.

Middle Childhood/Middle Childhood and Adolescence

Studies using middle childhood or middle childhood and adolescent samples from clinical maltreatment samples (e.g., CPS, battered women's shelters, foster care), community samples, or both, found that psychological abuse or psychological maltreatment (after controlling for the other forms of maltreatment and demographic factors) uniquely predicted a series of negative outcomes including social-emotional problems (Crittenden et al., 1994; Herrenkohl, Herrenkohl, Egolf, & Wu, 1991) and not having friends at school (Hart & Brassard, 1991). Psychological abuse in the form of spurning, threatening, and/or verbal aggression has been found to predict interpersonal problems (Vissing, Straus, Gelles, & Harrop, 1991), negative response to treatment in foster care (Dance, Rushton, & Quinton, 2002), poor behavioral adjustment (Moore & Pepler, 1998), and delinquency/aggression (Eron, 1982; Vissing et al., 1991). Harsh parenting and hostility that combined mild physical punishment with psychological harshness, rejection, inconsistency, and uninvolved, nonnurturant parenting also showed strong relationships with conduct problems (Brody et al., 2003; Kim, Ge, Brody, Conger, & Gibbons, 2003), depression (Kim et al., 2003), and sibling and peer aggression and low peer acceptance (MacKinnon-Lewis, Starnes, Volling, & Johnson, 1997). Similarly, a study of a sample of children who had been maltreated and who were recruited for a week-long summer camp (Kaufman, 1991) found that those who met criteria for a formal diagnosis of depression had significantly higher physical abuse, emotional maltreatment (primarily psychological unavailability), and out-of-home placement severity scores than those who did not meet criteria. Degree of physical neglect and sexual abuse did not distinguish depressed from nondepressed children.

In longitudinal studies of disadvantaged high-risk families and community two-parent families, Maughan, Pickles, and Quinton (1995) established that maternal hostility in childhood (based on interview of mother and observation-based ratings of hostile and rejecting behavior) predicted contemporaneous teacher-rated behavior problems, diagnosed conduct disorders (established from parental interview), and poor adult adjustment (poor social functioning, problems at work, criminal history), whereas living in a family under stress from parental psychiatric disorders (including personality disorders and alcoholism) did not. With maternal hostility in the statistical model, parental psychiatric disorder, maternal lack of warmth, marital discord, and paternal hostility were not significant in predicting childhood conduct problems or continuity of problems into adulthood. Only parental criminality added to the prediction. Fifty percent of children, male and female, with hostile mothers in both the high-risk and the community samples had childhood conduct problems. The best-fitting model suggested that maternal hostility led to the development of conduct problems and, in turn, the presence of conduct problems in childhood predicted poor adult functioning. Holmes and Robins (1987) report similar findings for depression: Unfair, inconsistent punishments predicted depressive disorders independent of parental psychiatric disorder.

In two studies, psychological maltreatment was related to externalizing problems, but physical abuse and physical neglect were stronger predictors. Egeland, Yates, Appleyard, and van Dulman (2002) compared two groups of children identified as having been maltreated in the first 5 years of life on measures of conduct problems: those who were physically abused and those having a psychologically unavailable caregiver. Both groups had elevated rates of externalizing behavior in early elementary school, but only physical abuse predicted conduct disorder in adolescence. Using a comprehensive measure of psychological maltreatment, Higgins and McCabe (1998) found physical neglect to be a better predictor of externalizing problems than of psychological maltreatment.

Finally, verbal abuse appeared in 7 of the top 10 worst combinations of maltreatment, in terms of outcome, for a clinical sample of children and adolescents who reported experiencing verbal abuse when reporting on and evaluating their own maltreatment experiences and rating their feelings of enjoyment in life and their future expectations (Ney, Fung, & Wickett, 1994). Verbal aggression also was found to be related to poorer academic achievement, lower self-worth, and perceptions of oneself as less socially accepted, academically competent, and well-behaved in a study of Canadian fifth graders who responded to a questionnaire assessing only this form of maltreatment (Solomon & Serres, 1999).

Adolescence/Young Adulthood

Evidence for the effects of psychological maltreatment during adolescence is provided by many studies, both longitudinal and cross-sectional in design. Across studies utilizing adolescent samples, it appears that the most detrimental forms of psychological maltreatment are emotional neglect alone and emotional neglect in combination with verbal abuse (usually spurning and terrorizing in nature). The great majority of these studies assessed several forms of abuse and/or neglect, finding that psychological maltreatment made a unique contribution to problematic outcomes, even in the presence of other types of maltreatment.

Brunner, Parzer, Schuld, and Resch (2000) found emotional neglect to be the best predictor of dissociative symptoms of three forms of maltreatment; however, their category of emotional and psychological neglect included spurning acts as well and thus may not represent solely the effects of emotional neglect. In studies of several forms of maltreatment—including emotional neglect—focusing on individuals who have attempted suicide (Lipschitz et al., 1999; Lyon et al., 2000) and psychopathology (Lochner et al., 2002), emotional neglect emerged as a significant predictor of suicide attempts (along with threats of separation from parents in Lyon et al., 2000), and occurred at significantly greater levels among participants diagnosed with obsessive-compulsive disorder and trichotillomania. In this latter study, emotional neglect, and not psychological abuse, was associated with the disorders examined.

When assessing other forms of maltreatment including sexual and physical abuse, and, in some cases, exposure to family violence, several studies have found that both emotional abuse and neglect are predictors of negative outcomes. Brown (1984) found that emotional abuse (assessed with a scale that included both spurning and denying emotional responsiveness items) was significantly related to delinquency in adolescents, whereas physical abuse was not. Results of a study of sex offenders in which the offenses were perpetrated against animals and humans (Fleming, Jory, & Burton, 2002) indicated that those adolescents who had committed sex offenses against animals experienced higher levels of emotional abuse and neglect than those who committed sex offenses against humans (there were no differences among the two groups for other forms of abuse); sex offenders also were more likely to come from families with more conflictual relationships and styles of communicating, including behaviors that would be considered spurning, such as yelling and screaming. Wolfe and McGee (1994) assessed five forms of abuse and neglect using the ROME, finding that both psychological abuse and neglect (defined as the absence of constructive parenting) were predictive of general adjustment problems in adolescent boys and girls, especially when there was an increase or stable high level over time.

Verbal abuse alone has been identified as a predictor of social phobia (Magee, 1999); a factor that increases odds of alcohol and tobacco use (Moran, Vuchinich, & Hall, 2004); and a predictor of delinquency, aggression, interpersonal problems (Vissing et al., 1991), and dating violence (Lavoie et al., 2002; using a measure that assessed harsh parenting, including one item on physical aggression). However, although all of these studies measured exposure to physical violence, with one assessing sexual abuse as well (i.e., Moran et al., 2004), none assessed emotional neglect, which leaves open the possibility that this was a factor driving results.

A few studies of adolescents have examined parental rejection, assessing both a lack of warmth and nurturance (e.g., denying emotional responsiveness) and, in some cases, the presence of parental hostility (e.g., spurning, terrorizing). None of these studies, however, accounted for the effects of other forms of maltreatment, either because they did not assess other forms or because they did not systematically look at these effects. Using the PARQ, Campo and Rohner (1992) found that parental rejection predicted substance use among adolescents and young adults in their sample. Miller and Baruch (1948) studied maternal rejection, including the verbal expression of this through spurning and terrorizing acts, and identified a dramatically larger percentage of rejected children and adolescents who developed allergies in comparison to those who were not rejected (98.4% of the allergy group were rejected; 24.3% of the nonallergy group were rejected). In a study of adolescents with thrown-away experiences (defined as spending at least one night away from home after being told to do so), Ringwalt, Greene, and Robertson (1998) found these experiences of rejection to be associated with several negative outcomes including drug use, theft, carrying of weapons, assault, and suicide attempts.

In research utilizing a longitudinal sample and focusing on outcomes in adolescence/young adulthood, Johnson and colleagues (Johnson, Cohen, Kasen, Smailes, & Brook, 2001; Johnson, Cohen, Smailes et al., 2001; Johnson, Smailes, Cohen, Brown, & Bernstein, 2000) found that—when controlling for other forms of abuse and neglect, as well as demographic characteristics such as age and gender, parental psychiatric disorder, and co-occurring psychiatric disorders— emotional neglect and verbal abuse are both associated with personality disorder symptoms or diagnoses in adolescence and early adulthood.

Discussion of Empirical Findings

As can been seen from this brief review of the empirical evidence, there is very strong evidence that hostile/verbally aggressive parenting (*spurning* and *terrorizing* APSAC categories) has been uniquely linked with conduct problems, delinquency, anxiety disorders, depression, suicidal behavior, and personality disorders; and its impact is independent of parental mental illness/personality disorder, criminality, and interparental violence even though it occurs at higher rates within populations experiencing these problems (Maughan et al., 1995). The impact of hostile/verbally aggressive parenting is particularly strong from the first year or two of life through middle childhood (Wolfe & McGee, 1994). There is also considerable evidence in the intimate partner violence literature demonstrating its negative impact on adult mental health, social functioning, and parenting (e.g., Levendosky & Graham-Bermann, 2000). Using representative samples of 101 world cultures from the Yale Human Relations Area Files, Rohner and Rohner (Rohner, 1975; Rohner & Rohner, 1980) have demonstrated the cross-cultural validity of this form of psychological abuse and its developmental impact as well.

Denying emotional responsiveness also is strongly supported as a clearly identifiable form of parenting that is particularly devastating in the infant-toddler and preschool years and then again during adolescence. At the youngest ages it is associated, in longitudinal studies, with a devastating drop in IQ score, language delays, attachment disorders, and early onset internalizing and externalizing problems despite infant competence at birth and in the first few months of life. Experimental studies with nonhuman primates further underscore the devastating impact of this form of maltreatment early in life and its role in the development of lifelong psychopathology. In a series of well-conducted cross-sectional and longitudinal studies, emotional neglect has been associated with a long list of emotional and behavior problems in adolescence. There is strong cross-cultural support for this subtype as well (Rohner, 1975; Rohner & Rohner, 1980).

Why would *denying emotional responsiveness* be so devastating early in life and then again in adolescence? In infancy, the child's environment really consists of the mother/caregiver. She is the source of emotional, cognitive, and social stimulation, and mother–child interactions shape the developing brain (Schore, 1994; Sroufe, 1996) and lay the foundation for the child's emotional regulation, language development, sense of self and other, mastery motivation, and moral development. Without caregiver support, the infant is on his or her own, allocating resources that could be spent mastering the social and object world to internal state regulation and safety concerns. This lack of psychological nurturance sets the infant up for future developmental problems, as the foundation required for mastery of developmental tasks is impaired. Adolescence and young adulthood is also a very vulnerable transition time of moving from dependency to independent functioning, especially for those who have never had the supportive care that builds self-confidence in one's own efforts. There are several possible reasons why *denying emotional responsiveness* may become particularly salient in the adolescent years. During adolescence, parents may begin to view their children as more emotionally mature and self-reliant than they really are because of their physical appearance. In addition, parents may not know how to appropriately show affection and caring once their children no longer look and act like children, leaving them without a way to communicate their love. Adolescents also may not appear to need the emotional support of parents as they become more involved with peers, or parents may believe that adolescents should be able to take care of themselves; however, as is clear from research on adolescence, parental involvement and emotional connection remain critical factors throughout these years.

There is less research on *isolating* per se. Insularity and lack of social support appear to be characteristic of all maltreating families, at least those at lower income levels (Pianta et al., 1989). They are likely tied to parental personality and emotional problems that interfere not only with good parent–child relationships but also with adult relationships as well (Pianta et al., 1989; Polansky et al., 1981). There is little research on the effects of *isolating* parental behavior on children beyond preschool. In infancy, *isolating* is closely tied to psychologically unavailable caregiving (see Spitz, 1945). Such caregivers often leave infants in cribs and playpens, strap them into infant seats, or lock them in rooms so they don't have to interact with them. Clearly, some of the dramatic adverse effects of institutional rearing on infants and toddlers are due to isolating, as seen in the detailed descriptive accounts of care in these reports.

The subtype of *exploiting/corrupting* has little research support. There is little research on modeling, permitting, and encouraging antisocial behavior by parents and its relationship to adverse outcomes. There is a large body of research showing that having a criminal parent places a child at increased risk of antisocial personality disorder—a relationship that may reflect genetic variance (e.g., Maughan et al., 1995) rather than encouragement by the parent. There is a robust literature showing that a lack of parental monitoring and supervision by the family is related to engaging in antisocial behavior and that interventions to increase monitoring reduce antisocial behavior (e.g., Patterson, 1982). Lack of monitoring and supervision of children might better be seen as a manifestation of hostile/verbally aggressive and noncontingent parenting, in which a parent, locked in a coercive relationship with a noncompliant child, abandons any attempt to guide and control the child (Patterson, Reid, & Dishion, 1992). It could also be a manifestation of psychologically unavailable parenting, in which the parent is largely indifferent to the child's involvement in antisocial behavior. More research is needed on this subtype as it overlaps with supervision.

Similarly, no studies were found that focused on modeling, permitting, or encouraging developmentally inappropriate behavior (i.e., infantalization, parentification) or restricting/interfering with cognitive development. There is relevant literature on restricting/undermining psychological autonomy, referred to by the term *psychological control* (Barber, 1996). Studies in this area assess constructs involving love withdrawal, constraining verbal expressions, guilt induction, and erratic emotional behavior. This body of research has been done largely with community samples, and there are modest but significant relationships between psychological control measures and internalizing problems (and sometimes externalizing problems). More research is needed, as this parenting style is clearly not optimal. However, the current evidence is not sufficient, in our opinion, to clearly label it as maltreatment.

Finally, no studies were found on *mental health, medical, educational neglect.* It is anticipated that in the next few years their may be a number of studies on the effects of children not receiving an education, even when enrolled in home-schooling.

CONCLUSIONS AND RECOMMENDATIONS FOR FUTURE WORK

Through a review of current definitions and measures of psychological maltreatment, it becomes obvious that there is much agreement among researchers with regard to which parental behaviors generally constitute this form of abuse/ neglect. Most disagreement relates to whether a behavior should be called psychological maltreatment or another form of abuse and neglect, which subtype of psychological maltreatment it falls under, or how severe a behavior has to be to be called psychological maltreatment as opposed to poor parenting. The review of instruments, summarized in Figure 7.2, indicated great variability with regard to comprehensiveness, ages assessed, and psychometric characteristics. In general, observational measures, social worker ratings, and record reviews are the most developed instruments, whereas interviews and parent/self-report instruments need the most work if they are to become useful clinical and research measures. Empirical evidence strongly supports the psychological maltreatment subtypes of *spurning* and *terrorizing* (hostile/verbally aggressive parenting), *denying emotional responsiveness* (psychologically unavailable caregiving or emotional neglect), and *isolating* in early childhood. There is little research on parental behavior grouped under *exploiting/corrupting* and *mental health, medical and educational neglect.*

The chapter authors believe that comprehensive research definitions for psychological maltreatment should include the following characteristics:

1. Theoretical justification of psychological maltreatment as a socially sanctioned behavior is based on societal standards of care and an ever increasing body of knowledge on developmental psychopathology and the role that all forms of maltreatment, singularly or in combination, play in poor developmental outcomes. All of the definitions reviewed above assume implicitly or explicitly that children have species-based needs for minimally adequate psychological care if they are to attain minimal levels of adult competence.

2. Any child screened or assessed for a specific form of maltreatment should also be screened for all forms of child abuse and neglect (Barnett et al., 1993; Moran et al., 2002; Sternberg et al., 2004; Zuravin, 1991). If not, negative outcomes influenced primarily by one form of maltreatment could be attributed to another. This also allows for greater precision in the description of children's experiences and, thus, their relationship to outcomes and would facilitate agreement over time on which behaviors to classify as psychological maltreatment, which as neglect, and which as other forms of maltreatment.

3. The perpetrator's behavior needs to be assessed independently from endangerment or harm to the child, although both need to be assessed as part of any comprehensive system (this is our reading of the general consensus of researchers in the issue of *Development and Psychopathology,* 1991, 3[1], devoted to the topic of psychological maltreatment). Even better would be the development of assessment schemes that describe the dysfunctional parent–child relationship (Egeland, 1991; Glaser, 2002), which could be done by expanding on frameworks that already exist (e.g., Ainsworth, Blehar, Waters, & Wall, 1978; Crittenden, 2001). The authors of this chapter are impressed by the continuity in parenting styles reported over years for psychologically unavailable caregiving and hostile/verbally aggressive parenting (e.g., Pianta et al., 1989; Maughan et al., 1995) in the absence of intervention, suggesting that the relationship and not discrete parental acts should be the focus of research. Although there may be a brief time lag (weeks to months) between the onset of psychological maltreatment and signs of children's developmental delay or distress, the evidence reviewed suggests that children quickly respond to the care they receive and sensitive measures can assess their immediate distress (e.g., facial coding, physiological responses during caregiver–child interactions, teacher reports) even if it may take a year or more for diagnosable disorders to appear, depending on the developmental period the child is in.

4. Research criteria have to be closely tied to criteria used by CPS, yet independent, given the variability with which states, provinces, and other governmental agencies define and respond to maltreatment, especially psychological maltreatment (Hamarman et al., 2002).

5. Multiple sources and measures of maltreatment need to be used in order to obtain a comprehensive picture of the child's experiences (Kaufman, Jones, Stieglitz, Vitulano, & Mannarino, 1994; Sternberg et al., 2004) and to determine how sources of information should be weighted at each age (e.g., self-reports of internalizing problems in children are given more weight than parent reports, whereas teacher and parent reports are given more weight for externalizing problems). Observational measures appear to be particularly powerful at capturing the relationship in an unbiased way and being comprehensive in covering many aspects of psychological maltreatment.

6. Information on other negative life events children have experienced, known to be related to poor developmental outcomes, needs to be collected routinely. Such factors include parent psychiatric problems, poverty, exposure to neighborhood violence, placement in foster care, and caregiver deaths (Barnett et al., 1993; Egeland, 1991; Sternberg et al., 2004). These factors, singularly or in combination with maltreatment, may account for variance in child outcomes, and their effects need to be understood in order to make judgments of service need, for example, and to contextualize and strengthen. Doing so may weaken the discriminant power of a classification system or it may strengthen it (see Maughan et al., 1995, for an example of the latter).

7. Information on protective factors, especially the role of supportive relationships, organization of the home environment, and opportunities to develop competence need to be collected as well, both to improve our understanding of development (Egeland, 1991; McCord, 1983; Rohner & Rohner, 1980; Sternberg, Lamb, & Dawud-Noursi, 1998) and to assist in making placement and treatment decisions for children who are being psychologically maltreated by one parental figure and yet receive support, if not protection, from another.

8. Information needs to be collected on the duration, frequency, and periodicity of maltreatment experienced (Barnett et al., 1993). Periodicity, as reflected in inconsistent and unpredictable disciplinary practices, is related to particularly poor outcomes in offspring (e.g., Glueck & Glueck, 1950; McCord, McCord, & Zola, 1959) but is inadequately covered by the measures reviewed above.

9. The age of the child at the time of the event needs to be noted as precisely as possible, such that developmental vulnerability to different forms of maltreatment can be carefully studied with measures sensitive to the developmental challenges that are most salient for the child at the time (Baily & Baily, 1986; Barnett et al., 1993; Brassard et al., 1987; Egeland et al., 1983; Garbarino et al., 1986; McGee & Wolfe, 1991; Schore, 1994). Definitions may need to reflect developmental changes and needs that can only be identified through careful research. Some of these relationships are beginning to emerge but more research is needed.

10. As has long been done with child sexual abuse, the relationship between the perpetrator and the target child needs to be specified (Sternberg et al., 2004) and psychologically maltreating behavior committed by non–parental figures assessed even if it would not typically be dealt with by CPS (e.g., abuse by teachers; Moran et al., 2002). This would allow for a more comprehensive picture of child's victimization experiences and the relative impact of maltreatment by different perpetrators on a child's development.

11. The classification of maltreatment experiences should be mutually exclusive and nonhierarchical; in other words, all forms of maltreatment should

be noted with no assumption made that one form outranks or subsumes another in the absence of strong theoretical and empirical evidence to the contrary, as we do not yet have the knowledge to make determinations regarding which aspects of parental behavior are the most harmful. Measures that allow for the coding of multiple forms of maltreatment for the same act (e.g., MCS, CECA) are preferred, as they allow for a more complete description of children's experiences. An example from the MCS is the coding of both emotional maltreatment and physical abuse when a child is confined with tightly bound rope that causes rope burn, bruises, or cuts but only emotional maltreatment if there is no tissue damage.

The major issue for researchers, as well as for clinicians and policy makers, in the definition of psychological maltreatment is severity. Where should the line be drawn between maltreatment and poor parenting? Parent or child report on screening measures—sometimes one question—as in Johnson, Cohen, Smailes, et al. (2001), has strong predictive validity in groups, but classification of individual cases with such measures has not been established. Some research groups appear to have made clear and predictive classifications of parent–child dyads as psychologically maltreating, but these were based on multiple sources of information at one time (Claussen & Crittenden, 1991; Maughan et al., 1995) or a series of laboratory and home visits over a number of years (Pianta et al., 1989). The exact criteria used are not clear from research reports, but developing decision making algorithms is an obvious next step for researchers.

Integrally related are issues of parental intent and evidence of harm. While arguing against the inclusion of intent in criteria for psychological abuse, Moran et al. (2002) nonetheless noted that it was a clear aspect of many of the narratives they classified as abuse. Hamarman and Bernet (2000) have argued that intent and likelihood of potential harm should be the determining variables in decision making in cases of emotional abuse. Whereas the research definitions reviewed above do not include intent in the criteria, it certainly plays a role in legal decision making and, thus, cannot be ignored. Research on the relationship between a victim's perception of the perpetrator's intent and harm would be useful. Similarly, except for the NIS and APSAC definitions and the MCS and Child Maltreatment Log instruments, none of the other definitions or instruments assesses harm or includes it in decisions about whether or not psychological maltreatment has occurred. Psychological maltreatment has not been assumed to be harmful in the absence of evidence of harm, as in the case of sexual abuse (Hart, Brassard, Binggeli, & Davidson, 2002). This review of the literature makes a strong case for psychological maltreatment in the forms of *denying emotional responsiveness* and *spurning/terrorizing,* at all ages, and *isolating* in early childhood being damaging under most circumstances; maybe it should be assumed that these forms are inherently harmful based on the existing evidence. Whether harm actually occurs seems to be mediated by individual characteristics and resources, which doesn't change the nature of the parental behaviors that occur initially. If you hit your child, and he or she does not have a negative response other than time-limited tissue damage, that does not excuse it or mean it did not happen. The same is true with psychological maltreatment.

In compiling the information to write this chapter, the authors were impressed by the quality of the definitional and empirical work that has been done to date in the psychological maltreatment field; there is a strong foundation on which to make empirically supported policy recommendations and guide future research. It is the hope of the authors that the information in this chapter will contribute to high-quality, clinically meaningful future research that informs theory, assessment, and policy and, most important, helps to improve individuals' lives.

REFERENCES

Ainsworth, M.S., Blehar, M.C., Waters, E., & Wall, S. (1978). *Patterns of attachment: A psychological study of the strange situation.* Oxford, England: Lawrence Erlbaum Associates.

American Humane Association. (1980). *Definitions of the national study data items and response categories: Technical report #3.* Denver, CO: Author.

American Professional Society on the Abuse of Children. (1995). *Guidelines for psychosocial evaluation of suspected psychological maltreatment in children and adolescents.* Chicago, IL: Author.

American Psychiatric Association. (1994). *Diagnostic and statistical manual of mental disorders* (4th ed.). Washington, DC: Author.

Baily, R.T., & Baily, W.H. (1986). *Operational definitions of child emotional maltreatment.* Augusta, ME: Department of Social Services.

Barber, B.K. (1996). Parental psychological control: Revisiting a neglected construct. *Child Development, 67,* 3296–3319.

Barnett, D., Manly, J.T., & Cicchetti, D. (1993). Defining child maltreatment: The interface between policy and research. In D. Cicchetti & S.L. Toth (Eds.), *Child abuse, child development and social policy* (pp. 7–73). Norwood, NJ: Ablex.

Bifulco, A., Brown, G.W., Neubauer, A., Moran, P.M., & Harris, T. (1994). *The Childhood Experience of Care and Abuse (CECA) interview: Training manual.* London: University of London, Royal Holloway.

Binggeli, N.J., Hart, S.N., & Brassard, M.R. (2001). *Psychological maltreatment of children: The APSAC study guides 4.* Thousand Oaks, CA: Sage Publications.

Bowlby, J. (1966). *Maternal care and mental health.* New York: Schocken Books.

Brassard, M.R., Germain, R.B., & Hart, S.N. (Eds.) (1987). *Psychological maltreatment of children and youth.* New York: Pergamon Press.

Brassard, M.R., Hart, S.N., & Hardy, D. (1993). The Psychological Maltreatment Rating Scales. *Child Abuse & Neglect, 17,* 715–729.

Brody, G.H., Ge, X., Kim, S.Y., Murry, V.M., Simons, R.L., Gibbons, F.X., et al. (2003). Neighborhood disadvantage moderates associations of parenting and older sibling problem attitudes and behavior with conduct disorders in African-American children. *Journal of Consulting and Clinical Psychology, 7*(2), 211–222.

Brown, S.E. (1984). Social class, child maltreatment, and delinquent behavior. *Criminology, 22*(2), 259–274.

Brunner, R., Parzer, P., Schuld, V., & Resch, F. (2000). Dissociative symptomatology and traumatogenic factors in adolescent psychiatric patients. *Journal of Nervous and Mental Disease, 188*(2), 71–77.

Burnett, B.B. (1993). The psychological abuse of latency age children: A survey. *Child Abuse & Neglect, 17,* 441–454.

Caldwell, B., & Bradley, R. (1984). *Home Observation for Measurement of the Environment: Administration manual.*. Little Rock: University of Arkansas at Little Rock.

Campo, A.T., & Rohner, R.P. (1992). Relationships between perceived parental acceptance-rejection, psychological adjustment, and substance abuse among young adults. *Child Abuse & Neglect, 16,* 429–440.

Chang, L., Schwartz, D., Dodge, K.A., & McBride-Chang, C. (2003). Harsh parenting in relation to child emotional regulation and aggression. *Journal of Family Psychology, 17*(4), 598–606.

Child Abuse Prevention and Treatment Act of 1974, PL 93-247, 42 U.S.C. § 5101 *et seq.*

Cicchetti, D. (Ed.). (1991). Psychological maltreatment [Special issue]. *Development and Psychopathology, 3*(1).

Claussen, A.H., & Crittenden, P.M. (1991). Physical and psychological maltreatment: Relations among types of maltreatment. *Child Abuse & Neglect, 15,* 5–18.

Corson, J., & Davidson, H. (1987). Emotional abuse and the law. In M.R. Brassard, R. Germain, & S.N. Hart (Eds.), *Psychological maltreatment of children and youth* (pp. 185–202). New York: Pergamon Press.

Crittenden, P. (2001). *CARE-Index: Coding Manual.* Miami, FL: Family Relations Institute.

Crittenden, P.M., Claussen, A.H., & Sugarman, D.B. (1994). Physical and psychological maltreatment in middle childhood and adolescence. *Development and Psychopathology, 6,* 145–164.

Dance, C., Rushton, A., & Quinton, D. (2002). Emotional abuse in early childhood: Relationships with progress in subsequent family placement. *Journal of Child Psychology and Psychiatry and Allied Disciplines, 43*(3), 395–407.

Davis, P.W. (1996). Threats of corporal punishment as verbal aggression: A naturalistic study. *Child Abuse & Neglect, 20*(4), 289–304.

Demaré, D. (1995). *Childhood Maltreatment Questionnaire (CMQ).* Winnipeg, Canada: University of Manitoba, Department of Psychology.

Dubowitz, H., Papas, M.A., Black, M.M., & Starr, R.H. (2002). Child neglect: Outcomes in high-risk urban preschoolers. *Pediatrics, 109*(6), 1100–1107.

Dykeman, B.F. (2003). The effects of family conflict resolution on children's classroom behavior. *Journal of Instructional Psychology, 30*(1), 41–46.

Egeland, B. (1991). From data to definition. *Development and Psychopathology, 3,* 37–43.

Egeland, B., & Erickson, M. (1987). Psychologically unavailable caregiving. In M.R. Brassard, R. Germain, & S.N. Hart (Eds.), *Psychological maltreatment of children and youth* (pp. 110–120). New York: Pergamon Press.

Egeland, B., Jacobvitz, D., & Sroufe, L.A. (1988). Breaking the cycle of abuse. *Child Development, 59,* 1080–1088.

Egeland, B., & Sroufe, L.A. (n.d.). *Observation measures from the Maternal Child Interaction Research Project.* Available from the authors, University of Minnesota, Minneapolis.

Egeland, B., Sroufe, L.A., & Erickson, M. (1983). The developmental consequences of different patterns of maltreatment. *Child Abuse & Neglect, 7,* 459–469.

Egeland, B., Yates, T., Appleyard, K., & van Dulman, M. (2002). The long-term consequences of maltreatment in the early years: A developmental pathway model to antisocial behavior. *Children's Services: Social Policy, Research, and Practice, 5*(4), 249–260.

Eron, L.D. (1982). Parent–child interaction, television violence, and aggression in children. *American Psychologist, 37*(2), 197–211.

Fleming, W.M., Jory, B., & Burton, D.L. (2002). Characteristics of juvenile offenders admitting to sexual activity with nonhuman animals. *Society and Animals, 10*(1), 31–45.

Garbarino, J., & Gilliam, G. (1980). *Understanding abusive families.* Lexington, MA: Lexington Books.

Garbarino, J., Guttman, E., & Seely, J.W. (1986). *The psychologically battered child.* San Francisco: Jossey-Bass.

Giovannoni, J., & Becerra, R. (1979). *Defining child abuse.* New York: Free Press.

Glaser, D. (1993). Emotional abuse. In C. Hobbs & J. Wynne (Eds.), *Child abuse* (pp. 251–267). London: Balliere Tindall.

Glaser, D. (2000). Child abuse and neglect and the brain—A review. *Journal of Child Psychology and Psychiatry and Allied Disciplines, 41*(1), 97–116.

Glaser, D. (2002). Emotional abuse and neglect (psychological maltreatment): A conceptual framework. *Child Abuse & Neglect, 26,* 697–714.

Glueck, S., & Glueck, E. (1950). *Unraveling juvenile delinquency.* New York: Commonwealth Fund.

Greenspan, S.I., DeGangi, G., & Wieder, S. (2001). *The Functional Emotional Assessment Scale (FEAS) for infancy and childhood: Clinical and research applications.* Bethesda, MD: Interdisciplinary Council on Developmental and Learning Disorders.

Hamarman, S., & Bernet, W. (2000). Evaluating and reporting emotional abuse in children: Parent-based, action-based, focus aids in clinical decision making. *Journal of American Academy of Child and Adolescent Psychiatry, 39,* 928–930.

Hamarman, S., Pope, K.H., & Czaja, S.J. (2002). Emotional abuse in children: Variations in legal definitions and rates across the United States. *Child Maltreatment, 7*(4), 303–311.

Harlow, H.F., & Harlow, M.K. (1971). Psychopathology in monkeys. In H.D. Kimmel (Ed.), *Experimental psychopathology: Recent research and theory* (pp. 203–229). San Diego, CA: Academic Press.

Hart, S.N. (1985). *Mental health neglect: Standards and procedures for legal and social services.* Working paper available from Indiana University, College of Education, the Office for the Study of the Psychological Rights of the Child.

Hart, S.N., & Brassard, M.R. (1990). *Final report (stages one and two): Developing and validating operationally defined measures of emotional maltreatment: A multi-modal study of the relationships between caretaker behaviors and child characteristics across three developmental levels* (Stage 1: Grant, N.O. DHHS 90CA1216). Washington, DC: U.S. Department of Health and Human Services, National Clearinghouse on Child Abuse and Neglect.

Hart, S.N., & Brassard, M.R. (1991). Psychological maltreatment: Progress achieved. *Development and Psychopathology, 3*(1), 61–70.

Hart, S.N., Brassard, M.R., Binggeli, N.J., & Davidson, H.A. (2002). Psychological maltreatment. In J.E.B. Myers, L. Berliner, J. Briere, C.T. Hendrix, C. Jenny, & T.A. Reid, (Eds.), *The APSAC handbook on child maltreatment* (2nd ed., pp. 79–117). Thousand Oaks, CA: Sage Publications.

Hart, S.N., Germain, R., & Brassard, M.R. (1983). *Proceedings summary on the International Conference on Psychological Abuse of Children and Youth.* Indianapolis: Indiana University, Office for the Study of the Psychological Rights of the Child.

Hart, S.N., Germain, R., & Brassard, M.R. (1987). The challenge: To better understand and combat psychological maltreatment of children and youth. In M.R. Brassard, R. Germain, & S.N. Hart (Eds.), *Psychological maltreatment of children and youth* (pp. 3–24). New York: Pergamon Press.

Herrenkohl, R.C., Egolf, B.P., & Herrenkohl, E.C. (1997). Preschool age antecedents of adolescent assaultive behavior: Results from a longitudinal study. *American Journal of Orthopsychiatry, 67*(3), 422–432.

Herrenkohl, R.C., Herrenkohl, E.C., & Egolf, B.P. (1991). *Methods of disciplining children—Revised.* Unpublished instrument available from R.C. Herrenkohl, Center for Social Research, Lehigh University, 10 West Fourth Street, Bethlehem, PA 18015.

Herrenkohl, R.C., Herrenkohl, E.C., Egolf, B.P., & Wu, P. (1991). The developmental consequences of child abuse. The Lehigh Longitudinal Study. In R.H. Starr, Jr., & D.A. Wolfe

(Eds.), *The effects of child abuse and neglect: Issues and research* (pp. 57–81). New York: Guilford Press.

Herrenkohl, R.C., Herrenkohl, E.C., & Toedter, L. (1982). *Procedures for interviewing families about their child discipline practices.* Unpublished instrument available from R.C. Herrenkohl, Center for Social Research, Lehigh University, 10 West Fourth Street, Bethlehem, PA 18015.

Herrenkohl, E.C., Herrenkohl, R.C., Toedter, L., & Yanushefski, A.M. (1984). Parent-child interactions in abusive and non-abusive families. *Journal of the American Academy of Child Psychiatry, 23*(6), 641–648.

Herrenkohl, R.C., & Russo, M.J. (2001). Abusive early child rearing and early childhood aggression. *Child Maltreatment, 6*(1), 3–16.

Hien, D., Matzner, F., First, M., Spitzer, R., Williams, J., & Gibbon, M. (1999). *Structured clinical interview for DSM-IV childhood diagnoses.* Unpublished interview.

Higgins, D.J., & McCabe, M.P. (1998). Parent perceptions of maltreatment and adjustment in children. *Journal of Family Studies, 4*(1), 53–76.

Higgins, D.J., & McCabe, M.P. (2003). Maltreatment and family dysfunction in childhood and subsequent adjustment of children and adults. *Journal of Family Violence, 18*(2), 107–120.

Holmes, S.J., & Robins, L.N. (1987). The influence of childhood disciplinary experience on the development of alcoholism and depression. *Journal of Child Psychology and Psychiatry, 28*(3), 399–415.

Johnson, J.G., Cohen, P., Gould, M.S., Kasen, S., Brown, J., & Brook, J.S. (2002). Childhood adversities, interpersonal difficulties, and risk for suicide attempts during late adolescence and early adulthood. *Archives of General Psychiatry, 59*(8), 741–749.

Johnson, J.G., Cohen, P., Kasen, S., Smailes, E., & Brook, J.S. (2001). Association of maladaptive parental behavior with psychiatric disorder among parents and their offspring. *Archives of General Psychiatry, 58*(5), 453–460.

Johnson, J.G., Cohen, P., Smailes, E.M., Skodol, A.E., Brown, J., & Oldham, J.M. (2001). Childhood verbal abuse and risk for personality disorders during adolescence and early adulthood. *Comprehensive Psychiatry, 42*(1), 16–23.

Johnson, J.G., Smailes, E.M., Cohen, P., Brown, J., & Bernstein, D.P. (2000). Associations between four types of childhood neglect and personality disorder symptoms during adolescence and early adulthood: Findings of a community-based longitudinal study. *Journal of Personality Disorders, 14*(2), 171–187.

Kairys, S.W., Johnson, C.F., & American Academy of Pediatrics Committee on Child Abuse and Neglect. (2002). The psychological maltreatment of children—technical report. *Pediatrics, 109*(4), 1–3.

Kaler, S.R., & Freeman, B.J. (1994). Analysis of environmental deprivation: Cognitive and social development in Romanian orphans. *Journal of Child Psychology and Psychiatry, 35*(4), 769–781.

Kaufman, J. (1991). Depressive disorders in maltreated children. *Journal of the American Academy of Child and Adolescent Psychiatry, 30*(2), 257–265.

Kaufman, J., Jones, B., Stieglitz, E., Vitulano, L., & Mannarino, A.P. (1994). The use of multiple informants to assess children's maltreatment experiences. *Journal of Family Violence, 9*(3), 227–248.

Kaufman, J., & Zigler, E. (1989). The intergenerational transmission of child abuse. In D. Cicchetti & V. Carlson (Eds.), *Child maltreatment: Theory and research on the causes and consequences of child abuse and neglect* (pp. 129–150). New York: Cambridge University Press.

Kempe, C., Silverman, F., Steele, B., Droegemueller, W., & Silver, H. (1962). The battered child syndrome. *Journal of the American Medical Association, 181,* 17–24.

Kim, I.J., Ge, X., Brody, G.H., Conger, R.D., & Gibbons, F.X. (2003). Parenting behaviors and the occurrence and co-occurrence of depressive symptoms and conduct problems among African-American children. *Journal of Family Psychology, 17*(4), 571–583.

Kingree, J.B., Phan, D., & Thompson, M. (2003). Child maltreatment recidivism among adolescent detainees. *Criminal Justice and Behavior, 30*(6), 623–643.

Korbin, J., Coulton, C., Lindstrom-Ufuti, H., & Spilsbury, J. (2000). Neighborhood views on the definition and etiology of child maltreatment. *Child Abuse & Neglect, 24,* 1509–1527.

Krugman, R.D., & Krugman, M.K. (1984). Emotional abuse in the classroom. *American Journal of Diseases in Children, 138,* 284–286.

Landau, H.R., Salus, M.K., Stiffarm, T., & Kalb, N.L. (1980). *Child Protection: The role of the courts.* Washington, DC: Government Printing Office.

Laury, G.V., & Meerloo, J.A. (1967). Mental cruelty and child abuse. *Psychiatric Quarterly Supplement, 41*(2), 203–254.

Lavoie, F., Hebert, M., Tremblay, R., Vitaro, F., Vezina, L., & McDuff, P. (2002). History of family dysfunction and perpetration of dating violence by adolescent boys: A longitudinal study. *Journal of Adolescent Health, 30*(5), 375–383.

Levendosky, A.A., & Graham-Bermann, S.A. (2000). Behavioral observations of parenting in battered women. *Journal of Family Psychology, 14*(1), 80–94.

Lipschitz, D., Winegar, R.P., Nicolaou, A.L., Hartnick, E., Wolfson, M., & Southwick, S.M. (1999). Perceived abuse and neglect as risk factors for suicidal behavior in adolescent inpatients. *Journal of Nervous and Mental Disease, 187*(1), 32–39.

Litrownik, A.J., Newton, R., Hunter, W.M., English, D., & Everson, M.D. (2003). Exposure to family violence in young at-risk children: A longitudinal look at the effects of victimization and witnessed physical and psychological aggression. *Journal of Family Violence, 18*(1), 59–73.

Lochner, C., du Toit, P.L., Zungu-Dirwayi, N., Marais, A., vanKardenburg, J., Seedat, S., et al. (2002). Childhood trauma in obsessive-compulsive disorder, trichotillomania, and controls. *Depression and Anxiety, 15,* 66–88.

Lourie, M.D., & Stefano, L. (1978). *On defining emotional abuse. Child abuse and neglect: Issues in innovation and implementation. Proceedings of the Second Annual National Conference on Child Abuse and Neglect.* Washington, DC: Government Printing Office.

Lyon, M.E., Benoit, M., O'Donnell, R.M., Getson, P.R., Silber, T., & Walsh, T. (2000). Assessing African-American adolescents' risk for suicide attempts: Attachment theory. *Adolescence, 35,* 121–134.

Lyons-Ruth, K., Connell, D.B., & Zoll, D. (1989). Patterns of maternal behavior among infants at risk for abuse: Relations with infant attachment behavior and infant development at 12 months of age. In D. Cicchetti & C. Carlson (Ed.), *Child maltreatment: Theory and research on the causes and consequences of child abuse and neglect* (pp. 464–493). New York: Cambridge University Press.

MacKinnon-Lewis, C., Starnes, R., Volling, B., & Johnson, S. (1997). Perceptions of parenting as predictors of boys' sibling relationships and peer relations. *Developmental Psychology, 33*(6), 1024–1031.

Magee, W. (1999). Effects of negative life experiences on phobia onset. *Social Psychiatry and Psychiatric Epidemiology, 34*(7), 343–351.

Magura, S., & Moses, B.S. (1986). *Outcome measures for child welfare services: Theory and applications.* Washington, DC: Child Welfare League of America.

Manly, J.T., Kim, J.E., Rogosch, F.A., & Cicchetti, D. (2001). Dimensions of child maltreatment and children's adjustment: Contributions of developmental timing and subtype. *Development and Psychopathology, 13,* 759–782.

Maughan, B., Pickles, A., & Quinton, D. (1995). Parental hostility, childhood and adult social functioning. In J. McCord (Ed.), *Coercion and punishment in long-term perspectives* (pp. 34–58). New York: Cambridge University Press.

McCord, J. (1983). A forty year perspective on effects of child abuse and neglect. *Child Abuse & Neglect, 7,* 265–270.

McCord, W., McCord, J., & Zola, I.K. (1959). *Origins of crime: A new evaluation of the Cambridge-Somerville youth study.* New York: Columbia University Press.

McGee, R.A., & Wolfe, D.A. (1991). Psychological maltreatment: Towards an operational definition. *Development and Psychopathology, 3,* 3–18.

McGee, R.A., Wolfe, D.A., &Wilson, S.K. (1990). *A record of maltreatment experiences.* Unpublished manuscript.

McGee, R.A., Wolfe, D.A., Yuen, S.A., Wilson, S.K., & Carnochan, J. (1995). The measurement of maltreatment: A comparison of approaches. *Child Abuse & Neglect, 19*(2), 233–249.

Merbert, C., & Straus, M.A. (2002). *Picture-Card Version for Young Children of the Parent-to-Child Conflict Tactics Scales.* Retrieved January 17, 2006, from http://pubpages.unh.edu/~mas2/CTS33%20WEB%20DESCRIPTION.htm

Miller, H., & Baruch, D.W. (1948). Psychosomatic studies of children with allergic manifestations: I. Maternal rejection: A study of 63 cases. *Psychosomatic Medicine, 10*(5), 275–278.

Moore, T.E., & Pepler, D.J. (1998). Correlates of adjustment in children at risk. In G.W. Holden, R.A. Geffner, & E.N. Jouriles (Eds.), *Children exposed to marital violence: Theory, research, and applied issues* (pp. 157–184). Washington, DC: American Psychological Association.

Moran, P.M., Bifulco, A., Ball, C., Jacobs, C., & Benaim, K. (2002). Exploring psychological abuse in childhood: I. Developing a new interview scale. *Bulletin of the Menninger Clinic, 66*(3), 213–240.

Moran, P.B., Vuchinich, S., & Hall, N.K. (2004). Associations between types of maltreatment and substance use during adolescence. *Child Abuse & Neglect, 28,* 565–574.

National Center on Child Abuse and Neglect. (1981). *Executive summary: National study of the incidence and severity of child abuse and neglect.* Washington, DC: Author.

National Research Council. (1993). *Understanding child abuse and neglect.* Washington, DC: National Academies Press.

Ney, P.G., Fung, T., & Wickett, A.R. (1994). The worst combinations of child abuse and neglect. *Child Abuse & Neglect, 18*(9), 705–714.

Olivan, G. (2003). Catch-up growth assessment in long-term physically neglected and emotionally abused preschool age male children. *Child Abuse & Neglect, 27*(1), 103–108.

Patterson, G.R. (1982). *Coercive family process.* Eugene, OR: Castalia Press.

Patterson, G.R., Reid, J.B., & Dishion, T.J. (1992). *Antisocial boys.* Eugene, OR: Castalia Press.

Pianta, R., Egeland, B., & Erickson, M.F. (1989). The antecedents of maltreatment: Results of the Mother-Child Interaction Project. In D. Cicchetti & V. Carlson (Eds.), *Child maltreatment: Theory and research on the causes and consequences of child abuse and neglect* (pp. 203–253). New York: Cambridge University Press.

Polansky, N., Chalmers, M.A., Buttenweiser, E., & Williams, D.P. (1981). *Damaged parents: An anatomy of child neglect.* Chicago, IL: University of Chicago Press.

Portwood, S.G. (1999). Coming to terms with a consensual definition of child maltreatment. *Child Maltreatment, 4*(1), 56–68.

Putnam, F.W. (1993). Dissociative disorders in children: Behavioral profiles and problems. *Child Abuse & Neglect, 17*(1), 39–45.

Repetti, R.L., Taylor, S.E., & Seeman, T.E. (2002). Risky families: Family social environments and the mental and physical health of offspring. *Psychological Bulletin, 128*(2), 330–366.

Ringwalt, C.L., Greene, J.M., & Robertson, M.J. (1998). Familial backgrounds and risk behaviors of youth with thrown away experiences. *Journal of Adolescence, 21*(3), 241–252.

Rohner, R.P. (1975). *They love me, they love me not: A worldwide study of the effects of parental acceptance and rejection.* New Haven, CT: HRAF Press.

Rohner, R.P., & Neilsen, C.C. (1978). *Parental acceptance and rejection: A review and annotated bibliography of research and theory* (Vol. 1, W6-006). New Haven, CT: Human Relations Area Files, Inc.

Rohner, R.P., & Rohner, E.C. (1980). Antecedents and consequences of parental rejection: A theory of emotional abuse. *Child Abuse & Neglect, 4,* 189–198.

Rohner, R.P., Saavedra, J.M., & Granum, E.O. (1978). Development and validation of the Parental Acceptance-Rejection Questionnaire. *Catalog of Selected Documents in Psychology (MS 1635), 8,* 7–8.

Sackett, G.P. (1965). Effects of rearing conditions on the behavior of the rhesus monkey. *Child Development, 36,* 855–868.

Schaefer, C. (1997). Defining verbal abuse of children: A survey. *Psychological Reports, 80,* 626.

Schore, A.N. (1994). *Affect regulation and the origin of the self.* Mahwah, NJ: Lawrence Erlbaum Associates.

Sedlak, A.J., & Broadhurst, D.D. (1996). *Third national incidence study of child abuse and neglect: Final report.* Washington, DC: U.S. Department of Health and Human Services.

Shaffer, D., Fisher, P., Lucas, C.P., Dulcan, M.K., & Schwab-Stone, M.E. (2000). NIMH Diagnostic Interview Schedule for Children IV (NIMH DISC-IV): Description, differences from previous versions, and reliability of some common diagnoses. *Journal of the American Academy of Child and Adolescent Psychiatry, 39*(1), 28–38.

Solomon, C.R., & Serres, F. (1999). Effects of parental verbal aggression on children's self-esteem and school marks. *Child Abuse & Neglect, 23*(4), 339–351.

Spillane-Grieco, E. (2000). From parent verbal abuse to teenage physical aggression? *Child and Adolescent Social Work Journal, 17*(6), 411–430.

Spitz, R.A. (1945). Hospitalism: An inquiry into the genesis of psychiatric conditions in early childhood. *The Psychoanalytic Study of the Child, 1,* 53–74.

Sroufe, L.A. (1996). *Emotional development: The organization of emotional life in the early years.* New York: Cambridge University Press.

Sternberg, K.J., Knutson, J.K., Lamb, M.E., Baradaran, L.P., Nolan, C., & Flanzer, S. (2004). The Child Maltreatment Log: A computer-based program for describing research samples. *Child Maltreatment, 9*(1), 30–48.

Sternberg, K., & Lamb, M. (1991). Can we ignore context in the definition of child maltreatment. *Development and Psychopathology, 3*(1), 87–92.

Sternberg, K., Lamb, M., & Dawud-Noursi, S. (1998). Using multiple informants to understand domestic violence and its effects. In G.W. Holden, R.A. Geffner, & E.N. Jouriles (Eds.), *Children exposed to marital violence: Theory, research, and applied issues* (pp. 121–156). Washington, DC: American Psychological Association.

Straus, M.A. (1979). Measuring intrafamily conflict and violence: The Conflict Tactics Scales. *Journal of Marriage and the Family, 41,* 75–88.

Straus, M.A., & Field, C.J. (2003). Psychological aggression by American parents: National data on prevalence, chronicity, and severity. *Journal of Marriage and Family, 65,* 795–808.

Straus, M.A., & Hamby, S.L. (1997). Measuring physical and psychological maltreatment of children with the Conflict Tactics Scales. In G. Kaufman Kantor & J.L. Jasinski (Eds.), *Out of the darkness: Contemporary perspectives on family violence.* Thousand Oaks, CA: Sage Publications.

Straus, M.A., Hamby, S.L., Finkelhor, D., Moore, D.W., & Runyan, D. (1998). Identification of child maltreatment with the Parent-Child Conflict Tactics Scales: Development and psychometric data for a national sample of American parents. *Child Abuse & Neglect, 22*(4), 249–270.

Straus, M.A., Kinard, E.M., & Williams, L.M. (2001). *The Multidimensional Neglectful Behavior Scale, Form A: Adolescent and Adult-Recall Version.* Retrieved January 17, 2006, from http://pubpages.unh.edu/~mas2/Mul.htm

Suomi, S.J., Eisele, C.D., & Grady, S. (1975). Depressive behavior in adult monkeys follow-ing separation from family environment. *Journal of Abnormal Psychology, 84,* 576–578.

Trocme, N. (1992). *Focus on neglect: Development of an expert-based index of child neglect.* Paper presented at the IPSCAN Conference, Chicago.

Trocme, N. (1996). Development and preliminary evaluation of the Ontario Child Neglect Index. *Child Maltreatment, 1*(2), 145–155.

Thompson, A.E., & Kaplan, C.A. (1999). Emotionally abused children presenting to child psychiatry clinics. *Child Abuse & Neglect, 23*(2), 191–196.

U.S. Department of Health and Human Services. (1981). *Study findings: National study of the incidence and severity of child abuse and neglect* (DHHS Publication No. OHDS 81-30325). Washington, DC: Government Printing Office.

U.S. Department of Health and Human Services. (1988). *Study findings: Study of national incidence and prevalence of child abuse and neglect* (DHHS Publication No. ADM 20-01099). Washington, DC: Government Printing Office.

Vissing, Y.M., Straus, M.A., Gelles, R.J., & Harrop, J.W. (1991). Verbal aggression by par-ents and psychosocial problems of children. *Child Abuse & Neglect, 15,* 223–238.

Wolfe, D., & McGee, R. (1994). Dimensions of child maltreatment and their relationship to adolescent adjustment. *Development and Psychopathology, 6*(1), 165–182.

Zuravin, S.J. (1991). Research definitions of child physical abuse and neglect: Current prob-lems. In R. Starr & D. Wolfe (Eds.), *The effects of child abuse and neglect: Issues in research* (pp. 100–128). New York: Guilford Press.

8

In Search of Construct Validity

Using Basic Concepts and Principles of Psychological Measurement to Define Child Maltreatment

DAVID WATSON

THE GOAL of this chapter is to provide child maltreatment researchers with a brief introduction to basic concepts and principles of psychological measurement. This topic can seem confusing, even intimidating at times, in part because of the large number of potentially relevant concepts. Within the broad domain of validity, for instance, one encounters a bewildering array of terms, including *concurrent validity, content validity, construct validity, criterion validity, discriminant validity, external validity, face validity, incremental validity,* and *predictive validity* (e.g., Anastasi & Urbina, 1997; Kaplan & Saccuzzo, 2001; Murphy & Davidshofer, 2001).

To place these concepts into a meaningful context, it is helpful to sketch a very brief outline of the evolution of psychometric thinking over the course of the 20th century. This thinking has revolved around the interplay between two broad concepts—reliability and validity. Reliability can be defined as the consistency of the scores that are obtained across repeated assessments (Anastasi & Urbina, 1997; Kaplan & Saccuzzo, 2001; Murphy & Davidshofer, 2001). Reliability was the dominant concern among psychometricians and test developers during the first half of the 20th century, largely because it appeared to be a more straightforward concept that was easier to evaluate than validity. As will be discussed subsequently, however, this apparent straightforwardness was deceptive. In fact, as this chapter shows, classical reliability theory was based on some very shaky assumptions that are unlikely to be met in many areas of psychological research. Moreover, it eventually was discovered that maximizing reliability actually can be counterproductive and can lead to the development of less interesting and useful measures (the "attenuation paradox"; see Loevinger, 1954, 1957).

Accordingly, reliability gradually lost its position of preeminence and was supplanted by validity as the conceptual centerpiece of measurement. In the current *Standards for Educational and Psychological Testing,* validity is defined as "the degree to which evidence and theory support the interpretation of test scores entailed by proposed uses of tests. Validity is, therefore, the most fundamental consideration in developing and evaluating tests" (American Psychological Association, 1999, p. 9). Throughout most of the 20th century, psychometricians recognized several distinct types of validity, including content validity, criterion validity, and construct validity. A major breakthrough occurred in the 1990s, however, when it was recognized that all other types of validity simply represent aspects of the all-encompassing process of construct validity (American Psychological Association, 1999; Messick, 1995). Thus, according to the current *Standards for Educational and Psychological Testing,* "Validity is a unitary concept. It is the degree to which all the accumulated evidence supports the intended interpretation of test scores for the proposed purpose" (American Psychological Association, 1999, p. 11). It is noteworthy, moreover, that this expanded conceptualization of construct validity also subsumes all of the major types of reliability evidence, including both internal consistency and stability. As Messick put it, "construct validity is based on an integration of any evidence that bears on the interpretation or meaning of the test scores" (1995, p. 742). Consequently, construct validity—a concept that originally was articulated by Cronbach and Meehl (1955)—gradually has emerged as the central unifying concept in contemporary psychometrics.

Another key insight was the recognition that construct validity is not simply a process of evaluating the properties of an already-developed test. Rather, it serves as the most appropriate basis for creating and refining new assessment instruments. In other words, construct validity considerations also should guide the entire process of scale construction. This viewpoint originally was articulated by Loevinger (1957) and it subsequently has been refined by many others (e.g., Clark & Watson, 1995; Messick, 1995). Loevinger argued that there are three basic stages in the process of construct validation, which she labeled substantive, structural, and external. This remains a useful way to organize this topic, and this framework is adopted in the material that follows in an effort to show that it can be applied to establish research definitions of child maltreatment.

In the material that follows, the term *item* is used generically as a unit of analysis pertaining to the measurement of maltreatment. As such, *item* is silent with respect to the source of the datum represented. Items could reflect scores from chart reviews, components from administrative data, self-reports by victims, self-reports by parents or perpetrators, or even ratings of parent–child behavior.

SUBSTANTIVE VALIDITY: DEVELOPMENT OF AN INITIAL ITEM POOL

The substantive phase is the first—and, in many respects, the most important—stage in the scale development process. Key aspects of this phase include a) conceptualization of the construct, b) reviewing the extant literature, and c) creation of the initial item pool.

Conceptualization of the Construct

The substantive stage of construct validation primarily addresses issues related to the traditional psychometric concept of content validity. The critical first step is to develop a precise and detailed conception of the target construct to be assessed. Test developers, of course, always have at least a sketchy understanding of what it is they are trying to measure, but many fail to take the important next step of fleshing out the nature and scope of this construct more precisely. Clark and Watson (1995) recommend writing a brief, formal description of the target construct, which can be very useful in crystallizing one's conceptual model. Among other things, this can help to clarify the breadth of the desired instrument. Suppose, for example, that one is interested in developing a new measure of maltreatment in very young children. Is the goal to develop an instrument that is relatively narrow in scope (e.g., one that focuses specifically on the experience of sexual abuse), or is it to construct a much broader measure of maltreatment (e.g., one that also assesses physical abuse and neglect)? These types of issues should be confronted at the very outset of scale development.

Literature Review

To articulate the target construct as clearly and thoroughly as possible, it is necessary to review the existing literature to see how others have approached the same assessment problem. Initially, this review should include previous attempts to assess both the same construct and any closely related concepts. Subsequently, the review should be broadened to encompass less-related concepts to help define the conceptual boundaries of the target construct. For instance, suppose that one is interested in creating a measure that assesses the extent to which child victims perceive themselves to be responsible for their maltreatment. One initially might focus on perceptions of responsibility regarding circumstances of physical and sexual abuse. However, a thorough review of the literature might reveal that it also is important to clarify the relations between these types of abusive experiences and the child's perceived responsibility for 1) neglect and 2) parental conflict. In this way, an investigator can begin to develop a predicted pattern of convergent and discriminant relations at the very outset of scale development (see Clark & Watson, 1995).

A comprehensive literature review is important for several reasons. First, such a review serves to clarify the nature and range of the content of the target construct. Second, a literature review often helps to identify problems with existing measures (i.e., confusing instructions, poorly functioning item content, or problematic response formats) that can be avoided in one's own instrument. Finally—and most importantly—a thorough review indicates whether the proposed scale is actually needed. If good measures of the target construct already exist, why create another? The burden of proof is on the prospective developer of a new test to articulate clearly how this proposed instrument represents a theoretical and/or empirical advance over existing measures; in the absence of such proof, it is preferable to avoid contributing to the needless proliferation of assessment instruments.

Creation of the Item Pool

Once the scope and range of the content domain have been tentatively identified, one can begin the actual task of item writing (see Clark & Watson, 1995, for a discussion of basic principles of item writing). No existing data analytic technique can remedy significant deficiencies in the item pool; consequently, the creation of the initial item pool is an absolutely critical stage in scale development. The basic goal at this stage is to sample systematically all content that is potentially relevant to the target construct. As Loevinger put it, *"The items of the pool should be chosen so as to sample all possible contents which might comprise the putative trait according to all known alternative theories of the trait"* (1957, p. 659; emphasis in original). Two key implications of this principle are that the initial item pool 1) should be broader and more inclusive than one's own theoretical view of the target construct and 2) should include content that ultimately will be shown to be unrelated to the core construct. The logic underlying this principle of overinclusiveness is simple: Subsequent psychometric analyses can identify weak, unrelated items that should be dropped, but they are powerless to detect relevant content that should have been included but was not.

Thus, this principle of overinclusiveness ultimately serves the goal of comprehensiveness, which is a key consideration in establishing the content validity of a measure (see Foster & Cone, 1995; Haynes, Richard, & Kubany, 1995; and Messick, 1995). For example, in developing a measure of neglect, it is important to assess the full range of events that can be subsumed within this domain. That is, neglect can encompass a wide array of experiences, such as the failure to supervise properly, denial of basic care (e.g., food, clothing, shelter), failure to seek necessary health care, educational neglect (e.g., truancy, failure to arrange special education services), and inattention to appropriate hygiene (see Knutson & Schartz, 1997; Sedlak & Broadhurst, 1996).

Another key consideration is representativeness, which is the degree to which the item pool provides an adequate sample of each of the major content areas within the domain of the target construct (Clark & Watson, 1995; Haynes et al., 1995). To ensure that each important aspect of the construct is assessed adequately, some psychometricians recommend that formal subscales be created to assess each major content area within a domain. These content scales have been labeled "homogeneous item composites," or HICs, by Hogan (1983; see also Hogan & Hogan, 1992). For instance, the author and his colleagues are in the process of developing a new self-report instrument that is designed to yield a multidimensional measure of depressive symptoms. They began by creating an overinclusive pool of 117 items. In creating this pool, their basic strategy was to include multiple markers to define all of the symptom dimensions that potentially could emerge in subsequent structural analyses. To ensure that sufficient markers were included for each potential dimension, they rationally organized the candidate items into 13 HICs, each of which contained 8–14 symptoms. Furthermore, to determine the boundaries of this domain, they included 63 anxiety symptoms that were grouped into seven additional HICs (see Watson et al. 2006, for more details).

This process of establishing domain boundaries represents a crucial step in the articulation and development of a new measure. In the area of neglect, for example, a key issue involves the potential inclusion of items that can be linked to economic disadvantage (see Chapter 5). That is, to what extent is it important to distinguish between events that impinge on a child that are specifically attributable to a parent versus those experiences that reflect broader socioeconomic problems in the surrounding community? Put differently, to what extent does the specific causal agent matter in the experience of neglect? This important issue can be examined by systematically sampling different types of content in the initial item pool.

A final consideration is relevance (e.g., Haynes et al., 1995; Messick, 1995), which is the requirement that all of the item content in the finished instrument should fall within the boundaries of the target construct. Although this requirement may seem incompatible with the earlier principle of overinclusiveness, it is not. The principle of overinclusiveness simply stipulates that some marginally relevant content should be included in the initial item pool to help specify the boundaries of the construct domain. Subsequent psychometric analyses then can determine these limits and identify construct-irrelevant content that ultimately should be discarded.

Although this property of content relevance may sound easy to attain in principle, it often is more difficult to achieve in practice. A key problem here is the dynamic nature of content validity (Haynes et al., 1995). As the understanding of the target construct evolves, content that previously was subsumed within the domain of the construct may now fall outside of its boundaries. Put differently, content that is initially judged to be construct-relevant later can be viewed as irrelevant. An excellent example of this dynamic process can be seen in the assessment of depression and anxiety symptoms. Prior to the 1980s, most test developers failed to make a sharp conceptual distinction between these constructs. Because of this, many older depression measures contain significant anxiety-related content and vice versa (see Clark & Watson, 1991; Gotlib & Cane, 1989). This irrelevant content now is judged to be problematic, as it lessens the discriminant validity of these instruments.

Similar considerations apply to the assessment of child maltreatment. Analyses of case record data consistently reveal substantial comorbidity among different forms of maltreatment, such that relatively few "pure" cases of neglect, physical abuse, and sexual abuse can be identified (e.g., Sullivan & Knutson, 1998, 2000). This pervasive comorbidity complicates the issue of content validity, as it makes it more difficult to establish the range of content that should be included in various types of maltreatment measures. Ultimately, the content of a measure should reflect the nature and breadth of the target construct. For example, if the goal is to develop a specific index of sexual abuse—rather than a broader measure of maltreatment—then it is problematic to include content related to these other forms of maltreatment in the final instrument.

Haynes et al. (1995) offered a number of useful suggestions for evaluating and improving the content validity of measures (see, e.g., their appendix on p. 247 of their article). In particular, they emphasize the importance of obtaining detailed feedback from expert judges with specific expertise in the construct domain. In the assessment of child maltreatment, this would involve obtaining judgments of content comprehensiveness, representativeness, and relevance from researchers and clinicians actively working in this area. As one example, experts were used to help define child maltreatment in a series of meetings convened by the National Institute of Mental Health, the National Institute of Child Health and Human Development, the National Institute of Justice, and the Administration on Children, Youth and Families during the 1990s (see Sternberg et al., 2004). Haynes et al. (1995) also recommended obtaining feedback from representatives of the targeted population, but this can be problematic and difficult to implement in the area of child maltreatment (e.g., Berger, Knutson, Mehm, & Perkins, 1998).

STRUCTURAL VALIDITY: METHODS OF ITEM SELECTION

The examination of the structural phase is organized around two key topics: 1) methods of item selection and 2) estimates of test reliability. This first section introduces the key concept of structural fidelity and then discusses four basic strategies of item selection: 1) rational/theoretical, 2) criterion-keying, 3) internal consistency, and 4) item response theory.

Structural Fidelity

Now consider the structural component of construct validation. The basic principle in this stage is structural fidelity (Loevinger, 1957; see also Messick, 1995). This is the idea that the internal structure of the scale (i.e., the correlations among its component items) should be fully consistent with what is known about the internal organization of the underlying construct. Given that most constructs are posited to be homogeneous and internally consistent, this principle typically means that the selected items also should be homogeneous and internally consistent (although exceptions to this rule are considered later in this chapter). Because of this, the structural component also subsumes traditional forms of reliability evidence. Consequently, in discussing this aspect of construct validity, it is best to begin by discussing basic methods of item selection and then turn to a consideration of major forms of reliability.

The Rational-Theoretical Approach

The choice of an item selection strategy has crucial implications for everything that follows; it needs to be carefully matched to the goals of scale development and to one's theoretical conceptualization of the target construct (see Clark & Watson, 1995). Although there are countless specific variations, it is useful to recognize four basic item selection strategies. The first strategy can be called the rational-theoretical approach. This item selection strategy is extraordinarily easy to implement. In this approach, the test developer creates an item pool that reflects his or her theoretical conceptualization of the target construct. The developer then simply assumes that this conceptualization is entirely satisfactory; consequently, all of the original items are retained in the final instrument without any attempt to refine it. Thus, the hallmark of this strategy is that no items are modified or dropped from the initial pool.

There are two obvious problems with this strategy—one is theoretical and the other is pragmatic. The theoretical problem is that this strategy is profoundly unscientific. The essential feature of the scientific method is that scientists must subject their ideas to empirical testing under conditions in which there is a strong likelihood of disconfirmation; this is what distinguishes science from other forms of human inquiry, such as philosophy. In marked contrast, however, test developers who employ this strategy simply assume that their ideas are correct without testing them empirically.

The pragmatic problem is that it is highly unlikely that one's initial conceptualization will, in fact, be entirely satisfactory and free from significant errors. Accordingly, the resulting scale will faithfully mirror any flaws in this initial conceptualization. Note, moreover, that theoretical consensus is lacking in many areas of assessment, such that rationally based measures can be expected to differ from one another in important ways. For instance, differing theoretical notions exist regarding what constitutes acceptable parental discipline versus child maltreatment. More specifically, disciplining children by striking them with objects is viewed as abuse by some investigators but not by others (for a discussion, see Baumrind, Larzelere, & Cowan, 2002; Gershoff, 2002). These differing theoretical models naturally would lead to the development of very different assessment instruments (and to very different estimates of the prevalence of maltreatment; see Knutson & Selner, 1994). Without subjecting such instruments to empirical scrutiny, it is impossible to resolve these theoretical disputes.

Despite these problems, test developers continue to use this strategy. For instance, Foa, Kozak, Salkovskis, Coles, and Amir (1998) described the development of a new self-report measure of obsessive-compulsive disorder (OCD), the

Obsessive-Compulsive Inventory (OCI). After describing the development of the initial item pool, Foa et al. simply stated that "seven subscales were constructed to represent the major symptoms of OCD" (1998, p. 208). There is no mention of any structural analyses, nor is there any indication that items were dropped during the item selection process; consequently, it appears that item selection proceeded entirely on rational grounds. This, in turn, helps to explain why the OCI has significant psychometric problems (see Wu & Watson, 2003). The most serious problem is the very poor discriminant validity of the original Checking and Doubting scales. In two large samples, Wu and Watson (2003) obtained correlations of .81 and .78 between these scales; after being corrected for attenuation due to unreliability, the correlations between these scales approached unity ($r = .96$ and $.95$, respectively), establishing that they actually assess a single underlying construct. To their credit, Foa and her colleagues subsequently corrected this problem when they created the revised OCI (OCI–R; Foa et al., 2002). To create this new version of the instrument, Foa et al. subjected the OCI items to rigorous structural analyses, which identified six underlying dimensions rather than the hypothesized seven. Accordingly, the original Doubting scale was dropped, thereby eliminating its problematic relation to the Checking scale.

Criterion-Based Methods

Meehl's (1945) "empirical manifesto" provided the theoretical stimulus that ushered in the heyday of empirical test construction during the 1940s and 1950s. In this method, the test developer administers the item pool to two groups that differ on the target variable of interest. To create a measure of depression, for instance, one would administer the items to two groups of respondents—one group that has depression and one group that does not. Similarly, a measure of sexual abuse would be constructed by giving items to participants who have been abused versus participants who have not. Items then are retained for the final scale if the participants in these two criterion groups respond to them differently (i.e., if they empirically differentiate the two groups of respondents).

The criterion method quickly became popular among test developers. It was easy and straightforward to use, and it usually created tests that possessed reasonable predictive validity. With widespread use, however, the limitations of this approach quickly became evident. At a conceptual level, these measures proved unsatisfactory because they failed to yield psychologically interpretable instruments that could help to advance psychological theory (Cattell, 1946; Loevinger, 1957). More pragmatically, criterion-keyed instruments such as the California Psychological Inventory (CPI; Gough, 1987) and the revised version of the Minnesota Multiphasic Personality Inventory (MMPI-2; Butcher, Dahlstrom, Graham, Tellegen, & Kaemmer, 1989) suffer from two crippling problems that render them unsatisfactory for most assessment purposes. First, the items comprising empirically keyed scales tend to be extremely heterogeneous, so that these scales lack internal coherence. Butcher et al. (1989), for instance, obtained coefficient alphas of only .34 and .39 for the MMPI-2 Paranoia scale in large samples of men and women, respectively. Similarly, several of the CPI scales have internal consistency reliabilities only in the .35–.60 range (see Gough, 1987, Table 19). Second, many of these criterion-keyed scales are very highly correlated and, therefore, have poor discriminant validity. For example, the CPI Dominance scale correlated .70 or greater with the Sociability, Self-acceptance, and Independence scales in two large normative samples (see Gough, 1987, Table 20).

These problems, in turn, reflect two interrelated flaws in the underlying rationale for this method. First, it is unreasonable to expect that the criterion groups will differ only on the target variable of interest. For instance, respondents who experience depression will not simply be more depressed than those in the nondepressed group: Beyond depression, they also can be expected to report a broad range of psychopathology, including greater anxiety and an increased level of somatic complaints (see Clark & Watson, 1991; Mineka, Watson, & Clark, 1998). Similarly, as noted earlier, the empirical data consistently demonstrate substantial comorbidity among different forms of maltreatment, including neglect, physical abuse, and sexual abuse (e.g., Sullivan & Knutson, 1998, 2000). This again means that it is highly unlikely that groups of individuals who have been maltreated will differ simply on the target variable of interest. For example, a criterion group composed of individuals who have been sexually abused also will show substantially elevated levels of neglect and physical abuse—as well as various types of maltreatment-related problems—thereby producing heterogeneity in the content of criterion-keyed scales.

Second, because of this comorbidity, many of the criterion groups that are used to create these scales will themselves overlap because of inherent links between the target constructs. This, in turn, means that 1) many of the same individuals could be used to form criterion groups for sexual abuse, physical abuse, and neglect and 2) many of the same items would be selected for each type of scale. This, then, helps to explain the very poor discriminant validity of many empirically keyed scales.

In light of these problems, psychometricians long have discouraged the use of criterion-keyed methods. Nevertheless, these methods continue to be used by test developers. Clark and Watson (1995), for example, identified a set of 41 scale-development papers that were published from 1989 through 1994; 7 of these articles (17%) relied primarily on criterion groups for item selection.

Internal Consistency Methods

Since high speed computers became widely available in the 1990s, the most widely used method for item selection in scale development is some form of internal consistency analysis (see Clark & Watson, 1995). This usually involves the use of some type of factor analysis to identify clusters of interrelated items (Clark

& Watson, 1995; Floyd & Widaman, 1995). A less common approach is to use corrected item–total correlations to identify and eliminate items that do not correlate substantially with the target construct.

Regardless of the specific method that is used, the basic goal in this approach is to select items that are moderately intercorrelated with one another. Clark and Watson (1995) recommend that the average interitem correlation generally should fall in the .15–.50 range. This wide range is provided because the optimal value necessarily varies with the generality versus specificity of the target construct. If one is measuring a relatively broad construct such as parental neglect, a lower mean correlation (e.g., a value in the .15–.30 range) likely will be optimal. In contrast, when measuring a narrower construct such as a specific domain of neglect (e.g., failure to seek appropriate health care), a higher mean intercorrelation (e.g., in the .30–.50 range) likely is needed. Once again, the key principle is structural fidelity: The magnitude of the item intercorrelations should faithfully reflect the internal organization of the underlying construct.

Item Response Theory

Scales created using item response theory (IRT; Embretson, 1996; Reise & Waller, 2003; Santor & Ramsey, 1998; Waller & Reise, 1989) still are relatively uncommon but are likely to become much more prevalent in the future with the increasing availability of sophisticated computer software. IRT is based on the assumption that test responses reflect levels of an underlying trait and, moreover, that the relation between the response and the trait can be described for each item by a monotonically increasing function called an item characteristic curve (ICC). Individuals with higher levels of the trait have higher expected probabilities for answering the item in the keyed direction (e.g., quantitatively gifted individuals are more likely to get a math problem correct), and the ICC provides the precise value of these probabilities for each level of the trait.

The emphasis in IRT is on identifying those items that are likely to be most informative for each individual test respondent, given his or her level of the underlying trait. For instance, an item reflecting a very mild and common form of neglect may provide useful information when administered to individuals who have experienced relatively low levels of maltreatment (who may or may not endorse it), but likely will be much less informative if given to an individual with an established history of severe maltreatment (because we know in advance that he or she almost certainly will endorse it). From an IRT perspective, the optimal item is one that the individual has a 50% probability of endorsing in the keyed direction because this conveys the maximum amount of new trait-relevant information for that person.

In comparison to other item selection approaches, IRT offers two important advantages. First, IRT enables the test developer to specify the trait level at which a given item is maximally informative. This information, in turn, can be used to identify a set of items that yield precise, reliable assessments across the entire range of the trait. Put differently, IRT-based scales offer an improved ability to discriminate among individuals at the extreme ends of the trait distribution (e.g., among those both very high and very low in maltreatment). Second, IRT methods allow one to estimate an individual's trait level without having to rely on a fixed, standard set of items. This property permits the development of computer-adaptive tests, in which assessment is focused primarily on the subset of items that are maximally informative for each individual respondent (e.g., more extreme, infrequent, difficult items for severely maltreated individuals versus milder, more common, easier items for others). Because of this, computer adaptive tests are extremely efficient and can yield the same amount of trait-relevant information using far fewer items than conventional measures (typically providing item savings of 50% or more; see Embretson, 1996; Waller & Reise, 1989).

STRUCTURAL VALIDITY: RELIABILITY EVIDENCE

The choice of scale construction method clearly can have a profound influence on the reliability of the resulting instrument. Most notably, internal consistency methods generally yield more homogeneous measures than rational and empirical approaches. In order to explicate the construct validity process more fully, various forms of reliability evidence are considered in greater detail in the following sections. Specifically, three common methods for assessing reliability are discussed: internal consistency, test–retest reliability, and interrater reliability. All of these methods are best viewed as indicators of the consistency of measurement across various conditions rather than reliability per se. Indeed, they may either overestimate or underestimate the true level of reliability (as it is strictly defined) under certain assessment conditions.

Overview of Reliability

In order to understand some of the material that follows, it is helpful to review briefly the central assumptions of classical reliability theory (see Anastasi & Urbina, 1997; Kaplan & Saccuzzo, 2001; Murphy & Davidshofer, 2001; Rushton, Brainerd, & Pressley, 1983; Watson & Tellegen, 2002). According to the logic that originally was articulated by Spearman (1910), any observed score can be decomposed into two independent components: the true score and measurement error. The true score (e.g., the individual's true level of intelligence) is assumed to be completely stable and invariant over time; it therefore should be perfectly correlated across different assessment conditions. In contrast, measurement error is assumed to be entirely random; consequently, this component should fluctuate chaotically and be entirely uncorrelated across different assessment conditions.

These assumptions further explain two crucial features of classical reliability theory. First, as we have seen, reliability and error were equated with consistency (i.e., the extent to which indicators of the construct are correlated across different assessments) and inconsistency (i.e., a lack of correlation across assessments), respectively. Accordingly, regardless of the specific method that is used, reliability estimates will increase in value as the assessed indicators of the construct (e.g., different items within a scale; different administrations of the same test over time; parallel forms of a test) become more highly intercorrelated. Second, reliability generally should increase as more and more assessments are aggregated together. Because random errors are, by definition, uncorrelated across assessments, they should increasingly cancel each other out as more observations are averaged. Rushton et al., for instance, stated that "there is always error associated with measurement. When several measurements are combined, these errors tend to average out, thereby providing a more accurate picture of relationships in the population" (1983, p. 19).

Internal Consistency
When is Homogeneity Desirable?

As stated earlier, structural fidelity is the guiding consideration in evaluating the internal consistency of an instrument: The correlations among the items should faithfully mirror the internal organization of the underlying construct. Given that most constructs are posited to be homogeneous and internally coherent, this principle typically means that the selected items also should be homogeneous and internally coherent. There are exceptions, however. These exceptions involve cases in which the items are designed to be causal indicators (i.e., causal contributors to some cumulative index) rather than effect indicators (i.e., parallel indicators of an underlying construct) (see Smith & McCarthy, 1995). This commonly is the case in the measurement of stress and trauma. For example, Simms, Watson, and Doebbeling (2002) created a Severe Exposures Index (SEI) to assess combat-related trauma in deployed Gulf War veterans. The SEI consisted of three items: "come under small arms fire," "exposure to nerve gas," and "exposure to mustard gas or other blistering agents." In this case, there is no expectation or requirement that these items should be significantly intercorrelated—for instance, that individuals who came under small arms fire also were more likely to be exposed to nerve gas. Rather, these items simply are seen as causal contributors that jointly create a cumulative index of combat-related trauma.

Similar considerations apply to measures of child maltreatment in which the overriding consideration is to create a cumulative index of traumatic exposure. For example, there is no necessary expectation that various discrete acts of sexual abuse—such as fondling or penetration of different areas of the child's body (see Sternberg et al., 2004, Table 2)—covary significantly with one another.

Homogeneity simply is not a relevant psychometric property in this type of measure.

Establishing the Homogeneity of a Measure

In most cases, however, the goal of assessment is to measure one thing (i.e., the target construct)—and only one thing—as precisely as possible. Unfortunately, an inspection of the contemporary literature makes it quite evident that this goal remains poorly understood by test developers and users. The most obvious problem is the belief that item homogeneity can be established simply by demonstrating that a scale shows an acceptable level of internal consistency reliability, as estimated by traditional indices such as coefficient alpha (Cronbach, 1951) or K-R 20 (Kuder & Richardson, 1937). Psychometricians long have discouraged the practice of using these conventional reliability indices to establish the homogeneity of a scale (Clark & Watson, 1995; Cortina, 1993; Schmitt, 1996). To understand this point, it is necessary to distinguish between internal consistency and homogeneity or unidimensionality. Internal consistency refers to the overall degree to which the items that make up a scale are interrelated, whereas homogeneity and unidimensionality indicate whether the scale items assess a single underlying factor or construct (Clark & Watson, 1995; Cortina, 1993; Schmitt, 1996). Thus, internal consistency is a necessary but not sufficient condition for homogeneity. Put differently, a scale cannot be homogeneous unless all of its items are interrelated, but a scale can contain many interrelated items and still not be unidimensional. Because the goal of assessment typically is to measure a single construct systematically, the test developer ultimately is pursuing scale homogeneity rather than internal consistency.

Unfortunately, K-R 20 and coefficient alpha are measures of internal consistency rather than homogeneity and so are of little use in establishing the unidimensionality of a scale. Moreover, they are imperfect indicators of internal consistency because they actually are a function of two separate parameters: 1) the number of scale items and 2) the average correlation among these items (Clark & Watson, 1995; Cortina, 1993; Schmitt, 1996). That is, one can achieve a high coefficient alpha by 1) having many items or 2) highly intercorrelated items or 3) some combination of the two. This obviously complicates things, because the number of items is irrelevant to the issue of internal consistency. In practical terms, this means that as the number of items becomes quite large, it is exceedingly easy to achieve a high reliability estimate. In fact, Cortina (1993) suggests that coefficient alpha is virtually useless as an index of internal consistency for scales containing 40 or more items.

Accordingly, the average interitem correlation (which is a straightforward measure of internal consistency) is more useful than coefficient alpha (which is not) in establishing construct validity. Consequently, test developers should work toward a target mean interitem correlation rather than trying to achieve a specified level of alpha. As discussed earlier, this average interitem correlation generally should fall in the range of .15–.50 (see also Clark & Watson, 1995).

To complicate things further, a scale can have an acceptable mean interitem correlation and still not be unidimensional. This occurs when many high item correlations are averaged with many low ones (Clark & Watson, 1995; Cortina, 1993; Schmitt, 1996). Cortina (1993), for instance, constructed an 18-item scale composed of two independent 9-item clusters. The items that made up each group were highly homogeneous and in each case had an average interitem correlation of .50. However, these groups were created to be statistically independent of one another, such that items in the different clusters were completed uncorrelated with one another. Obviously, this scale was not unidimensional, but instead reflected two independent dimensions; nevertheless, it had a coefficient alpha of .85 and an average interitem correlation of .24.

Thus, one cannot ensure unidimensionality simply by focusing on the mean interitem correlation; rather, it is necessary to examine the distribution and range of these correlations as well. Consequently, the author's earlier guideline must be amended to state that virtually all of the individual interitem correlations should fall somewhere in the range of .15–.50. In other words, unidimensionality is achieved when almost all of the interitem correlations are moderate in magnitude and cluster narrowly around the mean level. In practical terms, the easiest way to establish the homogeneity of a scale is to show that all of its items have a significant loading (a value of .35 and higher; see Clark & Watson, 1995) on the first unrotated factor in a principal factor analysis. A more stringent approach—which is recommended by Schmitt (1996)—is to use confirmatory factor analysis to test the fit of a single factor model.

The Attenuation Paradox

Throughout this discussion, I have emphasized that the interitem correlations should be moderate in magnitude. This may seem puzzling to some readers, given that estimates of internal consistency increase in value as the average interitem correlation increases. Obviously, therefore, one can maximize coefficient alpha by retaining items that are very highly correlated with others in the pool. Is it not desirable, therefore, to maximize reliability by retaining highly intercorrelated items in the final scale?

No, it is not. This is the crux of the classic attenuation paradox in psychometrics: Increasing internal consistency beyond a certain point actually lessens the construct validity of a scale (see Boyle, 1991; Clark & Watson, 1995; Loevinger, 1954, 1957). This paradox occurs for two reasons. First, strongly correlated items also are highly redundant with one another. Once one of them is included in a scale, the others contribute virtually no incremental information. For example, an individual who endorses the item, "My father sometimes punched me when he was angry with me," almost certainly will also endorse the item, "My father used to hit me when he was mad at me." Once one has asked the first item, there is no point in asking the second, because the answer already is evident. More generally, a scale will yield far more information—and, hence, be a more interesting and valid measure of a construct—if it contains differentiated items that are only moderately correlated. Second, attempts to maximize internal consistency almost invariably produce scales that are quite narrow in content; if this content is narrower than the target construct, then the validity of the scale is compromised. To return to the earlier example, a scale that simply were to contain a series of items assessing whether or not the father struck the child when angry would lack comprehensiveness as a measure of parental physical abuse and, therefore, would not be a valid measure of this construct.

The Problem of Short Forms

This discussion of the attenuation paradox should make it clear that the goal of assessment is to maximize validity rather than reliability. It was this realization, in fact, that eventually led psychometricians to embrace validity as the conceptual centerpiece of measurement. This tension between reliability and validity also plays a crucial role in the process of shortening an existing measure (for an extended discussion of short forms, see Smith, McCarthy, & Anderson, 2000). As has already been discussed, conventional indices of internal consistency are influenced by scale length—all other things being equal, longer scales yield higher reliability estimates. Consequently, the developers of short forms face an obvious dilemma: All other things being equal, shortening a scale necessarily will lower its reliability.

There is, however, a seemingly easy way out of this problem. One can maintain reliability by narrowing the scope of the measure and retaining only the most highly intercorrelated items from the original scale. In other words, one can counteract the effect of shortening the scale by increasing the magnitude of the average interitem correlation. Unfortunately, many short form developers choose this option. For instance, when they created the OCI–R, Foa et al. (2002) also shortened the six remaining scales to only three items apiece. Nevertheless, the reliability of these short forms generally remained impressively high; in fact, Foa et al. (2002, Table 4) reported several coefficient alphas of .90 or greater. It should be noted that in the case of a 3-item scale, an alpha of .90 reflects an average interitem correlation of .75, which is well above the guideline set earlier.

Thus, here is a clear, practical application of the attenuation paradox. Faced with the problem of reduced scale length, many short form developers choose to maximize reliability (by raising the average interitem correlation) at the expense of validity. This approach is wrongheaded. By narrowing the scope of the short form, the test constructor has substantially changed the nature of this measure and, therefore, compromised its construct validity. In the area of child maltreatment, it is easy to see how this process of narrowing the breadth of a measure could substantially lessen its construct validity. Suppose, for instance, that an investigator created a short-form measure of parental neglect by retaining only items related to the denial of basic care (e.g., food, clothing, shelter) and by dropping all other types of items (e.g., educational neglect, failure to supervise properly). This narrower scale no longer would represent a valid, clinically useful measure of parental neglect. Again, the goal of assessment should be to maximize validity (by retaining the full scope of the item content as much as possible) rather than reliability.

Alpha as an Index of Reliability

As stated earlier, conventional indices such as coefficient alpha are best viewed as indicators of the consistency of measurement across various conditions rather than reliability per se. Indeed, it is well known that alpha actually can either overestimate or underestimate the true level of reliability under different assessment conditions (see Becker, 2000; Green, 2003; Osburn, 2000; Schmidt, Le, & Ilies, 2003; Schmitt, 1996). Alpha overestimates reliability when there are systematic errors of measurement. Unlike random errors, systematic measurement errors are significantly correlated across different assessments. Consequently, they are misclassified as part of the "true score" component in classical reliability theory (which, as noted earlier, equates the true variance with consistency in measurement).

Two kinds of measurement errors are worth noting. The first are response biases such as acquiescence and social desirability (see Watson & Tellegen, 2002; Watson & Vaidya, 2003). Social desirability refers to a tendency for respondents to consciously or unconsciously distort their responses to make them more consistent with prevailing cultural norms (e.g., Paulhus & Reid, 1991; Watson & Vaidya, 2003). Acquiescence can be broadly defined as "an individual-difference variable to agree or disagree with an item regardless of its content" (Russell, 1979, p. 346); in other words, acquiescence causes individuals to provide similar responses to a diverse array of item content. In the area of child maltreatment, a related type of bias involves individual differences in the tendency to label experiences as normative or abusive (e.g., Bower & Knutson, 1996; Bower, Knutson, & Winebarger, 2001). That is, given the same set of childhood experiences, one respondent might define them as abusive, whereas another might see them as normative and describe them quite differently. Although all of these response biases represent errors of measurement that reduce the validity of an instrument, they can be expected to increase the magnitude of the interitem correlations, thereby spuriously raising coefficient alpha.

Transient error represents another potentially important type of systematic error that can be a problem when assessment is confined to a single occasion (Becker, 2000; Green, 2003; Osburn, 2000; Schmidt et al., 2003). Transient error reflects the influence of time-limited factors, such as the current mood of the respondent. As Green put it,

Respondents have moods, feelings, and mental states that affect their scores on a measure at a particular time, and these transient influences are likely to vary from week to week or even day to day and thus produce changes in the measure's scores when readministered. (2003, p. 88)

Generally speaking, transient errors can be expected to produce inconsistency across different occasions but consistent responses within the same assessment. Consequently, transient errors inflate values of coefficient alpha when they are based on a single occasion (for ways to address this problem, see Green, 2003; Schmidt et al., 2003). It is important to note, moreover, that the wording of items can influence their susceptibility to transient error. For example, Prescott et al. (2000) showed that participants' current mood influenced their responses to items that were phrased in evaluative terms (e.g., "harsh discipline") but not those referring to discrete behavioral acts (e.g., being hit by objects, being punched). These findings are consistent with other results indicating that current levels of depression can influence retrospective descriptions of certain childhood experiences (Brewin, Andrews, & Gotlib, 1993; Lewinsohn & Rosenbaum, 1987).

Conversely, alpha underestimates the true reliability of a measure that is heterogeneous and multidimensional (Cronbach, 1951; Osburn, 2000; Schmitt, 1996). As discussed earlier, classical reliability theory equates inconsistency with measurement error. Sometimes, however, inconsistency reflects the heterogeneity of item content, rather than error per se. Schmitt (1996) provides an excellent illustration of this situation. Suppose, for instance, that a test is composed of two highly homogenous item groups, such that the within-cluster correlations are all .80; suppose, furthermore, that these clusters are only moderately related to one another, such that the cross-cluster item correlations are only .30. These relatively low cross-cluster correlations (which actually reflect item heterogeneity, not error) will be misclassified as measurement error in the calculation of coefficient alpha, thereby making it a biased underestimation of the true reliability of the measure. This underestimation bias, incidentally, explains the nonsensical finding that correlations that are corrected for attenuation sometimes exceed 1.00 when coefficient alpha is used to estimate reliability (see Osburn, 2000; Schmitt, 1996).

Test–Retest Reliability

Classical reliability theory arose out of work on intelligence and related cognitive abilities (Spearman, 1910). Accordingly, it was assumed that basic dimensions of individual differences essentially are invariant over time, such that any observed change could be attributed to measurement error (Anastasi & Urbina, 1997; Kaplan & Saccuzzo, 2001; Murphy & Davidshofer, 2001). This assumption was incorporated into the concept of test–retest reliability, which is computed by correlating scores on the same test across two assessments separated by a specified time interval. As Murphy and Davidshofer have noted: "The rationale behind this method of estimating reliability is disarmingly simple. Because the same test is administered twice . . . differences between scores on the test and scores on the retest should be due solely to measurement error" (2001, p. 114). Kaplan and Saccuzzo further clarify that "This type of analysis is of value only when we measure 'traits' or characteristics that do not change over time" (2001, p. 106). Thus, classical psychometrics assumed that the true score components of trait measures were perfectly stable over time, so that the magnitude of observed change could be used to estimate the size of the random error component.

Temporal stability data can provide very interesting and useful information about virtually any measure, regardless of the particular construct that is being assessed. However, as the quotation from Kaplan and Saccuzzo (2001) suggests, retest correlations only represent clear, unambiguous indices of reliability when it is reasonable to assume that there has been no actual change on the assessed variable, such that the underlying true score remains perfectly invariant. For many areas of psychological research, this assumption is unreasonable for one of two reasons. First, many important psychological constructs—for example, moods and emotions—are inherently unstable and fluctuate substantially over time. For example, Lee Anna Clark and the author of this chapter developed the Expanded Form of the Positive and Negative Affect Schedule (PANAS-X; Watson & Clark, 1994), which assesses a wide range of current mood states. Clark and Watson have amassed a broad range of evidence establishing that the PANAS-X scales are sensitive to multiple influences. For instance, scores on several of the negative mood scales are elevated during episodes of stress and show significant decreases during exercise; conversely, positive mood scores increase during exercise and in response to a broad range of social activities. The temporal instability of these scales obviously is not problematic, nor is it reflective of measurement error. Indeed, these theoretically meaningful effects have helped to establish the construct validity of these scales.

Second, even very stable constructs may still show some true change that is not attributable to measurement error, particularly when the retest interval is quite lengthy. The personality literature provides an excellent illustration of this point. Various lines of evidence have established that personality traits are not static, nondevelopmental constructs; rather, they show meaningful change over time. Perhaps the most compelling evidence is that retest correlations for personality traits systematically decline as the elapsed time interval increases (e.g., Cattell, 1964a, 1964b; Roberts & DelVecchio, 2000). This finding is difficult to explain using the assumptions of classical reliability theory. If the underlying true scores are perfectly stable, and errors are randomly distributed across assessments, then reliability estimates should be unaffected by the length of the retest interval. This finding makes perfect sense, however, if one assumes that true change is possible, because change is more and more likely to occur with increasing retest intervals (Anastasi & Urbina, 1997; Murphy & Davidshofer, 2001).

Cattell (1964a, 1964b; Cattell, Eber, & Tatsuoka, 1970) emphasized this point more than 3 decades ago, arguing for the importance of distinguishing between dependability and stability. Cattell defined dependability as "the correlation between two administrations of the same test *when the lapse of time is insufficient for people themselves to change* with respect to what is being measured" (Cattell et al., 1970, p. 30; emphasis in original). In contrast, he defined stability as the correlation between two administrations of a test across a retest interval that is long enough for true change to occur (Cattell et al., 1970). This distinction is crucial: It makes it quite clear that dependability data provide an unambiguous index of reliability, whereas stability correlations do not.

Retest data can—and should—play an important role in the construct validation of child maltreatment measures. The possibility of true change can be ruled out for many such measures, so that any response inconsistencies over time clearly can be attributed to measurement error. Suppose, for instance, that one assesses child sexual abuse by asking about the occurrence of various physical acts (e.g., fondling or penetration of different areas of the body) in a sample of young adults on two different occasions. Given that all experience of abuse necessarily occurred in the past (i.e., during childhood), no true change is possible between Time 1 and Time 2. Consequently, retest correlations in this type of design necessarily would be measures of dependability rather than stability, regardless of the elapsed time span between the two assessments.

However, this situation clearly and unambiguously applies only to measures of specific events and behaviors. Any items that require significant interpretation or inference from the respondent (e.g., that ask whether parental discipline was harsh, or whether certain behaviors were desired or deserved) can be expected to fluctuate in response to current mood and other transient influences (Brewin et al., 1993; Lewinsohn & Rosenbaum, 1987; Prescott et al., 2000). Whether these fluctuations represent error depends on the goal of the assessment and the nature of the target construct. If the goal is to measure subjective responses to childhood experiences (e.g., the participants' perceptions of their parents' disciplinary practices), then such fluctuations are not necessarily problematic. In contrast, if the assessment is designed to provide objective evidence of actual maltreatment, then temporal instability is undesirable and represents measurement error.

Good retest data are lacking for many maltreatment measures (for recent reviews of this literature, see Aalsma, Zimet, Fortenberry, Blythe, & Orr, 2002; Fergusson, Horwood, & Woodward, 2000). The data that are available, however, are sufficient to raise some significant concerns about the reliability of many of these measures. Aalsma et al. (2002) examined the temporal consistency of self-rated childhood sexual abuse in a sample of 217 adolescents; they obtained a retest correlation of only .64 across a 7-month interval. They noted, moreover, that 21.7% of their respondents reported inconsistent abuse histories across the two occasions (i.e., they described significant sexual abuse at one assessment but not the other); this number actually exceeded the number of participants who consistently reported the experience of abuse at both assessments (20.3%). Similarly, Fergusson et al. (2000) used an interview to measure childhood sexual abuse and physical punishment in a large young adult sample; the participants initially were assessed at age 18 and then retested at age 21. Again, more respondents provided inconsistent abuse histories (9.3% and 11.1% for sexual abuse and physical punishment, respectively) than described consistent histories of abuse (4.7% and 6.2%, respectively). Finally, Sanders and Becker-Lausen (1995) obtained a retest correlation of only .71 on their child punishment subscale across a retest interval of 6–8 weeks.

These unimpressive numbers are hardly surprising, because ample evidence exists to show that retrospective judgments are subject to various errors and distortions (e.g., Bradburn, Rips, & Shevell, 1987; Kahneman, 1999; Robinson & Clore, 2002; Ross, 1989; Watson & Tellegen, 2002). For instance, several studies have shown that retrospective ratings are influenced by the respondents' mood state at the time of assessment (e.g., Brewin et al., 1993; Prescott et al., 2000; Schwarz & Strack, 1999; Stone, Shiffman, & DeVries, 1999). In addition, retrospective judgments are subject to recency effects, such that more recent experiences have a greater influence than more distant ones (Schwarz & Sudman, 1994; Stone et al., 1999). Other evidence indicates that respondents may reconstruct and redefine past experiences to make them more congruent with their current life situation (Ross, 1989). Although much of this literature is based on rather mundane experiences, similar considerations apply to more serious life events. For example, several studies of posttraumatic stress disorder have found that respondents' descriptions of precipitating events change substantially over time (King et al., 2000; Roemer, Litz, Orsillo, Ehlich, & Friedman, 1998; Southwick, Morgan, Nicolaou, & Charney, 1997).

These data indicate that maltreatment researchers need to pay greater attention to the retest reliability of their measures. For reasons already discussed, retest evidence is particularly important when 1) items require subjective inferences from the respondents and 2) maltreatment is assessed retrospectively.

Interrater Reliability

This examination of interrater reliability focuses on three main topics. The first section discusses basic analytic methods for assessing the level of interrater reliability. The second section provides guidelines for interpreting observed levels of interrater agreement. The final section summarizes key factors that can be expected to influence levels of interrater reliability.

Methods of Assessing Agreement

Interrater reliability can be defined as the level of agreement between two judges who are asked to rate the same phenomenon (e.g., whether there is evidence of abuse in an individual's case file). The assessment of interrater reliability involves design and data analytic complexities that are not seen with other types of reliability; it, therefore, is a topic that is difficult to summarize briefly. A brief overview of some basic issues and considerations is provided here.

The initial complication is that there are several different ways to compute interrater reliability, depending on the nature of the design. Two issues are critically important in the selection of the appropriate index. The first is whether the judgment is categorical (e.g., a dichotomous judgment of whether an individual meets diagnostic criteria for major depression) or continuous (e.g., rating the severity of depressive symptoms on a 7-point Likert scale). A number of different coefficients are available for categorical judgments (see Green, 1981; Zwick, 1988). Since its introduction more than 40 years ago, the most popular index for categorical judgments has been Cohen's (1960) kappa, which allows one to correct for chance-level agreement.

When judgments are continuous, some type of correlation coefficient can be used. This leads to the second issue, which is whether or not the same judges have rated all of the participants. Suppose, for instance, that two clinicians—Drs. Smith and Jones—rate the current level of depression in an entire sample of adolescents. In this simple design, it is possible to use the standard Pearson product–moment correlation. Alternatively, suppose that three different clinicians were used to make these judgments in randomly alternating pairs; for instance, some participants were rated by Smith and Jones, but others by Smith and Brown, and still others by Jones and Brown. In this case, it would be inappropriate to use a Pearson correlation; instead, one must compute an intraclass correlation (see Cicchetti, 1994; Fleiss & Cohen, 1973).

These two types of correlations can yield very different results under certain conditions. Most notably, intraclass correlations are influenced by differences in both rank order and level/severity; in contrast, Pearson correlations are influenced only by the former and are unaffected by the latter (see Cicchetti, 1994). Suppose, for instance, that Smith and Jones show complete agreement in their rank ordering of the participants (i.e., they rate the same individuals as most and least depressed), but that Smith consistently rates them as more depressed than does Jones. In this case, the Pearson correlation would approach +1.00 (reflecting the strong level of rank order agreement), whereas an intraclass correlation would be substantially lower (reflecting this level difference in rated severity). As Cicchetti put it,

> The product moment correlation places the maximum limit on what the intraclass correlation coefficient can be. Thus, the intraclass correlation coefficient can be no higher than the product–moment correlation and will be lower than the product–moment correlation depending on the extent to which there is a systematic bias (or higher mean values) for one examiner's set of evaluations in relation to that of another. (1994, pp. 286–287)

Consequently, the intraclass correlation is a more sensitive measure of interrater agreement (see Cicchetti, 1994).

Guidelines for Evaluating Agreement

Several authors have proposed very similar guidelines for evaluating obtained values of kappa and intraclass correlations (Cicchetti, 1994; Cicchetti & Sparrow, 1981; Fleiss, 1981; Landis & Koch, 1977). According to these guidelines, values below .40 can be classified as poor, those in the .40–.59 range as fair, those in the .60–.74 range as good, and those of .75 and greater as excellent.

Factors Influencing the Level of Agreement

Reliability ordinarily is seen as an inherent property of a particular measure: That is, superior measures yield better reliability estimates than inferior instruments. The situation is much more complicated in the case of interrater agreement, because many other considerations are involved. To be sure, the measure itself remains important: For instance, some diagnostic interviews simply are better (e.g., because of clearer instructions or more precise scoring criteria) than others. Nevertheless, several other factors also are important and can be expected to influence the overall level of interrater agreement.

Four additional factors are highlighted here. First, interrater agreement is highly influenced by the prevalence or base rate of the variable in the sample (Shrout, Spitzer, & Fleiss, 1987; Uebersax, 1987; Williams et al., 1992). Generally speaking, it is much easier to obtain strong interrater agreement when the base rate of the phenomenon is high (e.g., when 20% of the sample has been maltreated) than when it is low (e.g., when 2% of the sample was maltreated). This is particularly true when using kappa. As noted earlier, kappa corrects for the level of agreement that would be expected by chance. When base rates are low, the level of chance agreement is very high, so that it becomes quite difficult to out-perform chance (see also Meehl & Rosen, 1955). Base rate considerations are critically important in maltreatment research, given that many specific forms of maltreatment likely will occur relatively infrequently, even in high-risk samples.

Second, interrater agreement varies as a function of the degree of independence between the judges (see Williams et al., 1992). In this regard, researchers have employed a wide variety of designs to assess interrater reliability, some of which provide a greater level of independence than others. All other things being equal, greater independence in the judgments will be associated with lower agreement. For instance, Williams et al. (1992) used the very conservative retest method to assess the reliability of psychiatric diagnoses. In this method, each individual is interviewed separately by two different clinicians on two different occasions. This method promotes a maximum level of independence and generally can be expected to yield lower estimates of interrater reliability. In contrast, another common approach is to videotape or audiotape an interview conducted by the first clinician, which then is scored separately by a second. In this method, the judgments obviously are far less independent, because both clinicians now have access to the same pool of information (including probing, skip-outs, and so forth). Not surprising, this method yields higher estimates of interrater agreement than does the retest method (see Williams et al., 1992).

Third, interrater agreement will vary as a function of the training and competency of the judges (Williams et al., 1992). This perhaps is the aspect that most distinguishes this topic from other forms of reliability. When discussing either internal consistency or retest reliability, it is reasonable to describe the reliability of a measure. This makes little sense when discussing interrater reliability, because even the best, most carefully constructed instrument can be sabotaged by poorly trained or incompetent judges. Because of this, one cannot establish interrater reliability simply by citing comparable data from the past (e.g., previous evidence of interjudge agreement from the same laboratory); rather, interrater agreement must constantly be reestablished in each new sample and with each new set of judges.

Finally, some phenomena simply are easier to rate than others. Generally speaking, characteristics that are easily observable in others (i.e., those with clear, frequent behavioral manifestations) yield better interrater agreement than do variables that are more internal or subjective or that require a greater level of inference on the part of the judge (Funder, 1995; Watson, Hubbard, & Wiese, 2000). In the area of maltreatment, for example, it seems reasonable to suggest that it would be easier to rate behaviors that are present (e.g., specific occurrences of physical and sexual abuse) than those that are absent (e.g., instances of parental neglect). More generally, the Realistic Accuracy Model (RAM) proposed by Funder (1995) offers a useful conceptual framework for understanding the level of interrater agreement that reasonably can be expected. According to RAM, accuracy in judging traits depends on the "availability, detection, and utilization of relevant behavioral cues" (Funder, 1995, p. 656). In other words, the level of interrater agreement can be expected to vary as a function of the quality and quantity of construct-relevant information that is available to the judge. According to RAM, the validity of judges' ratings is influenced by a number of specific processes, including characteristics of the judge, of the target, and of the construct itself.

EXTERNAL VALIDITY

The final stage of construct validation moves beyond the test itself and considers how it relates to other variables. This external phase subsumes three basic considerations: convergent validity, discriminant validity, and criterion validity.

Convergent Validity

The concept of convergent validity was formally introduced into psychometrics by Campbell and Fiske (1959). Convergent validity is assessed by examining the relations among different purported measures of the same construct (e.g., Anastasi & Urbina, 1997; Kaplan & Saccuzzo, 2001; Murphy & Davidshofer, 2001). This type of evidence is crucial in the establishment of construct validity. If it can be shown that different indicators converge substantially, this significantly strengthens one's confidence that they actually do assess the target construct. According to Campbell and Fiske, these convergent correlations "should be significantly different from zero and sufficiently large to encourage further examination of validity" (1959, p. 82).

What does "sufficiently large" mean in this context? Campbell and Fiske were quite vague on this point, and their vagueness was entirely appropriate. In contrast to other types of construct validity evidence, one cannot offer simple guidelines for evaluating when convergent correlations are sufficiently high to support the validity of a measure. This is because the magnitude of these correlations will vary dramatically as a function of various design features. The single most important factor is the nature of the different measures that are used to examine convergent validity. In their original formulation, Campbell and Fiske (1959) largely assumed that investigators would examine convergence across fundamentally different assessment methods. In one analysis, for example, they examined the associations between trait scores assessed using 1) peer ratings and 2) a word association task (see their Table 2). In another analysis, they investigated the convergence among free behavior, role playing, and projective test scores (see their Table 8). DeGarmo, Reid, and Knutson (see Chapter 11) argue for the importance of multimethod approaches in maltreatment research and use structural equation modeling to examine the relations among self-report, observational ratings, and laboratory tasks.

In recent years, investigators have interpreted the concept of "method" much more loosely. For example, in the contemporary literature, it is commonplace for researchers to establish convergent validity by reporting correlations among different self-report measures of the same target construct. This practice is not problematic. Clearly, however, it creates a very different situation from the one originally envisioned by Campbell and Fiske (1959). Most notably, convergent correlations will be substantially higher when they are computed within the same basic method (e.g., between different self-report measures of child maltreatment) than when they are calculated across very different methods (e.g., between self-rated versus caseworker-rated maltreatment). This, in turn, means that the same level of convergence might support construct validity in one context but challenge it in another. Suppose, for instance, that one obtained a .40 correlation between two self-report measures of child neglect. Given this finding, it would be difficult to maintain that both of these instruments actually assessed the same construct. In contrast, a .40 correlation between self- versus caseworker-ratings of child neglect would be far more encouraging and likely would enhance the construct validity of these measures.

Discriminant Validity

Discriminant validity is assessed by examining how a measure relates to purported indicators of other constructs (e.g., Anastasi & Urbina, 1997; Kaplan & Sacuzzo, 2001; Murphy & Davidshofer, 2001). This concept also was formally articulated by Campbell and Fiske (1959), who introduced it in the context of a multitrait–multimethod matrix. This type of matrix can be created whenever one assesses two or more constructs in at least two different ways. For interpretative purposes, the matrix can be decomposed into two basic subcomponents: 1) the two monomethod triangles and 2) a single heteromethod block. For instance, Watson, Suls, and Haig (2002) assessed six different traits (self-esteem, neuroticism, extraversion, openness, agreeableness, and conscientiousness) using two different methods (self-ratings and peer-ratings) (see their Table 2). One monomethod triangle contained all of the correlations among the self-ratings; the second included all of the associations among the various peer-ratings. Finally, the heteromethod block contained all of the correlations between the self- versus peer-ratings.

As outlined by Campbell and Fiske, a multitrait–multimethod matrix yields three basic types of discriminant validity evidence (1959, pp. 82–83). First, each of the convergent correlations should be higher than any of the other values in its row or column of the heteromethod block. For instance, self-rated self-esteem should correlate more strongly with peer-rated self-esteem than with peer-rated extraversion or peer-rated openness. Similarly, self-reported neglect should correlate more strongly with caseworker ratings of neglect than with caseworker ratings of physical or sexual abuse. This requirement is rather minimal and usually is achieved quite easily. For example, all six traits examined by Watson et al. (2002) passed it without difficulty. Failure to achieve discriminant validity at this level typically signals a serious problem with either 1) one or more of the measures or 2) the construct itself (see Cronbach & Meehl, 1955).

The second type of discriminant validity evidence is that the convergent correlations should exceed all of the values in the monomethod triangles. As Campbell and Fiske put it, a variable should "correlate higher with an independent effort to measure the same trait than with measures designed to get at different traits which happen to employ the same method" (1959, p. 83). For instance, caseworker-rated neglect should correlate more strongly with self-reported neglect than with caseworker-rated physical abuse or caseworker-rated sexual abuse. This is a much stronger test of discriminant validity that is far more difficult to pass than the first; for instance, several of the traits examined by Watson et al. (2002) fail this criterion.

Failure to achieve discriminant validity at this level is not necessarily catastrophic. A key consideration here is the true level of correlation among the assessed constructs. In this regard, it must be emphasized that the most interesting tests of discriminant validity involve analyses of constructs that are known to be strongly related. For example, Watson and Clark (1992) reported several multitrait–multimethod matrices to examine relations among measures of fear, sadness, hostility, and guilt. It is well-established that measures of these negative affects are strongly interrelated, so it is hardly surprising that the monomethod triangles in these analyses included a number of substantial correlations. Of course, the presence of these strong monomethod correlations makes it very difficult to pass this second test, particularly when one uses very different assessment methods (e.g., self- versus peer ratings) that can be expected to yield relatively modest convergent correlations. This likely will be a significant consideration in many areas of maltreatment research, in light of the substantial comorbidity between different types of child maltreatment (e.g., Sullivan & Knutson, 1998, 2000).

According to Campbell and Fiske, the final consideration in discriminant validity is whether "the same pattern of trait interrelationship be shown in all of the heterotrait triangles" (1959, p. 83). The key issue here is the extent to which these heterotrait correlations reflect 1) true trait interrelations versus 2) the complicating influence of method variance. If the pattern of associations remains relatively consistent across all of the heterotrait triangles (e.g., fear and guilt are strongly related in every instance), then it is reasonable to conclude that these associations are true, accurate reflections of the links between the underlying constructs. Conversely, if the patterns show substantial discrepancies across the various triangles, then method variance likely is implicated. This type of evidence is best examined using confirmatory factor analysis, which allows one to model both construct-based and method-based factors (see Byrne, 1994; Kline, 1998; Watson et al., 2002). For example, the trait-based factors might represent different forms of maltreatment (e.g., neglect, physical abuse, sexual abuse), whereas the method-based factors would reflect different assessment approaches (e.g., self-reports, observational ratings, laboratory tasks; see Chapter 11 for more information).

Criterion Validity

Finally, criterion validity is assessed by relating a measure to important nontest variables. This type of evidence often is further subdivided into concurrent validity (which involves relations with nontest criteria that are assessed at the same time as the measure) and predictive validity (which examines associations with criteria that are assessed at some point in the future) (Anastasi & Urbina, 1997; Kaplan & Saccuzzo, 2001; Murphy & Davidshofer, 2001). Evidence of criterion validity is important for two reasons. The first is purely pragmatic: Measures that have no established links to nontest variables are of little interest to most researchers.

Second, criterion validity evidence is critically important in clarifying the inferences that can be drawn from test scores and, therefore, plays a crucial role in establishing the construct validity of a measure. As an example, Watson and Clark (1993) described the development and validation of a self-report personality scale. As part of this process, they provided a wide range of criterion validity evidence. Among other things, they found that high scores on this scale were associated with 1) heavier and more problematic use of alcohol, marijuana, and other drugs; 2) more casual sexual activity, including a greater number of different sex partners; 3) lower levels of self-reported spirituality and religiosity; and 4) poorer grades in both high school and college. Without knowing anything else about this instrument, one already can make a reasonably good guess about the trait that it measures. In this case, the assessed trait is disinhibition, which "reflects broad individual differences in the tendency to behave in an undercontrolled versus overcontrolled manner" (Watson & Clark, 1993, p. 506). These behavioral correlates are quite consistent with this conceptualization and, therefore, enhance the construct validity of the instrument. In other instances, criterion data may be inconsistent with the prevailing conceptualization of the construct (either because a predicted pattern was not found or because an unexpected correlate has emerged); such inconsistencies indicate a significant problem that must be addressed.

CONCLUSION

A large number of psychometric concepts have been discussed in this chapter. All of these different types of evidence now are viewed as aspects of the broader process of construct validation. In other words, they all simply are pieces in the larger puzzle that is construct validity. This focus on construct validity has fundamentally changed our understanding of many of these concepts. Most notably, it now is clear that they need to be applied flexibly to match the theoretical specifications of the target construct. Put differently, the same set of psychometric data may enhance the validity of one measure but challenge the validity of another, depending on the nature of the target construct.

For instance, temporal stability is an absolutely crucial consideration if the goal of assessment is to obtain objective evidence of childhood maltreatment. As discussed earlier, the retest reliabilities of some childhood abuse measures are surprisingly low, suggesting that they contain a substantial amount of measurement error. On the other hand, change is to be expected—and instability is not inherently problematic—when one is assessing subjective responses to childhood experiences (e.g., the participants' reactions to their parents' disciplinary practices). Similarly, although evidence of homogeneity is essential in establishing the construct validity of many measures, it is irrelevant when the goal of assessment is to create a cumulative index of traumatic experiences (e.g., the occurrence of child sexual abuse); here, there is no necessary expectation or requirement that different manifestations of maltreatment be interrelated. As one final example, a particular level of convergent validity may be very encouraging in one context (e.g., between self-reported and caseworker-rated neglect) but indicate significant problems in another (e.g., between two self-report measures of neglect).

This emphasis on construct validity also underscores the need to develop clear, precise definitions of the key constructs in the area of child maltreatment. For instance, it will be exceedingly difficult to develop a reliable and valid measure of parental neglect without having a clear, detailed conceptualization of what this construct entails. This statement should not be misunderstood to mean that all important theoretical issues and disputes must be resolved prior to the start of scale development and data collection. Indeed, the scale development process offers a very powerful mechanism for sorting through these disputes and resolving them. As originally articulated by Loevinger (1957), the key point is to incorporate all of these different theoretical schemes into the initial item tool so that they can be subjected to empirical scrutiny. To return to an earlier example, a key issue in the area of neglect involves the potential inclusion of items that can be linked to economic disadvantage (see Chapter 5). This important issue can be examined by systematically sampling different types of content in the initial item pool and then observing how they behave in subsequent analyses. Thus, psychological measurement involves a constant interplay between theoretical expectations and empirical data.

REFERENCES

Aalsma, M.C., Zimet, G.D., Fortenberry, J.D., Blythe, M., & Orr, D.P. (2002). Reports of childhood sexual abuse by adolescents and young adults: Stability over time. *Journal of Sex Research, 39,* 259–263.

American Psychological Association. (1999). *Standards for educational and psychological testing.* Washington, DC: Author.

Anastasi, A., & Urbina, S. (1997). *Psychological testing* (7th ed.). New York: Macmillan.

Baumrind, D., Larzelere, R.E., & Cowan, P.A. (2002). Ordinary physical punishment: Is it harmful? Comment on Gershoff (2002). *Psychological Bulletin, 128,* 580–589.

Becker, G. (2000). How important is transient error in estimating reliability? Going beyond simulation studies. *Psychological Methods, 5,* 370–379.

Berger, A.M., Knutson, J.F., Mehm, J.G., & Perkins, K.A. (1988). The self-report of punitive childhood experiences of young adults and adolescents. *Child Abuse & Neglect, 12,* 251–262.

Bower, M.E., & Knutson, J.F. (1996). Attitudes toward physical discipline as a function of disciplinary history and self-labeling as physically abused. *Child Abuse & Neglect, 20,* 689–699.

Bower, M.E., Knutson, J.F., & Winebarger, A. (2001). Disciplinary history, adult disciplinary attitudes, and risk for abusive parenting. *Journal of Community Psychology, 29,* 219–240.

Boyle, G.J. (1991). Does item homogeneity indicate internal consistency or item redundancy in psychometric scales? *Personality and Individual Differences, 12,* 291–294.

Bradburn, N.M., Rips, L.J., & Shevell, S.K. (1987). Answering autobiographical questions: The impact of memory and inference on surveys. *Science, 236,* 157–161.

Brewin, C.R., Andrews, B., & Gotlib, I.H. (1993). Psychopathology and early experience: A reappraisal of retrospective reports. *Psychological Bulletin, 113,* 82–98.

Butcher, J.N., Dahlstrom, W.G., Graham, J.R., Tellegen, A., & Kaemmer, B. (1989). *Minnesota Multiphasic Personality Inventory (MMPI-2). Manual for administration and scoring.* Minneapolis: University of Minnesota Press.

Byrne, B.M. (1994). *Structural equation modeling with EQS and EQS/Windows.* Thousand Oaks, CA: Sage Publications.

Campbell, D.T., & Fiske, D.W. (1959). Convergent and discriminant validation by the multitrait-multimethod matrix. *Psychological Bulletin, 56,* 81–105.

Cattell, R.B. (1946). *Description and measurement of personality.* Yonkers-on-Hudson, NY: World Book.

Cattell, R.B. (1964a). Beyond validity and reliability: Some further concepts and coefficients for evaluating tests. *Journal of Experimental Education, 33,* 133–143.

Cattell, R.B. (1964b). Validity and reliability: A proposed more basic set of concepts. *Journal of Educational Psychology, 55,* 1–22.

Cattell, R.B., Eber, H.W., & Tatsuoka, M.M. (1970). *Handbook for the Sixteen Personality Factor Questionnaire (16PF).* Champaign, IL: Institute for Personality and Ability Testing.

Cicchetti, D.V. (1994). Guidelines, criteria, and rules of thumb for evaluating normed and standardized assessment instruments in psychology. *Psychological Assessment, 6,* 284–290.

Cicchetti, D.V., & Sparrow, S.S. (1981). Developing criteria for establishing interrater reliability of specific items: Applications to assessment of adaptive behavior. *American Journal of Mental Deficiency, 86,* 127–137.

Clark, L.A., & Watson, D. (1991). Tripartite model of anxiety and depression: Psychometric evidence and taxonomic implications. *Journal of Abnormal Psychology, 100,* 316–336.

Clark, L.A., & Watson, D. (1995). Constructing validity: Basic issues in objective scale development. *Psychological Assessment, 7,* 309–319.

Cohen, J. (1960). A coefficient of agreement for nominal scales. *Educational and Psychological Measurement, 20,* 37–46.

Cortina, J.M. (1993). What is coefficient alpha? An examination of theory and applications. *Journal of Applied Psychology, 78,* 98–104.

Cronbach, L.J. (1951). Coefficient alpha and the internal structure of tests. *Psychometrika, 16,* 297–334.

Cronbach, L.J., & Meehl, P.E. (1955). Construct validity in psychological tests. *Psychological Bulletin, 52,* 281–302.

Embretson, S.E. (1996). The new rules of measurement. *Psychological Assessment, 8,* 341–349.

Fergusson, D.M., Horwood, L.J., & Woodward, L.J. (2000). The stability of child abuse reports: A longitudinal study of the reporting behavior of young adults. *Psychological Medicine, 30,* 529–544.

Fleiss, J.L. (1981). *Statistical methods for rates and proportions* (2nd. ed.). New York: Wiley.

Fleiss, J.L., & Cohen, J. (1973). The equivalence of weighted kappa and the intraclass correlation coefficient as measures of reliability. *Educational and Psychological Measurement, 33,* 613–619.

Floyd, F.J., & Widaman, K.F. (1995). Factor analysis in the development and refinement of clinical assessment instruments. *Psychological Assessment, 7,* 286–299.

Foa, E.B., Huppert, J.D., Leiberg, S., Langner, R., Kichic, R., Hajcak, G., et al. (2002). The Obsessive-Compulsive Inventory: Development and validation of a short version. *Psychological Assessment, 14,* 485–496.

Foa, E.B., Kozak, M.J., Salkovskis, P.M., Coles, M.E., & Amir, N. (1998). The validation of a new obsessive-compulsive disorder scale: The Obsessive-Compulsive Inventory. *Psychological Assessment, 10,* 206–214.

Foster, S.L., & Cone, J.D. (1995). Validity issues in clinical assessment. *Psychological Assessment, 7,* 248–260.

Funder, D.C. (1995). On the accuracy of personality judgment: A realistic approach. *Psychological Review, 102,* 652–670.

Gershoff, E.T. (2002). Corporal punishment by parents and associated child behaviors and experiences: A meta-analytic and theoretical review. *Psychological Bulletin, 128,* 539–579.

Gotlib, I.H., & Cane, D.B. (1989). Self-report assessment of depression and anxiety. In P.C. Kendall & D. Watson (Eds.), *Anxiety and depression: Distinctive and overlapping features* (pp. 131–169). San Diego, CA: Academic Press.

Gough, H.G. (1987). *California Psychological Inventory Administrator's Guide.* Palo Alto, CA: Consulting Psychologists Press.

Green, S.B. (1981). A comparison of three indexes of agreement between observers: Proportion of agreement, G-index, and kappa. *Educational and Psychological Measurement, 41,* 1069–1072.

Green, S.B. (2003). A coefficient alpha for test–retest data. *Psychological Methods, 8,* 88–101.

Haynes, S.N., Richard, D.C.S., & Kubany, E.S. (1995). Content validity in psychological assessment: A functional approach to concepts and methods. *Psychological Assessment, 7,* 238–247.

Hogan, R.T. (1983). A socioanalytic theory of personality. In M. Page (Ed.), *1982 Nebraska Symposium on Motivation* (pp. 55–89). Lincoln: University of Nebraska Press.

Hogan, R.T., & Hogan, J. (1992). *Hogan Personality Inventory Manual.* Tulsa, OK: Hogan Assessment Systems.

Kahneman, D. (1999). Objective happiness. In D. Kahneman, E. Diener, & N. Schwarz (Eds.), *Well-being: The foundations of hedonic psychology* (pp. 3–25). New York: Russell Sage Foundation.

Kaplan, R.M., & Saccuzzo, D.P. (2001). *Psychological testing: Principles, applications, and issues* (5th ed.). Belmont, CA: Wadsworth/Thomson Learning.

King, D.W., King, L.A., Erickson, D.J., Huang, M.T., Sharkansky, E.J., & Wolfe, J. (2000). Posttraumatic stress disorder and retrospectively reported stressor exposure: A longitudinal prediction model. *Journal of Abnormal Psychology, 109,* 624–633.

Kline, R.B. (1998). *Principles and practice of structural equation modeling.* New York: Guilford Press.

Knutson, J.F., & Schartz, H.A. (1997). Physical abuse and neglect of children. In T.A. Widiger, A.J. Frances, H.A. Pincus, R. Ross, M.B. First, & W. Davis (Eds.), *DSM-IV Sourcebook: Volume 3* (pp. 713–804). Washington, DC: American Psychiatric Association.

Knutson, J.F., & Selner, M.B. (1994). Punitive childhood experiences reported by young adults over a 10-year period. *Child Abuse & Neglect, 18,* 155–166.

Kuder, G.F., & Richardson, M.W. (1937). The theory of the estimation of test reliability. *Psychometrika, 2,* 151–160.

Landis, J.R., & Koch, G.G. (1977). The measurement of observer agreement for categorical data. *Biometrics, 33,* 159–174.

Lewinsohn, P.M., & Rosenbaum, M. (1987). Recall of parental behavior by acute depressives, remitted depressives, and nondepressives. *Journal of Personality and Social Psychology, 52,* 611–619.

Loevinger, J. (1954). The attenuation paradox in test theory. *Psychological Bulletin, 51,* 493–504.

Loevinger, J. (1957). Objective tests as instruments of psychological theory. *Psychological Reports, 3,* 635–694.

Meehl, P.E. (1945). The dynamics of structured personality tests. *Journal of Clinical Psychology, 1,* 296–303.

Meehl, P.E., & Rosen, A. (1955). Antecedent probability and the efficiency of psychometric signs, patterns, or cutting scores. *Psychological Bulletin, 52,* 194–216.

Messick, S. (1995). Validity of psychological assessment: Validation of inferences from persons' responses and performances as scientific inquiry into score meaning. *American Psychologist, 50,* 741–749.

Mineka, S., Watson, D., & Clark, L.A. (1998). Comorbidity of anxiety and unipolar mood disorders. *Annual Review of Psychology, 49,* 377–412.

Murphy, K.R., & Davidshofer, C.O. (2001). *Psychological testing: Principles and applications* (5th ed.). Upper Saddle River, NJ: Prentice Hall.

Osburn, H.G. (2000). Coefficient alpha and related internal consistency coefficients. *Psychological Methods, 5,* 343–355.

Paulhus, D.L., & Reid, D.B. (1991). Enhancement and denial in socially desirable responding. *Journal of Personality and Social Psychology, 60,* 307–317.

Prescott, A., Bank, L., Reid, J.B., Knutson, J.F., Burraston, B.O., & Eddy, J.M. (2000). The veridicality of punitive childhood experiences reported by adolescents and young adults. *Child Abuse & Neglect, 24,* 411–423.

Reise, S.P., & Waller, N.G. (2003). How many IRT parameters does it take to model psychopathology items? *Psychological Methods, 8,* 164–184.

Roberts, B.W., & DelVecchio, W.F. (2000). The rank-order consistency of personality traits from childhood to old age: A quantitative review of longitudinal studies. *Psychological Bulletin, 126,* 3–25.

Robinson, M.D., & Clore, G.L. (2002). Belief and feeling: Evidence for an accessibility model of emotional self-report. *Psychological Bulletin, 128,* 934–960.

Roemer, L., Litz, B.T., Orsillo, S.M., Ehlich, P.J., & Friedman, M.J. (1998). Increases in retrospective accounts of war-zone exposure over time: The role of PTSD symptom severity. *Journal of Traumatic Stress, 11,* 597–605.

Ross, M. (1989). Relation of implicit theories to the construction of personal histories. *Psychological Review, 96,* 341–357.

Rushton, J.P., Brainerd, C.J., & Pressley, M. (1983). Behavioral development and construct validity: The principle of aggregation. *Psychological Bulletin, 94,* 18–38.

Russell, J.A. (1979). Affective space is bipolar. *Journal of Personality and Social Psychology, 37,* 1161–1178.

Sanders, B., & Becker-Lausen, E. (1995). The measurement of psychological maltreatment: Early data on the Child Abuse and Trauma Scale. *Child Abuse & Neglect, 19,* 315–323.

Santor, D.A., & Ramsay, J.O. (1998). Progress in the technology of measurement: Applications of item response models. *Psychological Assessment, 10,* 345–359.

Schmidt, F.L., Le, H., & Ilies, R. (2003). Beyond alpha: An empirical examination of the effects of different sources of measurement error on reliability estimates for measures of individual differences constructs. *Psychological Methods, 8,* 206–224.

Schmitt, N. (1996). Uses and abuses of coefficient alpha. *Psychological Assessment, 8,* 350–353.

Schwarz, N., & Strack, F. (1999). Reports of subjective well-being: Judgmental processes and their methodological implications. In D. Kahneman, E. Diener, & N. Schwarz (Eds.), *Wellbeing: The foundations of hedonic psychology* (pp. 61–84). New York: Russell Sage Foundation.

Schwarz, N., & Sudman, S. (1994). *Autobiographical memory and the validity of retrospective reports.* New York: Springer-Verlag.

Sedlak, A.J., & Broadhurst, D.D. (1996). *Third national incidence study of child abuse and neglect: Final report.* Washington, DC: U.S. Department of Health and Human Services, Administration for Children and Families, Administration on Children, Youth, and Families, National Center on Child Abuse and Neglect.

Shrout, P.E., Spitzer, R.L., & Fleiss, J.L. (1987). Quantification of agreement in psychiatric diagnosis revisited. *Archives of General Psychiatry, 44,* 172–177.

Simms, L.J., Watson, D., & Doebbeling, B.N. (2002). Confirmatory factor analyses of post-traumatic stress symptoms in deployed and non-deployed veterans of the Gulf War. *Journal of Abnormal Psychology, 111,* 637–647.

Smith, G.T., & McCarthy, D.M. (1995). Methodological considerations in the refinement of clinical assessment instruments. *Psychological Assessment, 7,* 300–308.

Smith, G.T., McCarthy, D.M., & Anderson, K.G. (2000). On the sins of short-form development. *Psychological Assessment, 12,* 102–111.

Southwick, S.M., Morgan, C.A., Nicolaou, A.L., & Charney, D.S. (1997). Consistency of memory for combat-related traumatic events in veterans of Operation Desert Storm. *American Journal of Psychiatry, 154,* 173–177.

Spearman, C. (1910). Correlation calculated from faulty data. *British Journal of Psychology, 3,* 271–295.

Sternberg, K.J., Knutson, J.F., Lamb, M.E., Bradaran, L.P., Nolan, C., & Flanzer, S. (2004). The Child Maltreatment Log: A PC-based program for describing research samples. *Child Maltreatment, 9,* 30–48.

Stone, A.A., Shiffman, S.S., & DeVries, M.W. (1999). Ecological momentary assessment. In D. Kahneman, E. Diener, & N. Schwarz (Eds.), *Well-being: The foundations of hedonic psychology* (pp. 26–39). New York: Russell Sage Foundation.

Sullivan, P.M., & Knutson, J.F. (1998). The association between child maltreatment and disabilities in a hospital-based pediatric sample. *Child Abuse & Neglect, 22,* 271–288.

Sullivan, P.M., & Knutson, J.F. (2000). Maltreatment and disabilities: A population-based epidemiological study. *Child Abuse & Neglect, 24,* 1257–1274.

Uebersax, J.S. (1987). Diversity of decision-making models and the measurement of interrater agreement. *Psychological Bulletin, 101,* 140–146.

Waller, N.G., & Reise, S.P. (1989). Computerized adaptive personality assessment: An illustration with the Absorption scale. *Journal of Personality and Social Psychology, 57,* 1051–1058.

Watson, D., & Clark, L.A. (1992). Affects separable and inseparable: On the hierarchical arrangement of the negative affects. *Journal of Personality and Social Psychology, 62,* 489–505.

Watson, D., & Clark, L.A. (1993). Behavioral disinhibition versus constraint: A dispositional perspective. In D.M. Wegner & J.W. Pennebaker (Eds.), *Handbook of mental control* (pp. 506–527). New York: Prentice-Hall.

Watson, D., & Clark, L.A. (1994). *The PANAS-X: Manual for the Positive and Negative Affect Schedule–Expanded Form.* Unpublished manuscript, University of Iowa, Iowa City.

Watson, D., Hubbard, B., & Wiese, D. (2000). Self–other agreement in personality and affectivity: The role of acquaintanceship, trait visibility, and assumed similarity. *Journal of Personality and Social Psychology, 78,* 546–558.

Watson, D., O'Hara, M.W., Simms, L.J., Kotov, E.R., Chmielewski, M., McDade-Montez, et al. (2006). *Development and validation of the Iowa Depression and Anxiety Scales (IDAS).* Manuscript submitted for publication.

Watson, D., Suls, J., & Haig, J. (2002). Global self-esteem in relation to structural models of personality and affectivity. *Journal of Personality and Social Psychology, 83,* 185–197.

Watson, D., & Tellegen, A. (2002). Aggregation, acquiescence, and trait affectivity. *Journal of Research in Personality, 36,* 589–597.

Watson, D., & Vaidya, J. (2003). Mood measurement: Current status and future directions. In J.A. Schinka & W. Velicer (Eds.), *Comprehensive handbook of psychology. Volume 2: Research methods* (pp. 351–375). New York: Wiley.

Williams, J.B.W., Gibbon, M., First, M.B., Spitzer, R.L., Davies, M., Borus, J., et al. (1992). The Structured Clinical Interview for DSM-III-R (SCID). II. Multisite test–retest reliability. *Archives of General Psychiatry, 49,* 630–636.

Wu, K.D., & Watson, D. (2003). Further investigation of the Obsessive-Compulsive Inventory: Psychometric analysis in two nonclinical samples. *Journal of Anxiety Disorders, 17,* 305–319.

Zwick, R. (1988). Another look at interrater agreement. *Psychological Bulletin, 103,* 374–378.

III

CURRENT APPROACHES TO MEASUREMENT

ONE OF THE CRITICAL FACTORS confronting a child maltreatment researcher is how to measure the occurrence of that maltreatment. Stated in another way, what source of information should be used to determine whether a research subject has experienced circumstances of maltreatment, and what source of information can be used to actually detail the circumstances of that maltreatment? In some ways, issues concerning the source of information have been pivotal in the critiques of maltreatment research, and choosing a source of information is one of the more important questions confronting a researcher. In Section III, the three dominant approaches to assessing the occurrence of maltreatment are described, and relevant research is reviewed.

In Chapter 9, Portwood reviews a large number of self-report measures that have been used to assess the experiences of children as well as the acts of parents or other child maltreatment perpetrators. By detailing the evidence regarding these commonly used measures, Portwood provides the reader with some guidance as to which self-report measures might be useful in a research context; however, the chapter also provides critical information that should caution scholars who confine their research efforts to self-report methodologies.

One of the central criticisms leveled at maltreatment research has been the widespread practice of delegating the operational definition of abuse to a community agency or child protective services (CPS). Yet, the use of administrative data and CPS records remains the most common strategy for defining maltreatment or describing samples of children who have been maltreated and children in control or comparison groups. In Chapter 10, Runyan and English describe empirical work based on several different approaches for abstracting and coding CPS records for indices of child maltreatment. The chapter provides some guidance as to how that source of information can be used effectively in child maltreatment research as well as information regarding the limitations associated with that source (i.e., CPS records).

It is often assumed that child maltreatment reflects events that are not directly accessible to investigators. In Chapter 11, DeGarmo, Reid, and Knutson describe several strategies in which researchers approximate a more direct assessment of physical abuse and neglect by directly observing parenting in structured interactions, in analogs of parenting circumstances, and by a first-hand assessment of the circumstances of the child's life. By integrating multiple sources of information using structural equation modeling, Chapter 11 also provides an example of how investigators can develop a multimethod/multisource approach to operationally defining their maltreatment constructs.

Taken together, the three chapters of this section are designed to give researchers and students an overview of the strengths and limitations of the three major sources of information regarding child maltreatment as well as some guidance as to how a multimethod/multisource approach might be incorporated in future research. It is clear that there is no single ideal source of information regarding maltreatment, thus a goal of this section is to increase awareness of the different approaches and stimulate scholars to expand their approaches in efforts to describe the maltreatment of their research subjects.

9

Self-Report Approaches

SHARON G. PORTWOOD

BECAUSE CHILD MALTREATMENT typically occurs in private, such that it is not measurable by observation, researchers have primarily relied on victim and/or perpetrator self-reports or other documentation of its occurrence. This tendency to rely on self-reports has been particularly pronounced with regard to childhood sexual abuse (Holmes, 1995). Unfortunately, both self-reports and formal records are susceptible to potential inaccuracies. Also, it is widely recognized that official reports of child abuse and neglect (e.g., through child protection agencies; the police) seriously underrepresent the actual number of abuse cases (Sedlak & Broadhurst, 1996). In addition to concern that official definitions and record-keeping practices fail to reflect the child's experiences accurately, there is also concern that reported cases differ from those that are not identified to authorities (Straus, Hamby, Finkelhor, Moore, & Runyan, 1998). In order to capture cases not included in official records, researchers must rely on reports from victims, perpetrators, or, in rare cases, witnesses.

Historically, there has been extreme variation across studies in how child maltreatment is measured. In a review of 617 articles published in *Child Abuse & Neglect* between 1979 and 1989, Straus (1992) found that 86% of the studies documented in the articles did not use an instrument to measure any variable; by the late 1980s, two thirds of studies still employed no quantitative measures. Nonetheless, researchers have frequently employed self-report measures to classify participants into "abuse" and "no abuse" groups. A majority of early studies based the identification of an individual as abused or nonabused on his or her "yes" or "no" response to a single question regarding childhood abuse history (Aalsma, Zimet, Fortenberry, Blythe, & Orr, 2002). Even in recent studies, some authors have relied on a single item to classify participants, noting that while the item has no known validity or reliability, it does appear to have some face validity. Contrary to assertions that such measures are adequate for research purposes, there is a critical need to utilize measures with sound and well-established psychometric properties in order to advance the study of child maltreatment (National Research Council, 1993).

The purpose of this chapter is to provide a background for evaluating self-report approaches to child maltreatment research.[1] Although self-report approaches may also encompass individual face-to-face and telephone interviews, the focus of this chapter is on the use of written measures to classify respondents into abuse categories. Following an overview of the benefits and limitations of these self-report approaches, a sampling of existing measures for use with children, adolescents, and adults are reviewed. Special considerations applicable to each of these populations also are discussed.

AN OVERVIEW OF SELF-REPORT APPROACHES TO MEASURING CHILD MALTREATMENT

It is a fundamental principle of scientific research that before adopting a particular instrument for use in a study, a researcher should first evaluate the available validity and reliability studies to determine whether appropriate data exist to support the instrument's intended application. Unfortunately, adequate psychometric support is often unavailable for self-report measures of child abuse and neglect. In fact, many measures that purport to measure child maltreatment do not actually serve this purpose. For example, researchers cannot rely on the title of the instrument to indicate that it measures the construct of interest. As noted by Milner,

> In the worst case, a test will not actually measure the construct suggested by its title and should not be used. On the other hand, even well-developed instruments only approximately measure the construct under investigation. So even the best and most widely respected instruments have measurement error. (1989, p. 91)

Many of the factors that contribute to measurement error in assessing abuse are definitional in nature. Fundamentally, there is a question of whether abuse can be defined as the occurrence of specific acts or whether the perception of those acts should be considered. In fact, it can be argued that any classification of a particular act as maltreatment is a matter of perception; it is simply a matter of *whose* perception is used—that of the child, the researcher, lawmakers, or child protection agencies. In fact, data have demonstrated that individuals hold unique concepts of what constitutes abuse or neglect based on their personal and professional experiences and characteristics (Portwood, 1998, 1999). Some studies (e.g., Bower & Knutson, 1996; Rausch & Knutson, 1991) have demonstrated that individuals who report having experienced specific behaviors that might be categorized as abusive tend not to characterize themselves as abused. Thus, questions that ask respondents whether they were abused may produce less

---

[1]For an overview of self-report measures of child abuse and neglect appropriate for clinical use, see Miller and Veltkamp (1995). For an overview of self-report measures applicable to a broader range of criminal victimization of children, see Hamby and Finkelhor (2001).

valid data than questions assessing discrete events (Berger, Knutson, Mehm, & Perkins, 1988).

Not only an act itself but also the frequency and severity of the act may be deemed relevant to an act's classification as abuse. Again, however, both of these determinations are a matter of perception. For example, how many times must an act such as screaming at a child occur, and/or what must the nature of screaming be for it to be considered abusive? Ammerman (1998) suggested that molecular indices (e.g., the number of times a particular act occurs) are preferable to broader based categorizations (e.g., suspected abuse in a child service agency report) given that the former employ more reliable definitions than the latter and, thus, results are more replicable. Although gathering and reporting highly specific data facilitate both communication among researchers and comparisons between studies, reaching this level of specificity is enormously challenging. For example, neglect often is indicated by a pattern of behavior rather than by a single incident, making it particularly difficult to assess through self-reports (Hamby & Finkelhor, 2001).

The complex nature of child maltreatment, along with the lack of scales that cover all major forms of maltreatment—physical abuse, sexual abuse, psychological and emotional abuse and neglect—requires researchers to make an initial determination of the scope of experiences they will examine in their study. A majority of existing self-report measures focus on physical and/or sexual abuse; however, data indicate that the vast majority of child maltreatment cases involve child neglect (National Clearinghouse on Child Abuse and Neglect Information, 2001), which is infrequently assessed. Moreover, many self-report measures fail to provide respondents with clear definitions of the behaviors of interest. For example, given that spanking and other forms of physical discipline are legal, it may be difficult to distinguish those acts that constitute physical abuse (Hamby & Finkelhor, 2001). Likewise, defining sexual abuse as "any sexual activity against one's will" may prompt respondents to exclude certain acts that would appropriately be considered abusive, such as an act in which the age differential between parties renders the act abusive regardless of whether the child victim consented. Research with victims of sexual abuse has shown expressly that victims may not identify themselves as such, despite reporting experiences that are legally defined as rape (Koss, Gidicz, & Wisniewski, 1987).

Given the need for definitional clarity of the central constructs in child maltreatment, achieving an appropriate balance between brevity and content validity also presents special challenges to self-report approaches. As noted by Straus et al., an instrument must be

> Brief enough to be applicable in situations that permit only limited testing time . . . and long enough to achieve an adequate sampling of the universe of content (content validity) and enough observations, such as enough items, to achieve an adequate level of reliability." (1998, p. 251)

To ensure that respondents can complete a measure successfully, items must be worded and formatted such that they are easy to understand. To this end, it is recommended that questionnaires be written at less than an eighth-grade reading level for adults and older adolescents and at less than a fifth-grade reading level for younger adolescents (Hamby & Finkelhor, 2001). Adequate research from which to determine younger children's ability to complete self-administered questionnaires on abuse and neglect is not available; however, a questionnaire could be read aloud in order to facilitate its use with early readers or nonreaders.

Another primary concern with self-report questionnaires is their susceptibility to response distortions, including content responsive faking (i.e., when the respondent attempts to minimize or to exaggerate problems) and content nonresponsivity (i.e., when the respondent is unable or unwilling to respond to the substantive content of the item). Clearly, where, as in the case of child maltreatment, there is a motivation for participants to distort their responses, the test should have measures to detect these distortions (Milner, 1989). However, relatively few measures contain validity (e.g., lie) scales, and response biases are rarely assessed.

Despite their limitations and the special challenges that self-report approaches pose, they do offer some clear advantages to researchers. Most importantly, some researchers (e.g., Hamby & Finkelhor, 2001) contend that standardized self-report questionnaires elicit the most accurate reports of childhood victimization. At their best, standardized self-report questionnaires address a wide range of potentially abusive and neglectful experiences, employ clear and specific definitions, and produce normative data that researchers can then use to make meaningful comparisons between groups. Although an interview may provide more extensive information regarding the nature and duration of abuse than a questionnaire, this method is time-consuming, and its reliability has been poorly evaluated. In fact, data establish that the interview process can be contaminated by interviewer bias and/or social response bias (Milner, Murphy, Valle, & Tolliver, 1998). Moreover, it is essential that an individual have adequate clinical training and education before conducting an interview with a victim or potential victim of child maltreatment (Knight et al., 2000), whereas self-report questionnaires may be administered by a broader range of research personnel as well as in group settings (under appropriate circumstances).

Ultimately, the value of any self-report approach depends on its intended purpose. In selecting a self-report measure of child maltreatment, researchers should consider the underlying purpose for assessment and the relative implications of Type I versus Type II misclassification errors (i.e., sensitivity and specificity of the instrument). For example, during an initial screening, the goal is typically to minimize false negatives in order to avoid missing any actual cases, particularly if the goal is to provide services to those in need. However, in a study of prevalence, the researcher may choose to take a more conservative approach, minimizing the number of false positive classifications.

SELF-REPORT APPROACHES
WITH CHILDREN AND ADOLESCENTS

Although perhaps the most obvious way to assess child maltreatment is to make direct inquiries of the child, such approaches present a number of serious methodological, legal, and ethical dilemmas. As a result, only a few studies have asked children directly about abuse (Amaya-Jackson, Socolar, Hunter, Runyan, & Colindres, 2000).[2] At the outset, as with all self-reports, there is simply no guarantee that the child will provide accurate information. Children may distort their responses intentionally due to a desire to protect their abuser and/or to avoid embarrassment. Moreover, cognitive factors, such as memory function and comprehension, influence the quality of children's self-reports, even when children want to cooperate. Age, gender, and educational level may all account for variance in the accuracy of reports to the extent that they impact the child's ability to complete the research instrument. Thus, it is essential that constructs of interest be clearly defined in language that children can understand, a task that is particularly difficult with regard to sexual experiences. Recognizing respondents' limitations, victimization questions directed at young children tend not only to employ simpler language but also to be less specific and less extensive. Despite concerns with accuracy, there is a growing body of research to suggest that school-age children can provide good self-reports. In fact, in evaluating very young children's ability to give forensic interviews in cases of sexual abuse, it has been shown that children as young as age four are more than 90% accurate in their self-reports (Hamby & Finkelhor, 2000).

In addition to concerns with accuracy, child and adolescent self-report measures give rise to a host of ethical concerns regarding the potential risk to the respondent. Principal among the risks involved in asking children for self-reports of child abuse and neglect in a research context are 1) the potential risks of such direct questioning traumatizing the child and 2) perceived or actual negative consequences to children and families as a result of being reported to child protective services (CPS). A threshold question is "When is the child old enough to be approached for research participation?" In an informal poll, child maltreatment researchers indicated that age 12 represented an appropriate age for asking children about perceptions of abuse and neglect experiences (Knight, et al., 2000). However, even at age 12, consent issues are complex.

Whereas standard informed consent procedures assume that a parent or guardian will protect his or her child's interests, in the case of child maltreatment research, the consenting parent may be a perpetrator or have conflicted allegiances

---

[2]More common are studies that address the traumatic experiences of children in general or other clinical sequelae of child maltreatment. Because the self-report measures utilized in these studies (e.g., Briere's [1996] Trauma Symptom Checklist for Children) do not ask about abuse specifically, they have not been addressed in this chapter.

between the child and the abuser. In these circumstances, the U.S. Department of Health and Human Services (DHHS; 2004) regulations for the protection of human subjects provide that an institutional review board "may waive the [parent/guardian] consent requirements . . . provided an appropriate mechanism for protecting the children who will participate as subjects in the research is substituted." However, the regulations do not provide specific guidance as to what protection mechanisms are, in fact, appropriate, instead stating that this determination "would depend upon the nature and purpose of the activities described in the protocol, the risk and anticipated benefit to the research subjects, and their age, maturity, status, and condition" (45 C.F.R. § 46.408[c]).

Unfortunately, the current literature provides little guidance for researchers on how to respond in a legally and ethically appropriate manner when abuse is reported by participants (Amaya-Jackson et al., 2000). Not only must researchers be informed about and adhere to applicable reporting obligations when abuse or—in many jurisdictions—even potential or suspected abuse is reported, but also they must disclose these obligations to research participants. In the case of children, there is concern that even when an explanation is offered, children may not understand these obligations and their ramifications (e.g., the limits to confidentiality), particularly in the case of developmentally delayed children (Knight, et al., 2000). Likewise, parents or caregivers must be clearly informed as to what will happen if the child discloses maltreatment. However, advising the reporting obligations of the researcher will increase the likelihood of sampling bias if, as is widely assumed, parents are more likely to refuse to participate under these circumstances. (For additional discussion of ethical considerations, see Chapter 14.)

In response to the ethical and methodological issues involved in gathering children's self-reports of maltreatment, some researchers have begun to employ an audio computer-assisted self-interview technique, in which the child hears the question and answer choices through a headset, then responds by touching the computer screen. For example, the Longitudinal Studies of Child Abuse and Neglect (LONGSCAN)[3] project has employed the Audio-Computer Assisted Self Interview (A-CASI), which was designed to be compatible with children's cognitive abilities at age 12 and older. Not only does the A-CASI offer privacy protections (e.g., participants can be interviewed in their homes using headphones and a laptop computer), but also the format is less invasive in that participants can skip questions regarding behaviors to which they have not been exposed. Because the researchers in this study were blind to the data, this method also respected the limits of confidentiality. LONGSCAN researchers also included a question asking whether the respondent wished to speak with either the

[3]As the basis for LONGSCAN, Runyan et al. (1998) formed a consortium conducting five cohort studies of maltreatment and its consequences in five states, which involved collecting information from CPS records, state central registry data, parent self-reports of sexual abuse, Department of Social Services involvement, family variables, and discipline practices.

interviewer or someone else about the abuse; in the event of a positive response, the system notified the interviewer (Knight, et al., 2000). Although A-CASI is expensive and requires face-to-face contact with respondents in order to instruct them on its use, research indicating that adult and adolescent respondents disclose more sensitive information through this method suggests that its use will increase in child maltreatment research (Hamby & Finkelhor, 2001).

Although computer-based techniques hold promise for future research, the majority of researchers have relied on written measures for eliciting self-reports from children. Given that such measures necessarily assume a certain level of reading ability and/or comprehension, they have been used primarily with older children and/or adolescents. However, children as young as age six have provided self-reports for research purposes.

Sample Measures

Following is a brief presentation of several measures available for the purposes of classifying children and, more often, adolescents as abused. For additional information, readers are directed to Amaya-Jackson and colleagues' (2000) review of self-report survey and interview measures that were used in original research studies from 1960 through June 1999 to assess either sexual or physical abuse as an outcome or risk factor.

Assessing Environments III Questionnaire

The Assessing Environments III (AEIII) questionnaire is composed of 164 true–false items designed to elicit information on specific content domains and characteristics of the childhood environment that have been associated with abuse in the clinical literature (Berger et al., 1988). The instrument's authors documented test–retest reliability coefficients ranging from .61 to .89 for the 15 subscales: Physical Punishment, Father [aggressive and antisocial tendencies], Mother [depressed or psychological problems], Peer Relationships, Perception of Discipline, Shared Parenting, Positive Orientation to Education, Age Inappropriate Demands, Marital Discord, Isolation, Community Involvement, Potential Economic Stress, Negative Family Atmosphere, Positive Parental Contact, and Parental Rejection. Only four scales were below .75. Validity also was demonstrated through the AEIII's ability to distinguish between the responses of abused and nonabused adolescents. The Physical Punishment (PP) scale—comprised of 12 items that ask respondents to indicate the occurrence of specific disciplinary acts ranging in severity from mild (e.g., spanking) to potentially injurious (e.g., punching) to acts that have been identified in the literature as forms of abusive parenting (e.g., hitting with objects)—perhaps has been used most widely. To classify participants as abused or nonabused, the Berger (1981) criterion (cited in Rausch & Knutson, 1991) may be applied to designate those participants affirming five or more items on the PP scale as physically abused. A more conservative standard of requiring affirmation of four or more abusive events to classify a participant as abused has been found to produce a low rate of false positives (11.5%) but a high rate of false negatives (65%) (Prescott et al., 2000).

Child Sexual Abuse Scale

Aalsma et al. (2002) developed the Child Sexual Abuse Scale (CSA) in response to their need for a brief self-report measure of child sexual abuse that could assess a wide range of behaviors and psychosocial attitudes in a single study. The CSA was administered to adolescents who were instructed to respond to four items— "Someone tried to touch me in a sexual way against my will," "Someone tried to make me touch them in a sexual way against my will," "I believe that I have been sexually abused by someone," "Someone threatened to tell lies about me or hurt me unless I did something sexual with them"—relative to events occurring before they were 12 years old. This cutoff age was based on the results of focus groups indicating a consensus among adolescents that child sexual abuse involved acts before the age of 12, as well as a desire to limit conflicts regarding consensual sexual experiences. Scores of 0–4 were used to reflect the total number of items endorsed by respondents. In addition, the authors used the scale to create a dichotomous variable of child sexual abuse, with the first group defined as those endorsing a single item and the second group defined as those who endorsed two or more items. The authors reported "excellent" internal reliability at both baseline (alpha = .81) and 7-month follow-up (alpha = .84). However, they also noted "considerable instability" in CSA scale scores over a 7-month period, which they attributed to inconsistent reports of abuse. Nonetheless, using the CSA scale, it was possible to predict group membership based on the number of items endorsed 89% of the time for consistent reporters and 40% of the time for inconsistent reporters. Those adolescents who endorsed two or more CSA scale items were five times more likely to be consistent reporters of CSA.

Childhood Trauma Questionnaire

The Childhood Trauma Questionnaire (CTQ; Bernstein & Fink, 1998) has been recognized as a promising measure of several types of abuse, and it possesses strong psychometric properties, including convergent validity and reliability, both internally and across time. The 28 CTQ items are designed to assess emotional neglect, emotional abuse, physical neglect, physical abuse, and sexual abuse retrospectively among adolescents age 12 and older, and adults. Each type of maltreatment is assessed with five items; three additional items assess respondents' tendency to minimize or to deny abusive experiences. Respondents rate each statement, based on when they were growing up, on a 5-point Likert scale from *never true* to *very often true*. Factor analyses have confirmed a consistent five-factor structure. Test–retest reliability ranges from .79 to .86 over an average of 4 months, and internal consistency reliability coefficients range from a median of .66 for the Physical Neglect subscale to a median of .92 for the Sexual Abuse subscale across a range of samples. The usefulness of the CTQ for research purposes is further supported by consistent findings in regard to its psychometric properties when used with a racially mixed community sample. It should be noted that internal consistency for the Sexual Abuse subscale has been found to be particularly strong, whereas internal consistency for the Physical Neglect subscale has been relatively weak (Scher, Stein, Asmundson, McCreary, & Forde, 2001).

Conflict Tactics Scales

The Conflict Tactics Scales (CTS; Straus,1979, 1990) present respondents with a list of actions that a family member might have taken in a conflict, beginning with items low in coerciveness (e.g., discussing the issue) and gradually expanding to more aggressive acts (e.g., hitting). Respondents then indicate the number of times each action occurred during the specified time period. The measure includes scales on Reasoning, Psychological Aggression, and Physical Assault, and a scoring manual is available (Straus, 1995). The Very Severe Violence (VSV) scale frequently has been used to assess whether or not a respondent experienced childhood physical abuse (Straus & Gelles, 1990). The VSV scale addresses a series of acts that could have resulted in physical injury, including being kicked, bit or hit with a fist, beat up, or burned or scalded; or having had someone use a knife or gun on the respondent. In assessing child maltreatment, the CTS has been used primarily with adults as a retrospective measure of their parents' behavior, but a number of studies have also collected CTS data from children ranging in age from 6 to 17 years (Straus et al., 1998). Although the author has provided data indicating that the CTS works well as a measure of child maltreatment (for a review, see Straus & Hamby, 1997), he also notes several important limitations, many of which stem from the fact that the CTS originally was designed for use with partners in marital, cohabiting, or dating relationships. For example, Straus noted that whereas some items were not really applicable to parent–child relationships, other important parental behaviors were not included.

Parent–Child Conflict Tactics Scales

The Parent–Child Conflict Tactics Scales (CTSPC) measure the extent to which a parent has engaged in specific acts of aggression, physical and psychological, without regard to whether the child was actually injured. The CTSPC has been deemed by Straus and others to be better suited to measuring child abuse and neglect than the original CTS; in fact, the CTSPC was expressly developed to address some of the limitations of the CTS as a measure of child maltreatment (Straus et al., 1998). The three core CTSPC scales contain 22 items. The Nonviolent Discipline scale assesses four disciplinary practices (explanation, time out, deprivation of privilege, substitute activity) that may be used as alternatives to corporal punishment; the Psychological Aggression scale measures verbal and symbolic acts by the parent intended to cause psychological distress to the child; and the Physical Assault scale addresses 13 acts, ranging in severity, with supplemental questions on discipline in the previous week included to elicit a more accurate estimate of the number of behaviors. A supplemental Neglect scale assesses failure to engage in behaviors that satisfy the developmental needs of a child (e.g., failure to provide adequate food or supervision); and an experimental Sexual Abuse scale presents questions related to unwanted sexual touch and forced sexual contact (not limited to acts perpetrated by parents). Although designed for brief (6–8 minutes, increasing to 10–15 minutes when supplemental questions are included) and easy self-administration, the CTSPC also can be administered as a face-to-face or telephone interview. When used with pre-adolescents, the test authors state that an interview format should be used and each item asked about the mother and the father. The self-administered format can be used with adolescents or retrospectively with adults. Promising preliminary psychometric data on the CTSPC for a nationally representative sample of 1,000 U.S. children, along with its ease of administration, suggest that it has practical value for research and clinical screening purposes. However, the CTSPC has been criticized as insufficiently clear on many scales; for example, spanking and other forms of legal physical discipline are included on the Physical Violence scale (Hamby & Finkelhor, 2001).

Parental Punitiveness Scale

Epstein and Komorita (1965) developed the Parental Punitiveness Scale (PPS) as a means of assessing parents' disciplinary responses to children's physical, verbal, and indirect aggression in five primary situations (aggression toward parents, teachers, siblings, peers, and inanimate objects), as perceived by the children. The authors constructed 45 items representing aggression in various situations with four response alternatives to indicate how the child felt that his or her father and mother would respond: have a long talk with me, take away my television, send me to bed without supper, whip me. Internal consistency between the mother and father versions were .92 and .93, respectively.

Traumatic Events Questionnaire–Adolescent Version

The Traumatic Events Questionnaire–Adolescent Version (TEQ–A) contains 46 items designed to elicit details of traumatic experiences in six categories, including Sexual Abuse, Physical Abuse, Witnessing Violence in the Home, Witnessing or Being the Victim of Community Violence, and Accidental Physical Injuries. Winegar and Lipschitz (1999) found high rates of agreement among psychiatrically hospitalized adolescents' reports of childhood sexual abuse (88%, $k = .57$) and physical abuse (83%, $k = .58$) on the TEQ–A and collaborating sources, including information from clinicians, medical records, and CPS reports.

There was less agreement for reports of witnessing home violence (75%, k = .82); however, overall results supported the validity of adolescent self-report measures of abuse. In a second study, hospitalized adolescents provided consistent responses on the TEQ–A and the CTQ; however, the CTQ, which uses cutoff scores to identify cases, produced higher rates of physical and sexual abuse than did the TEQ–A, which relies on multiple yes/no screening questions and a multiple choice format to assess abuse status (Lipschitz, Bernstein, Winegar, & Southwick, 1999).

RETROSPECTIVE SELF-REPORT APPROACHES WITH ADULTS

Deficits in memory are of particular concern when using retrospective measures of childhood abuse history with adults. For example, studies have found that a substantial percentage of women in therapy, ranging from 20% to 60%, report periods of forgetting some or all episodes of childhood sexual abuse (Brewin & Holloway, 1997). In fact, symptoms associated with a history of childhood abuse, such as posttraumatic stress disorder, may be associated with particular impairments or distortions of memory. Not only may unconscious processes (e.g., repression of traumatic events in childhood) interfere with the recollection of childhood abuse, but, given society's disapproval of various forms of family violence, adults who are asked to report their own childhood experiences also might be sensitive to issues of social desirability (Widom & Shepard, 1996).[4] When asked to recall early childhood events, respondents may redefine their or others' behavior in the context of their later life circumstances and/or current situations, as well as their current knowledge. Simply put, what retrospective self-report questionnaires actually measure are adults' memories of abuse; the accuracy of those memories and, in fact, whether they are real or imaginary, constitutes a separate question.

Although repression, dissociation, infantile amnesia, suggestibility, and/or typical "forgetting" processes or other mnemonic fallacies may all account for adults' failure to provide accurate maltreatment histories, studies have shown reasonable accuracy in adult self-reports of childhood physical abuse compared with official case records documenting abuse (Widom & Shepard, 1996) and earlier documented observations of parent–child interactions (Prescott et al., 2000). Although Paivio (2001) established the stability of retrospective self-reports of childhood abuse over six months using the CTQ with a clinical sample, Prescott et al.'s (2000) data indicated that retrospective self-reports of physical abuse may be influenced by the emotional status and contemporary mood of the respondent. In regard to childhood sexual abuse, Widom and Morris (1997) found some

---

[4]For a discussion of self-report measures developed to assess childhood sexual abuse and neglect in an interview format, which might be adapted to a written questionnaire, see Widom and Morris (1997) and Weeks and Widom (1998).

gender differences in reporting. Although women provided more retrospective self-reports than did men, overall, there appeared to be substantial underreporting across genders.

Sample Measures

In addition to the AEIII, CTQ, and CTS, discussed in the preceding section, various measures have been employed to assess adults' self-reports of childhood maltreatment. However, as illustrated in this chapter, many of these measures were developed in connection with specific studies and lack research into their psychometric properties.

Childhood Experience of Care and Abuse Questionnaire

Smith, Lam, Bifulco, and Checkley (2002) developed the Childhood Experience of Care and Abuse Questionnaire (CECA.Q) as an alternative to the more time-consuming Childhood Experience of Care and Abuse interview (CECA) for screening individuals for purposes of research or estimation of adversity rates within populations. In addition to basic demographic information, including family composition, individual sections of the CECA.Q address physical abuse and sexual abuse, as well as measures of antipathy and neglect by either parent. The focus is on experiences prior to age 17. Research incorporating a 3-year follow-up supported the reliability and validity of the CECA.Q for use in research on clinical populations. In addition, results from the CECA.Q showed a high level of agreement with interview results, which often reveal higher rates of abuse than questionnaires.

Life Experiences Questionnaire

The Life Experiences questionnaire was adapted by Sacco and Farber (1999) from two questionnaires previously used in research on abuse (Bryer, Nelson, Miller, & Krol, 1987; Chu & Dill, 1990) for purposes of eliciting adults' reports of the manner in which they had been disciplined by their parents. Respondents are requested to indicate the extent of violence perpetrated by friends, other family members, and a variety of acquaintances. The test authors define physical abuse as

> Serious acts of physical aggression, such as kicking, punching, stabbing, burning, being hit with fists or with a foreign object such as a belt, or any other physical acts of aggression that resulted in marks left on the individual's body. (Sacco & Farber, 1999, p. 1196)

It is notable that spanking, shaking, or slapping with an open hand were expressly excluded from this definition, provided they did not result in physical marks or injury.

Self-Report of Childhood Abuse Physical

For purposes of their 1996 study, Widom and Shepard developed the Self-Report of Childhood Abuse Physical (SRCAP) to supplement retrospective assessments of childhood physical abuse obtained using the CTS. The SRCAP elicits responses to six items: "beat or really hurt you by hitting you with a barehand or fist", "beat or hit you with something hard like a stick or baseball bat", "injure you with a knife, shoot you with a gun, or use another weapon against you", "hurt you badly enough so that you needed a doctor or other medical treatment", "physically injure you so that you were admitted to a hospital", and "beat you when you didn't deserve it" (1996, p. 415). A dichotomous variable was used to indicate whether the respondent had 1) any or 2) none of these experiences. Principal components analysis revealed a two-factor solution that accounted for 63% of the variance (Cronbach's alpha = .75). A comparison of measurement results to correlates of official reports of childhood physical abuse further indicated high construct validity.

Sexual Experiences Questionnaire

Sacco and Farber (1999) expanded and adapted the Sexual Experiences Survey (DiTomasso & Routh, 1993) to garner reports of sexual experiences in childhood. Adult respondents are asked to characterize each experience as forced, somewhat forced, or voluntary. The questionnaire authors utilized the Sexual Experiences Questionnaire (SEQ) to classify respondents as sexually abused when they reported either forced or somewhat forced sexual experiences in childhood. Participants who reported childhood sexual contact with adults were categorized as abused regardless of their severity ratings.

The Wyatt Sex History Questionnaire

The Wyatt Sex History Questionnaire (WSHQ; Wyatt, Lawrence, Vodounon, & Mickey, 1992) was designed as a semistructured, face-to-face interview comprised of 478 items related to both retrospective and current data regarding incidents of nonconsensual sexual abuse. Questions focus on sexual socialization, age of onset, frequency, circumstances of consensual and nonconsensual sexual experiences, and consequences, both initial and long-term. For purposes of the interview, child sexual abuse was defined as "sexual behavior prior to age 18 by someone of any age or relationship to the participant" (Wyatt et al., 1992, p. 54). Two additional exclusion criteria were employed to distinguish sexual abuse from experimentation before age 12 and consensual sexual activity with peers: Incidents in which the perpetrator was more than 5 years older than the participant were considered abusive, as was any contact that was nonconsensual, regardless of perpetrator age. Wyatt and colleagues also developed a 398-item version of the

WSHQ that includes questions related to health correlates of sexual abuse (e.g., HIV/AIDS). Comparisons of telephone and face-to-face interviews prompted the test authors to recommend against telephone interviews, which afforded more opportunities for exaggeration and less specificity. Additional psychometric data on the reliability and validity of the WSHQ are being obtained.

SELF-REPORT APPROACHES WITH ADULT CAREGIVERS
Self-Reports to Identify Abusive Parenting

Self-report measures also have been employed with adults as caregivers to assess their abusive or potentially abusive behavior toward the children in their care. In fact, some researchers (e.g., Ammerman, 1998) contend that there has been an overreliance on reports from mothers despite evidence that reports from mothers are skewed and biased in child maltreatment populations. Caregiver reports of abuse and neglect are potentially problematic not only due to potential inaccuracies as a result of the respondents' lacking complete and/or accurate knowledge of the child's experiences but also because caregivers may intentionally distort their responses in order to avoid social judgments or, in more extreme cases, to avoid legal and/or CPS intervention. Regardless of whether parents have abused their children, they may attempt to conceal or to minimize their personal and family problems during assessment or screening. Less frequently, parents may exaggerate their problems as a result of psychopathology, as a cry for help, or because of other factors (Milner & Crouch, 1997). As a result of "faking good" or "faking bad" in caregiver self-reports, commentators have emphasized the need for the inclusion of scales to detect response distortions.

Despite these concerns, several national studies have shown that caregiver self-reports produce higher estimates of child abuse and neglect than children's protective services, police, or medical records; in fact, there is some evidence that caregivers will report more parent-to-child violence than will children. Moreover, proxy reports from caregivers may offer the best option for identifying abuse when very young children's language ability is so limited that they cannot provide self-reports of their own experiences (Hamby & Finkelhor, 2000). Following are examples of several caregiver self-report measures.

Child Abuse Potential Inventory

The Child Abuse Potential (CAPI) Inventory (Milner, 1986, 1994), a 160-item questionnaire, was designed for the purpose of and is widely used for screening for child physical abuse. Target respondents are parents and other caregivers who have been reported to CPS for physical abuse (Milner, 1989). In addition to a physical abuse scale, the CAPI Inventory contains six factor scales: Distress, Rigidity, Unhappiness, Problems with Child and Self, Problems with Family, and Problems from Others. Also included are three validity scales—a Lie scale, a Random Response scale, and an Inconsistency scale—which are used to form three indices of validity, a Faking-Good index, a Faking-Bad index, and a Random Response index. Overall, these validity scales have been found to provide an adequate level of detecting distorted responses (Milner & Crouch, 1997). A technical manual contains information on the development, structure, reliability, and validity of the CAPI Inventory. Details on scale score interpretation are found in an interpretative manual. In addition, several reviews of the applications and limitations of the CAPI Inventory are available (e.g., Hart, 1989; Kaufman & Walker, 1986; Melton, 1989; Melton & Limber, 1989; Milner et al., 1998). Studies have established that high scores on the CAPI Inventory are related to problems with parent–child interactions and that high-scoring individuals report using more harsh discipline and less positive parenting techniques. Overall, studies indicate high validity and an ability to classify respondents correctly according to physical abuse/nonabuse (Robertson & Milner, 1987). Nonetheless, the CAPI Inventory may not be reliable with all populations; for example, Blinn-Pike and Mingus (2000) found that alpha reliabilities were low for the Abuse Scale (.65) and low to moderate for the six CAPI subscales (.59–.74) in an adolescent sample.

Measure of Parenting Style

The Measure of Parenting Style (MOPS; Parker et al., 1997), which was developed from the Parental Bonding Instrument, contains 15 items. Scales assess Parental Overcontrol, Parental Indifference, and Parental Abuse. The MOPS can be administered to each caregiver independently. Respondents rate individual statements regarding perception of early family experiences on a 4-point scale ranging from *not true at all* to *extremely true.* Crohnbach's alphas for the subscales range from .76 to .93. In order to validate the MOPS, Parker and colleagues conducted a lengthy clinical interview, including questions on physical, emotional, and sexual abuse on 152 participants. Responses were categorically rated as either *no abuse, possible abuse,* or *definite abuse.* The abuse scores for subsets of participants in each of these categories were significantly different from each other, with higher scores associated with greater exposure to abuse. However, it should be noted that the MOPS has been validated only against another self-report measure of abuse (i.e., clinical interview) rather than independently corroborated evidence of abuse (Dalgleish et al., 2003).

Revised Version of Parental Punitiveness Scale

A revised version (Blane et al., 1988; Miller, Smyth, & Mudar, 1999) of Epstein and Komorita's Parental Punitiveness Scale (PPS; 1965) asks mothers to endorse various disciplinary strategies—changing the situation (for children 3–7 years of age), ignoring or doing nothing, taking away privileges, having a long talk with the child, yelling, spanking with an open hand, spanking/hitting with a belt or switch—in response to ten different hypotheticals in which a child misbehaves (e.g., child not doing something he or she was told to do; stealing something that belonged to mother or another child; kicking or hitting mother, teacher, or babysitter). A Severe Physical Violence subscale is computed by summing the number of situations for which the respondent endorses spanking or hitting the child with a belt or switch.

Self-Reports of Other Parenting Characteristics

When eliciting self-reports from parents, researchers also have tended to examine characteristics associated with abusive behavior in the literature rather than abuse itself. Parent characteristics associated with physical abuse include life stress, loneliness, depression, anxiety, parenting attitudes, locus of control, and conflict resolution. In regard to child sexual abuse, self-report measures have focused on assertiveness, social anxiety, self-esteem, empathy, sexual interest, sexual dysfunction, and family functioning. It is important to highlight that although studies employing such measures have detected many mean scale score differences between offenders and nonoffenders, these have frequently been accompanied by group overlap, such that the risk of false positives is substantial. Thus, although a test may discriminate between various groups of abusive parents and comparison groups, it does not necessarily follow that the test can successfully discriminate child maltreating caregivers on an individual basis (i.e., that the test is appropriate for classifying parents as abusive or nonabusive) (Milner, 1989). Such approaches may be less appropriate for empirical studies of child maltreatment than for purposes of evaluating the effectiveness of prevention and treatment interventions.

Adult–Adolescent Parenting Inventory-2

The Adult–Adolescent Parenting Inventory (AAPI-2; Bavolek & Keene, 1999) was designed to assess parenting attitudes and practices among adolescents and adults. At this writing it is marketed for purposes of identifying high-risk child rearing and parenting practices that could result in physical abuse, emotional abuse, or neglect (see also http://www.nurturingparenting.com). The AAPI-2 assesses risk for five parenting constructs associated with child maltreatment: Inappropriate Expectations of Children's Development and Growth, Empathy/Awareness of Child Needs, Use of Corporal Punishment, Reversal of Parent–Child Roles (i.e., expecting the child to "parent" the adult), and Suppression of Child Independence and Power Through Strict Obedience. Respondents are asked to endorse 40 items using a 5-point Likert scale ranging from *strongly agree* to *strongly disagree*. Scores then can be compared with normative data to determine degree of risk for abuse. The AAPI-2 is designed for use with adolescents as young as age 13. The self-report questionnaire is written at a fifth-grade reading level; alternatively, it can be administered verbally to nonreaders. Preliminary analyses to establish the reliability of the AAPI-2 with a sample of African American and European-American parents produced coefficient alpha reliability for the four summated scales measuring parenting knowledge and attitudes ranging from .64 to .76 (Cain, Washington, Wilson, & Combs-Orme, 2001).

Parenting Stress Index

The Parenting Stress Index (PSI; Abidin, 1995) consists of 120 items aimed at assessing three sources of stress: parent-related stress, child-related stress, and general life stress. The PSI produces a Total Stress score, a Parent Domain Stress score, a Child Domain Stress score, and a Life Stress score. The PSI also includes additional subscale scores that can be calculated within the parent and child domains, as well as scales to detect response distortions. Although not specifically developed as a measure of child maltreatment, the PSI has been used to measure parent- and child-related stress in both abusive parents and parents deemed to be at high risk for physical abuse. Studies indicate that at-risk and physically abusive parents score higher on the PSI than do comparison parents, and they have established a correlation between PSI scores and child abuse potential. However, data are not available on the sensitivity and specificity of the PSI for classifying abusers versus nonabusers. In fact, high PSI scores are not unique to physically abusive parents, such that reliance on PSI scores to indicate abuse threatens to result in relatively high rates of false positives among some nonabusive parent groups (Milner et al., 1998).

CONCLUSION

Among the priorities identified by the National Research Council Panel on Research on Child Abuse and Neglect in 1993, in an effort to advance the scientific study of child maltreatment, was the development of reliable and valid research instruments. In the case of self-report approaches designed to classify victims or perpetrators along dimensions of abuse, many questions remain unanswered, particularly with regard to the reliability and validity of available measures. The lack of a well-developed body of psychometrically sound instruments continues to constrain researchers' ability to classify participants as "abused" or "nonabused." Even fewer tools are available to assist researchers in adequately differentiating subgroups of child abuse victims (e.g., physically abused, neglected, multiply traumatized). Although a handful of self-report measures with sound psychometric properties are available, the use of adequate tools for child maltreatment research remains the exception rather than the norm, and there is a continuing need both to develop and to validate self-report measures for use with children, adolescents, adult victims, and caregivers. In particular, there is a need to continue validation of existing measures across diverse populations.

REFERENCES

Aalsma, M.C., Zimet, G.D., Fortenberry, J.D., Blythe, M., & Orr, D.P. (2002). Reports of childhood sexual abuse by adolescents and young adults. *The Journal of Sex Research, 39,* 259–263.

Abidin, R.R. (1995). *Parenting Stress Index–Manual* (3rd ed.). Odessa, FL: Psychological Assessment Resources.

Amaya-Jackson, L., Socolar, R.R.S., Hunter, W., Runyan, D.K., & Colindres, R. (2000). Directly questioning children and adolescents about maltreatment: A review of survey measures used. *Journal of Interpersonal Violence, 15,* 725–759.

Ammerman, R.T. (1998). Methodological issues in child maltreatment research. In J. Lutzker (Ed.), *Handbook of child abuse research and treatment* (pp. 117–132). New York: Plenum Press.

Bavolek, S.J., & Keene, R.G. (1999). *Adult Adolescent Parenting Inventory (AAPI-2).* Park City, UT: Family Development Resources.

Berger, A.M. (1981). *An examination of the relationship between harsh discipline in childhood, later punitiveness toward children, and later ratings of adjustment.* Unpublished doctoral dissertation, The University of Iowa, Iowa City.

Berger, A.M., Knutson, J.F., Mehm, J.G., & Perkins, K.A. (1988). The self-report of punitive childhood experiences of young adults and adolescents. *Child Abuse & Neglect, 12,* 251–262.

Bernstein, D.P., & Fink, L. (1998). *Childhood Trauma Questionnaire: A retrospective self-report manual.* San Antonio, TX: Harcourt Assessment.

Blane, H.T., Miller, B.A., Leonard, K.E., Nochajski, T.H., Bowers, P.M., & Gondoli, D. (1988). *Intra- and intergenerational aspects of serious domestic violence and alcohol and drugs.* Washington, DC: National Institute of Justice.

Blinn-Pike, L., & Mingus, S. (2000). The internal consistency of the Child Abuse Potential Inventory with adolescent mothers. *Journal of Adolescence, 23,* 107–111.

Bower, M.E., & Knutson, J.F. (1996). Attitudes toward physical discipline as a function of disciplinary history and self-labeling as physically abused. *Child Abuse & Neglect, 20,* 689–699.

Brewin, C.R., & Holloway, R. (1997). Clinical and experimental approaches to understanding repression. In J.D. Read & D.S. Lindsay (Eds.), *Recollections of trauma: Scientific evidence and clinical practice* (pp. 145–163). New York: Plenum Press.

Briere, J. (1996). *The Trauma Symptom Checklist for Children.* Florida: Psychological Assessment Resources, Inc.

Bryer, J.B., Nelson, B.A., Miller, J.B., & Krol, P.A. (1987). Childhood sexual and physical abuse as factors in adult psychiatric illness. *American Journal of Psychiatry, 144,* 1426–1430.

Cain, D.S., Washington, T.A., Wilson, E.E., & Combs-Orme, T. (2001). Reliability of parenting instruments with African-American and European-American parents. Retrieved January 12, 2004, from http://sswr.org/papers2001.330.htm

Chu, J., & Dill, D. (1990). Dissociative symptoms in relation to childhood physical and sexual abuse. *American Journal of Psychiatry, 147,* 887–892.

Dalgleish, T., Yiend, J., Tchanturia, K., Serpell, L., Hems, S., deSilva, P., et al. (2003). Self-reported parental abuse relates to autobiographical memory style in patients with eating disorders. *Emotion, 3,* 211–222.

DiTomasso, M., & Routh, D. (1993). Recall of abuse in childhood and three measures of dissociation. *Child Abuse & Neglect, 17,* 477–485.

Epstein, R., & Komorita, S.S. (1965). The development of a scale of parental punitiveness toward aggression. *Child Development, 36,* 129–142.

Hamby, S.L., & Finkelhor, D. (2000). The victimization of children: Recommendations for assessment and instrument development. *Journal of the American Academy of Child & Adolescent Psychiatry, 39,* 829–840.

Hamby, S.L., & Finkelhor, D. (2001, March). Choosing and using child victimization questionnaires. *OJJDP juvenile justice bulletin.* Washington, DC: U.S. Department of Justice, Office of Juvenile Justice & Delinquency Prevention.

Hart, A.N. (1989). Review of the Child Abuse Potential Inventory, Form IV. In J.C. Conoley & J.J. Kramer (Eds.), *The tenth mental measurements yearbook* (pp. 152–153). Lincoln, NE: Buros Institute of Mental Measurement.

Holmes, T.R. (1995). History of child abuse: A key variable in client response to short-term treatment. *Families in Society: The Journal of Contemporary Human Services, 76,* 349–359.

Kaufman, K.L., & Walker, C.E. (1986). The Child Abuse Potential Inventory. In D.J. Keyser & R.C. Sweetland (Eds.), *Test critiques* (Vol. 5, pp. 55–64). Kansas City, MO: Test Corporation of America.

Knight, E.D., Runyan, D.K., Dubowitz, H., Brandford, C., Kotch, J., Litrownik, A., et al. (2000). Methodological and ethical challenges associated with child self-report of maltreatment. *Journal of Interpersonal Violence, 15,* 760–775.

Koss, M., Gidicz, C., & Wisniewski, N. (1987). The scope of rape: Incidence and prevalence of sexual aggression and victimization in a national sample of higher education students. *Journal of Consulting and Clinical Psychology, 55,* 162–170.

Lipschitz, D.S., Bernstein, D.P., Winegar, R.K., & Southwick, S.M. (1999). Hospitalized adolescents' reports of sexual and physical abuse: A comparison of two self-report measures. *Journal of Traumatic Stress, 12,* 641–654.

Melton, G.B. (1989). Review of the Child Abuse Potential Inventory, Form IV. In J.C. Conoley & J.J. Kramer (Eds.), *The tenth mental measurements yearbook* (pp. 153–155). Lincoln, NE: Buros Institute of Mental Measurements.

Melton, G.B., & Limber, S. (1989). Psychologists' involvement in cases of child maltreatment: Limits of role and expertise. *American Psychologist, 44, 1225–1233.*

Miller, B.A., Smyth, N.J., & Mudar, P.J. (1999). Mothers' alcohol and other drug problems and their punitiveness toward their children. *Journal of Studies on Alcohol, 60,* 632– 642.

Miller, T.W., & Veltkamp, L.J. (1995). Assessment of sexual abuse and trauma: Clinical measures. *Child Psychiatry and Human Development, 26,* 3–10.

Milner, J.S. (1986). *The Child Abuse Potential Inventory: Manual* (2nd ed.). Webster, NC: Psytec.

Milner, J.S. (1989). Applications and limitations of the Child Abuse Potential Inventory. *Early Child Development and Care, 42,* 85–97.

Milner, J.S. (1994). *Assessing physical child abuse risk: The Child Abuse Potential Inventory. Clinical Psychology Review, 14,* 547–583.

Milner, J.S., & Crouch, J.L. (1997). Impact and detection of response distortions on parenting measures used to assess risk for child physical abuse. *Journal of Personality Assessment, 69,* 633–650.

Milner, J.S., Murphy, W.D., Valle, L.A., & Tolliver, R. (1998). Assessment issues in child abuse evaluations. In J. Lutker (Ed.), *Handbook of child abuse research and treatment* (pp. 75–115). New York: Plenum Press.

National Clearinghouse on Child Abuse and Neglect Information. (2001). *Child maltreatment 2001: Summary of key findings.* U.S. Department of Health and Human Services. Retrieved June 20, 2003, from http://www.calib.com/nccanch/pubs/factsheets/canstats .cfm

National Research Council. (1993). *Understanding child abuse and neglect.* Washington, DC: National Academies Press.

Paivio, S.C. (2001). Stability of retrospective self-reports of child abuse and neglect before and after therapy for child abuse issues. *Child Abuse & Neglect, 25,* 1053–1068.

Parker, G., Roussos, J., Hadzi-Pavlovic, D., Mitchell, P., Wilhelm, K., & Austin, M.P. (1997). The development of a refined measure of dysfunctional parenting and assessment of its relevance in patients with affective disorders. *Psychological Medicine, 27,* 1193–1203.

Portwood, S.G. (1998). The impact of individuals' characteristics and experiences on their definitions of child maltreatment. *Child Abuse & Neglect, 22,* 437–452.

Portwood, S.G. (1999). Coming to terms with a consensual definition of child maltreatment. *Child Maltreatment, 4,* 56–68.

Prescott, A., Bank, L., Reid, J.B., Knutson, J.F., Burraston, B.O., & Eddy, J.M. (2000). The veridicality of punitive childhood experiences reported by adolescents and young adults. *Child Abuse & Neglect, 24,* 411–423.

Rausch, K., & Knutson, J.F. (1991). The self-report of personal punitive childhood experiences and those of siblings. *Child Abuse & Neglect, 15,* 29–36.

Robertson, K.R., & Milner, J.S. (1987). An inconsistency scale for the Child Abuse Potential Inventory. *Psychological Reports, 60,* 699–703.

Runyan, D.K., Curtis, P., Hunter, W.M., Black, M.M., Kotch, J.B., Bangdiwala, et al. (1998). LONGSCAN: A consortium for longitudinal studies of maltreatment and the lifecourse of children. *Aggression and Violent Behavior: A Review Journal, 3,* 275–285.

Sacco, M.L., & Farber, B.A. (1999). Reality testing in adult women who report childhood sexual and physical abuse. *Child Abuse & Neglect, 23,* 1193–1203.

Scher, C.D., Stein, M.B., Asmundson, G.J.G., McCreary, D.R., & Forde, D.R. (2001). The Childhood Trauma Questionnaire in a community sample: Psychometric properties and normative data. *Journal of Traumatic Stress, 14,* 843–857.

Sedlak, A.J., & Broadhurst, D.D. (1996). *Third national incidence study of child abuse and neglect: Final report.* Washington, DC: U.S. Department of Health and Human Services.

Smith, N., Lam, D., Bifulco, A., & Checkley, S. (2002). Childhood Experience of Care and Abuse Questionnaire (CECA.Q): Validation of a screening instrument for childhood adversity in clinical populations. *Social Psychiatry and Psychiatric Epidemiology, 37,* 572–579.

Straus, M.A. (1979). Measuring intrafamily conflict and violence: The Conflict Tactics Scales. *Journal of Marriage and Family, 41,* 75–88.

Straus, M.A. (1990). The Conflict Tactics Scales and its critics: An evaluation and new data on validity and reliability. In M.A. Straus & R.J. Gelles (Eds.), *Physical violence in American families: Risk factors and adaptations to violence in 8,145 families* (pp. 49–73). New Brunswick, NJ: Transaction Publishers.

Straus, M.A. (1992). Sociological research and social policy: The case of family violence. *Sociological Forum, 7,* 211–237.

Straus, M.A. (1995). *Manual for the Conflict Tactics Scales.* Durham: Family Research Laboratory, University of New Hampshire.

Straus, M.A., & Gelles, R.J. (Eds.). (1990). *Physical violence in American families: Risk factors and adaptations to violence in 8,145 families.* New Brunswick, NJ: Transaction Publishers.

Straus, M.A., & Hamby, S.L. (1997). Measuring physical and psychological maltreatment of children with the Conflict Tactics Scales. In G. Kaufman Kantor & J.L. Jasinski (Eds.), *Out of the darkness: Contemporary research perspectives on family violence* (pp. 119–135). Thousand Oaks, CA: Sage Publications.

Straus, M.A., Hamby, S.L., Finkelhor, D., Moore, D.W., & Runyan, D. (1998). Identification of child maltreatment with the Parent-Child Conflict Tactics Scales: Development and psychometric data for a national sample of American parents. *Child Abuse & Neglect, 22,* 249–270.

U.S. Department of Health and Human Services Protection of Human Subjects Regulations, 45 C.F.R. § 46.408 (2004).

Weeks, R., & Widom, C.S. (1998). Self-reports of early childhood victimization among incarcerated adult male felons. *Journal of Interpersonal Violence, 13,* 346–361.

Widom, C.S., & Morris, S. (1997). Accuracy of adult recollections of childhood victimization: Part 2. Childhood sexual abuse. *Psychological Assessment, 9,* 34–46.

Widom, C.S., & Shepard, R.L. (1996). Accuracy of adult recollections of childhood victimization: Part 1. Childhood physical abuse. *Psychological Assessment, 8,* 412–421.

Winegar, R.K., & Lipschitz, D.S. (1999). Agreement between hospitalized adolescents' self-reports of maltreatment and witnessed home violence and clinician reports and medical records. *Comprehensive Psychiatry, 40,* 347–352.

Wyatt, G.E., Lawrence, J., Vodounon, A., & Mickey, M.R. (1992). The Wyatt Sex History Questionnaire: A structured interview for female sexual history taking. *Journal of Child Sexual Abuse, 1,* 51–68.

10

Measuring Child Abuse and Neglect Using Child Protective Services Records

DESMOND K. RUNYAN AND DIANA J. ENGLISH

RESEARCH EXAMINING child maltreatment is complicated by a number of ethical, legal, and methodological constraints that make it one of the most difficult types of research to undertake (Socolar, Runyan, & Amaya-Jackson, 1995). The difficulties faced by investigators conducting research on child maltreatment include the fact that many researchers rely solely on official case records to operationally define maltreatment and the fact that legal definitions of maltreatment used by the states vary. In addition, a number of practice and policy variations exist within state and local agencies that affect how maltreatment cases are defined or grouped. Another difficulty is that laws addressing mandatory reporting of suspected maltreatment may result in adult and child research participants being reported for additional social services or legal interventions if the participants reveal new information about what might have happened within the family. Ethical guidelines for research require informed consent, with careful attention to respect for participants, and nonmalfeasance, the avoidance of doing harm (King & Churchill, 2000). As a result, research using child protective services (CPS) records to define and measure maltreatment instead of asking participants directly about their experiences has become a common practice—a practice that is itself subject to specific methodological and ethical challenges that must be considered in evaluating current measures and approaches. This chapter addresses the definitional and measurement issues that complicate research in the area of child maltreatment when administrative data are used. Discussion of relevant ethical and reporting issues that have been addressed elsewhere (see Kalichman, 1993; Runyan, 2000; Chapter 14 by Simmel and colleagues) will be deferred. In discussing these issues, the chapter authors present original data from a multisite longitudinal study of child abuse and neglect (Longitudinal Studies of Child Abuse and Neglect [LONGSCAN]) as a means of illustrating many of the definitional and measurement challenges inherent in this type of research. In doing so, the authors hope to call attention to both the strengths and limitations of using CPS records in research on child maltreatment and to suggest potential ways that information from these records can be used to inform future research on defining and measuring child abuse and neglect experiences.

BACKGROUND

In much of the published research on child maltreatment, maltreatment typically has been treated as a categorical dichotomous variable (indicating the presence or absence of maltreatment) and/or as a single type of child abuse or neglect, despite the heterogeneous nature of maltreatment and the frequent comorbidity among maltreatment types (Crouch & Milner, 1993; Manly, Cicchetti, & Barnett, 1994; Paget, Philip, & Abramczyk, 1993; Silverman, Reinherz, & Giaconia, 1996; Tebbutt, Swanston, Oates, & O'Toole, 1997). Although some attention has been paid to the multidimensional nature of child maltreatment, researchers have not agreed on a systematic procedure for describing a child's maltreatment experiences, especially from a longitudinal perspective (Cicchetti & Manly, 2001; Kinard, 1994). In 1993, a National Academy of Sciences panel systematically reviewed child abuse and neglect research and identified a number of inadequacies in the knowledge base (National Research Council [NRC], 1993). Importantly, as noted by Chalk (see Chapter 2), the panel explicitly cited the absence of clear definitions of child maltreatment as a major deterrent to advancing knowledge in this area and recommended the development of standardized research definitions and instruments.

In the decade since the publication of the NRC report, several attempts have been made to develop standard definitions and coding schemes of child maltreatment experiences. These have included the National Incidence Studies (NIS; Sedlak & Broadhurst, 1996; U.S. Department of Health and Human Services [DHHS], 1981, 1988), the Maltreatment Classification System (MCS; Barnett, Manly, & Cicchetti, 1993), the Record of Maltreatment Experiences (ROME; McGee, Wolfe, & Wilson, 1990) and the Child Maltreatment Log (CML; Sternberg et al., 2004), all of which were designed to bring uniformity to information derived from a variety of official sources of information on child maltreatment. Each of these systems for classifying information from official records has made a significant contribution to research in child maltreatment, improving the tools available to researchers using administrative data. However, these methods are not without their limitations. These limitations will be discussed in the sections that follow.

AN OVERVIEW OF APPROACHES
TO DEFINING AND CLASSIFYING CHILD ABUSE
AND NEGLECT USING CPS AND ADMINISTRATIVE DATA
The National Incidence Studies

How much child maltreatment occurs each year in the United States? The NIS (DHHS, 1981, 1988; Sedlak & Broadhurst, 1996), mandated by Congress, were commissioned by the DHHS with the goal of estimating the incidence of child abuse and neglect in the population. To date, there have been three studies: The first NIS (NIS-1) was conducted in 1979 and 1980 and published in 1981, the second NIS (NIS-2) was conducted in 1986 and 1987 and published in 1988, and the third and most recent NIS (NIS-3) was conducted between 1993 and 1995 and published in 1996. Although CPS data provide estimates of the number of cases of child abuse and neglect reported to and investigated by CPS agencies, the three NIS studies were designed to go beyond the estimates provided by CPS by including information from a variety of professionals who are mandated to report child maltreatment (e.g., health care professionals, teachers, day care providers, police, hospital personnel) but who, for a variety of reasons, might not do so. As such, the studies were designed to estimate the incidence of child abuse and neglect based on both CPS and non-CPS sources by random sampling of a range of mandated reporters across different counties in the United States.

As part of these studies, uniform definitions of child maltreatment were developed in order to standardize the abuse label. Specifically, NIS-2 and NIS-3 used two sets of standardized definitions of abuse and neglect: 1) Under the Harm Standard, children identified to the study were considered to be maltreated only if they had already experienced harm from abuse and neglect; and 2) under the Endangerment Standard, children who experienced abuse and neglect that put them at risk of harm also were included as having experienced maltreatment. NIS-1 used only the Harm Standard. In addition, all cases included in the studies had to meet a number of definitional standards regarding the child's age, residence, custody status, time of maltreatment, and purposive and avoidable acts or omissions, as well as requirements concerning the allowable nature of the abusive acts or omissions that could be included, the perpetrator of these acts/omissions, and the degree of harm to the child. The broad categories of maltreatment included in the studies were physical abuse, sexual abuse, emotional abuse, physical neglect, emotional neglect, and educational neglect.[1] All cases submitted to the studies were screened for conformity to these definitional standards and only those that fit the standards were counted. In addition, for each child thought to meet the study requirements, project staff rated the degree to which the abuse or

---

[1]In the NIS studies, the following types of abuse are further divided into subcategories (listed in parentheses): sexual abuse (intrusion, genital molestation, and other or unknown); emotional abuse (close confinement—tying or binding, other close confinement, verbal or emotional assault, other or unknown abuse); physical neglect (refusal of health care, delay in health care, abandonment, expulsion/refusal of runaway, other custody-related maltreatment, inadequate supervision, and other physical neglect); educational neglect (permitted chronic truancy, other truancy/failure to enroll, and inattention to special educational need); emotional neglect (inadequate nurturance/affection, chronic/extreme spouse abuse, permitted drug/alcohol abuse, permitted other maladaptive behavior, refusal of psychological care, delay/failure of psychological care, and other inattention to emotional needs); and other types (involuntary neglect, general or unspecified neglect, other or unspecified maltreatment, chemically dependent newborns, and nonmaltreatment cases). Each type of abuse or neglect is also coded as to whether the abuse/neglect is committed or permitted by the specified perpetrators (there are different perpetrator requirements for the Harm and Endangerment Standards).

neglect situation met each of the two sets of definitional standards (Harm and Endangerment) and each of the individual aspects of the standards. Following this evaluation, overall assessments were made under each of the definitional standards, and a child was considered maltreated if "there was reasonable cause to believe that the child had experienced maltreatment that met all of the requirements of the definitional standard in question" (Sedlak & Broadhurst, 1996, p. 2–20). Based on this procedure, interrater reliability was found to be quite high (95% overall, 98% for the Harm standard, and 99% for the Endangerment standard in the NIS-3) (Sedlak & Broadhurst, 1996). In addition, the incidence rates of child maltreatment were found to be significantly higher in each of the studies than those typically found using administrative data from CPS alone, suggesting that such administrative datasets do not include a substantial portion of children who have been harmed or endangered by abuse and neglect.[2]

Although the NIS definitions have not been widely used in research studies, they do provide a set of standard definitions for the field. In addition, they have been used as part of the basis for an effort led by the Centers for Disease Control and Prevention to develop uniform definitions of maltreatment for surveillance purposes (see, e.g., Leeb, Melanson, Simon, Arias, & Paulozzi, 2004).

The Maltreatment Classification System

Around the same time that the NIS-2 was being conducted, Barnett et al. (1993) developed the MCS, a standardized coding scheme for use with administrative data. The MCS was designed as a systematic framework for quantifying aspects of children's maltreatment experiences among multiple dimensions thought to be related to children's developmental outcomes across a variety of domains of functioning. Specifically, the MCS includes operational definitions of each subtype of abuse and neglect, with provisions for coding multiple subtypes, and with recognition of the frequency of co-occurrence or comorbidity among subtypes. In addition, the MCS includes several dimensions of maltreatment in addition to subtype that are expected to affect children's development. These dimensions include the timing of the maltreatment (i.e., age of onset, frequency, chronicity, and developmental period), the relationship of the perpetrator to the victim, the occurrence of separation from the perpetrator and placement of the victim outside the home, and the severity of maltreatment incidents. Moreover, these dimensions can be captured both within and across subtypes and were designed specifically to add "depth and breadth to maltreatment assessment that is lacking in use of CPS labels alone" (Manly, 2005, p. 426).

---

[2]See Sedlak & Broadhurst (1996) for a review. In the NIS-3, CPS investigated only 28% of the recognized children who met the Harm Standard (in the NIS-2 the corresponding proportion was 44%), less than half of children who met the Endangerment Standard recognized by any source except police and sheriffs' departments, and only 26% of the seriously injured and 26% of the moderately injured children in the study.

Although the MCS was originally designed as a means of coding information from CPS records in a way that would minimize variability across reporters and regions, because it does not rely on CPS labels but rather on information contained in case records, it has been applied not only to CPS records but also to other case record data as well, such as treatment records, medical records, and foster care placement histories (Manly, 2005). In addition, since publication of the MCS, the system has been used in a variety of studies examining characteristics of child maltreatment experiences and their associations with a variety of child outcomes (e.g., Cicchetti & Toth, 1995; Manly, Kim, Rogosch, & Cicchetti, 2001). The results from these studies have supported the predictive validity of the subtypes and dimensions of maltreatment used in the MCS in explaining aggressive behavior, adolescent delinquent behavior, peer rejection and aggression, prosocial behaviors, internalizing and externalizing behavior problems, and dimensions of personality (Manly et al., 2001). In addition, several studies have suggested that the MCS has high interrater reliability (with Kappa statistics ranging from .86 to .98) and demonstrates adequate reliability and validity in classifying maltreatment incidents (Bolger & Patterson, 2001; Bolger, Patterson, & Kupersmidt, 1998; Cicchetti & Rogosch, 2001; Manly et al., 1994; Manly et al., 2001; Smith & Thornberry, 1995).

The Record of Maltreatment Experiences

A third system for describing children's maltreatment experiences was developed by McGee and colleagues in 1990. ROME, like the MCS, was developed as a tool to code information derived from CPS records. In developing the instrument, the authors selected items for inclusion based on expert consensus regarding acts of physical and sexual abuse, exposure to domestic violence, and acts of psychological maltreatment. In addition, the instrument was designed to identify perpetrators including biological mothers, biological fathers, and other perpetrators, and to measure the frequency and severity of maltreatment experiences.

Although the ROME includes a broad range of maltreatment experiences and some research has supported the validity and utility of this methodology in examining the interplay among dimensions of maltreatment (e.g., McGee et al., 1990), several shortcomings of the instrument have been noted, including the fact that the instrument provides little information about perpetrator identity and developmental level at the time of reported events and does not provide details on injuries resulting from maltreatment or treatment for those injuries (see, e.g., Sternberg et al., 2004).

The Child Maltreatment Log

Another approach to characterizing information on child maltreatment was undertaken by the Research Subcommittee of the Federal Interagency Task Force on Child Abuse and Neglect. Beginning in 1994, the committee organized a series of meetings, with the aim of identifying core variables that could be used by researchers to describe children's maltreatment experiences and co-occurring events that might be relevant to research on maltreatment. As a result of these meetings, a computer program—the CML—was developed as a tool for standardizing information collected from a variety of sources on the experiences and circumstances of children included in studies of child maltreatment (Sternberg et al., 2004). Once developed, the CML was used in pilot field tests using CPS records (English, Graham, Clark, & Brummel, 2002), which resulted in further modifications of the program.

The final version of the CML (see Sternberg et al., 2004) is a computerized data entry system that can be used by researchers and practitioners to develop a systematic and detailed record of a child's maltreatment experiences. Unlike other methods developed for classifying CPS data, the CML does not limit users to a specific data collection format but rather encourages the use of information from a variety of informants and measures so that a comprehensive record of a child's maltreatment experiences can be created. Because the instrument was designed to serve the needs of researchers from a variety of disciplines, the CML encourages the collection of data at the most basic level, "with few inferences made by the person recording the data" (Sternberg et al., 2004, p. 38). To that end, the CML is child-centered rather than perpetrator-centered. There are separate scales for collecting information about perpetrators, actions, frequency of actions, injuries, treatment, sources of information, and informants. Furthermore, because the CML asks users to specify the data sources used, the instrument allows for examination of the role of sources and informants in collecting data about children's experiences, permitting "the creation of a database that affords the greatest possible freedom to researchers who can create higher order constructs empirically" (Sternberg et al., 2004, p. 38).

Although the CML is a relatively recent contribution to the literature and thus has not been widely used in research studies of child maltreatment, the instrument provides a means of describing children's maltreatment experiences in a comprehensive and objective way, "thereby making it possible to improve our understanding of maltreatment and its correlates" (Sternberg et al., 2004, p. 42). Specifically, the instrument allows for entering and aggregating data from multiple sources and across multiple events, types and dimensions of maltreatment, and perpetrators, allowing for an examination of comorbidity or overlap among maltreatment types and analysis of demographic, cultural, and developmental variables relevant to the short- and long-term consequences of abuse and neglect. Furthermore, because the instrument provides a framework for aggregating data across different studies and methodologies, it provides a means of creating a common core of variables that can be used to improve and foster secondary analyses of research data (see Sternberg et al., 2004, for a complete description of the CML and its potential uses).

Summary and Discussion

In recent years, several attempts have been made to develop standardized definitions and tools for coding child maltreatment experiences. Although each of these efforts has made significant contributions to the child maltreatment literature, it is important to note that each also has its limitations. Although the NIS definitions have provided standard definitions that can be used in research, these definitions, as some have noted, rely on interview data from a range of sources that are not available to state and local health departments, thus limiting their application to public health contexts (e.g., surveillance) (Leeb et al., 2004). Similarly, although the MCS and ROME provide a standard system of coding information from official records (e.g., CPS records), the findings of the NIS demonstrate that such records most likely only represent a fraction of children harmed or endangered by abuse and neglect. In addition, because both the MCS and ROME are used in the context of administrative records, they cannot address issues regarding bias in such records, different standards for reporting and different definitions used in different jurisdictions, different processes for substantiation of cases, and different levels of quality of information available in records from different sources. Furthermore, as noted by Sternberg et al. (2004), the MCS does not allow researchers to describe acts of omission, neglect, and sexual abuse in as much detail as physical abuse, does not encode much information about children's exposure to domestic violence (which is considered to be child maltreatment in some jurisdictions), does not adequately distinguish between acts and the potential or actual injuries that result from them, and can be unduly influenced by the amount of information available in different records. Similarly, as noted previously, the ROME provides little information about perpetrators and children's developmental levels at the time of reports and does not provide for a specific detailing of injuries or treatment/intervention for those injuries (Sternberg et al., 2004). Finally, although the CML provides a tool to bring some measure of uniformity to data collected about child maltreatment from a variety of sources and can be used to test a variety of hypotheses about child maltreatment, as noted by the authors, the instrument does not resolve issues regarding statutory requirements, public policy, and social influences that complicate research in child maltreatment. In addition, the CML does not eliminate the need for researchers to establish the reliability of their data or reduce the labor involved in collecting high-quality data. Lastly, although the CML provides a framework for research in child maltreatment and a tool for testing a variety of hypotheses about classification and definitions, it does not provide an empirically based taxonomy of maltreatment types. Rather, it provides a means of gathering information in a useful and standardized way so that the data can be used to inform the development of such empirically guided classification efforts.

Because of the limitations inherent in many of the methods discussed for defining and classifying child maltreatment experiences, the chapter authors believe that the best approach to research in child maltreatment is a multiple-method, multiple-source approach. When information from a variety of sources and methods is aggregated, the limitations of any one method or approach can be attenuated by the strengths provided by other approaches and other sources of information. The remainder of this chapter presents an overview of a consortium of studies designed to address many of these issues by gathering information on child maltreatment from a variety of sources and using a variety of methodologies. The results from some analyses conducted by the consortium are then presented to examine some of the issues involved with (or some of the limitations of) using CPS records and administrative data in research on child abuse and neglect.

LONGSCAN

At the same time that several of the methodologies discussed were being developed and used in research studies in child maltreatment, an established consortium of longitudinal studies, LONGSCAN, was struggling with the issues of recording and standardizing records of child maltreatment across participant samples in five states. After reviewing available methods for classifying maltreatment, the LONGSCAN team concluded that working to expand and operationalize the MCS (Barnett et al., 1993) would be the most effective way for LONGSCAN to collect and code official data on child maltreatment across multiple sites and multiple dimensions of maltreatment. Merely recording maltreatment information derived from official records in a structured and standardized manner is a major task. However, developing methods for standardized assessments of severity and chronicity of maltreatment and establishing the way in which complex or multiple events should be categorized as to principal type of abuse adds additional levels of complexity, which remain as important considerations. In addition, different sources of data may be incomplete or two reports of the same event may appear to conflict in the details presented or even in whether the events are regarded as maltreatment. As a result, the LONGSCAN consortium undertook a series of analyses to examine some of these definitional issues and to attempt to resolve some of the dilemmas that have been a major barrier to the classification of the maltreatment experiences of children when CPS data are used to operationalize maltreatment. In the sections that follow, the LONGSCAN project and the approach taken by the LONGSCAN team to classifying child maltreatment are described. A series of analyses conducted by LONGSCAN to examine definitional issues is then presented, followed by a summary of the findings and limitations of this research.

Overview of the LONGSCAN Study

In 1989, an agency that was then the National Center on Child Abuse and Neglect (NCCAN) and is now the Office on Child Abuse and Neglect in the Children's

Bureau of the Administration on Children, Youth and Families called for the development of a major multisite study of the antecedents and consequences of child abuse and neglect. LONGSCAN, a consortium of five longitudinal studies of child abuse, was developed in response to that NCCAN solicitation. To develop a large database with prospects for generalization, LONGSCAN was designed to be a coordinated, multiple site, prospective study that emphasized the use of shared standard measures, common definitions, jointly developed interview protocols for specific child ages, joint interviewer training, and a common data entry system across five complementary studies, each proposed to last 20 years. As part of the design of the project, caregivers and their children were to be interviewed at enrollment, at age 4 if this was not the baseline enrollment, and then at child ages 6, 8, 12, 14, 16, and 18 years. The LONGSCAN cohorts were enrolled beginning in 1991.

The five LONGSCAN sites, spread across the country, are referred to by their geographical locations (East, South, Midwest, Northwest, and Southwest) as an additional means of protecting participant identity. The collaborating studies developed systematically different samples that represented a continuum of maltreatment experiences, from children at risk for maltreatment to children reported for maltreatment, and from children characterized by substantiated maltreatment to children placed in foster care (Runyan et al., 1998). Table 10.1 provides a brief description of the LONGSCAN samples. LONGSCAN has been described in a number of publications (e.g., Runyan et al., 1998; see also English, 2005) and thus will only be summarized here. Briefly, the LONGSCAN consortium is coordinated at the University of North Carolina School of Medicine and Injury Prevention Research Center by a staff of social scientists, epidemiologists, and statisticians who are responsible for developing the measurement batteries, human participants protocols, and a joint database of participant responses from all of the sites and for overseeing collaborative analyses of the data.

The University of North Carolina School of Public Health directs one of the component studies. For this study, 243 children were selected at 4 years of age out of a larger statewide cohort of infants identified at birth as being at high risk for adverse development because of young maternal age, medical conditions, or prematurity or because of concerns expressed by nurses in hospital nurseries about observed parenting interactions. At age 4, 140 children from this cohort had already been reported to social services agencies for suspected abuse or neglect. LONGSCAN enrolled 50% of these reported children and then matched them with children of the same age, race, and family composition who had not been reported for maltreatment. These matched groups have been followed since that time. The final sample of 243 included the addition of 31 children from the original birth cohort who were added to the sample at age 6 to compensate for children lost to follow-up.

In order to expand the LONGSCAN sample to include a comparison between children who were reported for maltreatment and whose maltreatment

Table 10.1. Brief description of Longitudinal Studies of Child Abuse and Neglect (LONGSCAN) samples

	Eastern (N = 282)	Midwestern (N = 245)	Southern (N = 243)	Southwestern (N = 330)	Northwestern (N = 254)	Total (N = 1,354)
Cohort birth year	1988– 1991	1991– 1994	1986– 1987	1989– 1991	1988– 1994	1986– 1994
Race (%)						
African American	92.9	53.5	63.0	37.6	20.5	53.3
White	5.0	13.1	35.8	28.5	50.0	26.2
Hispanic	0.4	13.9	0.0	16.7	2.8	7.2
Mixed	1.1	17.1	1.2	15.8	24.0	11.9
Other	0.7	2.4	0.0	1.5	2.8	1.5
Gender (%)						
Male	52.1	46.9	45.3	47.3	50.8	48.5
Female	47.9	53.1	54.7	52.7	49.2	51.5
Maltreatment status at recruitment[a] (%)						
Maltreated	24.1	60.8	34.2	100	100	65.3
At risk	36.5	—	56.8	—	—	17.8
Control	39.4	39.2	9.0	—	—	16.9

[a]Maltreatment status at recruitment has been simplified for the purposes of this table. The samples of children vary systematically within site with regard to risk status and exposure to maltreatment.

was substantiated and those who were reported for maltreatment but whose maltreatment was not substantiated, the Washington State Department of Social and Health Services recruited a second cohort of children who were 4 years of age or younger at the time of a report to CPS. Those children whose intake risk assessment indicated either a moderate or high risk at CPS intake were recruited for the study (referred to as the Northwest sample of LONGSCAN). About 35% of the parents whose children were eligible gave permission for their children to be enrolled in LONGSCAN. The children enrolled in this sample (N = 254) were similar on key characteristics to those who were not enrolled. This cohort consisted of about 60% of children who were substantiated for maltreatment and 40% who were unsubstantiated by CPS on the original maltreatment report.

Along a continuum of children reported to social services, the LONGSCAN researchers also were interested in identifying a cohort of children who were substantiated for maltreatment but for whom services might or might not have been offered. In the Midwest, the Juvenile Protective Association of Chicago organized a study of children substantiated by CPS and offered family service help by a group of private, nonprofit service agencies and two comparison groups: 1) children substantiated for maltreatment by CPS but whose families were not referred for treatment by a nonprofit agency, and 2) a group of children identified as neighbors of the substantiated participants, matched for age. This sample (N = 245) was restricted by the local collaborating LONGSCAN agency to children under

1 year of age at the time of recruitment. As this sample (referred to as the Midwest sample) was recruited prospectively, beginning in 1991, with all children under the age of 1 at the time of recruitment, it represents the youngest sample within LONGSCAN.

As the LONGSCAN researchers sought to develop the ideal cohort for a study examining the impact of abuse or neglect, they felt they also needed to include young children who were removed from their families and placed into foster care as a result of maltreatment. A sample was found of children who were part of an existing short-term prospective study of young children who had all been placed in foster care before age 4 because of child maltreatment. This sample (N = 330), coordinated by investigators at San Diego State University (referred to as the Southwest sample), was extended as a source of research data by enrolling the children into the LONGSCAN study as they reached their fourth birthdays. Approximately 40% of the children had returned home by their fourth birthdays, so this constituent study provides a natural comparison between children remaining in foster care, children living with relatives, and children who have been reunited with their parent(s).

The fifth and final LONGSCAN sample consists of young children who were identified by a medical center as being at risk for maltreatment (referred to as the East sample). Children in this sample were identified as having been drug- or HIV-exposed in utero or as having been referred for failure to thrive in a pediatric clinic in Baltimore. A third group of children was matched by age from the well-child clinics in the same inner city neighborhoods. This sample (N = 282) represents an at-risk sample that may never have been involved with CPS, as the referral of HIV- or drug-exposed infants to CPS was not a standard practice in that jurisdiction at the time of recruitment.

The LONGSCAN data collection procedures and interviews of the children and their parents systematically change as the children age. The details of all of the instrumentation are beyond the scope of this chapter, but a full index of the research measures used for each interview is available on the internet at www.iprc.unc.edu/longscan. The outcome measures used to examine the impact of maltreatment on child development are described in this section.

Although the spectrum of risk for maltreatment before age 4 distinguished the samples at initial recruitment into the LONGSCAN study, since 1991 the consortium has been collecting extensive data about family functioning, schooling, employment, family composition, neighborhood environments, subsequent involvement with social services, and the nature of any subsequent child maltreatment in an identical way for each of the five cohorts of children. As the children now approach 16 and 18 years of age, the characteristics that distinguished their early lives from each other no longer distinguish the cohorts in terms of outcomes (Runyan, 2005, unpublished data). Indeed, the absence of differences between some of the cohorts can already be seen in some of the results presented in the sections that follow for age 8 outcomes. As a result, for many LONGSCAN analyses, it has been possible to group the children into a single sample using control variables to assess the significance of specific sites.

LONGSCAN's Approach to Classifying Child Maltreatment

Because LONGSCAN is a five-site study being conducted longitudinally in five states, LONGSCAN researchers faced the challenge of establishing reliable data on the exposure of the children in the study to various forms of child maltreatment in the different jurisdictions represented by the different sites (because legal and policy definitions of maltreatment differ across different jurisdictions). In order to accomplish this, the LONGSCAN investigators developed a multiple method, multiple-source approach to collecting data on exposure to child maltreatment.[3] Specifically, data from the children and parents are being regularly collected in standardized ways: Researchers have collected caregiver reports of the use of discipline at child age 8 as well as youth self-reports of physical abuse, sexual abuse, and neglect at ages 12 and 16 and plan to collect an extensive lifetime history of maltreatment exposure as each child participant enters adulthood. LONGSCAN researchers also needed to develop an approach to systematically coding the information available from CPS. To this end, as part of the LONGSCAN study, they have been conducting periodic systematic reviews of official CPS records. Because access to CPS records systematically varies across sites (in the two western sites, the investigators have real-time access to all new reports of maltreatment, whereas in the other locations access and review of records has to be regularly requested and approved), researchers have established a protocol for review of CPS records requiring that reviews be conducted at least every 2 years and include a comprehensive review of all records for the child's lifetime; therefore, records that might have been misplaced or unavailable at an earlier review might be coded on subsequent reviews. In addition, a process has been established whereby records are coded at both the child- and report-levels.

Reliably coding CPS data posed specific challenges, as the form, content, and completeness of records varied across the different states and counties from which the samples were collected. The LONGSCAN researchers thus developed a protocol for collecting and then recoding the maltreatment allegations documented in the CPS narrative records. In addition to recording the determination of type of abuse or neglect identified by CPS intake workers when a CPS referral first entered the system, LONGSCAN staff reviewed the allegations for every new CPS report and coded those allegations as to type of abuse using two alter-

---

[3]Although the LONGSCAN group has collected data on child maltreatment using a variety of methods and plan to combine this information in future work, the data presented here are based only on the information gathered from CPS records.

nate coding systems. This methodology provided an opportunity to contrast the two coding systems in their utility for predicting outcomes when compared with CPS classification of maltreatment, and it suggests future strategies for the field in terms of achieving comparable data across multiple input sources. The two coding systems examined by LONGSCAN were a modified version of the MCS, developed by Barnett et al. (1993), and the coding system used by the NIS-2 (DHHS, 1988). Each of these systems has a specified approach to coding severity, chronicity, and type of maltreatment, as detailed in this chapter.

The Modified Maltreatment Classification System

The MCS, originally developed by Barnett et al. (1993), was adopted and modified in 1994 for use in the LONGSCAN Study (and subsequently called the Modified Maltreatment Classification Scheme [MMCS]).[4] The dimensions of maltreatment included in the MCS are severity of incidents within each type of maltreatment, the frequency and chronicity of maltreatment reports, the length of time of CPS involvement, the developmental period during which the maltreatment occurred, the type and number of placements outside the home, and the alleged perpetrators of the incident. In the MMCS, LONGSCAN researchers retained type, severity, frequency, and alleged perpetrator variables. However, LONGSCAN did not specifically code to developmental periods as specified in the MCS but did collect information on the dates of referrals so that the timing of maltreatment could be derived from the LONGSCAN dataset using child age. Data on both substantiation and child placement were derived from other CPS record sources. Finally, LONGSCAN researchers did not collect chronicity data based on length of time a CPS record was open for service. Rather, because research in recent years has suggested that the length of time a CPS case is open may be more of a reflection of CPS system issues (e.g., priorities, resources) than a child's experience of maltreatment (see Drake & Pandey, 1996; English, Brummel, Coghlan, Novicky, & Marshall, 1998), chronicity was defined as the extent and continuity of a child's CPS involvement with either recurrent new reports and/or substantiations or continued CPS services since birth.

Although the original MCS uses specific anchors for the lowest and highest levels of severity (e.g., no harm, hospitalization, death) for each type of abuse or neglect and requires the user to interpolate severity codes for intermediate levels of harm, such as bruises or broken bones, the MMCS adds more specificity to the intermediate severity codes. In particular, the MMCS specifies the codes for specific intermediate levels of harm (e.g., broken bones; injuries requiring medical care) by type of maltreatment and disaggregates the inclusive Neglect code in

---

[4]The LONGSCAN version of the MCS, the MMCS, is publicly available at http://www.iprc .unc.edu/longscan.

Table 10.2.   Example of type and severity coding on the
Modified Maltreatment Classification System (MMCS)

Neglect: Failure to provide food

Each subcategory within a subtype may have severity levels
1 (low) through 5 (high). Each severity code has specific
meaning:

   Severity 1: Caretaker does not provide regular meals.
   Severity 2: Caretaker does not ensure that food is
   available.
   Severity 3: Child experiences pattern of frequently missed
   meals.
   Severity 4: Child fails to grow because of poor nutrition.
   Severity 5: Child is hospitalized or dies from starvation.

the MCS. This is done so that cases of neglect can be characterized as failure to supervise, failure to provide, educational neglect, medical neglect, or exposure to violence in the home. An example of the classification of severity rating for the subtype Neglect—Failure to Provide Food is provided in Table 10.2. (Severity ratings for other subtypes are similar, with severity level examples consistent with maltreatment types.)

The NIS-2 Coding System

A second system used by LONGSCAN to classify information from CPS records was the coding system used in the NIS-2 (and subsequently in the NIS-3). As described earlier, this coding system provides specific definitions for harm and endangerment, as well as definitions for different types (and subtypes) of abuse and neglect, including physical abuse, sexual abuse, physical neglect, educational neglect, and emotional neglect. In addition, the NIS coding system requires that a number of additional definitional standards be met regarding a child's age, residence, custody status, time of maltreatment, and purposive and avoidable acts/ omissions. For the different types of abuse and neglect coded, specific information is gathered with respect to perpetrators, injuries, and age and sex of the child, as well as information concerning a number of child characteristics, family characteristics, and perpetrator characteristics. For the purpose of the LONGSCAN study, researchers were interested in using the NIS definitional standards as a means of coding and classifying CPS records in terms of the types and subtypes of abuse and neglect experienced by different children. Severity is described for each form of maltreatment on a scale of 1–6 (1 is fatal, 2 involves life-threatening injury or hospitalization, 3 is moderate injury with observable consequences, 5 is no harm or threat of harm, and 6 is reserved as unknown), with rater interpretation of severity being left more to judgment and with less specificity than with the MMCS codes.

Ongoing Review of CPS Records

Because each of the LONGSCAN study sites are in different jurisdictions, the process of continuing ongoing review of CPS records for new allegations has required different procedures for each site. In the two western sites, access to records is continuous, but systematic review of these records is undertaken by a staff member every 2 years. In the other sites, negotiations between the investigators and the local social services agencies have been recurrent and new permission is required each time a review is undertaken. To date, these negotiations have been successful and quite regular, but they are also the reason that the interval between record reviews is 2 years (to allow for time for the negotiations to occur).

Multiple Types of Maltreatment

LONGSCAN also faced the challenge of how to assign a maltreatment type code to allegations that included multiple forms of maltreatment. The multiple possible combinations of physical abuse, sexual abuse, psychological abuse/neglect, and multiple types of neglect suggest an enormous number of coding categories. Research indicating that the effects of maltreatment on child outcomes vary by the type of maltreatment has led some researchers to argue that the effects of different types and subtypes of maltreatment should be examined separately (e.g., Kinard, 2001; Lau et al., 2005; Manly et al., 1994). The problem with this approach, however, is that it ignores the substantial comorbidity among the different types of maltreatment and raises questions about how one develops a hierarchy for deciding which type of maltreatment should be regarded as the most serious or most determinative of adverse outcomes. For example, how should one characterize the severity of maltreatment experienced by the child (i.e., which type of maltreatment to code) when there are multiple types with differing levels of severity? Is one high-severity sexual abuse incident such as penetration more important or significant for a child's development than 20 low-level severity allegations of neglect, such as failure to provide regular meals? How should an investigator code the chronicity, frequency, and age of onset or developmental period in which a child first experiences maltreatment in order to assess impact? Does examination of chronicity, frequency, severity, age of onset, or type of maltreatment add to our understanding of maltreatment over traditional approaches? Is it worth the extra time and effort to recode maltreatment information into multiple dimensions of maltreatment?

Confirmation of the importance of these questions quickly accumulated during the earliest data collection phases of the LONGSCAN study. For example, among 545 children with completed data collection at ages 4, 6, and 8 years of age, there were 1243 reports and more than 1900 different allegations of various forms of maltreatment from birth to age 8. One way to address these questions is to empirically compare different methods of coding maltreatment dimensions and test their ability to predict adverse outcomes among maltreated children. The LONGSCAN study, with its relatively large sample of youth who have been maltreated and longitudinal data collected in multiple states, has been able to provide data to compare reports classified using different systems of coding and to examine the predictive ability of the systems with respect to child outcomes. In a special issue of the journal *Child Abuse & Neglect* (Volume 29, July 2005), the LONGSCAN investigators undertook multiple examinations of the dimensions of maltreatment definitions. The major findings of these papers pertinent to research definitions of maltreatment are summarized in the next section of this chapter.

CONCORDANCE AMONG DIFFERENT CODING SYSTEMS

When the LONGSCAN group conceived of a project to examine the performance of alternative approaches to the coding of maltreatment, it used a subsample of participating children who met the following specific criteria: 1) the child and parent both completed the age 4 and age 8 data collection interviews so that there were data about the family members and the cognitive and behavioral functioning of the children, 2) there was a reported allegation of maltreatment that occurred before the age 8 interview, and 3) CPS records had been searched by a LONGSCAN reviewer for each child from birth through the date of the age 8 interview. The researchers excluded all children enrolled in LONGSCAN who had never been reported for abuse or neglect for these analyses because they had no CPS records to examine. These criteria produced a sample of 545 children and their primary caregivers out of the total sample of 806 children who had completed age 8 interviews at the time of these analyses. The four-site attrition rate (excluding the Midwest site, which was not used in these analyses because of the small number of completed interviews at the time the analyses were initiated) between baseline and the age 8 data collection effort and interview for the overall LONGSCAN sample was 16.7% (185 of 1,109 children enrolled in the four sites of the project). Attrition analyses, comparing the two groups of children (those who dropped out of the LONGSCAN study and those who did not) on race/ethnicity, gender, and various caregiver measures (i.e., the Vineland Screener [Sparrow, Carter, & Cicchetti, 1993], the Battelle Developmental Inventory Screening Test [Battelle Screener; Newborg et al., 1998], a measure of caregiver depression, years of parent education, and the Child Behavior Checklist [CBCL; Achenbach, 1991]) indicated no significant differences between the groups at the interview baseline or at the age 8 interview. Table 10.3 presents sample characteristics for the subsample of LONGSCAN children used in the concordance analyses.

Table 10.3. Longitudinal Studies of Child Abuse and Neglect (LONGSCAN) concordance analysis sample characteristics at age 4 (N = 545)

Characteristic	%	N	Mean	Median
Child gender				
Male	49.2	268		
Female	50.8	277		
Child ethnic status				
Majority status	31.9	174		
Minority status	68.1	371		
Child age (years)			8.2	8.1
Caregiver marital status				
Married	34	185		
Single/never married	37	202		
Separated	10	52		
Divorced	18	96		
Widowed	2	10		
Caregiver education (years)			11.8	12.0
Family income (U.S. $)ª				$15K–$19.9K
Family geographic location (site)				
East	12	66		
South	10	56		
Southwest	40	217		
Northwest	38	206		

ªThe range for the upper category of income was truncated, so it is not appropriate to report a mean for this variable.

Sample Characteristics

Sixty-six percent of the sample was of minority ethnic status (i.e., Black, Hispanic, Mixed Race, Asian, and American Indian). The sample was nearly equally divided between boys and girls (51% boys). The range of educational attainment of the participating primary maternal caregivers was broad, ranging from less than high school completion to completion of graduate school. On average, caregivers used for these analyses had 12 years of education; 31% of the caregivers reported post–high school education. Participating families had a median income of between $15,000 and $19,999 per year at the time that the child was enrolled in the study (1990–1995).

Procedure

One or two trained reviewers at each site abstracted data for each allegation, the conclusion of any investigation, and information about any services or interven-

tions that resulted. Reviewers completed a structured coding form, using specified pages from the CPS records that included the face sheet and the intake form,
and recorded the original CPS classification of the case. They then completed the
fields required to score the record according to the criteria for the MMCS and for
the NIS-2 research coding systems. Because of the difficulties involved in accessing records in the field and resource limitations, no effort was made to have independent coding for the NIS-2 and the MMCS categorizations of records; the
records were coded when they were located and reviewed, and all information
needed for assessing the original CPS classification and developing codes for each
of the research systems was collected at the same time. The collection of the data
for the alternative research classification systems was not originally intended to
produce a comparison between the systems, so no effort was undertaken to build
in independence.

As noted previously, two sites had continuous access to CPS records. The
maltreatment data collection training required a minimum of 2 days each time
a new staff member was hired to conduct the reviews. Training involved both
didactic presentations and a requirement that the interviewer demonstrate at
least 90% concordance on all the major elements with a gold standard reviewer
on 10 records selected from across all five LONGSCAN sites. The gold standard
reviewer was a MSW coinvestigator at the Coordinating Center who helped develop the expanded coding specifications for the MMCS. This investigator also
organized the original and repeated training of the interviewers at all of the sites
and sent out a selection of records from each of the sites to all of the other sites
for review to assess scoring consistency. The test records were two social services
records selected by each site where allegations of maltreatment had been recorded. Each site copied two actual Department of Social Services records from
one of the LONGSCAN participants at their site that were legible and for which
all identifying information was redacted. The selected records had to contain at
least one maltreatment allegation and provide a set of specified pages from the
CPS records, including the reported allegation and a face sheet that specified the
age and gender of the child and the identity (i.e., role in the family) of the
responsible family. These records were then sent to the Coordinating Center, and
copies of the packets of 10 records were sent to all of the active record reviewers.
The test records were coded by each record reviewer, using the LONGSCAN data
entry coding system, and their scoring reports were then sent to the statistical
unit of the Coordinating Center for analyses.

Record reviewers not achieving a 90% concordance rate on all data elements were retrained and retested until they reached the required standard. In
addition, all active record reviewers were (and continue to be) required to repeat
the scoring procedures at least once every 2 years so that coder drift could be
assessed and retraining conducted if the score fell below 90% concordance. (The
2-year window reflects the periodicity of the record reviews, as most records are
reviewed promptly at the start of every record review period. During each record

review period, two new records are obtained for review from each site for each major training session of record reviewers.) Trainings were scheduled such that record reviewers for multiple sites could attend them; some were held at the Coordinating Center and some were conducted in cities involved in the research. The gold-standard trainer and each record reviewer entered the records into a special version of the LONGSCAN data entry system, and the concordance rate was calculated across all fields of the record review form, including dates, types of maltreatment, and severity. Record reviewers may or may not have been child interviewers, depending on the resources and staffing available to each LONGSCAN site, but the record reviews and child interviews were never contemporaneous and most sites, at most of the periods of time in which records were reviewed, trained staff who were not child interviewers were used for the record review task. Because of limited staff resources, it was not always possible to require completely independent assessments of child functioning and record reviews, but this was achieved for most children.

Child Outcome Measures

The LONGSCAN researchers' efforts to study alternate maltreatment classification systems required assessment of child development at age 4 and at age 8. Developmental outcomes of interest included behavioral, adaptive, and physical and emotional functioning of the children at age 8 years. The researchers used the child's baseline developmental and behavioral status before new experiences of maltreatment and examined change as it related to new maltreatment experiences. Although latent effects of earlier maltreatment before age 4 might thus confound these analyses, for this exploratory study of alternate coding systems, the researchers postulated that measures of functioning at age 4 would partially control for the impact of maltreatment and other adverse life events prior to entry into LONGSCAN. In this way, the investigators attempted to isolate changes in the functioning of the children that might be tied to new experiences of maltreatment.

In line with the researchers' multiple-method principles, they selected, as outcomes, measures obtained by parent report, by child report, and by interviewer assessment. Child behavior was assessed at ages 4 and 8 using the Total Problems, Internalizing Problems, and Externalizing Problems scales of the CBCL (Achenbach, 1991). The validity and reliability of this 113-item instrument have been well described (Achenbach, 1991). The Internalizing Problems scale combines three subscales: the Social Withdrawal, Somatic Complaints, and Anxiety/Depression scales. The Externalizing Problems scale combines the Delinquent Behavior and Aggressive Behavior subscales. T-scores less than 60 are considered in the normal range, whereas T-scores above 63 are considered in the clinical range, and scores of 61–63 are considered borderline (Achenbach, 1991).

The Socialization and Daily Living Skills subscales of the Vineland Screener were used to assess child adaptive behavior at age 8. The Vineland Screener (Sparrow et al., 1993) is an abbreviated version of the Vineland Adaptive Behavior Scales (Sparrow, Balla, & Cicchetti, 1984) developed exclusively for research use and administered to the child's caregiver. The authors of the instrument reported interrater reliability coefficients of .98 with lay interviewers, and correlations between the full Vineland and Vineland Screener of the Daily Living Skills and Socialization subscales of 0.92 and 0.93, respectively (Sparrow et al., 1993).

LONGSCAN used the Trauma Symptom Checklist for Children-Alternative Version (TSCC-A; Briere, 1996) to assess child emotional functioning at age 8. The TSCC-A is a child report instrument of posttraumatic distress and related psychological symptoms designed for use with child victims of traumatic events. The alternative version includes five subscales (Anxiety, Depression, Anger, Posttraumatic Stress, and Dissociation). Higher scores reflect greater symptomatology. T-scores of 65 or greater are considered clinically significant.

Approach to Data Analyses

The LONGSCAN investigators theorized that the effects of maltreatment experienced prior to the time of the age 4 interview already would have influenced the measures of child functioning at age 4. This assumption provided a conservative bias; to the extent that there might be late or latent effects from earlier maltreatment, the relationships between child functioning and any new maltreatment would be less apparent. This conservative approach seemed appropriate for these exploratory analyses because measures of child development in very early childhood have shown poor correlation with measures of later cognitive functioning (Committee on Children With Disabilities, 2001).

To control for the effects of maltreatment prior to the child's enrollment in LONGSCAN, the child's T-score on the age 4 CBCL Total Problems scale was used in models predicting age 8 scores on the CBCL Total Problems, Internalizing Problems, and Externalizing Problems scales and—because no baseline TSCC-A data were available—in the models predicting scores on the five TSCC-A scales, to control for the effects of maltreatment prior to the child's enrollment in LONGSCAN, as no baseline TSCC-A. For models predicting scores on the Vineland Screener Socialization and Daily Living Skills subscales, researchers used the Personal–Social Skills and Adaptive Behavior domain scores from the Battelle Screener administered at age 4 (Newborg et al., 1988) to control for developmental effects from earlier maltreatment. Thus, the analyses were designed to be able to assess change in child behavior by using the baseline CBCL as a baseline for changes in CBCL scores at follow-up; the statistical modeling was designed to examine change in mental health status from baseline and examine whether that change was linked to any maltreatment exposure that occurred between the baseline assessment and the age 8 assessment.

Research Questions

Reports versus Substantiations

Before proceeding with an examination of concordance among the classification schemes used by CPS, the NIS-2 coding system, and the MMCS, the LONGSCAN investigators first addressed another issue that has been controversial in maltreatment research. Namely, should substantiated referrals or just allegations of maltreatment be used as the basis of analysis? Although many studies of maltreatment use substantiated allegations as the measure of maltreatment (e.g., Runyan & Gould, 1985), several recent studies have questioned the use of only substantiated cases in child maltreatment research (see Drake & Pandey, 1996; English et al., 1998). The LONGSCAN group examined this issue in the LONGSCAN sample (Hussey et al., 2005) by comparing social, emotional, and behavioral functioning of the sample participants without reports of maltreatment, participants with reports that had not been substantiated, and participants with reports that were substantiated. After controlling for potential confounding variables, including reports of maltreatment prior to enrollment in LONGSCAN at age 4, Hussey et al. (2005) found no significant differences between children with substantiated versus unsubstantiated reports between the ages of 4 and 8 on any of the outcomes of interest, suggesting that the differences between groups with respect to substantiation may have reflected the investigative process rather than the actual experiences of the children. Hussey et al. did describe significant differences in outcomes, however, between the groups of LONGSCAN children who had never been reported for maltreatment and those who were reported at some point in their lives (both substantiated and unsubstantiated cases), indicating that reported children showed significantly worse outcomes than nonreported children. Based on the Hussey et al. findings and results from other studies (e.g., Drake & Pandey, 1996; English et al., 1998, Leiter & Johnsen, 1997), the LONGSCAN researchers thus decided to use allegations of maltreatment recorded as having been made to CPS in the jurisdictions of the LONGSCAN consortium, instead of substantiations of maltreatment by CPS, as the basis of judging that maltreatment had occurred to a child enrolled in LONGSCAN for concordance analyses. Because the MMCS and NIS-2 codes are established on a specified set of limited pages from the records, and entire CPS records are not required, there did not appear to be any differences between substantiated and alleged maltreatment reports in the information available to code the type of maltreatment.

Concordance in Maltreatment Definitions Between Coding Schemes

The LONGSCAN investigators next addressed the issue of concordance in maltreatment definitions across the three classifications of maltreatment type considered—the original CPS designation, the NIS-2 codes, and the modified MCS codes (MMCS). Each of these codes were compared using both Kappa statistics to assess agreement beyond chance and receiver operating characteristic (ROC) curve analysis (Fletcher, Fletcher, & Wagner, 1996). CPS maltreatment type was coded using a checklist. The major categories for this variable were Physical Abuse, Sexual Abuse, Neglect, and Emotional Maltreatment. Allegations that did not fit one of these types were not considered reports; nonreport categories included *None given, Dependency, Caretaker absence/incapacity, Moral/legal/educational, Abuse (unspecified),* and *Don't know.* The researchers excluded 387 reports with no valid CPS allegation type codes. Clearly, if no CPS allegation was contained in the record, it could not be recoded by the other systems. In addition, 167 reports with multiple types of allegations coded by CPS were excluded because there was no systematic way to decide which allegation should be used in the comparison of the CPS and research codes without biasing the agreement by assuming concordance. An additional 163 reports were dropped because no valid MMCS type of maltreatment could be applied to the CPS narrative (as it was impossible to find sufficient information to ascertain the nature of the allegation), yielding 1263 reports as the total number of reports for these analyses.

Because the use of an ROC curve for analysis requires that one measure be designated as the standard to which the others can be compared, the LONGSCAN researchers had to select one of the measures as the criterion. Because of its extensive development, level of specification, and the researchers' efforts to ensure that this instrument described the events recorded in the case files, the researchers decided that the MMCS would be regarded as the gold standard, or the criterion against which each of the other coding strategies could be compared.[5] In this ROC curve analysis, the sensitivity (classification of reports as abuse when the MMCS classification system determined that there was abuse) and specificity (reports not classified as abuse when there was no abuse coded using the MMCS system) were calculated. The researchers contrasted the sensitivity and false positive rates of both the original CPS classification and the NIS-2 classification to the MMCS classification. In an ROC curve analysis comparing two different measures on sensitivity and specificity, without consideration of cost or difficulty, the preferred test is the test that is graphically closer to 100% sensitivity and 100% specificity (i.e., a 0% false positive rate). In its simplest form, the visual inspection of the relative positions of alternative tests compared with a gold standard will identify how closely the tests perform. More sophisticated examinations can then be undertaken to compare the area under the curve when each of the possible tests has a variety of possible cutpoints or determinations as to when the test

---

[5]When little data exist to specify which measure is best designated as a standard, the face validity and content validity of the measures can be used to select one, but the analyses also can be iteratively performed with each of the potential candidates used as the gold standard in order to graphically represent the level of agreement between measures. Thus, it is not critical that the gold standard be the best measure as long as the shortcomings of each measure are understood and the limitations of using a less-than-gold standard are appreciated, because the figures for sensitivity and specificity will be depressed by a less-than-gold standard (Fletcher, Fletcher, & Wagner 1996).

is positive (Fletcher, Fletcher, & Wagner, 1996). The researchers' alternate approach to establishing the relations between the two alternative coding schemes was to examine agreement using the Kappa statistic. The Kappa statistic is close to 1 if there is agreement in all of the reports and 0 if none of the reports are classified as the same type by the two coding systems (Sim & Wright, 2005). The researchers did not attempt a weighted Kappa but looked for agreement between the primary type of maltreatment for each report determined by CPS and the type of maltreatment determined by the MMCS. When there was more than one MMCS abuse or neglect type that could be derived from a single CPS report, LONGSCAN researchers assigned a single, predominant type of maltreatment allegation coded under the MMCS system to each report. They developed an algorithm to determine the predominant type for each report: The type of maltreatment allegation with the highest severity rating was assigned. As the MMCS severity codes for physical and sexual maltreatment were intended to be parallel insofar as possible, selection of the highest severity rating generally resulted in a ranking with face validity. When two MMCS types were coded as having equivalent severity, researchers selected the type coded with the combination of both the highest severity and the greatest frequency. This approach allowed them to assign a primary form of maltreatment for nearly all of the cases. In those few cases in which the severity and frequency codes were identical, type was assigned according to the conventional hierarchical ordering of sexual abuse, physical abuse, neglect, and emotional abuse (see Lau et al., 2005). Although the researchers recognize that using this convention has limitations, they needed to make some ordering possible in cases in which both frequency and severity were equal, and they felt that using this hierarchy would be a reasonable solution for the seven cases of tied severity and frequency and would be preferable to dropping these cases (which would have the effect of inflating the estimate of concordance).

Comparison of Different Coding and Definitional Schemes in Predicting Outcomes

In addition to examining concordance, the LONGSCAN investigators also wanted to compare the ability of the different coding systems to predict children's functioning at age 8. A total of 10 measures of functioning at age 8 were predicted with nearly identical regression models for each type of maltreatment (i.e., physical abuse, sexual abuse, neglect, and emotional maltreatment experienced after age 4). The researchers used as outcome variables the CBCL Internalizing Problems, Externalizing Problems, and Total Problem scores; Vineland Daily Living Skills and Socialization scores; and the TSCC-A Depression, Anxiety, and Posttraumatic Stress scores.

In the regression analyses for each outcome, the researchers first entered a block that described the demographics of the child and a baseline value of either the baseline CBCL score or Batelle Screener score. The choice of the baseline control variable was related to the outcome; the age 4 CBCL Behavior Problems score was used as a control in the age 8 models in which the CBCL provided the outcome, and the baseline Battelle Screener score was used as a control for the Vineland Screener scales. Next, researchers entered in a second block a control variable for site and in a third block the type of maltreatment according to one or the other coding systems (i.e., the presence or absence of a specific maltreatment type as noted in the original CPS allegation, the presence of a specific maltreatment type as recorded by the NIS-2 coding system, or the presence of that same maltreatment type as recorded by the MMCS). These maltreatment-type codes were dichotomous and the outcome variables were the scale scores for the 10 different outcomes measures derived from either the CBCL, the Vineland Screener, or the TSCC-A. The models were held constant for each outcome with the sole exception that the researchers systematically varied the maltreatment variable in each model using each of the three coding systems. For example, to examine the impact of physical abuse, the researchers sequentially substituted the CPS variable indicating whether an allegation of physical abuse had been made with the NIS-2 variable for a physical abuse allegation and then the MMCS allegation of physical abuse variable, while keeping the remaining variables— child demographics, site, and baseline functioning measures—unchanged in the models.

Results

The results from these analyses—organized by major findings—are presented in the following section and in Tables 10.4, 10.5, and 10.6.

Significant Agreement Between the Research Coding Systems

Agreement between the MMCS codes and CPS recorded allegations based on the predominant type coded from the MMCS, for each reported allegation of child abuse or neglect in the social services records, is presented in Table 10.4. The LONGSCAN researchers found that the overall agreement rate between the MMCS predominant allegation type of physical abuse and CPS recorded allegations for physical abuse was 82%. Agreements between the MMCS and CPS designations for sexual abuse, neglect, and emotional abuse were 90%, 85% and 37%, respectively. Some major areas of disagreement also were noted. Nine percent of reports assigned a MMCS code of physical abuse (because the record included data that indicated that physical abuse should be coded) had been recorded by CPS as neglect. Similarly, 9% of cases to which an MMCS code of sexual abuse was assigned had been recorded by CPS as neglect, with no sexual abuse determination noted in the CPS record. The code of emotional abuse was rarely used by CPS as a major category, which may be related to the difficulty of assigning this type as an explanation. However, the total number of cases meet-

Table 10.4. Type of maltreatment allegation designated by child protective services (CPS) by predominant type of narrative-based allegation, coded by Longitudinal Studies of Child Abuse and Neglect (LONGSCAN)[a] for 1,263 maltreatment reports from CPS records

CPS codes	Modified Maltreatment Classification System (MMCS) codes[b]				
	Physical abuse	Sexual abuse	Neglect	Emotional	Total
Physical	222	1	36	16	275
Sexual	8	101	32	2	143
Neglect	25	10	663	35	733
Emotional	4	0	11	36	51
Other[c]	12	0	40	9	61
Total	271	112	782	98	1,263

[a]The predominant type of maltreatment alleged when multiple types were coded was determined using the following algorithm: The type with highest severity (excluding emotional maltreatment, as severity is coded using a different scheme) was assigned; then the type with highest severity and frequency when two types were coded with equal severity was assigned; then, if no type was coded more frequently than any other, type was assigned in the following hierarchy: sexual abuse, physical abuse, neglect, and then emotional abuse.

[b]Of 163 reports excluded from this table because LONGSCAN coders were unable to code the report as one of these four types using MMCS, CPS classified 22 (14%) as physical abuse, 29 (18%) as sexual abuse, 87 (53%) as neglect, 2 (1%) as emotional maltreatment, and 23 (14%) as some other type.

[c]Other type categories used by CPS included dependency, caretaker absence/incapacity, moral/legal/educational, and unspecified abuse.

ing MMCS criteria and being assigned a code for emotional abuse in the MMCS was 98, whereas only 51 cases of emotional abuse were recorded by CPS. Among all of the reported maltreatment, only 36 cases were coded by both CPS and the MMCS as emotional abuse. Overall, CPS and the MMCS classified cases as the same type of maltreatment in 81% of reports, with 19% of reports being classified differently by CPS and the MMCS coding system.

The NIS-2 and CPS codes similarly agreed for 81% of reports, although it is important to note that these levels of agreement clearly were enhanced by the process of collecting data for all three systems by the same record reviewers at the same time. The LONGSCAN researchers also found a very high level of agreement between the NIS-2 and the MMCS codes for all types of maltreatment. For physical abuse, the Kappa statistic was 0.981. The agreement between CPS and the MMCS system for physical abuse was much lower, with a sensitivity of 74%, a specificity of 95%, and a positive predictive value of 81%. A similarly high level of agreement between the NIS-2 and MMCS codes for sexual abuse was also found (Kappa = 0.961). CPS codes for sexual abuse had much greater misclassification when assessed against the MMCS. Despite the influence of the method of case review previously noted, the agreement between the NIS-2 and the MMCS codes for neglect was not as strong as for physical abuse, with a Kappa statistic of 0.743.

The type of abuse with the least agreement was emotional abuse. CPS recorded an allegation in just 51 reports of maltreatment. The MMCS codes for emotional maltreatment added another 239 reports that met research criteria for this type of maltreatment. The sensitivity was just 16% for a CPS report identifying emotional maltreatment as the type of maltreatment, and the Kappa statistic for agreement between the CPS and MMCS codes was low at 0.224. In contrast, the agreement between the NIS-2 and MMCS codes for emotional abuse was relatively high, with a Kappa of 0.722 (see Table 10.5).

Regression Analyses Predicting Child Outcomes

In an attempt to refine the measurement of maltreatment, the LONGSCAN researchers also used hierarchical regression models to compare the relative ability of the three different coding systems (as applied to new maltreatment reports) to predict child functioning at age 8, controlling for status before the reports. Clearly, as investigators, the LONGSCAN researchers had no a priori need to prefer one coding system over another. This is in contrast to the CPS system, which is likely to have policy or legal constraints that favor some "diagnoses" over others. To the extent that these constraints alter the determination of the nature of a case by CPS agencies, CPS data are unlikely to be satisfactory as a means of surveillance or as descriptions of the epidemiology of child maltreatment.

Although the LONGSCAN researchers recognize that determining categories of maltreatment exposure by impact is circular reasoning, their approach to these analyses was purely exploratory. Specifically, the goal of these analyses was to explore the relative usefulness of these different coding systems in predicting outcomes by comparing them in parallel regression models. However, these data illustrate the problem with studies that rely solely on CPS as the source of data about what children have experienced. The researchers' efforts to assess exposure to maltreatment will thus require multiple sources of data from parents, the children themselves, and CPS records; and the LONGSCAN researchers plan to pursue these more detailed analyses in the future.[6] As such, these analyses were designed solely as a means of examining the relative utility of CPS data in predicting outcomes.

For these analyses, 10 outcome variables and four exposure variables, each measured by the three alternative coding systems, resulted in a total of 120 separate regression equations. In the LONGSCAN researchers' analyses, they focused on three specific questions:

---

[6]Data from the first LONGSCAN site to complete youth self-reports found little agreement between child reports and CPS reports, suggesting that relying on CPS data alone may misrepresent children's experiences. Other studies have suggested that less than 5% of the maltreatment acknowledged by parents is ever reported to CPS (Theodore, Chang, Runyan, Hunter, Bangdiwala, & Agans, 2005), again suggesting the importance of a multiple-method, multiple-source approach.

Table 10.5. Sensitivity, specificity, positive predictive value, and Kappa statistics for child protective services (CPS) and Second National Incidence Study (NIS-2) coding of abuse allegations using the Modified Maltreatment Classification System (MMCS) as the gold standard

Type	Sensitivity (%)	Specificity (%)	Positive predictive value[a](%)	Kappa[b]
CPS physical abuse	74	95	81	
NIS-2 physical abuse	98	100	99	0.981
			(0.975 substantiated cases)	
CPS sexual abuse	87	95	65	
NIS-2 sexual abuse	92	100	97	0.961
			(0.971 substantiated cases)	
CPS neglect	82	76	83	
NIS-2 neglect	84	93	94	0.743
			(0.785 substantiated cases)	
CPS emotional abuse	16	99	87	0.224
NIS-2 emotional abuse	72	96	85	0.722
			(0.207 substantiated cases)	

[a]Positive predictive value is the probability that the type of maltreatment coded by the CPS system or by the NIS-2 system will be the same type as coded by the MMCS system.

[b]Kappa statistics were calculated for all 1,920 records of maltreatment coded by NIS-2 and the MMCS. CPS comparisons were limited to 1,426 records with a single valid CPS code.

1. In the third hierarchical block, does entry of the maltreatment code for type of maltreatment into the regression model result in a significant increase in overall variance explained (R2 change)?

2. Is the unstandardized regression coefficient for the maltreatment type code statistically significant in the final regression model containing all control variables?

3. Are there regression models with a statistically significant amount of the variance explained by one of the coding systems not matched by the other two coding systems?

The regression results for the MMCS and NIS-2 coding systems were very similar—results that were not unexpected given that the LONGSCAN record reviewers simultaneously coded for both systems. (Data found in the record reviews for either coding process were likely to find their way into the codes for the other process.)[7] Demographic and control variables explained about 12% of the variance in composite and individual CBCL and Vineland Screener scores and

---

[7]It is important to note, however, that structured coding with a codebook and formal training are always going to beat a more haphazard process, as might occur with CPS workers who are making coding decisions that may have no impact on their own actions to help families and for which there may be overarching policy considerations and implications.

Table 10.6. Comparing child protective services (CPS), Modified Maltreatment Classification Scheme (MMCS), and Second National Incidence Study (NIS-2) coding of specific allegations of maltreatment after age 4, looking at block 3 R^2 Change, final model β values, and post-hoc comparisons

	CPS		MMCS		NIS-2	
	R^2 Change	β	R^2 Change	β	R^2 Change	β
CBCL[a] Internalizing Problems						
Physical abuse	.002	-2.088	.001	-1.184	.001	-1.247
Sexual abuse	.006	4.645*	.022***	8.289***	.017***	7.314***
Neglect	.003	1.476	.001	0.665	.003	1.316
Emotional maltreatment	.014**	7.108***	.004	2.511	.001	1.414
CBCL Externalizing Problems						
Physical abuse	.001	-2.046	.002	-2.085	.003	-2.261
Sexual abuse	.003	3.339	.030***	10.293***	.020***	8.615***
Neglect	.001	1.554	.000	-0.275	.000	0.000
Emotional maltreatment	.001	0.677	.002	2.573	.003	2.815
CBCL Total Problems						
Physical abuse	.005*	-3.612**	.003	-2.365	.004	-2.605
Sexual abuse	.004	3.075	.028***	9.861***	.020***	8.469***
Neglect	.001	1.570	.000	0.395	.001	0.979
Emotional maltreatment	.003	2.895	.004	3.109*	.002	2.547
Vineland Daily Living Skills						
Physical abuse	.005	3.960	.010*	6.846*	.012**	7.451**
Sexual abuse	.001	-2.918	.000	1.742	.000	-0.466
Neglect	.000	0.000	.000	0.000	.000	0.687
Emotional maltreatment	.003	4.428	.001	-1.470	.004	-3.728
Vineland Socialization						
Physical abuse	.000	-0.329	.001	1.817	.002	2.417
Sexual abuse	.001	-2.918	.006	-6.697	.005	-5.916
Neglect	.007*	-4.810**	.001	-1.751	.002	-2.508
Emotional maltreatment	.001	1.776	.000	-0.618	.009*	-5.268

Note: There were no significant findings for the TSCC-A (Trauma Symptom Checklist for Children-Alternative Version) scales; therefore, these have been excluded.

[a]CBCL, Child Behavior Checklist (Achenbach, 1991)   [b]Vineland (Sparrow, Carter, & Cicchetti, 1993)

*$p < .05$.   **$p < .01$.   ***$p < .001$.

thus, child outcomes. Physical abuse predicted higher CBCL Total Problems scores whereas neglect, both failure to provide and failure to supervise, predicted poorer Vineland Screener Socialization scores but had no apparent impact on a child's behavioral functioning. The codes for sexual abuse predicted more behavior problems for each coding system. Although statistically significant, use of either of the research codes for physical abuse only modestly contributed to the variance in Vineland Screener Daily Living Skills scores, whereas sexual abuse accounted for most of the variance in child functioning outcomes at age 8.

Sexual abuse, classified by any of the coding systems, predicted higher CBCL Internalizing Problems scores. CBCL Externalizing Problems and Total Problems scores were affected by sexual abuse only when the sexual abuse was coded by the MMCS or NIS-2 systems; CPS determination of sexual abuse had no apparent impact on either of these scores.

Physical abuse explained a significant amount of the variance in CBCL Total Problems scores regardless of which of the three systems was used to determine physical abuse exposure. Vineland Screener Daily Living Skills scores appeared to be affected by a history of physical abuse only when the abuse was coded by one of the research systems; there was no apparent impact for physical abuse when the abuse was coded by CPS.

Emotional maltreatment, when coded by the MMCS, explained some of the variance in CBCL Total Problems scores, but the R squared change was modest at best. A CPS emotional maltreatment determination explained only variance in the CBCL Internalizing Problems score. The MMCS and the NIS-2 codes of sexual abuse were both better predictors of CBCL Internalizing Problems and CBCL Total Problems Scores than CPS coding; the effect size was larger when coded by the MMCS, as can be seen in Table 10.6.

Neglect Determinations and Child Outcomes at Age 8

The LONGSCAN researchers did not find a significant effect of neglect at age 8 on either the Vineland Screener or the CBCL scales using either of the research coding systems. They did find that the CPS classification of the original allegation as neglect was predictive of worse outcomes on the Vineland Screener, but this may well be because the same forms of maltreatment that the research coding systems regarded as physical abuse and sexual abuse were classified as neglect in the CPS records. Dubowitz et al. (2005) addressed the failure of neglect, as defined by both the MMCS and the NIS-2 systems, to predict child outcomes within LONGSCAN and offered a number of hypotheses for the failure of the study to find an apparent impact of neglect. One likely suggestion is that in many jurisdictions, social services personnel may code allegations of sexual or physical abuse by a boyfriend or other person who is not a household member as neglect by the resident caregiver because he or she allowed the child to be mistreated.

284 Runyan and English

Summary and Discussion of Findings

Though the lack of uniform research definitions of maltreatment remains an issue if a researcher is confined to using CPS records to define maltreatment, the LONGSCAN researchers found agreement between the original CPS classification of reports and two different research classification systems for reviewing CPS records for some forms of maltreatment. Overall, the percent agreement (concordance) between the original CPS classifications and the research classifications using the MMCS was in the 80–90% range for physical abuse, sexual abuse, and neglect. Much greater disagreement was found among emotional maltreatment reports, with potentially significant misclassification. The ROC curve analyses and the Kappa statistics confirmed close agreement between the two alternative research definition coding systems as they were used in LONGSCAN. For each type of maltreatment, the sensitivity and specificity of the NIS-2 codes were very close to the MMCS codes, although high levels of agreement would be expected given the simultaneous coding and the collection of data from the records, which remains as a limitation of this study. Importantly, however, the LONGSCAN data emphasize the lack of concordance between the original determinations of categories of maltreatment by CPS and what was learned by record review. This is most likely due to the fact that the LONGSCAN record abstractors had specific coding manuals for both coding systems, and both systems used the form of abuse with the greatest severity code as the major form of maltreatment. In contrast, the coding decisions made by CPS agency staff in daily practice are typically without the same systematic training and provision of coding manuals to guide decisions.

This work, a secondary analysis of data collected by LONGSCAN to compare the predictive ability of the original CPS classifications and two research definition systems in explaining subsequent child functioning, represents a novel addition to the current discussion about the need to improve research definitions. The data have serious limitations as discussed previously, as they were not collected to produce a comparison of coding methods. However, what these data do demonstrate is that serious misclassification of maltreatment is likely if CPS data are not used cautiously to describe children's maltreatment experiences.

One might ask if there is any utility to the use of CPS data on exposure to maltreatment. The LONGSCAN data call into question whether conclusions based on official data can be used to examine trends in the epidemiology of maltreatment or to compare patterns of official statistics across jurisdictions. Systematically recoded CPS data does appear to be useful in that there were differences in child outcomes by exposure to physical abuse and sexual abuse, and CPS records are available for children offered services. Recoded CPS data may thus prove to be useful in assessments of the impact of child welfare interventions.

Many children are reported to CPS with allegations that specify more than one form of maltreatment. Clearly, one of the differences this presents is that the apparent harms, or planned interventions, may need to be linked to a specific type of maltreatment. Investigators may need to decide which of several allegations is most important.

How to Deal with Determining the Predominant Type of Maltreatment

Parallel LONGSCAN analyses have been undertaken to examine if an empirical approach can help determine how reports or cases should be classified when multiple types of maltreatment are reported longitudinally and/or concurrently. In the analyses presented in this chapter, the researchers classified the type of maltreatment that they considered the most important by weighting severity. They compared the severity codes for each reported type and generated a predominant type based on the highest severity score. Ties in severity score were broken by using the most frequent type of abuse or neglect. Where a tie still existed, it was broken by weighting active forms of maltreatment over more passive forms (i.e. physical and sexual abuse were judged to be more dominant than emotional abuse or neglect when all else was equal). Lau and other LONGSCAN colleagues (2005) examined this issue in greater depth. In the Lau et al. study, the classification scheme used previously in this chapter, herein called the Severity/Frequency Classification scheme for type (SFT), was compared with two other methods of type of maltreatment classification. The other two classification schemes were the Hierarchical Type (HT) and the Expanded Hierarchical Type (EHT). The HT scheme was based on the assumption that when co-occurring types of maltreatment are experienced, active forms of abuse such as sexual abuse are more detrimental than passive forms such as neglect (see, e.g., DePanfilis & Zuravin, 2001; Levine, Doueck, Freeman, & Compaan, 1998, for a discussion). The EHT scheme differentiated multiple maltreatment type combinations from "pure" or single subtypes. In the EHT scheme, six type categories were derived, including *sexual abuse only, sexual abuse plus other types of maltreatment, physical abuse only, neglect only, physical abuse and physical neglect,* and *emotional maltreatment only.* The latter category seems to be seldom used; data suggests that the CPS agencies LONGSCAN is working with do not identify emotional maltreatment except in combination with other types of maltreatment. The very few emotional maltreatment only referrals contained egregious allegations of emotional maltreatment. Although the HT approach has more commonly been used in maltreatment research, there is little empirical evidence to suggest which method of organizing single or co-occurring types of maltreatment best predicts child outcomes.

The same analytical approach used in the other LONGSCAN analyses referenced in this chapter also was used in the examination of the predictive utility of different classification schemes (English, Bangdiwala, & Runyan, 2005; Hussey et al., 2005; Lau et al., 2005). Hierarchical regression analyses examined whether the HT, SFT, and EHT schemes differentially predicted child emotional, behavioral, and adaptive functioning. The EHT scheme actually produced the strongest set of predictive models of child outcomes and predicted more child outcomes than either the HT scheme or the SFT scheme to classify cases with multiple allegations of maltreatment. These analyses confirmed that the co-occurrence of multiple types of maltreatment was significantly related to child outcomes and that classification of maltreatment types must account for multiple types of maltreatment whether within one episode (e.g., a report to CPS) or across multiple episodes/reports of maltreatment over time. Each of the systems examined in this study predicted child outcomes, but different schemes predicted different levels of outcomes. The HT scheme gave primacy of effect to the active abuse categories compared with the passive forms. However, the system that differentiated single versus combined types—the EFT scheme—provided finer discriminations in terms of predicting emotional, behavioral, and adaptive outcomes for children at age 8. This study confirms the importance of examining profiles of maltreatment to help better understand the consequences of individual types of maltreatment and combinations or co-occurring types of maltreatment on child outcomes. It also highlights the problem of using a single type of maltreatment allegation as is coded most frequently in CPS records. Careful examination of records to ascertain all of the forms of maltreatment a child has experienced would appear to be supported by these findings.

Accounting for Chronicity of Child Maltreatment Experiences

Examination of different approaches to defining a child's maltreatment experiences over time, including age of onset of alleged maltreatment, has been identified as an important element in the description of a child's maltreatment experiences (Manly, 2005). In order to explore the utility of different definitions of maltreatment, English, Graham, Litrownik, Everson, and Bangdiwala (2005) developed descriptions of maltreatment based on a child's experiences within specified developmental periods (e.g., 0–18 months, 19–36 months). The broad developmental definition used in this set of analyses was developed to correspond to Erikson's 1963 classification of initial stages of psychosocial development—infancy, toddlerhood, preschool, and early school age—and a calendar definition (within each calendar year of life from birth through age 8). In addition, descriptions of a child's experiences of maltreatment across time included concepts of extent (the number of units or periods of maltreatment experienced within the developmental and calendar definitions) and continuity (whether there were any gaps or maltreatment-free periods within the defined developmental and calendar units).

This analysis and its findings emerged as among the most complex and difficult to interpret of the various analyses undertaken by LONGSCAN. Further work will be needed as the LONGSCAN children age to continue to clarify the impact of chronic maltreatment that extends over multiple developmental stages. The overall analytical approach was to contrast different definitions of chronic-

ity to determine their differential utility in accounting for different child outcomes. These analyses took age, gender, and minority status demographics into
account. Block-wise hierarchical regression analyses for each of the ten outcomes
of interest were conducted for each of the three chronicity definitions. Demographics were entered into the first block. The chronicity variable was entered
into the second block so that variance associated with this variable could be accounted for next. Age of onset was entered into the third block to give priority
to pattern rather than time at which the pattern began. Finally, income and site
were entered into the last block in the final model. The most useful definition of
chronicity, in terms of its ability to predict child behavioral and emotional functioning, varied by specific outcome. A developmental definition, counting the
number of developmental stages of the child's life that maltreatment had been
reported, was found to have the most balanced sensitivity (increased percent of
variance explained) across the three domains of outcome. The developmental definition predicted child outcomes across social, emotional, and behavioral functioning of the child, whereas a simple classification based on age and frequency
predicted outcomes in just two of three outcome domains of interest across outcomes. Among other significant findings, both the total number of maltreatment
reports and the continuity of maltreatment across developmental stages of the
child's life—from infancy to middle childhood, up through age 8—contributed
respectively to the prediction of behavior and emotional trauma symptoms. Consideration of the number of major developmental stages involved and the continuity across stages together were more useful than a simple enumeration of number of reports (English, Graham, et al., 2005).

CONCLUSIONS AND RECOMMENDATIONS

Overall, the exploration of a more detailed description of a child's experiences of
maltreatment conducted by the LONGSCAN group confirms and extends the
findings and recommendations of other researchers (Bolger & Patterson, 2001;
Drake & Pandey, 1996; Manly et al., 1994). First, if a child's well-being or functioning is a criterion of interest, then the important distinction appears to be
whether a child has been reported for maltreatment, not whether the allegation
of maltreatment has been substantiated. As noted earlier, many factors influence
whether a CPS referral is substantiated, and if a referral is not substantiated that
does not mean the child has not been maltreated, nor does it mean a child is
doing well.

Second, researchers have long suggested that use of CPS designations of type
of maltreatment is flawed (NRC, 1993). Although findings of concordance
between CPS and other methods of classifying type of maltreatment reached 80%
or higher for physical and sexual abuse, that still leaves as many as one in five
CPS cases potentially misclassified for these types of abuse. In addition, the
LONGSCAN researchers have noted that the majority of apparent emotional mal-

treatment is unclassified in the CPS typology. At the very least, the findings by Runyan et al. (2005) suggest that maltreatment researchers cannot rely on CPS designation of type of maltreatment as the best summary of the child's experiences. These and other findings suggest that maltreatment researchers, at this time, must go beyond use of CPS classification of physical abuse, sexual abuse, neglect, and emotional abuse until the issue of problems of classification of maltreatment by CPS is adequately addressed.

Finally, the examination of the dimensions of maltreatment by the LONGSCAN group has demonstrated that maltreatment experiences are very complex and will not yield to a simplistic definitional scheme. When examined longitudinally, maltreatment classifications may take into account multiple allegations within one episode or multiple episodes over time. Evaluating different methods of classifying or describing a child's maltreatment experiences based on child functioning is one way to test the usefulness of different characterizations of maltreatment. The utility of this approach will be tested again when LONGSCAN researchers examine child outcomes related to CPS and child, parent, and adult retrospective reports of maltreatment and have to reconcile type and severity across various sources of information.

Overall, the exploration of definitions of maltreatment examined by the LONGSCAN group confirms that record review of CPS records for determinations of exposure to child abuse or neglect will need to be approached very carefully. The concordance between unexamined official records and any systematic coding system is such that the usefulness of records may be in question if they have not been systematically recoded. The two research coding systems used by LONGSCAN largely agreed with each other. Clearly, training and a procedures manual can produce more reliable coding. The LONGSCAN researchers' premise that examining child outcomes permits a more in-depth examination of individual dimensions of maltreatment has allowed them to make some recommendations about coding severity and dealing with concurrent multiple reports. However, these recommendations are limited in that the researchers conducted a series of secondary analyses on data already collected and did not test alternative coding systems "head-to-head" in a blinded and independent comparison. Thus, future research will need to explore these issues further.

In summary, the LONGSCAN researchers' analyses demonstrate that CPS classifications of maltreatment are not good enough, and researchers will need to use more complex classification schemes to accurately describe the maltreatment experiences of children. Furthermore, the data suggest that if researchers' interest is in examining child well-being, reliance on CPS classification of substantiation is not an adequate measure. Indeed, there is so much slippage in classification between CPS use and more rigorous efforts to classify experiences that one may call CPS-based national trend data on declines in sexual abuse or increases in neglect into question (DHHS, 2005; Jones & Finkelhor, 2003). Finally, examinations of various definitions of type, subtype, severity, and chronicity of different forms of maltreatment suggest that the way these dimensions are defined will make a difference in researchers' understanding of the effects of maltreatment on child outcomes overall as well as within different outcome types. Looking at one set of longitudinal change data in one study with outcomes at age 8 has just scratched the surface.

Careful recoding of CPS records will be needed to accurately describe the experiences of children in the system. Research types of quality control and coding manuals with careful attention to training of coders will be needed by CPS data systems if conclusions about trends and changes are to become useful. Investigators seeking to use CPS record data will need to recognize the limitations of official records and make plans to augment or recode the data. Because the LONGSCAN researchers recoded simultaneously to two different systems without setting up independent coding, they can attest that there appear to be some modest differences depending on which system is used, but they cannot make a definitive recommendation as to which system is superior on the basis of their data. However, use of either research coding system appears to be superior to the use of raw CPS records alone.

Finally, LONGSCAN researchers' analyses suggest that the best approach to using official data is most likely an approach that uses these data in combination with other methods and sources of information. Because CPS records and other official sources of information appear to reflect only a small fraction of all maltreatment cases, to accurately characterize a child's maltreatment experiences will require a multimethod, multisource approach, as suggested by other contributors to this volume. The LONGSCAN study is using such an approach and will be able to more fully explore an examination of children's maltreatment experiences as these data from multiple sources become available over time.

REFERENCES

Achenbach, T.M. (1991). *Manual for Child Behavior Checklist/4-18 and 1991 profile.* Burlington: University of Vermont, Department of Psychiatry.

Barnett, D., Manly, J.T., & Cicchetti, D. (1993). Defining child maltreatment: The interface between policy and research. In D. Cicchetti & S.L. Toth (Eds.), *Advances in applied developmental psychology: Child abuse, child development and social policy* (pp. 7–73). Norwood, NJ: Ablex Publishing Corp.

Bolger, K.E., & Patterson, C.J. (2001). Developmental pathways from child maltreatment to peer rejection. *Child Development, 72,* 549–568.

Bolger, K.E., Patterson, C.J., & Kupersmidt, J.B. (1998). Peer relationships and self-esteem among children who have been maltreated. *Child Development, 69,* 1171–1197.

Briere, J. (1996). *Trauma Symptom Checklist for Children: Professional manual.* Odessa, FL: Psychological Assessment Resources, Inc.

Cicchetti, D., & Manly, J.T. (2001). Editorial: Operationalizing child maltreatment: Developmental processes and outcomes. *Development and Psychopathology, 13,* 755–757.

Cicchetti, D., & Rogosch, F.A. (2001). The impact of child maltreatment and psychopathology on neuroendocrine functioning. *Development and Psychopathology, 13,* 783–804.

Cicchetti, D., & Toth, S.L. (1995). A developmental psychopathology perspective on child abuse and neglect. *Journal of the American Academy of Child & Adolescent Psychiatry, 34,* 541–565.

Committee on Children with Disabilities. (2001). Developmental surveillance and screening of infants and young children. *Pediatrics, 108,* 192–195.

Crouch, J.L., & Milner J.S. (1993). Effects of child neglect on children. *Criminal Justice and Behavior, 20,* 49–65.

DePanfilis, D., & Zuravin, S.J. (2001). Assessing risk to determine the need for services. *Children and Youth Services Review, 23,* 3–20.

Drake, B., & Pandey, S. (1996). Understanding the relationship between neighborhood poverty and specific types of child maltreatment. *Child Abuse & Neglect, 20,* 1003–1018.

Dubowitz, H., Pitts, S.C., Litrownik, A.J., Cox, C.E., Runyan, D.K., & Black, M.M. (2005). Defining child neglect based on child protective services data. *Child Abuse & Neglect, 29,* 493–511.

English, D.J., (Ed.). (2005). LONGSCAN [Special issue]. *Child Abuse & Neglect, 29*(7).

English, D.J., Bangdiwala, S.I., & Runyan, D.K. (2005). The dimensions of maltreatment: Introduction. *Child Abuse & Neglect, 29,* 441–460.

English, D., Brummel, S.C., Coghlan, L.K., Novicky, R.S., & Marshall, D.B. (1998). *Decision-making in child protective services: A study of effectiveness. Phase II: Social worker interviews.* Olympia: Washington State Department of Social and Health Services.

English, D.J., Graham, J.C., Clark, T.K., & Brummel, S. (2002). *Pilot test of Child Maltreatment Data Log and comparison to another maltreatment coding scheme: Final report.* Unpublished report, Office of Children's Administration Research, Children's Administration, Department of Social and Health Services, Washington State.

English, D.J., Graham, J.C., Litrownik, A.J., Everson, M., & Bangdiwala, S.I. (2005). Defining maltreatment chronicity: Are there differences in child outcomes? *Child Abuse & Neglect, 29,* 575–595.

Erickson, E. (1963). *Childhood and Society* (2nd ed.). New York: W.W. Norton & Company.

Fletcher, R., Fletcher, S., & Wagner, E. (1996). *Clinical epidemiology: The essentials* (3rd ed.). Baltimore: Lippincott Williams & Wilkins.

Hussey, J.M., Marshall, J.M., English, D.J., Knight, E.D., Lau, A.S., Dubowitz, H., et al. (2005). Defining maltreatment according to substantiation: Distinction without a difference? *Child Abuse & Neglect, 29,* 479–492.

Jones, L.M., & Finkelhor D. (2003). Putting together evidence on declining trends in sexual abuse: A complex puzzle. *Child Abuse & Neglect, 27,* 133–135.

Kalichman, S.C. (1993). *Mandated reporting of suspected child abuse: Ethics, law, and policy.* Washington, DC: American Psychological Association.

Kinard, E.M. (1994). Methodological issues and practical problems in conducting research on maltreated children. *Child Abuse & Neglect, 18,* 645–656.

Kinard, E.M. (2001). Characteristics of maltreatment experience and academic functioning among maltreated children. *Violence and Victims, 16*(3), 323–337.

King, N.M.P., & Churchill, L.R. (2000). Ethical principles guiding research on child and adolescent subjects. *Journal of Interpersonal Violence, 15*(7), 710–724.

Lau, A.S., Leeb, R.T., English, D., Graham, C., Briggs, E.C., Brody, K.E., et al. (2005). What's in a name? A comparison of methods for classifying predominant type of maltreatment. *Child Abuse & Neglect, 29,* 533–551.

Leeb, R.T., Melanson, C., Simon, T., Arias, I., & Paulozzi, L. (2004). *Child maltreatment surveillance: Uniform definitions and recommended data elements* (version 1.0). Unpublished report. Centers for Disease Control and Prevention, U.S. Department of Health and Human Services.

Leiter, J., & Johnsen, M.C. (1997). Child maltreatment and school performance declines: An event–history analysis. *American Educational Research Journal, 34*(3), 563–589.

Levine, M., Doueck, H.J., Freeman, J.B., & Compaan, C. (1998). Rush to judgment? Child protective services and allegations of sexual abuse. *American Journal of Orthopsychiatry, 68,* 101–107.

Manly, J.T. (2005). Advances in research definitions of child maltreatment. *Child Abuse & Neglect, 29,* 425–439.

Manly, J., Cicchetti, D., & Barnett, D. (1994). The impact of subtype, frequency, chronicity, and severity of child's maltreatment on social competence and behavior problems. *Development and Psychopathology, 6,* 121–143.

Manly, J.T., Kim, J.E., Rogosch, F.A., & Cicchetti, D. (2001). Dimensions of child maltreatment and children's adjustment: Contributions of developmental timing and subtype. *Development and Psychopathology, 13,* 759–782.

McGee, R.A., Wolfe, D.A., & Wilson, S.K. (1990). *A record of maltreatment experiences.* Unpublished manuscript, University of Western Ontario, Canada.

National Research Council. (1993). *Understanding child abuse and neglect.* Washington, DC: National Academies Press.

Newborg, J., Stock, J.R., Wnek, L., Guidubaldi, J., Svincki, J., Dickson, J., et al. (1988). *Battelle Developmental Inventory with recalibrated technical data and norms: Screening test examiner's manual* (2nd ed.). Allen, TX: DLM, Inc.

Paget, K.D., Philip, J.D., & Abramczyk, L.W. (1993). Recent developments in child neglect. *Advances in Clinical Child Psychology, 15,* 121–174.

Runyan, D.K. (2000). The ethical, legal and methodological issues surrounding directly asking children about child abuse. *Journal of Interpersonal Violence 15*(7), 675–681.

Runyan, D.K. (2005). [LONGSCAN cohorts: Differences over time]. Unpublished raw data.

Runyan, D.K., Curtis, P., Hunter, W.M., Black, M.M., Kotch, J.B., Bangdiwala, S., et al. (1998). LONGSCAN: A consortium for longitudinal studies of maltreatment and the life course of children. *Aggression and Violent Behavior, 3*(3), 275–285.

Runyan, D.K., & Gould, C.L. (1985). Foster care for child maltreatment: Impact on delinquent behavior. *Pediatrics, 75,* 562–568.

Runyan, D.K., Leeb, R., Dubowitz, H., English, D., Cox, C., & Knight, E. (2005). Describing maltreatment: Do child protective service reports and research definitions agree? *Child Abuse & Neglect, 29,* 461–477.

Sedlak, A.J., & Broadhurst, D.D. (1996). *Third national incidence study of child abuse and neglect: Final report.* Washington, DC: U.S. Department of Health and Human Services.

Silverman A.B., Reinherz H.Z., & Giaconia, R.M. (1996). The long-term sequelae of child and adolescent abuse: A longitudinal community study. *Child Abuse & Neglect, 20*(8), 709–723.

Sim, J., & Wright, C.C. (2005). The kappa statistic in reliability studies: Use, interpretation, and sample size requirements. *Physical Therapy, 85*(3), 257–268.

Smith, C.A., & Thornberry, T. (1995). The relationship between child maltreatment and adolescent involvement in delinquency. *Criminology, 33,* 451–481.

Socolar, R., Runyan, D.K, & Amaya-Jackson, L. (1995). Methodological and ethical issues related to studying child maltreatment. *Journal of Family Issues, 16*(5), 565–586.

Sparrow, S.S., Balla, D.A., & Cicchetti, D.V. (1984). *Vineland Adaptive Behavior Scales: Interview edition, survey form manual.* Circle Pines, MN: American Guidance Service.

Sparrow, S.S., Carter, A.S., & Cicchetti, D.V. (1993). *Vineland Screener: Overview, reliability, validity, administration, and scoring.* New Haven, CT: Yale University Child Study Center.

Sternberg, K.J., Knutson, J.F., Lamb, M.E., Baradaran, L.P., Nolan, C.M., & Flanzer, S. (2004). The Child Maltreatment Log: A computer-based program for describing research samples. *Child Maltreatment, 9,* 30–48.

Tebbutt, J., Swanston, H., Oates, R.K., & O'Toole, B.I. (1997). Five years after child sexual abuse: Persisting dysfunction and problems of prediction. *Journal of the American Academy of Child and Adolescent Psychiatry, 36*(3), 330–339.

Theodore, A.D., Chang, J.J., Runyan, D.K., Hunter, W.M., Bangdiwala, S.I., Agans, R. (2005). Epidemiologic features of the physical and sexual maltreatment of children in the Carolinas. *Pediatrics, 115,* 331–337.

U.S. Department of Health and Human Services. (1981). *Study findings: National study of the incidence and severity of child abuse and neglect* (DHHS Publication No. OHDS 81-30325). Washington, DC: Government Printing Office.

U.S. Department of Health and Human Services. (1988). *Study findings: Study of national incidence and prevalence of child abuse and neglect* (DHHS Publication No. ADM 20-01099). Washington, DC: Government Printing Office.

U.S. Department of Health and Human Services. (2005). *Child maltreatment 2003* (Administration for Children and Families). Washington, DC: Government Printing Office.

11

Direct Laboratory Observations and Analog Measures

In Research Definitions of Child Maltreatment

DAVID S. DEGARMO, JOHN B. REID, AND JOHN F. KNUTSON

SINCE THE 1970S, child maltreatment has been a topic of intense concern to policy makers and the general public, as well as to juvenile judges; child services professionals; and social, developmental, and prevention scientists. As reflected in other chapters in this volume, there are many complex definitional, theoretical, methodological, and contextual issues that must be detailed and understood if researchers are to develop powerful integrative models of child maltreatment, its developmental course and sequelae, and the potentially malleable antecedents and mediators involved. The development of precisely targeted preventive and clinical interventions necessary to reduce the unacceptable prevalence of child maltreatment hinges on the precision with which critical variables are measured and the degree to which they approximate the circumstances under which maltreatment can occur. Despite the substantial development in theory and research methods relevant to child maltreatment, there still remain difficult obstacles to the development of scientific methodology of sufficient rigor to lead to continued and substantial progress in this area.

The purpose of this chapter, therefore, is to discuss the roles of observational and laboratory measurements in research on child maltreatment (with a specific focus on child physical abuse and neglect), to identify and describe some powerful and specific methods, and to make recommendations (with illustrations) about when and where these methods can be utilized most effectively. Because of the large number and types of constructs that must be measured in a comprehen-

Research directly reported in this chapter was supported, in part, by Grant MH 61731, funded by the National Institute of Mental Health (NIMH) and the Administration on Children, Youth and Families, John F. Knutson, Principal Investigator; Grant HD 42115 funded by the National Institute of Child Health and Human Development, David S. DeGarmo, Principal Investigator; Grants P20 DA 017592 and P30 46690, funded by the National Institute on Drug Abuse (NIDA) and NIMH, respectively, John B. Reid, Principal Investigator; and Grant MH 40859 funded by NIMH and NIDA, C. Hendricks Brown, Principal Investigator. The facilitation of the research by Paul Spencer (Oneida County Department of Social Services), Barry Bennett, Cheryl Whitney, Marc Batey, Mark Schmidt, and Wayne McCracken (Iowa Department of Human Services) is gratefully acknowledged.

sive model of maltreatment and because naturalistic and laboratory methods are typically expensive, a tactical framework is required to inform the optimal (i.e., most cost-effective) integration of such measures in model tests.

The authors of this chapter first discuss a set of general challenges and obstacles to measurement in the maltreatment area, for which observational and laboratory measures may be useful. Second, a conceptual framework for the development of measurement and analytic models is described. Third, the use of observational and analog measures is described, giving examples of naturalistic and structured observations and analog laboratory tasks. More specifically, the chapter authors employ constructs derived from these various approaches to illustrate the study of linkages among theoretical constructs measuring child neglect and physical abuse.

CHALLENGES AND OBSTACLES TO THE MEASUREMENT OF NEGLECT AND MALTREATMENT

It is clear that the circumstances of physical abuse and neglect involving direct encounters between parents and children are not likely to be displayed in the presence of a research team. As a result, many critical aspects of child maltreatment are not directly measurable, and maltreatment researchers are forced to utilize variables that are only approximations of the variables of interest. Hence, if one is interested in investigating the conditions under which physical abuse or neglect occur or the manner in which they occur, proxy variables have to substitute for direct indices of the events. This is, of course, not the only circumstance in social and behavioral science in which the phenomena of interest are not directly assessed; therefore, strategies to operationalize other phenomena can provide some guidance to maltreatment researchers. Nevertheless, some of the common strategies for measuring events do not work well in maltreatment research. For example, in some contexts in which investigators cannot directly measure the behaviors of target participants, they can turn to informants regarding the events of interest. Thus, people who have direct and intimate knowledge of the behaviors of interest (e.g., roommates, spouses) can serve as informants. In the context of maltreatment, informants who have direct knowledge often are not readily available or may be unwilling to provide data. This is, in part, attributable to the insularity of the maltreating families (e.g., Wahler, 1980), in that these private behaviors are not readily accessible to, or are intentionally hidden from, the typical informant. In addition, there are strong proscriptions against many of the behaviors of interest, putting potential informants at social or legal risk.

Another reason for the difficulty in measuring child maltreatment is that the actual abusive event often occurs quickly and with extreme emotion. In the case of the parent–child interactions in which physical abuse is embedded, it is unlikely that the participants are able to track, or even remember, the specifics of rapidly unfolding and often highly emotional transactions. This last point has important implications for the development of theoretical and assessment models that inform the development of prevention and intervention efforts for child maltreatment. Although some form of parent training or education is becoming nearly a mandatory requirement for maltreating biological parents of children in foster care (Barth et al., 2005), little is known about its quality and effectiveness in this context.

It is becoming clear that parent training interventions that have been precisely informed by careful and detailed observations of the parenting interactions of families in the mental health and juvenile justice systems are highly effective in reducing both the behavior problems of children and the harsh discipline practices of their parents (Reid, Patterson, & Snyder, 2002; Webster-Stratton, Reid, & Hammond, 2004). At least as much detailed knowledge about the parent–child interactions in maltreating families probably will be required if highly effective parent training and support programs for this population are to be developed. Observational assessments of parent–child interactions before and after randomized intervention trials have provided the level of detail in assessing parenting changes to facilitate the iterative development and improvement of parenting interventions over successive studies (again, see Reid et al., 2002; Webster-Stratton et al., 2004). If intervention strategies based on the next generation of models in the area of maltreatment are to be rigorously assessed in randomized trials, it is absolutely necessary that key assessments blind to condition developed. Therefore, when possible, parent or child reports, or any informant data from family, friends, or caseworkers who are aware of the intervention condition, cannot be the sole source of data to evaluate outcomes in controlled trials. Ideally, these sources would not be used at all in evaluating proximal intervention outcome effectiveness.

The field of research on deficient parenting and children's behavior in non-intervention studies relies heavily on a single method and single source data, typically self-report. Although self-report indices of physical abuse and neglect have been used profitably, there are many reasons why self-report measures can be compromised. Certainly self-report measures of child maltreatment are vulnerable to all of the problems that are inherent in self-report measures used in other domains of social science and medical research. However, self-report measures in maltreatment research occasion a number of somewhat unique problems.

The first problem with using self-report measures in maltreatment research relates to the fact that reporting of events relevant to maltreatment can be a function of the mood state of the respondent (see Kuyken & Brewin, 1995; Lewinsohn & Rosenbaum, 1987; Prescott et al., 2000). This may be more of a problem in retrospective reports than in the reporting of contemporaneous events; however, empirical evidence on that possibility is lacking at the present time. Second, when reporting contemporaneous events, parents and other family members may be concerned that the self-report of some acts might place them in jeopardy of legal consequences; these family members may thereby be motivated to deny, minimize, or reframe their reports. Third, several multimethod studies of family interactions have demonstrated that dispositional characteristics of individuals (e.g., negativity, irritability, depression) can lead to reporting biases and inflated association among variables in monomethod models. As a consequence, these monomethod models may obtain lower predictive validity (Bank, Dishion, Skinner, & Patterson, 1990; Bank & Patterson, 1992; Lorenz, Conger, Simons, Whitbeck, & Elder, 1991). With shared method variance and shared source variance increasing the apparent covariation among variables, the presumed links between maltreatment variables and putative outcomes could be inflated. In addition, there is some evidence in maltreatment research that maltreating parents demonstrate systematic and negative biases in reporting on the behavior of their children (Reid, Kavanagh, & Baldwin, 1987).

Thus, the problems of single-source data and the need for multimethod/ multisource constructs forces the maltreatment researcher to consider innovative strategies that are not compromised by a single-source and single-method approach. Yet, another factor that must be considered in the context of assessing physically abusive and neglectful parenting is the fact that parenting, whether ideal or deficient, involves dynamic interpersonal processes—parenting is not a static event. Moreover, the child's response to that parenting is not static. Thus, operational definitions of the circumstances of maltreatment should attempt to capture some aspects of that dynamic quality of the events. Observational methodologies and analog tasks that represent an approximation of the events or populations of interest are well-suited for that task. Moreover, these methodologies and tasks can be effective individually or in combination with other methods.

It is because of the many methodological issues inherent to self-report indices that maltreatment researchers often turn to the use of administrative data such as official agency records of documented neglect or abuse. As is the case with self-reports, there are a number of reasons why administrative data are of limited utility in operationally defining constructs pertaining to maltreatment. In particular, there are differences among jurisdictions in determining standards for parenting that reflect either policy and statutory differences or merely differences that are attributable to the caseload and implementation differences among locales (e.g., Alter, 1985; Deitrich-MacLean & Walden, 1988; Dukes & Kean, 1989; Giovannoni & Becerra, 1979; Misener, 1986; O'Toole, Turbett, & Nalepka, 1983; Snyder & Newberger, 1986; Wolock, 1982). In addition, as noted by Finkelhor and Hotaling (1984) in their consideration of the levels of information regarding maltreatment and in the findings of the National Incidence Studies (e.g., Sedlak & Broadhurst, 1996), only a portion of the circumstances of deficient parenting and physical abuse that occur are even known by the child protection agencies that establish the administrative data. Thus, even when administrative data are excellent, there is likely to be a significant number of false negative classifications in the control or comparison groups that would be derived from administrative data, even among those families known to the agencies for some level of maltreatment.

Related to administrative classifications, another set of conceptual and methodological issues in maltreatment research concerns whether the maltreatment is considered to be categorical or continuous. The authors of this chapter believe that this issue can be addressed by the thoughtful use of observational and analog measures. Of course, maltreatment research is not the only domain in which there is some dispute as to whether the focus of the research reflects an underlying discontinuity or some quantitative difference on a scalable dimension. For example, there is considerable continuing debate regarding whether some forms of psychopathology are best represented by continuous models or categorical models (see Widiger & Clark, 2000). In 1997, Greenwald, Bank, Reid, and Knutson proposed a discipline-mediated model of physical abuse that conceptualized abuse as being at the extreme of a continuously measured pattern of physical discipline. Similarly, circumstances of neglect can be conceptualized as a reflection of an inadequate rate or intensity of some parenting acts that are distributed on a continuous scale (e.g., degree of supervision, dental care, hygiene). Furthermore, in terms of statistical properties, multiple indicator models that combine, for example, observational frequency count data, self-reported scale scores, and scales derived from analog lab tasks obtain more properties of continuous variables than do individual items with limited response formats, such as reliance on Likert scales only.

Analogs for testing hypotheses regarding clinical phenomena or clinical populations are usually developed when the researcher cannot conduct research directly on the phenomenon of interest or the target population. Thus, analogs can be seen as approximations of the populations or the events of interest. Although analog approximations can be criticized for their artificiality and the degree to which they depart from the phenomena of interest, Kazdin (1978) noted that virtually all of the research in experimental psychology can be considered analogs of the target problems. Moreover, Kazdin also noted that because of the potential for experimental control of variables, it is the case that analog tests are not necessarily weak tests of hypothesized relationships. Indeed, there is an important literature in which critical clinical questions were effectively addressed using analog tests (e.g., Cook & Minneka, 1989; Öhman, & Mineka, 2001; Widom, 1977). In a context in which the dynamic parent–child interactions of abuse or neglect are unlikely to be directly assessable or experimentally manipulable, analog tests of hypotheses can be useful and important tests of hypothesized relations.

Therefore, for all of the reasons discussed, it is extremely important to include and/or integrate "objective" measures using multimethod assessment strategies in research conducted on inept parenting practices and more severe child neglect and maltreatment. It is important to note that although the authors of this chapter are making a distinction between direct observational approaches and analog approaches in this chapter, that distinction is for heuristic purposes only. The authors recognize that the observational methodologies are also analogs in that the observational process itself makes the test an analog of what might transpire if the observer were not present or if the participants were not in a laboratory environment. In that context, one could consider the work reviewed in this chapter to vary on three dimensions pertaining to setting, participants, and measures and the degree to which the conditions approximate the natural circumstances under which physical abuse and neglect are thought to occur.

In considering these dimensional aspects of research and the degree to which an analog is an approximation of the natural circumstance, the researcher is confronted with a decision as to the sorts of constructs in the child maltreatment domain that are best suited for a direct observational approach. For example, the natural habitat setting for high-risk families can provide behavioral assessments that capture the dynamic aspects of parent–child interactions; this approach has associated with it a very high cost (e.g., fiscal cost for staff, travel, and time for set up as well as cost to families at home) but potentially a high payoff regarding actual sampling of individual and interpersonal behavioral repertoires compared with more clearly analog approaches in which the setting, samples, and behavioral assessments are more removed from the natural circumstances of occurrence. The latter, of course, are associated with lower costs and greater control, but probably less detail with respect to the interpersonal processes involved. It is the belief of the authors of this chapter that optimal strategies may include both natural habitat and more analog approaches in obtaining data on high-risk families or high-risk behaviors that are difficult to observe in naturalistic settings. In the section that follows, the theoretical underpinnings and the rationales for developing a conceptual and analytical framework for testing models of maltreatment and neglect using a multiple-method approach are examined.

A THEORETICAL AND ANALYTICAL FRAMEWORK FOR INTEGRATING OBSERVATIONAL AND ANALOG PROCEDURES

The goal of this chapter is to illustrate how a more comprehensive measurement strategy can aid a researcher and, ultimately, the field of neglect and maltreatment by providing more rigorous evaluations of family processes. Each researcher is faced with the choices of balancing costs of collecting data with payoff for more valid and reliable assessment tools. Our goal is to develop multiple-method strategies that are more efficient than tradition single source data and, therefore, more cost-effective because they maximize convergent and predictive validity. Even with the best-quality sampling strategies of maltreating families or prevention samples of families at risk for maltreatment, the costs to the field are far greater for designing policies with research based on measures and assessment protocols susceptible to sources of unreliability. Focusing on neglect, poor supervision skills, and abusive physical discipline, the authors of this chapter integrate multiple measurement strategies to evaluate theoretically specified associations. These strategies include analog procedures and information derived from them, interview data from insider and outsider perspectives (e.g., teacher report) and, more importantly, direct observation ranging from global assessments of environmental conditions to highly specified coding systems (using trained coders) of discrete behaviors.

The theoretical basis for measuring constructs with multiple sources of data is that traits and enduring patterns of behavior should be detectable across a variety of settings with a variety of methods (Campbell & Fiske, 1959). As previously discussed, multiple methods provide increased reliability and validity by reducing potential threats of monomethod bias and reporting bias due to dispositional characteristics. For family interactions, multiple informants and multiple sources provide the added advantage of including insider as well as outsider perspectives, rather than relying on one person's point of view. This is not to say that self-report measures are inherently biased, distorted, or of no use, but that they need to be augmented by a conceptual triangulation or convergence of data (see Maxfield, Weiler, & Widom, 2000; Widom, 1988).

For high-risk and low base-rate events such as abuse and neglect, a requirement for comprehensive models is that they should be able to capture the social-interactional aspects of maltreatment. Because physical abuse and neglect involve a transaction between a victim and a perpetrator, usually embedded in daily or routine patterns of relevant interactions, the interactional context becomes critical. The reporting agents most aware or familiar with maltreating transactions are the participants. Because transactions may be highly emotional, escalate quickly, and have legal implications, a comprehensive measurement strategy must address the ability or willingness of the interactants to provide valid information. At the same time insider perspectives are valuable sources of data; each individual may also bring relevant trait variables to the mix that can limit individual reports in the assessment of maltreating behaviors (e.g., children who are highly oppositional or who have developmental delays or physical disabilities; parents who are chronic substance users, suffer from depression, or have limited parenting skills). An interactional perspective by definition requires not only an examination of the process and outcomes but must also include characteristics of the individuals engaging in the interaction as well (DeGarmo & Forgatch, 1999; Reid et al., 2002).

Further consideration is needed on the context and structure of any behavioral assessment. The role of direct observation procedures is to measure directly, and in real time, behaviors and interactions of interest in either natural or laboratory settings. Although expensive and intrusive, direct observations in family homes have been useful in assessing social interactions of the sort often studied in the area of maltreatment (e.g., parent–child interactions after school, over dinner, during chores, and at bedtime) and can be coded in detail, with remarkable precision (Reid, 1978; Reid, Baldwin, Patterson, & Dishion, 1988). The observations can be quantified in terms of rates, durations, and intensities for individual behaviors such as negative or positive physical or verbal behaviors of interest, as well as for complex social-interactional sequences of interest (Reid, 1978, 1986). Naturalistic observations conducted in family homes have been shown to be highly reliable (see Reid, 1978; Reid et al., 1988), to discriminate among independently classified groups of parents and children (e.g., maltreating parents, parents of children referred because of externalizing problems, community controls) (Reid, 1986; Kavanagh, Youngblade, Reid, & Fagot, 1988), and to have good predictive validity over periods as long as 10 years (Prescott et al., 2000; Reid et al., 2002). In addition to being useful for classification and precise behavioral descriptions, direct observation methods in natural settings and in the laboratory (observing family problem-solving tasks) have been excellent for measuring targeted behavior and interactional changes in response to intervention (e.g., DeGarmo & Forgatch, 2004; Patterson & Forgatch, 1995; Stoolmiller, Eddy, & Reid, 2000; Taplin & Reid, 1977; Webster-Stratton et al., 2004).

A useful less expensive, though less precise, alternative to microsocial observations in real time is the use of ratings of family behavior and interactions. The ratings are conducted by independent observers after observing social interactions in the home or laboratory or on videotapes. They provide more global information than microsocial codes but are direct and unbiased if the observers are kept blind to condition. As is the case with behavioral coding systems, and with proper training, the ratings can be quite reliable, with good construct and predictive validity (Melby & Conger, 2001; Weinrott, Reid, Bauske, & Brummett, 1981). Such ratings can be made by anyone—interviewers, recruiters, or laboratory staff—who comes into systematic contact with a study participant. Because of all these characteristics, direct observational ratings have been used increasingly to provide behavioral indicators for multimethod constructs (e.g., Greenwald et al., 1997; Melby, Conger, Ge, & Warner, 1995).

Home observations, using both microsocial coding and rating systems, have been extremely useful in developing multiagent, multisource models of coercive parent–child interactions (e.g., Capaldi, Forgatch, & Crosby, 1994; Greenwald et al., 1997; Patterson, Reid, & Dishion, 1992; Reid et al., 2002), and there are many well-established systems, depending on specific research requirements (e.g., Reid et al., 1988; Rusby, Estes & Dishion, 1991). They are, however, quite expensive. Since the 1970s, laboratory tasks have been developed to examine a number of dimensions of parent–child interactions (e.g., problem solving, structured and unstructured play) that have been extremely useful for developing observational measures for the development of a wide range of theoretical constructs related to negative or coercive and positive or prosocial parenting practices and for measuring the proximal effects of interventions on parenting and child behavior (e.g., Forgatch & DeGarmo, 2002; Martinez & Forgatch, 2001).

More recently, observational methods for observing children in structured playgroups have been developed for the measurement of subtle forms of relational aggression among children (Putallaz, Kupersmidt, Coie, McKnight, & Grimes, 2004), an innovation that has rich implications for operationalizing and objectively measuring forms of psychological abuse. In addition, observations of problem solving in young couples have been used profitably to provide observational, quantitative measures of actual physical and verbal attacks in developing multimeasure, multiagent models of partner aggression (see Capaldi, Kim, & Shortt, 2004; Capaldi, Shortt, & Crosby, 2003). Because child exposure to domestic violence is subsumed under neglect in some jurisdictions (Coohey, 2003), the strategy of Capaldi and colleagues can be incorporated effectively in studies of that aspect of neglectful parenting. For assessing attachment and related constructs in the interactions of mothers and toddlers, at least three observational coding systems are in wide use (Ainsworth, Blehar, Waters, & Wall, 1978; Crittenden, 1995; Fagot, 1997). Though less expensive and intrusive than home-based procedures, they are still not inexpensive and require consistent training and assessment of observers as well as specialized equipment and data management. Although it is becoming more common to use observational measures to anchor multimethod constructs in the study of coercive and abusive interactions, integrating observational scores with self-report, other report, and official records (see Greenwald et al; 1997; Knutson, DeGarmo, & Reid, 2004; Reid et al., 2002) is a tactic that is not widespread at the present time. Because of this, rather than just reviewing examples of observational and analog approaches to the study of maltreatment, in the present context the chapter authors decided there would be heuristic value in providing examples with original data in which integration of analogs and observational methods could be accomplished. Thus, by using a theoretical framework to guide the model specification, the chapter authors will attempt to show how observation and analog strategies can be used to operationally define some central constructs of maltreating parenting.

DIRECT OBSERVATIONS AND ANALOGS OF HARSH DISCIPLINE AND NEGLECT

To illustrate the use of direct observation and analog methods, the chapter authors describe how the methods can be integrated into theoretical constructs using structural equation modeling (SEM) to test a conceptual model of deficient parenting and poor child outcomes. Specifically, a model will be tested that is based on a conceptual framework as to how neglectful parenting and ineffective supervision of a child covaries with the propensity for severe discipline and how these factors are collectively associated with the development of child aggression and antisocial behavior. For the central maltreatment constructs, the authors use direct observation and analog tests as indicators. The specific model that has been adopted for this illustrative example was explicated and tested by Knutson, DeGarmo, et al. (2004).

The initial evaluation of the theoretical model developed by Knutson, DeGarmo, et al. (2004) was accomplished in a population-based preventive intervention study of 762 families from at-risk neighborhoods characterized by high rates of juvenile delinquency. For the purposes of the present chapter, a few comments regarding that research are necessary to understand the notions behind our use of the model to illustrate the use of analog and direct observational methods in defining maltreatment. The analyses used to test the model were based on two developmental cohorts of first- and fifth-graders assessed over a 5-year period who had been enrolled in a universal prevention project (Linking the Interests of Families and Teachers [LIFT]; Reid, Eddy, Fetrow, & Stoolmiller, 1999). In a test of the model detailing how social disadvantage influenced the development of antisocial behavior through neglectful parenting and punitive discipline, Knutson, DeGarmo, et al. (2004) were able to develop multimethod indices of care neglect, supervisory neglect, punitive discipline, and children's aggression that incorporated both self-report, direct observational methods, and reports from informants (e.g., teachers). Although the LIFT study provided rich data for studying family processes using multiple-method approaches, the sampling and measurement designs were not specifically developed to target neglect and maltreatment. As a result, relatively few of the participants in the sample could be expected to manifest significant levels of either neglect or harsh discipline. Thus, although the Knutson, DeGarmo, et al. (2004) study provided some documentation of the potential utility of direct observational methods in establishing circumstances of maltreatment, the base rate of maltreatment in that study was in the normative range, and no analog measures were included. In the illustration that follows, a portion of the theoretical model is replicated using a selection of analog and/or direct observational measures to assess care neglect, supervisory neglect, and harsh discipline in a cohort of impoverished families either at risk for neglectful and physically abusive parenting or identified as physically abusive or neglecting.

The sample employed for this illustration consisted of 218 consecutively recruited families who were participating in a multisite longitudinal study of neglectful parenting. One hundred fifty-five families were recruited from the small urban and rural areas of eastern Iowa, and sixty-three families were recruited from rural counties in northern Wisconsin. The sample included children between the ages of 4 and 8; 46% were girls. Details about the sample and the recruitment process are available in Knutson, DeGarmo, Reid, and Koeppl (2005). For the purpose of the illustration, this sample offered the advantage that it was recruited to better capture the continuum of parental neglect and maltreatment. Using multiple sources of data, the core constructs in the following example include care neglect, poor supervision and tracking, angry and abusive discipline, and child aggression. In addition to some parent reports, the indicators of the theoretical constructs use several measures derived from analog procedures, direct observation of parent–child interaction by trained coders. Essentially, the goal of the illustration is to show how these analog and observational indices can be used in multimethod tests of a theoretical model.

Development of a Neglect Risk Index: Trained Observer Ratings and Parent Report

The chapter authors first focus on the development of a parental neglect index that does not rely on administrative data. This approach serves the purpose of increasing replicability that is threatened by potential nonstandard criteria across agencies and jurisdictions as well as increasing the potential for validity by providing a continuous scaling of neglect using greater specification. Such an approach is based on the testable assumption that there is likely to be more variability than homogeneity in parenting practices within socioeconomic strata and that a continuum of parenting, ranging from highly skilled and effective to highly inept and abusive, will be manifested. Some support for this assumption is reflected in data derived from previously developed measures that have shown great utility and offer considerable advantage over other indices when assessing families in socially disadvantaged contexts (e.g., Home Observation for Measurement of the Environment [HOME]; Caldwell & Bradley, 1978, modified by the Project on Human Development in Chicago Neighborhoods [Selner-O'Hagan, Leventhal, Brooks-Gunn, Bingenheimer, & Earls, 2004]). However, new methodologies may be used to amplify those approaches. For example, some of the information that is obtained by interview or from administrative data should be obtained directly in the context of other direct observational approaches (e.g., in-home observations) when conditions permit. Thus, when procedures call for direct contact with families in their homes, a direct observation of household risks (e.g., accessible toxins, accessible drugs, inadequate sleeping arrangements, insufficient plumbing, and inadequate hygiene) should be made directly by researchers rather than relying on administrative data. In the LIFT study (Knutson, DeGarmo, et al., 2004), the assessment of parental care neglect was relatively limited and comprised a summative index using six items rated by a home visitor and from teacher observations (e.g., child's hygiene). Here, an expanded neglect index will be attempted by employing specific exemplars of care-neglect (e.g., child does not have a toothbrush) and household environmental conditions that would occasion social (e.g., household is overly crowded or there is inadequate illumination) and physical (e.g., unsafe stairs, inadequate plumbing, animal feces present, accessible pharmaceuticals) risks to a child.

Items from the index of care and environmental neglect described by Knutson, DeGarmo, et al. (2004) and selected for this illustration are presented in Table 11.1, blocked by source (i.e., parent in-home interview and observer ratings). Items were all scored in a direction to indicate neglect and then summed. Items were chosen based on their inclusion in the research literature or recom-

Table 11.1.   Items for developing environmental and care neglect risk index

Parent report during interview	Observer ratings during home visit
Care neglect	Care neglect
Child plays without supervision	Child never or rarely sees doctor
Child leaves home area often	Child does not bathe regularly
Child is home alone	Child does not brush teeth in morning
	Child does not brush teeth in evening
Environmental neglect	Child does not eat breakfast
House is cramped or crowded	Child is not required to check in
Less than 100 square feet of space per person	Inadequate after school care
	Teen babysitters
Drugs or alcohol paraphernalia lying about	Excessive frequency of babysitter
	Duration of babysitter
Garbage lying about	Child eats dinner elsewhere
House is clean	No rules regarding television
House is cluttered	No rules for child's behavior
House is not overly noisy—inside noise	No curfew on school nights
House is not overly noisy—outside noise	No curfew on weekends
	No rules for when child is in car
House or apartment is free from dangers	Child belongs to clubs and/or organizations
House has adequate furniture	Child visits museums
TV is on majority of the day	Child reads together with parent
House has at least two pictures or types of art	
House is not dark or monotonous	Environmental neglect
Poor condition of houses on face block	Electricity interrupted
Poor condition of street on face block	Water interrupted
Industrial land uses of properties on the face block	Sewage interrupted
	Heat interrupted
Heavy volume of traffic on face block	Heat interrupted for more than a day
Private or public dwelling	Physical problem with house or apartment
Safe and friendly neighborhood	Called or need to call landlord to fix something

Source: Knutson, DeGarmo, & Reid, 2004.

mendations from the Interagency Task Force on Defining Child Maltreatment (see Sternberg et al., 2004) and were obtained from parent interviews and also from observer ratings of the home environment. In selecting this summative risk index, the authors considered item relevance or face validity, avoided operational confounding with other constructs, and considered the importance of comprehensiveness as suggested by Turner and Wheaton (1995). Although it is also important to consider the significance of the content items in relation to age and cultural variations in the sample, in this illustration the sample was somewhat age-restricted to permit item inclusiveness. The index approach was also chosen with the assumption that not all items would covary or converge in a psychometric sense (Dillon & Goldstein, 1984; see also Chapter 8) although personality characteristics or environmental stressors might cause negative life events to co-occur (for example, one would not expect that a child would experience every event on a neglect index). Finally, not all the items define continuous properties. With that in mind, greater utilization of items with different scaling properties can be accomplished by rescoring to indicate the presence or absence of risk in the summative index.

The distributional properties of the neglect index are shown in Figure 11.1. The parent-reported index is the top panel, the observer rated index the middle, and the total neglect index is plotted at the bottom. Figure 11.1 reflects impor-

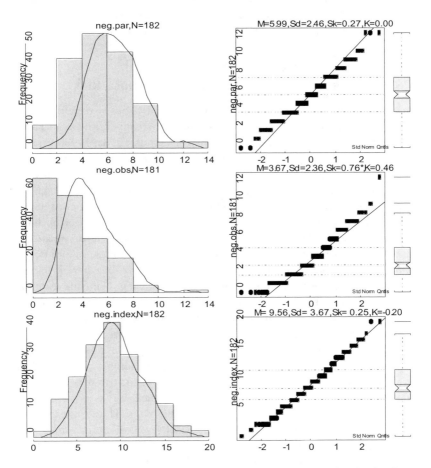

Figure 11.1. Parent interview (top panel), trained observer (middle panel), and total neglect (bottom panel) index of the Iowa–Wisconsin maltreatment study. (*Key:* M, mean; Sk, skew; K, kurtosis; Sd, standard deviation; neg. par, neglect parent report; neg. obs, neglect observer report; neg. index, combined reporters of neglect.)

tant differences in variance, range, and normality of the summative index as well as the potential importance of combining direct observations with parental report. Note that the observer index is significantly skewed and that the range and standard deviation is greater for the total neglect index than for a single agent alone. Note that even though this is a highly socially disadvantaged sample (all participants received assistance from state agencies), there is a very adequate range in neglect captured at a continuous level. Also note that, in Table 11.1, the care neglect items are more frequently reported by the parent interview items, and the environmental neglect items are more frequently reported by the objective observer. In this case it is not so much that self-report is potentially biased, but rather that self-report and observer ratings maximize the range of material assessed along the continuum of neglect. An examination of the predictive validity of the neglect index follows a discussion of analog procedures.

Development of Analogs of Severe Physical Discipline and Abuse Risk

A number of different approaches to assessing physically abusive parenting in an analog context have been attempted. Although there are interesting animal analog studies of maltreatment (e.g., Maestripieri & Carroll, 1998a; 1998b; Suomi, 1978), a consideration of the animal analogs and the controversies they occasion (e.g., Cicchetti, 1998; Mason, 1998) is beyond the scope of the present chapter. Among the first studies to employ a laboratory analog test pertaining to physical abuse was a study by Passman and Mulhern (1977) that was designed to test the hypothesis that punitive discipline of children would be a function of child-related and situational stress. In that work, mothers and children participated in simultaneous laboratory tasks. The mothers worked on a console to earn points while remotely monitoring their child's performance on a puzzle task. Essentially, the mothers were to do their own work while helping their child learn the puzzle by applying response consequences to the child's errors. The dependent measure in this case was the magnitude of the response-cost that was applied in response to child errors. Stress in the task was operationalized as the interruptions imposed by the task on the mother. In many ways, this analog procedure bore a close resemblance to "Aggression Machine" paradigms widely used in aggression research in the early 1970s (e.g., Baron, 1974; Baron & Eggleston, 1972). Passman and Mulhern (1977) argued that the severity of the parental response to child errors was an analog of severe discipline. Thus, this early analog work placed physical abuse in the context of severe discipline, much like other models that view abuse as extreme discipline rather than a parental act that is categorically different (e.g., Greenwald et al., 1997).

In related work, Vasta and Copitch (1981) tested a hypothesized relation between aversive arousal and willingness to use physical discipline with children. In this work, the participants were university students who were to monitor and influence the behavior of a child. Similar to the work of Passman and Mulhern

(1977), Vasta and Copitch showed that young adults reacted to child failures with increasing aversive choices as a function of aversive arousal. Thus, using both analog participants (university students) and an analog of the disciplinary context (correcting the child), Vasta and Copitch tested hypotheses that placed physical abuse in the context of discipline that has been carried too far and used laboratory disciplinary choices to serve as the index of abuse risk.

One model of child maltreatment that has been advanced by a number of theorists considers evocative behaviors of children that set the stage for excessively punitive discipline (e.g., Gil, 1970; Herrenkohl, Herrenkohl, & Egolf, 1983; Kadushin & Martin, 1981). A number of analog tasks have been developed that measure the disciplinary preferences of adults and parents as a function of the child attributes that evoke the more severe forms of discipline. One strategy that has been adopted has been to provide written or oral vignettes of child transgressions to participants and ask the participants how they would respond if they were charged with the responsibility to discipline the depicted child. Although some studies (e.g., Berger, 1981) have not found the written vignette approach to be effective in evoking a range of disciplinary choices in young adults, Rodriguez and Sutherland (1999) were able to use a written vignette analog to determine the context in which parents would elect to use more severe and potentially injurious discipline. In such analog work, variables (i.e., child transgressions) that are thought to increase risk for the occurrence of physical abuse are evaluated by their association with more severe disciplinary choices.

A number of studies have used visual stimuli instead of written vignettes to provide a depiction of children engaging in potentially irritating behaviors that were either frankly deviant or normative for the age of the depicted children. In such studies, various forms of child behavior have been hypothesized to evoke more punitive disciplinary strategies, and more punitive disciplinary strategies by participants have been assumed to be a reflection of a risk for physical abuse. One of the early studies that used visual images to evoke discipline was conducted by Zaidi, Knutson, and Mehm (1989). In that research, slide images of children engaging in a range of potentially irritating behaviors were presented to young adults who described different disciplinary histories. Participants who came from more punitive disciplinary backgrounds were more willing to endorse physical discipline and potentially injurious discipline in response to those visual images of child transgressions. Moreover, the Zaidi et al. study also demonstrated that different classes of child transgressions (e.g., destructive, dangerous, rule violating) were differentially effective in evoking the more severe disciplinary reactions. Thus, Zaidi and colleagues' research provided data that were consistent with transgenerational models of maltreatment as well as some of the interactional models of maltreatment using visual analogs of child misbehavior and disciplinary choices of adults in response to those scenes.

The Zaidi et al. (1989) paradigm has been used profitably by a number of researchers who tested various hypotheses regarding personal attributes and contextual attributes hypothesized to influence risk for maltreatment. For example,

Knutson and Bower (1994) tested the hypothesized relation between childhood experiences with severe discipline, ratings of the normative nature of those experiences, and the probability that participants would respond with more intense and potentially injurious discipline. Bower-Russa, Knutson, and Winebarger (2001) extended that research, showing that the attitudinal attributes of participants derived from their childhood experiences mediated their willingness to escalate their discipline in response to a hypothesized persistence of the child's transgression.

In a recent study of parents of deaf children and children with typical hearing, Knutson, Johnson, and Sullivan (2004) demonstrated that parents of deaf children were appreciably more likely to endorse the use of physical discipline in response to the depictions of child transgressions in the slide-based analog task used in the Zaidi et al. (1989) research. Thus, testing the hypothesis that parents of deaf children were more likely to resort to physical discipline and thereby increase the risk for physical abuse (see Knutson, Johnson, et al., 2004; Sullivan & Knutson, 1998; 2000), the researchers showed that the parents of deaf children were much more likely to endorse physical discipline and escalate that discipline in response to the depicted child behaviors.

As noted earlier, drawing on the Greenwald et al. (1997) work, physically abusive parenting can be conceptualized as embedded in a dynamic pattern of exchanges between a parent and a child. Although the visual depictions of the analog task seem to be very engaging and successful in evoking severe disciplinary preferences, the task does not truly capture the interactive nature of the circumstances of parenting. Indeed, repeat transgressions and behavior that is refractory to initial disciplinary responses can be conveyed to participants as a question as to what the participant would do if the child were to persist in the behavior after the initial disciplinary tactic had been selected (see Knutson & Bower, 1994; Knutson, Schartz, & Zaidi, 1991; Zaidi et al., 1989). An alternative strategy would be to use video stimuli to capture the more dynamic attributes of child behavior and parental responses.

In one video analog task, Zaidi et al. (1989) used "point-of-view" filming of children engaging in a range of irritating behaviors. By using point-of-view filming, it is as if the participant is in an encounter with the depicted child. By filming multiple scenes related to a single behavioral event (e.g., refusing to eat), various patterns of child behaviors in response to discipline can be presented by altering the sequences that are shown to the participant. Thus, sequences of child behaviors can be presented in such a way that the child's behavior becomes either more or less severe in response to discipline. In this paradigm, the escalation of discipline in response to increasingly aversive child transgressions can be assessed rather than asking the adult to imagine the child behavior persisting following discipline. Similar to the slide-based analog task of parenting, with the video analog task, the disciplinary choice is the outcome measure. When Knutson and Bower (1994) used this analog task, they documented an increased risk for escalation in discipline by young adults who had punitive childhood histories and noted that scenes associated with child destructive behavior were most provocative of escalation.

Fagot (1992) also used video depictions of child behavior to induce disciplinary responses in parents of young children. In her work, the laboratory task was validated against other indices of discipline, including direct observation, self-report, and parental daily reports obtained by telephone. In a second study, the 20-minute video measure of coercive discipline was a significant predictor of the aggressive behavior of the participant parents' children. Thus, the Fagot (1992) and Knutson and Bower (1994) studies together provide evidence that the video analog task can be an effective strategy for assessing coercive discipline by parents in a cost-effective and relatively brief test.

In all of these analog tasks, hypotheses related to the occurrence of physical abuse were evaluated using approximations of the sorts of child transgressions that are thought to increase risk for abuse among some populations. In addition, by selecting participants on the basis of various backgrounds or setting circumstances, hypotheses regarding proximal and distal influences on potentially abusive discipline could be tested. It is important to note that although no physical abuse was actually measured in any of the studies, in all of the studies the findings obtained were quite consistent with theoretical formulations or existing data with clinical samples. In short, although researchers are rarely able to directly measure how parents might respond to the more severe and irritating child misbehaviors, by presenting parents or other participants with stimuli that approximate those misbehaviors, and obtaining disciplinary responses to those misbehaviors, some researchers have been able to test hypothesized relations between participant attributes and target attributes that could determine the occurrence of physical abuse.

In 2001, Bower-Russa et al. described an analog task that depicts a mother's response to a hypothetical child transgression. In this task, the mother's reaction is displayed, but the child and the associated transgression is not. Thus, participants were asked to respond to the appropriateness of the mother's disciplinary strategy as a function of various child behaviors. In this work, the suitability of discipline is evaluated as an indicator of the mother's tendency to use physical discipline. Similar to other analog research, Bower-Russa et al. (2001) showed that willingness to endorse physical discipline was related to childhood experiences and attitudes that treat severe physical discipline as normative.

The video analog tasks that have been used provide some evidence that parental propensities to use severe physical discipline and, perhaps, be at risk for being physically abusive can be measured. There is some evidence of validity, as reflected in the theoretical consistency of the work (e.g., Knutson et al., 2005; Zaidi et al., 1989) as well as of the utility of analog tests of coercive parenting in predicting children's aggression (e.g., Fagot, 1992). The procedures that have been described to date have used both slide images and video scenes quite productively, but in an era of highly realistic video and computer games, it would seem likely that more truly interactive analogs will be available to researchers soon.

MODELING MULTIPLE-METHOD PROCEDURES INVOLVING ANALOG PROCEDURES FOR TESTING MAIN EFFECTS

In this next illustration, the Iowa–Wisconsin sample is used to specifically illustrate the use of multiple-method approaches involving both analog and direct observational procedures. The authors first introduce ineffective supervision as a distinct construct from neglectful care. They then discuss analog procedures for abusive parenting and, finally, model theoretical associations for each of the specified constructs.

Effective Supervision and Tracking

Neglectful parenting usually is conceptualized as an act of omission or a failure to meet various basic needs of the child. As such, there have not been any studies in which analog measures have been developed to measure a parent's inadequacy with respect to the provision of care, such as a failure to provide adequate clothing, medical care, food, and shelter. In some respects, these are indices of care that can be measured directly and would be generally accessible to the researcher. Other aspects of neglect, such as inadequate supervision and monitoring, would be less directly observable to a researcher. Thus, similar to punishment and other forms of parent–child interactions, supervisory neglect might be amenable to an analog approach.

In the last few years, the chapter authors have attempted to develop a construct of *supervisory neglect* using two indices of concordance between the responses of parents and their children in reporting the child's participation or engagement in a host of common and less common acts. The first index asks parents and children to indicate the child's involvement in a host of activities that are depicted in slide images using the Children's Experience and Excitement Scale (CEES; Selner, 1992; Selner & Knutson, 1990). In this task, the child is asked to view 44 slides depicting children engaging in activities that range from sleeping and riding a bicycle to loading a revolver and jumping from a 3-meter diving board. For each slide, the child is asked whether he or she has ever engaged in the depicted behavior. If the child indicates that the activity has been performed, the examiner changes to the next slide image. If the child indicates that he or she has not engaged in the depicted activity, he or she is asked if there was ever an opportunity to do so. The same slides are shown to the mother, who is asked to indicate whether her child has ever engaged in the depicted activity. If the mother responds negatively, she is asked whether the child has had the opportunity to participate in the depicted activity. The degree to which the mother and child reports correspond is taken as an index of supervision and tracking. It is based on the assumption that the parent who is effective at supervising the child is more likely to be able to report opportunities to engage in various activities in a manner that is congruent with the child's report.

The second supervision indicator is derived from the congruence of the independent reports of the parent and child on the Children's Reinforcement Survey Scale (RSS; Clement & Richard, 1976). Using the RSS in a structured interview, the child indicates the people with whom he or she spends the most time, the activities in which he or she most commonly participates, the locations in which he or she most commonly spends time, the toys he or she uses most frequently, and his or her ten favorite foods. The children also are interviewed about activities they would like to do more often, places at which and people with whom they would like to spend more time, and things they do not own but desire. Then, without having an opportunity to talk with the child about those topics, the parent completes the self-report form of the RSS. Again, the degree to which the mother and child reports correspond is taken as an index of supervision and monitoring. It is based on the assumption that the parent who is effective at supervising the child is more likely to be aware of the child's preferences as well as his or her activities and the people with whom the child spends time.

Angry and Abusive Discipline

Four indicators were used for specifying the angry and abusive discipline latent variable. The first indicator was a parent-report composite of two scales: Abusive Discipline, and Inconsistent and Harsh Discipline. The Abusive Discipline scale included 10 items in a summative index. The items indicated whether the parent had used unusual punishment such as locking the child in a closet or tying the child up or if the child had incurred bruises or broken bones or required a trip to the emergency room specifically as a result of discipline. The second parent-reported scale directly paralleled 11 items in the Inconsistent and Harsh Discipline scale tested with the LIFT sample (Knutson, DeGarmo, et al., 2004). In that study, parental report of getting angry when punishing the child was in the Harsh Discipline Index.

Two indicators were obtained from analog procedures. One indicator used Likert-type responses ranging from *not angry* to *very angry* in response to 28 photo slides in the Analog Parenting Task as described by Zaidi et al. (1989). The slides depict a child engaging in appropriate, inappropriate, rule-breaking, and dangerous activities. Another indicator utilized responses to nine video scenarios and combined (a) the frequency with which the parent chose physical discipline and (b) the escalation in severe physical and angry discipline as a response to a hypothetical circumstance in which the depicted child continued to display the behavior in spite of the adult's initial disciplinary efforts. Procedures are described fully in Knutson and Bower (1994).

The fourth indicator was a microsocial observational measure—the frequency count of aversive and negative physical behaviors initiated by the mother and directed to the child during a 40-minute structured laboratory interaction task. The Interpersonal Process Code (IPC) was used to index the frequency of maternal aversive and physically negative behaviors. Three main dimensions coded concurrently compose the IPC: *activity* (the global context or setting in which the interactions occur), *content* (a description of each verbal, nonverbal, and physical behavior), and *affect* (the emotional tone accompanying each content code). Only *content* and *affect* codes were used to score mothers' aversive physical behaviors (e.g., contempt, anger, hitting with hand, hitting with an object, pinching, ear flicking, kicking, grabbing, restraining, spitting, shoving). For the *content* codes in the maltreating study, the percent agreement was .89 and kappa was .80 for intercoder reliability. Kappa is a coefficient calculating agreement above chance. For *affect* codes, percent agreement was .93 and kappa was .78.

Four models are used for this illustration as to how analog and direct observational measures can be used to define maltreatment. The chapter authors used SEM to develop the illustrations because SEM is particularly suited for multimethod, multitrait data matrices. In general, SEM assumes multivariate normality and is a latent variable regression technique that simultaneously combines factor analyses and path analyses. One advantage is the ability to partial measurement error of constructs and to control for method or agent bias. For the models shown here, a progression is followed that introduces new indicators or methods to show how those added indicators enhance or detract from the models. Indicators from the prior models are shaded gray to emphasize the unique aspect of each step. Again, the general structure of the models is based on the Knutson et al. (2004) study and a general theoretical notion that neglect and harsh discipline contribute to the development of aggressive behavior.

The first model specifies the expected relations among neglect, supervision, abusive discipline, and child aggression. However, typical of most traditional research in the area, the first model relies on parent report of neglect and severe physical and abusive discipline. The criterion variable was a latent factor of child aggression. The factor's first indicator was a measure of the child's aggressive responses to four social vignettes. The index score could range from 0 to 8 and summed the child's endorsement of either behavioral retaliation, hostile intent of the child in the scenario, or both, across the four vignettes (range = 0–7; M = 1.68, SD = 1.76). The second indicator was a summative index of dichotomous items rated by the interviewer in the home and at the laboratory visit. Seven items comprised the checklist of items rescored to indicate aggression: *child struck parent, positive to interviewer, cooperative, angry-irritable, screamed or yelled, noncompliant,*

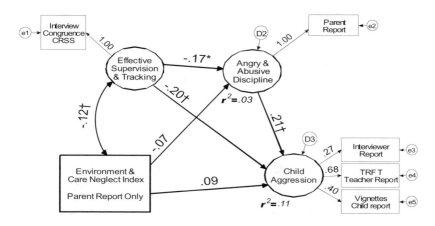

Figure 11.2.   Iowa–Wisconsin Maltreatment: Model of parent report of neglect and angry and abusive discipline. Chi-square = 2.14; *df* 6; *p* = .91; Comparative Fit Index = 1.00.

and *friendly to parents*. The third indicator was the Aggression T-score from the Teacher Report Form (TRF) of the Child Behavior Checklist (CBCL) long form (Achenbach, 1991, 1992). Results of the first model are presented in Figure 11.2 in the form of standardized beta coefficients. For visual clarity, in this and subsequent models, controls for age and sex of child are not shown. All models were estimated with control variables and substantively identical results were obtained.

The model obtained excellent fit to the data, $\chi^2(6)$ = 2.14, p = .91, CF I = 1.00. The factor loadings were fixed at 1.0 for the single item factors. The loadings for the aggression factor obtained acceptable ranges for communalities in defining the underlying latent construct. Results of the first model provide marginal support for a majority of the hypothesized relationships. Neglect was marginally associated with poor supervision (r = −12, p < .10), supervision marginally predicted lower levels of aggression (ß = −.20, p < .10) and significantly predicted discipline as expected (ß = −.17, p < .05), and, finally, abusive discipline marginally predicted lower levels of aggression (ß = .21, p < .10). Eleven percent of the variance was explained in the aggression factor, which utilized no method overlap with the other predictors.

In the next step, the chapter authors entered the contribution of analog measures. (Again, please note that the measures used in the previous step are grayed out in each new figure.) First, for the supervision factor, the analog procedures for measuring congruence were added. Second, for the discipline factor, the analog escalation response to the Analog Parenting Task, as described by Knutson and Bower (1994) and Zaidi et al. (1989); the parents' anger responses to the pictorial representations of children's behavior on the analog task; and the IPC obser-

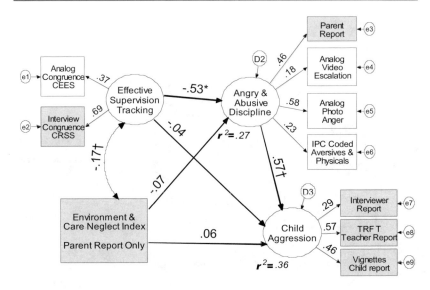

Figure 11.3. Model after adding analog and observational measures of angry-abusive discipline and analog measure of supervision and tracking. Gray areas are measures included in the previous model. Chi-square = 20.81; df 31; p = .922; Comparative Fit Index = 1.00. (Key: CEES, Children's Experience and Excitement Scale; CRSS, Children's Reinforcement Schedule Survey; TRF, Teacher Report Form.)

vational scores for aversive and negative physical behaviors of the mother were now included. Results of testing the same hypotheses with the added analog and observational indicators are presented in Figure 11.3.

The model again obtained excellent fit to the data, $\chi2\,(31) = 20.81, p = .92$, CFI = 1.00, however, there were variations in the substantive results. The correlation path from neglect to supervision increased in magnitude but remained of marginal significance ($r = -.17, p < .10$), the path from the newly specified supervision factor showed greater prediction to discipline ($\beta = -.53, p < .05$), and, finally, the standardized path from discipline to aggression was much greater in magnitude but remained marginally significant ($\beta = .57, p < .10$). Note that the marginal effect of supervision and tracking was now mediated by the angry and abusive discipline factor once the analog and observational indicators were added. Also, inspection of the factor variances indicated there was marginal significance for both the child aggression factor ($VAR = .16, SE = .10, p < .10$) and the discipline factor ($VAR = .12, SE = .06, p < .06$), thus contributing to the lack of significance for the strong path of .57 from discipline to child aggression. The analog indicator of abusive escalation did not obtain a rule of thumb value of greater than .30, but it did contribute marginally significant communality to the other indicators and, therefore, was retained as theoretically specified. Upon integrating analog and observational measures, the explained variance in aggression

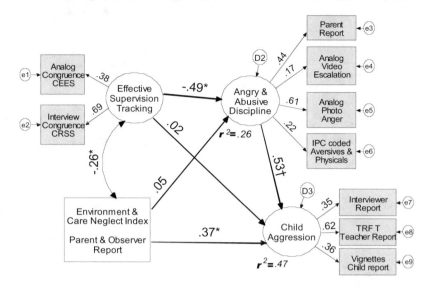

Figure 11.4. Iowa–Wisconsin Maltreatment Study: Model after adding observer ratings to neglect index. Gray areas are measures included in the previous model. (*Key:* CEES, Children's Experience and Excitement Scale; CRSS, Children's Reinforcement Schedule Survey; TRF, Teacher Report Form.)

was threefold in Figure 11.3 relative to the model in Figure 11.2 that did not include the analog indicators.

In the subsequent model, the total neglect index score, as a combination of parent and observer items, was entered. Results are presented in Figure 11.4. Note the first marked difference is the contribution of the total neglect index to the prediction of child aggression ($\beta = .37$, $p < .05$), also adding more than 10% additional explained variance. Similarly, using no method overlap, the path from neglect to effective supervision and tracking now obtained significance ($r = -.26$, $p < .05$). This model underscores the notion presented in Figure 11.1 regarding the continuous nature of the neglect index maximizing sources of data in predicting latent variables using observation, analog procedures, and teacher report.

In the last tested model, parent-reported aggression was added as another independent source of data for measuring child aggression. Although parents who are reporting their own parenting practices may not be adequate or objective judges, they do have unique access to some child behaviors and thus can provide a unique contribution as an insider reporter of child behavior across settings beyond the classroom and the laboratory. Note also the latent factor of child aggression represents the shared communality and, therefore, agreed *convergence* of parent, teacher, coder, and child as sources of data. Results are shown in Figure 11.5.

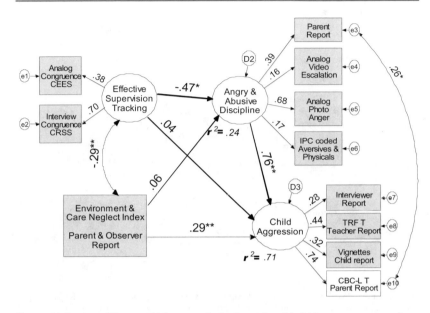

Figure 11.5. Iowa–Wisconsin Maltreatment Study: Optimal model: Adding parent communality to aggression factor, controlling for measurement error. Gray areas are measures included in the previous model. Chi-square = 30.21; *df* 39; *p* = .84; Comparative Fit Index = 1.00. (*Key:* CEES, Children's Experience and Excitement Scale; CRSS, Children's Reinforcement Schedule Survey; TRF, Teacher Report Form; CBCL, Child Behavior Checklist.)

In Figure 11.5, the restricted error covariance for the parent-report indicator of discipline and the parent-report indicator of aggression was freed and estimated. Any dispositional or situational reporting bias of the parent is partialled out in the error term correlation. The final results provide an optimal evaluation of the theoretical model. The path from angry and abusive discipline (ß = .76, *p* < .01) is now significant at an alpha level of .05, and the factor variance for child aggression is now significant using one additional source of data (*VAR* = 21.21, *SE* = 6.50, *p* < .001). Further, the explained variance was increased roughly seven- to eight-fold for each of the respective underlying constructs when compared with the results of the model in Figure 11.2, which relied on parent report only. Thus, results indicated that the multiple source operationalization of the theoretical constructs was optimized by using all potential sources of data in regard to factor variance and predictive validity.

The distributional properties of the abusive discipline factor also were inspected, and it was found that similar to the neglect index, the maltreating risk sample obtained adequate variance in abusive discipline for standard normal theory analyses, even when considering just the parent report. However, the multiple-method factor score obtained a lower standard error of the mean and greater continuous distributional properties, as did the neglect index. The standard error of the mean was .057 for the parent-report factor of two scales and was .038 for the multiple-method factor score of aggression. Given the rare sampling of identified maltreating families and families at high risk, researchers using analog and observational methods are likely to reach radically different conclusions from those relying on self-report alone.

MODERATING EFFECTS
USING ANALOG PROCEDURES: A REPLICATION

The final illustration in this chapter focuses on a hypothesis that an underlying predisposition for negativity or anger may moderate or *amplify* the detrimental impact of abusive parenting. Amplifying effects of coercive or abusive interactions can be trait-like characteristics or can be situationally induced by acute stressors such as divorce or job loss (Patterson & Forgatch, 1990; Robertson, Elder, Skinner, & Conger, 1991). Here analog-based measures are examined as moderators of harsh and severe physical discipline. Again, the key advantage to utilizing analog procedures is that they can enhance the continuous assessment of an underlying theoretical construct. If this is true, then the power can be increased to detect statistical interactions or moderating effects (see McClelland & Judd, 1993).

The Oregon Divorced Father Study

For this illustration, two independent samples are employed using distinct but conceptually related analog approaches. The first is the maltreating study previously described, and the second is the first 114 fathers assessed in the first cohort of the Oregon Divorced Fathers Study (ODFS), an ongoing representative sample of divorced fathers and their children. Fathers who were recently divorced were recruited through public court records. The response rate of 46% was very favorable compared with the literature on court-records studies of divorce. A comparison of available sociodemographic and neighborhood characteristics of participants and nonparticipants revealed no significant differences, suggesting that the recruited sample is representative of recently divorced fathers from the community sampled. The data presented in this chapter are for fathers with available teacher-reported data regarding their children ($n = 67$). This reduction in sample size is due to the fact that obtaining teacher data requires that fathers have legal custody of and access to their children and have children of school age.

One advantage to the ODFS is the use of multimethod data. There is virtually no empirical literature on the study of a continuum of severe abuse and neglect to more mild harsh and coercive discipline involving observations of father–child interactions for residential or nonresidential divorced fathers. In fact, there are many cultural and scientific myths that are perpetuated by a handful of inadequately designed nonrepresentative studies and poor reviews of the available literature (Braver & O'Connell, 1998; Parke & Brott, 1999). Many of these myths result in detriment to fathers' well-being, their custody efforts, and the well-being of children. What is sorely needed is a better empirical base of findings using multiple-method designs and representative populations (Lamb, 1997; Tamis-LeMonda & Cabrera, 1999). Although the ODFS sample is not at high risk for maltreatment, it is a representative sample of families whose children are at risk for the development of problem behaviors (Amato & Keith, 1991; Hetherington, Bridges, & Insabella, 1998). The sample covers a considerable range of parenting styles and families of differing socioeconomic status. The design employs multimethod procedures including analog parenting tasks. The analog procedure used in the ODFS is the KidVid analog parenting task. The development of the KidVid was based, in part, on prior research with analog paradigms by Fagot and colleagues to examine gender effects of video stimuli, and, in part, on Fagot's analog research on the assessment of parents' skill at discriminating risky and aversive behaviors of children using both pictorial still presentations (Fagot, Kronsberg, & MacGregor, 1985) and video scenarios (Kronsberg, Schmaling, & Fagot, 1985). The video scenes involve children in the elementary school–age ranges. The videotapes were professionally produced by a team of parenting experts from Oregon Social Learning Center, professional actors, and a video production company. Short scenes depicting child behaviors lasting a few seconds are presented to the parent, who then records his or her response to the scene in the interscene interval. The scenes include common parenting situations in which children behave appropriately or inappropriately. Examples include situations in which children may or may not misbehave while doing the dishes, feeding the dog, playing with siblings, or watching television. One set of measures assesses the parents' tracking skills and ability to appropriately discriminate between aversive and prosocial child behaviors. Another set of measures focuses on the parents' discipline strategies using microsocial codes and global impressions of discipline.

For this illustration, only the available tracking skills data are reported, operationalizing the misidentification of negative behaviors by the parent as an analog-based measure of a negative biasing trait or predisposition for antisocial and coercive parenting. Specifically, a team of licensed and certified behavior therapists and staff supervisors were asked to come to consensus on the identification of positive, negative, and neutral child behaviors in the video scenes. The term *false negatives* was used to operationalize fathers who incorrectly identified positive or neutral behaviors as negative. Therefore, the higher the number of false child negatives identified, the greater the likelihood the parent may perceive and respond to the child as needing punishment.

To examine the moderating effects, ordinary least squares (OLS) regression models were used following techniques outlined for testing statistical interaction (Cohen & Cohen, 1983). First, first-order variables were entered as centered predictors of child aggression. The predictors were reports of abusive discipline in

Table 11.2.   Analog measures as moderators of abusive and harsh physical discipline predicting child aggression

	Model 1	Model 2
Iowa–Wisconsin Maltreatment Study		
Child age	–.15	–.15
Child gender	.05	.04
Abusive discipline	.08	.08
Video analog physicals and escalation	–.05	–.03
Photo analog anger response	.54**	.51**
Video analog anger × abusive discipline	—	.14*
Photo analog anger × abusive discipline	—	–.09
R^2	.33	.35
Oregon Divorced Fathers Study		
Child age	.06	.08
Child gender	–.09	–.10
Harsh physical discipline	.10	.12
KidVid analog false negatives	.19†	.26*
KidVid analog × harsh physical discipline	—	.22*
$R^2$$R^2$	.04	.09

†$p \leq .09$; *$p \leq .06$;**$p \leq .001$.

the Iowa–Wisconsin study and reports of harsh discipline (e.g., slapping, hitting, yelling, scolding) in the divorced father study. The analog procedures involve both the escalation measure and the anger-response measure from the analog task in the Iowa–Wisconsin study and from the KidVid child negatives in the ODFS sample. In the second model, second-order product terms of the centered predictors were entered. Results for regressing the aggression Child Behavior Checklist T-score for the Iowa–Wisconsin sample and for regressing the TRF Externalizing T-score for the ODFS sample are presented in Table 11.2 using standardized coefficients.

Results of Model 1 indicate there was a strong main effect for the analog measure in the Iowa–Wisconsin study (ß = .54, p < .001), and this effect was marginally replicated in the Oregon sample of divorced fathers (ß = .19, p < .09). Results of the second OLS model showed a significant amplifying effect of one of the analog measures on abusive discipline in the Iowa–Wisconsin sample (ß = .14, p < .05) and a moderating effect of the KidVid on harsh discipline reported in the ODFS sample (ß = .22, p < .05). Therefore, with relatively small samples, a significant moderating effect using analog procedures was replicated across independent multiple-method samples that varied substantially in their risk status. To examine the robustness of the finding, a plot of the interaction effect is shown in Figure 11.6.

The plots were generated with the SPLUS software program and show the conditioning analog measure in the top row of the two respective panels. Within

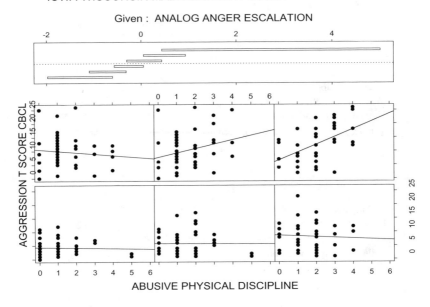

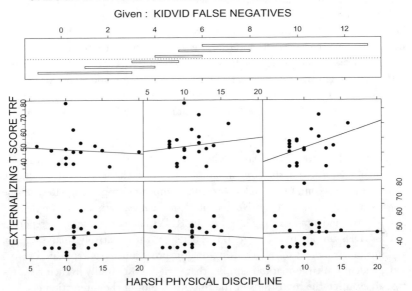

Figure 11.6. Iowa–Wisconsin Maltreatment Study and Oregon Divorced Fathers Study (Cohort 1): Moderating effect of analog measures across two studies. Conditioning or moderating effect of analog measures on the relationship of discipline and aggression across two studies.

each panel there are 6 subpanels. Each of these subpanels is a scatter plot of the effect of abusive discipline predicting child aggression. These boxes are also known as the overlapping "shingles" in the distribution of anger or father ratings of child negatives. They read from left to right in the bottom row and then left to right in the top row. Therefore, they read as the conditioning effect of the analog measure on the relation of discipline predicting aggression. So in the bottom left-hand box of both studies there is a flat slope, but moving left to right through the top row of each panel, the effect is amplified in the higher end of anger escalation and child negative ratings. Visually plotting the effect shows that neither of the conditioning effects were a result of outliers; OLS regression diagnostics also confirmed this.

DISCUSSION

It is the view of the chapter authors that there is no single methodology that is perfect for operationally defining child maltreatment. Although theory and empirical antecedents can dictate the specifics of a research definition of maltreatment, other exigencies ranging from budget constraints to statutory limitations on access to records often can determine how investigators establish research definitions of maltreatment. The studies reviewed in this chapter and the data from the illustrative examples support a view that research on maltreatment can be advanced by adopting a multimethod/multisource approach to operationally defining circumstances of neglect, poor supervision, and harsh and punitive discipline. Indeed, in high-risk samples and normative moderate-risk samples, observational and analog paradigms can result in measures that have excellent statistical properties for testing hypotheses using contemporary statistical methods. As shown in this chapter, convergence among multiple sources of data provided greater specification among related but distinct concepts in the study of maltreatment, the underlying latent factors provided enhanced predictive validity, and factors with more continuous properties provided more power for detecting moderating effects. Thus, it is quite feasible to go beyond administrative data and parent report in establishing valid indices of deficient parenting.

Although some research on maltreatment is appropriately limited in scope or focus, to a large extent most researchers aspire to contributing to a comprehensive model of maltreatment involving distinct domains of deficient parenting. The way that such a comprehensive model is developed will dictate, to a large extent, how the events of focus are operationalized. At the least, any model of maltreatment, or any model of a subtype of maltreatment, will necessarily be relatively complex.

Models that influence the chapter authors' approach to this chapter have a number of components. First, models must be longitudinal in nature. Although the previous illustrations not longitudinal in design, the data were taken from projects that are longitudinal. One is rarely concerned only with the discrete event of maltreatment, but rather the event in concert with contextual factors in which it is embedded, its antecedents and, importantly, its proximal and distal sequelae. With that in mind, the chapter authors lean toward comprehensive models that not only include sampling periods over the life course of the victim but also at least some relevant continuous and antecedent periods in the life-course of the perpetrators and relevant others. In that framework, interests in hypothesized transgenerational considerations also can be placed in a longitudinal context. As with any phenomenon that unfolds over longer periods of time, threats to validity in the form of limits to recall or retrospective bias (e.g., Brewin, Andrews, & Gotlib, 1993; Kuyken & Brewin, 1995; Lewinsohn & Rosenbaum, 1987; Prescott et al., 2000) are critical. In that context, analog and observational methods can be excellent for defining and anchoring the measurement of important processes relevant to child maltreatment, such as parental supervision and tracking, harsh discipline, and even supportive interactions and warm encouragement.

Analog measures are not common in contemporary research on deficient parenting and, further, observational methodology is rarely applied in studies of maltreatment. However, research using analogs based on photographic images (Zaid et al., 1989) and video-clip stimuli (Knutson & Bower, 1994; Kronsberg et al., 1985) have shown that these procedures can be an extremely useful supplement to studying in vivo socialization processes (Fagot et al., 1985). Not only do the analog procedures provide methodological advantages in terms of statistical properties for measuring parents at risk for maltreatment, but they are also beneficial in measuring subjects that are often difficult to observe in vivo. When utilizing validated laboratory procedures that provide a rich context for observing behaviors of focus, research supplemented by analog procedures can ultimately be more cost effective than the amount of time needed for sampling low base-rate events in naturalistic settings (Patterson et al., 1992; Reid et al., 1988).

Not only do observations of parent–child interactions and analog derivations describe the topography of parent–child relations, but also they are sensitive as measures of change and mediation (Reid et al., 2002). The family processes most proximal to child maltreatment are embedded in historical, current, and future contexts that require other well-known and well-developed measurement methodology. Constructs such as parental and child psychopathology, social and economic disadvantage, and family structure and community characteristics, all of which can have direct and indirect effects on parenting and maltreatment, must include state of the art diagnostic and demographic measures so that the constructs measured by observational and analog methods can be mapped on to relevant epidemiological, developmental, and clinical constructs in literatures across the life course. For example, Reid (1986) reported results of a home observational study of the interactions in three groups of families: nondistressed mothers and their children, mothers of children with conduct problems but no evidence of physical abuse, and mothers and their children referred for physical abuse. Children in the abuse group demonstrated a mean of .75 aversive behaviors a minute compared with .38 for the nonabused children with conduct problems and .21 for nondistressed controls.

Given demonstrated effect sizes for reductions in aversive behaviors for at-risk samples, suppose that a group of children who have been maltreated and their mothers were randomly assigned to parent training and control conditions and the intervention was successful (i.e., the children in the treatment condition dropped to the levels of the nondistressed children, and the controls remained at baseline levels). This would be an exciting finding, even more so if that reduction was followed by a significant reduction ten years later in the conduct disorder diagnoses in the intervention group compared with the controls. The results of such a trial become of much greater interest to students of maltreatment, not to mention to policy makers, and would be of great benefit to society (see Stoolmiller et al., 2000 for a discussion of cost-benefit analyses of effective behavioral interventions).

Although direct observation and laboratory precision represent a gold standard in intervention research as well as developmental and epidemiological research, it is the opinion of this chapter's authors that in an ideal research environment, all constructs would be measured using multiple methods and agents, anchoring each where possible with such objective measures. The least fallible operationalization of underlying constructs is essential to any appropriate test of the most basic to the most complex theoretical propositions (Turner, 1989; Zeller & Carmine, 1980). Measurement becomes more valuable in evaluating prevention or treatment designs. Optimal measurement will result in more effective screening of families at risk and provide better diagnosis of targets for behavioral intervention. At the same time, because of the expense of observational methods and the need to relate family processes to more macro-variables and processes (e.g., poverty, family history and structure, psychopathology, educational attainment, substance use, delinquency, health risking behaviors or suicide), it is necessary to pick observational or analog variables carefully in the tests of longitudinal conceptual models. As Brown and Lia (1999) suggested, such models evaluated with observational and analog measures of deficient parenting would include potential mediators and moderators that could be targeted for interventions and measured directly in randomized controlled intervention trials.

REFERENCES

Achenbach, T.M. (1991). *Manual for the Teacher's Report Form and 1991 Profile.* Burlington: University of Vermont, Department of Psychology.

Achenbach, T.M. (1992). *Revised Child Behavior Checklist.* Burlington: University of Vermont, Department of Psychology.

Ainsworth, M.D.S., Blehar, M.C., Waters, E., & Wall, S. (1978). *Patterns of attachment: A psychological study of the Strange Situation.* Hillsdale, NJ: Lawrence Erlbaum Associates.

Alter, C.F. (1985). Decision-making factors in cases of child neglect. *Child Welfare, 64*(2), 99–111.

Amato, P.R., & Keith, B. (1991). Parental divorce and the well-being of children: A meta-analysis. *Psychological Bulletin, 110,* 26–46.

Bank, L., Dishion, T., Skinner, M., & Patterson, G.R. (1990). Method variance in structural equation modeling: Living with "glop." In G.R. Patterson (Ed.), *Depression and aggression in family interaction* (pp. 247–279). Mahwah, NJ: Lawrence Erlbaum Associates.

Bank, L., & Patterson, G.R. (1992). The use of structural equation modeling in combining data from different types of assessment. In J.C. Rosen & P. McReynolds (Eds.), *Advances in psychological assessment* (Vol. 8, pp. 41–74). New York: Plenum Press.

Baron, R.A. (1974). Aggression as a function of the victim's pain cues, level of prior anger arousal, and exposure to an aggressive model. *Journal of Personality and Social Psychology, 29,* 117–124.

Baron, R.A., & Eggleston, R.J. (1972). Performance on the "aggression machine": Motivation to help or to harm? *Psychonomic Science, 26,* 31–322.

Barth, R.P., Landsverk, J., Chamberlain, P., Reid, J., Rolls, J., Hurburt, M., et al. (2005). Parent training in child welfare services: Planning for a more evidence-based approach to serving biological parents. *Research on Social Work Practice, 15,* 353–371.

Berger, A. (1981). *An examination of the relationship between harsh discipline in childhood, later punitiveness toward children and later ratings of adjustment.* Unpublished doctoral dissertation, University of Iowa.

Bower-Russa, M.E., Knutson, J.F., & Winebarger, A. (2001). Disciplinary history, adult disciplinary attitudes, and risk for abusive parenting. *Journal of Community Psychology, 29*(3), 219–240.

Braver, S., & O'Connell, D. (1998). *Divorced dads: Shattering the myths.* New York: Tarcher Puttnam.

Brewin, C.R., Andrews, B., & Gotlib, I.H. (1993). Psychopathology and early experience: A reappraisal of retrospective reports. *Psychological Bulletin, 113,* 82–98.

Brown, C.H., & Lia, J. (1999). Principles for designing randomized preventive trials in mental health: An emerging developmental epidemiology paradigm. *American Journal of Community Psychology, 27,* 673–710.

Caldwell, B.M., & Bradley, R.H. (1978). *Home observation and measurement of the environment.* Little Rock: University of Arkansas Press.

Campbell, D.T., & Fiske, D.W. (1959). Convergent and discriminant validation by the multi-trait-multimethod matrix. *Psychological Bulletin, 56,* 81–105.

Capaldi, D.M., Forgatch, M.S., & Crosby, L. (1994). Affective expression in family problem-solving discussions with adolescent boys: The association with family structure and function. *Journal of Adolescent Research, 9,* 28–49.

Capaldi, D.M., Kim, H.K., & Shortt, J.W. (2004). Women's involvement in aggression in young adult romantic relationships: A developmental-contextual model. In K. Bierman & M. Putallaz (Eds.), *Aggression, antisocial behavior, and violence among girls: A developmental perspective* (pp. 223–241). New York: Guilford Press.

Capaldi, D.M., Shortt, J.W., & Crosby, L. (2003). Physical and psychological aggression in at-risk young couples: Stability and change in young adulthood. *Merrill-Palmer Quarterly, 49,* 1–27.

Cicchetti, D. (1998). Child abuse and neglect—Usefulness of the animal data: Comments on Maestripieri and Carroll (1998). *Psychological Bulletin, 123,* 224–230.

Clement, P., & Richard, R. (1976). Identifying reinforcers for children: A children's reinforcement survey. In E. Mash & R. Terdal (Eds.), *Behavior therapy assessment: Diagnosis, design and evaluation* (pp. 207–216.). New York: Springer.

Cohen, J., & Cohen, P. (1983). *Applied multiple regression/correlation analysis for the behavioral sciences.* Hillsdale, NJ: Lawrence Erlbaum Associates.

Coohey, C. (2003). Defining and classifying supervisory neglect. *Child Maltreatment, 8,* 145–156.

Cook, M., & Mineka, S. (1989). Observational conditioning of fear to fear-relevant versus fear-irrelevant stimuli in Rhesus monkeys. *Journal of Abnormal Psychology, 98,* 448–459.

Crittenden, P. (1995). *The Preschool Assessment of Attachment: Coding Manual.* Miami, FL: Family Relations Institute.

DeGarmo, D.S., & Forgatch, M.S. (1999). Contexts as predictors of changing maternal parenting practices in diverse family structures: A social interactional perspective to risk and resilience. In E.M. Hetherington (Ed.), *Coping with divorce, single parenting and remarriage: A risk and resiliency perspective* (pp. 227–252). Hillsdale, NJ: Lawrence Erlbaum Associates.

DeGarmo, D.S., & Forgatch, M.S. (2004). Putting problem solving to the test: Replicating experimental interventions for preventing youngsters' problem behaviors. In R.D. Conger, F.O. Lorenz, & K.A.S. Wickrama (Eds.), *Continuity and change in family relations: Theory, methods, and empirical findings* (pp. 267–290). Mahwah, NJ: Lawrence Erlbaum Associates.

Deitrich-MacLean, G., & Walden, T. (1988). Distinguishing teaching interactions of physically abusive from nonabusive parent–child dyads. *Child Abuse & Neglect, 12*(4), 469–479.

Dillon, W.R., & Goldstein, M. (1984). *Multivariate analysis: Methods and applications.* New York: Wiley.

Dukes, R.L., & Kean, R.B. (1989). An experimental study of gender and situation in the perception and reportage of child abuse. *Child Abuse & Neglect, 13*(3), 351–360.

Fagot, B.I. (1992). Assessment of coercive parent discipline. *Behavioral Assessment, 14,* 387–406.

Fagot, B. (1997). *Training manual for the Interactive Code—Revised.* Unpublished instrument. (Available from the Oregon Social Learning Center, 160 East 4th Avenue, Eugene, OR, 97401)

Fagot, B.I., Kronsberg, S., & McGregor, D. (1985). Adult responses to risky behavior. *Merrill-Palmer Quarterly, 31,* 385–395.

Finkelhor, D.H., & Hotaling, G.T. (1984). Sexual abuse in the National Incidence Study of Child Abuse and Neglect: An appraisal. *Child Abuse & Neglect, 8*(1), 23–32.

Forgatch, M.S., & DeGarmo, D.S. (2002). Extending and testing the social interaction learning model with divorce samples. In J.B. Reid, G.R. Patterson, & J. Snyder (Eds.), *Antisocial behavior in children and adolescents: A developmental analysis and model for intervention* (pp. 235–256). Washington, DC: American Psychological Association.

Gil, D.G. (1970). *Violence against children.* Cambridge, MA: Harvard University Press.

Giovannoni, J.M., & Becerra, R.M. (1979). *Defining child abuse.* New York: Free Press.

Greenwald, R.L., Bank, L., Reid, J.B., & Knutson, J.F. (1997). A discipline-mediated model of excessively punitive parenting. *Aggressive Behavior, 23,* 259–280.

Herrenkohl, R., Herrenkohl, E., & Egolf, B. (1983). Circumstances surrounding the occurrence of child maltreatment. *Journal of Consulting and Clinical Psychology, 51*(3), 424–431.

Hetherington, E.M., Bridges, M., & Insabella, G.M. (1998). What matters? What does not? Five perspectives on the association between marital transitions and children's adjustment. *American Psychologist, 53*(2), 167–184.

Kadushin, A., & Martin, J.A. (1981). *Child abuse: An interactional event.* New York: Columbia University Press.

Kavanagh, K.A., Youngblade, L., Reid, J.B., & Fagot, B.I. (1988). Interactions between children and abusive versus control parents and children. *Journal of Clinical Child Psychology, 17,* 137–142.

Kazdin, A.E. (1978). Evaluating the generality of findings in analogue therapy research. *Journal of Consulting and Clinical Psychology, 46*(4), 673–686.

Knutson, J.F., & Bower, M.E. (1994). Physically abusive parenting as an escalated aggressive response. In M. Potegal & J.F. Knutson (Eds.), *The escalation of aggression in dyads and groups: Biological and social processes.* (pp. 195–225). Hillsdale, NJ: Lawrence Erlbaum Associates.

Knutson, J.F., DeGarmo, D.S., & Reid, J.B. (2004). Social disadvantage and neglectful parenting as precursors to the development of antisocial and aggressive child behavior: Testing a theoretical model. *Aggressive Behavior, 30*(3), 187–205.

Knutson, J.F., DeGarmo, D.S., Reid, J.B., & Koeppl, G. (2005). Care neglect, supervisory neglect and harsh parenting in the development of children's aggression: A replication and extension. *Child Maltreatment, 10*(2), 92–107.

Knutson, J.F., Johnson, C.R., & Sullivan, P.M. (2004). Disciplinary choices of mothers of deaf children and mothers of normally hearing children. *Child Abuse & Neglect, 28,* 925–937.

Knutson, J.F., Schartz, H.A., & Zaidi, L.Y. (1991). Victim risk factors in the physical abuse of children. In R. Baenninger (Ed.), *Targets of violence and aggression.* (pp. 103–157). Amsterdam: Elsevier/North Holland.

Kronsberg, S., Schmaling, K., & Fagot, B.I. (1985). Risk in a parent's eyes: Effects of gender and parenting experience. *Sex Roles, 13*(5/6), 329–341.

Kuyken, W., & Brewin, C.R. (1995). Autobiographical memory functioning in depression and reports of early abuse. *Journal of Abnormal Psychology, 104,* 595–591.

Lamb, M. (1997). *The role of fathers in child development.* New York: Wiley.

Lewinsohn, P.M., & Rosenbaum, M. (1987). Recall of parental behavior by acute depressives, remitted depressives, and nondepressives. *Journal of Personality & Social Psychology, 52*(3), 611–619.

Lorenz, F.O., Conger, R.D., Simons, R.L., Whitbeck, L.B., & Elder, G.H. (1991). Economic pressure and marital quality: An illustration of the method variance problem in the causal modeling of family process. *Journal of Marriage and the Family, 53,* 375–388.

Maestripieri, D., & Carroll, K.A. (1998a). Child abuse and neglect: Usefulness of the animal data. *Psychological Bulletin, 123,* 211–223.

Maestripieri, D., & Carroll, K.A. (1998b). Risk factors for infant abuse and neglect in group-living rhesus monkeys. *Psychological Science, 9,* 143–149.

Martinez, C.R., Jr., & Forgatch, M.S. (2001). Preventing problems with boys' noncompliance: Effects of a parent training intervention for divorcing mothers. *Journal of Consulting and Clinical Psychology, 69,* 416–428.

Mason, W.A. (1998). Words, deeds, and motivations: Comment on Maestripieri and Carroll (1998). *Psychological Bulletin, 123,* 231–233.

Maxfield, M.G., Weiler, B.L., & Widom, C.S. (2000). Comparing self-reports and official records of arrests. *Journal of Quantitative Criminology, 16*(1), 87–110.

McClelland, G.H., & Judd, C.M. (1993). Statistical difficulties of detecting interactions and moderator effects. *Psychological Bulletin, 114*(2), 376–390.

Melby, J.N., & Conger, R.D. (2001). The Iowa family rating scales: Instrument summary. In P.K. Kerig & K.M. Lindahl (Eds.), *Family observational coding systems: Resources for systematic research* (pp. 33–58). Mahwah, NJ: Lawrence Erlbaum Associates.

Melby, J.N., Conger, R.D., Ge, X., & Warner, T.D. (1995). The use of structural equation modeling in assessing the quality of marital observations. *Journal of Family Psychology, 9,* 280–293.

Misener, T.R. (1986). Toward a nursing definition of child maltreatment using seriousness vignettes. *Advances in Nursing Science, 8*(4), 1–14.

Öhman, A., & Mineka, S. (2001). Fears, phobias, and preparedness: Toward an evolved model of fear and fear learning. *Psychological Review, 108,* 483–522.

O'Toole, R., Turbett, P., & Nalepka, C. (1983). Theories, professional knowledge, and diagnosis of child abuse. In D. Finkelhor, R.J. Gelles, G.T. Hotaling, & M.A. Straus (Eds.),

The dark side of families: Current family violence research (pp. 349–362). Beverly Hills, CA: Sage Publications.

Parke, R.D., & Brott, A.A. (1999). *Throwaway dads: The myths and barriers that keep men from being the fathers they want to be.* New York: Houghton Mifflin.

Passman, R.H., & Mulhern, R.K. (1977). Maternal punitiveness as affected by situational stress: An experimental analogue of child abuse. *Journal of Abnormal Psychology, 86*(5), 565–569.

Patterson, G.R., & Forgatch, M.S. (1990). Initiation and maintenance of process disrupting single-mother families. In G.R. Patterson (Ed.), *Depression and aggression in family interaction* (pp. 209–245). Hillsdale, NJ: Lawrence Erlbaum Associates.

Patterson, G.R., & Forgatch, M.S. (1995). Predicting future clinical adjustment from treatment outcome and process variables. *Psychological Assessment, 7,* 275–285.

Patterson, G.R., Reid, J.B., & Dishion, T.J. (1992). *A social interactional approach: Antisocial boys* (Vol. 4). Eugene, OR: Castalia.

Prescott, A., Bank, L., Reid, J.B., Knutson, J.F., Burratson, B.O., & Eddy, J.M. (2000). The veridicality of punitive childhood experiences reported by adolescents and young adults. *Child Abuse & Neglect, 24,* 411–423.

Putallaz, M., Kupersmidt, J.P., Coie, J.D., McKnight, K., & Grimes, C.L. (2004). A behavioral analysis of girls' aggression and victimization. In M. Putallaz & K.L. Bierman (Eds.), *Aggression, antisocial behavior, and violence among girls: A developmental perspective.* Volume 1: Duke Series in Child Development and Public Policy. New York: Guilford Press.

Reid, J.B. (Ed.). (1978). *A social learning approach to family intervention. II. Observation in home settings.* Eugene, OR: Castalia.

Reid, J.B. (1986). Social-interactional patterns in families of abused and nonabused children. In C. Zahn Waxler, E.M. Cummings, & R. Iannotti (Eds.), *Altruism and aggression: Biological and social origins* (pp. 238–255). New York: Cambridge.

Reid, J.B., Baldwin, D.V., Patterson, G.R., & Dishion, T.J. (1988). Observations in the assessment of childhood disorders. In M. Rutter, A.H. Tuma, & I.S. Lann (Eds.), *Assessment and diagnosis in child psychopathology* (pp. 156–195). New York: Guilford Press.

Reid, J.B., Eddy, J.M., Fetrow, R.A., & Stoolmiller, M. (1999). Description and immediate impacts of a preventive intervention for conduct problems. *American Journal of Community Psychology, 27*(4), 483–517.

Reid, J.B., Kavanagh, K.A., & Baldwin, D.V. (1987). Abusive parents' perceptions of child problem behaviors: An example of parental bias. *Journal of Abnormal Child Psychology, 15,* 457–466.

Reid, J.B., Patterson, G.R., & Snyder, J. (Eds.). (2002). *Antisocial behavior in children and adolescents: A developmental analysis and model for intervention.* Washington, DC: American Psychological Association.

Robertson, E.B., Elder, G.H., Jr., Skinner, M.L., & Conger, R.D. (1991). The costs and benefits of social support in families. *Journal of Marriage and the Family, 53,* 403–416.

Rodriguez, C.M., & Sutherland, D. (1999). Predictors of parents' physical disciplinary practices. *Child Abuse & Neglect, 23,* 651–657.

Rusby, J.C., Estes, A., & Dishion, T. (1991). *The Interpersonal Process Code (IPC).* Oregon Social Learning Center, Eugene.

Sedlak, A.J., & Broadhurst, D.D. (1996). *Third national incidence study of child abuse and neglect: Final report.* Washington, DC: U.S. Department of Health and Human Services.

Selner, M.E. (1992). *The role of childhood sensation seeking and parental supervision in the emergence of childhood psychopathology.* Unpublished doctoral dissertation, University of Iowa.

Selner, M.E., & Knutson, J.F. (1990, May). *The development of the Children's Experience and Excitement Scale.* Paper presented at the Midwestern Psychological Association Meeting, Chicago.

Selner-O'Hagan, M.B., Leventhal, T., Brooks-Gunn, J., Bingenheimer, J.B., & Earls, F.J. (2004). The Homelife Interview from the Project on Human Development in Chicago Neighborhoods: Assessment of parenting and home environment for 3- to 15-year olds. *Parenting: Science and Practice, 4,* 211–214.

Snyder, J.C., & Newberger, E.H. (1986). Consensus and difference among hospital professionals in evaluating child maltreatment. *Violence and Victims, 1*(2), 125–129.

Sternberg, K.J., Knutson, J.F., Lamb, M.E., Bradaran, L.P., Nolan, C., & Flanzer, S. (2004). The Child Maltreatment Log: A PC-based program for describing research samples. *Child Maltreatment, 9,* 30–48.

Stoolmiller, M., Eddy, J.M., & Reid, J.B. (2000). Detecting and describing preventive intervention effects in a universal school-based randomized trial targeting delinquent and violent behavior. *Journal of Consulting and Clinical Psychology, 68*(2), 296–306.

Suomi, S. (1978). Maternal behavior by socially incompetent monkeys: Neglect and abuse of offspring. *Journal of Pediatric Psychology, 3,* 28–34.

Sullivan, P.M., & Knutson, J.F. (1998). The association between child maltreatment and disabilities in a hospital-based pediatric sample. *Child Abuse & Neglect, 22,* 271–288.

Sullivan, P.M., & Knutson, J.F. (2000). Maltreatment and disabilities: A population-based epidemiological study. *Child Abuse & Neglect, 24,* 1257–1273.

Tamis-LeMonda, C.S., & Cabrera, N. (1999). *Perspectives on father involvement: Research and policy* (Social Policy Report Volume XIII, No. 2). Ann Arbor, MI: Society for Research in Child Development.

Taplin, P.S., & Reid, J.B. (1977). Changes in parent consequences as a function of family intervention. *Journal of Consulting & Clinical Psychology, 45*(6), 973–981.

Turner, J.H. (1989). *Theory building in sociology: Assessing theoretical cumulation.* Newbury Park, CA: Sage Publications.

Turner, R.J., & Wheaton, B. (1995). Checklist measurement of stressful life events. In S. Cohen, R.C. Kessler, & L.U. Gordon (Eds.), *Measuring stress: A guide for health and social scientists* (pp. 29–57). New York: Oxford University Press.

Vasta, R., & Copitch, P. (1981). Simulating conditions of child abuse in the laboratory. *Child Development, 52*(1), 164–170.

Wahler, R.G. (1980). The insular mother: Her problems in parent–child treatment. *Journal of Applied Behavior Analysis, 13*(2), 207–219.

Webster-Stratton, C., Reid, M.J., & Hammond, M. (2004). Treating children with early onset conduct problems: Intervention outcomes for parent, child, and teacher training. *Journal of Clinical Child and Adolescent Psychology, 33*(1), 105–124.

Weinrott, M.R., Reid, J.B., Bauske, B.W., & Brummett, B. (1981). Supplementing naturalistic observations with observer impressions. *Behavioral Assessment, 3,* 151–159.

Widiger, T.A., & Clark, L.A. (2000). Toward DSM-V and the classification of psychopathology. *Psychological Bulletin, 126,* 946–963.

Widom, C.S. (1977). A methodology for studying noninstitutionalized psychopaths. *Journal of Consulting & Clinical Psychology, 45,* 674–683.

Widom, C.S. (1988). Sampling biases and implications for child abuse research. *American Journal of Orthopsychiatry, 58*(2), 260–270.

Wolock, I. (1982). Community characteristics and staff judgments in child abuse and neglect cases. *Social Work Research and Abstracts, 18*(2), 9–15.

Zaidi, L.Y., Knutson, J.F., & Mehm, J.G. (1989). Transgenerational patterns of abusive parenting: Analog and clinical tests. *Aggressive Behavior, 15,* 137–152.

Zeller, R.A., & Carmine, E.G. (1980). *Measurement in the social sciences: The link between theory and data.* New York: Cambridge University Press.

IV

SOCIAL POLICY ISSUES

ALL CLASSIFICATION and definitional systems exist in social and policy contexts. The social contexts include public sentiment about the relationship of government to families, opinions about child discipline, and beliefs about appropriate relationships within the family as well as, on a larger scale, the personnel or organizational framework of a child welfare system and the business processes of that system. Social contexts can have considerable variability in how concrete, or codified, they are or are not. Social contexts also may have considerable variability among individuals and across social systems. For example, it is quite possible that the good citizens of a rural community might not agree with the equally good citizens of urban centers about how to discipline children. The policy contexts, by comparison, are often somewhat easier to describe. They include federal, state, and local laws and statutes and the interpretive policy directives and practice guidance that both refine the definitions of child maltreatment and operationalize them. Adding to the challenge of defining and classifying child abuse and neglect are the applications those definitions will be put in the service of, as described elsewhere in this volume. The need for legal definitions, agency or practice definitions, and research definitions compound the variations created by the contexts. In short, simplistically, the creation of classification systems and definitions cannot be done in a contextless vacuum.

The chapters in Section IV focus on these context issues, describing the kinds of contextual issues that can be considered as definitions are developed. In Chapter 12, Porter, Antonishak, and Reppucci examine the impact of divergent purposes of setting (i.e., legislation, services, research) on the development of definitions. Casting a definitional wide net in legislation allows, and promotes, local flexibility and responsiveness in policy while creating a lack of both specificity and sensitivity unsettling to researchers. If policy and law utilize definitions that define thresholds for government intervention in family life and minimal standards for burdens of proof in court, researchers more frequently seek to anchor their definitional schema in child development theory, or ecological models of family functioning, or empirically derived paradigms. It is no wonder, then, that differences exist. The chapter concludes with an implicit challenge for researchers, describing four tasks that researchers must accomplish if research, and the definitions that drive the categorization of child abuse and neglect that underpin the

330 Social Policy Issues

research, are to be useful to child protective services workers, prosecutors, and policy makers. In Chapter 13, Flanzer, Yuan, and English look at another part of the context—the impact of information technology (IT) on defining and classifying child abuse and neglect. At the very least, they suggest, IT can streamline the exchange of information, communication, and automated data collection at the local, or agency, level. Once data has been collected, IT systems can provide analysis tools and build information systems that will have impacts on generalizable knowledge, powering meta-analytic techniques, large sample sizes, and data archives. All of these contribute to the possibility of creating greater definitional concordance across the various policy and social contexts that will improve both basic and applied research and support evidence-informed practice. In Chapter 14, Simmel, Flanzer, and Webb add yet another layer to the task of defining child abuse and neglect—that of conducting research with children, about children—in ethical ways. Unsolicited disclosures of past and present abuse; very specific federal regulations regarding permission and assent for children to participate in research; and tensions, as well as special regulations, unique to research with children who are members of special populations such as foster care, are just some of the ethical issues specific to child abuse and neglect research that are highlighted in this chapter. This section concludes with Chapter 15 by Feerick and Snow, which summarizes common themes in the book and outlines an agenda for future research. In this chapter, the authors address the key question: Where do we go from here?

12

Policy and Applied Definitions of Child Maltreatment

MARYFRANCES R. PORTER,
JILL ANTONISHAK, AND N. DICKON REPPUCCI

OVER THE PAST THREE DECADES, increasing attention has been paid to the definitions of, and outcomes associated with, various forms of child maltreatment. Although the majority of contributions to this book are focused on detailing empirical definitions of child maltreatment, this chapter examines ambiguities in empirical and policy definitions. Because levels of definitional specificity and reliability, as well as the bases for validity, differ depending on the purpose for which a definition was designed, the divergent purposes of child protective legislation, child protective services (CPS), and empirical research in child abuse and neglect can impede the development of a universal definition of child maltreatment (Aber & Zigler, 1981; Barnett, Manly, & Cicchetti, 1993; Dubowitz, Black, Starr, & Zuravin, 1993; Shonkoff, 2000). For example, at the federal level, definitions are designed to broadly establish the government's ability to intervene with the family. Legal definitions focus on the caregiver's conduct. Mandated reporting laws define abuse in order to delineate specific indicators for service providers to report specific abuse. Caseworkers define abuse based on circumstances within a given family, whereas research definitions focus on the implications of maltreatment for developmental outcomes. In addition, broad policy definitions of child maltreatment, paired with significant variation in definitions, standards, and practices between localities, may have the deleterious effects of potentially increasing the workloads of child protection caseworkers and resulting in inconsistent, if not inaccurate, decision making. These broad definitions also may create barriers for researchers invested in influencing policy definitions and improving local standards and practices.

This chapter reviews the purposes of current federal and state policy definitions of child maltreatment and the ways in which these definitions are tested

Work on this chapter was supported by a grant from the National Institute of Mental Health (Grant F31-MH65711-01) to the first author.

Correspondence should be directed to N. Dickon Reppucci, University of Virginia, Department of Psychology, Post Office Box 400400, Charlottesville, Virginia 22904-4400; e-mail: ndr@virginia.edu.

in criminal and domestic/family courts. Furthermore, the origins of policy definitions are examined and the way in which empirical and policy definitions may inform each other to strengthen child protection is highlighted. Next, this chapter focuses on applying policy definitions to CPS practices. Several challenges in the development of applied definitions are highlighted. These include the way in which decisions are made in the process of identifying maltreatment as well as the conflicting roles of caseworkers to define abuse for investigatory purposes and/or to target families who need services. The chapter concludes with a few suggestions for collaborations among policy makers, agencies, and researchers that may clarify definitional ambiguities and strengthen the overarching objectives of protecting children and promoting healthy families.

CHILD MALTREATMENT DEFINITIONS AT THE FEDERAL AND STATE LEVELS

The core legislative debates regarding defining child maltreatment concern establishing a threshold for when government may intervene in the family and prosecute abusers. In order to elucidate the legal requirements for substantiating a case of maltreatment, the following sections provide a review of federal policy definitions and statutes at the state level and in the legal system. The authors then comment on how policy definitions diverge from research definitions and how these definitions may inform each other to strengthen child protection.

Federal and State Policy Definitions

In response to medical recognition of the battered child syndrome in the 1960s (Kempe, Silverman, Steele, Droegemueller, & Silver, 1962) and increasing public concern over child maltreatment, as evidenced by the rapid proliferation of child abuse reporting laws, Congress passed the Child Abuse Prevention and Treatment Act (CAPTA; PL 93-247) of 1974 to establish the government's legal ability to intervene to protect children from maltreatment, prosecute abusers, authorize funding, and establish a regulatory framework and infrastructure for CPS (see Barnett et al., 1993, for a comprehensive review of the origins and evolution of child maltreatment legislation). CAPTA's current definition of child maltreatment reads as follows:

> At a minimum, any recent act or failure to act on the part of a parent or caretaker, which results in death, serious physical or emotional harm, sexual abuse or exploitation, or an act or failure to act which presents an imminent risk of serious harm.

Deliberately broad and vague, this definition established a minimum standard for state statutes. However, legislators have since struggled with the lack of specificity of child maltreatment definitions. Given the overburdened child protection system, some advocates recommend that case substantiation should be based on physical evidence or observable injury (e.g., bruising). Such specificity would allow for a more precise determination of abuse and would limit the number of cases that fall under the purview of CPS but would necessarily exclude cases without physical evidence (e.g., some cases of neglect or psychological maltreatment). Political trends, cases in the popular media, and consideration of overburdened CPS agencies often have reignited this debate about the specificity of definitions (English, 1998). Federal child abuse legislation has evolved since the passing of CAPTA in 1974 and was rewritten in 1988 as part of the Child Abuse Prevention, Adoption and Family Services Act of 1988 (PL 100-294), but the definitions of child maltreatment have been relatively consistent.

Reviewing the numerous state statutes is beyond the scope of this chapter, but a U.S. Department of Health and Human Services (DHHS; 2003) review reported that states generally define the term *maltreatment* as "harm or threatened harm" to a child vis-à-vis nonaccidental physical or mental injury, actual or attempted sexual abuse/exploitation, and/or "inflicting," "allowing to be inflicted," or "knowingly, intentionally, or negligently causing" harm/injury. Most states delineate four subtypes of maltreatment: *physical abuse, neglect, sexual abuse/ exploitation*, and *psychological maltreatment*. When distinguished from physical abuse, *neglect* is often further defined as deprivation of basic needs including adequate food, clothing, shelter, or medical care. Many states identify financial limitations, reasonable corporal punishment, and/or religious/customary traditions as possible exceptions to the maltreatment definitions. Most states do not define psychological or emotional maltreatment, but when they do, they typically require evidence of harm in the form of mental illness or impairment of the child's ability to function (see Giovannoni, 1991, for a detailed discussion of policy considerations in defining psychological maltreatment).

Legal Definitions and Substantiation

To substantiate a reported case of maltreatment, caseworkers assess whether child maltreatment has occurred or is imminently likely to occur. Meeting the burden of proof means that a case has met the legal definition of maltreatment. Standards to substantiate a report of maltreatment vary by state. Twenty-three states use a standard of "preponderance of evidence," "material evidence," or "clear and convincing evidence" that maltreatment occurred or could imminently occur, and nineteen states use a less rigorous standard of either "credible evidence" or "probable cause" (DHHS; 2003). If the burden of proof is met, families are required to comply with agency directives regardless of criminal charges. If the family refuses to comply with agency directives, the case may be brought to family/domestic court, where the validity of an agency's judgment is tested against the state's statutes and the federally defined limits of the government's right to act as parens patriae (*Prince v. Massachusetts*, 1944).

The standard of proof required by state policies becomes more stringent based on the degree of governmental intrusion in individual or familial rights. In criminal court, which poses the highest risk to individual liberties, the state must prove "beyond a reasonable doubt" that maltreatment occurred. In family or domestic court, states use the "clear and convincing evidence" standard of evidence to terminate parental rights (regardless of criminal prosecution). When states' interventions are less intrusive, less rigorous standards of proof are used, implying an acceptance that false positives generally are better than the risk of false negatives.

In addition to establishing evidentiary requirements regarding the jurisdiction of the government or the guilt of an accused offender, many court judgments have refined or expanded the ways in which localities interpret child welfare policies. For example, in *In the Matter of Shane T* (1988), a family/domestic court clarified a New York State statute that necessitated that a victim sustain physical injuries in order for maltreatment to be substantiated. The court ruled that a child's stomachaches resulting from his father's perpetual taunting constituted a physical injury and thus justified agency intervention. Child maltreatment policies also have been expanded by courts; for example, although such was not the intent of the original statutes, definitions of neglect in Illinois, California, and New York were expanded to include children who have witnessed domestic violence, regardless of demonstrable harm to the child because the abusive parent failed to consider the child's well-being (Weithorn, 2001).

Research Definitions and Public Policy

Policy definitions of child maltreatment seldom appear to be based on research regarding the short- and long-term consequences of maltreatment, service provision, termination of parental rights, and foster care placement for children and families. Rather, policy is often influenced by public outcry arising from media attention to sensational cases (Reid, 1997; Wilson & Morton, 1997) and shifts in popular political views regarding how much the government should be involved in families (see Barnett et al., 1993). Bevan, advocating for greater social science involvement in policy, suggested

> Many . . . would probably be surprised if not disturbed to realize that policy hardly ever exists in a totally explicit, completely rational, clearly formulated, and fully comprehensive set of statements. Policy is more often than not nothing more than what a particular bureaucrat elects to do about a particular matter at a particular time. (1980, p.787)

Although researchers' participation in the policy process has improved, research definitions of child maltreatment rarely are applied to policy definitions because the political reality poses a challenge for researchers hoping to develop integrated definitions of abuse. Bevan (1980) argued that researchers need to better understand the policy process and take into account the social, political, and economic reality of society within limits. Researchers can work with policymakers as a top-down strategy or continue research with families and children from a bottom-up approach, but both approaches are essential to ensuring the dissemination of research-to-policy definitions (Reppucci, 1985), especially regarding which types of parental behaviors within a developmental context adversely affect children (see also Barnett et al., 1993; Emery & Laumann-Billings, 1998; Kaufman & Zigler, 1996).

CHILD MALTREATMENT DEFINITIONS AT THE APPLIED LEVEL

Unlike policy makers, CPS caseworkers face the actual decisions about when it is appropriate to intervene with families and when the local laws will support them in requiring families to comply with treatment plans. To understand the inherent problems in operationalizing policy definitions, this section provides a discussion of the definitional ambiguity involved in decision making and risk assessment as well as the ambiguity arising from caseworkers fulfilling dual roles with often divergent purposes: to provide needed services and to investigate and substantiate maltreatment. Throughout this section, the authors make note of the growing body of research evaluating the efficacy of administrative practices within social services agencies, directing the decision-making process, and informing the ways in which services are provided.

Definitions of Maltreatment Reflected by Agency Procedures, Decision-Making Strategies, and Risk Assessment

Agency policies and procedures regarding exactly how reported cases are processed and substantiated vary sometimes dramatically from locale to locale (DHHS; 2003). Because broad federal and state statutes do not provide specific demarcations of when harm crosses over from nonmaltreating to maltreating, decisions regarding whether an act constitutes maltreatment rely heavily on risk assessment, the presumed credibility of information sources, the personal judgment of the caseworker, and standards set by agency supervisors (see Wilson & Morton, 1997, for a comprehensive review). Personal judgment may override more objective assessments of maltreatment; one study found that workers' urgency ratings at intake were more accurate in identifying which cases were ultimately substantiated than an empirically derived likelihood model (Wells & Anderson, 1992). In English's (1997) review of research on CPS decisions, she found that caseworkers' perceptions of their roles, as well as agencies' policies and procedures (including screening practices, thresholds for substantiation, work load, budget limitations, and the duration and depth of investigations), affected their decisions about whether a given case was substantiated. Furthermore, definitions of child maltreatment may be inextricably tied to the assessment of risk for imminent harm— a task at which we are inherently and humanly flawed (Meehl, 1954). Although evaluations of individual agency criteria for substantiation may demonstrate that definitions are applied consistently by caseworkers, even subtle differences between agency definitions make interagency comparisons challenging in the same way that comparing research findings among research laboratories using different assessment tools is problematic, even when definitions and assessment tools are based on common underlying theories.

Wells (1997) found that some screening procedures systematically resulted in a lack of case substantiation, indicating not only a need for the standardization of substantiation criteria but also of the general decision-making process. The need for objective and specific guidelines for decision making in CPS practice is well appreciated by policy makers, caseworkers, researchers, and advocates, as evidenced by the adoption of decision-making tools in some localities (see Milner, Murphy, Valle, & Tolliver, 1998, for descriptions of empirically derived measures, and DHHS, 2001, for instruments used in localities). The general purpose of these tools is to ensure comprehensive risk assessments and to target limited resources to investigations for children at highest risk for maltreatment (English, 1997). Two main types of decision-making tools are generally used. The risk factors included in *consensus-based tools* are typically decided on by a group of experts, such that a standard set of risk factors may be considered by caseworkers at different decision points. The risk factors included in *actuarial-based tools* also begin as a list of risk factors generated by a group of experts, but then a retrospective review of case files determines which risk factors have the strongest correlations with critical outcomes (e.g., re-referrals, subsequent out-of-home placements) (Freitag & Wordes, 2001). DHHS (2003) reported that 42 states use risk assessment tools, and there is emerging evidence that similar methods do decrease the number of children re-reported to agencies (e.g., Freitag & Wordes, 2001; Wiebush, Freitag, & Baird, 2001).

Although standardized decision-making tools may improve the decision-making process, the practice of using risk factors as the basis of these tools introduces another layer of ambiguity in the practical definition of maltreatment. Several caseworker handbooks list specific indicators associated with maltreatment, which include risk factors that may be used in initial screenings to estimate the safety of the child and in investigations to rule out maltreatment (e.g., DePanfilis & Salus, 2003; Dubowitz & DePanfilis, 2000; Filip, McDaniel, & Schene, 1992; U.S. Department of Justice, 1996). However, there is little agreement concerning the critical variables to consider when assessing safety or risk of maltreatment (DePanfilis, 1997; Reid, 1997), and many of the risk factors are described without citation, making it difficult to determine their origins. Even when empirical origins may be assumed, parental or environmental risk factors derived from correlational research are misapplied when used as the basis for making dichotomous decisions regarding whether maltreatment has occurred in an individual case (Barnett et al., 1993).

Ultimately, a diagnostic model focused on need, not risk or legal determinations of guilt, may more clearly facilitate service delivery by abandoning traditional conceptions of risk assessment and instead assessing each family's specific strengths and weaknesses (Kaufman & Zigler, 1996). Such a system would likely, in turn, reduce risk by establishing a social support system sensitive to changing levels of risk (Barnett et al., 1993; Kaufman & Zigler, 1996). However, although researchers familiar with child development, ecological models, and best practices champion this direction (see Melton, Thompson, & Small, 2001), policy makers have yet to adopt this model by providing the resources or infrastructure to support it in practice.

The Impact of Caseworkers' Roles on Definitions of Maltreatment

From the initial report through case closure, caseworkers balance the dual roles of service provider and investigator. Although the ultimate goals of service provision and investigation are to ensure child welfare, service providers may define maltreatment as poor parenting practices with negative effects on child development, whereas investigators define maltreatment based on a legal burden of proof. These often contradictory purposes, paired with variability in agency procedures, only compound the problems caseworkers face in operationalizing maltreatment definitions.

Several scholars (e.g., Melton, Thompson, & Small, 2001) have suggested that agencies draw a line between conducting family assessments aimed at service planning, and investigations, aimed at gathering evidence, for substantiation of maltreatment allegations. States are moving toward conducting family assessments and demarcating the roles of child protection agencies and the police. As of April 2003, 20 states identified at least one locale as offering an alternative response to a standard investigation (e.g., family assessments in which the caseworker makes an evaluation of the family's needs and works closely with them in service planning). Several states have published evaluations indicating that these initiatives are successful in reducing the duration of family involvement with agencies, increasing family participation in community services, and maintaining child safety (see DHHS, 2003, for a more detailed review of the CPS policies and practices nationwide). To the extent that developmental research may inform legislative policy and legal decisions, with a focus on identifying levels of family need rather than caregiver guilt or the presence of maltreatment, the disparity between service provision and investigation definitions may be lessened.

CONCLUSIONS

Although policy definitions are useful for guiding legal jurisdiction, court decisions useful for defining guilt, and empirical definitions useful when describing study populations and outcomes, these definitions fail to provide concrete guidelines for individual caseworkers. Agencies are responsible for 1) "diagnosing" children who are abjectly harmed, who are victims of morally reprehensible acts, or who suffer inhumane and/or potentially harmful nonaccidental acts of their caregivers; 2) providing evidence to be used for prosecuting maltreating caregivers; and 3) providing a safe, protected environment for children. In order for definitions of maltreatment (coming from empirical research or legislative policy) to be useful at the applied level, they must have the specific, logistical goals of the caseworker in mind. As broad policy definitions are ineffectual in the field, so are definitions constructed too narrowly for other purposes.

This assessment of the current policy and applied definitions of child maltreatment suggests the following ways that researchers can strengthen the practice of CPS:

- Researchers should work to develop a developmentally sensitive, descriptive model of maltreatment based on evaluating service needs, not merely risk or guilt (see Barnett et al., 1993, for a discussion of methodological issues when conducting research with the goal of creating a classification system), with the goal that definitions and practices may become more standard across localities.

- Researchers should explore novel methods of disseminating research findings so that policy makers, courts, agencies, and the public can easily access and understand which parenting practices, family dynamics, and environmental factors are developmentally damaging for children, and which protective factors are important to consider in assessing need and determining definitions.

- Investigators should strengthen collaborations with agencies and caseworkers such that their logistical needs and administrative limits are addressed.

- Researchers and others should continue to develop and investigate options for managing caseworkers' service provision and investigative roles to narrow the gap between the purposes of the roles and/or more clearly separate the service provision and investigation activities.

Policy makers, courts, and caseworkers face a demanding dilemma in ensuring child welfare and prosecuting abusers within the context of the public agenda. This chapter has focused on some of the ambiguities inherent in policy and applied definitions of child maltreatment. Hopefully this chapter, and the book as a whole, will help to promote greater collaboration among researchers, policy makers, and practitioners to expand our society's capacity to strengthen families and foster healthy development in children.

REFERENCES

Aber, J.L., & Zigler, E. (1981). Developmental considerations in the definition of child maltreatment. In R. Rizley & D. Cicchetti (Eds.), *Developmental perspectives on child maltreatment. New directions for child development* (pp.1–29). San Francisco: Jossey-Bass.

Barnett, D., Manly, J.T., & Cicchetti, D. (1993). Defining child maltreatment: The interface between policy and research. In D. Cicchetti & S.L. Toth (Eds.), *Child abuse, child development, and social policy: Vol. 8. Advances in applied developmental psychology* (pp.7–72). Norwood, NJ: Ablex Publishing.

Bevan, W. (1980). On getting in bed with a lion. *American Psychologist, 35,* 779–789.

Child Abuse Prevention, Adoption and Family Services Act of 1988, PL 100-294, 42 U.S.C. §§ 5101 *et seq.*

Child Abuse Prevention and Treatment Act of 1974, PL 93-247, § 88 Stat. 4, codified as amended at 42 U.S.C. § 5101-5120 (1996).

DePanfilis, D. (1997). Is the child safe? How do we respond to safety concerns? In T.D. Morton & W. Holder (Eds.), *Decision making in children's protective services: Advancing the state of the art* (pp. 86–102). Atlanta, GA: The National Resource Center on Child Maltreatment.

DePanfilis, D., & Salus, M. (2003). *Child protective services: A guide for caseworkers* (DHHS Publication No. 20-10265). Washington, DC: U.S. Department of Health and Human Services.

Dubowitz, H., & DePanfilis, D. (Eds.). (2000). *Handbook for child protection practice.* Thousand Oaks, CA: Sage Publications.

Dubowitz, H., Black, M., Starr, R., & Zuravin, S. (1993). A conceptual definition of child neglect. *Criminal Justice & Behavior, 20,* 8–26.

Emery, R.E., & Laumann-Billings, L. (1998). An overview of the nature, causes, and consequences of abusive family relationships. *American Psychologist, 53,* 121–135.

English, D.J. (1997). Current knowledge about CPS decision making. In T.D. Morton & W. Holder (Eds.), *Decision making in children's protective services: Advancing the state of the art* (pp. 40–52). Atlanta, GA: The National Resource Center on Child Maltreatment.

English, D.J. (1998). The extent and consequences of child maltreatment. *Future of Children,* 8(1), 39–53.

Filip, J., McDaniel, N., & Schene, P. (1992). *Helping in child protective services: A competency-based casework handbook.* Denver, CO: American Humane Association.

Freitag, R., & Wordes, M. (2001). Improved decision making in child maltreatment cases. *Journal of the Center for Families, Children, & the Courts, 3,* 75–84.

Giovannoni, J. (1991). Social policy considerations in defining psychological maltreatment. *Development and Psychopathology, 3,* 51–59.

In re Shane T., 544, A.2d. 1295 (1988).

Kaufman, J., & Zigler, E.F. (1996). Child abuse and social policy. In E.F. Zigler, S.L. Kagan, & N.W. Hall (Eds.), *Children, families and government: Preparing for the twenty-first century* (pp. 233–255). New York: Press Syndicate of the University of Cambridge.

Kempe, C.H., Silverman, F.N., Steele, B.F., Droegemueller, W., & Silver, H.K. (1962). The battered child syndrome. *Journal of the American Medical Association, 181,* 17–24.

Meehl, P. (1954). *Clinical versus statistical prediction: A theoretical analysis and a review of the evidence.* Minneapolis: University of Minnesota Press.

Melton, G.B., Thompson, R.A., & Small, M.A. (Eds.). (2001). *Toward a child-centered, neighborhood-based child protection system: A report of the Consortium on Children, Families, and the Law.* Westport, CT: Praeger Publishers.

Milner, J.S., Murphy, W.D., Valle, L.T., & Tolliver, A.M. (1998). Assessment issues in child abuse evaluation. In J.R. Lutzker (Ed.), *Handbook of child abuse research and treatment* (pp. 75–115). New York: Plenum Press.

Prince v. Massachusetts, 321 U.S. 158 (1944).

Reid, G. (1997). Case selection. In T.D. Morton & W. Holder (Eds.), *Decision making in chil-dren's protective services: Advancing the state of the art* (pp. 76–85). Atlanta, GA: The National Resource Center on Child Maltreatment.

Reppucci, N.D. (1985). Psychology in the public interest. In A.M. Rogers & C.J. Scheirer (Eds.), *The G. Stanley Hall lecture series* (Vol. 5, pp. 121–156). Washington, DC: Ameri-can Psychological Association.

Shonkoff, J.P. (2000). Science, policy, and practice: Three cultures in search of a shared mis-sion. *Child Development, 71,* 181–187.

U.S. Department of Health and Human Services, Administration for Children and Families, Children's Bureau, and Office of the Assistant Secretary for Planning and Evaluation. (2001). *National study of child protective services systems and reform efforts: Literature review.* Washington, DC: U.S. Government Printing Office.

U.S. Department of Health and Human Services, Administration for Children and Families, Children's Bureau and Office of the Assistant Secretary for Planning and Evaluation. (2003). *National study of child protective services systems and reform efforts: Findings on local CPS practices.* Washington, DC: U.S. Government Printing Office.

U.S. Department of Justice, Office of Juvenile Justice and Delinquency Prevention. (1996, June). *Recognizing when a child's injury or illness is caused by abuse: Portable guides to investi-gating child abuse* (NCJ Publication No. 16-0838). Washington, DC: Author.

Weithorn, L.A. (2001). Protecting children from exposure to domestic violence: The use and abuse of child maltreatment. *Hastings Law Journal, 53,* 1–156.

Wells, S., & Anderson, T. (1992). *Model building in child protective services intake and investiga-tion: Final report.* Washington, DC: American Bar Association.

Wells, S.J. (1997). Screening in child protective services: Do we accept a report? How do we respond? In T.D. Morton & W. Holder (Eds.), *Decision making in children's protective services: Advancing the state of the art* (pp. 67–75). Atlanta, GA: The National Resource Center on Child Maltreatment.

Wiebush, R., Freitag, R., & Baird, C. (2001, July). *Preventing delinquency through improved child protection services* (NCJ Publication No. 187759). Washington, DC: U.S. Department of Justice, Office of Juvenile Justice and Delinquency Prevention, Office of Justice Pro-grams.

Wilson, D., & Morton, T.D. (1997). Issues in CPS decision-making. In T.D. Morton & W. Holder (Eds.), *Decision making in children's protective services: Advancing the state of the art* (pp. 1–11). Atlanta, GA: The National Resource Center on Child Maltreatment.

13

The Impact of Information Technology on Defining and Classifying Child Abuse and Neglect

SALLY M. FLANZER, YING-YING T. YUAN, AND DIANA J. ENGLISH

IN TIMES OF RISING EXPECTATIONS, all available resources need to be maximally applied to support understanding how the design and delivery of child welfare services are accomplished and what effects they are having. Information technology (IT) and its resulting products of data and information are among the resources that support both the mission and the critical operations of child protective services (CPS) practices. IT is a critical and essential infrastructure resource but can be an expensive investment in both dollars and staff time. As an investment, IT needs to be maximized just as investments in hiring and training staff and building good facilities are. Broadly defined, IT includes not only the automated information systems that are used to track clients and services in child welfare agencies but also many automated tools. These tools include common business applications such as word processing programs, spreadsheet programs, and e-mail as well as somewhat less commonly used software applications (e.g., statistical analysis packages). Technology includes mobile telephones, camera integration with communications, laptop computers, and so forth. Over the next decade, technology designed specifically for child welfare systems and technology usage in child welfare systems are expected to increase. The parallel anticipation is that there will be increased access to information for child welfare practitioners, managers, providers, researchers, and perhaps even clients.

This chapter begins with an overview of the use of IT in child welfare services and by examining some of the contributions that IT can make to child welfare research as a consequence of the benefits IT makes to child welfare service system operations in general. Regardless of technological advances, the impact of the definitions of those elements that comprise the information that is developed with IT merit consideration. Because definitions of child maltreatment exist in law, and variations in law are present in different jurisdictions, some variation exists in child maltreatment definitions; therefore, the creation of generalizable knowledge as an outcome of research must be considered in light of those variations. The authors of this chapter describe how IT can assist researchers by disclosing or creating patterns and features common across the definitions that are used by workers and researchers in IT-assisted data collection and analysis. The use of commonly and locally collected data can allow workers to study patterns over time for a large number of cases and allow researchers to do the same on an even larger scale. Indeed, the extensive data—collected over a number of years from numerous locations—that are now available have never before been accessible to researchers.

The chapter then discusses some approaches to examining variation in observations; additional features of information systems that can be useful in developing more comprehensive understandings of classifications made by workers, data analysis approaches to further deconstructing or reconstructing data categories, and advances in data merging that create greater analytic potential for the primary data as well as newly created datasets. The chapter concludes with a discussion of some issues of privacy and confidentiality that may arise.

THE USE OF INFORMATION TECHNOLOGY IN CHILD WELFARE: AN OVERVIEW

Since the 1980s, there has been continual growth in the use of automated information systems to record and maintain case- and agency-level data. The child welfare field presently uses IT at different points organizationally and structurally to input, create, maintain, categorize, define, and extract data. IT functions can be used on both the input and output side of data collection and analysis. There are three primary uses of IT on the input side. First, IT can be a work management aid; the creation of accessible on-line electronic case file records is one example. Second, as an accountability system, IT can simplify case handling by enabling caseworkers to track and note who is responsible for which parts of service planning or delivery. Third, as a communication system, IT can streamline case handling by allowing users to forward important case information, send automated reminders, schedule follow-ups for services, or send "tickler" messages to prompt review of changes made by others with access to the same client records. The primary uses of the output capabilities of IT are to fulfill requirements for reporting administrative data and perform quality improvement (intramural) and extramural research through grants, contracts, or cross-program efforts.

As an input tool, IT has brought word processing, calendaring of work, and access to data records to the fingertips of most child welfare workers. Although paper files and individual worker files still exist, the organizing and recording of work efforts already are influenced by IT and will be influenced to a greater degree in the future. The most recent wave of development has put these data on the desks and laptop computers of workers. This has led not only to increased access by workers, but also to increased availability of data for research as well. Finally, the Internet has changed the manner in which much communication is conducted. Although workers are not yet routinely communicating with their clients over the Internet, this possibility can be envisioned. Indeed, just a few years ago, banking on-line was not even envisioned by most people in the United States. In fact, in 1997, the penetration rate for on-line access was only 18% (U.S. Department of Commerce, 1998), but by 2003, 63% of U.S. adults were online. (Madden, 2003). Although demographic differences in usage persist, parents with children living at home, regardless of race and income, tend to be more electronically connected than those with no children at home (Madden, 2003).

Accepting reports alleging child abuse or neglect through the Internet is being discussed in some jurisdictions; however, at this time only New Mexico has a web-based reporting system, and that is available only to mandated reporters from the Albuquerque Public Schools (S. McLeod, personal communication, February 10, 2004). Arizona, Florida, and Texas (as well as several other states) accept faxed reports; Florida even posts its fax form on a web site (http://www.dcf.state.fl.us/abuse/howtoreport.shtml). Greater connectivity of data among public agencies and between public and private nonprofit agencies is definitely becoming the trend.

The greatest impetus for the application of IT in child welfare was increased federal funding for states to implement automated case management systems. For a 3-year period starting in 1995, states were eligible for increased federal participation in developing a Statewide Automated Child Welfare Information System (SACWIS; U.S. Department of Health and Human Services [DHHS], 1998). Basically, a SACWIS is a comprehensive case management tool to support the foster care and adoptions case management practices of social workers. States were encouraged to add complementary functionality to their SACWIS to support child protective and family preservation services, thereby providing a unified automated tool to support most, if not all, child welfare services. In addition, states had the option of incorporating other programs into their SACWIS, such as emergency assistance from Temporary Assistance to Needy Families (TANF), juvenile justice, and child care. By law, a SACWIS is required to support the reporting of data to the Adoption and Foster Care Analysis Reporting System (AFCARS) and to the extent practicable the National Child Abuse and Neglect Data System (NCANDS). Furthermore, a SACWIS system is expected to have bidirectional interfaces with a state's Title IV-A (TANF) and Title IV-D (Child Support) systems. (For additional information on SACWIS, see http://www.acf.hhs.gov/programs/cb/dis/sacwis/about.htm.)

Additional impetus for the use of IT in a child welfare context occurred with the passage of the Adoption and Safe Families Act (ASFA) in 1997 (Title IV-E of the Social Security Act). As required by this legislation, the federal government initiated a series of annual reports on the outcomes achieved by state child welfare agencies. In addition, the federal government designed a system of reviewing state child welfare practices. The review system, the Child and Families Services Review (CFSR), relies heavily on key indicator data about a variety of case- and system-level outcomes initially collected as part of a state self-assessment and then assessed by the analysis of administrative data collected through the SACWIS. The federal CFSR team and peer reviewers then conduct intensive site visits to review the actual practices being implemented by each state agency. Both the CFSR (for additional information about the CFSR, see http://www .acf.hhs.gov/programs/cb/cwmonitoring/index.htm#cfsr) and a federally reported annual report on child welfare outcomes (for additional information about the annual report, see http://www.acf.hhs.gov/programs/cb/stats_research/index.htm #cw) have utilized state data reported to the Children's Bureau through AFCARS (for additional information about AFCARS, see http://www.acf.hhs.gov/programs/ cb/systems/index.htm#afcars) and NCANDS (for additional information about NCANDS, see http://www.acf.hhs.gov/programs/cb/systems/index.htm#ncands). Both AFCARS and NCANDS collect automated case-level data reported in a common format to the Children's Bureau. State variations in definitions and responsibilities are addressed in guidance on how to crosswalk state-specific terms to the federal terms. Without IT, this level of monitoring, review, and reporting would not be practical.

The reliance of the federal government on administrative data for its annual reports is ample demonstration of the increased importance of automation in producing data at the state and federal levels. This accomplishment, primarily within the last decade, places child welfare in advance of most social services programs. There are no comparable data on services for older adults, adult protective services, services for people with disabilities, or mental health services. At the same time, however, this richness of data has been met with concerns by researchers because of the variability in definitions among states. The Third National Incidence Study (NIS-3; Sedlak & Broadhurst, 1996; for additional information about the NIS, see http://nccanch.acf.hhs.gov/pubs/statsinfo/nis3.cfm), the most recent of three studies on the incidence of maltreatment conducted by the National Center on Child Abuse and Neglect, presented an example of this concern, discussed the impact of interstate variability on generalizability, and used uniform coding.

The data for the National Incidence Studies are based on samples of counties and achieve an estimate of abused or neglected children known to the public CPS agencies and the professional community. As with all estimates, the data must be used cautiously. First, they are supplied by state child protection agencies and professionals, and each state has its own laws regarding what constitutes maltreatment, its own definitions of instances of physical or sexual abuse and of neglect, and different investigative practices (Courtney, Dworsky, Zinn, & Piliavin, 2003). In each of the earlier studies, as well as the current study, NIS-4, there is quite a bit of standardization. (For more information about NIS-4, see https://www.nis4.org/contact.asp.) Coders are trained in reading and translating raw case data to the NIS codification. Sentinels choose from study-defined, set categories of maltreatment that best match their observations.

VARIATIONS IN OBSERVATIONS

The following section focuses on some approaches to examining variations in observations of child maltreatment. The acts and events, commissions and omissions, of parents and other caregivers in reference to their children have weight as freestanding features of the experiences children have. Understanding these events and acts takes on added importance in the child welfare system because these events and acts have service and legal implications for children and families.

Across states, there are differences in both the categorization of data, whether notations in case records or direct observations of behaviors, and the legal and policy consequences of those categorized behaviors. At times, it may be unclear exactly what determines the consequences: law, policy, or categorization systems. The variations across states and localities are not great in terms of the most extreme classifications or the most obvious or most commonly illegal behaviors. Rather, there are variations as to whether certain very specific actions are included in the statutory definitions. Some states have very expansive but relatively general definitions, whereas other states have highly specific definitions (DHHS, 2003). Even with the most egregious and least varied categorizations, it may be said that child welfare systems are not operating within a framework of a uniform or consistent set of definitions or observational and diagnostic techniques. The reasons behind this variation lie in the developmental stage of the study of child maltreatment as a science, the locus of responsibility for child abuse and neglect being essentially a state and local function, and the community as a reference point for behaviors that are considered acceptable. These variations and differences become quite important to researchers because confidence in the findings of their research rests on assumptions of comparability of the data on which their research is conducted (i.e., replicability of research findings), and these assumptions require concordance of the inputs.

Although differences across states can be one source of lack of concordance, within states there also can be variation (Wolock, 1982). Each state child welfare system operates within a common set of definitions of terms established in state law, policy, and procedure. Even child welfare systems that are county-administered operate under common state law. Despite common state law, however, there is still room for variability among agencies.

All child workers receive some training in applying their diagnostic skills in the context of state regulations, agency policy, and intake procedures to understanding what has happened to a child or what may happen to a child in terms of actions that will harm the child. States have various preservice and in-service training programs (many of them funded by the federal Child Welfare Training Program of Title IV of the Social Security Act) to teach workers how to do their jobs. It is the case, however, that caseworkers come to the job from a variety of backgrounds. The General Accounting Office (2003) cited evidence from a national child welfare workforce study (Child Welfare League of America, 1999) indicating that fewer than 15% of child welfare agencies require caseworkers to hold either bachelor's or master's degrees in social work. This diversity compels the use of as many decision guides (many of them electronic) as possible to standardize best practices and good supervision. Supervision, then, becomes another tool for training on the job. One role of supervision is to increase the consistency, commonalities, and comparability of these observations, judgments, and assessments by workers within an agency and within units of an agency. Before data were automated and available for review by many people, supervisors might not have been able to compare the observations of their workers with observations by workers in other units. Even now, it is not clear whether the use of automated data has percolated down to actually changing practices or creating common practices, except for providing the opportunity for the comparison of outcomes across units in some states.

Given the general recognition of individual worker variability, unit variability, and state variability, researchers are faced with the task of determining how comparable collected data actually are. There are various ways this can be accomplished—fields can be examined for comparability and consistency, random samples of data elements can be drawn and case records can be examined for consistency and reliability of data input, or caseworkers can be interviewed.

For example, in one study, researchers wanted to verify the accuracy of the ethnicity code in the automated data system before conducting an analysis of ethnic differences in case outcomes. In this case, a random sample of cases was selected from the automated system, and either case records were reviewed or the assigned social workers were interviewed to verify the accuracy of the ethnicity code. The researchers found that the electronic designation of ethnicity was 95% accurate and thus felt confident generalizing results across ethnic groups in the larger analyses utilizing the administrative data (D. English, personal communication, February 12, 2004).

Usually, child welfare agencies provide guidelines on the kinds of information that should be documented in narrative fields. Researchers can use the detail provided in the guidelines to develop checklists of case characteristics and subsequently hand-code data to add to the administrative data used in each analysis. For example, in one study, researchers wanted to develop more specific details on the maltreatment incident reported to CPS and the relationships between specific dimensions of maltreatment and the CPS finding decision (English, Graham, Brummell, & Coghlan, 2002). Typically, in automated systems, CPS workers designate the type of maltreatment in a check-box format utilizing four major categories of maltreatment (i.e., sexual abuse, physical abuse, neglect, and emotional maltreatment). However, research studies indicate that many referrals include multiple allegations, even though electronically the case is assigned to only one type. In this study, the researchers recoded each case utilizing an alternative maltreatment classification scheme. Differential outcomes for CPS findings were found based on which definition, that is, which classification scheme (CPS or researcher-defined), was used in the analysis (English et al., 2002).

IT can play an important role in helping to work around these variations to achieve concordance of data and/or research findings and an understanding of whether these variations are meaningful. The relation of research-to-practice and practice-to-research requires not only concordance among the practice-derived inputs but also across them to the foundations of the findings (i.e., among the outputs) as well. Building an evidence base requires this kind of assumption of comparability. IT-supported manipulations enable researchers to establish these definitional assumptions, but with these opportunities come burdens. The primary burden is designing a system that achieves a balance and a good fit across existing legal and policy definitions and the actual events that occurred to the individuals involved.

INFORMATION SYSTEMS DESIGN APPROACHES

From the perspective of definitions of child abuse and neglect, the primary issue related to systems design is the level of detail at which data will be collected and, then, the level at which that collection will be automated and, perhaps, sorted. Recognizing that most child welfare agencies maintain paper files on cases but that this practice may diminish as a data collection device over time, agencies and practitioners are faced with questions about what to automate. It behooves researchers to become part of this conversation as members of the community of endusers because the benefits of this automation to researchers are not insignificant. Most child welfare systems have decided that they will collect both narrative and coded information, and most are keeping both paper and electronic files (T. Hay, personal communication, February 12, 2004). The coded information will be at a level of specificity that would serve to inform the researchers as well as the practitioners or service providers. For example, most child welfare information systems have copied the paper lists of terms they previously used to describe the characteristics of abuse or neglect, allowing the worker to check off on the automated systems whether these terms apply. Most IT systems also include narrative fields for more detail. Whether researchers make use of this information to create generalizable knowledge depends, at a minimum, on the variability previously mentioned and the face validity, specificity, and sensitivity of the collected categories. It may be that the inclusion of narrative information allows workers to avoid making categorical decisions, accumulating data that will not be useful for creating generalizable knowledge over time. The narrative may, however, provide other researchers additional cues or clues useful in further categorization.

Agencies are building additional protocols into their information systems that prompt or guide workers on what to consider when reporting on their observations. These standardized protocols may be used as tools for recording observations directly or from case notes. Sometimes these protocols are called risk assessment tools or structured decision-making tools; whether theoretically constructed or empirically derived, they exist as part of an electronic dataset. Although designed as a practitioner aid, these guiding protocols could benefit researchers as well by establishing a priori analytic variable options with greater specificity and that are amenable to research. There also is an increasing trend for child welfare agencies to adopt standardized measures as part of their assessment process. Scores at the individual item level and overall scores are entered into the electronic case files in numeric or narrative fields. This type of information can be very useful for research purposes and is ripe for empirical evidence about its reliability and validity.

For example, in 2000, the state of Washington adopted a screening process for all children entering foster care that were identified as likely to remain in foster care for longer than 30 days (Office of the Children's Administration Research, 2001). The screening protocol consisted of rapid assessment tools measuring child developmental and behavioral health and functioning as well as family issues related to the reason for placement. A profile was developed for each child, and the information from the screening tool was used in case planning. The data for each child is entered into the electronic case management system. This screening process is an example of how an electronic data system can enhance both practice and research. On a practice level, the data are entered into the system, and for some measures, electronic profiles are produced. The data are available for easy review by the assigned social worker or for transfer to service providers who are involved with providing treatment for the child. For research purposes, the data for each child can be aggregated at the community, region, and/or state level. These data, in turn, can be used by researchers to address a variety of research questions. For example, they could be used to examine service effectiveness or the relationships between service components and outcomes. They also could be used to examine a variety of other important research questions about the needs of children in foster care, the relationships between needs and services, and the effectiveness of the services. At the state level, worker variation in input is reduced, and researchers can proceed to analysis with minimal interim steps. Interim steps, however, are sometimes necessary. The following section describes approaches to data analysis when immediate analysis is not possible because of variability in data.

DATA ANALYSIS APPROACHES

Given the variability in definitions and data collection prior to analysis, researchers are faced with a task of reconciliation—creating or collapsing data into useable categories, creating, in effect, usable definitions. There are two basic approaches to resolving or harmonizing differences in terminology and categorization. The first is to essentially deconstruct the report or label into its essential and distinct elements. The second is to reconstruct labels or sets of events into a taxonomy based on theory or on empirically derived relations. Automation utilizes both reconstructive and deconstructive techniques and has made both increasingly possible, providing the ability to aggregate or to compare across otherwise disparate descriptions. This technologically driven (and supported) ability to nullify (or at least approach resolution of) the tension between a priori and ad hoc definitions has tremendous power. (See examples later in this chapter.) It may be a bigger boon for the research community than it is for the practice community, but it is not a detriment to either.

Deconstructive techniques undo the labels, ignore classification systems, and disregard preset typologies. These techniques depend on the availability of a sufficient amount of rather descriptive data. An event can be described in terms of its many elements—the actual behavior and its intensity and chronicity, the immediate consequences of the behavior, and the subsequent events related to the behavior.

For example, a "physical abuse" incident from a case narrative could be deconstructed into the following elements:

- The child was hit by an ashtray thrown by the father.
- This had occurred at least once before.
- The child's eyebrow area was bruised.
- The child was taken to the hospital by the mother.
- No stitches were required.
- The doctor found additional bruises on the child's back, which the mother said were from the father hitting the child with a belt.
- The doctor confirmed that this might be the cause.
- No additional medical attention was needed.

Although some preparatory work exists in creating the construct, deconstruct, or mapping rules, researchers do not need to physically locate the records and seek out specific pieces of information when the information is available electronically. Even the narrative data are more accessible.

Analysis, then, of these separated elements is likely to yield greater insight across cases. To improve the quality of practice, supervisors might use this approach once the electronic case files are available. By collecting data that allows them to look at similar events across cases, they can adjust interventions based on outcomes. Quality improvement, in this sense, is continuous evaluation. Reviewing case record database entries looking for patterns of response to individual elements across cases for any single worker or across workers within work units would be as useful for supervision and monitoring as for research and evaluation purposes.

Another example of both the importance and feasibility of this type of deconstructive effort is demonstrated by some work being conducted in the Longitudinal Studies of Child Abuse and Neglect (LONGSCAN) research project.

LONGSCAN is a consortium of federally funded research studies operating with common procedures (Hunter & Knight, 1998; or see http://www.iprc.unc.edu/longscan). First funded in 1990, the consortium has five sites and a university-based coordinating center. Each site is conducting a separate and unique research project on the etiology and impact of child maltreatment. Although each project can stand alone on its own merits, through the use of common assessment measures, similar data collection methods and schedules, and pooled analyses, LONGSCAN is a collaborative effort that is truly greater than the sum of its parts (see, e.g., http://www.iprc.unc.edu/longscan/ for LONGSCAN website). In addition to the specific focus of the individual sites, the coordinated LONGSCAN design permits a comprehensive exploration of many critical issues in child abuse and neglect on a combined sample of sufficient size for unprecedented statistical power and flexibility. Built into the LONGSCAN design is also the ability to replicate and extend findings across a variety of ethnic, social, and economic subgroups.

In the LONGSCAN study, a child's maltreatment experience is classified in two ways: 1) the CPS designation based on CPS records and 2) by classification using the Maltreatment Classification Scheme (MCS) developed by Barnett, Manly, and Cicchetti (1993). Recent analyses of the correspondence between CPS designations and classification using the MCS revealed differences in classifications of maltreatment type (Runyan et al., 2003). Regardless of whether one system is superior to the other or not, it appears clear that a researcher can arrive at disparate conclusions based on the method used to classify the event rather than on the event itself. Although in the past almost all researchers used the CPS designation, it is now possible and reasonably economical to develop different classification systems to fit the particular research question.

Using a deconstructive approach, the event itself and its ancillary features can be manipulated independently. (See the description of the Child Maltreatment Log [CML] elsewhere in this volume for a personal computer version of an IT-driven deconstructive research tool and Sternberg et al., 2004.) Using the information about differences based on classification scheme, empirical evidence can create the organizing principles, if any are desired. This deconstruction, de-layering, or unhooking from legal or agency labels can be done for analytic purposes on either narrative or item-entry records; at almost any systemic level from micro to macro; and within and across geographic, political, legislative, and cultural boundaries.

Reconstructive techniques translate, transmute, or relabel finite entities into a common grid or categorization system. These techniques also can be called *mapping*. For example, data may be collected in terms of many different types of behaviors or observed effects. These entities can be collapsed into larger new or existing categories for specific purposes or grouped into entirely new sets. One example would be to collapse the terms *sexual exploitation, sexual penetration,* and *sexual molestation* into sexual abuse. Another example would be to collapse the terms *death due to abuse, brain damage, skull fracture due to abuse, subdural hematoma due to abuse, internal injuries due to abuse, burns/scalding due to abuse, cuts/bruises/welts due to abuse, human bites due to abuse, tying/close confinement, sprains/dislocations due to abuse,* or *torture* all to the more general label of physical abuse. Those events are, then, the descriptors of the definition of physical abuse. This reconstruction is a "collapse up" process. Another example might be to group events by severity, creating a category based on either physical injury or emotional trauma. In addition, a mapping process may be used to translate information from a variety of data sources, each with their own labels or definitions, into a categorical structure based on their essential commonalities. Mapping, in this way, recodes information that means the same thing, despite its different origins, onto a common field or grid.

Once decisions are made as to what larger order coding structures will be used and for what purpose, if data are already recorded at the more finite level, computer programs can be written to map terms into the new schema. Statistical packages exist that permit this kind of recoding and computation of new variables. This can be done for any number of purposes, using any number of classification schemes. Automation allows the primary resources to be spent on decision making related to the appropriate classifications and in a more purposive, global (large application) way rather than on the actual work of recoding data records. Both of these approaches, deconstructive and reconstructive, through automation, significantly enhance researchers' analytic opportunities for everything from pattern discernment to hypothesis testing. However, no analytic package or technique can succeed beyond the limits of the data entered.

In addition to these opportunities for small and large basic research, new analytic models can be created for site-adjusted program development, replications, and testing hypothesis-driven service models in applied research designs. Once the data are in an information system, they can be retrieved and used in any number of ways. They can, of course, always be reported at the level at which they are entered or maintained. A case record can be printed out, or records can be reported using particular rules of analysis. For example, a selection rule that specified that all cases that had been in foster care for more than 12 months after a specific date could be used to search the information system for those cases and then report on specific attributes of the cases. Or, a rule could be created that collapsed data on the basis of any single analytic variable. In some ways, one might argue, the information system makes the debate about definitions unnecessary, presuming excellent detail and specificity at the data input level and sound reasoning at the analytic framework output level. However, the data fields included in the information system may not cover all of the necessary variables, and researchers may still need to grapple with how to use data in a particular theoretical perspective. With IT, they have the opportunity to see those gaps more clearly.

More sophisticated analyses, such as hazards analysis, event history analysis, survival analysis, and modeling or analyses involving relational databases also can be applied to data that have been entered as uniquely defined and manipulable elements. Of course, prior to any application, the properties of the data need to be reviewed and analyzed to meet basic IT quality standards. Data quality routines precisely assess the quality of the data in terms of missing values, skewed distributions of data, and data entry errors. But for logic, rationality, and appropriateness, thoughtful human consideration is required.

APPROACHES FOR MERGING DATASETS

Analysis across databases is another example of data manipulation made possible by IT. Drake and Jonson-Reid (1999) provide a specific example as they describe an analytic dataset constructed from administrative datasets that combine data on a larger scale but about finite groups of people. The larger picture of the use and impact of administrative data for child maltreatment as a field, they believe, suggests that despite the arguable strengths and weaknesses of administrative data per se, the wealth of data alone creates an imperative for the increased use of such data, and that this increased use is both "desirable and inevitable." The article concludes with a discussion of the benefits of this kind of analytic work to researchers and practitioners in the long run, especially with the development of historical archives that will allow future researchers "unprecedented freedom in pursuing longitudinal designs" for superior research and enhanced research-to-policy-to-practice transformations. The IT capacity for fast, high-volume data matching—longitudinally, cross-sectionally, by variable, or probabilistically—provides astounding research opportunities.

Merged datasets, made possible by the commonalities deliberately created by a mapping, matching, or recoding process, may be the most value-added aspect of an IT-supported research process. Whether this merging occurs in the context of meta-analysis or crosswalked datasets, more data does contribute to power and analytic confidence. With increased power, rigor, and confidence, IT certainly supports the research enterprise. Use of IT-derived data allows for analyses of very large and very rich datasets that might include thousands of cases and hundreds of variables. These large datasets can support bivariate and multivariate analyses, allowing for the examination of relations that have not been possible in the past. Consideration of the immeasurably wider possible impacts on the dissemination of research findings and the application of findings on research-to-practice and practice-to-outcomes is where this entire pursuit brings us—practically and intellectually. The sheer ability to create common meanings, regardless of the legal or agency definition, has tremendous implications for research, generalizable knowledge, the applicability of research findings, and the translation of valid and reliable research findings into evidence-based change at a variety of levels on practices in diverse communities.

IT also enables researchers to access other data sources more easily. Perhaps the most common example of this is the use of census data. Only a little more than a decade ago, before the beginning of the Internet, the use of census data was limited to a number of special locations with access to the data or to others who could receive automated files of the data in various formats. Now these data are, for the most part, available to anyone who is on the Internet. Researchers can integrate census data at the census track level or at a larger geopolitical level for additional analyses. It also is possible to access other national study databases to compare state-specific or sample case-specific characteristics to larger national samples. This ability to crosswalk, or interdigitate, datasets without complete merging adds tremendous analytic potential.

Finally, IT allows for information on clients found within access to other databases on a selected group of clients. Some examples might be crosswalking data from other state systems that service child welfare clients, for example, state drug and alcohol services, economic services, birth records, and arrest and conviction data. There is recognition that sharing data on specific clients is of huge potential use for researchers and practitioners, but that this also has implications for privacy and confidentiality.

ISSUES OF PRIVACY AND CONFIDENTIALITY

The many benefits of increased access to data will require attention to balancing interests in accessing data with interests in maintaining data confidentiality and personal privacy. These issues have gained prominence in large part due to the opportunities presented by technology. The issues that now arise go beyond the most basic and long-standing privacy and confidentiality concerns. Amdur and Bankert cited these 1993 definitions of privacy and confidentiality:

> Privacy can be defined in terms of having control over the extent, timing, and circumstances of sharing oneself (physically, behaviorally, or intellectually) with others. Confidentiality pertains to the treatment of information that an individual has disclosed in a relationship of trust and with the expectation that it will not be divulged to others in ways that are inconsistent with the understanding of the original disclosure without permission. (2002, p.169)

Researchers generally operate with an awareness and sensitivity to the potential impact of breaching privacy and confidentiality of research participants and generally are careful to avoid disclosing individuals as members of a child maltreatment group, whether victims or perpetrators. In most cases, researchers are expected to balance their obligations to report maltreatment with their responsibilities to protect privacy and maintain confidentiality, except when explicit statutory exceptions exist. This being said, the chapter authors were unable to find an example of researchers being included in statutory lists of "privileged" communications (i.e., attorneys or the clergy, as in Delaware; or licensed psychologists, professional counselors, or social workers, as in Georgia and Missouri; S. Slappey, personal communication, February 11, 2004). However, the passage of the Health Insurance Portability and Accountability Act (HIPAA; PL 104-

191) of 1996, though designed to protect health information specifically, has brought heightened caution regarding privacy and confidentiality to all research activities based on individually identifiable personal information. Child maltreatment data especially contains necessary and important personal information. This information should be treated carefully and respectfully, should not be freely distributed, and should be maintained only as long as required. Deliberate data-handling and security strategies mitigate the enhanced risk of inadvertent disclosure provided by the ability to merge datasets and to create triangulation analytic routines that might be able to identify a person, despite the fact that, in each dataset, the person's individually identifiable data has been removed.

Technology has created these enhanced abilities. First, more individuals have access to computer power that can perform more sophisticated analyses of data. Second, more individuals can gain access to electronic datasets, either through established routes or, potentially, through underground routes of the Internet (despite some restrictions on data use that require the user to be working at a computer that has no outside access to the Internet). This combination creates the potential for both more creative analyses and increased risk of breaches of confidentiality and invasion of privacy. For example, if one gained access to a vital statistics dataset with birth records and then linked it to a child maltreatment dataset that did not contain names or birth dates or addresses but did contain counties of residence, the chance of finding the name of a child who has been maltreated would be seriously increased.

There are several approaches that are being implemented to guard privacy and maximize electronic data confidentiality. For example, archives designed specifically to encourage secondary analysis and common data usage have moved to restrict access to datasets in some cases and suppress the content of datasets in others. The Children's Bureau and the National Data Archive on Child Abuse and Neglect (for additional information about the data archive, see http://www .ndacan.cornell.edu) do both. The dataset from the National Survey of Child and Adolescent Well-Being, which contains the results of a large number of individual scored tests, exists in three versions—each containing different amounts of individual data and because of the access to different amounts of individually identifiable data, each requiring a different license, or use, agreement. The first version is a "general" release of "scrubbed" data (data from which all personal identifiers, small cells [e.g., counties have been merged up to a standard minimum population], or sensitive information have been removed); the second is a licensed "restricted" release (with personal identifiers removed); and the third is available only by submitting requests to the data archive managers, who will link the data in its most identifiable form to data sent to them by researchers to produce an anonymous merged dataset.

Another approach designed to protect confidentiality of data and individual privacy is to suppress data. When small cell sizes of rare events offer sufficient potential for matching or data-triangulation identification, IT routines can be used to collapse up the cells; that is, the cells can be folded into larger units until cell sizes or other identifiable information are in more inclusive blocks. For example, geocodes or census tracks might be taken up to the county level, or counties might be grouped so that all small counties appear as one unit. Birth dates could be grouped by 6-month intervals; the specificity of whether a child was 3 years and 6 months old or 3 years and 7 months old is probably not essential information. In other words, protecting the privacy of individuals whose data were collected for one purpose but used for another and safeguarding the confidentiality of that data is paramount.

Coding and encryption are other avenues to limiting the identifiability of data. The Office of Human Research Protections (OHRP) of the DHHS has clarified that information should be considered identifiable regardless of who holds the code that can link information to individuals. The code or link holder may be the researcher, the data provider organization, or some third party. The ability to identify an individual who has "an unusual constellation of characteristics" (Institute of Medicine, 2000, p. 45) is not addressed in OHRP regulations. But, the fact that "indirect inferences can be made by computer analyses and linking several databases" (Institute of Medicine, 2000, p. 45) presents real threats of disclosure and risk of harm.

IT also makes continuous review of data possible. This capability is especially important when adverse events or increased risk to clients is a possible consequence of participation in the research protocol. (Readers particularly interested in this aspect of the research process are referred to Chapter 14 of this volume.)

Of additional importance is that under the most recent amendment to the Office of Management and Budget circular A-110 (1999), public access to research data is available under some circumstances through the Freedom of Information Act. In addition, child abuse and neglect data collected in federally supported activities are maintained in the archives for public use. The rules governing the use of these datasets are not fully established.

SUMMARY AND CONCLUSIONS

Despite ethical and privacy concerns, but with them clearly in mind, strategies for making data more available are sought and funded and hold significant analytic promise for understanding, preventing, and treating child maltreatment. IT makes possible a uniform data approach that creates definitional categories exclusive enough to be useful to researchers, even when individual data entry and individual research designs are quite varied. IT enhances the possibilities of comparative studies and creates a climate for a more reliable and valid understanding of existing variation. Uniformly constructed (or possible) databases are powerful resources for any field.

The development and implementation of electronic datasets offers immense potential for research in the field of child protective and child welfare services.

Replicable solutions to basic research issues such as sample selection and the description of populations as well as to more complex analytical approaches such as developing models to predict outcomes for families served in the system are increasingly possible.

IT cannot and will not solve every definitional dilemma or, alone, improve the interpretation and application of research findings. There are still limitations. However, with datasets as large as 100,000 cases (not uncommon in large child welfare administrative databases these days), it is possible both to select a sample with complete data and to compare the selected dataset with larger datasets on key variables to determine whether the selected dataset is comparable and the findings, therefore, generalizable.

Child maltreatment is an acknowledged national issue. There are important variations in policies and practices that shape the experiences of children who are maltreated. These differences lead to the recognition that both basic and applied research are essential to support evidence-based practice. Technology allows researchers to envision a new "information paradigm." This paradigm would continue to develop increasingly refined techniques to maximize the creation and use of large datasets as an end in itself, for meta-analysis, and as a means of identifying what other research tools are applicable to address those questions that have not yet been addressed. Although not solving the definitional dilemmas, IT allows researchers to pursue knowledge building despite the lack of uniform definitions. The IT engine (to mix the metaphor) should now be harnessed by child maltreatment researchers to move the field forward.

REFERENCES

Amdur, R.J., & Bankert, E.A.. (2002). *Institutional review board: Management and function.* Boston: Jones and Bartlett.

Barnett, D., Manly, J.T., & Cicchetti, D. (1993). Defining child maltreatment: The interface between policy and research. In D. Cicchetti & S. Toth (Eds.), *Advances in applied developmental psychology: Child abuse, child development, and social policy* (pp. 7–73). Norwood, NJ: Ablex.

Child Welfare League of America. (1999). *Minimum education required by state child welfare agencies, percent, by degree type, 1998,* State Child Welfare Agency Survey. Washington, DC: Author.

Courtney, M., Dworsky, A., Zinn, A., & Piliavin, I. (2003). TANF families and the child protective system: Evidence from Illinois and Wisconsin. *Focus, 22*(3), 27 *et seq.*

Drake, B., & Jonson-Reid, M. (1999). Some thoughts on the increasing use of administrative data in child maltreatment research. *Child Maltreatment 4*(4), 308–315.

English, D.J., Graham, J.C., Brummell, S.C., & Coghlan, L.K. (2002). *Final report: Factors that influence the decision not to substantiate a CPS referral. Phase I: Narrative and empirical analysis.* Grant No. 90-CA-1590, Washington, DC: U.S. Department of Health and Human Services, Administration for Children and Families, Children's Bureau, Office of Child Abuse and Neglect.

General Accounting Office. (2003). *Child welfare: HHS could play a greater role in helping child welfare agencies recruit and retain staff* (GAO Publication No. 03-357). Washington, DC: Author.

Health Insurance Portability and Accountability Act (HIPAA) of 1996, PL 104-191, 42 U.S.C. §§ 201 *et seq.*

Hunter, W.M., & Knight, E. (Eds.). (1998). *LONGSCAN research briefs: Vol. 1.* Washington, DC: National Clearinghouse on Child Abuse and Neglect.

Institute of Medicine. (2000). *Protecting data privacy in health services research.* Washington, DC: National Academies Press.

Madden, M. (2003). America's Online Pursuits. *Pew Internet and American Life Project.* Retrieved February 7, 2006 from http://www.pewinternet.org/pdfs/PIP_Online_Pursuits_Final.pdf

Office of Children's Administration Research. (2001, January). *Kidscreen evaluation report.* Seattle: Washington State Department of Social and Health Services, Children's Administration.

Office of Management and Budget. (1999). *Office of Management and Budget Circular A-110.* Retrieved from http://www.whitehouse.gov/omb/circulars/a110/a1100.html

Runyan, D.K., Cox, C.E., Dubowitz, H., Newton, R.R., Upadhyaya, M., Kotch, J. B., et al. (2003). Describing maltreatment: Do child protective services reports and research definitions agree? *Child Abuse & Neglect, 29* (5), 461–477.

Sedlak, A.J., & Broadhurst, D.D. (1996). *Third national incidence study of child abuse and neglect: Final report.* Washington, DC: U.S. Department of Health and Human Services.

Sternberg, K.J., Knutson, J.F., Lamb, M.E., Baradaran, L.P., Nolan, C., & Flanzer, S. (2004). The Child Maltreatment Log: A PC-based program for describing research samples. *Child Maltreatment, 9,* 30–48.

Title IV-A of the Social Security Act, Temporary Assistance to Needy Families (TANF), Personal Responsibility and Work Opportunity Reconciliation Act of 1996. 42 U.S.C., part A.

Title IV-D of the Social Security Act, Child Support. 42 U.S.C. § 620.

U.S. Department of Commerce, National Telecommunications and Information Administration. (1998). *Falling through the Net II: New data on the digital divide.* Retrieved February 10, 2004, from http://www.ntia.doc.gov/ntiahome/net2/falling.html

U.S. Department of Health and Human Services, Administration for Children and Families and the Office of the Assistant Secretary for Planning and Evaluation. (2003). *National study of child protective services systems and reform efforts: Review of state CPS policy.* Washington, DC: U.S. Government Printing Office.

U.S. Department of Health and Human Services, Administration on Children, Youth and Families. (2006). *Child maltreatment 2004.* Washington, DC: U.S. Government Printing Office.

U.S. Department of Health and Human Services, Office of State Systems, Administration for Children and Families. (1998). *State technical assistance information about the Information Technology Consortium and its technical assistance efforts to states* (OSS-ACF-IM Publication No. 98-003). Washington, DC: U.S. Government Printing Office.

Wolock, I. (1982). Community characteristics and staff judgments in child abuse and neglect cases. *Social Work Research and Abstracts. 18*(2), 9–15.

14

A New Look at Ethical Issues in Child Maltreatment Research

CASSANDRA SIMMEL, SALLY M. FLANZER, AND MARY BRUCE WEBB

IN THE DECADE since the National Research Council (NRC) published *Understanding Child Abuse and Neglect* (1993), the diverse field of child maltreatment research, indeed, has responded to the call for more comprehensive, targeted, and rigorous research. For example, witness the field's transformation toward the more frequent use of rigorous methodological procedures such as random assignment of research subjects and conducting nationwide longitudinal and multisite program evaluation studies. Moreover, several states now are partnering with university-based researchers to house comprehensive state-based child welfare data records for the dual benefit of researchers and states. Similarly, the Children's Bureau (CB) of the U.S. Department of Health and Human Services (DHHS) has created a repository at the National Data Center for Child Abuse and Neglect at Cornell University for all CB-funded grants on maltreatment research; these data are then housed for public use. Progress has been made as well on designing "methods, procedures, and resources that can resolve ethical problems associated with recruitment of research subjects; informed consent; privacy, confidentiality, and autonomy; assignment of experimental and control research participants; and debriefings" (NRC, 1993, p. 36).

Although these activities are very exciting, they are accompanied by a new set of risks to both subjects and researchers that were unforeseen 10 years ago. Conducting random assignment evaluation studies with foster youth, for instance, raises concerns about potentially withholding treatment for a very vulnerable population that may have no other treatment options available to it. Consider another example: Secondary analysis of data that were collected under the auspices of a completely different research team may yield possible suspicions about abuse or neglect in a given sample that were undetected by the original research team. If so, then who is responsible for filing a child abuse report? The original team? The new research team, even though that team likely will not have any identifying information about the research subjects? Is there a statute of limitations for the ethical responsibility of the researchers involved in collecting the data as well as for all future researchers who may use the dataset? Current research teams have begun to investigate more deeply research subjects' histories of victimization. Many studies now frequently directly question subjects—including minors—about their knowledge of their victimization. Although these techniques are certainly valuable in terms of adding to the knowledge base about maltreatment, are researchers causing harm to the minor subjects by addressing these topics? Is this line of questioning too invasive and threatening for the (young) subjects?

Child maltreatment is a multiply determined phenomenon, with many diverse and varied pathways as precursors. Similarly, maltreatment researchers are a diverse group, which presents both strengths and challenges. Although the interdisciplinary nature of the child abuse field can be a real strength, as the NRC report pointed out, this diversity in the field may also lead to excessive "fragmentation" (1993, p. 46). The respective missions of these research professions indicate the diversity in research definitions of child maltreatment. Basic researchers, for example, work, in part, to advance knowledge of child and youth populations, which in turn can advance identification, prevention, and intervention efforts. They possess an ethical obligation to advance the field based on rigorous and comprehensive scientific inquiry. From a slightly different perspective, child welfare system researchers conduct research to enhance programmatic and policy-level changes. Their ethical obligation includes creating immediate and potentially large-scale modifications in the services they implement. Legal entities, in general, focus more on the criminality of child abuse and neglect. As such, law-related research may aim to reduce prevalence rates and to identify effective punishment or rehabilitative techniques for families involved with the court system. Other specific areas of legal research entail studying micro-level factors in the courtroom, such as the efficacy of child abuse victims as witnesses in courtroom proceedings (Ceci & Bruck, 1998; Saywitz, Goodman, & Lyon, 2002). Finally, public health researchers may adopt an epidemiological approach and attempt to identify trends and changes in the demographics and prevalence rates of child abuse and neglect and also in the families involved in the child welfare system.

Uncertainty around uncovering suspicions of abuse and whether to report these suspicions is likely to emerge for virtually all investigators researching children, youth, and families, not just for researchers who focus specifically on maltreatment (Kalichman, 1999). For example, studies involving the etiology of psychopathology in children may elicit responses indicating past or current abuse. Thus, researchers need to know their reporting obligations as well as how maltreatment may interface with their intended research topics. As Putnam, Liss, and Landsverk noted,

> Many researchers who are not specifically interested in or looking for disclosures of maltreatment are nonetheless faced with this eventuality at some point in the course of their research. Research with children and adolescents that focuses on their behaviors, feelings, social life, or their health is likely to elicit disclosure of maltreatment by some subjects. As a matter of principle, every researcher studying children and adolescents should be aware of the legal and ethical issues activated by unsolicited

disclosures of maltreatment in the course of data collection on other questions. (1996, p. 114)

The child and youth research community is, therefore, contending with an evolving set of ethical quandaries that are intertwined with contemporary research procedures and with the subjective nature of defining child maltreatment. Whereas this volume as a whole deals with how such definitions are constructed and applied, the ethical course of action when confronted with child maltreatment is a process of consideration in a multilayered context. Indeed, even the development of maltreatment-focused questions—and knowing how and when to ask such questions—is greatly affected by ethical issues. In addition, the direct querying of children and youth, as opposed to relying on child welfare agency records and information, opens new layers of ethical risks.

Definitions of maltreatment exist with utility in various settings—legal, state agency, policy, research, and treatment. This chapter looks at how ethical considerations utilize a specifically defined event as maltreatment and how this affects the research process and the research participant, which in turn may be affected by specific contexts. In addition to reviewing current legal standards around enrolling vulnerable research subjects, this chapter also explores emerging issues and how the ethical dilemmas have changed as child maltreatment research has become more sophisticated. To illustrate these changes, examples of contemporary child abuse and neglect research projects that have addressed the new ethical challenges in measurement development, data collection, data handling, and analysis are provided. Last, close attention is paid to the complexities faced by researchers who directly study children residing in foster care who, because of the circumstances engendering their entry into substitute care, constitute a particularly vulnerable research population.

On a final note, the chapter authors would like to underscore that they are presenting a range of ethical issues that have emanated from the conduct of research on this highly sensitive topic. The research studies described herein are presented to depict the range of solutions that various researchers have utilized to contend with these ethical dilemmas, either real or potential. As such, the authors are not validating or endorsing one strategy or school of thought over another; they are simply attempting to present the very real struggles that all child maltreatment researchers must face at some point in their careers.

ETHICAL ISSUES SPECIFIC TO CHILD MALTREATMENT RESEARCH

All research conducted with federal funds, and much research funded by other sources, must comply with a set of federal regulations (45 C.F.R. 46) protecting the individuals who participate in the research and the information that is collected about them. Though many feel the regulations were designed primarily to address biomedical research, they apply equally to social and behavioral research.

Oversight of individual researchers' compliance with these regulations falls to an institutional review board (IRB), a group convened at host research institutions to review, approve, and/or modify research protocols regarding the ethical treatment of human research subjects. IRB committees are mandated by federal law (National Research Act of 1974, PL 93-348) and are required to exist in institutions that conduct research involving human subjects and that receive federal funding for such research. Oversight of IRBs is provided by the Office of Human Research Protections (OHRP), formerly the Office of Protection from Research Risks (OPRR) (Sieber, 1994).

An important historical event in the development of human participant protections was the publication of *The Belmont Report* (National Commission for the Protection of Human Subjects of Biomedical Research, 1979). This report identified three fundamental principles for considering the ethics of research and to be applied in making considered moral judgments about research. The report, named for a conference center outside of Baltimore, Maryland where the authoring committee wrote it, was commissioned by Congress in 1974 "to investigate the ethics of research and to study how research was conducted and reviewed in U.S. institutions; it was also charged with determining the basic ethical principles that should govern research with humans" (Institute of Medicine, 2003, p. 30). The report "provides an analytical framework composed of principles and their applications that will help resolve ethical problems arising from research" (Amdur & Bankert, 2002, p. 4). Namely, the three principles identified in the report are respect for people, beneficence, and justice. Although neither these specific principles nor *The Belmont Report* is specifically mentioned in the federal regulations, the ethical principles are operationalized in the regulations. Respect for people is fundamental to the informed consent process, beneficence guides the consideration of the risk and benefit of participating in research, and justice speaks to the selection of subjects and their risks and benefits by participating in research. The national commission that wrote *The Belmont Report* was convened in a climate of particular concern over two now notorious experiments that shed light on this chapter's focus on research with vulnerable populations. In addition, the naming of the commission followed the publication of the seminal article in 1966 by Henry Beecher on the ethical flaws in human participant protection and ethical research in the United States. Brief descriptions of the two particular studies ought to be sufficient to cause every present day researcher to exercise thoughtfulness.

First, in the Willowbrook Study, which took place from 1956 to 1972, children who were residents of the Willowbrook School for the Retarded (Staten Island, New York) were injected with a form of hepatitis. Parents had to consent to the study in order to have their children admitted to the only available local school. Second, in the infamous Tuskegee, Alabama study, begun in 1932, U.S. Public Health Service physicians followed several hundred African-American men who had syphilis. Subjects were not informed of the study's intentions, nor were they provided with a newly found effective treatment—penicillin. The study was not discontinued until 1973 (Institute of Medicine, 2003, p. 63).

A chief responsibility of IRBs is to evaluate all aspects of proposed research protocols and assess the appropriateness of research teams' ethical approaches. Researchers, in turn, are advised to make modifications requested by their respective IRB committees. Yet, because each research setting has its own IRB—each composed of a unique set of professionals—the assessment of ethical approaches is quite subjective and variable. It is not uncommon for one university to approve a research study while a neighboring university, whose IRB is composed of an entirely different panel of professionals, prohibits an identical plan. In fact, this subjectivity of opinions is recognized in the federal guidelines.

Federal regulations regarding ethics are concerned both with the physical (i.e., medical) risks to human research subjects as well as the psychological risks attendant to them that jeopardize the confidentiality of subjects' data or the privacy of their participation in the research. The federal regulations define *risk* in ways that include potential harm and define *harmful* as anything that might "reasonably place [the individual] at risk of criminal or civil liability or be damaging to the subjects' financial standing, employability, insurability, reputations, or be stigmatizing" (45 C.F.R. 46 § 101). Subpart D of this regulation deals especially with children as research subjects and the special considerations applied to them for respect, beneficence, and justice in selection as subjects (Sieber, 1994). Certainly, these risks will be considered during review by IRBs. However, prior to such reviews, researchers should consider these risks and potential harms and have plans for minimizing them procedurally. Ideally, IRBs should be viewed as guides to facilitate researchers' adoption of ethically appropriate research standards (Sieber, 1994).

OVERVIEW OF CONSENT AND ASSENT PROCEDURES

Although obtaining informed consent from research subjects is legally mandated in all research on humans, it is not specifically mandated with minors (i.e., while the legal adult caregiver must provide informed consent, it is not legally required of the youth participant). Federal regulations strongly advise, however, that children and youth should formally "assent" to their participation in research projects. Securing assent from minor subjects, although not legally binding, does demonstrate the principle of respect that is outlined in the aforementioned federal regulations and fulfills the obligation to allow subjects the informed option of involvement.

Formal assent is generally obtained from minors who are older than 7 or 8 years. From the perspective of IRBs, virtually all minors are described as having diminished autonomy, which is why the acquisition of consent from a legal caregiver is necessary as well. In addition, it is important to bear in mind that children have limited capacity to comprehend research procedures and they may be uniquely sensitive to the inherent power differential between them and adult researchers (Putnam et al., 1996). Both of these factors may obscure minors' full understanding of the risks of their involvement in research projects.

The assent process does not supersede the obtaining of consent from parents, in that parents are still the legal entity responsible for permitting children and youths' involvement in research. However, there should be concordance between the parents' and the minor's respective views on the youths' participation. That is, a minor can prohibit involvement in a research project, despite the parents' provision of permission to participate (King & Churchill, 2000; Sieber, 1994). Differentiating the respective parties' intents to participate is sometimes a matter of perception, and it may be difficult to gauge whether a child is responding to parental pressure (Attkisson, Rosenblatt, & Hoagwood, 1996).

INFORMED CONSENT
PROCEDURES WITH SPECIAL POPULATIONS

For research involving children and youth who may be at risk of involvement in abusive situations with their biological caregivers, seeking both consent and assent thus entails extenuating circumstances that necessitate careful precautions on behalf of researchers. Researchers must be sensitive both to their perceived role by the minor participant and to the fact that subjects may take this opportunity to disclose their circumstances to the interviewer (Putnam et al., 1996; Sieber, 1994). This propensity to disclose, however, may greatly depend on the age of the minor involved.

For minors who no longer reside with biological caregivers and are in substitute care, the acquisition of consent from legal caregivers presents a new quandary. This population constitutes an especially vulnerable group that requires further research safeguards, particularly when providing informed assent. In most circumstances pertaining to foster children, the biological parents are no longer eligible to provide legal permission on behalf of their children. Thus, there is a question as to who holds the legal authority over foster children. If this legal authority has had only brief contact with a minor, can they evaluate whether the research project is in the child's best interest? Substitute caregivers (i.e., foster parents) possess limited legal oversight over the children in their care. For instance, foster parents generally do not have the authority to permit medical services and treatments. Thus, designating an adult who can authorize a foster child's involvement in a research project may be left to a child advocate/Guardian Ad Litem (GAL), child welfare worker, or a judge, depending on the state in which the research is carried out (Liss, 1994; Sieber, 1994). The importance of having a legal authority advocating for the best interests of a foster child in a research project notwithstanding, relying on alternative adults for legal consent may be cumbersome. Moreover, judges and other court representatives are generally both quite busy and somewhat unfamiliar with research protocols and procedures.

Seeking permission from a judge may thus present obstructions in conducting a research project. Relying on child welfare workers or advocates such as GALs raises issues around whether their knowledge of a particular child's capabilities is adequate and/or whether they truly represent the child's best interests (Kinard, 1985). In addition, such advocates may be overly protective of foster children's involvement in any activities they deem as foreign. It also should be noted that there are wide variations in states' and counties' rules regarding who can provide consent for foster children's research participation. In some locales, it may be a dependency court judge; in others it may be a GAL. The inclusion of biological parents, though they may not possess legal jurisdiction over their children at the time, also may vary. At times it may be necessary to get informal approval from biological parents even though they do not have the legal authority to provide consent.

Enrolling foster youth in research projects requires consideration of the vulnerability of abused and neglected youth. Namely, their cognitive abilities may be especially compromised and underdeveloped in comparison with their age-similar peers, and the power differential in the interviewer–minor participant relationship may be exacerbated by the prior victimization that the participant has endured (Kinard, 1985; Putnam et al., 1996). As Kinard noted,

> Particular attention must be given to convincing abused children that they have the freedom of choice (to participate or not) since their life experiences may have taught them that failure to conform to parental expectations is likely to increase the risk of abuse. (1985, p. 304)

An additional consideration to bear in mind when conducting research with foster children is the receptivity of social services agencies in being studied. It is quite likely that social services agencies may feel that they—not the foster children in their jurisdiction—are the ones underneath the metaphorical microscope and that their professional conduct will be scrutinized by researchers (Attkisson et al., 1996). For example, the Multi-Site Evaluation of Foster Youth Programs, an evaluation project being conducted under the auspices of the Children's Bureau, is a study of foster youth who are preparing to leave the foster care system. In this congressionally mandated project, 1,400 youth who reside in four different regions across the country are assigned to either treatment or control conditions for the receipt of specific preparatory services geared toward independent living following emancipation from foster care. Although foster youth represent an extremely at-risk population with respect to immediate and long-term outcomes across numerous psychosocial domains, they are a vastly understudied group (Courtney, 2000). To date, no random assignment study has ever been conducted on this population that looks specifically at the effectiveness of independent living services on youths' subsequent functioning. Thus, the CB and the contractors charged with conducting this project have confronted numerous ethical issues in planning this project. Germane to the relationship between researchers and social services agencies, the research team debated whether to ask youth subjects about current abuse that they might be experiencing. Keeping in mind that the youth in this project are all in out-of-home care (e.g., foster homes or group homes), current validations of abuse would implicate the substitute caregivers or settings (who are not otherwise involved in the study). In the absence of empirical evidence about how frequently foster youth are abused by out-of-home caregivers, the team decided to investigate this domain. The chapter authors are not aware of any other studies that even approach directly investigating such a sensitive topic. The research team, therefore, had to grapple with several difficult issues, such as weighing the benefits of gaining knowledge about out-of-home care victimization against the risks of losing subjects because child welfare workers would not want to frighten foster parents about the collection of this type of information. In part, research questions of this nature have implications for agencies' relationships with their foster care providers and how the agencies regulate and license these homes. In order to break new ground in research studies with foster youth, the team decided to wait until the minors were over the age of 18 years (during the follow-up phase of the study) before seeking information about abusive events that might have occurred while they were in foster care. This example demonstrates the challenges that must be faced when delving into unknown topic areas with sensitive populations, areas that have previously been ignored and/or avoided by researchers.

A second issue that arose on this project, which also relates to working with social services agencies, concerned conducting a random assignment study, which can invoke fear on behalf of child welfare workers and administrators. For an at-risk group—foster youth—that is already devoid of resources, the appearance of denying services to them is not a welcome suggestion. To address this issue, sites selected into the random assignment study were those that had waiting lists for services. Using overenrolled sites is important in this type of research for several reasons. First, it allows the researcher to randomly assign youth subjects to treatment and nontreatment conditions, which enables the examination of the effects of the agency intervention. Second, this approach also eases the child welfare workers' and agency practitioners' anxiety around prohibiting services to foster youth. With this method, it is already known that some foster youth will be denied specific services; the study just formalizes the process.

A related issue of concern to researchers is the use of state- or county-level administrative data. Although administrative and case records may be accessed under some circumstances without signed informed consent, the policies and regulations governing access to records may be at odds with IRB concerns. In the case of the National Survey of Child and Adolescent Well-Being (NSCAW), for example, most states had legal provisions that allowed for access to administrative and case records, and the NSCAW design took advantage of these provisions by using administrative data for sampling and for conducting caseworker (i.e., the people responsible for abstracting information from case records) interviews prior to contacting respondents. This initial contact with the caseworkers allowed for significant efficiencies in data collection because the caseworker contact usually was necessary for obtaining information for locating the respondents. The IRB, however, would not allow retention of individual-level data collected from caseworkers unless consent formally was granted at a later time. Although NSCAW was allowed to use the caseworker information to conduct non–response analyses, the records had to be destroyed at that point unless consent had been obtained from the respondents (Dowd, 2004).

SHOULD RESEARCHERS SERVE AS MANDATED REPORTERS?

Whether researchers should serve as mandatory reporters is a question that is not without controversy. On the one hand, many would regard the safety and protection of children as the ultimate priority. On the other hand, there are researchers who place a higher premium on the integrity of the research process and on their commitment to protecting the confidentiality of all of the research subjects in their projects (Kalichman, 1999; Liss, 1994). In the absence of clear federal guidelines about a researcher's role in deciding whether to report suspected abuse, a continuum of actions has been adopted by the research community. The following paragraphs highlight and examine the varied methods that not only have been used by researchers but that also have been approved by their respective IRBs. It is important to note that the chapter authors are not endorsing any one method but simply highlighting the range of actions put forth by researchers.

Informed consent procedures for parents, regardless of whether the research is focused on maltreatment or on some other aspect of child and youth functioning, must specify that subsequent discovery of suspected abuse will override the confidentiality agreements researchers have with subjects. It also should be noted that the uncovering of suspected abuse may derive from interviews with parents as well as from interviews with children and youth. This exception to confidentiality raises concerns for researchers on two levels. First, parents may not comprehend that their children may disclose information regarding abuse and so may not be fully aware of the risks inherent in their children's participation. Researchers have to walk a fine line between being candid and genuine and yet not unnecessarily alarming families. Similarly, if disclosures of abuse were to be uncovered, it is nearly impossible for a researcher to identify to the participant beforehand the numerous scenarios that might result based on this disclosure. Investigations—and any subsequent response—by child protective services (CPS) and Departments of Social Services are based on a number of factors (e.g., age of child; type of abuse; timing of abusive event), and a researcher cannot predict how the process will unfold, especially before consent has even been granted and no information is known (Putnam et al., 1996). A second concern for researchers is that the mandate to report instances of suspected abuse may thwart participation of prospective families. Some argue that a priori notification of this confidentiality exception may compel families to voluntarily seek assistance on their own, regardless of the research project (Putnam et al., 1996); unfortunately, this may result in a number of false positives of abuse in research studies (Kalichman, 1999; Kotch, 2000). Conversely, other researchers fear that the looming threat of researchers' reporting may strongly dissuade individuals from engaging in particular research studies (Kotch, 2000). Thus, a selection bias—or a large number of false negatives—may result as well. At present, except for descriptive information from NSCAW, the chapter authors do not know of any studies looking specifically at the impact of reporting on research subjects' potential propensity to decline involvement. Although the NSCAW data revealed that notification of reporting procedures to the families involved in this project—a population that is involved with the child welfare system—did *not* dissuade subsequent participation, this topic is strongly deserving of further scientific inquiry.

At one end of the spectrum in contending with a researcher's role in mandated reporting, Kotch (2000) described a strategy for securing the privacy of respondents' answers, thereby nullifying the possibility of making a report to CPS. This procedure involved keeping interviewers blind to the responses of sensitive questions posed in a questionnaire booklet to their youth subjects. These booklets were then sealed and delivered to the research project office, where the data were entered by a separate team that could not match up the responses to the respondents' identifying information. Kotch argued that this method is necessary in order to preserve the confidentiality of the data collected and to maintain the integrity of the research process.

Sieber suggests that "a simple solution to the reporting mandate would be for researchers to claim that they are not helping professionals and, hence, not bound by the reporting mandate" (1994, p. 3). One of the flaws in this position, as she further contends, is that research subjects may view the researcher as the one and only person whom they can trust and, therefore, may be more apt to make disclosures to the researcher. In other words, a minor participant may not previously have divulged to anyone anything about her current or prior victimization because she had never before been queried about such events. Sieber also notes that making all researchers mandated reporters may result in lower participation rates or in subjects covering up information. Requiring such a mandate would also obscure the boundaries between being a researcher and a practitioner.

The complexities involved with whether researchers should be mandated reporters are further complicated by the varying definitions that respective research communities utilize. Moreover, even when child maltreatment is not the direct focus of a study, suspicions may arise. This raises the question, should only specific categories of researchers be mandated reporters, or should all researchers be required to report suspected abuse? The Child Abuse Prevention and Treatment Act (CAPTA; PL 93-247) of 1974 was the first federal mandate that required states to formulate designations of certain professionals as mandated (required) or discretionary (optional) reporters (Liss, 1994; Sieber, 1994; Steinberg,

Pynoos, Goenjian, Sossanabadi, & Sherr, 1999). Whereas professionals belonging to primarily "helping professions" (e.g., physicians, psychologists, social workers) and those working in child-oriented environments (e.g., teachers, child care providers) were among the pool of mandated reporters, Liss noted that "there is no case law to lend guidance with respect to a researcher's obligation to subjects in terms of the reporting of child abuse or the resultant breach of confidentiality" (1994, p. 134).

The widespread use of secondary datasets engenders new ethical quandaries. Public use datasets, funded by federal agencies, are now readily available, even while aspects of the studies may still be underway. Hence, secondary researchers may indeed be contending with potential abuse incidents that are current, not historical. Thus, where does this leave researchers when they uncover child maltreatment in their empirical investigations or in the analyses of secondary datasets? Central to this question is the context in which the researcher is conducting his or her work. That a researcher is generally acting in the capacity as a *psychological* researcher or *social work* researcher and not just as a *researcher* (Liss, 1994) indicates an ethical obligation under his or her own professional standards and responsibilities (Kalichman, 1999). Moreover, in states that mandate a discretionary form of child abuse reporting, such professionals

> In addition to mandated reporting when they are in their professional roles, . . . have the discretion to report child abuse and neglect cases that 'have come to their attention in their nonprofessional capacities' as defined within the codification of the rules and regulations of their profession. (Liss, 1994, p. 138)

A challenge for multisite studies is maintaining a standard protocol while also responding to legal requirements that vary across communities and conforming to standards imposed by local IRBs. The variation in requirements can affect comparability of data across sites; for example, differences in consent procedures may affect the responses of subjects in unknown ways. NSCAW provides an example of a successful resolution of these potentially conflicting interests. By negotiating from the planning stages of the survey with participating agencies as well as with the IRBs for both the central field office and the local communities, NSCAW was able to establish a set of uniform procedures for consent and assent, as well as criteria for mandatory reporting, that took into account the likely concerns and requirements of each site. Once these protocols were established, a second round of negotiations resulted in buy-in from all partners about responses to interview items that would result in mandatory reports. Although specific mechanisms for reporting differed across agencies, decisions about what would be reported were made in advance, and interviewers were trained in both the local procedures as well as the common framework for mandatory reporting. Individual items in the computerized questionnaires were flagged for review if a response suggested maltreatment; a flagged response indicating maltreatment resulted in a review by the central field office of the entire questionnaire for that child, and reports were made from that office if necessary. For observed maltreatment, as distinguished from concerns arising from responses to items in the questionnaires, interviewers were trained to report directly to the local agencies. For other types of endangerment (chiefly, suicidal ideation or threats), items were immediately flagged for interviewers, and they were trained to inform a responsible adult in the household and to make sure the child was safe before leaving the home (Dowd, 2004; Dowd et al., 2002).

EMERGING ISSUES AMONG RESEARCHERS: HOW THE FIELD HAS CHANGED SINCE THE INCEPTION OF CHILD MALTREATMENT RESEARCH INVESTIGATIONS

Regardless of whether children are the direct subjects of research, information about their family backgrounds and legal circumstances constitutes quite sensitive material. Such material may include details surrounding abuse and/or neglect allegations, the parents' legal status, and mental health and/or substance abuse issues. As is the case with all research subjects, extreme caution should be applied in protecting research subjects, analyzing data and interpreting results, and archiving data and records.

There are other considerations that also have ethical implications for both the collection of child maltreatment data and the analysis of the data collected. These include the use of sensitive questions with special populations, considerations of the veracity of the reports of maltreatment, issues about delayed disclosure and reporting, and issues about third-party reporting and disclosure. Some of these risks exist specifically because of the new large sample sizes used in child maltreatment research, and others exist because of new information technology–supported analytic capabilities.

Use of Sensitive Questions with Children in Foster Care

Data collection with foster children is a uniquely complicated undertaking. As previously mentioned, the assent/consent issues involved, the complexities of engaging the multiple parties (i.e., child welfare workers, judges, foster parents) of the "system" who are inextricably linked with foster children's lives, and the circumstances surrounding their abuse may all hamper foster children's participation. Further, in the experience of the chapter authors, foster children often feel stigmatized for being in foster care and may not care to associate with a study that addresses this topic. On the one hand, conducting detailed interviews with foster children about their lives is innovative as it provides avenues for researchers to explore domains of vulnerable children's lives that rarely have been examined. Such research can further elucidate the distinctions between types of maltreatment and the ramifications of maltreatment as well as the legal or systemic implications of disruption to the parent–child relationship. On the other hand, data collection of this nature must be painstakingly cautious and sensitive.

For example, in selecting the measures to be used in the Multi-Site Evaluation of Foster Youth Programs, the research team gave primary consideration as to whether minors should be queried about the circumstances involving their abuse histories. For research purposes, this material was critical to understanding the interaction between these past events and the youths' ability to effectively avail themselves of independent living program services. However, the research team was wary of broaching a topic that might result in upsetting the youth, particularly when the interviewers were contractors (as is customary in large-scale research/evaluation projects) and not experienced clinicians who have the clinical acumen to ameliorate respondent discomfort. In the end, it was decided that such information should be sought because the benefits to the research and child welfare communities outweighed the risks involved. However, safeguards were put in place to facilitate interviewers' handling of respondents' negative reactions. Also, based on feedback from the respective IRBs involved, some questions were eliminated because they were deemed too risky altogether.

A second example is based on the Termination of Parental Rights (TPR) Project being conducted by the Children's Bureau—an exploratory study of the impact of the termination of parental rights on older youth in foster care. This study, being conducted in several states, entails focus groups and interviews with child welfare workers, juvenile court judges, foster parents, and youth who have undergone TPR. Originally, in developing the project, the research team planned on interviewing both youth whose parents had had their rights terminated and those who were close to having this legal designation. However, the IRB involved disapproved of the idea of interviewing youth whose parents were close to having their rights terminated because there was too much risk involved in what would be disclosed to the youth. In other words, the IRB was worried that the research team would unwittingly divulge sensitive case information to the youth before these events had occurred. This IRB was aware that foster youth are not always supplied with critical and timely information about their circumstances. Therefore, the project proceeded according to this modification in research protocol: Focus groups were held with foster youth whose parents' rights had already been terminated about the circumstances of their legal relationship with their biological caregivers. However, during the data collection phase, it became clear to the research team that many of the youth simply did not understand that their legal ties to their biological families had been severed. Either they were completely unaware that this legal designation had occurred, or they were at a loss as to its meaning and implications. This information, according to the respondents in this project, had not been explained to them by their child welfare workers. Therefore, instead of the participant disclosing personal information to the researchers, the researchers inadvertently conveyed this information to the young subjects.

Veridicality of Reports

The move to achieve uniformity or standardization in definitions has led researchers toward more structured and unambiguous ways of collecting information about maltreatment. This movement toward standardized definitions also raises concerns about veridicality, or the accuracy and truthfulness of respondents' information. Respondents in data collection efforts are relied on to be truthful, genuine, honest and accurate—to give reports that are veridical. Though researchers are committed to accuracy, only the respondents can be responsible for the truthfulness of their reports. Conformity to definition—whether they be research, agency, or legal—relies on veridicality.

Respondents' truthfulness and accuracy, however, may vary considerably in both of these dimensions. Their reports may be untrue—they may obfuscate or lie to cause or prevent "punishment," or their reports may be inaccurate—unmatched to the definition being employed. Thus, veridicality presents an analytic dimension for researchers that relates to the methodological dilemmas of Type I (false positive) and Type II (false negative) errors. Extending this analogy to the concept of accuracy or concordance between the researcher and the respondent (either child or parent) allows researchers to assess the mismatch of the definitions used by researchers and those used either by research respondents or CPS workers who classify the cases (creating the administrative records). The matrix depicted in Figure 14.1 outlines the concordance possibilities; such a matrix carries important contextual importance analytically and to an IRB. Furthermore, the concordance between parent and child respondents—an additional concern for maltreatment researchers—also can be evaluated. These concordance possibilities are illustrated in Figure 14.2.

Respondents may vary in their understanding of questions or items as well as in the ways they choose to respond and in their motivations to present information in a particular way. In particular, when interviewing children, investigators need to take into account their developmental stages and their varying levels of cognitive ability. Younger children may have difficulty distinguishing between what is real and what is imagined, or they may be more likely to respond in ways that they think will please the investigator. Children with limited cog-

Research definition of child maltreatment	Respondent accurate	Respondent inaccurate
Accurate	*Match*	Mismatch
Inaccurate	Mismatch	*Match*

Figure 14.1.   Concordance possibilities for research definition of child maltreatment and respondent's definition.

Child report	Parent report accurate	Parent report inaccurate
Accurate	Match	Mismatch
Inaccurate	Mismatch	Match

Figure 14.2. Concordance possibilities for parent respondent and child respondent.

nitive ability may simply misunderstand what is being asked of them. At the same time, these children may be perceived as more vulnerable, and minimizing their reports is not a favorable course of action. For children and adults, the possibility exists for deliberately false reports in which there is some sort of secondary gain to the respondent—perhaps a desire for attention or revenge or a perception of an advantage in custody disputes. Data collectors, themselves, may be responsible for inaccurate reports because individuals hearing certain responses or observing households may misinterpret what they have heard or seen. For example, the word *beating* is used in some cultural groups to denote spanking, but it may sound like a more violent encounter to the untrained ear; similarly, households that are disorganized or that do not meet some subjective view of cleanliness or neatness may appear to some as evidence of neglect. Investigators must carefully consider the likelihood of eliciting false reports through their research protocols and factor this into their decisions about what actions to take. Direct questioning of respondents, particularly children, about the occurrence of maltreatment is relatively new, and the instruments and procedures for collecting such information have only a limited history of use; it may not always be clear how to interpret the information that is obtained.

Frequently, anecdotally, researchers may desire to take action on suspicion of abuse or neglect "to be on the safe side." This kind of action is not without negative consequences that may concern an IRB: A breach of confidentiality and trust is a serious matter in itself, and the potential for disruption and emotional upheaval in the lives of children and families who are confronted with accusations of maltreatment, whether through official reports or through referral to services, is a very real threat for some.

Delayed Reporting

In addition to concerns about veracity of reports, certain research questions and data collection strategies present the opportunity for locating or disclosing positive examples of abuse and suspicions of abuse after the events have occurred or even after the data collection phase of the study is complete.

The discovery of previously unreported events that meet legal and/or research definitions of abuse or suspicions of abuse prompts a series of decisions for the researcher. Some of these decisions are related to concerns mentioned in previous sections of this chapter, such as the veracity of the reports. But the researcher also faces a decision point related to mandatory reporting. In some cases, the identification of possible abuse may occur months or even years after the data have been collected. In fact, it may be possible that the research participant is no longer a minor. Given the potential time lag, the researcher might need to decide if mandatory reporting procedures still apply. The researcher also has to grapple with the reality that CPS may not act on a report that is old or dated. Should the researcher base her actions on how CPS is *likely* to respond? Because of the complexities involved with filing an abuse report, there are significant questions a researcher must address about how to create a calculus that includes some principle of timeliness and how to weigh the harms or potential harms against the benefit of services that might result from reporting or the harm that might result from lack of reporting (especially if reporting is a gatekeeper for access to services) at the time the abuse is discovered. These kinds of ethical questions exist regardless of the size of the dataset or the analytic plan but are fundamentally seated in the definitions that the researcher is employing and the fit of those definitions to the events being described.

Regardless of researchers' status as mandated reporters, case law, rather than statute, generally defines the applicable window during which reporting would be expected or during which it would be a reporter's responsibility. Adults who themselves become aware that they were victims of abuse generally have 3 years after they have reached their majority age (i.e., the age at which the state no longer considers them a child or minor) to bring civil action for abuse that occurred when they were children. The 3 years does not include the time between the alleged event and their reaching their majority age. Some states have legislation pending regarding this issue specifically. There are, to the best of the chapter authors' knowledge, no usual and customary procedures for considerations related to elapsed time for researchers.[1]

Particular research strategies do, however, mitigate the ability of a researcher to identify individuals about whom reports might be made and may, then, obviate the researcher from this dilemma. Although earlier in this chapter the chapter authors discussed how researchers in the past decade meet or avoid the mandate to report, an additional example is offered here of data collection and analysis strategies that constrain researchers' options for responding to delayed, or historical, disclosure. This example presents reporting dilemmas and solutions in which the interface of law and protocol creates both the disclosure and prescribed or delimited responses by the researcher.

The Third National Incidence Study (NIS-3) of Child Abuse and Neglect was conducted from 1994 to 1995, under contract from the DHHS (Sedlak &

---

[1] For more information about particular state statutes and case law, contact the National Clearinghouse on Child Abuse and Neglect Information, 1-800-394-3366, http://nccanch.acf.hhs.gov

Broadhurst, 1996).[2] The NIS-3 used two sources of information to estimate the total national incidence of child maltreatment: 1) CPS records for those cases investigated by child welfare agencies, and 2) reports from community professionals or "sentinels" (i.e., teachers or hospital workers who were likely to see and recognize children who were maltreated but who may or may not have made official reports). Sentinel reporters were instructed to routinely fulfill their professional reporting obligations and were told that a report to the study did not constitute an official agency report in any way. When sentinel reporters submitted the data collection form to the research contractor, they included information by which they could be identified in case the contractor needed to verify or clarify some piece of information necessary to the processing or coding activity. That identifying information was removed within 10 days of receipt, leaving no link between the NIS report and the sentinel reporter. The analysis first matched the reports by sentinels to those cases known to agencies, eliminating duplication of cases. By recoding both datasets into the same definitional classification system, the research team was able to assess cases of abuse and neglect that did not appear in agency records but that met the same definitions or acceptance criteria. (A more detailed explanation of the process of creating common definitions and matching appears in Chapter 13 of this volume.) The ethical issue raised by this methodology was that the researchers were in a situation in which they could potentially know of cases that were recognized by professionals but that were not reported to the authorities.

At the time the NIS data were being collected, it was not known which of the sentinel reports had and had not been reported to CPS. The coded event (assigned to the correct NIS-3 definition category) became the analytic unit for the database. Only at this point was the research team aware of those reports that existed only through sentinel reports and that were not duplicated on CPS data forms. Only these children who are not known to CPS but who are countable would be eligible for reporting to CPS (i.e., creating a decision point regarding reporting for the researchers). This decision point in terms of the research teams' ability to report occurred approximately 18 months following the data collection period (A. Sedlak, personal communication, November 18, 2003), and no link remained between the data entry and the sentinel to the child; therefore, no report to CPS was possible.

Third-Party Sources: When to Report

One of the newest innovations in child abuse and neglect research is a data collection strategy that asks children about their maltreatment histories. This methodology raises many concerns, including definitional issues and ethical issues

---

[2]For more information about the NIS-3, see http://nccanch.acf.hhs.gov/pubs/statsinfo/nis3.cfm

ranging from what might be the effects on children of recalling and disclosing these events to what it means to ask children to inform on their parents in an intersection with human subject protection issues related to gathering information about one party from another (i.e., third-party information). Certainly, a great deal of sensitivity and caution are necessary when one asks children to talk about events that may be defined as abusive and that were perpetrated predominantly by their parents.

Asking children directly is not without controversy. Runyan found it "paradoxical that maltreatment, one of the key exposures of interest, could not be ascertained from the people most likely to know whether these experiences had occurred" (2000, p. 675). One longitudinal study, the LONGSCAN (Longitudinal Studies of Child Abuse and Neglect)[3] project, addresses this issue. LONGSCAN is a consortium of researchers who are conducting longitudinal studies in five sites, focusing on the correlates and consequences of child maltreatment. The collective researchers also employ common measures that involve direct interviewing and assessment of children (as well as their caregivers) beginning at age 4. In early waves of interviewing subjects, researchers did not ask questions that would "automatically require reporting" (Runyan, 2000, p. 676), but as the children grew older, the researchers in LONGSCAN concluded that "12-year-old children were most likely old enough to understand the consent process and be asked about maltreatment" directly (Runyan, 2000, p. 677). To the best of the chapter authors' knowledge, no empirical research has yet been published on the impact of this decision or on the quality of children's self-reports or their concordance to other report sources (i.e., parents or agencies). NSCAW, described previously, has preliminary data to suggest that parents do not refuse participation following an explicit consenting process that describes the possibility of being reported for suspected maltreatment, nor do they withdraw from the study if a report is made. Many questions remain unanswered regarding using children's self-reports in research. For example, when children self-report, naming their parents as alleged perpetrators, do children define the events in ways that are accurate and accurately interpreted by the researcher? Do children tell their parents that they have disclosed this event to researchers? Do children risk "retributive punishment" from parents following such a disclosure, despite confidentiality practices on the part of the researchers? The situation is ripe for empirical pursuit.

It is also unknown how IRBs consider the implications of children sharing information about their parents. Child maltreatment research, in which children themselves are the research subjects, certainly comes under the pervue of Subpart D of the federal regulations. That part, as detailed earlier in this chapter, defines a child by age and outlines that the affirmation of agreement to participate must be solicited from the child and the parent or guardian (45 C.F.R. 46 § 402), with special requirements for the participation of children who are wards of the state

---

[3]For more information about LONGSCAN, see http://www.sph.unc.edu/iprc/longscan/

(§ 409). Also, as described previously, IRBs have some flexibility to waive some of these consent procedures if the waiving of them protects the subjects. However, this does not address whether IRBs will consider the information disclosed by the child about the parent third-party information. Abiding by these regulations regarding consents meets one set of ethical standards (for participation) but creates other ethical issues (those of third-party data).

To illustrate a third-party scenario, consider the following hypothetical situation. Johnny, age 12, is being interviewed by a researcher regarding the way in which Johnny's parents discipline him. The researcher reads a vignette describing a boy like Johnny who skips school one spring day. Johnny is asked to pick which of three scenarios best describes how his parents would handle the situation. Johnny picks none of the researcher's options, but says, "When I did that last year, my father beat me with his belt, locked me in my room, and I didn't get any dinner. He thought that would teach me a lesson. Last week, when he heard I had been at the mall and not in class, he just shoved me around a little." The researcher, who was not inquiring about maltreatment may, as the responses accumulate, feel that Johnny is at risk of maltreatment. What should the researcher do, and to what extent does an IRB even consider the possibility of this kind of disclosure?

It is not the *fact* of knowing something about a third party that is at issue. It is that the information that is disclosed is both private and individually identifiable. In the context of child maltreatment, the disclosure and accompanying report to CPS when maltreatment has occurred, or is suspected, underscores the concept of potential harm or risk of harm to the participants (the parents) both dignitary (the indignity of being the object of a child abuse investigation) and possible legal penalties should maltreatment be substantiated. Given the present interpretation of guidance regarding the regulation, the National Institutes of Health, the OHRP, and IRBs across the country would be asked to consider whether the potential for disclosure creates a situation that demands prior informed consent of the third party (those likely to be put at risk of harm) because having private and identifiable information about them becomes part of the research record. Most IRBs would engage in a process of informed consent if the intention is to solicit this kind of information (i.e., informing the parent that they will be asking the child about disciplinary practices in the home) because the parent is now a third party about whom information is being collected and that information poses some potential risk for that third party. IRBs may request this consent process if they feel there is even a reasonable possibility of this kind of information surfacing.

Because parents are required to give permission for their child to participate in child maltreatment research and because they are the individuals most likely to be disclosed "about" during that research, they are usually made aware of the consequences of certain types of disclosures—intentional or unintentional. As discussed earlier in this chapter, IRBs commonly require that the informed consent/assent/permission process include information about the risk of CPS involvement. A researcher can rightfully ask if parents understand what that might mean. In addition, a researcher could easily ask if parents and children are operating from the same definitions of abusive or neglectful events (e.g., appropriateness of physical punishment) from which the researchers are operating. Do parents define what they did, and what the child reported, in ways that are congruent with the way in which researchers will categorize the events; and what congruence, then, exists with actionable CPS definitions? It is a very complicated chain of applied translations.

All of this also occurs in a state of tension and imbalance between promoting the safety of the child and the very nature of allegations about parent perpetrators that may prove to be nonfactual. Although information about third parties often is used to provide background information or context to understanding the circumstances or environments of the identified subjects—in this case the child informants—these disclosures have more significance in child maltreatment research because of the decision point they create for the researcher. These disclosures may compromise third-party privacy and put the third party (e.g., parents) at risk of harm. These disclosures are not a function of data handling or data security. They are, in some ways, an intended consequence of the data collection strategy (i.e., child informants) and deserve to be given ethical consideration as such by the researcher and the IRB.

Special Challenges of New Data Collection Technologies

Although new technologies have expanded greatly the possibilities for the types of information that can be obtained and stored, they also have presented new challenges for maltreatment researchers. For example, computer-assisted technologies now allow sensitive information to be collected and coded in such a way that a respondent's input can be completely masked from the researchers, thus providing additional assurances of privacy and confidentiality to the respondent. Although not having access to the information would appear to release the researcher from any legal obligation to report situations that may compromise the well-being of children, the ethical issues of disclosure remain. For example, children may not understand the limits of technology and may expect that the revelation of information, even in a computerized or other private format, in the presence of an adult will result in assistance from that adult (Black & Ponirakis, 2000). The age of the child and the type of information being elicited may govern the investigator's decisions about how to treat this kind of information.

The LONGSCAN project offers an example of one contemporary technological approach. Computer-assisted interviews conducted with children are designed to provide a sense of privacy. Children's responses, however, are not necessarily private. For younger children, in which the measures focus on general development and functioning, the computer program flags responses that may indicate a threat or danger to the child so that the interviewer can follow up with appropriate action. For children age 12 and above, however, the information is treated differently. For these children, a lengthy computerized interview is conducted that captures self-reported details about the children's experiences of maltreatment. During this interview, the computer program elicits specific information about whether the respondent wishes to have any of his or her private information disclosed or if he or she would like to obtain assistance related to any of the items that have been presented in the interview protocol (Kotch, 2000). The investigators have argued (and their IRBs have concurred) that autonomy and respect for older children is an important consideration and that the children themselves should decide whether their personal information is disclosed.

The consent process, of course, must reflect the investigator's decisions about how to handle self-administered questionnaires, computerized or not; such formats are likely to raise an expectation of privacy that may not in fact exist, and it is important that any exceptions be made explicit and understandable to children.

Researchers must constantly weigh the balance between confidentiality considerations and their obligations to protect children, without any hard and fast rules to guide their decision making. How far is the researcher obliged to go in protecting child subjects? Another contemporary research example, from a project sponsored by the Department of Justice, highlights the tensions between confidentiality guarantees and the social obligations of adult researchers in projects with child subjects. In 1998, the Office of Juvenile Justice and Delinquency Prevention oversaw the development of the Survey of Youth in Residential Placement (SYRP).[4] The survey provided data on, among other things, the occurrence of abuse or neglect while a youth was in residential placement. The SYRP was administered via an audio computer-assisted self-interview (ACASI) format, using strict anonymity procedures. No one connected with the study, including field staff, ever knew identifying information about the youth who participated. None of the interview answer data could be opened until all statistical weighting was completed and the records were completely de-identified (the research team could not even tell which facility the interview came from). Because a participant could have been in danger of retribution from staff or residents if it became known that he or she had endorsed abuse, the legal requirements, the survey methodology, and some practical considerations appeared to argue for a fairly straightforward decision that ensuring children's safety was beyond the capability of the research team. The research team, however, actively sought a design that provided some assistance (i.e., protection) to youth who might be entrapped in abusive situations but that did not put the research team in a position requiring a report or in violation of the Department of Justice regulations. In the end, facilities were required to allow their participating youth—if he or she so desired—access to an unmonitored conversation with a counselor, hired by the research contractor for

---

[4]For more information about the SYRP, see http://www.ncjrs.org/html/ojjdp/annualreport99/ch6_e.html)

the duration of the data collection period, at an 800 telephone number. Youth were told they could call if they had questions about the study, if they had any concerns, or if they wanted to talk about the issues that the survey had touched on. In this way, a report by the counselor on a youth would not come about because of the youth's answers to the survey but rather from a disclosure made during the telephone conversation with the counselor. This strategy allowed the research team to abide by the Department of Justice's confidentiality protections but also to sleep at night, knowing that youth had some opportunity to seek help if they desired it (A. Sedlak, personal communication, November 18, 2003).

Once a researcher has addressed the informed consent process issues and considered their responses to handling potentially actionable information disclosed in the data collection process, there remain additional ethical deliberations regarding the researcher's responsibilities in regard to information that may become known as the result of analyses or analytic processes. The consideration of information that becomes known as result of analysis was addressed, partially, in the previous section on delayed reporting. Here, new information that emerges primarily as a result of an analytic process—the power provided by new technologies to interdigitate or crosswalk datasets at the time of collection; in the planned analyses; and later, using archived datasets, in yet unknown ways—with its attendant new requirement for ethical consideration, is considered. (See also Chapter 13 of this volume by Flanzer, Yuan, and English).

Briefly, several data handling procedures can be instituted to protect researchers from inadvertent disclosures that might occur during analyses. These strategies range from suppressing data to masking it. Small data cells can be combined to produce larger cells representing larger units of analyses for the same data. In suppressing data, researchers must consider the effects that the creation of these new variables or cells may have on analytic potential. The chapter authors, however, believe that careful suppression of data—erring on the side of lower risk to the research participant rather than increased benefit to the researcher—is almost always more beneficial in the risk–benefit calculation. Masking data, perhaps by creating categories of less specific information, is another option. When the inclusion of specific variables or details increases the likelihood of breach of confidentiality or loss of privacy but less detail would not affect the interpretation of the data, masking should be considered. For example, the dates of recurrent incidents of abuse may be converted to the length of time between recurrences with minimal loss of analytic potential if the research question is one about the relationship of services delivered during the time elapsed between incidents. In addition, as described in Chapter 13 by Flanzer and colleagues, coding and encryption are other data handling strategies that provide an ethical, at best, and an IRB-approvable, at a minimum, plan for confidentiality and privacy. Finally, restricted-release procedures for archived data, in which access to data is limited to specific groups of researchers or others and its use is carefully monitored, are becoming increasingly common, and IRB exemptions for secondary data analyses are becoming less likely.

Large-scale datasets that are made available for use by the public, particularly those derived from federal or state databases, are vulnerable to being exploited by researchers and nonacademic users. One such example underscores this vulnerability. In the mid 1990s, a journalist investigated whether a federal database contained serious errors and general insufficiency. His investigation aimed to match entries of child fatalities from an archived dataset to county death records in his state—obviously highly sensitive material. When confronted with his findings and allegations of errors, federal staff were relieved that intentional data masking strategies had successfully protected the privacy of those families whose cases met the criteria for inclusion in the archived dataset. The data did not, nor were they intended to, represent every child death in any county during a specific time period. Regardless of the intent of the journalist's pursuit, his lack of sensitivity to the families in his state is worth consideration. Although public records exist about children who die from many causes and public records exist about children who die while in the custody of the public child welfare system, attempts to match the two sets of data, looking for those that appear in one and not the other, intended to discredit the thoroughness of the child welfare agency, seems, at least potentially, an invasion of a family's privacy. The federal agency had, in fact, created a public use file data-record format that guarded against just such matching-based disclosures. In other words, by masking data, the agency intended to protect the privacy of individuals whose data was collected for one purpose from being used for other purposes in ways that compromised both confidentiality and privacy without significant loss of detail and utility of the archived dataset. That, in summary, is the ethical concern. Can privacy and confidentiality be protected without diminishing data quality and utility? Investing federal research funds in data collection ethically obligates the "collector" to use the data in ethical ways. Masking data, or similar strategies, that protect the privacy and confidentiality of the subjects and their information is an ethical choice and exhibits ethical behavior on the part of the data collector/analyst/researcher. Finding the ethical balance is, of course, the challenge.

One federal tool that is used to protect research subjects is the Certificate of Confidentiality. Certificates of Confidentiality are available to any researcher, regardless of funding source, from the National Institutes of Health for protection against the subpoena of data. That is, the certificate ensures that the names of and information about subjects in a particular study are protected; a researcher cannot be compelled, even with a subpoena, to release them. Yet, as Sieber noted, "whether any waiver [sic, certificate] protects the researcher who discovers child abuse is debatable," (1994, p. 13) and there is no mention in the certificate of the researchers' obligation regarding reporting of abuse. In fact, Sieber further notes that this debate exists within the DHHS: The National Institutes of Health assert that researchers are exempt from reporting based on this certificate, whereas the National Center on Child Abuse and Neglect (now the Office on Child Abuse and Neglect) has taken the opposite viewpoint. Although the Certificate of Confidentiality can be broken to report abuse without penalty to the researcher, it makes no mention as to whether a researcher would be held responsible for not reporting abuse discovered or disclosed in the course of conducting research. However, in addition to obtaining a Certificate of Confidentiality, some researchers have worked with their states to request a formal written exemption from the reporting mandates for specific research investigations (Sieber, 1994).

CONCLUSION

The changes that have occurred in child maltreatment research since the mid-1990s also have engendered a parallel set of ethical challenges in terms of enrolling vulnerable youth and families into projects and with respect to data collection, analysis, and archiving procedures. As the research community has broadened over the years and because research on child maltreatment has aimed to become more rigorous, new complexities have emerged that necessitate thoughtful, sensitive, and consistent responses on behalf of researchers. Definitions of child maltreatment have become more refined over the years, which has also brought about new opportunities for undertaking research. Although distinct groups of researchers may be looking at abuse differently from one another or in isolated contexts, all researchers must contend with a number of issues: 1) how to discuss exclusions to confidentiality during the consent/assent process; 2) what to do with sensitive information, if anything, should it be disclosed to a researcher during the course of data collection; 3) the unique circumstances of research with children residing in foster care; 4) the delayed discovery of abuse that may be identified in archived datasets; and 5) the use of advanced technologies in collecting personal data from children and youth. In addition, it is not at all uncommon for the discovery of abuse to happen in nonmaltreatment research as well.

Although this chapter outlines the ethical quandaries that many in the research community face, the chapter authors also recognize that there is an absence of explicit federal guidelines in place to address these challenges. Thus, they propose the following remedies and strategies for contending with these ethical challenges.

First, with respect to research subjects' perspectives, the field is in need of investigations that explore how the subject of maltreatment is presented to subjects in research studies. Subjects could be debriefed following the conclusion of data collection and queried about how they interpreted the maltreatment topic. What definition did they adopt? How do these definitions of abuse compare with those used by researchers? How well did they understand the consent form, and what effect did the reporting requirement have on them? It might also be helpful to ascertain information from those who decline participation based on this reporting mandate. Was the reporting requirement, in fact, the primary deterrent?

Second, related to state variations in interviewing youth, the field needs clearer directions about how to work with special populations of youth. Certain youth may be eligible to provide their own consent to participate if they are legally emancipated from their caregivers. However, how do researchers treat youth—such as homeless youth—who are distinct from their parents but not *legally* separated from them? Moreover, this legal distinction is bound to vary from state to state, and it is unclear how and when youth can provide their own consent.

Third, related to the perspective of university IRBs, it would be helpful to measure the variation in IRB understanding of child maltreatment research. Gauging the knowledge base of the varied faculty members—who come from disparate academic disciplines—may shed light on what they actually know versus what they believe or fear. For many faculty members, conducting research with children and families involved in child abuse may be an entirely foreign subject area and may seem too evocative or threatening an idea to even entertain. Armed with this information, researchers could work with their respective IRBs in advance to prepare them for the atypical nature of this research and what the likely barriers—and attendant solutions—might be.

Finally, with respect to researchers, the field needs to formally address the progression of ethical dilemmas that have emerged in the 1990s and, perhaps, refine protocols that were formulated before the current generation of research studies began. Upon writing this chapter, it is striking to the chapter authors just how varied the ethical issues are in child abuse research, how many divergent resolutions exist to contend with these issues, and how the dilemmas are entangled with research definitions. It is clear that the ethical and definitional issues need to be refined so that researchers can ensure the safety and protection of children, youth, and families involved in their projects.

REFERENCES

Amdur, R.J., & Bankert, E.A. (2002). *Institutional review board: Management and function.* Boston: Jones and Bartlett.

Attkisson, C.C., Rosenblatt, A., & Hoagwood, K. (1996). Research ethics and human subjects protection in child mental health services research and community studies. In K. Hoagwood, P. Jensen, & C.B. Fisher (Eds.), *Ethical issues in mental health research with children and adolescents* (pp. 43–57). Mahwah, NJ: Lawrence Erlbaum Associates.

Beecher, H. (1966). Ethics and clinical research. *New England Journal of Medicine, 274,* 1354–1360.

Black, M.M., & Ponirakis, A. (2000). Computer-administered interventions with children about maltreatment: Methodological, developmental, and ethical issues. *Journal of Interpersonal Violence, 15*(7), 682–695.

Ceci, S.J., & Bruck, M. (1998). Suggestibility of the child witness: A historical review and synthesis. *Psychological Bulletin, 113,* 403–439.

Child Abuse Prevention and Treatment Act of 1974, PL 93-247, 42 U.S.C. § 5101 *et seq.*

Courtney, M.E. (2000). Research needed to improve the prospects for children in out-of-home placement. *Children and Youth Services Review, 22*(9–10), 743–761.

Dowd, K.L. (2004). Human subjects issues in the national survey of child and adolescent well-being. In S.B. Cohen & J.M. Lepowski (Eds.), *Proceedings of the Eighth Conference on Health Research Methods* (MD DHHS Publication No. 04-1013, pp. 189–194). Hyattsville, MD: National Center for Health Statistics.

Dowd, K.L., Kinsey, S., Wheeless, S., Thissen, R., Richardson, J., Mierzwa, F., et al. (2002). *National survey of child and adolescent well-being: Introduction to the wave I general and restricted release data.* Retrieved January 25, 2006, from http://www.ndacan.cornell.edu/NDACAN/Datasets/UserGuidePDFs/092_Intro_to_NSCAW_Wave_1.pdf

Federal Policy for the Protection of Human Subjects, The Common Rule, 45 C.F.R. 46 § 101. Subpart D, § 402; § 46.409. (1991).

Institute of Medicine (IOM) Committee on Assessing the System for Protecting Human Research Participants. (2003). *Responsible research: A systems approach to protecting research participants.* Washington, DC: National Academies Press.

Kalichman, S.C. (1999). *Mandated reporting of suspected child abuse: Ethics, law, and policy* (2nd ed.). Washington, DC: American Psychological Association.

Kinard, E.M. (1985). Ethical issues in research with abused children. *Child Abuse & Neglect, 9,* 301–311.

King, N.M.P., & Churchill, L.R. (2000). Ethical principles guiding research on child and adolescent subjects. *Journal of Interpersonal Violence, 15*(7), 710–724.

Kotch, J.B. (2000). Ethical issues in longitudinal child maltreatment research. *Journal of Interpersonal Violence, 15*(7), 696–709.

Liss, M.B. (1994). Child abuse: Is there a mandate for researchers to report? *Ethics & Behavior, 4*(2), 133–146.

National Commission for the Protection of Human Subjects of Biomedical and Behavioral Research. (1979). The Belmont report: Ethical principles and guidelines for the protection of human subjects of research. Washington, DC: U.S. Government Printing Office.

National Research Act of 1974, PL 93-348.

National Research Council. (1993). *Understanding child abuse and neglect.* Washington, DC: National Academies Press.

Putnam, F.W., Liss, M.B., & Landsverk, J. (1996). Ethical issues in maltreatment with children and adolescents. In K. Hoagwood, P. Jensen, & C.B. Fisher (Eds.), *Ethical issues in mental health research with children and adolescents* (pp. 113–132). Mahwah, NJ: Lawrence Erlbaum Associates.

Runyan, D.K., (2000). The ethical, legal, and methodological implications of directly asking children about abuse. *Journal of Interpersonal Violence, 15*(7), 675–681.

Saywitz, K.J., Goodman, G.S., & Lyon, T.D. (2002). Interviewing children in and out of court: Current research and practice implications. In J.E.B. Meyers, L. Berliner, J. Briere, C.T. Hendrix, C. Jenny, & T.A, Reid (Eds.). *The APSAC handbook on child maltreatment* (2nd ed., pp. 349–377). Thousand Oaks, CA.: Sage Publications.

Sedlak, A.J., & Broadhurst, D.D. (1996). *Third national incidence study of child abuse and neglect: Final report.* Washington, DC: U.S. Department of Health and Human Services.

Sieber, J.E. (1994). Issues presented by mandatory reporting requirements to researchers of child abuse and neglect. *Ethics & Behavior, 4*(1), 1–22.

Steinberg, A.M., Pynoos, R.S., Goenjian, A.K., Sossanabadi, H., & Sherr, L. (1999). Are researchers bound by child abuse reporting laws? *Child Abuse & Neglect, 23,* 771–777.

15

Conclusions and Future Research Directions

MARGARET M. FEERICK AND KYLE L. SNOW

THE EARLIER CHAPTERS in this volume make the case that a scientifically driven examination of definitions of child maltreatment and development of a classification system is necessary to support the field of child maltreatment research and help it to move forward. Both the preface and forewords to this book provide some important historical context for the development of this volume, a context that represents a convergence of factors that is unique in the field since the landmark National Research Council (NRC; 1993) report calling for rigorous study of child abuse and neglect. However, this book is neither the first (see, e.g., Cicchetti & Manly, 2001; Giovannoni & Becerra, 1979) nor likely the last effort to inform the field's activities in a move toward better definition and classification systems. The question this concluding chapter attempts to address is, In what ways does this volume move the field forward toward a research-based definition and classification system for child maltreatment? The answer to this question is framed by first examining the themes that emerge across several chapters in the book, especially those themes that highlight the current state of the art in thinking about definitions of maltreatment. Second, because part of the goal of this volume is to move the field forward, suggestions for future work to be completed are extracted from various chapters and, where appropriate, recommendations are made on how to realize these goals. With this foundation, the critical need for undertaking a research-driven effort at defining and classifying child abuse and neglect experiences is revisited and placed in the larger policy and practice contexts that are central to the field of child maltreatment.

EMERGING THEMES

The introductory chapters of this volume provide a rich historical and social context for contemporary measures and definitions of child maltreatment. These chapters highlight the tension between research definitions and legal and sociocultural definitions that have been in place since the beginnings of societal concern about child maltreatment. Consistent with the intent of this volume, the authors in these introductory chapters call for efforts to develop scientifically based research definitions of key constructs, and they indicate (implicitly or explicitly) that it is essential that these efforts feed back into and inform social and legal conceptualizations to move the policy, practice, and research aspects of child maltreatment work forward. The authors also agree that such endeavors need to be systematic and researchers likely will require a period of time to develop a more rigorous research-driven approach to the definition of maltreatment.

As Haugaard argues in Chapter 3, definitions of maltreatment historically have been based on the behaviors of the perpetrators, a focus that was made early on in the development of the field and that has led to a focus on types of maltreatment that are then connected to specific child outcomes. This approach has changed slightly to accommodate multiple forms of maltreatment, which have only recently (i.e., in the past decade) been treated as potentially interacting, as opposed to additive, experiences. This view of child maltreatment, embraced by clinicians and researchers alike, effectively has limited the incentives and recognition for alternative conceptualizations. For example, efforts at standardized classification and measurement schemes that challenge the current state-based definitions (e.g., the National Child Abuse and Neglect Data System, NCANDS) have met with stark resistance. Yet the field must confront this resistance directly on the strength of sound scientific data and emerging theoretical perspectives on the nature of child maltreatment.

None of the chapters in this volume, however, offer any guidance about how to reconcile differences between research-based definitions and their social and legal counterparts. The implications of possible differences in definitions across different arenas of usage raise serious concerns from research, legal, and ethical standpoints. As pointed out by several authors (see Chapters 2, 3, 4, and 12), there are differences across systems in how definitions of maltreatment are used. For example, in the legal context, it is critical not only to indicate that an act occurred, but also to identify the responsible party in order to take legal action. A similar but slightly less stringent criterion is set for social services adjudication, in which, for example, the act and probable responsible agents need to be identified to justify removal of a child from his or her home. From a research perspective, it may be less important to be able to definitively identify the responsible party or parties and more important to specify the experience itself, especially in efforts to understand developmental pathways and trajectories for child development. How should society respond, then, if research definitions that emerge are dramatically different from those currently in use, especially within the legal system? Will the legal system adjust to the new definitions? If not, does the potential discrepancy in definitions used by different systems leave open legal loopholes in which accused perpetrators can claim that their acts, although legally identified as maltreatment, have not been so identified in the research community? Certainly, if such differences exist, then researchers will need to reexamine methods that rely on reviews of child protective services (CPS) records to identify abuse and neglect. Likewise, what are the ethical and legal responsibilities of researchers who, using research-based definitions to identify maltreatment, un-cover suspected cases of maltreatment not currently identified within the legal or CPS systems? Most critically, how will the relationships between legal and research definitions evolve over time during the scientific discovery process, dur-ing which definitions are developed, evaluated, revised, and utilized? Indeed, as attested to by many of the chapters in this volume, the scientific discovery process of research definitions likely will take considerable time, even though research on child maltreatment (as a field) has certainly evolved to be capable of taking the next step.

The contributors to this book also reiterate the central definitional themes articulated by the NRC (1993): endangerment versus harm, severity of the act(s), frequency of acts, intent to harm, developmental level, and cultural sensitivity. Throughout chapters in Section II of this volume, attention is paid both to the actions of parents/caregivers and the consequences of those actions (e.g., harm, injuries) as important components of maltreatment definitions. The authors in Section II make the argument that, without a coupling of act and consequences, many parenting behaviors in which there is neither intent nor harm to the child may be identified as maltreatment. This is an important consideration because many parenting behaviors may appear to be maltreatment when taken out of con-text (e.g., restraining a child in a chair for a period of minutes) and when there is general agreement that the practice (in this case, giving the child a time-out) is not harmful and may in fact be a beneficial parenting strategy to handle diffi-cult behaviors. In this framework, the early work by Garbarino (1977) placing child maltreatment into the larger context of unhealthy parenting behaviors may serve as an important model in conceptualizing maltreatment. Despite the strengths of Garbarino's approach, however, several authors point out that there is still a need to identify a set of candidate maltreatment behaviors and a set of likely potential consequences of those behaviors, and the identification of behav-iors and consequences should be driven by theory and research on child develop-ment to avoid the arbitrariness the approach is intended to reduce. The NRC (1993) argued that the fundamental role of conceptual frameworks is to guide measurement and data collection. Such frameworks are only tenable, however, in the presence of valid and reliable measurement.

The contributors to this volume also have attempted to reconcile the debate between categorical and continuous definitions of child maltreatment. Each of the chapter authors in Sections II and III indicates that at the extremes of a hypothesized continuum, indications of maltreatment are reasonably clear. It is in identifying the points of demarcation along the continuum that researchers struggle, especially the point that divides poor parenting from harmful parent-ing, for example. Conceptualizing maltreatment as a continuous rather than di-chotomous variable (or set of variables) also has implications for the measures that are used and the ways in which the data derived from multiple informants and multiple sources are combined. Here developments in statistics, including the increased use of latent and instrumental variable approaches, will become increasingly important to researchers in the field, especially to the degree that data reduction techniques impose certain assumptions on the measures contributing to the derived measure or measures. Therefore, in planning to use such statistical approaches, researchers need to develop measurement approaches that are more efficient and effective in reliably and accurately classifying the maltreatment experiences of individuals who have experienced maltreatment.

Individual chapters in Section III of this volume provide overviews of the different approaches to measurement used by child maltreatment researchers. Although the authors provide some compelling, positive rationales for using particular approaches, they also point out many of the inadequacies that the next generation of measurement approaches must overcome.

Direct observation of maltreatment events is often not possible, so researchers must often rely on proxy measures. Although proxies may be adequate for some research purposes, such as the construction of groups of individuals with certain common experiences (assuming these experiences are adequately defined), they do not provide data rich enough to understand the dynamic unfolding of maltreatment events during the course of parent–child interactions, which ultimately limits the field's capacity to understand the immediate antecedents of maltreatment and therefore develop effective intervention and prevention strategies.

One common proxy is to use self-report, either from the adult or the child (or from an adult recollecting his or her own childhood). Many of these measures of child abuse and neglect lack adequate psychometric support, especially in terms of validity and accuracy measures. Of course, self-report measures must deal with any number of complications to prove their utility, including the distinction between the occurrence of an act and an individual's perception of the act. Among retrospective self-report measures, the distinction between actual and perceived experiences is exacerbated by the adequacy of memory. The problems of perception and memory are critical if such measures are also to provide information to researchers about timing, duration, and other important characteristics of the events. There is also the challenge of using developmentally and culturally appropriate language in a way that does not undermine the construct being assessed. Finally, in addition to the problems encountered with child self-report measures, researchers using parental self-report measures must contend with potential concerns about the impact of disclosure of potentially punishable actions from parents. Still, self-report measures remain a mainstay in the tools used to measure child maltreatment. As Portwood argues in Chapter 9, the best self-report measures would address a range of maltreatment experiences, use clear definitions, and produce normative data that allow for comparisons across groups.

The potential first-person biases introduced to measures of child maltreatment based on self-report are, in theory, limited through the use of outside or third-party reporting. Such is the case with administrative and case records methods that result from CPS investigations, or in rare studies, medical record reviews based on medical examinations. Although such records may avoid problems encountered in first-person reporting, they are not insulated completely from the potential for biases, such as may exist in an agency's determination to open a case record (in CPS) or an individual's decision to seek medical treatment (as is the case for medical record review), or in how a determination is made that a record indicates maltreatment as opposed to a wide range of other antecedent events (e.g., accidental injury).

A critical consideration in developing measures of child maltreatment must be given to the ethical treatment of human participants, in particular, the responsibility to protect those participants from harm. There is still some concern that asking individuals about possible abuse experiences may retraumatize them, and in some cases plant false memories of abuse. These concerns are particularly strong for professionals working with young children and/or individuals with disabilities. Although there is data to speak to these concerns, the concerns remain entrenched to differing degrees in the legal and practice communities and so must be considered (Ceci & Bruck, 1995). In addition, from a research perspective, studies of child maltreatment must obtain approval from local institutional review boards (IRBs) as well as meet grant reviewers' demands regarding the ethical treatment of human participants in research. Frequently, meeting these demands requires the development and use of consent forms that include information about the way in which disclosures of abuse will be handled (increasingly these lead to referrals to local reporting agencies). Although these ethical and human participants' requirements make conducting child maltreatment research challenging, especially in terms of obtaining accurate data on perpetration and victimization (and incidence and prevalence), it is still critical to obtain this information, especially from high-risk samples who may be particularly concerned about being reported for child maltreatment and/or prompting a CPS investigation. Some studies, such as those on teenage sexuality, collect anonymous data. These studies use a unique methodology to collect and handle children's information in an ethical manner. It might be useful for child abuse and neglect researchers to consider these methods of data collection.

Although ethical issues make conducting research on child maltreatment particularly challenging, these issues should not prevent researchers from measuring these constructs (i.e., child abuse and neglect) or doing the kind of sampling that is necessary for generalizable results. The important questions to address are, How much error do these constraints create, and how best should researchers deal with this error?

FUTURE DIRECTIONS

Several chapters in this volume note that there are two linked problems with the current variability with which constructs in child maltreatment are defined. First, the variability itself, although problematic, has been partitioned into several channels based on the dominant approach represented by each definition. For example, although reliance on raw CPS data alone may not be a common approach across the field, there has been movement toward general acceptance of CPS data as one source of relevant data. What compounds this variability, however, is the general lack of specificity present in many operational definitions of critical constructs. It is in this context that a rigorous effort at developing a classification system for child maltreatment is necessary.

One of the primary purposes of a classification system is to improve communication about the objects and the areas of interest; classification systems that are simple, dichotomous, and unidimensional are the easiest about which to communicate. But those simple communication classification systems are often reified into public policy and law. Thus, it is important to recognize that classification is also a sociopolitical process; that is, it leads people to organize and think about the world in certain ways. Once a classification system is established in a policy or legal context, it is difficult for scientists to depart from that framework and to think beyond the legalistic model/definition. But, from a scientific point of view, the main reason to focus on classification issues, as these issues pertain to child maltreatment, is to improve predictions regarding etiology, treatment, and behaviors. When scientists engage in classification research, they are not really trying to develop a better communication system, although such a system may emerge; they are interested in treating the etiologies of abuse and neglect, in dealing with the behaviors and the outcomes, in predicting the future for children or adults, or in preventing negative consequences. This situation requires more complex classification systems. Typically the goals of communicability and complexity are in conflict. Scientifically, however, without some measure of complexity, the result is a poorly defined, simplistic model.

In developing a classification system, the first step is to specify constructs and attributes. This step entails the conceptualization of the phenomena under study (see Chapters 1 and 8). The next step is to develop operational definitions of these constructs and develop methods to accurately and reliably measure them (see the chapters in Sections II and III). Throughout these complimentary processes, the goal is to achieve and then maintain internal reliability of the system while at the same time maintaining coverage. From a developmental perspective, this is particularly challenging because, as several chapters in this volume indicate, there may be varying definitions of maltreatment based on the age of the child involved. A classification system that does not consider the development of the child and the implications of that development may lose coverage of important maltreatment events. Finally, the classification system must be assessed for external validation. Cluster analysis and other statistical techniques may prove to be critical to this validation but must be used with caution insofar as some methods, without being informed by theory or conceptualization, will form groups of any attribute; it is important to decide whether the groups are useful. Given the legal aspects of child maltreatment, a classification system will have to be assessed for its utility in law enforcement and other applied settings. However, because such a system would ultimately be the basis for mobilizing social and human services (and possibly medical and mental health services as well), the classification system must also provide clinical validity to ensure that services are effectively targeted where they are needed.

The classification of child maltreatment is complicated, however, by the fact that the child is inherently nested within a variety of contextual influences. Child abuse and neglect are problems that exist both within the child and in relation to a set of circumstances; they are multilevel social models. The key is to operationalize all the different levels to understand what contributes to child functioning. The question then, from a classification point of view, is which attributes at each level of those models are most important to measure? Then, researchers need to look at the interrelationships among different levels. Finally, researchers need to determine if there is a comprehensible model that integrates all the information and reduce variables at each level. In an ideal world, researchers would examine only a handful of variables at a time, and the summary variables among them would be most helpful. Because child abuse is a field dominated by advocates who are trying to get children out of certain situations, it is natural to set up a research problem using the child as the unit of analysis. But, with a multilevel process, this is not the only way to set up a study. Researchers could also predicate other types of studies at different levels of analyses, including the household level, the family level, and the community level. In such studies, researchers would approach definitions, sampling, and measurement schemes differently depending on the level of analysis. Similarly, public policy approaches would potentially differ at each level, as well.

In addition to multiple levels of study, there are a range of interested parties that rely on definitions of child maltreatment to make legal decisions or to provide services. Often, these definitions are based on differing levels of scientific rigor and a different set of motivations. For example, in the legal system, concern is in identifying children who are maltreated and identifying a particular perpetrator or perpetrators. How should children be classified or identified to meet legal requirements? From a treatment or intervention perspective, the definitions need to be more specific to define domains for knowing what kinds of services are appropriate; often, specific kinds of services may be tied to specific kinds of treatments or responses. The broadest definitions of conditions or activities that might harm children may be useful for advocacy and, perhaps, for public policy. Child abuse and neglect is a sociopolitical issue; at a specific child/family clinical level the details of abuse or neglect may not be important. The attention drawn to the need to do something to protect children may be the most important aspect of the work in child abuse and neglect. Finally, at the research level, definitions may focus more at understanding variation in experiences and their consequences over time.

Still, the authors in this volume and elsewhere have identified what may be considered a reasonably agreed-on collection of attributes to measure and incorporate into a classification system. These include severity of harm; nature of the act(s) or type (or subtype) of maltreatment; timing, such as age of onset, frequency, duration, and chronicity; relationship to the perpetrator(s); number of perpetrators; and developmental level of the child.

A classification system for child maltreatment requires clear definitions, as noted above, but also must rely on psychometrically sound measurement strategies. Not only are the conceptual definitions in use in need of refinement, but extant measures are also prone to inadequacies as well. As discussed by Knutson and Heckenberg in Chapter 4 and Portwood in Chapter 9, self-report measures are often lacking in adequate reliability or validity, suggesting the worse-case scenario of measuring an unknown construct (albeit a named construct) without reliability or validity. The authors in Chapters 10 through 12, as well as in Chapters 4 through 7, summarize the state of measurement and data collection on child maltreatment. Each chapter points out severe limitations in the current state of measurement. Clearly, more attention must be paid to developing valid and reliable measures. Ideally, these would be constructed in concert with efforts at refining definitions or developing classification schemes. Often in the behavioral and social sciences, researchers tend to shape their research questions to accommodate scientifically reasonable tools rather than identify key constructs and questions and build tools to accurately measure and address them.

At the September 2000 meeting focused on defining and measuring child abuse and neglect, the assembled experts identified a number of measurement needs, all of which are echoed in the chapters of this volume. First, there is a need to develop better measures of family functioning, in general, and of the caregiver–child relationship and the quality of that relationship, more specifically. As Dubowitz (Chapter 5) points out, often neglect and abuse exist on a continuum of normative functioning; the only way to reliably and accurately identify dysfunctional family interaction patterns then is to be able to accurately and reliably measure these patterns across a continuum of quality. Also, given the cultural variability in parenting practices and family functioning, measures of these factors must themselves be culturally sensitive. Second, there is a need to develop better ways to measure constructs within a classification model that can be used outside of record reviews but that ideally would be reconcilable with these sources of data. Third, given the importance of child developmental status, and the possibility of child maltreatment occurring from birth through early adulthood, measures must be developed to be age- and/or developmentally appropriate across the childhood years. Finally, given the prominent role of CPS in directing attention at children who have experienced maltreatment, measures of the responses of children and families to CPS involvement that go beyond re-reporting will become increasingly important to developmental studies that may ultimately inform prevention and intervention approaches to at-risk families and/or children.

Several of the chapters in this book point out the emergence of multimethod, multisource strategies in operationally defining key constructs in child maltreatment. These have been in large part strategies developed to overcome the limitations of relying on single-method, single-source data. However, although such approaches potentially limit the drawbacks of any single approach, the degree to which these multiple sources of information can be validated and reconciled presents a potential limitation to their successful application. Indeed, multiple-method, multi-information approaches assume that enduring patterns of behavior occur across a variety of settings (e.g., Campbell & Fiske, 1959) and would potentially be witnessed by a range of individuals within a given setting. However, in the study of child maltreatment, especially, there is often disagreement among the various sources of information. For example, self-report may or may not be corroborated by direct physical examination, which may or may not coincide with the statements of others, be they witnesses or case investigators. Reconciling this typical mixture of indicators of abuse or lack thereof poses a serious threat to the use of such approaches. Thus, even while the use of multiple sources of information and multiple methods is endorsed by nearly all of the authors, there continues to be a need for the development of strategies for successfully integrating these data in classifying abuse and neglect.

Finally, the editors of this volume echo the call made by Knutson and Heckenberg in Chapter 4 for the research community to be more demanding of how studies are reported, especially the level of detail provided within operational definitions. This is not simply an issue for researchers or journal editors or for those who hope to translate research to practice, but rather it demands a comprehensive effort by all parties to bring the level of specification in definitions used in research to a point in which replication is possible (see Morris et al., 1994, for a similar discussion relevant to the learning disabilities field). In doing so, even if the specific operationalizations differ across studies, at the very least, researchers and consumers of research will be able to consider multiple studies simultaneously and with full appreciation for the findings. In this way, the measure and method become almost inextricably linked together in the field of child maltreatment research, so efforts to improve the accuracy of the measure also require a simultaneous consideration of the methods being used to obtain the measure.

Even while explicitness in language must be achieved, the field needs to examine the words and phrases it uses, which often become overly cumbersome in their explicitness, especially in communication with nonresearchers, for whom fine-grained linguistic analysis of terminology is not as important as clarity. This is, of course, the central challenge of any classification scheme and one that will need to be addressed if researchers are to have credibility in guiding the practice and legal communities.

In conclusion, whether the evolution of child maltreatment research called for in this book will raise to the level of a scientific revolution or paradigm shift (Kuhn, 1996) remains to be seen; however, it is clear that a time of reexamination is required to break free of the historical approaches previously taken and to reconsider these early assumptions in the light of contemporary research. Certainly, all fields of research are prone to conceptual inertia. The question remains whether the chapters in this book will provide the necessary opposing force to alter this path. The likelihood of such a dramatic shift will require the efforts of researchers to create innovative definitions and measurement approaches as well as the support of grantmakers and journal editors.

REFERENCES

Campbell, D.T., & Fiske, D.W. (1959). Convergent and discriminant validation by the multitrait-multimethod matrix. *Psychological Bulletin, 56,* 81–105.

Ceci, S.J., & Bruck, M. (1995). *Jeopardy in the courtroom: A scientific analysis of children's testimony.* Washington, DC: American Psychological Association.

Cicchetti, D., & Manly, J.T. (Eds.). (2001). Operationalizing child maltreatment: Developmental processes and outcomes [Special issue]. *Development and Psychopathology, 13*(4).

Garbarino, J. (1977). The human ecology of child maltreatment: A conceptual model for research. *Journal of Marriage and the Family, 39,* 721–735.

Giovannoni, J., & Becerra, R. (1979). *Defining child abuse.* New York: Free Press.

Kuhn, T.S. (1996). *Structure of scientific revolutions* (3rd ed.). Chicago: University of Chicago Press.

Morris, R., Lyon, G.R., Alexander, D., Gray, D.B., Kavanagh, J., Rourke, B.P., et al. (1994). Proposed guidelines and criteria for describing samples of persons with learning disabilities. *Learning Disability Quarterly, 17*(2), 106–109.

National Research Council. (1993). *Understanding child abuse and neglect.* Washington, DC: National Academies Press.

INDEX

Page references to figures, tables, and footnotes are indicated by *f, t,* and *n,* respectively.